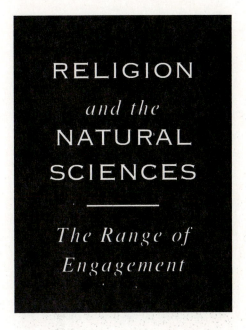

RELIGION
and the
NATURAL
SCIENCES

———

The Range of Engagement

JAMES E. HUCHINGSON
FLORIDA INTERNATIONAL UNIVERSITY

HBJ
Harcourt Brace Jovanovich College Publishers
Fort Worth   Philadelphia   San Diego   New York   Orlando   Austin   San Antonio
Toronto   Montreal   London   Sydney   Tokyo

Editor-in-Chief   Ted Buchholz
Acquisitions Editor   David Tatom
Developmental Editor   Tracy Napper
Senior Project Editor   Kay Kaylor
Production Manager   Erin Gregg
Designer   Nick Welch

Acknowledgments and illustration credits appear on pages 412–15, which constitute a continuation of the copyright page.

ISBN: 0-03-052253-6

Library of Congress Catalog Card Number: 92-81266

Printed in the United States of America

3456789012 016 987654321

PREFACE

No one can doubt that we live in a time of extreme specialization. By concentrating our attention laser-like we may enjoy power and clarity, but we succeed in illuminating only a very small part of the world. Specialization has given us the modern university with its multiplicity of divisions, including schools or colleges, departmental disciplines, subdisciplines and individual specialties. The modern ideal is that all these efforts at precise focus should combine in a sharing process and give rise to a vast network of unified knowledge. But in large measure this synthesis has not taken place. Professional academicians continue to take Voltaire's advice to "cultivate your own garden" in splendid isolation from one another.

Generalists are those who prefer the broad beam of the searchlight to the precision of the laser. They are often found in eclectic academic fields—American Studies, Environmental Studies, Liberal Studies, and Religious Studies—where they work to reknit the isolating consequences of analysis by supplying the common webbing snipped apart by the drive to specialize. This task is conducted in recognition of the fact each of these areas is so rich in interdisciplinary potential that it cannot be explored adequately by any single method of scholarship.

The labors involved in the assembly of a book of readings in contemporary science and religion take place in this context. Nowhere has specialization proceeded further than in the natural sciences and in theology. The task of assembling an anthology in either area would be formidable enough, but to try and bring them together is especially daunting. Textbooks of readings in established disciplines are easily organized according to long-standing traditions, fixed subdisciplines, important issues and questions, and appropriate methodologies. Not so in the studies of science and religion where the dialogue is varied, wide ranging, and in some ways changing constantly. Also, the fact that history cherishes the myth that the two sides are natural enemies has not helped relate them in positive, meaningful ways. Any project hoping to connect the two must supply the categories of connection found primarily, although not exclusively, in philosophy. Now we have three balls to juggle: the natural sciences, religion, and the go-between—philosophy.

The book's subtitle, *The Range of Engagement*, suggests the extremes of interaction between science and religion. "Engagement" is both a military figure of speech—as when opposing forces engage one another—and a relational figure of speech—as when a man and a woman enter into a long-term relationship of mutual commitment to common interests and goals. Additionally, students of science and religion should find dialogue engaging, stimulating in its own right, whatever the consequences may be for culture and life.

All this should lead the reader to expect a book that is not a rigidly organized collection of articles. In accord with the principle of parsimony, I have chosen the way that keeps the outline as simple and economical as possible. The first half of the book (Parts I–III) is an introduction to the discussion of science and religion. Here the reader learns why any debate at all occurs and what resources exist for responding to it. The second half (Parts IV–VI) deals with specific issues that arise in the individual sciences, from astronomy and physics to biology and ecology.

Part I, "The Range of Engagement," introduces students to the ways science and religion have been understood to relate. The selections are intended to provide a conceptual framework for the examination of specific issues in following parts.

Part II, "Words, Images, and Stories," examines a very important human invention—language—and the paramount role it plays in both science and religion, especially in terms of poetic devices, such as metaphor, and creative stories, including myth.

Part III, "The Two-Storied Universe," provides a series of selections that share a common understanding of God (Supernature) and the world (Nature) found in traditional monotheism. The introductory piece by C. S. Lewis describes clearly what this understanding is. The other selections explore problems arising from a model of deity that places God beyond the world of creation but in a position to influence it. Two related topics are included here. One concerns Albert Einstein's strong reservations about the compatibility of science and the existence of a supernatural and personal God. The other concerns the place of miracle in a world defined by science as resistant to any possible violation of its integrity by a transcendent source.

Part IV, "The Cosmos," begins a survey of the various natural sciences that are of direct interest to religion and cosmology—the scientific study of the origin and structure of the universe. Students are made aware that theologians are drawn to the macrocosmos—to the Big Bang model of cosmic birth and to the subsequent evolution of the cosmos, because both appear to suggest the involvement of some intelligent agency in its development. At the other end of the range of size, the microcosmic, students are shown how the bizarre and spooky world of quantum physics encourages speculation about the relation of Eastern religion to modern science.

Part V, "Life," moves from the study of stars and particles to the investigation of living things in the biological sciences. The continuing public debate between creationism and evolution is, of course, included here. Equally important, however, are the often neglected alternatives in the dispute. Examples of these moderating positions are included as well. An excellent example of recent biological thought, which because of its broad implications spills over into humanistic and religious concerns, is the comprehensive science of sociobiology. Sociobiology attempts to integrate social behavior with evolutionary explanation through the science of genetics; it raises specific questions concerning the status of moral action and its sources and justification, to which philosophical and theological ethicists take strong exception. Several of the selections address these issues and the underlying methodological assumptions of sociobiology that support them.

Finally, Part VI, "Ecos and Gaia," explores recent religious thought about the environmental crisis and the role of planet Earth as a symbol and emerging model for theological discourse. Central to this discussion is the question of anthropology: How are we to define our species so we are in the best positon to treat the natural environment in the most responsible way? Two major alternatives are examined. The exclusion model says that humankind has been given special status in partial transcendence of nature and special responsibility for the management of nature. The inclusion model sees us as integrated into the natural order with responsibilities to conform to the requirements of its living community. Process and feminist critiques are included in the discussion of this latter perspective. Similar ideas carry over into *Gaia*, the popular characterization of the planet as a living entity. Several selections describe this image and critically examine its adequacy.

The simplicity of the arrangement and the nature of the selections are intended to make *Religion and the Natural Sciences* available to as wide an audience as possible— including students from the sciences and technology, the professions, the humanities and liberal studies, and theology. The large number of shorter selections gives the instructor considerable leeway in choosing issues pertinent to his or her course. Some selections are relatively simple; others are more challenging. Several are taken from recent novels, short stories, and poetry in hopes of involving students in issues that could otherwise easily dissolve into an impenetrable, esoteric fog. Many selections are taken from well-known authors, others from authors of lesser fame. I used the standards of clarity of style and relevance of content to make these choices. They are not perfect, and anyone acquainted with the tremendous variety and range of published material in these fields will find some of their favorites included here and others missing. It is hoped the balance serves the greater good.

These remarks also serve to explain what should be obvious by now. The range of engagement is limited to the natural sciences and excludes the behavioral or social sciences (psychology, anthropology, sociology) simply because, unless the editor suffers from ency-clopedic delusions, a single volume cannot pretend to address all of these adequately.

I have restricted the coverage primarily to the Judeo-Christian tradition, because it would be impossible to do justice to both Western and Eastern thought within the scope of one book. More importantly, perhaps, is the fact the issues raised between science and religion have taken place primarily within the cultural tradition of the West, with its rich heritage of Jewish and Christian sources. In addition, feminism is represented through the inclusion of several selections that focus on feminist concerns and on con-cerns about environment, areas where discussion has been most animated.

I have included extensive introductions to each part that show how the various selections are related and that lay out the problems they intend to address. This effort at integration continues in the "Questions for Study" and "Questions for Reflection" that follow each selection. Extensive cross-references of major concepts are provided in the "Networkings." Finally, an annotated bibliography titled "Suggestions for Further Reading" is included to provide the interested reader with additional basic resources for each part. These pedagogical devices will prove useful for the identification of common topics in a wide variety of selections. The "Glossary" is intended to help clarify new terms and concepts. Technical terms have been held to a minimum—no mean task in science and theology.

I want to acknowledge those who have helped me negotiate each of the many steps along the way. They include my spouse Olga and my son Andrew, who have endured my absence at home on numerous weekends as I labored to complete these tasks; Barbara Dunevitz and Patricia De Mar for their efficient secretarial support and constant encouragement; and Jo-Anne Weaver, Tracy Napper, and Kay Kaylor of Harcourt Brace Jovanovich for their very professional guidance. In a real sense, I have been their apprentice in the basics of the art of assembling a resource text.

Finally, I should recognize the contributions of the reviewers. I was pleased with their praise, but I truly benefited from their criticisms and suggestions. Their careful reading of the manuscript resulted in a more accurate, intelligent, and relevant book. They are Paul Anderson, *Seattle Central Community College*; Robert Boyd, *Texas Christian University*; Rose Ann Christian, *Towson State University*; Carlo Filice, *SUNY Geneseo*; Patrick Green, *University of Alabama, Tuscaloosa*; George Mavrodes, *University of Michigan*; William Nietmann, *Northern Arizona University*; Karl Peters, *Rollins College*; William Reese, *SUNY, Albany*; John Sallstrom, *Georgia College*; Gerald Smith, *University of the South*; Robert Trundle, *Northern Kentucky University*; Rodney Vliet, *Pacific Christian College*; and Steve Voss, *San Jose State University*.

James E. Huchingson

CONTENTS

PART I

The Range of Engagement

THE BOLD SPIRIT OF OUR MODERN AND SECULAR AGE IS CAPTURED IN THE MASSIVE SOARING LINES OF THE SKYSCRAPER. THE CHURCH IS SHAPED ALONG TRADITIONAL LINES IN ACCORDANCE WITH THE JUDEO-CHRISTIAN VIEW OF THE WORLD. THIS JUXTAPOSITION SHOWS HOW RELIGION HAS MADE IMPORTANT CONTRIBUTIONS TO THE RISE OF SCIENCE AND TECHNOLOGY WHILE ALSO STANDING IN TENSION WITH THEM.

Science and religion are popularly known for their tempestuous relationship. The chronicle of the antagonistic encounter between these two authorities of considerable stature in Western culture includes accounts of the challenges of Copernicus, Kepler, and Galileo to the dogmatic views of the medieval church as well as the heated controversies generated by Darwin's theories on the origins and evolution of life.

This popular characterization of the warfare of science and religion is very incomplete. The readiness to do battle on the part of outspoken crusaders on both sides overshadows other less dramatic but equally significant ways that science and religion can and do relate. The selections in Part I explore this extended range of interaction.

The selections in the first section, "Surveying the Possibilities," examine a number of the most important ways science and religion are understood to relate. The second section, "Making Connections," focuses on a subset of these possibilities, those that emphasize similarity in method and perspective. The selections included in the last section of Part I, "Affirming Differences," are arguments for the claim that science and religion are distinct and independent enterprises posing no legitimate threat to one another.

In the first selection, "Ways of Relating Science and Religion," Ian Barbour presents a spectrum of possibilities for interaction as well as a rich description of each. These options, *Conflict, Independence, Dialogue,* and *Interaction,* provide an overture to the many complex issues we will encounter in the remainder of this book.

Barbour's discussion reveals that science and religion are concerned with far more than facts and their interpretation. On the intellectual side, they seek a total explanation of things, sometimes known as metaphysics, and employ rational and empirical methods for achieving this understanding. On the normative side, these two major human enterprises are concerned with values, loyalty to ideals and communities, and other essential, even ultimate, human needs. In the end, truth is bifocal; it satisfies both dimensions, the rational-empirical and the normative, in order to achieve depth of insight. The remaining selections in Part I focus on the interplay between the two enterprises in the science-religion encounter.

Mary Midgley's "Mixed Antitheses" elaborates further on these relationships but from a different approach. Midgley illustrates the complexity involved in comparing science and religion. She offers a useful index of contrasting terms, or *antitheses,* which are frequently employed by those who subscribe to the opinion that science is decidedly superior to religion. Midgley notes that many of these antitheses are in true opposition. They clearly show, rhetorically at least, that science is preferable to religion. Others, however, are ambiguous. Indeed, some terms pair up as complements rather than opposites, making it impossible to choose the column describing scientific attitudes over the one describing religious attitudes.

For example, if science is not "superstition" and "wish fulfillment" and religion is, then choosing science over religion is no contest. But why, without further justification, would one prefer "hard" over "soft," "progress" over "tradition," "quantity" over "quality," or "realism" over "reverence" even if the first of each of these pairs generally describes science and the second religion?

Harold Schilling offers a useful schematic for understanding similarities in the methods and aims of science and religion. Both enterprises, he suggests in the third selection, "The Threefold and Circular Nature of Science and Religion," engage in observation and the gathering of evidence (the first circle), theorizing or generalizing on this empirical material (second circle), and finally applying resulting theories or concepts skillfully to practical endeavors (third circle). In addition, the specific outcomes of activities in each circle are fed back to those of earlier circles for verification and reinforcement. Schilling sees that, while science and religion differ radically in content and specific goals, they share a general approach for achieving understanding and changing the world. This similarity in method makes dialogue possible and desirable.

In the fourth selection, "Radical Faith and Western Science," the theologian H. Richard Niebuhr examines the notion of authority in science by employing concepts taken from the study of religion. Religion has always struggled with faith in terms of its proper object, God, and other objects that compete for its loyalty. The lessons of this struggle can be profitably applied to other institutions, like science, which may not have been aware that the problem of faith is ever their problem. Niebuhr claims that science, like religion, can be successful only if it has an unyielding loyalty to its task and community.

Niebuhr uses concepts such as *henotheism* and "the closed society" to demonstrate the struggles shared by religious and scientific communities. The actions of a community are often determined by some absolute center of loyalty. Henotheism is unwavering dedication to this absolute center wherein all other values are submitted to its ends. In the modern world the state or nation (nationalism) and the absolute quest for reliable truth (scientism) are examples of henotheism. Henotheism is dangerous because it leaves no room for self-criticism. Dedication is singular: the reigning object or value takes on the character of an idol. Everything is submitted instrumentally to the fulfillment of that idol.

Niebuhr understands that science often works to demote the "little gods" of henotheism by its commitment to truth (however unpopular and harsh), its commitment to the universal, and its relentless criticism of claims to truth based on questionable motives and methods. For Niebuhr, any science that serves as the critic of potentially exclusive systems of thought is an ally of radical monotheism.

In the fifth selection, "On the Relationship of Theology and Science," the German theologian Hans Küng begins his discussion of the relationship between science and religion with a similar point. Neither enterprise should insist that it and it alone possesses an exclusive and correct understanding of reality such that, while it enjoys the privilege of criticizing other sources of knowledge in its terms, these other sources of knowledge cannot in turn criticize it. This "dogmatic interpretation" is another example of Niebuhr's closed society orientation. Science and theology have their proper tasks, says Küng. They may supplement or inform each other, but neither may declare itself to be the superior authority whose job is to certify the truth claims of the other.

Küng, however, does make an important distinction that favors theology. Neither science nor theology can claim to be a "comprehensive, systematic world view" that makes all other perspectives obsolete or superfluous. But theology is universal in that it is interested finally in ultimate questions of human identity and destiny, "an ultimate why and wherefore, whence and whither," which science cannot touch. This interest, Küng seems to say, makes the discoveries of science relevant to theology in ways that theology is not relevant to science.

The final two selections advocate the absolute distinction between the attitudes and interests of science and those of religion based primarily upon the separation between the objective and the existential, the observer and the participant.

In the sixth selection, "Theories in Science and Religion" taken from *Creationism on Trial,* Langdon Gilkey speaks from the dock in his role as an expert witness for the prosecution during the landmark Little Rock trial of 1980–1981. As a result of that trial, an Arkansas statute that permitted evolutionary theory and creationism to be taught side by side in public school science classes was declared unconstitutional in Federal court. He answers questions on the important differences between science and religion in the areas of theory and authority.

Gilkey's opinion is clearly that each approach is independent of the other. Science, he says, pursues an explanation of the events of the world in terms of the operations of fixed, blind, automatic laws of nature that govern existence. It does so by using a method that emphasizes the absolute objective detachment of the investigator. In sharp contrast, religion seeks explanations that have to do with questions of human meaning, questions of destiny and purpose and moral conduct, especially as these explanations end finally in the reality of God. The method of religion is personal and involved, that is, "existential."

The final selection, "I and You" from Buber's classic, *I and Thou,* focuses first on the utter distinction between two fundamental modes of relationship—I and Thou (or "You")—and I and It—and second on the illustration of these two applied to an encounter with a nonhuman object—a tree.

Buber's account is based on the ways we relate to others, both human and nonhuman. The I-It encounter "goes over the surface of things" to generate knowledge and control. The I-You "stands in relation" to the other in open, active, mutually vulnerable address, which is a far different experience. The two modes represent respectively the scientific and technological and the existential and potentially religious. Buber speaks of God as the "eternal You." The reader is left to decide how Buber understands the two approaches to come together in the contemplation of the tree.

Together, Gilkey and Buber argue eloquently for an approach to the interaction of science and religion that establishes an absolute sanctuary for each enterprise, a safe haven from possible attacks. Nevertheless, this insistence on independence also frustrates efforts to establish the integrity and wholeness of knowledge and experience, whether the object of attention is World War II or a tree in the forest.

Those who are of the opinion that science and religion share common admirable purposes, or at least are on speaking terms, affirm that each enterprise possesses a rational-factual and a normative or valuing component. Both contribute to a fully satisfying understanding of the world and our place in it. Others, however, are of a different opinion. They sharply demarcate the methods and goals of science and religion, assigning special functions to each so as to assure their mutual independence. On the one hand, the challenge is to avoid reducing one enterprise to the other—science to religion in the form of natural theology or religion to science as an antiquated approach to explaining natural phenomena. On the other hand, the challenge is to avoid complete compartmentalization by assigning matters of the heart to religion and matters of the head to science where each has nothing to contribute to the other.

SURVEYING THE POSSIBILITIES
WAYS OF RELATING SCIENCE AND RELIGION
IAN BARBOUR

Ian Barbour has a degree in theology from Yale University and a Ph.D. in physics from the University of Chicago. He teaches in both fields at Carlton College in Minnesota. Barbour has written extensively in the area of science and religion. *Issues in Science and Religion* is his best-known book and a classic in its own right. This selection is taken from his most recent book, *Religion in an Age of Science,* volume one of the distinguished Gifford lectures that he delivered in 1989.

The first major challenge to religion in an age of science is the success of the methods of science. Science seems to provide the only reliable path to knowledge. Many people view science as objective, universal, rational, and based on solid observational evidence. Religion, by contrast, seems to be subjective, parochial, emotional, and based on traditions or authorities that disagree with each other. . . .

In order to give a systematic overview of the main options today, I have grouped them . . . under four headings: *Conflict, Independence, Dialogue,* and *Integration.* Particular authors may not fall neatly under any one heading; a person may agree with adherents of a given position on some issues but not on others. . . . After surveying these four broad patterns, I will suggest reasons for supporting *Dialogue* and, with some qualifications, certain versions of *Integration.*

Any view of the relationship of science and religion reflects philosophical assumptions. Our discussion must therefore draw from three disciplines, not just two: *science* (the empirical study of the order of nature), *theology* (critical reflection on the life and thought of the religious community), and *philosophy,* especially epistemology (analysis of the characteristics of inquiry and knowledge) and metaphysics (analysis of the most general characteristics of reality). Theology deals primarily with religious beliefs, which must always be seen against the wider background of religious traditions that includes formative scriptures, communal rituals, individual experiences, and ethical norms. I will be particularly concerned with the epistemological assumptions of recent Western authors writing about the relationship between science and religious beliefs.

CONFLICT

Scientific materialism is at the opposite end of the theological spectrum from biblical literalism. But they share several characteristics that lead me to discuss them together. Both believe that there are serious conflicts between contemporary science and classical religious beliefs. Both seek knowledge with a sure foundation—that of logic and sense data, in the one case, that of infallible scripture, in the other. They both claim that science and theology make rival literal statements about the same domain, the history of nature, so that one must choose between them.

I will suggest that each represents a misuse of science. Both positions fail to observe the proper boundaries of science. The scientific materialist starts from science but ends by making broad philosophical claims. The biblical literalist moves from theology to make claims about scientific matters. In both schools of thought, the differences between the two disciplines are not adequately respected.

In a fight between a boa constrictor and a wart-hog, the victor, whichever it is, swallows the vanquished. In scientific materialism, science swallows religion. In biblical literalism, religion swallows science. The fight can be avoided if they occupy separate territories or if, as I will suggest, they each pursue more appropriate diets.[1]

Scientific Materialism

Scientific materialism makes two assertions: (1) the scientific method is the only reliable path to knowledge; (2) matter (or matter and energy) is the fundamental reality in the universe.

The first is an *epistemological* assertion about the characteristics of inquiry and knowledge. The second is a *metaphysical* or ontological assertion about the characteristics of reality. The two assertions are linked by the assumption that only the entities and causes with which science deals are real; only science can progressively disclose the nature of the real.

In addition, many forms of materialism express *reductionism*. Epistemological reductionism claims that the laws and theories of all the sciences are in principle reducible to the laws of physics and chemistry. Metaphysical reductionism claims that the component parts of any system constitute its most fundamental reality. The materialist believes that all phenomena will eventually be explained in terms of the actions of material components, which are the only effective causes in the world. Analysis of the parts of any system has, of course, been immensely useful in science, but I will suggest that the study of higher organizational levels in larger wholes is also valuable. Evolutionary naturalism sometimes avoids reductionism and holds that distinctive phenomena have emerged at higher levels of organization, but it shares the conviction that the scientific method is the only acceptable mode of inquiry.

Let us consider the assertion that the scientific method is the only reliable form of understanding. Science starts from reproducible public data. Theories are formulated and their implications are tested against experimental observations. Additional criteria of coherence, comprehensiveness, and fruitfulness influence choice among theories. Religious beliefs are not acceptable, in this view, because religion lacks such public data, such experimental testing, and such criteria of evaluation. Science alone is objective, open-minded, universal, cumulative, and progressive. Religious traditions, by contrast, are said to be subjective, closed-minded, parochial, uncritical, and resistant to change. We will see that historians and philosophers of science have questioned this idealized portrayal of science, but many scientists accept it and think it undermines the credibility of religious beliefs.

Among philosophers, *logical positivism* from the 1920s to the 1940s asserted that scientific discourse provides the norm for all meaningful language. It was said that the only meaningful statements (apart from abstract logical relations) are empirical propositions verifiable by sense data. Statements in ethics, metaphysics, and religion were said to be neither true nor false, but meaningless pseudo-statements, expressions of emotion or preference devoid of cognitive significance. Whole areas of human language and experience were thus eliminated from serious discussion because they were not subject to the verification that science was said to provide. But critics replied that sense data do not provide an indubitable starting point in science, for they are already conceptually organized and theory-laden. The interaction of observation and theory is more complex than the positivists had assumed. Moreover, the positivists had dismissed metaphysical questions but had often assumed a materialist metaphysics. Since Wittgenstein's later writings, the linguistic analysts argued that science cannot be the norm for all meaningful discourse because language has many differing uses and functions.

Most of Carl Sagan's TV series and book, *Cosmos,* is devoted to a fascinating presentation of the discoveries of modern astronomy, but at intervals he interjects his own philosophical commentary, for example, "The Cosmos is all that is or ever was or ever will be."[2] He says that the universe is eternal or else its source is simply unknowable. Sagan attacks Christian ideas of God at a number of points, arguing that mystical and authoritarian claims threaten the ultimacy of the scientific method, which he says is "universally applicable." Nature (which he capitalizes) replaces God as the object of reverence. He expresses great awe at the beauty, vastness, and interrelatedness of the cosmos. Sitting at the instrument panel from which he shows us the wonders of the universe, he is a new kind of high priest, not only revealing the mysteries to us but telling us how we should live. We can indeed admire Sagan's great ethical sensitivity and his deep concern for nuclear survival and environmental preservation. But perhaps we should question his unlimited confidence in the scientific method, on which he says we should rely to bring in the age of peace and justice.

The success of molecular biology in accounting for many of the basic mechanisms of genetics and biological activity has often been taken as a vindication of the reductionist approach. Thus Francis Crick, codiscoverer of the structure of DNA, wrote, "The ultimate aim of the modern movement in biology is in fact to explain *all* biology in terms of physics and chemistry."[3] I will argue . . . that there is in the biological world a hierarchy of levels of organization. This would lead us to accept the importance of DNA and the role of molecular structures in all living phenomena, but it would also allow us to recognize the distinctiveness of higher-level activities and their influence on molecular components.

Jacques Monod's *Chance and Necessity* gives a lucid account of molecular biology, interspersed with a defense of scientific materialism. He claims that biology has proved that there is no purpose in nature. "Man knows at last that he is alone in the universe's unfeeling immensity, out of which he emerged only by chance."[4] "Chance alone is the source of all novelty, all creation, in the biosphere." Chance is "blind" and "absolute" because random mutations are unrelated to the needs of the organism; the causes of individual variations are completely independent of the environmental forces of natural selection. Monod espouses a thoroughgoing reductionism: "Anything can be reduced to simple, obvious mechanical interactions. The cell is a machine. The animal is a machine. Man is a machine."[5] Consciousness is an epiphenomenon that will eventually be explained biochemically.

Monod asserts that human behavior is genetically determined; he says little about the role of language, thought, or culture in human life. Value judgments are completely subjective and arbitrary. Humanity alone is the creator of values; the assumption of almost all previous philosophies that values are grounded in the nature of reality is undermined by science. But Monod urges us to make the free axiomatic choice that knowledge itself will be our supreme value. He advocates "an ethics of knowledge," but he does not show what this might entail apart from the support of science.

I submit that Monod's reductionism is inadequate as an account of purposive behavior and consciousness in animals and human beings. There are alternative interpretations in which the interaction of chance and law is seen to be more complex than Monod's portrayal and not incompatible with some forms of theism. The biochemist and theologian Arthur Peacocke gives chance a positive role in the exploration of potentialities inherent in the created order, which would be consistent with the idea of divine purpose (though not with the idea of a precise predetermined plan).[6] At the moment, however, we are interested in Monod's attempt to rely exclusively on the methods of science (plus an arbitrary choice of ethical axioms). He says that science proves that there is no purpose in the cosmos. Surely it would be more accurate to say that science does not deal with divine purpose; it is not a fruitful concept in the development of scientific theories.

As a last example, consider the explicit defense of scientific materialism by the sociobiologist Edward O. Wilson. His writings trace the genetic and evolutionary origins of social behavior in insects, animals, and humans. He asks how self-sacrificial behavior could arise and persist among social insects, such as ants, if their reproductive ability is thereby sacrificed. Wilson shows that such "altruistic" behavior enhances the survival of close relatives with similar genes (in an ant colony, for example); selective pressures would encourage such self-sacrifice. He believes that all human behavior can be reduced to and explained by its biological origins and present genetic structure. "It may not be too much to say that sociology and the other social sciences, as well as the humanities, are the last branches of biology to be included in the Modern Synthesis."[7] The mind will be explained as "an epiphenomenon of the neural machinery of the brain."

Wilson holds that religious practices were a useful survival mechanism in humanity's earlier history because they contributed to group cohesion. But he says that the power of religion will be gone forever when religion is explained as a product of evolution; it will be replaced by a philosophy of "scientific materialism."[8] (If he were consistent, would not Wilson have to say that the power of science will also be undermined when it is explained as a product of evolution? Do evolutionary origins really have anything to do with the legitimacy of either field?) He maintains that morality is the result of deep impulses encoded in the genes and that "the only demonstrable function of morality is to keep the genes intact."

Wilson's writing has received criticism from several quarters. For example, anthropologists have replied that most systems of human kinship are not organized in accord with coefficients of genetic similarity and that Wilson does not even consider cultural explanations for human behavior.[9] In the present context, I would prefer to say that he has described an important area of biology suggesting some of the constraints within which human behavior occurs, but he has overgeneralized and extended it as an all-encompassing explanation, leaving no room for the causal efficacy of other facets of human life and experience. . . .

Each of these authors seems to have assumed that there is only one acceptable type of explanation, so that explanation in terms of astronomical origins or biochemical mechanisms or evolutionary development excludes any other kind of explanation. Particular scientific concepts have been extended and extrapolated beyond their scientific use; they have been inflated into comprehensive naturalistic philosophies. Scientific concepts and theories have been taken to provide an exhaustive description of reality, and the abstractive and selective character of science has been ignored. The philosopher Alfred North Whitehead calls this "the fallacy of misplaced concreteness." It can also be described as "making a metaphysics out of a method." But because scientific materialism starts from scientific ideas, it carries considerable influence in an age that respects science.

Biblical Literalism

A variety of views of scripture and its relation to science have appeared throughout the history of Christian thought. Augustine held that when there appears to be a conflict between demonstrated scientific knowledge and a literal reading of the Bible, the latter should be interpreted metaphorically, as in the case of the first chapter of Genesis. Scripture is not concerned about "the form and shape of the heavens"; the Holy Spirit "did not wish to teach men things of no relevance to their salvation."[10] Medieval writers acknowledged diverse literary forms and levels of truth in scripture, and they gave figurative and allegorical interpretations to many problematic passages. Luther and the Anglicans continued this tradition, though some later Lutherans and Calvinists were more literalistic.

Biblical interpretation did play a part in the condemnation of Galileo. He himself held that God is revealed in both "the book of nature" and "the book of scripture"; the two books could not conflict, he said, since they both came from God. He maintained that writers of the Bible were only interested in matters essential to our salvation, and in their writing they had to "accommodate themselves to the capacity of the common people" and the mode of speech of the times. But Galileo's theories did conflict with a literal interpretation of some scriptural passages, and they called into question the Aristotelian system that the church had adopted in the Thomistic synthesis. At the 350th anniversary of the publication of the *Dialogues,* Pope John Paul II said that since then there has been "a more accurate appreciation of the methods proper to the different orders of knowledge." The church, he said, "is made up of individuals who are limited and who are closely bound up with the culture of the time they live in. . . . It is only through humble and assiduous study that she learns to dissociate the essentials of faith from the scientific systems of a given age, especially when a culturally influenced reading of the Bible seemed to be linked to an obligatory cosmology."[11] In 1984, a Vatican commission acknowledged that "church officials had erred in condemning Galileo."[12]

In Darwin's day, evolution was taken mainly as a challenge to design in nature and as a challenge to human dignity (assuming that no sharp line separates human and animal forms), but it was also taken by some groups as a challenge to scripture. Some defended biblical inerrancy and totally rejected evolution. Yet most traditionalist theologians reluctantly accepted the idea of evolution—though sometimes only after making an exception for humanity, arguing that the soul is inaccessible to scientific investigation. Liberal theologians had already accepted the historical analysis of biblical texts ("higher criticism"), which traced the influence of historical contexts and cultural assumptions on biblical writings. They saw evolution as consistent with their optimistic view of historical progress, and they spoke of evolution as God's way of creating.

In the twentieth century, the Roman Catholic church and most of the mainline Protestant denominations have held that scripture is the human witness to the primary revelation, which occurred in the lives of the prophets and the life and person of Christ. Many traditionalists and evangelicals insist on the centrality of Christ without insisting on the infallibility of a literal interpretation of the Bible. But smaller fundamentalist groups and a large portion of some major denominations in the United States, such as the Southern Baptists, have maintained that scripture is inerrant throughout. The 1970s and 1980s have seen a growth of fundamentalist membership and political power. For many members of "the New Right" and "the Moral Majority," the Bible provides not only certainty in a time of rapid change, but a basis for the defense of traditional values in a time of moral disintegration (sexual permissiveness, drug use, increasing crime rates, and so forth).

In the Scopes trial in 1925, it was argued that the teaching of evolution in the schools should be forbidden because it is contrary to scripture. More recently, a new argument called "scientific creationism" or "creation science" has asserted that there is scientific evidence for the creation of the world within the last few thousand years. The law that was passed by the Arkansas legislature in 1981 required that "creationist theory" be given equal time with evolutional theory in high school biology texts and classes. The law specified that creationism should be presented purely as scientific theory, with no reference to God or the Bible.

In 1982, the U.S. District Court overturned the Arkansas law, primarily because it favored a particular religious view, violating the constitutional separation of church and state. Although the bill itself made no explicit reference to the Bible, it used many phrases and ideas taken from Genesis. The writings of the leaders of the creationist movement had made clear their religious purposes.[13] Many of the witnesses against the bill were theologians or church leaders who objected to its theological assumptions.[14]

The court also ruled that "creation science" is not legitimate science. It concluded that the scientific community, not the legislature or the courts, should decide the status of scientific theories. It was shown that proponents of creation science had not even submitted papers to scientific journals, much less had them published. At the trial, scientific witnesses showed that a long evolutionary history is central in almost all fields of science, including astronomy, geology, paleontology, and biochemistry, as well as most branches of biology. They also replied to the purported scientific evidence cited by creationists. Claims of geological evidence for a universal flood and for the absence of fossils of transitional forms between species were shown to be dubious.[15] In 1987, the U.S. Supreme Court struck down a Louisiana creationism law; it said the law would have restricted academic freedom and supported a particular religious viewpoint.[16]

"Creation science" is a threat to both religious and scientific freedom. It is understandable that the search for certainty in a time of moral confusion and rapid cultural change has encouraged the growth of biblical literalism. But when absolutist positions lead to intolerance and attempts to impose particular religious views on others in a pluralistic society, we must object in the name of religious freedom. Some of the same forces of rapid cultural change have contributed to the revival of Islamic fundamentalism and the enforcement of orthodoxy in Iran and elsewhere.

We can also see the danger to science when proponents of ideological positions try to use the power of the state to reshape science, whether it be in Nazi Germany, Stalinist Russia, Khomeini's Iran, or creationists in the United States. To be sure, scientists are inescapably influenced by cultural assumptions and metaphysical presuppositions—as well as by economic forces, which in large measure determine the direction of scientific development. The scientific community is never completely autonomous or isolated from its social context, yet it must be protected from political pressures that would dictate scientific conclusions. Science teachers must be free to draw from this larger scientific community in their teaching.

Creationists have raised valid objections when evolutionary naturalists have promoted atheistic philosophies as if they were part of science. Both sides err in assuming that evolutionary theory is inherently atheistic, and they thereby perpetuate the false dilemma of having to choose between science and religion. The whole controversy reflects the shortcomings of fragmented and specialized higher education. The training of scientists seldom includes any exposure to the history and philosophy of science or any reflection on the relation of science to society, to ethics, or to religious thought. On the other hand, the clergy has little familiarity with science and is hesitant to discuss controversial subjects in the pulpit. The remainder of this chapter explores alternatives to these two extremes of scientific materialism and biblical literalism.

INDEPENDENCE

One way to avoid conflicts between science and religion is to view the two enterprises as totally independent and autonomous. Each has its own distinctive domain and its characteristic methods that can be justified on its own terms. Proponents of this view say there are two jurisdictions and each party must keep off the other's turf. Each must tend to its own business and not meddle in the affairs of the other. Each mode of inquiry is selective and has its limitations. This separation into watertight compartments is motivated, not simply by the desire to avoid unnecessary conflicts, but also by the desire to be faithful to the distinctive character of each area of life and thought. We will look first at contrasting methods and domains in science and religion. Then we will consider their differing languages and functions.

Contrasting Methods

Many writers in the history of Western thought have elaborated contrasts between religious and scientific knowledge. In the Middle Ages, the contrast was between revealed truth and human discovery. It was said that God can be fully known only as revealed through scripture and tradition. The structures of nature, on the other hand, can be known by unaided human reason and observation. There was, however, some middle ground in "natural theology"; it was held that the existence (though not all the attributes) of God can be demonstrated by rational arguments, including the argument from the evidence of design in nature.

This epistemological dichotomy was supported by the metaphysical dualism of spirit and matter, or soul and body. But this dualism was mitigated insofar as the spiritual realm permeated the material realm. While theologians emphasized God's transcendence, most of them also referred to divine immanence, and the Holy Spirit was said to work in nature as well as in human life and history. St. Thomas held that God intervenes miraculously at particular times and also continually sustains the natural order. God as primary cause works through the secondary causes that science studies, but these two kinds of cause are on completely different levels.

In the twentieth century, Protestant *neo-orthodoxy* sought to recover the Reformation emphasis on the centrality of Christ and the primacy of revelation, while fully accepting the results of modern biblical scholarship and scientific research. (I will refer to him as Christ rather than Jesus, since we are dealing with a historical figure as understood within a tradition of theological interpretation.) According to Karl Barth and his followers, God can be known only as revealed in Christ and acknowledged in faith. God is the transcendent, the wholly other, unknowable except as self-disclosed. Natural theology is suspect because it relies on human reason. Religious faith depends entirely on divine initiative, not on human discovery of the kind occurring in science. The sphere of God's action is history, not nature. Scientists are free to carry out their work without interference from theology, and vice versa, since their methods and their subject matter are totally dissimilar. Here, then, is a clear contrast. Science is based on human observation and reason, while theology is based on divine revelation.[17]

In this view, the Bible must be taken seriously but not literally. Scripture is not itself revelation; it is a fallible human record witnessing to revelatory events. The locus of divine activity was not the dictation of a text, but the lives of persons and communities: Israel, the prophets, the person of Christ, and those in the early church who responded to him. The biblical writings reflect diverse interpretations of these events; we must acknowledge the human limitations of their authors and the cultural influences on their thought. Their opinions concerning scientific questions reflect the prescientific speculations of ancient times. We should read the opening chapters of Genesis as a symbolic portrayal of the basic relation of humanity and the world to God, a message about human creatureliness and the goodness of the natural order. These religious meanings can be separated from the ancient cosmology in which they were expressed.

Another movement advocating a sharp separation of the spheres of science and religion is *existentialism*. Here the contrast is between the realm of personal selfhood and the realm of impersonal objects. The former is known only through subjective involvement; the latter is known in the objective detachment typical of the scientist. Common to all existentialists—whether atheistic or theistic—is the conviction that we can know authentic human existence only by being personally involved as unique individuals making free decisions. The meaning of life is found only in commitment and action, never in the spectatorial, rationalistic attitude of the scientist searching for abstract general concepts and universal laws.

Religious existentialists say that God is encountered in the immediacy and personal participation of an I-Thou relationship, not in the detached analysis and manipulative control characterizing the I-It relationships of science. The theologian Rudolf Bultmann acknowledges that the Bible often uses objective language in speaking of God's acts, but he proposes that we can retain the original experiential meaning of such passages by translating them into the language of human self-understanding, the language of hopes and fears, choices and decisions, and new possibilities for our lives. Theological formulations must be statements about the transformation of human life by a new understanding of personal existence. Such affirmations have no connection with scientific theories about external events in the impersonal order of a law-abiding world.[18]

Langdon Gilkey, in his earlier writing and in his testimony at the Arkansas trial, expresses many of these themes. He makes the following distinctions: (1) Science seeks to explain objective, public, repeatable data. Religion asks about the existence of order and beauty in the world and the experiences of our inner life (such as guilt, anxiety, and meaninglessness, on the one hand, and forgiveness, trust, and wholeness, on the other). (2) Science asks objective how questions. Religion asks personal why questions about meaning and purpose and about our ultimate origin and destiny. (3) The basis of authority in science is logical coherence and experimental adequacy. The final authority in religion is God and revelation, understood through persons to whom enlightenment and insight were given, and validated in our own experience. (4) Science makes quantitative predictions that can be tested experimentally. Religion must use symbolic and analogical language because God is transcendent.[19]

In the context of the trial, it was an effective strategy to insist that science and religion ask quite different questions and use quite different methods. It provided methodological grounds for criticizing the attempts of biblical literalists to derive scientific conclusions from scripture. More specifically, Gilkey argued that the doctrine of creation is not a literal statement about the history of nature but a symbolic assertion that the world is good and orderly and dependent on God in every moment of time—a religious assertion essentially independent of both prescientific biblical cosmology and modern scientific cosmology.

In some of his other writings, Gilkey has developed themes that we will consider under the heading of Dialogue. He says there is a "dimension of ultimacy" in the scientist's passion to know, commitment to the search for truth, and faith in the rationality and uniformity of nature. For the scientist, these constitute what Tillich called an "ultimate concern." But Gilkey states there are dangers when science is extended to a total naturalistic philosophy or when science and technology are ascribed a redemptive and saving power, as occurs in the liberal myth of progress through science. Both science and religion can be demonic when they are used in the service of particular ideologies and when the ambiguity of human nature is ignored.[20]

Thomas Torrance has developed further some of the distinctions in neo-orthodoxy. Theology is unique, he says, because its subject matter is God. Theology is "a dogmatic or positive and independent science operating in accordance with the inner law of its own being, developing its distinctive modes of inquiry and its essential forms of thought under the determination of its given subject-matter."[21] God infinitely transcends all creaturely reality and "can be known only as he has revealed himself," especially in the person of Christ. We can only respond in fidelity to what has been given to us, allowing our thinking to be determined by the given. In science, reason and experiment can disclose the structure of the real but contingent world. Torrance particularly appreciates Einstein's realist interpretation of quantum physics, and he defends realist epistemology in both science and theology.

Differing Languages

An even more effective way of separating science and religion is to interpret them as languages that are unrelated because their functions are totally different. The logical positivists had taken scientific statements as the norm for all discourse and had dismissed as meaningless any statement not subject to empirical verification. The later *linguistic analysts,* in response, insisted that differing types of language serve differing functions not reducible to each other. Each "language game" (as Wittgenstein and his successors called it) is distinguished by the way it is used in a social context. Science and religion do totally different jobs, and neither should be judged by the standards of the other. *Scientific language* is used primarily for prediction and control. A theory is a useful tool for summarizing data, correlating regularities in observable phenomena, and producing technological applications. Science asks carefully delimited questions about natural phenomena. We must not expect it to do jobs for which it was not intended, such as providing an overall world view, a philosophy of life, or a set of ethical norms. Scientists are no wiser than anyone else when they step out of their laboratories and speculate beyond strictly scientific work.[22]

The distinctive function of *religious language,* according to the linguistic analysts, is to recommend a way of life, to elicit a set of attitudes, and to encourage allegiance to particular moral principles. Much of religious language is connected with ritual and practice in the worshiping community. It may also express and lead to personal religious experience. One of the great strengths of the linguistic movement is that it does not concentrate on religious beliefs as abstract systems of thought but looks at the way religious language is actually used in the lives of individuals and communities. Linguistic analysts draw on empirical studies of religion by sociologists, anthropologists, and psychologists, as well as the literature produced within religious traditions.

Some scholars have studied diverse cultures and concluded that religious traditions are *ways of life* that are primarily practical and normative. Stories, rituals, and religious practices bind individuals in communities of shared memories, assumptions, and strategies for living. Other scholars claim that religion's primary aim is the transformation of the person. Religious literature speaks extensively of experiences of liberation from guilt through forgiveness, trust overcoming anxiety, or the transition from brokenness to wholeness. Eastern traditions talk about liberation from bondage to suffering and self-centeredness in the experiences of peace, unity, and enlightenment.[23] These are obviously activities and experiences having little to do with science.

George Lindbeck compares the linguistic view with two other views of religious doctrines:

1. In the *propositional* view, doctrines are truth claims about objective realities. "Christianity, as traditionally interpreted, claims to be true, universally valid, and supernaturally revealed."[24] If doctrines are true or false, and rival doctrines are mutually exclusive, there can be only one true faith. (Neo-orthodoxy holds that doctrines are derived from the human interpretation of revelatory events, but it, too, understands doctrines as true or false propositions.) The propositional view is a form of realism, for it believes that we can make statements about reality as it exists in itself.

2. In the *expressive* view, doctrines are symbols of inner experiences. Liberal theology has held that the experience of the holy is found in all religions. Since there can be diverse symbolizations of the same core experience, adherents of different traditions can learn from each other. This view tends to stress the private and individual side of religion, with less emphasis on communal aspects. If doctrines are interpretations of religious experience, they are not likely to conflict with scientific theories about nature.

3. In the *linguistic* view, which Lindbeck himself advocates, doctrines are rules of discourse correlated with individual and communal forms of life. Religions are guides to living; they are "ways of life which are learned by practicing them." Lindbeck argues that individual experience cannot be our starting point because it is already shaped by prevailing conceptual and linguistic frameworks. Religious stories and rituals are formative of our self-understanding. This approach allows us to accept the particularity of each religious tradition without making exclusive or universal claims for it. This is a nonrealist position. It does not assume a universal truth or an underlying universal experience; it sees each cultural system as self-contained. By minimizing the role of beliefs and truth claims, the linguistic view avoids conflicts between science and theology that can occur in the propositional view, yet it escapes the individualism and subjectivity of the expressive view.

The three movements we have been considering—neo-orthodoxy, existentialism, and linguistic analysis—all understand religion and science to be independent and autonomous forms of life and thought. Each discipline is selective and has its limitations. Every discipline abstracts from the totality of experience those features in which it is interested. The astronomer Arthur Eddington once told a delightful parable about a man studying deep-sea life using a net on a three-inch mesh. After bringing up repeated samples, the man concluded that there are no deep-sea fish less than three inches in length. Our methods of fishing, Eddington suggests, determine what we can catch. If science is selective, it cannot claim that its picture of reality is complete.[25]

The independence of science and religion represents a good starting point or first approximation. It preserves the distinctive character of each enterprise, and it is a useful strategy for responding to both types of conflict mentioned earlier. Religion does indeed have its characteristic methods, questions, attitudes, functions, and experiences, which are distinct from those of science. But there are serious difficulties in each of these proposals.

As I see it, *neo-orthodoxy* rightly stresses the centrality of Christ and the prominence of scripture in the Christian tradition. It is more modest in its claims than biblical literalism, since it acknowledges the role of human interpretation in scripture and doctrine. But in most versions it, too, holds that revelation and salvation occur only through Christ, which seems to me problematic in a pluralistic world. Most neo-orthodox authors emphasize divine transcendence and give short shrift to immanence. The gulf between God and the world is decisively bridged only in the incarnation. While Barth and his followers do indeed elaborate a doctrine of creation, their main concern is with the doctrine of redemption. Nature tends to be treated as the unredeemed setting for human redemption, though it may participate in the eschatological fulfillment at the end of time.

Existentialism rightly puts personal commitment at the center of religious faith, but it ends by privatizing and interiorizing religion to the neglect of its communal aspects. If God acts exclusively in the realm of selfhood, not in the realm of nature, the natural order is devoid of religious significance, except as the impersonal stage for the drama of personal existence. This anthropocentric framework, concentrating on humanity alone, offers little protection against the modern exploitation of nature as a collection of impersonal objects. If religion deals with God and the self, and science deals with nature, who can say anything about the relationship between God and nature or between the self and nature? To be sure, religion is concerned with the meaning of personal life, but this cannot be divorced from belief in a meaningful cosmos. I will also suggest that existentialism exaggerates the contrast between an impersonal, objective stance in science and the personal involvement essential to religion. Personal judgment does enter the work of the scientist, and rational reflection is an important part of religious inquiry.

Finally, *linguistic analysis* has helped us to see the diversity of functions of religious language. Religion is indeed a way of life and not simply a set of ideas and beliefs. But the religious practice of a community, including worship and ethics, presupposes distinctive beliefs. Against instrumentalism, which sees both scientific theories and religious beliefs as human constructs useful for specific human purposes, I advocate a critical realism holding that both communities make cognitive claims about realities beyond the human world. We cannot remain content with a plurality of unrelated languages if they are languages about the same world. If we seek a coherent interpretation of all experience, we cannot avoid the search for a unified world view.

If science and religion were totally independent, the possibility of conflict would be avoided, but the possibility of constructive dialogue and mutual enrichment would also be ruled out. We do not experience life as neatly divided into separate compartments; we experience it in wholeness and interconnectedness before we develop particular disciplines to study different aspects of it. There are also biblical grounds for the conviction that God is Lord of our total lives and of nature, rather than of a separate "religious" sphere. The articulation of a theology of nature that will encourage a strong environmental concern is also a critical task today. I will argue that none of the options considered above is adequate to that task.

DIALOGUE

In moving beyond the Independence thesis, this section outlines some indirect interactions between science and religion involving boundary questions and methods of the two fields. The fourth section, called Integration, will be devoted to more direct relationships when scientific theories influence religious beliefs, or when they both contribute to the formulation of a coherent world view or a systematic metaphysics.

Boundary Questions

One type of boundary question refers to the general presuppositions of the whole scientific enterprise. Historians have wondered why modern science arose in the Judeo-Christian West among all world cultures. A good case can be made that the doctrine of creation helped to set the stage for scientific activity. Both Greek and biblical thought asserted that the world is orderly and intelligible. But the Greeks held that this order is necessary and therefore one can deduce its structure from first principles. It is not surprising that they were stronger in mathematics and logic than in experimental science. Only biblical thought held that the world's order is contingent rather than necessary. If God created both form and matter, the world did not have to be as it is, and one has to observe it to discover the details of its order. Moreover, while nature is real and good, it is not itself divine, as many ancient cultures held. Humans are therefore permitted to experiment on nature.[26] The "desacralization" of nature encouraged scientific study, though it also—along with other economic and cultural forces—contributed to subsequent environmental destruction and the exploitation of nature.

We must be careful not to overstate the case for the role of Christian thought in the rise of science. Arab science made significant advances in the Middle Ages, while science in the West was often hampered by an otherworldly emphasis (although important practical technologies were developed, especially in some of the monastic orders). When modern science did develop in Europe, it was aided by the humanistic interests of the Renaissance; the growth of crafts, trade, and commerce; and new patterns of leisure and education. Yet it does appear that the idea of creation gave a religious legitimacy to scientific inquiry. Newton and many of his contemporaries believed that in their work they were "thinking God's thoughts after him." Moreover, the Calvinist "Protestant ethic" seems to have particularly supported science. In the Royal Society, the earliest institution for the advancement of science, seven out of ten members were Puritans, and many were clergy.

I believe the case for the historical contribution of Christianity to the rise of science is convincing. But once science was well established, its own success was sufficient justification for many scientists, without the need for religious legitimation. Theistic beliefs are clearly not explicit presuppositions of science, since many atheistic or agnostic scientists do first-rate work without them. One can simply accept the contingency and intelligibility of nature as givens and devote one's efforts to investigating the detailed structure of its order. Yet if one does raise wider questions, one is perhaps more open to religious answers. For many scientists, exposure to the order of the universe, as well as its beauty and complexity, is an occasion of wonder and reverence.

On the contemporary scene, we have seen that Torrance maintains the characteristic neo-orthodox distinction between human discovery and divine revelation. But in recent writings he says that at its boundaries science raises religious questions that it cannot answer. In pressing back to the earliest history of the cosmos, astronomy forces us to ask why those particular initial conditions were present. Science shows us an order that is both rational and contingent (that is, its laws and initial conditions were not necessary). It is the combination of contingency and intelligibility that prompts us to search for new and unexpected forms of rational order. The theologian can reply that God is the creative ground and reason for the contingent but rational unitary order of the universe. "Correlation with that rationality in God goes far to account for the mysterious and baffling nature of the intelligibility inherent in the universe, and explains the profound sense of religious awe it calls forth from us and which, as Einstein insisted, is the mainspring of science."[27]

The theologian Wolfhart Pannenberg has explored methodological issues in some detail. He accepts Karl Popper's contention that the scientist proposes testable hypotheses and then attempts to refute them experimentally. Pannenberg claims that the theologian can also use universal rational criteria in critically examining religious beliefs. However, the parallels eventually break down, he says, because theology is the study of reality as a whole; reality is an unfinished process whose future we can only anticipate, since it does not yet exist. Moreover, theology is interested in unique and unpredictable historical events. Here the theologian tries to answer another kind of limit question with which the scientific method cannot deal, a limit not of initial conditions or ontological foundations but of openness toward the future.[28]

Three Roman Catholic authors, Ernan McMullin, Karl Rahner, and David Tracy, seem to me to be advocates of Dialogue, though with varying emphases. McMullin starts with a sharp distinction between religious and scientific statements that resembles the Independence position. God as primary cause acts through the secondary causes studied by science, but these are on radically different levels within different orders of explanation. On its own level, the scientific account is complete and without gaps. McMullin is critical of all attempts to derive arguments for God from phenomena unexplained by science; he is dubious about arguments from design or from the directionality of evolution. Gaps in the scientific account are usually closed by the advance of science, and in any case they would only point to a cosmic force and not to the transcendent biblical God. God sustains the whole natural sequence and "is responsible equally and uniformly for all events." The theologian has no stake in particular scientific theories, including astrophysical theories about the early cosmos.[29]

Some theologians have taken the accumulating evidence for the Big Bang theory as corroboration of the biblical view that the universe had a beginning in time—which would be a welcome change after the conflicts of the past. McMullin, however, maintains that the doctrine of creation is not an explanation of cosmological beginnings at all, but an assertion of the world's absolute dependence on God in every moment. The intent of Genesis was not to specify that there was a first moment in time. Moreover, the Big Bang theory does not prove that there was a beginning in time, since the current expansion could be one phase of an oscillating or cyclic universe. He concludes, "What one cannot say is, first, that the Christian doctrine of creation 'supports' the Big Bang model, or, second, that the Big Bang model 'supports' the Christian doctrine of creation."[30] But he says that for God to choose the initial conditions and laws of the universe would not involve any gaps or violations of the sequence of natural causes. McMullin denies that there is any strong logical connection between scientific and religious assertions, but he does endorse the search for a looser kind of compatibility. The aim should be "consonance but not direct implication," which implies that in the end the two sets of assertions are not, after all, totally independent:

> The Christian cannot separate his science from his theology as though they were in principle incapable of interrelation. On the other hand, he has learned to distrust the simpler pathways from one to the other. He has to aim at some sort of coherence of world-view, a coherence to which science and theology, and indeed many other sorts of human construction like history, politics, and literature, must contribute. He may, indeed *must,* strive to make his theology and his cosmology consonant in the contributions they make to this world-view. But this consonance (as history shows) is a tentative relation, constantly under scrutiny, in constant slight shift.[31]

For Karl Rahner, the methods and the content of science and theology are independent, but there are important points of contact and correlations to be explored. God is known primarily through scripture and tradition, but he is dimly and implicitly known by all persons as the infinite horizon within which every finite object is apprehended. Rahner extends Kant's transcendental method by analyzing the conditions that make knowledge possible in a neo-Thomist framework. We know by abstracting form from matter; in the mind's pure desire to know there is a drive beyond every limited object toward the Absolute. Authentic human experience of love and honesty are experiences of grace; Rahner affirms the implicit faith of the "anonymous Christian" who does not explicitly acknowledge God or Christ but is committed to the true and the good.[32]

Rahner holds that the classical doctrines of human nature and of Christology fit well with an evolutionary viewpoint. The human being is a unity of matter and spirit, which are distinct but can only be understood in relation to each other. Science studies matter and provides only part of the whole picture, for we know ourselves to be free, self-conscious agents. Evolution—from matter to life, mind, and spirit—is God's creative action through natural causes, which reach their goal in humanity and the incarnation. Matter develops out of its inner being in the direction of spirit, empowered to achieve an active self-transcendence in higher levels of being. The incarnation is at the same time the climax of the world's development and the climax of God's self-expression. Rahner insists that creation and incarnation are parts of a single process of God's self-communication. Christ as true humanity is a moment in biological evolution that has been oriented toward its fulfillment in him.[33]

David Tracy also sees a religious dimension in science. He holds that religious questions arise at the horizons or limit-situations of human experience. In everyday life, these limits are encountered in experiences of anxiety and confrontation with death, as well as in joy and basic trust. He describes two kinds of limit-situations in science: ethical issues in the uses of science, and presuppositions or conditions for the possibility of scientific inquiry. Tracy maintains that the intelligibility of the world requires an ultimate rational ground. For the Christian, the sources for understanding that ground are the classic religious texts and the structures of human experience. All our theological formulations, however, are limited and historically conditioned. Tracy is open to the reformulation of traditional doctrines in contemporary philosophical categories; he is sympathetic to many aspects of process philosophy and recent work in language and hermeneutics.[34]

How much room is there for the reformulation of classical theological doctrines in the light of the findings of science? If the points of contact between science and theology refer only to basic presuppositions and boundary questions, no reformulation will be called for. But if there are some points of contact between particular doctrines and particular scientific theories (such as the doctrine of creation in relation to evolution or astronomy), and if it is acknowledged that all doctrines are historically conditioned, there is in principle the possibility of some doctrinal development and reformulation, not just correlation or consonance. What is the nature and extent of the authority of tradition in theology? The Thomistic synthesis of biblical and Aristotelian thought has held a dominant position in the Catholic tradition in the past, but with the help of recent biblical, patristic, and liturgical scholarship, Catholic theologians have made significant efforts to delineate the central biblical message with less dependence on scholastic interpretive categories (see section on Integration).

Methodological Parallels

The positivists, along with most neo-orthodox and existentialist authors, had portrayed science as *objective,* meaning that its theories are validated by clearcut criteria and are tested by agreement with indisputable, theory-free data. Both the criteria and the data of science were held to be independent of the individual subject and unaffected by cultural influences. By contrast, religion seemed *subjective.* We have seen that existentialists made much of the contrast between objective detachment in science and personal involvement in religion.

Since the 1950s, these sharp contrasts have been increasingly called into question. Science, it appeared, is not as objective, nor religion as subjective, as had been claimed. There may be differences of emphasis between the fields, but the distinctions are not as absolute as had been asserted. Scientific data are theory-laden, not theory-free. Theoretical assumptions enter the selection, reporting, and interpretation of what are taken to be data. Moreover, theories do not arise from logical analysis of data but from acts of creative imagination in which analogies and models often play a role. Conceptual models help us to imagine what is not directly observable.

Many of these same characteristics are present in religion. If the data of religion include religious experience, rituals, and scriptural texts, such data are even more heavily laden with conceptual interpretations. In religious language, too, metaphors and models are prominent, as discussed in my writing and in that of Sallie McFague, Janet Soskice, and Mary Gerhart and Allan Russell.[35] Clearly, religious beliefs are not amenable to strict empirical testing, but they can be approached with some of the same spirit of inquiry found in science. The scientific criteria of coherence, comprehensiveness, and fruitfulness have their parallels in religious thought.

Thomas Kuhn's influential book, *The Structure of Scientific Revolutions,* maintained that both theories and data in science are dependent on the prevailing paradigms of the scientific community. He defined a paradigm as a cluster of conceptual, metaphysical, and methodological presuppositions embodied in a tradition of scientific work. With a new paradigm, the old data are reinterpreted and seen in new ways, and new kinds of data are sought. In the choice between paradigms, there are no rules for applying scientific criteria. Their evaluation is an act of judgment by the scientific community. An established paradigm is resistant to falsification, since discrepancies between theory and data can be set aside as anomalies or reconciled by introducing *ad hoc* hypotheses.[36]

Religious traditions can also be looked on as communities that share a common paradigm. The interpretation of the data (such as religious experience and historical events) is even more paradigm-dependent than in the case of science. There is a greater use of *ad hoc* assumptions to reconcile apparent anomalies, so religious paradigms are even more resistant to falsification. . . .

The status of the observer in science has also been reconsidered. The earlier accounts had identified objectivity with the separability of the observer from the object of observation. But in quantum physics the influence of the process of observation on the system observed is crucial. In relativity, the most basic measurements, such as the mass, velocity, and length of an object depend on the frame of reference of the observer. Stephen Toulmin traces the change from the assumption of a detached spectator to the recognition of the participation of the observer; he cites examples from quantum physics, ecology, and the social sciences. Every experiment is an action in which we are agents, not just observers. The observer as subject is a participant inseparable from the object of observation.[37] Fritjof Capra and other adherents of Eastern religions have seen parallels here with the mystical traditions that affirm the union of the knower and the known, deriving ultimately from the participation of the individual in the Absolute.[38]

Michael Polanyi envisions a harmony of method over the whole range of knowledge and says that this approach overcomes the bifurcation of reason and faith. Polanyi's unifying theme is the personal participation of the knower in all knowledge. In science, the heart of discovery is creative imagination, which is a very personal act. Science requires skills that, like riding a bicycle, cannot be formally specified but only learned by example and practice. In all knowledge we have to see patterns in wholes. In recognizing a friend's face or in making a medical diagnosis, we use many clues but cannot identify all the particulars on which our judgment of a total pattern relies.

Polanyi holds that the assessment of evidence is always an act of discretionary personal judgment. No rules specify whether an unexplained discrepancy between theory and experiment should be set aside as an anomaly or taken to invalidate the theory. Commitment to rationality and universality, not impersonal detachment, protects such decisions from arbitrariness. Scientific activity is thus personal but not subjective. Participation in a community of inquiry is another safeguard against subjectivity, though it never removes the burden of individual responsibility.

Polanyi holds that all these characteristics are even more important in religion. Here personal involvement is greater, but not to the exclusion of rationality and universal intent. Participation in the historical tradition and present experience of a religious community is essential. If theology is the elucidation of the implications of worship, then surrender and commitment are preconditions of understanding. Responding to reductionism, Polanyi describes ascending levels of reality in evolutionary history and in the world today:

> Admittedly, religious conversion commits our whole person and changes our whole being in a way that an expansion of natural knowledge does not do. But once the dynamics of knowing are recognized as the dominant principle of knowledge, the difference appears only as one of degree.... It establishes a continuous ascent from our less personal knowing of inanimate matter to our convivial knowing of living beings and beyond this to knowing our responsible fellow men. Such I believe is the true transition from the sciences to the humanities and also from our knowing the laws of nature to our knowing the person of God.[39]

Several authors have recently invoked similar methodological parallels. The physicist and theologian John Polkinghorne gives examples of personal judgment and theory-laden data in both fields, and he defends critical realism in both cases. The data for a religious community are its scriptural records and its history of religious experience. Similarities exist between the fields in that "each is corrigible, having to relate theory to experience, and each is essentially concerned with entities whose unpicturable reality is more subtle than that of naive objectivity."[40] The philosopher Holmes Rolston holds that religious beliefs interpret and correlate experience, much as scientific theories interpret and correlate experimental data. Beliefs can be tested by criteria of consistency and congruence with experience. But Rolston acknowledges that personal involvement is more total in the case of religion, since the primary goal is the reformation of the person. Moreover, there are other significant differences: science is interested in causes, while religion is interested in personal meanings.[41]

Such methodological comparisons seem to me illuminating for both fields. . . . Here I will only note several problems in the use of this approach:

1. In the attempt to legitimate religion in any age of science, it is tempting to dwell on similarities and pass over differences. Although science is indeed a more theory-laden enterprise than the positivists had recognized, it is clearly more objective than religion in each of the senses that have been mentioned. The kinds of data from which religion draws are radically different from those in science, and the possibility of testing religious beliefs is more limited.

2. In reacting to the absolute distinctions presented by adherents of the Independence thesis, it would be easy to minimize the distinctive features of religion. In particular, by treating religion as an intellectual system and talking only about religious beliefs, one may distort the diverse characteristics of religion as a way of life, which the linguistic analysts have so well described. Religious belief must always be seen in the context of the life of the religious community and in relation to the goal of personal transformation.

3. Consideration of methodology is an important but preliminary task in the dialogue of science and religion. The issues tend to be somewhat abstract and therefore of more interest to philosophers of science and philosophers of religion than to scientists or theologians and religious believers. Yet methodological issues have rightly come under new scrutiny in both communities. Furthermore, if we acknowledge methodological similarities we are more likely to encourage attention to substantive issues. If theology at its best is a reflective enterprise that can develop and grow, it can be open to new insights, including those derived from the theories of science.

INTEGRATION

The final group of authors holds that some sort of integration is possible between the content of theology and content of science. There are three distinct versions of Integration. In natural theology, it is claimed that the existence of God can be inferred from the evidences of design in nature, of which science has made us more aware. In a theology of nature, the main sources of theology lie outside science, but scientific theories may affect the reformulation of certain doctrines, particularly the doctrine of creation. In a systematic synthesis, both science and religion contribute to the development of an inclusive metaphysics, such as that of process philosophy.

Natural Theology

Here arguments for the existence of God are based entirely on human reason rather than on historical revelation or religious experience. The "five ways" of Thomas Aquinas included several versions of *the cosmological argument*. One version asserted that every event must have a cause, so we must acknowledge a First Cause if we are to avoid infinite regress. Another version said that the whole chain of natural causes (finite or infinite) is contingent and might not have been; it is dependent on a being which exists necessarily. These are what we have called boundary questions, since they refer only to the existence and very general features of the world. *The teleological argument* may similarly start from orderliness and intelligibility as general characteristics of nature. But specific evidences of design in nature may also be cited. In this form the argument has often drawn from the findings of science.

The founders of modern science frequently expressed admiration for the harmonious correlations of nature, which they saw as God's handiwork. Newton said that the eye could not have been contrived without skill in optics, and Boyle extolled the evidences of benevolent design throughout the natural order. If the Newtonian world was the perfect clock, the deistic God was its designer. In the early nineteenth century, Paley said that if one finds a watch on a heath, one is justified in concluding that it was designed by an intelligent being. In the human eye, many complex parts are coordinated to the one purpose of vision; here, too, one can only conclude that there was an intelligent designer. Paley cited many other examples of the coordination of structures fulfilling functions useful to living organisms.

Hume had already made several *criticisms of the teleological argument*. He observed that the organizing principle responsible for patterns in nature might be within organisms, not external to them. At most the argument would point to the existence of a finite god or many gods, not the omnipotent Creator of monotheism. If there are evil and dysfunctional phenomena in the world, does one ascribe them to a being with less benevolent intentions? It was Darwin, of course, who dealt the most serious blow to the argument, for he showed that adaptation can be explained by random variation and natural selection. An automatic and impersonal process could account for the apparent design in nature.

Many Protestants ignored the debate, asserting that their religious beliefs were based on revelation rather than natural theology. Others advocated a *reformulation of the argument.* Design is evident, they said, not in the particular structures of individual organisms, but in the properties of matter and the laws of nature through which the evolutionary process could produce such organisms. It is in the design of the total process that God's wisdom is evident. In the 1930s, F. R. Tennant argued that nature is a unified system of mutually supporting structures that have led to living organisms and have provided the conditions for human moral, aesthetic, and intellectual life.[42] Reformulations of the teleological argument are common in Roman Catholic thought, where natural theology has traditionally held a respected place as a preparation for the truths of revealed theology.[43]

The British philosopher Richard Swinburne has given an extended defense of natural theology. He starts by discussing *confirmation theory* in the philosophy of science. In the development of science, new evidence does not make a theory certain. Instead, a theory has an initial plausibility, and the probability that it is true increases or decreases with the additional evidence (Bayes's Theorem). Swinburne suggests that the existence of God has an initial plausibility because of its simplicity and because it gives a personal explanation of the world in terms of the intentions of an agent. He then argues that the evidence of order in the world increases the probability of the theistic hypothesis. He also maintains that science cannot account for the presence of conscious beings in the world. "Something outside the web of physical laws" is needed to explain the rise of consciousness. Finally, religious experience provides "additional crucial evidence," Swinburne concludes, "On our total evidence, theism is more probable than not."[44]

The most recent rendition of the design argument is *the Anthropic Principle* in cosmology. Astrophysicists have found that life in the universe would have been impossible if some of the physical constants and other conditions in the early universe had differed even slightly from the values they had. The universe seems to be "fine-tuned" for the possibility of life. For example, Stephen Hawking writes, "If the rate of expansion one second after the big bang had been smaller by even one part in a hundred thousand million million, the universe would have recollapsed before it even reached its present size."[45] Freeman Dyson draws the following conclusion from such findings:

> I conclude from the existence of these accidents of physics and astronomy that the universe is an unexpectedly hospitable place for living creatures to make their home in. Being a scientist, trained in the habits of thought and language of the twentieth century rather than the eighteenth, I do not claim that the architecture of the universe proves the existence of God. I claim only that the architecture of the universe is consistent with the hypothesis that mind plays an essential role in its functioning.[46]

John Barrow and Frank Tipler present many other cases in which there were extremely critical values of various forces in the early universe.[47] The philosopher John Leslie defends the Anthropic Principle as a design argument. But he points out that an alternative explanation would be the assumption of many worlds (either in successive cycles of an oscillating universe or in separate domains existing simultaneously). These worlds might differ from each other, and we just happen to be in one that has the right variables for the emergence of life.[48] Moreover, some of these apparently arbitrary conditions may be necessitated by a more basic unified theory, on which physicists are currently working. . . .

The bishop of Birmingham, Hugh Montefiore, claims that there are many instances of design in the universe, including the Anthropic Principle and the directionality of evolution. Some of his other examples, such as James Lovelock's "Gaia Hypothesis" and Rupert Sheldrake's "morphogenetic fields," are much more controversial and have little support in the scientific community. Montefiore does not claim that these arguments prove the existence of God, but only that the latter is more probable than other explanations.[49]

Debates continue about the validity of each of these arguments, to which we will return in later chapters. But even if the arguments are accepted, they would not lead to the personal, active God of the Bible, as Hume pointed out, but only to an intelligent designer remote from the world. Moreover, few if any persons have actually acquired their religious beliefs by such arguments. Natural theology can show the existence of God is a plausible hypothesis, but this kind of reasoning is far removed from the actual life of a religious community.

Theology of Nature

A theology of nature does not start from science, as some versions of natural theology do. Instead, it starts from a religious tradition based on religious experience and historical revelation. But it holds that some traditional doctrines need to be reformulated in the light of current science. Here science and religion are considered to be relatively independent sources of ideas, but with some areas of overlap in their concerns. In particular, the doctrines of creation, providence, and human nature are affected by the findings of science. If religious beliefs are to be in harmony with scientific knowledge, some adjustments or modifications are called for. The theologian will want to draw mainly from broad features of science that are widely accepted, rather than risk adapting to limited or speculative theories that are more likely to be abandoned in the future.

Our understanding of the general characteristics of nature will affect our models of God's relation to nature. Nature is today understood to be a dynamic evolutionary process with a long history of emergent novelty, characterized throughout by chance and law. The natural order is ecological, interdependent, and multileveled. These characteristics will modify our representation of the relation of both God and humanity to nonhuman nature. This will, in turn, affect our attitudes toward nature and will have practical implications for environmental ethics. The problem of evil will also be viewed differently in an evolutionary rather than a static world.

For Arthur Peacocke, the starting point of theological reflection is past and present religious experience, together with a continuous interpretive tradition. Religious beliefs are tested by community consensus and by criteria of coherence, comprehensiveness, and fruitfulness. But Peacocke is willing to reformulate traditional beliefs in response to current science. He discusses at length how chance and law work together in cosmology, quantum physics, nonequilibrium thermodynamics, and biological evolution. He describes the emergence of distinctive forms of activity at higher levels of complexity in the multilayered hierarchy of organic life and mind. Peacocke gives chance a positive role in the exploration and expression of potentialities at all levels. God creates through the whole process of law and chance, not by intervening in gaps in the process. "The natural causal creative nexus of events is itself God's creative action."[50] God creates "in and through" the processes of the natural world that science unveils.

. . . Peacocke provides some rich images for talking about God's action in a world of chance and law. He speaks of chance as God's radar sweeping through the range of possibilities and evoking the diverse potentialities of natural systems. In other images, artistic creativity is used as an analogy in which purposefulness and open-endedness are continuously present. Peacocke identifies his position as *panentheism* (not pantheism). God is in the world, but the world is also in God, in the sense that God is more than the world. In some passages, Peacocke suggests the analogy of the world as God's body, and God as the world's mind or soul. I am sympathetic with Peacocke's position at most points. He gives us vivid images for talking about God's relation to a natural order whose characteristics science has disclosed. But I believe that in addition to images that provide a suggestive link between scientific and religious reflection, we need philosophical categories to help us unify scientific and theological assertions in a more systematic way.

The writings of the Jesuit paleontologist Teilhard de Chardin are another example of a theology of nature. Some interpreters take *The Phenomenon of Man* to be a form of natural theology, an argument from evolution to the existence of God. I have suggested that it can more appropriately be viewed as a synthesis of scientific ideas with religious ideas derived from Christian tradition and experience. Teilhard's other writings make clear how deeply he was molded by his religious heritage and his own spirituality. But his concept of God was modified by evolutionary ideas, even if it was not derived from an analysis of evolution. Teilhard speaks of continuing creation and a God immanent in an incomplete world. His vision of the final convergence to an "Omega Point" is both a speculative extrapolation of evolutionary directionality and a distinctive interpretation of Christian eschatology.[51]

In any theology of nature there are theological issues that require clarification. Is some reformulation of the classical idea of God's omnipotence called for? Theologians have wrestled for centuries with the problem of reconciling omnipotence and omniscience with human freedom and the existence of evil and suffering. But a new problem is raised by the role of chance in diverse fields of science. Do we defend the traditional idea of divine sovereignty and hold that within what appears to the scientist to be chance all events are really providentially controlled by God? Or do both human freedom and chance in nature represent a self-limitation on God's foreknowledge and power, required by the creation of this sort of world?

How do we represent God's action in the world? The traditional distinction of primary and secondary causes preserves the integrity of the secondary causal chains that science studies. God does not interfere but acts through secondary causes, which at their own level provide a complete explanation of all events. This tends toward deism if God has planned all things from the beginning so they would unfold by their own structures (deterministic and probabilistic) to achieve the goals intended. Is the biblical picture of the particularity of divine action then replaced by the uniformity of divine concurrence with natural causes? Should we then speak only of God's one action, the whole of cosmic history? These are some of the questions that a theology of nature must answer. . . .

Systematic Synthesis

A more systematic integration can occur if both science and religion contribute to a coherent world view elaborated in a comprehensive metaphysics. Metaphysics is the search for a set of general categories in terms of which diverse types of experience can be interpreted. An inclusive conceptual scheme is sought that can represent the fundamental characteristics of all events. Metaphysics as such is the province of the philosopher rather than of either the scientist or the theologian, but it can serve as an arena of common reflection. The Thomistic framework provided such a metaphysics, but one in which, I would argue, the dualisms of spirit/matter, mind/body, humanity/nature, and eternity/time were only partially overcome.

Process philosophy is a promising candidate for a mediating role today because it was itself formulated under the influence of both scientific and religious thought, even as it responded to persistent problems in the history of Western philosophy (for example, the mind/body problem). Alfred North Whitehead has been the most influential exponent of process categories, though theological implications have been more fully investigated by Charles Hartshorne, John Cobb, and others. The influence of biology and physics is evident in the process view of reality as a dynamic web of interconnected events. Nature is characterized by change, chance, and novelty as well as order. It is incomplete and still coming into being. Process thinkers are critical of reductionism; they defend organismic categories applicable to activities at higher levels of organization. They see continuity as well as distinctiveness among levels of reality; the characteristics of each level have rudimentary forerunners at earlier and lower levels. Against a dualism of matter and mind, or a materialism that has no place for mind, process thought envisages two aspects of all events as seen from within and from without. Because humanity is continuous with the rest of nature (despite the uniqueness of reflective self-consciousness), human experience can be taken as a clue to interpreting the experience of other beings. Genuinely new phenomena emerge in evolutionary history, but the basic metaphysical categories apply to all events.

Process thinkers understand God to be the source of novelty and order. Creation is a long and incomplete process. God elicits the self-creation of individual entities, thereby allowing for freedom and novelty as well as order and structure. God is not the unrelated Absolute, the Unmoved Mover, but instead interacts reciprocally with the world, an influence on all events though never the sole cause of any event. Process metaphysics understands every new event to be jointly the product of the entity's past, its own action, and the action of God. Here God transcends the world but is immanent in the world in a specific way in the structure of each event. We do not have a succession of purely natural events, interrupted by gaps in which God alone operates. Process thinkers reject the idea of divine omnipotence; they believe in a God of persuasion rather than compulsion, and they have provided distinctive analyses of the place of chance, human freedom, evil, and suffering in the world. Christian process theologians point out that the power of love, as exemplified in the cross, is precisely its ability to evoke a response while respecting the integrity of other beings. They also hold that divine immutability is not a characteristic of the biblical God who is intimately involved with history. Hartshorne elaborates a "dipolar" concept of God: unchanging in purpose and character, but changing in experience and relationship.[52]

In *The Liberation of Life,* Charles Birch and John Cobb have brought together ideas from biology, process philosophy, and Christian thought. Early chapters develop an ecological or organismic model in which (1) every being is constituted by its interaction with a wider environment, and (2) all beings are subjects of experience, which runs the gamut from rudimentary responsiveness to reflective consciousness. Evolutionary history shows continuity but also the emergence of novelty. Humanity is continuous with and part of the natural order. Birch and Cobb develop an ethics that avoids anthropocentrism. The goal of enhancing the richness of experience in any form encourages concern for nonhuman life, without treating all forms of life as equally valuable. These authors present a powerful vision of a just and sustainable society in an interdependent community of life.[53]

Birch and Cobb give less attention to religious ideas. They identify God with the principle of Life, a cosmic power immanent in nature. At one point it is stated that God loves and redeems us, but the basis of the statement is not clarified. But earlier writings by both these authors indicate their commitment to the Christian tradition and their attempt to reformulate it in the categories of process thought. Writing with David Griffin, for example, Cobb seeks "a truly contemporary vision that is at the same time truly Christian."[54] God is understood both as "a source of novelty and order" and as "creative-responsive love." Christ's vision of the love of God opens us to creative transformation. These authors also show that Christian process theology can provide a sound basis for an environmental ethics.

I am in basic agreement with the "Theology of Nature" position, coupled with a cautious use of process philosophy. Too much reliance on science (in natural theology) or on science and process philosophy (as in Birch and Cobb) can lead to the neglect of the areas of experience that I consider most important religiously. As I see it, the center of the Christian life is an experience of reorientation, the healing of our brokenness in new wholeness, and the expression of a new relationship to God and to the neighbor. Existentialists and linguistic analysts rightly point to the primacy of personal and social life in religion, and neo-orthodoxy rightly says that for the Christian community it is in response to the person of Christ that our lives can be changed. But the centrality of redemption need not lead us to belittle creation, for our personal and social lives are intimately bound to the rest of the created order. We are redeemed in and with the world, not from the world. Part of our task, then, is to articulate a theology of nature, for which we will have to draw from both religious and scientific sources. . . .

In articulating a theology of nature, a systematic metaphysics can help us toward a coherent vision. But Christianity should never be equated with any metaphysical system. There are dangers if either scientific or religious ideas are distorted to fit a preconceived synthesis that claims to encompass all reality. We must always keep in mind the rich diversity of our experience. We distort it if we cut it up into separate realms or watertight compartments, but we also distort it if we force it into a neat intellectual system. A coherent vision of reality can still allow for the distinctiveness of differing types of experience.

NOTES

1. For this parable I am indebted to Ted Peters, speaking at a symposium at the Lutheran School of Theology at Chicago on Nov. 17, 1988.
2. Carl Sagan, *Cosmos* (New York: Random House, 1980), p. 4. See also Thomas W. Ross, "The Implicit Theology of Carl Sagan," *Pacific Theological Review* 18 (Spring 1985): 24–32.
3. Francis Crick, *Of Molecules and Men* (Seattle: University of Washington Press, 1966), p. 10.
4. Jacques Monod, *Chance and Necessity* (New York: Vintage Books, 1972), p. 180.
5. Monod, BBC lecture, quoted in *Beyond Chance and Necessity*, ed. John Lewis (London: Garnstone Press, 1974), p. ix. This book includes a number of interesting critiques of Monod.
6. Arthur Peacocke, *Creation and the World of Science* (Oxford: Clarendon Press, 1979), chap. 3.
7. Edward O. Wilson, *Sociobiology: The New Synthesis* (Cambridge: Harvard University Press, 1975), p. 4.
8. Edward O. Wilson, *On Human Nature* (Cambridge: Harvard University Press, 1978), chaps. 8, 9.
9. See the essays by Marshall Sahlins, Ruth Mattern, Richard Burian, and others in *The Sociobiology Debate,* ed. Arthur Caplan (New York: Harper & Row, 1978).
10. Cited by Ernan McMullin, "How Should Cosmology Relate to Theology?" in *The Sciences and Theology in the Twentieth Century,* ed. Arthur Peacocke (Notre Dame: University of Notre Dame Press, 1981), p. 21.
11. *Origins: NC Documentary Service* 13 (1983): 50–51.
12. *Origins: NC Documentary Service* 16 (1986): 122. See Cardinal Paul Poupard, ed. *Galileo Galilei: Toward a Resolution of 350 Years of Debate, 1633–1983* (Pittsburgh: Duquesne University Press, 1987).
13. Henry Morris, ed., *Scientific Creationism,* 2d ed. (El Cajon, CA: Master Books, 1985). The text of the ruling, McLean v. Arkansas, together with articles by several of the participants in the trial, is printed in *Science, Technology & Human Values* 7 (Summer 1982).
14. See Langdon Gilkey, *Creationism on Trial* (Minneapolis: Winston Press, 1985); Roland Frye, ed., *Is God a Creationist: The Religious Case Against Creation-Science* (New York: Charles Scribner's Sons, 1983).
15. In addition to the reports on the trial mentioned above, see Philip Kitcher, *Abusing Science: The Case Against Creationism* (Cambridge, MA: MIT Press, 1982); Michael Ruse, *Darwinism Defended: A Guide to the Evolution Controversies* (Reading, MA: Addison-Wesley, 1982).

16. *Washington Post,* June 20, 1987, p. A1.
17. A good introduction is Karl Barth, *Dogmatics in Outline* (New York: Harper & Row, 1949). See also W. A. Whitehouse, *Christian Faith and the Scientific Attitude* (New York: Philosophical Library, 1952).
18. Rudolf Bultmann, *Jesus Christ and Mythology* (New York: Charles Scribner's Sons, 1958).
19. Gilkey, *Creationism on Trial,* pp. 108–16. See also his *Maker of Heaven and Earth* (Garden City, NY: Doubleday, 1959).
20. Gilkey, *Religion and the Scientific Future* (New York: Harper & Row, 1970), chap. 2. Also his *Creationism on Trial,* chap. 7.
21. Thomas Torrance, *Theological Science* (Oxford: Oxford University Press, 1969), p. 281.
22. Useful summaries are given in Frederick Ferré, *Language, Logic, and God* (New York: Harper and Brothers, 1961) and William H. Austin, *The Relevance of Natural Science to Theology* (London: Macmillan, 1976). See also Stephen Toulmin, *The Return to Cosmology* (Berkeley and Los Angeles: University of California Press, 1982), part 1.
23. Frederick Streng, *Understanding Religious Life,* 3d ed. (Belmont, CA: Wadsworth, 1985).
24. George Lindbeck, *The Nature of Doctrine: Religion and Theology in a Postliberal Age* (Philadelphia: Westminster Press, 1984), p. 22.
25. Arthur Eddington, *The Nature of Physical World* (Cambridge: Cambridge University Press, 1928), p. 16.
26. Alfred North Whitehead, *Science and the Modern World* (New York: Macmillan, 1925), chap. 1; Stanley L. Jaki, *The Road of Science and the Ways to God* (Chicago: University of Chicago Press, 1978).
27. Thomas Torrance, "God and the Contingent World," *Zygon* 14 (1979): 347. See also his *Divine and Contingent Order* (Oxford: Oxford University Press, 1981). Torrance also defends contingency *within* the created order (that is, the unpredictability of particular events), as evident in the uncertainties of quantum physics. Here the invocation of Einstein seems more dubious, since Einstein adhered to a determinist as well as a realist view of physics. He was confident that quantum uncertainties will be removed when we find the underlying deterministic laws, which he believed a rational universe must have.
28. Wolfhart Pannenberg, *Theology and the Philosophy of Science* (Philadelphia: Westminster Press, 1976).
29. Ernan McMullin, "Natural Science and Christian Theology," in *Religion, Science, and the Search for Wisdom,* ed. David Byers (Washington, DC: National Conference of Catholic Bishops, 1987). See also his "Introduction: Evolution and Creation" in *Evolution and Creation,* ed. Ernan McMullin (Notre Dame: University of Notre Dame Press, 1985).
30. Ernan McMullin, "How Should Cosmology Relate to Theology?" in *The Sciences and Theology in the Twentieth Century,* ed. Arthur Peacocke, p. 39.
31. Ibid., p. 52.
32. Karl Rahner, *Foundations of Christian Faith* (New York: Seabury, 1978); Gerald McCool, ed., *A Rahner Reader* (New York: Seabury, 1975); Leo O'Donovan, ed., *A*

World of Grace: An Introduction to the Themes and Foundations of Karl Rahner's Theology (New York: Seabury, 1980).

33. Karl Rahner, "Christology within an Evolutionary View of the World," *Theological Investigations,* vol. 5 (Baltimore: Helicon Press, 1966); also *Hominization: The Evolutionary Origin of Man as a Theological Problem* (New York: Herder and Herder, 1965).

34. David Tracy, *Blessed Rage for Order* (New York: Seabury, 1975); also *Plurality and Ambiguity* (San Francisco: Harper & Row, 1987).

35. Ian G. Barbour, *Myths, Models, and Paradigms* (New York: Harper & Row, 1974); Sallie McFague, *Metaphorical Theology: Models of God in Religious Language* (Philadelphia: Fortress Press, 1982); Janet Soskice, *Metaphor and Religious Language* (Oxford: Clarendon Press, 1985); Mary Gerhart and Allan Russell, *Metaphorical Process* (Fort Worth: Texas Christian University Press, 1984).

36. Thomas S. Kuhn, *The Structure of Scientific Revolutions,* 2d ed. (Chicago: University of Chicago Press, 1970).

37. Toulmin, *Return to Cosmology,* part III.

38. Fritjof Capra, *The Tao of Physics* (New York: Bantam Books, 1977).

39. Michael Polanyi, "Faith and Reason," *Journal of Religion* 41 (1961): 244. See also his *Personal Knowledge* (Chicago: University of Chicago Press, 1958).

40. John Polkinghorne, *One World: The Interaction of Science and Theology* (Princeton: Princeton University Press, 1987), p. 64. See also his *Science and Creation* (London: SPCK, 1988).

41. Holmes Rolston, *Science and Religion: A Critical Survey* (New York: Random House, 1987).

42. F. R. Tennant, *Philosophical Theology,* vol. 2 (Cambridge: Cambridge University Press, 1930).

43. See, for example, W. N. Clarke, S. J., "Is Natural Theology Still Possible Today?" in *Physics, Philosophy, and Theology: A Common Quest for Understanding,* eds. Robert J. Russell, William R. Stoeger, S. J., and George V. Coyne, S. J. (The Vatican: Vatican Observatory, and Notre Dame: University of Notre Dame Press, 1988).

44. Richard Swinburne, *The Existence of God* (Oxford: Clarendon Press, 1979), p. 291.

45. Stephen W. Hawking, *A Brief History of Time* (New York: Bantam Books, 1988), p. 291.

46. Freeman Dyson, *Disturbing the Universe* (New York: Harper & Row, 1979).

47. John Barrow and Frank Tipler, *The Anthropic Cosmological Principle* (Oxford and New York: Oxford University Press, 1986).

48. John Leslie, "How to Draw Conclusions from a Fine-Tuned Universe," in *Physics, Philosophy, and Theology,* ed. Russell et al.

49. Hugh Montefiore, *The Probability of God* (London: SCM Press, 1985).

50. Arthur Peacocke, *Intimations of Reality* (Notre Dame: University of Notre Dame Press, 1984), p. 63; see also *Creation and the World of Science.*

51. Pierre Teilhard de Chardin, *The Phenomenon of Man* (New York: Harper & Row, 1959). I have discussed Teilhard in "Five Ways of Reading Teilhard," *Soundings* 51

(1968); 115–45, and in "Teilhard's Process Metaphysics," *Journal of Religion* 49 (1969): 136–59.

52. Charles Hartshorne, *The Divine Relativity* (New Haven: Yale University Press, 1948).
53. Charles Birch and John B. Cobb, Jr., *The Liberation of Life* (Cambridge: Cambridge University Press, 1981).
54. John B. Cobb, Jr. and David Ray Griffin, *Process Theology: An Introduction* (Philadelphia: Westminster Press, 1976), p. 94. See also L. Charles Birch, *Nature and God* (London: SCM Press, 1965).

QUESTIONS FOR STUDY

1. What are the four essential ways in which science and religion can relate? Briefly describe each.

2. Although scientific materialism and biblical literalism are at opposite ends of the theological spectrum, Barbour discusses them together. Why?

3. Define *scientific materialism*. Give two examples of scientists who subscribe to this position.

4. What is the theology of neo-orthodoxy? How is it an example of Barbour's independence position?

5. Define "existentialism."

6. In what ways, historically, did religion contribute to the rise of Western science?

7. Define *natural theology*. How is it different from a "theology of nature"?

8. Describe process philosophy. Which of Barbour's four positions does it represent?

QUESTIONS FOR REFLECTION

1. Why would biblical literalism be more in conflict with science than other forms of biblical interpretation?

2. What is the point of the parable of the fishnet told by Arthur Eddington? In your estimate, is the point valid in arguing for the separation option?

3. If human existence is the experience of selfhood, how is science an important activity? That is, from the existentialist point of view, how can science matter?

4. If science and religion are in conflict, then dialogue is obviously impossible. If they are independent, then they have nothing in common to discuss and dialogue again is impossible. If they are integrated, then dialogue is unnecessary. How, then, can dialogue be a separate and distinct way in which science and religion might relate?

NETWORKING

Further remarks on *scientific materialism* may be found in Gish, Peacocke, and Haught and *biblical literalism* in Barbour (V), Schmidt, Gish, and Asimov. Ruse and Wilson, Peacocke, and Haught discuss *reductionism*. Schmidt describes *logical positivism and linguistic analysis*. Each selection in Part V, Section B is concerned with *sociobiology*. Updike focuses on the *neo-orthodox theology of Karl Barth*. The *I-Thou/It model* appears in Buber, Swimme, Tillich, McFague, and Berry. Both Polkinghorne and Haught defend their positions with the help of *Polanyi*. Bube, Lackey, Dyson, Updike, and Polkinghorne examine the methods of *natural theology*, which is closely associated with the *Anthropic Principle* in Dyson, Wald, Feinberg and Shapiro, and Polkinghorne. Barbour subscribes to *process philosophy* and finds comrades in Dyson and Cobb in this respect. For the *Big Bang*, see Jastrow, Geisler and Anderson, and Russell.

MIXED ANTITHESES
MARY MIDGLEY

Mary Midgley was formerly Senior Lecturer in Philosophy at the University of Newcastle in Tyre. This selection is taken from her 1987 book, *Evolution as a Religion*.

I have been arguing that the contrast between science and religion is unluckily not as plain, nor the relation between them as simple, as is often supposed, and have been discussing some elements which can equally form part of either. Thoughtful scientists have often mentioned this problem, but a great many of their colleagues, and of the public generally, cling to the reassuringly simple opposition. What often seems to happen is that a great number of different antitheses are mixed up here, and used rather indiscriminately, as each happens to be convenient, to give colour to the idea of a general crusade of light against darkness. We could group them roughly like this:

1	science	v.	superstition partiality error magic wish-fulfilment dogmatism blind conformism childishness
2	common sense science rationalism logic	v.	intuition mysticism faith
	materialism	v.	idealism animism vitalism mind–body dualism commonsense agnosticism
3	hard	v.	soft
	progress	v.	tradition
	determinism	v.	free will
	mechanism	v.	teleology
	empiricism	v.	rationalism metaphysics

scepticism	v.	credulity
reason	v.	feeling or emotion
objective	v.	subjective
quantity	v.	quality
physical science	v.	the humanities
realism	v.	reverence
specialism	v.	holism
prose	v.	poetry
male	v.	female
clarity	v.	mystery

...Which among these antitheses are really the ones we need, which of them give clear ground for a crusade? The ones in the first group seem the most promising for crusaders. In them science stands opposed to something undoubtedly bad. But in these cases it is certainly not the only opponent of the evils in question. Superstition and the rest find their opposites in clear thinking generally, and a particular superstition is as likely to be corrected by history or logic or common sense as by one of the physical sciences. The second group deals in ideas which are more ambitious, more interesting, but also much more puzzling, because we at once need definitions of the terms involved, and cannot easily give them without falling into confusion. The odd tendency of both rationalism and common sense to jump the central barrier is only one indication of the difficulties. In the third group, we have contrasts which are a good deal clearer. But they do not seem to provide material at all suitable for a crusade. They describe pairs of complementary elements in life and thought, both members of which are equally necessary, and indeed could scarcely be identified except in relation to each other as parts of a whole. We no longer want that truculent little 'v.' to divide them. They go very well together, and crusaders must avoid trying to set them at loggerheads. Thus it does not matter here that 'reason' appears on both sides; we no longer want to reduce all these contrasts to a single underlying shape. The lines of division cross each other. Different distinctions are needed for different purposes.

How hard it is to relate these various antitheses clearly can be seen in Bertrand Russell's very interesting and influential paper "Mysticism and logic." [New York: Barnes and Noble, Inc., 1917. P.1.] Russell's main enterprise here is an admirable attempt to move the whole debate into our group 3, to show apparently warring elements as both necessary and complementary:

Metaphysics, or the attempt to conceive the world as a whole by means of thought, has been developed, from the first, by the union and conflict of two very different human impulses, the one urging men towards mysticism, the other urging them towards science. ... In Hume, for instance, the scientific impulse reigns quite unchecked, while in Blake a strong hostility to science co-exists with profound mystic insight. But the greatest men who have been philosophers have felt the need both of science and of mysticism; the attempt to harmonize the two was what made their life, and what always must, for all its arduous uncertainty, make philosophy, to some minds, a greater thing than either science or religion. ... Mysticism, is, in essence, little more than a certain intensity and depth of feeling in regard to what is believed about the universe. . . . Mysticism is to be commended as an attitude towards life, not as a creed about the world. The metaphysical creed, I shall maintain, is a mistaken outcome of the emotion, although this emotion, as colouring all other thoughts and feelings, is the inspirer of whatever is best in Man. Even the cautious and patient investigation of truth by science, which seems the very antithesis of the mystic's swift certainty, may be fostered and nourished by that very spirit of reverence in which mysticism lives and moves.

Russell has got a lot of things right here. He has 'got in', as they say, many items from the right-hand column of our antitheses in legitimate relation to science. He has got in emotion and poetry, indeed he has got in Blake, with his criticisms of Newton. He sees that emotion is so far from being an opponent of science, or a menace to it, that emotion of a suitable kind is necessary for science, and that part of that emotion can quite properly be called 'reverence'. He sees that something of the sort is necessary for metaphysics too.

The word metaphysics here is not of course used in the abusive sense to mean mere empty vapouring. It is used in its proper sense of very general conceptual enquiry, covering such central topics as the relation in mind and matter, free will and necessity, meaning, truth and the possibility of knowledge, all in an attempt (as Russell rightly says) to make sense of the world as a whole. In this sense, naturally, views like materialism and empiricism, and also sceptical enquiries like those of Hume, Ayer and Popper are themselves part of metaphysics just as much as what they oppose or enquire into. When A. J. Ayer began his book *Language, Truth and Logic* with a chapter called 'The elimination of metaphysics', and went on to explain that the word was for him virtually equivalent to 'nonsense', he was, in any ordinary sense of that word, simply doing metaphysics himself—expounding one theory of meaning among many others. Empty vapouring is *bad* metaphysics. There is a lot of it about, but it cannot make the study unnecessary.

Russell, who had the advantage of having started his philosophical life as a disciple of Hegel, was not tempted, as Hume and his disciples were, to suppose that good metaphysics merely meant cutting down one's thoughts on such topics to a minimum. He knew that, far from that, even highly constructive metaphysicians like Plato and Heraclitus, Leibnitz and Hegel often had something very important to say, especially about mathematics. Yet he was now a convert to empiricism, and he wanted to set limits on the thought-architecture of these bold rationalists. His solution was, on the whole, to concentrate on the emotional function of this large-scale, constructive metaphysics, and on the intellectual function of science and of more sceptical philosophy. Thus mystical, constructive metaphysics was to supply the heart of the world-grasping enterprise, while science supplied the head. . . .

This is a bold and ingenious idea, but something has gone wrong with it. He has fitted the head of one kind of enquiry on to the heart of another. Constructive metaphysics has its own thoughts, and science its own motives. If the word *science* means what it seems to mean here—primarily the search for particular facts—then it is powered emotionally by the familiar motive of detailed curiosity. If it means the building of those facts into a harmonious, satisfying system, then it draws upon a different motive, the desire for intellectual order; which is also the motive for metaphysical endeavour.

Without this unifying urge, science would be nothing but mindless, meaningless collecting. At the quite ordinary scientific level, before any question of mystically contemplating the whole comes in, the system-building tendency, with its aesthetic criteria of elegance and order, is an essential part of every science, continually shaping the scrappy data into usable patterns. Scientific hypotheses are not generated by randomizers, nor do they grow on trees, but on the branches of these ever-expanding thought systems.

This is why the sciences continually go beyond everybody's direct experience, and do so in directions that quickly diverge from that of common sense, which has more modest systems of its own. And because isolated systems are always incomplete and can conflict with each other, inevitably in the end they require metaphysics, 'the attempt to conceive the world as a whole', to harmonize them.

To what are interestingly called *lay* people, however, these intellectual constructions present problems of belief which are often quite as difficult as those of religion, and which can call for equally strenuous efforts of faith. This happens at present over relativity, over the size and expansion of the universe, over quantum mechanics, over evolution and many other matters. Believers are—perhaps quite properly—expected to bow to the mystery, admit the inadequacy of their faculties, and accept paradoxes. If a mystical sense of reverence is, as Russell suggested, the right response to the vast and incomprehensible universe, then science itself require it, since it leads us on directly to this situation. It cannot therefore be right to call mysticism and science, as Russell does, two distinct, co-ordinate 'human impulses'. Mysticism is a range of human faculties; physical science, a range of enquiries which can, at times, call these faculties into action. But long before it does so, it has passed the limits of common sense, transcended experience and begun to ask for faith.

At this stage, there is often a real problem about what kind of thinking is going on, and whether it ought to be stopped. If, for instance, we ask whether the universe is finite, are we still talking about anything at all? If so, do we know what it is? The most general concepts used by any science—concepts like life, time, space, law, energy—raise serious headaches, affecting their use in actual problems. To resolve these, however, we often need not more facts but a better way of fitting these concepts into their neighbors, of stating the wider problems which surround them, of 'conceiving the world as a whole'. Science quite properly calls on the whole range of our cognitive faculties, but it is not alone in doing so, nor can it define their whole aim. It is a part of our attempt to understand the universe, not the whole of it. It opens into metaphysics.

QUESTIONS FOR STUDY

1. Midgley divides her antitheses into two columns and three groups. What is the major difference between the first group and the other two?

2. What do Bertrand Russell and Midgley mean by the term *metaphysics?*

3. How does Midgley argue for the claim that science "opens into metaphysics"? What is its "unifying urge"?

4. How does Midgley argue that science requires mysticism?

QUESTIONS FOR REFLECTION

1. Look up *metaphysics* and *mysticism* in the Glossary or a dictionary. Do the definitions have anything in common?

2. Choose several terms from the columns describing science and religion that, in your opinion, best contrast the two approaches. Choose several terms that support a close relationship between them.

NETWORKING

For *metaphysics,* see Popper and Dyson. For *metaphysics as world view, total explanation, myth, and root metaphor,* see Küng, MacCormack, Langer, Swimme, Lewis, Hick, Polkinghorne, Gish, and Berry.

MAKING CONNECTIONS
THE THREEFOLD AND CIRCULAR NATURE OF SCIENCE AND RELIGION
HAROLD K. SCHILLING

Harold Schilling was professor of physics and dean of the Graduate School at Pennsylvania State University. His long-standing view, that science and religion represent kindred spirits and ideals, is reflected in each of his several books and numerous articles on the subject.

SCIENCE IS THREEFOLD AND CIRCULAR

Science may be regarded as being threefold in nature and activity, as suggested by the three circles of [the following figure]. First (circle *a*), it is *empirically descriptive,* engaging in data gathering by observation and experimentation. Second (circle *b*), it is *theoretical,* producing symbolic structures or systems for purposes of correlation of concepts, generalization, explanation and prediction. Third (circle *c*), it is *transformative,* transforming man's natural and cultural environment by so-called "practical appli-

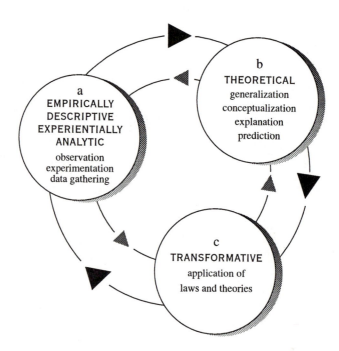

SCHEMATIC REPRESENTATION OF THREEFOLD AND
CIRCULAR NATURE OF SCIENCE AND RELIGION

cations" of scientific laws and theories. None of these terms is completely adequate or accurate in its connotations. To give concrete meaning to them let us look at some examples.

Consider the physics of gases. The part of it that provides information about the experimentally known behavior of gases is represented by circle *a*. Much of this information is formulated in the so-called gas laws, such as Boyle's Law and Charles' Law. These *laws* are expressed in mathematical equations which indicate how various measurable physical quantities are related to each other, and how they vary (change) together under different physical conditions. Thus Boyle's Law tells us approximately how the pressure of a confined gas varies with its volume, while the temperature is constant. Charles' Law shows how the volume and corresponding temperature vary while the pressure is held constant. The General Gas Law relates all three variables, i.e., the pressure, volume, and temperature, while the mass is constant. Such laws are useful in that they correlate and represent huge amounts of data. They provide information about both what has actually been observed, and what may be expected under specified conditions, i.e., for particular values of the pertinent variables.

Now physicists, like other scientists, are the kind of people who are not satisfied with having a lot of data about specific properties of gases, or even isolated laws that correlate data. What they want also is a way of correlating the laws so as to get an overall view of the behavior of gases. Moreover, what they want especially is a mathematical structure, or theory, from which to deduce the various known gas laws and predict the existence of others not yet known. Physicists feel that when they have provided such a theoretical structure they have *explained* both the data and the laws. It is this theorizing that is represented by circle *b*.

In building such theoretical structures the physicist often proceeds by imagining, i.e., hypothesizing, a "model" which he invests with certain postulated properties. He then works out a mathematical description (system of equations) of how the imagined model works. If from this mathematical system he can deduce the laws he wants to correlate, and it meets certain other criteria of acceptability, he has a satisfactory theory.

In the case of gases, a remarkably successful theory is the so-called Kinetic Theory, which pictures a gas as consisting of a huge number of molecules that are extremely small relative to the distances between them, that are in random motion, that maintain the pressure of the gas upon the containing walls through their impact upon them. Not only does this theory "explain" the gas laws per se, but it sheds light on the laws of thermodynamics, the more general science of heat.

Circle *c* stands for the application of the empirical information about gases and the theory of gases to particular concrete situations for the purpose of controlling or transforming the physical world. There is a vast body of gas technology, which at least in its modern manifestations is to a large extent the direct consequence of this threefold activity of the physics of gases.

Another example. Chemistry is empirical and directly descriptive (circle *a*) when it propounds the laws of chemical reactions in terms of observed, measured quantities, such as weights and volumes and combining proportions, and of empirically specifiable classes or species of substances, such as elements and compounds, or gases, liquids and solids. A case in point is the so-called Law of Lavoisier, which tells us that when a chemical reaction takes place in an enclosure no weight, or mass, is lost or gained in the process. This means that in the case of a chemical decomposition the sum of the weights of the resulting components equals the weight of the sample decomposed. Thus if water is decomposed the sum of the weights of the components hydrogen and oxygen equals the weight of the water decomposed.

This is a much more meaningful and empirically useful statement than the more general one that is often called the Principle of Conservation of "Matter." This is because the term *matter* used in the latter is itself not a quantitative term, and one cannot therefore properly speak of measuring the amount of it in a container. On the other hand it is clear what it means to measure its mass or weight. Actually, like all the empirical laws of science, this Law of Lavoisier is valid only approximately, since the weights before and after a chemical reaction never do in fact add up exactly. There is always at least a small "remainder," and this may be due either to "errors" in measurement, or, say, to the presence of another, but unsuspected, component. When we take this into account we can see that in the laboratory this law, if taken precisely, functions not as a description of an aspect of nature, but as a method, an investigative tool, for the discovery of unknowns. Therefore from this point of view it could be stated more explicitly as follows: "If in the course of a change we discover a decrease in the sum of the masses of the bodies enclosed in a container, we shall say that a body having a mass of exactly the difference between the two measured masses has gone from the container in which the change took place. We shall look for this fugitive body." Many a new chemical substance has been found this way. Now it is this kind of thinking that is symbolized by circle *a*.

Of course, the experimental situation with regard to chemical reactions cannot be described completely without recourse also to other laws, such as the Law of Proust, or the Law of Definite Proportions, and the Law of Dalton, or of Multiple Proportions. These are also formulated in terms of measurable quantities such as weight or mass, and of empirically identifiable chemical substances. Here we are still in circle *a*.

Now we enter circle *b*. The experimental laws of chemical reactions—and others— are correlated and explained by the grand and remarkably successful theoretical structure called the atomic and molecular theory, which *postulates* some entities called molecules, atoms, electrons and so on and assigns to them certain properties. The growth and developments of this potent theory provide one of the most interesting and informative chapters in the history of ideas, and illustrate many features of the evolution and nature of scientific theory in general.

Chemistry is one of the sciences that illustrate most obviously the transformative activity of circle *c*. It has become not only analytical and exploratory, but truly creative. It has not only studied many substances already in existence, but has produced many new ones, such as the novel plastics, to take only one example. It has profoundly affected our mode of life and physical environment in other ways—witness its contributions in the fields of nutrition and medicine.

There was a time when science was thought to include only circles *a* and *b*, its empirical and theoretical aspects, while *c* was regarded as engineering or technology— i.e., not "really" science at all. Today this is no longer the case. Many members of, say, the American Physical Society and American Chemical Society are engaged mainly in applying their sciences to technological problems, and yet consider themselves to be physicists or chemists, not engineers. It is becoming more and more difficult to distinguish between so-called "pure" and "applied" science.

The three components of science are, of course, inseparable and utterly interdependent. Each is meaningful only in relation to the others and to the whole. This is symbolized in the diagram by the circular arcs with arrows. Each circle is connected with each of the others by two such arcs, pointing in opposite directions to indicate action-and-reaction effects and feed-back relations. Those between circles *a* and *b* signify respectively the facts that, on the one hand, theory depends upon and comes out of observation and experimentation, and, on the other hand, observation and experimentation at their best are influenced, and often even guided, by theory. A theoretical structure endeavors to correlate and explain what one has seen. But what one sees is often affected or even determined to a considerable extent by the theoretical viewing screen through which one does the observing. Moreover, what one sets out to look for in the first place is often determined by what theory has led one to expect. We have here another case of circularity. Still another is depicted by the double connection between circle *b* and circle *c*. Theory is important in assaying the possibility of particular useful applications and indicates the direction they might well take. Conversely, theory is enlarged and enriched as one struggles with new problems in the attempt to apply it usefully. Circles *a* and *c* are similarly connected, signifying that observation and experiment often suggest or open up possibilities for useful applications without the mediation of theory; and conversely, technological needs and developments call for or suggest new areas for data gathering. The point of all this is that science is an indivisible unity. It thrives best when all three of its main components are thriving, and when there is a proper balance and interdependence among them. And for present purposes it should be stressed especially that science would be inconceivable without theory.

Although in its essentials this threefold sketch depicts the nature of all the basic sciences, there are significant differences of emphasis among them. Physics and astronomy are alike in their strong emphasis upon mathematical theory—and in their quest for the grand, all inclusive theory. But, for astronomy, circle *a* represents almost exclusively only observation and measurement, with virtually no experimentation. After all, astronomers cannot experiment with the planets or stars, i.e., intervene in their courses to manipulate them under control conditions. Nor is astronomy outstandingly transformative. Useful applications are very few indeed, and they are confined mostly to determining time and place (latitude and longitude). As we review the physical sciences, passing from physics and astronomy, through chemistry to meteorology, geology, mineralogy, and physical geography we find progressively less emphasis on precise measurements, controlled experimentation, and mathematical theory. In the biological and social sciences this trend persists and becomes even more pronounced. Moreover, the various particular science communities appear to have somewhat different viewpoints about the nature of science; that is to say, their philosophies of science are not all alike. Not only does this show up in different methodologies, but in different conceptions of basic purposes. Thus physical scientists lean more toward positivistic conceptions of theory, emphasizing their symbolic nature and predictive purpose, while the biologists seem to tend toward more realistic views about theory, regarding them as being more pictorially descriptive of nature itself.

It is therefore not too meaningful to speak of a "typical" science. They are all different in significant respects. Moreover, it is unsafe to generalize as to scientific methodology. Thus it is not true that experimentation is what characterizes all sciences. Nor do all of them think predominantly in quantitative terms.

With respect to all the sciences, however, the three circles of our diagram have this historical significance: that they represent different phases of their development. In their first stage the purely experiential, i.e., direct observation and simple data gathering, predominates. Only later do the more analytical and critical, interpretive and transformative activities put in their appearance. No doubt this is inevitable.

THE THREEFOLD AND CIRCULAR NATURE OF RELIGION

Turning now to religion, in many respects it also is portrayed rather well by the diagram. Certainly it too is threefold, with *a* the experiential or empirical component, *b* the theoretical or explanatory and interpretive one, and *c* the one that is transformative and pragmatic, or what is sometimes referred to as "applied religion" or "practical religion."[1] Here also we encounter the feedback interactions and circularities indicated by the dual connections between the component circles.

Theology is represented by circle *b*. It interprets and explains the faith experience of the religious community and is, therefore, largely determined by it as indicated by the arrow from *a* to *b*. On the other hand, by the concepts, doctrines and thought patterns theology develops, it profoundly affects, and partly determines, the religious life of the community (arrow from *b* to *a*). Moreover, both the life of faith and the enterprise of theology profoundly affect the transformative action of religion in the realm of ethics and morals, and in social action, while it in turn deeply affects them (opposite arrows). In a sense, then, theology (circle *b*) has a dual stance and purpose. Facing circle *a* it conceptualizes, interprets, criticizes and reacts upon the revelatory experience of the community of faith. Facing circle *c* it elaborates the implications of faith and belief for life and work, and points to the responsibilities and problems of the community in the transformation of the world.

An important aspect of theology's function has been to interpret the significance of Christian insights for succeeding generations, for different cultures, and for different situations. In so doing it asks what the situation really is in a given time and culture, relative to man's relation to God and existence. It asks what it means in practice, in that situation, to love God and one's neighbor, and what action is called for, and what duties thus devolve upon Christians in the world of affairs and in personal relations. This brings us to the relation of Christian theology to the transformative aspect of religion, symbolized by the dual connection between circles *b* and *c*. This function of theology is at least as important as the other. Here theology must analyze the ills besetting mankind, and its grave concerns and anxieties, both those that are universal and those that appear in particular situations. It must also be conscious of the great questions man asks, that reflect his ultimate concerns—for to love man significantly in the *agape* sense, one must be aware of his longings and predicaments. But more than that, theology asks which of man's questions are truly meaningful and of ultimate concern and which are not in the light of the Gospel, and what light the Gospel can shed upon the situation.

It is probably correct to say that, relative to the transformative function of religion, for a long time the primary concern of Christianity was the "salvation" of the individual "soul." Now by *salvation* I do not mean "being saved from eternal damnation and hell fire" in the once popular sense, but from the domination of sin, man's lower, egocentric self, and from the social and cosmic forces that are beyond his control and yet threaten his very existence and being. While the contemporary Church would certainly not discount the importance of personal salvation, it is preoccupied much more than formerly with the salvation of man in community and therefore with the problems of society at large. And theology has contributed in no small measure to the development of this wider point of view, and to the channeling of Christian action along appropriate lines (circle *c*). . . .

Much of the work of the Church that is indicated by circle *c* might aptly be called Christian technology. Under this heading come such activities as the improvement of man's physical environment and the acquisition of the necessities of life, proper food, clothing and shelter; the conquest of disease, ignorance, superstition, slavery, and tyranny; the support of efforts toward peace and the abolishing of war; the establishment of justice and fair practices in business affairs, in labor and management relations; the improvement of race relations; the support of good government. Home and foreign missions in their various aspects come under this heading, as do many other activities. In all these fields the Church has developed experts, among both its clergy and laity, who may well be regarded as the technologists of the Church for the transformation of the world. Parenthetically it should be remarked that much of this application of the gospel to real life needs to be effected within the Church itself. I refer to unjust social practices and other evils that are condoned or even engaged in by large sections of its membership, as well as to practices of the institutional Church itself. There is much to be done here.

It must be recognized, of course, that much of the Church's labor of love in the world is done by unsophisticated Christians with an intense love of neighbor, who are quite uninformed theologically. It might then be said that for them transformative, social action springs directly from the basic Christian faith and the sense of responsibility to God and man. This is why circle *c* is connected to both *a* and *b*. To put this into the faith language of the community, our love-action relative to our fellow men (circle *c*) is determined largely by our experience of God and man (circle *a*) and our theological beliefs about them (circle *b*). Also, conversely, our religious experience and theological conceptions are very much affected by our actions among men.

NOTE

1. It should be noted that I am not now using some of the terms in the diagram, e.g., *experimental* and *data gathering*. This indicates that science and religion are not parallel in all respects relative to the diagram. There *are* significant differences.

QUESTIONS FOR STUDY

1. Briefly describe the function of each of the three circles in Schilling's diagram.

2. How does the two-way interaction between the first two circles describe the scientific method?

3. Why does Schilling include circle *c* in his discussion of science?

4. Give one example of the application of the three circles to religion.

QUESTIONS FOR REFLECTION

1. In terms of Barbour's account in Selection 1, to which of Barbour's four positions does Schilling belong?

2. Use Schilling's diagram to explain how both science and religion might team together to respond to the dangers of genetic engineering or the environmental crisis.

3. What, if anything, would be wrong with the argument that, since science and religion share a common method or approach, religion is really only another form of science?

NETWORKING

Other selections about aspects of *method and explanation in science and religion* include Niebuhr, Barbour (Part I), Gilkey, Popper, and Geisler and Anderson.

RADICAL FAITH AND WESTERN SCIENCE
H. RICHARD NIEBUHR

H. Richard Niebuhr, one of the most respected American theologians of this century, was born in Missouri in 1894. In 1916 he was ordained a pastor in the German Evangelical Synod of North America. After earning a doctorate from Yale Divinity School in 1924, Niebuhr became president of Elmhurst College. By 1931 he had returned to Yale as professor of Christian ethics, a position he retained until his death in 1962. Among his acclaimed books are *The Kingdom of God in America, Christ and Culture,* and *The Responsible Self.*

A theologian must approach the question of the place of faith in Western science with a diffidence even greater than he feels when he poses the like question about politics. And that for at least two reasons. For one, all of us nonscientists in Western society, no matter what our special responsibilities, tend to participate more directly in political than in scientific life. Hence we can reflect critically on political principles with some immediacy though we are far from being political specialists. For another, politics seems more akin than science to religion and ethics; for in politics we also engage in that practical reasoning which accompanies our own behavior with its decisions, choices, and commitments or, in current terms, in these spheres we are concerned with values. In science, on the other hand, men engage in the theoretical reasoning that accompanies observation of the behavior of other beings, that is, of objects; they are concerned in this reasoning, we are accustomed to say, with facts rather than values. Nevertheless, in modern culture no one can escape some direct relation to science; though we do not participate in it intensely yet scientific ways of thought have influenced wide circles. Moreover, fact and value or theoretical and practical reasoning cannot be so divorced from each other that political, ethical, and religious men can reason without theorizing, observing, and being concerned with facts; or that scientific men can develop theory without making decisions and choosing values. Hence I venture to approach scientific activity and the scientific community with the question: Is there in them something akin to that trust-loyalty syndrome that is encountered in religion and of which there are recognizable elements in politics? And is the struggle of the various forms of faith also enacted in science?

OUR FAITH IN SCIENCE

As inquirers into faith and its relations it may strike us not, first of all, that scientists are believers but that they are *believed in*. Our twentieth century is an age of confidence in science. In our culture we tend to believe scientists as, we are told, in another age of faith men believed churchmen. To be sure, we call the content of what we now believe knowledge or science, but for the most part it is direct knowledge only for the scientific specialist while for the rest of us it is belief—something taken on trust. We cannot even say that we believe what we do, and what we call factual knowledge, because we know that if we put ourselves through the discipline of scientific inquiry we shall be able to convince ourselves directly of the content of our beliefs and so convert them into knowledge. This also we have been told; and this also we believe on authority and rarely put to the test. Our beliefs about atoms and their nuclei, about electrons, protons, and stranger particles, about fusion and fission, viruses and macromolecules, the galaxies and the speed of light, the curvature of space and gamma-rays, hormones and vitamins, the localization of functions in the brain and the presence of complexes in the subconscious, the functions of the liver and the activities of ductless glands—these seem to excel in variety, complexity, and remoteness from either personal experience or ratiocination all that earlier men believed about angels, demons, miracles, saints, sacraments, relics, hell, and heaven. Perhaps the distance between what scientists assert and what we ordinary men accept as the meaning of their statements is also greater than was the considerable distance between what churchmen said and what people heard and believed.

Why is this so much an age of trust in science? One reason seems to be that the scientists, or the technologists who are associated with them (a distinction which in our naïve beliefulness we often fail to make), have commended themselves to us by the signs they have wrought. Seeing is believing in all common-sense philosophy. Of course we have not seen, with the eye or the mind's eye, what the scientists have seen with the aid of experiment and in theory but we have seen wonderful signs which, we have been told, are the consequences of their understanding. We believe what physicists and engineers tell us about electricity, sound-waves and light-waves, because we have heard radio and seen television. We believe what the professors of nuclear physics say—or what their interpreters say they say—because we have seen not indeed atomic and hydrogen bomb blasts or nuclear-powered engines but pictures of them. Modern, so-called scientific, man is not too different from his forebears in this respect; unless he sees signs and wonders he is reluctant to believe and, as scientists are wont to complain today, he gets the wonder-worker mixed up now as of old with the seer and prophet. If he did not understand that Einstein somehow made the atomic bomb possible he would probably still listen to Edison with greater respect than he accords to Einstein.

Now, also, as of old there is a second ground for believing our authorities. We believe because they make predictions that come true. Once true and false prophets were distinguished from each other on the basis of the accuracy of their predictions; now science and pseudo-science are discriminated on similar grounds. We believe the astronomers because we have seen eclipses at the predicted hour; we believe meteorologists—somewhat—because storms and fair weather have ensued as they foretold; we believe our child psychologists because our children behave as was promised or threatened. We are somewhat skeptical about our economists because their predictions conflict and at critical junctures have misled us and so we may wonder whether their enterprise is truly a science. Prediction and fulfillment, we note, run through our daily experience from the turning of a light switch to a medical prognosis in the doctor's office; and we understand that they run through all scientific work in laboratory and study.

There is, however, a third ground of interpersonal trust. We believe what scientists tell us because they have been faithful to us; they have been loyal to the human community and its members in their administration of the particular domain for which they have responsibility. That domain, we believe, is the understanding of the natural world in which we live and of which we are a part. In administering that domain the scientific community has been on its guard against error and self-deception, and also against the lie. It has not abused the power its esoteric understanding gives it; it has not used the rest of us as instruments for the private purposes of a special class; it has not deceived us, who can easily be deceived about many things that lie beyond our knowledge.

We have come to have our great confidence in science, I think, because we encounter it not as an impersonal activity but as a community of men with a tradition and a discipline of faithfulness. And one aspect of this faithfulness has been its loyalty to the whole human community. This loyalty has been demonstrated in the effort of scientists to keep the commandment of not bearing false witness against any of their neighbors; they have maintained the implicit covenant into which they entered to communicate their knowledge truly in the whole human community. The ethics of science is not ruled only by respect for fact but by respect also for those to whom facts are communicated. The interpersonal faithfulness of the scientific community appears in this, that it is a truth-telling and not only a truth-seeking society of men. The interpersonal loyalty of the scientific community appears at another point. On the whole, despite the esoteric nature of much modern science and the great advantages which such knowledge bestows on its possessors, the layman has confidence that the specialist is keeping his explicit or implicit promise to use his knowledge, with its power, for the benefit of the whole human society and for each individual in it as though humanity and the individual had a value not derived from their relations to a nation or a caste, or some other special value-center. This confidence appears especially, it seems, in the relations of the layman to biological and psychological scientists and to physicians and psychiatrists. If he did not count on their loyalty to him simply as an existent human being participating in the realm of being he could not entrust himself to their ministrations as now he does. He trusts the scientist as loyal to him with an interpersonal loyalty in a universal human realm.

Reflecting on these things the lay beneficiary of science begins to appreciate the dilemmas in which the scientific community has been placed by the rise to supremacy of nationalist loyalty. He notes the uneasiness with which scientists accept the compulsion of secrecy in those phases of research that might give aid to a national enemy. The universal truthfulness of science has not yet been perverted, he believes, by the imposition of such secrecy, though a second step, moving from secrecy to the use of science for the deception of national enemies, would be such a perversion. Science primarily loyal to a nation, or to some other closed community, speaking truth only to the nation, seeking to benefit only the nation or a class—this would be science operating under henotheistic faith as the theologian sees it; it would be science that found value only in what is valuable to the national center and be loyal only to the national community and its members. That a faith or at least morality is tied up with modern science and that this faith may be either more universal or more provincial has been brought home to the layman by what he has heard of Nazi perversions of medicine and Communist pressures on inquires in genetics. He notes that problems of value and loyalty arise not only where nonscientists make use of scientific findings but where scientists themselves commit themselves to their tasks within a context. This problem of value and loyalty in science itself is not a scientific problem soluble by scientific means. It is, in theological terms, a question of faith.

At another point also the layman becomes aware of a conflict of faiths within science. He notes the possibility that science may find its center within itself and that it may use him, his nation, his friends, and whatever he values, as instrumental goods for the cause of science. His value and the value of all that he values would then be esteemed wholly by reference to knowledge itself or to "truth" as center of value. Whatever value anything has in that scheme would be its value for science, for instance as the illustration of scientific theory, or as the object of scientific observation and experiment. Such partial valuation, made for temporary purposes and quickly overruled by the consideration that the being in question has another value, is not disturbing. The layman can accept his own role or that of other valuable beings as guinea pigs, provided it is provisional and imposed only with consent. He accepts vivisection, which poses the question of a more than humanistic orientation, despite his faith for which animals have more than scientific value, provided it is carried on with some respect for the nonscientific value of the animal. But he suspects that there is a movement in science which operates on the basis of the principle that man and everything else was made for the increase of knowledge, that "truth" is the key-value and the center of values. Here he discerns the presence of a henotheism not unlike the one he finds in a religion that has turned inward and made its own principle of being into a god of faith.

When we suspect that such restricted orientations of value consciousness and loyalty prevail our confidence in science begins to falter. It is not wholly clear to us that the science in which we had conceived confidence is actually pervaded by universal faithfulness. The science which is subject to the skeptical attitude of the larger community is one in which such universal faith is in conflict with partial, closed-society evaluations and loyalties, whether these be the loyalties of nationalism or of scientism.

THE FAITHS OF SCIENCE

A second approach to our concerns about the presence in science of faith and of conflict between its forms seems possible to the theologian without presumption. Instead of beginning with his confidence in the scientists he may begin with his valuations of the scientific enterprise. As he reflects on this he becomes aware of the tendency, first of all, to begin with himself as the center of value—a tendency he suspects all men share with him, as his formulation of the law of original sin also leads him to expect. Insofar as this is his orientation whatever is good for him is really good; what is bad for him, in his best judgment, is really bad. He values and disvalues science and the sciences as they tend to serve his needs, to maintain his physical being, to preserve his personal intellectual synthesis of convictions and ideas, and to promote his large or small ego. He is willing to sustain the scientific enterprise so far as it serves these needs. He is not loyal to it; he has interests in it. Knowledge is valued so far as it is useful power in the service of the self-cause.

More frequently, at least in public demonstrations of his faith, this man approaches science as the kind of churchman or citizen for whom the value-center is the closed society of church or state. As a churchman the question about the value of science becomes for him the question about its value in relation to the church and to the principle of the church. If the principle of the church, on which it depends for its existence, is thought to be the creed the question will be: How are scientific beliefs related to the creed? Science and the sciences will be valued accordingly. If it can be shown or believed, as many have argued, that the basic condition for the rise of modern science was the medieval creed of the churches, then churchly henotheism values science if not as the church's child at least as its first cousin. If science is out of harmony with the creed it may still be regarded as an errant child that will eventually mend its ways. When its theories can be used for the support of the creed and the church it may be valued not as sinner but as saint.

When the principle of the church is conceived more ethically than creedally, more as a "spirit" informing the will than as a "spirit" presiding in the mind of the community, then sources of science in the humanitarian ethos of Christianity may be brought into view and it will be valued as a creation of neighbor-love. It will be appreciated and depreciated also in its present activities in accordance with its relation to love as the cause to be served. Then so-called applied science will be highly regarded insofar as it contributes to human welfare. The value of pure science will be questionable.

A closed-society Biblicist, who does not look beyond the Bible, in the direction toward which the Bible points, but centers on the Bible itself as the principle of the church or of Christianity, will value science by its relation to that book. He may prize archaeology of a certain sort as the chief of sciences. In the conflicts of religion and science the presence of such henotheistic faiths within the church has played a significant role, though it would be wrong to locate the source of all the conflicts *there* or to think that in religion only we are subject to the temptations of henotheism.

We make a similar faith evaluation of science today as members of national society. Historically, it seems that the alliances and conflicts between religion and science have been replaced by the alliances and conflicts between nation and science. But the latter also takes place under the aegis of a closed society. The utility of science in developing weapons and methods of national defense, in increasing the nation's economic wealth, power, and glory makes it highly valuable. Some reverence for it as the creation of the national genius may also occasionally be present, yet fundamentally it is appreciated as the instrument of national loyalty more than as the creation of the national genius. Hence also arises the use of a standard of evaluation, apparently most distasteful to many scientists, which prizes more highly the technical achievements science makes possible than science itself, and socially useful inquiries more than insights that have no foreseeable significance for national survival, power, and glory.

The external observer cannot but overhear the complaints of the scientific community against these evaluations of its worth and against the kinds of support or antagonism it must endure as a result of these various loyalties. The question which arises for an observer who has learned, not without aid from science, to be critical of his own narrowly based evaluations is whether the judgment science makes of other enterprises and the support it renders them is sometimes similarly founded on a closed-society orientation of its own; whether in the alliances and conflicts of political, religious, humanitarian, and scientific communities the last of these is indeed always on the side of the universal against the particularism present in the others. It seems to such an observer that at times in the scientific community, as in the religious, a creed may come to be regarded as the absolute principle on which science itself is thought to depend for its being and by reference to which all other human beliefs, and indeed the significance of all beings or phenomena, are judged. The mechanistic creed, for instance, seems to have played such a role in long periods in past centuries and for large sections of the scientific community. As in the case of the church the question about such a creed is not whether it is valuable but whether it is the ultimate standard by which all other beliefs are judged; whether it itself is made the object of commitment and devotion. Or, the closed-society faith of science can concentrate on scientific method as the church can concentrate on its own ethos. It does not seem entirely a figure of speech to say that sometimes for some of the devotees of science, if not for scientists themselves, the scientific method has become a god. It determines, if not all value, then at least all truth; what it reveals is held to be indubitably true, what is untrue for it is false. Sometimes the more enthusiastic believers seem to look to it also for the determination of the good and beautiful. Indeed a churchman would hardly dare to raise any questions about a phrase he has learned from his society to approach with a sense of reverence and feelings of the holy had he not heard from many a scientist statements like President Conant's: "It would be my thesis that those historians of science, and I might add philosophers as well, who emphasize that there is no such thing as *the* scientific method are doing a public service." I know some men for whom such a statement has the ring of blasphemy. For the observer the question is not whether there is a scientific method; the question is whether science can so concentrate on it that this one discipline immanent in men, this one "spirit" among the many "spirits" in our world, becomes for it an absolute, a center of devotion, and an ultimate cause.

Again, the scientific community in its alliances and conflicts with other communities gives evidence of the presence of a closed-society faith when it exalts truth as the central value and the final end to be pursued not simply by the scientific community or by man in his role of scientist, but by all men and always. Then it seems to rely on truth to bring forth justice, welfare, integrity, peace, and all other goods. Then man exists for the sake of truth and truth is not a part of a complex system of values in subjects and objects in a complex world of being. True knowledge then is no longer the limited cause which with true justice, true beauty, and true religion receives the devoted service of one special group among many in a community that has a center and a cause beyond all these vocational ends; it becomes the exclusive cause to which all others are thought to be secondary and inferior. In practice such exclusiveness may rarely be found; but it is not infrequently expressed in the confused words which equate truth with ultimate value and make science the sole devotee of truth.

A theologian would not be so aware of the prevalence in science of the kind of closed-society faith he has encountered in religion did not scientists themselves in their constant self-criticism call these things to his attention. Without such self-criticism in the scientific community he might be the more tempted to fall back on his own tendencies toward henotheistic thinking and would tend to oppose the faith of his religious in-group to that of a scientific out-group. But as he attends to the self-questionings of scientists he senses that the issues present in their enterprise have a similarity to those with which he is concerned in religion. He thinks that he discerns alongside of the tendencies toward closed-society orientation in science a fundamental movement that is like the radical monotheism he encounters in religion and of which he sees the presence in political issues.

Something like the radical faith in the principle of being as center of value and in the realm of being as cause, seems to the theologian to be present first of all in a negative form in the established habit of scientific skepticism toward all claims to absolute significance on the part of any finite being and of the absolute truth of any theory of being. In the endeavor of science to rid itself of all anthropomorphism and anthropocentrism, of all tendencies to regard man as the measure of all things, whether of their nature or their value, he notes the presence of movement like that of radical faith in religion. Conflicts of science with religion he sees have occurred at least as often between anthropocentric religion and a science that challenged such concentration on man as between science that started with human reason as the measure of all things and a religion that regarded this beginning as idolatrous. Scientific skepticism has dethroned also the efforts to define all things and processes in terms of number or after the model of the machine. In this negative movement of scientific skepticism something is present which is like that *via negativa* in the religion which denies the name of God to any limited form or power, not because it doubts the reality of the One beyond the many but because it believes in him.

More positively radical faith in that One seems present to the theological point of view in the confidence with which pure science seems to approach anything and everything in the world as potentially meaningful. It does not assert explicitly nor does it imply, as universal religion and ethics do, that whatever is, is good. But in its domain it appears to move with the confidence that whatever is, is worthy of attention. Like pure religion pure science seems to care for "widows and orphans"—for bereaved and abandoned facts, for processes and experiences that have lost meaning because they did not fit into an accepted framework of interpretation. Whatever is, in the world of being and becoming, is worthy of inquiry not because of its intrinsic worth nor yet because it is part of some familiar pattern of meanings, but because it *is*, because in its existence it participates in being and is related to the universal and the unitary. How it is so related pure science does not yet know; but it pursues knowledge with apparently unshakable confidence that relation there is and that something universal appears in each particular. Not all events or things are equally revelatory of universal meanings to be sure, but all are participant in them. In their words scientists may express great skepticism about the unity of the world of being, but the external observer continues to marvel at the confidence with which in patience and despite many defeats the quest for universally valid knowledge of the particular is carried on. Attention seems to be given to the most unlikely phenomena in the assurance that the relatedness of the apparently unrelated will appear, though at its appearance a transvaluation of all previous scientific values may be necessary.

There is a loyalty also in pure science that is like the fidelity associated in universal religion with radical faith in being. Science always involves commitment; the scientist devoting himself to his work must accept the arduous discipline of service to a cause. Usually that cause is simply called "knowledge" or "truth" to distinguish it from the causes served in religion, art, or politics. But when this is done a fundamental problem is obscured and the issues between science and religion or politics are confused. The cause of the pure scientist does not seem simply to be knowledge or truth but universal knowledge, universal truth. He carries on his work with "universal intent," as one who seeks a truth that is true of universal relations and true for all subjects in the universe. This cause is distinguished not only from the causes of religion, art, and politics but from commitments to knowledge with a particularistic intent, or from devotion to truth that might be true for some subjects only. The conflict of science with religion has been conflict less with the religious element in religion—with reverence for the holy, for instance—than with the dogmatic "truth-systems" of closed-society faith; its conflicts with politics have been with the dogmatic "truth-systems" of closed political societies as well as with their power interests. Science which makes universal truth its cause takes its place alongside universal religious faith and the politics that is guided by universal loyalty, not without tension to be sure, but with some community of spirit.

It would be possible, I believe, for someone more adequately equipped to carry this analysis of the forms of human faith into other spheres of activity than those of religion, politics, and science. The humanities and especially literature offer a rich field of inquiry not only into the problem of how faith is expressed in life but into the other problems of the forms of faith that are so expressed, and of their conflict. Such an inquiry would raise more directly than the present attempt has done the question of humanism. Is not the alternative to all pluralistic and henotheistic, to all individualistic and closed-society forms of faith, a humanistic confidence and loyalty? Speaking in Durkheim's terms, does not the issue lie between those whose god is the collective representation of a special group and those who trust in and are loyal to the collective representation of mankind as a whole?

There is a historical answer to that question. Modern humanism to a large extent is, as previously pointed out, a protest against henotheistic faith, especially in the realm of religion. It is a protest, in the name of a larger trust and more inclusive loyalty, against those forms of faith that put their confidence in some exclusive principle. Insofar as it is a protest against theism it is often a protest against henotheism disguised as monotheism. Historically, however, humanism is the affirmation of the value of all men and as the acceptance of the vow of loyalty to the whole human community has flourished only within the framework of radical monotheism. Symbolically speaking the revelation of the Son of man has occurred only within the context of the revelation of the principle of being as God.

Genuinely radical monotheism has included all that humanism includes and something more. It has affirmed not only all mankind but all being. It has involved men not only in battle against the wrongs that afflict men but set them into conflict with what is destructive and anarchic in all accessible realms of being. Its religion has found holiness in man, but also in all nature and in what is beyond nature. It has believed in the salvation of men from evil, but also in the liberation of the whole groaning and travailing creation. Its science has sought to understand men, yet for it the proper study of mankind has been not only man but the infinitely great and the infinitely small in the whole realm of being. Its art has reinterpreted man to himself but has also re-created for man and reinterpreted to him natural beings and eternal forms that have become for him objects of wonder and surprise.

Radical monotheism as the gift of confidence in the principle of being itself, as the affirmation of the real, as loyalty—betrayed and reconstructed many times—to the universe of being, can have no quarrel with humanism and naturalism insofar as these are protests against the religions and ethics of closed societies, centering in little gods—or in little ideas of God. But insofar as faith is given to men in the principle of being itself, or insofar as they are reconciled to the Determiner of Destiny as the fountain of good and only of good, naturalism and humanism assume the form of exclusive systems of closed societies. A radically monotheistic faith says to them as to all the other claimants to "the truth, the whole truth and nothing but the truth," to all the "circumnavigators of being" as Santayana calls them: "I do not believe you. God is great."

QUESTIONS FOR STUDY

1. Explain Niebuhr's statement: "It may strike us not . . . that scientists are believers but that they are believed in."

2. What three reasons does Niebuhr give for the fact that society places extensive trust in science?

3. What does Niebuhr mean when he says that "this problem of value and loyalty in science itself is not a scientific problem soluble by scientific means. It is, in theological terms, a question of faith."

4. Give two ways in which science sometimes defines itself as the absolute center of value or as a closed-society faith.

5. In what ways does science, in its attitudes and actions, express radical faith in the universal principle of being?

QUESTIONS FOR REFLECTION

1. Niebuhr uses the term *henotheism* several times in this selection. Read Niebuhr's essay "Radical Monotheism and Western Culture" in his book by the same name for a clear discussion of henotheism. How can the term accurately be applied to science?

2. Does science have absolute values, or is it dedicated completely to the skeptical attitude? Is this attitude itself absolute? Read Jacob Bronowski's *Science and Human Values* for a discussion of values and science, and compare Bronowski's reasoning with Niebuhr's essay.

3. Do you agree that we live in an age of trust in science? What events have shaken or reinforced this faith since Niebuhr composed his essay in 1957?

4. Are the attitudes of skepticism and universality in science actually expressions of a kind of religious faith as Niebuhr claims? If skepticism means chronic doubting and faith means commitment, how can the scientific skeptic be described as religious?

5. What, according to the author, is the "universal intent of science"? Is it similar to the "unifying urge" described by Midgley in the second selection?

NETWORKING

See Küng, Gilkey, and Cobb for *faith as trust*. For *God as the center of value and ultimate reality*, see Küng, Gilkey, Tillich, Bube, and Lackey.

ON THE RELATIONSHIP OF THEOLOGY TO SCIENCE
HANS KÜNG

Hans Küng is a distinguished but controversial Catholic theologian in the Institute for Ecumenical Research at the University of Tubingen. He has lectured and taught widely in the United States, including the Union Theological Seminary and the University of Chicago. His books include *The Church, On Being a Christian*, and *Does God Exist?*

In taking account of the modern outlook, does it still need to be stressed that theology may not pass over the other sciences and attempt itself to give *a total explanation of reality*. This is perhaps what representatives of "critical rationalism" fear, allergic as they are to the "theological heritage of philosophy," "theories of redemption," and to theology as a whole. That such fears are groundless may be seen from the fact that our theology has

- nothing against the ideals of accuracy, precision and efficiency, as upheld by the natural sciences, as long as the latter do not attempt without more ado to extend their methods from watches and computers to man's mind, which is neither a watch nor a computer.
- nothing against science's objectivity, neutrality and freedom from values, as long as neither its presuppositions nor its social obligations and consequences are ignored and commitment is not excluded.
- nothing against mathematization, quantifying and formalizing of problems, as long as no one is so lacking in a sense of humor as to assume that these methods serve to provide an exhaustive explanation of such phenomena as love and grace.
- obviously nothing against natural science as the basis, not only of technology and industry, but also of the modern world picture as a whole, as long as the methods proper to other sciences are permitted at the same time—the social and cultural sciences for instance and perhaps even philosophy and theology.
- in brief, nothing against critical rationality in science as a whole and in theology in particular, if this does not mean a certain kind of "critical rationalism," a rationality uncritical toward itself: a rationalism, that is, which makes a mystery of the rational, which seeks to deal with all questions of politics, aesthetics, morality and religion, only by methods appropriate to the natural sciences; and for this very reason, despite all its insistence on fallibility and revisability in regard to solutions of individual problems, it represents as a whole that kind of total dogmatic interpretation—claiming to be critical—with which it is always ready to reproach theology and which for its own part is no less open to the suspicion of ideology.

Should not theologians too be aware of their debt to the "tradition of critical thinking"? The boldest of them in antiquity, the middle ages and modern times have had no small part in the enlightenment of mankind in regard to mythologies, ideologies and obscurantism of all kinds. Yet they have little use for making a mystery of reason. Even according to Adorno-Horkheimer's "Dialectic of Enlightenment," the supposedly very intelligent social technicians are in fact anything but true enlighteners. They have made the principle of thinking behind the Enlightenment into an instrument of social organization and with its aid have set up that technological system of control which negates the very thing which the Enlightenment intended by way of freedom, equality and happiness. It should be added that the great initiators of the Enlightenment—philosophers like Descartes, Spinoza and Leibniz, Voltaire also, Lessing and Kant, then natural scientists like Copernicus, Kepler, Galileo and Newton—would never have thought of forthrightly denying any dimension beyond that of mathematical-natural scientific reason. In this sense these great rational thinkers—by no means members of a professional substructure, which also exists—are wrongly called "rationalists," representatives of an "ism," blind to the wholeness of reality.

"Critical rationalism" overlooks the complexity of reality. "The real can be met with in a variety of ways and consequently take on a very different character. The reality of the atomic physicist is different from that of the Platonic philosopher, the reality of ordinary life different from that of religious experience. Considered in regard to its content, reality is fissured; differences appear with every change of focus. Evidently there is not simply *one* solid reality, but many different planes of reality. But this means that we cannot and may not turn a particular aspect into absolute reality: that would only lead to a mutiny of the other aspects."

Obviously the development of the secular world and secular science presents an enormous *challenge to theology:* a challenge to critical theological introspection. The task today, which surpasses the powers of one generation of theologians, is no easier than that of the Greek and Latin Fathers of the second and third centuries or of Scholasticism confronted with Aristotelianism in the thirteenth century or of the Reformers of the sixteenth century. Today also the task can be effectively accomplished—as we are striving to do here—only against the background of this present world, as it really is, with the aid of the sciences and experiences of the present time, with an eye on the practice of the individual, of the Church, of society. The more therefore the theologian knows of this world, through the natural sciences, psychology, sociology, philosophy and—today less than ever to be forgotten—history, but most of all through his own experience, so much the better will he be able to fulfill his theological task.

Serious theology does not claim any elitist, privileged access to the truth. It claims only to be a scholarly reflection on its object with the aid of a method appropriate to this object, a method whose usefulness—as in other sciences—is to be proved by results. Theology can never be content to be graciously tolerated within a field where conclusions are notably inexact and lacking in binding force, as if "religious truth" were similar to "poetic truth." The rules of the game in theological science are not in principle different from those of the other sciences. It should not be thought that irrationality, unjustifiable reactions, subjective decisions are permissible here: arguments, information, facts, are not to be shut out; existing intellectual and social situations are not to be unconditionally authorized; there must be no partisan justification of certain dogmas, ideological structures, even forms of social domination. For serious theology it is not a question of rewarding simple faith or cementing an ecclesiastical system, but—always and everywhere—of seeking the whole and entire truth.

On the other hand, serious theology does not claim any complete, total possession of the truth, any monopoly of truth. It claims to be no more than scholarly reflection on its object from *one* particular standpoint, which is anyway one *legitimate* standpoint among others. Theology can never be a comprehensive, systematic world view, worked out down to the smallest details and rendering ultimately superfluous any further reflections of sociologists, psychologists, economists, jurists, medical experts and natural scientists. In theological science we cannot appeal to any authorities whatsoever to relieve us of the duty of attending to critical arguments, to evade the competition of ideas, to suppress temptations to doubt, to exclude the possibility of error on the part of certain persons or in certain situations. No science—theology no more than any other science— can take as its object *all* aspects of human life and action. But if, for scholars in other fields but likewise concerned with man, it is a question mainly of analysis of dates, facts, phenomena, operations, processes, energies, norms, for the theologian it is a question of *ultimate* interpretations, objectives, values, ideals, norms, decisions, attitudes. The often tormenting but perhaps nevertheless liberating questions about an ultimate why and wherefore, whence and whither, cannot—as we saw—be classified as emotional reactions and therefore not the legitimate object of our science. Hence the questions of theology do not touch merely a *part* of what men are and do. They touch the most fundamental *aspect* of *all* that men are and do. From this *one* aspect theology examines *all* the strata of human life and action; from the one basic aspect *everything* can find expression, from this aspect the theologian must face *all* questions.

QUESTIONS FOR STUDY

1. Does Küng believe that theology is superior to the sciences, that theology passes over the sciences as an explanation of reality?

2. In what four areas does theology "have nothing against science"?

3. What are the characteristics of the critical rationalism that Küng disfavors?

4. Does theology have privileged access to the truth?

QUESTIONS FOR REFLECTION

1. Küng insists that theology has nothing against science as long as science admits to certain limits. Name these limits.

2. Describe the kind of critical rationalism that Küng opposes. Who might be guilty of practicing it? Hint: Consider several representatives of the various ideologies or *isms* of our time.

3. Compare Küng's critical rationalism with H. Richard Niebuhr's understanding of henotheism and closed community loyalty. Do you see any resemblances?

4. Küng seems to define theology as a science. What passages support this claim? How is theology a science?

NETWORKING

Niebuhr, Gilkey, Einstein, Haught, Gish, and Peacocke also discuss *science and religion as authority and exclusive explanation.*

AFFIRMING DIFFERENCES
THEORIES IN SCIENCE AND RELIGION
LANGDON GILKEY

Now retired, Langdon Gilkey was Sailer Mathews Professor of Theology at the University of Chicago Divinity School. In his many books and articles he has shed considerable scholarly light on the mutual influence of religion and culture in the modern world.

In this selection, Gilkey testifies as an expert witness for the American Civil Liberties Union at the "creationist trial" in Little Rock, Arkansas, on December 7–9, 1981. He is responding to questions from the attorney for the ACLU, Tony Siano.

". . . Your statement seems to draw a sharp distinction between religious ideas or religious theories and scientific ideas or theories. Would you agree with that? If so, would you tell us your view—as a theologian—on the differences between scientific and religious propositions or theories?"

"This is as complex matter; I will try to be brief and yet clear. I think, though I am not sure, that what I say about science will be acceptable to philosophers of science." (Many scientists, I noted silently to myself, don't really know too much about the questions of what science is or is not!) "All theories—scientific, philosophical, and religious—seek to explain or make intelligible the varied stuff of experience; thus, all theories—and here we are concentrating on scientific and religious theories—have certain general characteristics in common: (1) all seek to explain experiences, and appeal to certain types of 'facts'; (2) all ask certain specific sorts or kinds of questions; (3) all are responsible to certain sorts of authorities; and, as a consequence, (4) all theories have certain specific kinds of character and obey certain definite rules or 'canons.' While both are theories in this sense, still scientific and religious theories differ markedly in each of these areas.

"First, then, science seeks to explain sensory experience, facts that can be shared by everyone anywhere or any place, facts available to anyone by 'looking' or observing—that is to say, objective, sharable, external, and repeatable facts or experiences, what we ordinarily call 'sense data.' Religion is interested in a different level of experiences and in different sorts of facts: experiences of the world as a whole, its order or beauty, its meaning or lack of meaning. And religion concentrates on facts of inner life: responsibility, conscience, right and wrong, guilt, anxiety, meaninglessness, despair on the one hand, or trust, new life, release, wholeness, centeredness, forgiveness, peace—even ecstasy—on the other. Thus, science moves entirely in the sphere of objective, public experience; religion is more apt to point to special, inward, unusual, shattering, or healing experiences.

"Correspondingly, science asks objective questions, questions directed at knowledge in its strictest sense. What sorts of things are there here, or in the world? What causes what? What sorts of invariable relations are there between events—what laws govern existence? If we do (a), then does (b) follow? Does it always follow? And if so, how can we explain that? Science asks *how* questions, questions about the character and processes of change. It seeks after laws of change, and thus it concentrates on material, universal, and necessary or automatic causes, structures, laws, and habits.

"Religion asks different sorts of questions, questions about meaning. Thus religious myths, symbols, doctrines, or teachings answer these sorts of questions. Why is there anything at all, and why are things as they are? Why am I here, and who am I? Who put me here and for what purpose? What is wrong with everything, and with me? And what can set it right again? What is of real worth? Is there any basis for hope? What ought I to be and do? And where are we all going?

"These are important questions, important for life because basic to life's meaning, direction, and purpose. If not answered in terms of a traditional religion, they must still be answered. Wherever they are answered, the theories or views answering them will turn out to be examples of religious speech. These are questions of ultimate origins, of the why of things, of good and evil, of the promise of healing and reunion, questions of hope. Reality is questioned with regard to purposes, to salvation—with regard to its meaning, not primarily its structures, with regard to its spiritual dimension, not its material causes—though in the end, the two cannot be completely separated. This is what all the great religions, and certain central aspects of all the great philosophers, talk about. Wherever you have these questions addressed, you have religious speech."

There was a noticeable pause while I tried to remember where I was. I looked at Tony, and fortunately he broke right in.

"Do both science and religion recognize some sort of authority, and are these authorities different?"

"Yes, in science, the authority—the basic criterion of science—is represented by logical coherence and experimental adequacy. And by experimental adequacy is meant that a theory has not yet been falsified by experiment and that insofar as that is the case in repeated experiments, it is confirmed—that it is characterized by coherence with other established theories, fruitfulness for further questions, and simplicity or elegance. In practice, this means the authority of the consensus of working scientists in that field. This consensus of the scientific community alone determines what proposed theories conform to the requirements of logic, of experimental adequacy, and of coherence and fruitfulness. This authority among the scientists is an *earned* authority, through training, experience, and excellence in the common work of the community.

"In religion, or at least in monotheistic religion, the final authority is God, or the point where our relation with God appears, and is recognized. This point is often called revelation, or its equivalent—some special touch with the divine where enlightenment occurs and insight is given (as, for example, in the Word of God given in the Israelite Covenant, in Jesus Christ and in the Scriptures or in the 'higher consciousness' of Yoga or of Buddhism). Secondarily, authority lies with those who have received or receive revelation: prophets and apostles, holy men and women, teachers; in their writings and in those who can interpret their writings; or, in other traditions, in a holy person, a yogin, or one who has had a special experience or special authority.

"Such authority resident in special persons is not necessarily solely external to the rest of us. Usually it is also subsequently validated in some way in *my own* experience wherein I, too, make relation with the divine, through prayer or hearing the Word, through sacrament, meditation, ritual, or obedient action. But in all of these, the authority is special, and the experience of illumination is special and not ordinary or 'public' in the usual sense of that word. In each case, the authority is of a special sort; it is *given*, not earned—and is usually regarded as given by the divine. Of course, the authority in a religion may be supplemented and buttressed by rational argument—as in much theology or apologetics; but that is generally a supplemental and not an originating authority, and it is rarely the basis for the acceptance of the truth of what is there asserted." . . .

"Can you, then, Doctor Gilkey, describe for us briefly what sorts of characteristics you find scientific theories to have?"

"First of all, a scientific theory seeks to explain the facts of experience by means of law—that is, universal patterns of behavior which are necessary (always happen), which are automatic and blind (not knowing or planning what they do). Or, as is often said, scientific laws are sets of invariable relations between events; if p, then q, and *always* if p, then q.

"Secondly, these laws can appeal to, or point to, only *natural* or *human* causes or powers, forces within the creaturely world, within the system of nature and of history. No supernatural force or cause from outside the system can be a part of a scientific explanation.

"Thirdly, the basic forces or factors referred to in a scientific explanation are quantitative, not qualitative, in character, and thus are they measurable, objective, and sharable. As a consequence, no scientific theory explains by means of purposes or intentions. None answers a 'why' question, except when in asking 'Why did this event happen,' we mean merely 'What were the proximate causes of that event?'

"Finally, a scientific theory or explanation starts with concrete, objective, sharable observations or data, and it is tested by them. A quite definite outcome is predicted that anyone can observe, a datum whose non-appearance would *falsify* the explanation. A scientific theory is not tested merely by seeming to 'make sense' or to provide an adequate and coherent explanation, but by a quite definite, observable experiment. Thus the language of science is quantitative, mathematical, precise; its referent is to quite universal patterns of behavior; it is limited to describing the impersonal system of relations between the things or entities around us."

"And religious speech or theories, what are they like?"

"In the West, religious language refers to God, an intelligent, purposive being or reality, one who is transcendent, that is, who is *not* part of the system of creaturely things but precisely their source and ground. Thus language about God, 'religious explanations' or theories, is personal and purposive ('God willed it' or 'intended it'), not necessary or determined; in referring to a transcendent being, this language is symbolic or analogical, not precise and univocal.

"Religious theories explain by speaking of God's actions or purposes, not of finite causes. Whenever finite things or persons are related to God, there is religious discourse or theories about them; wherever they are related merely to one another, one has 'secular' discourse, not religious discourse. Thus when we ask, How did *a* arise out of *b*? we are not asking a religious question of origins but a scientific question. When we ask how the whole system arose, and we give God as its origin, then we are *not* providing a scientific explanation but a religious one.

"The basic words here are qualitative, not quantitative; they have to do with purposes, God's purposes—with order and disorder, good and evil; religious explanations have to do with the meaning of things, the *why* of them, not the structure or the *how*. And, as we have seen, religious explanations are based on special sorts of experience, special insights or revelations, not objective, observable, sharable experiences. Religious theories or beliefs cannot, therefore, be falsified by evidence or by new evidence. When Paul said, 'Whether we live or die, we are the Lord's,' he was making a powerful religious statement: *Whatever* happens, God is there—and my faith in God holds.

"Religion, in other words, tends to answer—or to try to answer—our *ultimate* questions: questions of ultimate origins (where did it *all* come from?), of ultimate worth (what is the point or meaning, the *why* of life?), of ultimate destiny (where are we all going?). Religious answers thus provide confidence, hope, trust; they offer guidance and direction, the promise of healing, reconciliation, and fulfillment. They form the basis for our style of life, for our norms, for the shared beliefs that create community. Religious models are imprecise, untestable, often fuzzy, but they express immensely important issues, *the* important issues for our individual and communal existence.

"Science asks what happened, what made it happen, what universal habits are there in things—it seeks that sort of understanding, *how*, not *why*, understanding. It is precise, measurable, testable; thus it is relatively certain and reliable knowledge. But by the same token, science is *limited*; it asks only certain kinds of questions; it is limited to physical explanations, to objective issues, to understanding natural relations.

"As is plain, science and religion present to us very different forms of speaking or thinking, very different sorts of models or theories. To ask whether there is scientific evidence establishing or demonstrating scientifically a religious theory, for a theory or model speaking of God's creative action, is therefore an empty question. There *can* be evidence for a religious view, of course; but any amount of 'scientific evidence' (whatever that means) for a religious theory about God cannot make the theory scientific. It remains a religious theory or model for all the reasons we have stated, primarily because it speaks of God, God's power, God's intentions, and God's deeds.

"Science is, in short, *secular*; it deals with the worldly world: with nature and its forces, with human bodies, and—by extension into the social and psychological sciences—with social, historical, and possibly psychological forces. It cannot go beyond this 'secular' level because then it leaves the observable, sharable, quantitative, measurable, the natural or finite, level. Thus it leaves out a lot: my intentions, decisions, values, and commitments, as well as God's; it omits the human and the divine *person*.

"Thus, scientific discussions of origins are significantly different from religious discussions of origins. The first trace out the finite processes by which things arose and came to be; the second witnesses to the ultimate origin and purpose of these processes. Scientific accounts of development in astronomy, geology, and biology, are, therefore, not at all incompatible with religious views, even though they do not speak of God. The fact that science omits God is a result of the *limitation* of science, not of its atheism: Science is limited to finite causes and *cannot* speak of God without making God into a finite cause.

"Let me point out that this 'methodological non-theism' of science is not confined to natural science—or to evolutionary theory. It is characteristic of all modern academic disciplines. If I write a history of World War II for the History Department at the University of Chicago, I will discuss the historical causes: political, economic, psychological, and social causes, and the historical actions by men and women, that seem to me to have brought about that war. I will *not* say, as a historian, that God's judgment on Europe caused the war.

"When, however, I write a *theological* account of modern history, I will—and I have done so in my own works—speak not only of all these factors but also of our common sin and of God's judgment; and, I must add, I do not think the event of that war can be understood until this theological dimension is included. For those theological factors, hidden though they be to the inquiries of secular historians, are, I believe, really there and vitally effective in the march of events. And the task of philosophical theology is precisely to unify in some coherent way those two diverse and yet valid ways of speaking of the war. Nevertheless, that latter represents a *theological* interpretation, not an example of inquiries recognized by most historians as 'historical.' The same is true of the law. If I am a lawyer defending a client from the charge of the murder of John Doe, I cannot offer—even in this court in Arkansas—an 'explanation' of the murder that holds that God, and not my client, struck John Doe dead."

(I noticed that Judge Overton was by now intensely interested and was looking sharply at me, and so I enlarged on this theme.)

"That would not be an explanation or theory recognized by the court; our law in this sense is 'secular' in principle. Legal procedures are limited to explaining an event by natural, historical, or personal causes, and can only develop theories that explain by means of such causes. That limitation does not mean that judges, prosecutors, and defending lawyers do not believe in God; nor that God is not at work in our society or in Arkansas society; nor that the divine hand might not have been at work in and through this event; nor that there may be, as I believe there is, a divine foundation to any 'secular' law that is just. Nevertheless, again, despite these 'religious dimensions' to the law, God is not recognized as an *agent* in a legitimate *legal* explanation of events, any more than God can be an agent in a scientific or an historical explanation of events."

(I was relieved to hear the judge at this point mutter an almost inaudible grunt of agreement, so I continued.)

"To say that evolution 'excludes God' is, therefore, merely to say that it is a theory within natural science. It is not to say that this theory is essentially atheistic or represents atheism. It is because science is limited to a certain level of explanation that scientific and religious theories can exist side by side without excluding one another, that one person can hold both to the scientific accounts of origins and to a religious account, to the creation of all things by God—which accommodation this law definitely excludes."

Figuring I had by now made my point as clearly as it could be made, I stopped and subsided back into my chair.

QUESTIONS FOR STUDY

1. Gilkey claims that theories in science and religion are very different in accordance with four main features of any theory. Summarize these differences by charting the four features of a theory in two columns: one for scientific theories and the other for religious ones.

2. Explain what Gilkey means when he says that authority in science is "earned," but in religion it is "given."

3. Gilkey claims that religious statements cannot be falsified by evidence. What does he mean?

4. Are scientists, in their method, atheistic or merely nontheistic?

QUESTIONS FOR REFLECTION

1. Gilkey is testifying at a trial that tests the constitutionality of a state law permitting creationism to be taught in public schools. The judge overturned the law. What effect could Gilkey's testimony have had on his decision?

2. If God is the cause of the whole universe and science is in the business of examining causes, why cannot God be included in its investigations?

3. In Gilkey's illustration, a historian cannot identify God as a cause of World War II. However, a theologian may see the war as a judgment of God upon the world. Is Gilkey consistent in this position?

NETWORKING

For further discussion of *theory and authority in science and religion*, see Midgley, Niebuhr, Küng, Bube, and Gish. For *"how" and "why" questions*, see Buber and Bube. *Methodological nontheism in science* arises as an issue in Bube, Einstein, and Hick.

I AND YOU
MARTIN BUBER

Martin Buber (1878–1965) was born in Vienna, and was educated and taught in Germany prior to World War II. In 1938 he joined the faculty of the Hebrew University in Jerusalem where he remained for fifteen years. Buber published widely in existential philosophy and religion. He contributed to the Jewish mystical movement known as Hasidism. This selection is taken from what is probably his best known essay, *Ich und Du*. A note on the translation: Most translators render "du" and "thou" in an effort to preserve the intimate or familiar intention of the original. Walter Kaufman, who made this translation, prefers "you" to the antiquated "thou." For our purposes, we will consider the two terms interchangeable.

The world is twofold for man in accordance with his twofold attitude.

The attitude of man is twofold in accordance with the two basic words he can speak.

The basic words are not single words but word pairs.

One basic word is the word pair I-You.

The other basic word is the word pair I-It; but this basic word is not changed when He or She takes the place of It.

Thus the I of man is also twofold.

For the I of the basic word I-You is different from that in the basic word I-It.

Basic words do not state something that might exist outside them; by being spoken they establish a mode of existence.

Basic words are spoken with one's being.

When one says You, the I of the word pair I-You is said, too.

When one says It, the I of the word pair I-It is said, too.

The basic word I-You can only be spoken with one's whole being.

The basic word I-It can never be spoken with one's whole being.

There is no I as such but only the I of the basic word I-You and the I of the basic word I-It.

When a man says I, he means one or the other. The I he means is present when he says I. And when he says You or It, the I of one or the other basic word is also present.

Being I and saying I are the same. Saying I and saying one of the two basic words are the same.

Whoever speaks one of the basic words enters into the word and stands in it.

The life of a human being does not exist merely in the sphere of goal-directed verbs. It does not consist merely of activities that have something for their object.

I perceive something. I feel something. I imagine something. I want something. I sense something. I think something. The life of a human being does not consist merely of all this and its like.

All this and its like is the basis of the realm of It.

But the realm of You has another basis.

Whoever says You does not have something for his object. For wherever there is something there is also another something; every It borders on other Its; It is only by virtue of bordering on others. But where You is said there is no something. You has no borders.

Whoever says You does not have something; he has nothing. But he stands in relation.

We are told that man experiences his world. What does this mean?

Man goes over the surfaces of things and experiences them. He brings back from them some knowledge of their condition—an experience. He experiences what there is to things.

But it is not experiences alone that bring the world to man.

For what they bring to him is only a world that consists of It and It and It, of He and He and She and She and It.

I experience something.

All this is not changed by adding "inner" experiences to the "external" ones, in line with the non-eternal distinction that is born of mankind's craving to take the edge off the mystery of death. Inner things like external things, things among things!

I experience something.

And all this is not changed by adding "mysterious" experiences to "manifest" ones, self-confident in the wisdom that recognizes a secret compartment in things, reserved for

*initiated, and holds the key. O mysteriousness without mystery,
O piling up of information! It, it, it!*

*Those who experience do not participate in the world.
For the experience is "in them" and not between them and
the world.*
*The world does not participate in experience. It allows
itself to be experienced, but it is not concerned, for it
contributes nothing, and nothing happens to it.*

*The world as experience belongs to the basic word I-It.
The basic word I-You establishes the world of relation.*

*Three are the spheres in which the world of relation
arises.*
*The first: life with nature. Here the relation vibrates in
the dark and remains below language. The creatures stir
across from us, but they are unable to come to us, and the
You we say to them sticks to the threshold of language.*
*The second: life with men. Here the relation is manifest
and enters language. We can give and receive the You.*
*The third: life with spiritual beings. Here the relation is
wrapped in a cloud but reveals itself, it lacks but creates
language. We hear no You and yet feel addressed; we
answer—creating, thinking, acting: with our being we
speak the basic word, unable to say You with our mouth.*
*But how can we incorporate into the world of the basic
word what lies outside language?*
*In every sphere, through everything that becomes present
to us, we gaze toward the train of the eternal You; in each we
perceive a breath of it; in every You we address the eternal
You, in every sphere according to its manner.*

I contemplate a tree.
*I can accept it as a picture: a rigid pillar in a flood of light,
or splashes of green traversed by the gentleness of the
blue silver ground.*
*I can feel it as movement: the flowing veins around the
sturdy, striving core, the sucking of the roots, the breathing
of the leaves, the infinite commerce with earth and air—
and the growing itself in its darkness.*
*I can assign it to a species and observe it as an instance,
with an eye to its construction and its way of life.*

I can overcome its uniqueness and form so rigorously that I recognize it only as an expression of the law—those laws according to which a constant opposition of forces is continually adjusted, or those laws according to which the elements mix and separate.

I can dissolve it into a number, into a pure relation between numbers, and eternalize it.

Throughout all of this the tree remains my object and has its place and its time span, its kind and condition.

But it can also happen, if will and grace are joined, that as I contemplate the tree I am drawn into a relation, and the tree ceases to be an It. The power of exclusiveness has seized me.

This does not require me to forego any of the modes of contemplation. There is nothing that I must not see in order to see, and there is no knowledge that I must forget. Rather is everything, picture and movement, species and instance, law and number included and inseparably fused.

Whatever belongs to the tree is included: its form and its mechanics, its colors and its chemistry, its conversation with the elements and its conversation with the stars—all this in its entirety.

The tree is no impression, no play of my imagination, no aspect of a mood; it confronts me bodily and has to deal with me as I must deal with it—only differently.

One should not try to dilute the meaning of the relation: relation is reciprocity.

Does the tree then have consciousness, similar to our own? I have no experience of that. But thinking that you have brought this off in your own case, must you again divide the indivisible? What I encounter is neither the soul of a tree nor a dryad, but the tree itself.

QUESTIONS FOR STUDY

1. Describe briefly the distinction between I-You and I-It attitudes.

2. I-You encounters arise in three spheres. Describe them.

3. How may a tree be experienced as an I-It? An I-You? According to Buber, are the two approaches mutually exclusive in the case of the tree?

QUESTIONS FOR REFLECTION

1. Is the I-You attitude reserved for meetings with persons and the I-It for objects? Give an example of a possible I-It approach to another person.

2. Explain Buber's statement: "Whoever says You does not have something; he has nothing. But he stands in relation."

3. How is science an experience of the "surface of things?"

4. Buber seems frustrated with the dominance of the I-It approach: "O mysteriousness without mystery. O piling up of information! It, it, it!" While we would quickly point to science and technology as "I-It" enterprises, are there forms of religion which qualify as well? What would they be? Is it possible to address God as an It?

5. Buber says that relation (I-You) is reciprocity. He then speculates on the consciousness of the tree, which seems necessary for this reciprocity. Why should we not charge him with promoting primitive animism or pantheism (see *animism* and *pantheism* in the Glossary)?

6. Since beliefs fall into the category of the I-It, does it not follow that beliefs destroy I-Thou relationships between persons?

NETWORKING

Barbour (Part I), Gilkey, and Küng also advocate a *two approaches understanding of science and religion*. References to the *I-Thou/It relationship* may be found in Barbour (I), Swimme, Tillich, and Berry.

SUGGESTIONS FOR FURTHER READING

Barbour, Ian G. *Religion in an Age of Science: The Gifford Lectures*. Vol. 1. San Francisco: Harper and Row Publishers, 1990. An updated and more accessible version of Barbour's earlier classic survey, *Issues in Science and Religion* (Prentice-Hall, 1966). Either of these works is an excellent introduction to the study of science and religion.

Barnett, William. *Irrational Man: A Study in Existential Philosophy*. New York: Doubleday and Company, 1962. This book remains one of the most readable explications of an elusive philosophical movement that has had its disagreements with science and religion.

Bronowski, Jacob. *Science and Human Values*. New York: Harper and Row, 1965. A very readable examination of the act of discovery as it occurs both in the sciences and the humanities. First delivered as lectures at the Massachusetts Institute of Technology.

Buber, Martin. *The Writings of Martin Buber*. Translated by Will Herberg. New York: Meridian Books, 1956. An excellent representative anthology of Buber's work including selections from "I and Thou."

Gilkey, Langdon. *Maker of Heaven and Earth: The Christian Doctrine of Creation in the Light of Modern Knowledge*. New York: Doubleday and Company, 1959. Perhaps the clearest available exposition of the Judeo-Christian doctrine of God and world and how it is distinct from philosophical and scientific ideas.

Kleiver, Lonnie E. *The Shattered Spectrum: A Survey of Contemporary Theology*. Atlanta: John Knox Press, 1981. In the introductory chapter, the author traces the crises of theology to the rise of science and its impact upon society. The remainder of the book is a clear survey how the various schools of theology have responded to this situation. A good introduction to the major trends in theological thought.

Kuhn, Thomas S. *The Structure of Scientific Revolutions*. Chicago: University of Chicago Press, 1970. A controversial and important examination of the process of scientific discovery that questions the idea that science is pure objective inquiry with no social dimension.

Küng, Hans. *Does God Exist?: An Answer for Today*. Translated by Edward Quinn. New York: Doubleday and Company, 1980. Küng is a contemporary, and controversial, Catholic theologian. He addresses in considerable detail the various reasons for not believing in God provided by philosophy and sciences before presenting his own position.

Nagel, Ernest. *The Structure of Science*. New York: Harcourt, Brace, Jovanovich, Inc., 1961. This book remains one of the best philosophical accounts of the scientific enterprise. Difficult but very rewarding.

Perspectives on Science and Christian Faith: Journal of the American Scientific Affiliation. The American Scientific Affiliation. Although this journal approaches issues in science and religion from an unabashed Christian evangelical stance, one can frequently find thoughtful and objective articles on almost any topic.

Rolston, Holmes, III. *Science and Religion: A Critical Survey*. New York: Random House, 1987. A clear and insightful survey of the field of science and its engagement with religion. In many ways Rolston parallels Barbour and offers an alternative to him.

Whitehead, Alfred North. *Science and the Modern World*. New York: Macmillian Publishing Company, 1925. A twentieth century classic. Whitehead, the father of process philosophy, offers profound insight into the history of science and its relation to civilization. The book contains a good chapter on science and religion.

Zygon: Journal of Religion and Science. Joint Publishing Board of the Institute for Religion in an Age of Science and the Meadville Theological School. This premier journal in the field encourages dialogue between scientists, philosophers, and theologians. Since it was founded by Ralph W. Burhoe in 1966, the journal has published articles by some of the generation's most distinguished scientists and philosophers. Volume 22 contains the twenty-year indexes of all articles and reviews published during that period.

For further suggestions, see the footnotes at the end of the Barbour selection in this section.

PART II

Words, Images, and Stories

THE TRIBES OF ISRAEL STAND BEFORE THE TABLETS OF THE LAW OR TORAH GIVEN BY GOD THROUGH MOSES AT SINAI. THE SCULPTURE IS AN EXCELLENT EXAMPLE OF THE ROLE OF WORDS, IMAGES, AND STORIES IN THE LIFE OF A COMMUNITY.

"God made man because He loves good stories," says Elie Wiesel, essayist, novelist, and Nobel laureate. It appears that God passed this pleasure on to the human creature undiminished. After all, we are language-bearing animals who build much of our civilization out of words and express the meaning of our lives in stories.

Contemporary theologians, philosophers, and other students of culture are acutely aware of the importance of words and stories in shaping the lives of individuals and communities. Language is the natural element of human existence, just as water is for fish and air is for birds. We are so immersed in this stuff of our lives that most often we are unaware of its presence. That, most likely, is the way it should be. We never notice the air we breathe unless it is fouled or missing, in which case we seek some immediate remedy. It is the same with language. Unless some crisis of Babel, some consistent failure of speech; forces us to become conscious of that medium itself, we go on blithely assuming its reliable presence.

The rise of science and its kin, technology, have produced such a crisis. These successful enterprises use language to appraise empirical events, to convey information and instructions, and to produce some desired behavior or achieve some practical goal. Modern society depends so completely on these functions of language that its consciousness of other more traditional functions is reduced considerably. Language has always opened doors to new thoughts and new options for action. It has served as an X ray to probe the depths of human existence. Language evokes and provokes. It is the cohesive of human community. Language makes and keeps us human.

The readings in this section are intended to clarify the specific tasks carried out by language in science and religion and to recognize their similarities and differences within each domain. The first two selections of the section "words and images" examine the functions of language, especially paradox and metaphor, in science and religion. The third demonstrates how the vocabulary taken from the domain of science and technology provides new insights when applied to the other domain, religion. The two selections of the next section, "stories," explore the nature of myth and its power in attempts to draw upon the vision of science for religious purposes.

Roger Schmidt's contribution in the first selection is a straightforward attempt to outline the tasks of scientific and religious language. In "The Functions of Language in Science and Religion," he first identifies scientific speech as concerned primarily with empirical reality and therefore subject to procedures of verification. Then he shows that, given this somewhat narrow understanding of the role of language, statements about religious matters fail to qualify as meaningful, since, for the most part, they can neither be confirmed nor denied by an appeal only to empirical states of affairs. They are worse than false—they are altogether meaningless.

Schmidt builds on this effort to demarcate scientific and religious discourse into spheres of sovereignty and influence in his account of the important features of religious language. Religious terms are drawn from the common stock of human experience, but they point beyond their ordinary meaning to something ultimate, which is ineffable, that is, literally unspeakable. Religious discourse takes place at the edges of our ordinary experiences but is about the extraordinary. Such speech is, in the author's terms, "double-intentional," "paradoxical," "evaluative," and "revelatory."

The ubiquitous influence of the computer and mass media confirms that the primary function of words in our society is to convey information and instructions. The poetic use of words is relegated to some lesser role in our lives, to literature and perhaps politics, where it serves to entertain and persuade, but little else. Thus we might be surprised to discover that a great deal of what we say, even when conveying simple information, is based on poetic resemblances between different terms or referents such as analogies and metaphors.

In the second selection, "Metaphor in Science and Religion," Earl MacCormack explores the universal meaning of an important form of poetic speech—metaphor. A metaphorical statement in science is an imaginative and suggestive hypothesis to be explored by thought and experiment. Physicists speak of force and energy as if they were manifested as particles. They have particles of electricity called electrons, of electromagnetic energy called photons, and of gravity called gravitons. Particles "carry" various forces and energies between other particles and physical objects. Since these particles and forces are not available for direct inspection, they are known primarily through readings on instruments which must be interpreted. Metaphors are used to give scientists some satisfactory image of what they might be examining so that they may talk about it, exchange ideas, and suggest avenues for further research.

Theologians recognize that this kind of predicament is what makes metaphorical speech indispensable. Theology, after all, means "God-talk" and God is no more readily available for direct examination than minute particles and forces. The very nature of God's hiddenness, or "aseity," makes efforts to speak literally of the divine nature impossible. God is thus spoken of metaphorically in scripture as "King" or "Lord," "Shepherd," and "Father," and by theologians and philosophers as "cosmic mind" or "watchmaker" so that some sense can be made in the experience of the religious community of the role and will of the divine.

The root metaphor, is useful in efforts to characterize the cosmos as a whole. "The world is a machine or clock" and "the world is a living thing or organism" are potent root metaphors. MacCormack explores the powerful influence of such generalizations on thought and action.

R. Buckminster Fuller, author of the third selection, "Ever Rethinking the Lord's Prayer," is acknowledged to be one of the most creative and independent thinkers of the twentieth century. Fuller was a prodigious engineering genius who applied his inventive mind to numerous fields, including theology. He was also exceedingly innovative in his style of composition, so much so that his use of technical jargon defies comprehension. One might classify his writing style as technical gobbledygook at its worst, the nightmare of every instructor of freshman composition. Still, creative insight is the result of new and unusual combinations of words and ideas. When language intended for one domain, here the systems sciences, is employed in the context of another domain, prayer, the words take on new and surprising, if not perplexing, meaning. Granted, readers may have to reorient their perspectives to understanding the unfamiliar associations, but the reward for this perseverance is insight.

The fourth selection, "Understanding Myth" by Suzanne K. Langer, is a discussion of the nature, function, and dynamics of myth. The modern world has discredited the concept of myth, which has become synonymous with fantasy, false opinion, and the wish to escape reality by weaving dreamlike, happily-ever-after stories. Langer sees these as distortions of the essential functions of myths. She claims instead that myths are courageous, cognitive efforts to face the difficult and terrifying realities of life through symbolic narrative. The figures of a mythic story are not idiosyncratic representatives of the private imagination. They are figures signifying crises, problems, and threatening powers shared by the community as a whole. They embody considerable social insight.

Science rises against myth when somebody discovers that myths are not literal, not concerned with facts. This discovery encourages the conclusion that myths are false and science, which seeks to identify and account for facts, is true. As science progresses, myth necessarily retreats. Langer takes exception to this "silly conflict" for two reasons. One is that myth has other powers—primarily emotional or attitudinal, but also cognitive—which science lacks. Secondly, we must beware of trusting science to progress indefinitely. The same forces of exhaustion that overtook myth as an exclusive mode of truth may well deflate science too and give rise to yet another stage of thought and vision—perhaps even a new mythology.

In the last selection, "A Cosmic Creation Story," Brian Swimme confirms Langer's final point with his belief that a new mythology is required to meet the needs of rapidly changing times. He insists that something must be done to get the human species back on track and synchronized with the cosmos before it is too late. We need a transformation, and that can only come from a radical shift in the way we think. Presently, we think primarily in terms of facts and theories. We have forgotten how to tell stories. Consequently, we have lost our way.

The emerging narrative of an evolving cosmos will be the next cosmic story. It will be universal—intended not just for a single tribe or culture, but for all humankind. Swimme sees the day when evolutionary cosmology will combine with the mythic attitude to offer a dramatic narrative account of the coming-to-be of the world. The transformation he calls for will then occur. All humans will reconcile to the earth as "earthlings" and, through that identity, reconcile to the cosmos as well. Poets and artists, along with scientists, will make their special contributions to the shaping of this new story.

WORDS AND IMAGES
THE FUNCTIONS OF LANGUAGE IN SCIENCE AND RELIGION
ROGER SCHMIDT

Roger Schmidt teaches philosophy and religion at San Bernardino Valley College in California. This selection is taken from his popular introductory text, *Exploring Religion.*

———————————————

The scientific way of seeing and speaking provides knowledge or information about the world. It has, as its guiding principle, systematic and dispassionate description of the world and the construction of formal models that parallel the relationships operative in the natural and social worlds. It also demands that its propositions and models be empirically verifiable. The cognitive character of scientific discourse raises the question of whether religious statements provide information or knowledge about the world, and, if they do, how they are validated. At least superficially, religious statements appear to provide knowledge about what is real. For example, the Hindu teaching that souls are eternal is assertive, as is the Buddhist doctrine that denies the reality of personal immortality. The statement, I believe in God, assumes that there is something to which the word God applies. The Muslim confession of faith, "There is no God but Allah, and Muhammad is his prophet," declares not only that there is a God but that Muhammad has a prophetic relationship to him.

For those who take such affirmations seriously, they are not mere psychisms intended only to express human feelings or prompt certain attitudes. They are assertions about reality. Nevertheless, the validation of the cognitive claims of religious statements presents serious problems. In fact, the philosophical point of view known as logical positivism or logical empiricism regards all talk about God, Tao, and such ineffable religious experiences as nirvana to be cognitively meaningless, since such talk refers to things that cannot be empirically verified. How, for example, is the proposition that God exists, to be verified, since it is neither empirically verifiable nor true by definition? The positivist's solution is to argue that religious language is emotive rather than cognitive, an expression of feelings and psychic needs. In this view, while the assertion that God exists appears to be an informative statement, it is better understood as an emotive utterance or a statement of value rather than a statement of fact.

Because the rules of evidence operative in scientific methods of validation are not readily applicable to truth-claims regarding what a person or a people regard as holy, philosophers have insisted that religious statements are a form of belief rather than knowledge. Belief statements may be true, but they do not constitute knowledge until the evidence is so conclusive that all reasonable doubt is overcome. Although religionists may acknowledge that theological propositions, such as God exists, are not factually descriptive in the same way that "All crows are black" is, they may want to insist that religious statements do have a noetic or cognitive quality that is more than a subjective commitment.

Not surprisingly, in an age that desires a scientific seal of approval, religionists occasionally appropriate the language and methodology of science to demonstrate the truth of their claims. Conservative Christians, in particular, have selectively used the scientific approach to buttress their conviction that the biblical story is either factually descriptive or defensible indirectly through empirical evidence. For example, some biblical archaeologists diligently search for Noah's ark in order to corroborate the biblical text, while Christian astronomers attempt to provide evidence of the star that guided the Magi to Bethlehem. Scientists who are biblical creationists examine the fossil record and life's molecular structure in order to prove that the biblical account of creation is more plausible than evolution.

Christians are not alone in seeking the aura of scientific verification. Transcendental Meditation proponents regularly publish data intended to demonstrate empirically that meditation enhances health, and other religionists believe that biofeedback research offers empirical evidence of what sages and yogis have achieved through self-mastery.

The efforts of theologians and committed lay scientists to provide empirical evidence for their faith suggests that, although faith points to a mysterious and nonordinary dimension that is always beyond or something more than argument and evidence, belief in the holy is not unreasonable. Saint Augustine believed that faith seeks understanding; thus the noetic quality of religious language entails reasons, explanations, and evidence for the truth that is proclaimed.

We should note that contemporary behavioral and social scientists have, for the most part, retreated from logical positivism. They may concur that religious statements are beliefs rather than knowledge, but they are less likely to dismiss them as emotive and cognitively meaningless as the positivists do. J. Milton Yinger writes that "social scientists are less prone to assert all that is important about religion is available to the objective observer. This is, after all, an extra-scientific assumption, not itself demonstrable by scientific study.". . .

The scientific way of knowing is an incredible human accomplishment. No other approach has proved equally fruitful as a way of understanding our natural and social environments, and yet to remain deaf to other ways of appropriating the world is dehumanizing. The language and method of science, with its emphasis on objectivity, precision, quantification, and empirical verification, needs to be complemented by an openness to expressions of feelings, commitment, and wonder. Science and mathematics may help build skyscrapers, formulate actuarial tables, and send spaceships to the moon, but the language of the heart does not speak in numbers. The scientific mode describes impersonally and objectively what is known and neglects the personal and individual character of existence. Its content is a world known as an object—a world in which feelings and evaluations are secondary.

Implicitly, science involves a commitment to the value of truth; nevertheless, because it is so narrowly circumscribed by adherence to natural explanations and a sticking to the "facts," it is a limited mode of discourse. Science offers information about such vital concerns as the pollution of the environment, the depletion of natural resources, and the magnitude of modern weaponry. It can suggest ways that resources can be conserved or alternatives developed, but on questions of value, of priorities, of choosing between industrial expansion or conservation, polluted or restored environments, an escalated arms race or disarmament, it is silent. Human expression is not exclusively a vehicle for conveying information or stating what is true. Familiarity with other more intuitive, existential, evaluative, and revelatory ways of knowing and speaking offers a corrective to the limits of science.

The language of science describes a natural world, a cosmos, of infinite complexity and intricate interdependence. To ask, What is the ultimate meaning of this complexity, this interdependence? is to transpose scientific discourse into a religious inquiry. Does the universe, as mirrored by science, require a unifying force such as the Tao or a creative intelligence (God) to adequately account for it? Does the design of the cosmos suggest a designer? When such questions are raised, humans have moved beyond the empirical limitations of science in the direction of ultimacy. . . .

Religious language is not an exclusive vocabulary or separate language; it is a use of words in a distinctive way. It differs from other modes of discourse in that religious discourse points to the ultimate and nonordinary, whereas a scientific use of language refers to the natural world. Religious language is operative whenever the symbolic process points beyond itself to the ultimate. Four features of religious language are especially important in understanding religious ways of seeing and speaking: it is double-intentional, paradoxical, evaluative, and revelatory. . . .

Religious language arises out of the human attempt to speak of ultimate existence. It is double-intentional in the sense that humans employ words used to speak of ordinary reality in such a way that they point to a nonordinary reality. If the sacred were entirely like ourselves or other things in the natural world, direct, rather than double-intentional, speech would be possible. If, however, the holy is an ineffable and indefinable mystery that prompts humans to grope for words and symbols that point beyond the limits of language, then religious language must be double-intentional—that is, religious symbols must signify in the way that ordinary symbols do and, at the same time, must illuminate the ultimate as well. The twofoldness of human existence, our rootedness in the ordinary and our restless yearning for the nonordinary, is expressed through double-intentional metaphors. For example, in the Chinese classic, the *I Ching,* humans are seen as middle creatures stationed between heaven and earth. Here, *middle creature* is a double-intentional metaphor because it employs an experience common to all of us (that of being in between) in such a way that it points beyond the ordinary to our position in the cosmos. The imagery suggests that as middle creatures we unite in our being heaven and earth. Things can also be double-intentional; thus a Japanese garden, with its meticulously cared-for sand and solitary rocks, is a reminder that insights and transformed existence are manifested in silence.

Jesus was a master of double-intentionality, of talking about God in images of the ordinary. While conversing with a Samaritan (a member of a nonconforming Jewish sect) woman at a well, Jesus used the commonplace thirst for water as a metaphor for a spiritual thirst. In Jesus' metaphor the act of drinking water, which restores life to those who are thirsty, is compared by extension to a water that can forever quench a spiritual thirst. In another context, Jesus spoke of a shepherd's concern for a lost sheep in such a way that it served as an image of God's concern for the spiritually lost.

The language of Zen Buddhism is also rich in double-intentionality. The genius of Zen is that enlightenment or nirvana occurs within the ordinary. The truth of Zen is to be experienced and manifested in every aspect of the practical life; thus the graceful life of Zen is like a simple meal. A Buddhist metaphor compares the nonordinary and sudden character of enlightenment to an unruffled pond into which a frog jumps:

> *The old pond.*
> *A frog jumps in—*
> *Plop!*

Sacred acts, like sacred words, are double-intentional in that they must point to the holy through such familiar activities as eating, drinking, gesturing, and speaking. In sacred rites the commonplace must point in two directions—to itself and beyond itself to the transcendent and enduring. For example, the washing of hands, as a holy rite, must point at once to the here-and-now and to the ultimate. The double-intentional nature of holy rites brings the familiar and habitual in contact with the holy. Holy acts and, in particular, holy rites are moments in which the nonordinary breaks into the ordinary—moments when the tyranny of the trivial is broken. . . .

Religious language is at least implicitly paradoxical. A paradoxical use of language is one in which contradictions are brought together in such a way that, instead of simply negating each other or becoming an absurdity, they express a profound truth. This paradoxical feature of religious language is amusingly illustrated by a passage from James Weldon Johnson's book *God's Trombones,* a collection of Negro sermons formulated in verse. Johnson told of a preacher who, after reading a rather cryptic Bible passage to his congregation, "took off his spectacles, closed the Bible with a bang and by way of preface said, 'Brothers and sisters, this morning—I intend to explain the unexplainable— find out the undefinable—ponder over the imponderable—and unscrew the inscrutable.'" The preacher's conjoining of opposites is a vivid and explicit use of paradox.

Much of religious language is not, however, explicitly paradoxical. The statements that God exists or that the Noble Eightfold Path leads to enlightenment are not overtly paradoxical. The double-intentionality of the Buddhist Eightfold Path makes an analogy between a path, familiar in ordinary experience, to a spiritual path that leads to nirvana. Systematic analysis cannot completely remove an element of paradox in religious expressions, because sacred words and gestures must mediate between the known and the unknown, the instrumental and the ultimate, the speakable and the unspeakable, the temporal and the durative. The problem in speaking about nirvana is that nirvana is not a place and therefore, strictly speaking, no paths lead to it. Likewise, we are familiar with the existence of things, and the assertion that God exists is grammatically the same as the statement, Trees exist. The difficulty is that God is believed to be the ultimate ground of all things, the presupposition of existence. Can the ground of all things also be a thing?

Invariably, talk about the holy is driven to contradiction and paradox because it must speak of the infinite in terms of the finite. The sacred is always beyond the power of speech and the constrictions of definition, yet the other side of the paradox is that if the holy is to be known at all, it must be present in and through the symbolic or meaning-giving process. Humans and holiness meet in experience, and yet as Dionysus the Areopagite, a fifth-century Christian, wrote, "The simple, absolute and immutable mysteries of Divine Truth are hidden in the superluminous darkness." Religious expression forces language beyond its ordinary uses and employs paradoxical expressions to speak about the unspeakable. Nirvana, for instance, is spoken of as ultimate enlightenment and, paradoxically, as nothingness or no-thingness. The *Tao Te Ching,* a classic rich in paradox, says enigmatically that the Tao does nothing, "yet through it everything is done."

The double-intentional and paradoxical character of religious expression can be further illustrated by Abraham Heschel's remarks about the Jewish observance of Sabbath. In the Jewish tradition, Sabbath is a holy day—a day on which God draws near to his creation. Sabbath and Sabbath observance is a reminder of the two worlds, this world and the world to come. In Heschel's commentary, the joy of Sabbath is part of this world, while its holiness and peace are signals of the world to come. He wrote that "the seventh day in time is an example of eternity"; thus, paradoxically speaking, in Sabbath observance the eternal is drawn into time. . . .

Religious language focuses on matters of value rather than matters of fact. Evaluative religious discourse is evident in the providing of instructions for living, in making commitments, or in raising questions that require moral or ethical reflection. Ultimate values provide norms by which individual and group life is guided and judged. For example, a Jewish interpretation of the story of creation in Genesis suggests that in the taking of a single human life a whole world is destroyed; killing a person destroys not only a single life but all those that might issue from it. The rabbinical tradition continues, "If anyone saves a single person, Scripture credits him as though he had saved a whole world." The interpretation asks us to be sensitive to the ultimate value of each human life.

Evaluative religious language is often directive—that is, it commands or instructs. Traditionally, sacred duty is not so much reasoned moral deliberation as it is something commanded. The Ten Commandments are in the imperative form of "thou shall" or "thou shall not"; thus they prescribe Sabbath as a holy day and inveigh against adultery, lying, stealing, and murder. In the Gita, Arjuna is pictured as a warrior-prince, who, although obligated to lead his army in battle, was morally troubled because the war that he was to initiate pitted relatives against relatives, countrymen against countrymen. Arjuna told Krishna that he wished neither victory nor the slaying of his enemies. Lord Krishna responded by insisting that Arjuna's duty as a warrior-leader was to commence the struggle. The abandoning of duty, Krishna declared, would only bring evil to Arjuna and his people. The validation of religious directives, sacred duty, is thus usually associated with a divine authority, such as Krishna, or is mediated through a sacred person or holy book. We should note, however, that some people may question and reject traditional authority when it is in conflict with moral reflection or matters of conscience.

Certainly much that was traditionally taught concerning the male's spiritual and temporal rule of women has been modified or forthrightly repudiated by modern moral and theological arguments.

Unlike factual assertions, instructions or commandments are not, strictly speaking, either true or false. A more appropriate response to such directives is to question whether they are reasonable or unreasonable, performable or unperformable, legitimate or illegitimate. In the Sermon on the Mount, Jesus instructed his followers to love their enemies. The Buddha directed those who would serve him to do so by nursing the sick. Both assumed that their instructions could be carried out. The question was not whether Buddha's and Jesus' words were true, but whether they should be obeyed.

Evaluative discourse can be performative as well as directive—that is, words can be employed to do something. The taking of an oath, I do solemnly swear, is a thing done and not merely a description of reality. Performative statements change the situation; thus the words, I now pronounce you man and wife, directly change the relationship of the two parties, legally, morally, and perhaps spiritually. Mormons, for example, believe that marriages can be performed that are binding not only in time but for eternity. Since religious vocations require a commitment to a way of life, the context in which the commitment is made usually involves a ceremony in which a performative statement is made. For example, an initiate entering a Buddhist monastic community makes a threefold vow (I take refuge in the Buddha, I take refuge in the Teachings, I take refuge in the Community) in order to effect his or her passage from outsider to insider. . . .

The point has been made that religious language is double-intentional, paradoxical, and evaluative. Religious language is also revelatory—that is, the religious way of seeing and speaking is something that is both a sacred disclosure and an invitation to see and model the social and psychological aspects of human existence in respect to what is ultimately real. . . .

The way the world appears to us is not entirely within our control. This has profound implications for religious ways of seeing and speaking that are more intuitive and revelatory than rational and empirical. From a religious standpoint the sacred is revealed or discerned in manifestations that seem more given than exacted, more waited on and listened for than willed or mastered. In theistic traditions, for instance, God takes the initiative in making himself known; thus he speaks to Moses out of a burning bush and to Job through a whirlwind. The holy can be known in more muted hierophanies. God was revealed to Elijah in "a still, small voice," and enlightenment, the Zen Buddhist reminds us, can be experienced in everyday activities and in the soft sounds that well up in the silence of meditation. The revelatory character of religious knowledge also implies that religious language is, in some situations, regarded as given rather than as a conscious human creation; thus, for example, the words of Muhammad recorded in the Koran are believed to have originated with Allah rather than with the prophet.

Because revelation and enlightenment cannot be forced, experiences of holiness are usually described as spontaneous, momentary, and self-confirming. The Zen scholar, D.T. Suzuki, described the liberating and revelatory character of satori (enlightenment) as being a moment of direct seeing, an intuitive apprehension, of things as they are. The experience, he insisted, transforms our normal way of seeing so that time and eternity are one. Buddhist monks may spend years preparing for such an experience of ultimacy;

a good part of their time may be devoted to controlling their appetites and to countless hours of disciplined meditation. Yet paradoxically, when the unity of being that is satori is experienced, it is abrupt or sudden and, though sought and prepared for, always a joyous surprise and a mysterious and amazing gift. . . .

In one sense, religious ways of seeing and speaking are sacred disclosures, something given; but in a second sense, they are human creations that invite us to discover an emotionally and intellectually satisfying view of life. In this second sense, religious symbol systems are heuristic or revelatory models that serve as an invitation to discover and know what is ultimately real. Religious discourse, whether sacred disclosure or conscious creation, is an invitation to discover, as a presupposition of all existence, an ultimate order through which human life can be unified.

As noted previously, science provides a picture of reality by employing symbols to correspond to relationships between entities in the natural world. Religious symbol systems are also models or maps of reality. In this sense, religion, like science, is cognitive—that is, a way of perceiving or knowing. However, scientific and religious knowledge differ profoundly. Scientific knowledge is factually descriptive and empirically verifiable. In contrast, the cognitive claims of religion are not so much about matters of fact as they are heuristic models for discovering what is ultimately real, for shedding light about the whole of existence. Reality isn't just a matter of facts; the manner in which facts are interpreted and the patterns that they are judged to form depend in part on the conceptual models through which they are filtered. Religious ways of modeling or arranging what is known provide a context in which the facts and the ambiguities of human existence are integrated and interpreted.

Religious language counters the fragmentary and commonsense character of what we know with an explanation of the whole of things. Religious models attempt to help us see patterns that are already there, but to which we may have been blind. A story from India illustrates the fragmentary nature of human understanding and suggests what a picture of the whole is like. Several blind men came upon an elephant. One grabbed the elephant's tail, a second felt the tusks, while a third companion caught hold of the trunk. Others busied themselves with the elephant's legs and sides. The blind people attempted to describe what they had ventured upon. None of their descriptions were entirely false, but each was true only up to a point. What they lacked was a vision of the elephant's wholeness. It is a vision of ultimate wholeness—that is, a comprehensive cosmic order—that religious ways of seeing invite us to discover.

As invitation and discovery, heuristic or revelatory religious language is also evident in the way in which religious questions center on things that concern us ultimately. The religious use of the interrogative is a device through which humans question their position in the cosmos. We can, like the biblical Job, take our case to the court of God and ask Why? of the universe. The religious voice can be painfully honest, like that of the psalmist who asked, "Why dost thou stand afar off, O Lord? Why dost thou hide thyself in times of trouble?" The lamentation of the psalmist becomes, by extension, that of all humanity: Why must I suffer and die?

The test of religious questions is not simply whether they are answerable once and for all, but whether they are fruitful—that is, whether they lead from the ordinary to the nonordinary, from the instrumental to the ultimate. Perhaps Zen Buddhism more than any other tradition employs language playfully and humorously in order to serve the business of spiritual liberation. Questions (*koan*) and stories are cleverly used to transform and enlighten one's normal way of looking at things. For example, one Zen saying invites us to reverse our ordinary way of looking at things by suggesting it is the bridge that moves and the water that remains stationary.

Because Zen is so suspicious and critical of doctrinal discourse, it prefers linguistic forms that are enigmatic and revelatory. For example, the koan is a disconcerting form of questioning employed in the Rinzai Buddhist tradition. "What is the sound of one hand clapping?" and "Does a dog have the Buddha nature?" are two well-known examples. Koan are perplexing problems because they are questions for which there are many correct answers but, paradoxically, no single right answer. The aim of these puzzling questions is the cultivation of intuition and insight in preparation for satori, rather than the formulation of correct responses. The instrumental nature of the koan is evident in the thirteenth-century Zen master Ekai's understanding of them as guides: "I meant to use the koan as a man who picks up a piece of brick to knock at a gate, and after the gate is opened the brick is useless and is thrown away."

Koan, in a question and answer form, have been preserved as stories (*mondo*) that serve Zen students in their quest for liberation. Some of these stories invite a direct and intuitive understanding of Buddha's teaching that in the experience of ultimate existence the seeker must light his or her own way rather than look to others, including the Buddha, for deliverance. For example, on one occasion when a monk asked the master Ummon, "What is the Buddha?" he received the reply, "Dried dung." The point of this mondo is that a person must sometimes say "no" to the Buddha in order to become a Buddha or, as another master, Joshu, humorously put it, "Wash your mouth thoroughly if you say 'Buddha.'"

A religious question is unfruitful if it leads to shallowness; in fact, one of the objectives of the koan is to bring Buddhist students to a wariness and distrust of easy answers. Religious questions may be difficult to penetrate, even unanswerable, but they can be fruitful because they are valuable ways of remaining open to the possibilities of ultimate existence.

Like koan and mondo, religious language is often ambiguous, evocative, and contradictory. As revelatory or heuristic, religious language is intended to lure us beyond the fetters of literal-mindedness and the safety of the ordinary to an experience of the sacred. In the introduction to his play, *The Best Man,* Gore Vidal points out the difficulties that the storyteller faces: "It is infinitely harder to ask questions in such a way that the audience is led not to the answers (the promise of the demagogue) but to new perceptions."

QUESTIONS FOR STUDY

1. What is "objectivity" in science? How does the quest for objectivity help determine the kind of language used in science?

2. How do positivists argue that religious language is not "cognitively meaningful" but rather "emotive"?

3. In addition to examining facts, in what other ways can one achieve knowledge?

4. Religious language is double-intentional because it speaks about two realities. What are these realities?

5. In what sense are religious rituals, like religious language, double-intentional?

6. What is a paradox? Give an example of a paradoxical religious assertion and one example of an assertion that is not paradoxical.

7.   Schmidt says that instructions or commandments are not, strictly speaking, true or false. What does he mean?

QUESTIONS FOR REFLECTION

1. Argue for the position that only statements which can be empirically tested have any meaning and that all others are emotional or subjective. Does your argument contain only statements that are empirically verifiable? Is there any way around this problem?

2. Religion, especially mysticism, often claims that experience of the sacred (such as God, Nirvana, or the Tao) is ineffable. Define "ineffable." (See the Glossary.) Do you agree that some experiences cannot be communicated?

3. Why is it apparently impossible to have a language that describes the sacred in the same way as we have a language to describe the secular or worldly?

4. Paradox appears in modern physics in the notion of complementarity, wherein particles, such as electrons and photons, are described in incompatible images as both particles and waves. (See Part IV, "Beyond Language.") Does religion have its own forms of complementarity?

5. Schmidt claims that religious images often provide models for God. How is the term *model* used here? Can you describe several such models which religion has used to describe God or the sacred?

NETWORKING

Barbour (I) and Asimov also discuss *literalism in religion*. For the concept of *paradox,* see Capra. *Logical positivism* and *linguistic analysis* are treated by Barbour (I).

METAPHOR IN SCIENCE AND RELIGION
EARL R. MAC CORMACK

Earl MacCormack is science advisor to the governor and executive director of the North Carolina Board of Science and Technology. For twenty-five years he taught philosophy, most recently as Charles A. Dana Professor of Philosophy at Davidson College. Dr. MacCormack has a degree in engineering and a Ph.D. degree from Yale University in philosophy. He was a visiting scholar at the Massachusetts Institute of Technology and Fulbright Visiting Professor at the University of Madras in India.

For some time it has been seriously doubted that metaphor could be a legitimate device for the expression of genuine knowledge. Many philosophers believed that when arguments were weak, metaphor was invoked to serve as a distraction from obvious faults. It has been viewed as more expressive of emotive feelings than of cognitive information. Metaphor was acceptable in poetry and literature for there the purpose of the writer was to convey intense feelings about the nature of human existence. But when metaphor appeared in science or philosophy, efforts were immediately undertaken to eliminate it, for it was considered to be dangerous rather than beneficial. This attitude was part of the reason that philosophers objected to religious language, which was notorious in its use of metaphor. Religious language was thought to be emotive, not only because it could not be directly and publicly verified or falsified, but also because it employed metaphors. When positivists found that scientists also utilized such infamous linguistic devices, they strove to eliminate them by representing scientific language in formal logic. Without metaphor, however, scientists could not change the meanings of terms and suggest new hypotheses. That scientific terms necessarily change their meanings seriously undermined the view that scientific language could be unambiguous and precise.

The discovery that science needs metaphor does not by itself guarantee the legitimacy of the religious use of metaphor. It merely eliminates a negative argument; to object to religion solely because it uses metaphor is not a sufficient argument for the same criticism could be leveled at science. Nor does the scientific use of metaphor guarantee that metaphor is always a proper tool for the expression of knowledge. Some poetical metaphors may well express emotions rather than concepts. What we need is a theory that will differentiate among different uses of metaphor showing us which ones constitute knowledge claims and which ones seek to reveal deep human feelings and how these different functions are achieved. The development of a "tension theory" of metaphor by both philosophers and literary critics seeks to do just that—to offer an interpretation of the various forms and uses of metaphor. During the last decade philosophers have moved far beyond Aristotle's notion of metaphor as the use of one word to stand for another. They want to show just how it is possible for some metaphors to create meaning, for others to express analogies, and for still others to become "dead" as they enter our everyday usage, and it is to this theory that we must attend if we are to understand the similarities and differences of the scientific and religious uses of metaphor.

The essence of a tension theory is that if a metaphor is taken literally, it produces absurdity. When we first hear the metaphor or see it in writing we are genuinely shocked by it. The new word or the juxtaposition of old terms is quite unnatural and produces an emotional response in us. When it was found that "particles" which were thought to be irreducible atoms could be divided as in the case of the nucleus, scientists were surprised and the word "particle" took on a new and metaphorical meaning. Or talking about "particles" that travel faster than the speed of light is similarly shocking. When the early Christians claimed that "God" has become man in Jesus, the Jews who heard this were stunned because their notion of Yahweh assumed that God was completely different from man. To say that God is light does not claim that "God" is the physical phenomenon of photons. Even commonplace metaphors like "time flies" or to "see the point of a story" or to "hear from someone" when one received a letter all seem odd and strange when they are first used. Time does not literally "fly" in the sense that a bird does, nor do we literally "see" the point of a story in the sense of visual perception, nor do we "hear" in the auditory sense when we receive a letter. Tension is the emotional shock produced in the hearer by an intentional misuse of language. We are not comfortable seeing ordinary language used in this fashion and in the sense of surprising us and causing us to pause and consider what is meant by this strange juxtaposition of words, metaphors when they are new are the occasions for emotional responses.

All metaphors that produce legitimate tension consist of two referents. Often it is said that these two parts are the well-known and the less-well-known. The well-known has been called the "tenor" or underlying idea (principle subject) and the less-well-known the "vehicle" or imagined nature. This certainly fits the case of "particle" where the principle idea was that of solid irreducible atoms (tenor) and the imagined hypothesis was that these objects could be subdivided (vehicle). Yet the categories are not precise for not only does the old sense of particle take on a new meaning, but the new meaning of subatomic physics where "particles" do divide also retains many of the properties of the older notion of "particle" such as solidity. There is an interaction in all metaphors between the referents. Consider the metaphor "Man is a wolf." Here "man" takes on the qualities of wolf-like behavior such as grouping together in bands and preying on his fellow man in a rapacious manner. But "wolf" may also take on the characteristics of human behavior so that when we see wolves in zoos or in the wilderness, we think of them as possessing certain human qualities. When it was claimed that God was man in Jesus, certainly both the notion of God was altered as well as the notion of man. The advent of this metaphor led to the doctrine of the Trinity and to many theological doctrines of man that include the possibility of man participating in divinity through his own humanity. To say that "God is man" alters both our notion of God and our notion of man.

At this point we should note that when we describe a metaphor as possessing two referents, we do not necessarily mean that it is composed of two "words." The word "particle," for example, could be a metaphor in quantum mechanics because it referred both to its Newtonian use as a solid irreducible atom *and* to its new properties of divisibility and transmutation into energy. In other metaphors, such as "God is man" or "Man is a wolf," the two referents are explicit and consist of the juxtaposition of words not normally put together when they are first expressed. Our notion of metaphor as composed of two referents producing absurdity in the hearer extends to all grammatical forms including simile, synecdoche, metonymy, and catachresis just to name a few. We reject the old division between simile and metaphor on the grounds that both grammatical forms involve a comparison of the properties of both referents. To say that "Man is like a wolf" and "Man is a wolf" are different is only to claim that the first simile explicitly *asks* the listener to compare the two while the latter does the same thing implicitly. When one hears "Man is a wolf," he must consider the ways in which it might be possible for men to be *like* wolves and wolves to be *like* men. Simile as a grammatical form explicitly reminds us to compare the two referents. And if the juxtaposition of referents in a metaphor rested upon no likeness at all, then the metaphor would not just be strange, it would be unintelligible. There would be no way in which we could recognize one part as even possibly related to the other part.

Since taking metaphors literally produces absurdity and emotional shock, we must consider the metaphor "as if" it were true. Man is not a wolf and yet we consider what it would be like to be a wolf or for a wolf to be a man. This is what gives metaphor its hypothetical character; it is suggestive of new possibilities for meaning. The act of creating a new metaphor is the process of forming an imaginative hypothesis. Poets suggest new ways of viewing the world or of considering human feelings by their novel use of language. Some of the ideas they propose seem plausible to us while others seem foreign and remote. Some of their suggestions express the ways in which we feel and others do not. When the author of Psalm 23 wrote: "The Lord is my shepherd . . ." the suggestion that God protected his people like a shepherd who guards his sheep had deep meaning for those believing that God had delivered them from adversity. But for those like Job who had been afflicted and tormented, the suggestion of God as a shepherd was so irrelevant as almost to be offensive. Scientists also make suggestions some of which find confirmation, as in seventeenth century mechanics where it was proposed that action could take place at a distance. To Aristotelians the notion that movement could take place without a force or impetus in direct contact with the object moved was absurd. Yet this metaphorical suggestion came to be expressive of what later scientists actually believed to be the case in nature. Bodies could be in motion without an impressed force. Yet other suggestions also expressed in metaphors never did become expressive of confirmed experience. We have already seen that the "funiculus" as an explanation of why mercury rose to a height of 29.5 inches was discarded. The history of science is filled with metaphorical terms that have since been discarded. We are familiar with the overthrow of the phlogiston theory and the refutation of ether. There is nothing to stop us from *considering* that there is an invisible substance ether that is necessary for the propagation of light waves except scientific experiments that produce contrary evidence. There are still other scientific metaphors like the tachyon (a particle that travels faster than the speed of light) that remain speculative hypotheses; they are suggestions neither confirmed nor disconfirmed.

Interestingly, the "as if" quality of many metaphors disappears altogether after a time. What may start out as a suggestive juxtaposition of referents filled with tension ends up as a commonplace part of our ordinary language. We call these dead or faded metaphors. When we say that "time flies" no one is shocked or surprised and we all know what we mean by this. Yet when the metaphor was first uttered, it did occasion surprise, for time is not literally something that flies. But it is expressive of how we do feel about time. Often our experience is that time passes swiftly like the swift flight of a bird. Certainly there are other occasions when "time drags" to use another metaphor. However, when we want to express our feelings of the rapid passage of time, we say "time flies." This metaphor was so expressive of human feelings that it was used over and over again. What started out as a misuse of language, the juxtaposition of "time" with the verb "fly," becomes a proper use. Gradually, through the repeated use of the metaphor, "fly" takes on the connotation of "rapid passage" in addition to that of "physical movement through the air." Just when this transition takes place is difficult to ascertain, but a glance at dictionaries of different periods clearly shows that words do change their meanings. . . .

This is how a word like "particle" can move from a meaning that includes the properties of solidity and irreducibility to a meaning that includes divisibility and existence as a field of energy. The word still retains its concept of a definite entity as did the older concept so that "particle" in quantum mechanics is not completely different from the classical notion. Electrons and other subatomic particles are different from Newton's corpuscles in that they are not bits of matter and yet they are also still like them in that we can talk about them as single entities. We say that there are a discrete number of electrons orbiting the nucleus or that electrons jump from one energy level to another. Tension disappears in the metaphor as the "as if" quality is eliminated by the confirmation of the hypothesis.

In theology the concept of God has often had the status of a metaphor suggesting an hypothesis that is later widely accepted with the concurrent loss of tension. Since the reformation, Protestants have considered God as an absolute, transcendent being, invisible, immutable, all powerful and beneficent. Proposals by process theologians that God should be thought of as di-polar with one aspect absolute and another aspect relative and changing cause shock among those committed to the older meaning of the term. The new metaphorical suggestion has a tension that the older one has lost. Whether the suggestion will be adopted and the metaphor pass into ordinary theological usage will depend upon the confirmation that this hypothesis does or does not receive in the minds of believers. Without such acceptance, the metaphor of God as a di-polar being will remain only a suggestive hypothesis. Reinterpretations of theological terms resulting in the formation of new theological metaphors have occurred over and over again. Dogmatic theologians who claim that theology is relatively unchanging have only to look at the entries for "God" in an etymological dictionary to find the contrary. "God" has had "tribal," "legal," "metaphysical" and "psychological" characteristics. . . .

By conveying what is literal, ordinary language provides a firm platform from which to judge what is hypothetical. Only if we have some notion of the ordinary and commonplace can we have any sense of this suggestive. Thus, a metaphor offers not only an unusual grammatical usage, but it also suggests experience beyond the ordinary literal sense of everyday life. And among metaphors, there are some that are more suggestive than others. Those that are most speculative and hypothetical never do become reduced to ordinary discourse, but remain primarily suggestive and hypothetical. At this time, we are not sure whether the tachyon will remain a speculation that can be neither confirmed nor disconfirmed or whether empirical evidence will be found for it. In poetry, there are irreducible suggestive metaphors and it seems unlikely that we shall ever adopt them as modes of everyday conversation. John Donne wrote, "Yea plants, yea stones detest And love." Here is a case in which it is extremely unlikely that stones detesting and loving will be experienced by us as a testable phenomena. Certainly, when we look at a stone we may think of it as appearing as if it hated or loved, but there is little likelihood that we will ordinarily speak of "stones" as possessing the feelings of detesting and loving. There are numerous other metaphors like this one that are suggestive and appeal to our imaginations, but are remote from the everyday experiences of our lives. Literature abounds in them as do science and theology. It is doubtful that "force" as used either in Newtonian mechanics or quantum mechanics can be expressed in ordinary language. It certainly has an ordinary technical usage determined by theory, but this is not the same meaning as the "push" or "pull" that we think of when we use the word in everyday conversation. Similarly, we talk about God to each other, but we do not fully grasp all of the hypothetical possibilities for this term as suggested by various theological interpretations. The term "God" remains an emotional and controversial word because we cannot specify fully what we mean by it. It remains a tension-filled metaphor suggesting possibilities only some of which we can confirm. Not all of the metaphorical qualities of either silence or religion can be reduced to ordinary language. That some of the suggestive hypotheses can be experientially confirmed in each is of prime importance. Without this confirmation, each enterprise would remain purely speculative.

The difference between ordinary language and metaphor rests not only upon the tension produced by metaphors and absent from common discourse, but also upon the speculative and hypothetical nature of metaphor. Some metaphors die and do become part of the language of the marketplace, but other metaphors remain suggestive and tension-filled. And the method by which metaphors cease to be metaphors occurs through confirmation by experience; when a metaphor suggests a meaning that is often confirmed by experience, it is widely used and the terms (or term) composing it undergo a change in their semantical meaning (new lexical entries are added in dictionaries). . . .

The metaphors that we have considered thus far have all been used to express hypothetical concepts in scientific theories and in theological explanations. Words like "force" and "positron" found employment as suggestive of various experiments while theological terms like "God" and "love" were used to express aspects of human existence that are not fully comprehensible. Metaphor can also serve another function besides that of suggesting possible experiments and experience or expressing that which is only partially known. It can present an hypothesis that is much more fundamental and comprehensive in its application. This is its function as a "root-metaphor." A root-metaphor is the most basic assumption about the nature of the world or experience that we make when we try to give a description of it. Starting with the belief that the world is like a machine, we may then try to build a series of categories composed of physical laws which seek to explain just how it operates mechanically. Or, we may feel that the world is chaotic and meaningless and then we try to express this perception in novels and paintings. None of these assumptions are literally true; the world is not really a machine nor is it fully chaotic. However, the employment of a metaphor to express this most basic judgment about the world forces us to consider our surroundings *as if* they were machine-like or disorderly. The function of the root-metaphor is to suggest a primary way of viewing the environment or experience and this way of looking at things assists us in building categories or in creating art forms that will express this insight. Our very notions of what is true and what is meaningful rest upon our underlying assumptions about the nature of reality. Without such tentative statements about the nature of the world, knowledge would be impossible, for we would have no way of organizing our perceptions into a coherent whole. . . .

A root-metaphor is constructed by considering a commonsense notion and then generalizing it by applying it to things, experiences, and events beyond those that are ordinary. Applying the concept beyond immediate experience, new categories are constructed to assist in the process. If the common-sense notion is restricted in its applicability, then it is quickly discarded, but if it does apply to many experiences beyond those of common sense, then it may be adopted as a legitimate way of looking at the world. For example, all men are familiar with their own bodies as a basis of life. Taking this concept of organism, it is possible to speculate on whether the entire world can be understood according to this root-metaphor. We know literally that the world is not an organism, but we wonder whether a system of categories erected upon this hypothesis will be insightful and fruitful for an explanation. One characteristic of organisms is that they are in constant flux, they are born, live, and die. Certainly, the world changes and there are cyclic events like those of the organism. We note that higher organisms have intelligence. Does this mean by analogy that all parts of the world, not only lower organisms, but inanimate objects as well, have intelligence? If we are unwilling to admit this, then we try to show how such a category is limited and why only higher organisms have the function of thinking. With the category of "life" we may wish to show that "life" is nothing more than a special combination of chemicals and that the dividing line between animate and inanimate is not as obvious as it once seemed to be. And so the process goes; some categories will fit and others will not and still others will only partially describe all the phenomena. The root-metaphor is retained only so long as it provides a basis for a theory that we accept as explaining the world or part of it. No system of explanation founded upon a root-metaphor will be completely successful in encompassing all types of experience. Inevitably, there are competing ways of viewing the world, with different explanations. Some explanations better describe one type of phenomena than another and choices are made upon the basis of that elusive criterion of "adequacy." This is similar to the problem of deciding just why one theory is "better" than another one. In a few cases it is clear that the system of explanation does not fit the experience of most men and so is discarded. Taking a clue from the Freudian claim that dreams reveal much of the unconscious, one might be tempted to speculate that the world itself is a dream or an illusion. So empirically-minded are most westerners that this view of the physical universe is unacceptable even though for some forms of Buddhism and Hinduism it is quite normal.

For those who seek to explain the nature of reality itself, a root-metaphor may be applied as a world hypothesis as in the cases of considering reality as if it were an organism or a machine. Yet the scope of a root-metaphor may be much more limited, as it is in a discipline like science or even in a single literary work. The claim may be made that the root-metaphor of the discipline is also applicable as a world hypothesis and this has happened over and over again. However, this procedure often has led to severe disappointment when the root-metaphor used as a world hypothesis has been often convicted of distorting or ignoring much evidence that does not fit its categories. In the exuberance of finding meaningful categories that do describe phenomena in his discipline, the researcher may generalize beyond the limits of his knowledge. In the case of a single artistic work, the author genuinely hopes that the idea underlying his creation will have a universal quality. The novelist portrays characters that have traits common to us all, but to claim that all men conform exactly to his figures claims too much.

Both science and religion use root-metaphors as the basis for their whole enterprise, but the contents of the metaphors employed are different. To discern the differences, it will be necessary to look more closely at several types representative of each discipline.

A characteristic root-metaphor of scientific theory until the twentieth century was that of the world considered as a mechanism. Newton's mechanics along with the corpuscular theory that he and numerous others in the seventeenth century espoused provided many of the categories for theories erected upon the "world-as-a-mechanism" metaphor. This conceptual pattern viewed the universe as composed of a series of irreducible material atoms which interacted with each other according to precise mechanical laws. Although Newton admitted that there were gaps in this system of motion, succeeding mathematical physicists like LaGrange and LaPlace developed universal equations which they thought eliminated chance altogether and completely described the motion of all of the particles in the world. If one could establish the initial positions, times, and velocities of these particles, then it would be possible to predict with absolute certainty their locations and velocities at later times. This led to the belief that the universe was a closed, deterministic system.

So widespread was the acceptance of this root-metaphor and its systems of categories in the eighteenth and nineteenth centuries that men began to think of the universe as actually having this kind of deterministic reality. Theologians were so convinced of this world view that they sought to relate the mechanical order perceived in the world to theology. Their favorite device for doing this was the notion of a creator God who had designed the world with a purpose in similar fashion to the way in which a mechanic would build a machine.

When Einstein's special theory of relativity replaced the classical concept of mechanics, a great revolutionary shock was felt in the scientific world. Those who took Newtonian mechanics in its later formulations as the absolute description of the world had forgotten that all scientific theories have a tentative status. They forgot that the concept of the world as a mechanism was a root-metaphor, a suggestive way of viewing the world and not necessarily conclusive.

Although the root-metaphor of the world-as-a-mechanism was overthrown by the advent of relativity theory, its generalization into a world hypothesis had produced a reaction against this world view in the form of the nineteenth century romantic poets. Looking back to the heyday of mechanism, Whitehead noted that scientists of that ilk could have learned from poets like Wordsworth and Coleridge not only that such a conception of the world left no room for "feeling," but that it also assumed a separation between the knower and the known. It was not only Einstein who claimed that the position and perspective of the subject affected his perception of the object.

The road to Einstein's achievement had been prepared by physicists like Ernst Mach who had demonstrated many of the internal inconsistencies within Newtonian theory. In doing this, Mach and others were proposing an alternative root-metaphor. Instead of mechanism, they were advocating science as mathematics. Viewing the world as mathematical in nature is an ancient root-metaphor dating back at least to the early Greeks with their preoccupation with geometry and numbers. Through the centuries, the inheritance of Euclid has been to use deduction as the basis of all reasoning. Spinoza's *Ethics* is a well known attempt to philosophize utilizing the deductive method of geometry. The Pythagorean assumption that the world can be represented by numbers also remains with us today. Few would take the metaphor the-world-is-mathematical literally for that would all too obviously produce an absurdity, but it often does achieve a dogmatic status when defenders of this view claim that theories can only be composed of mathematics and that models or conceptual patterns which employ non-mathematical terms are illegitimate. Mach and Duhem both objected to theories which borrowed terms from the empirical world to build their structures. Their assertion was that the mathematical edifices of science properly represented the empirical world as confirmed by experiments.

A vastly different root-metaphor that we have already mentioned and which has been used in the construction of scientific theories is the conception of the world-as-an-organism. This is an ancient metaphor often used by primitive peoples in their mythology, but still used today, especially by those committed to a neo-evolutionary position. The process of evolution from inorganic to organic and then from relatively simple to relatively complex beings culminating in man and his society can be viewed as the development of an organism. The dividing line between organic and inorganic is almost impossible to make, especially with the recent successful analyses of DNA into its helical structure of triplet groupings of amino acids. Because of its earlier acknowledged association with mythology, few today take the-world-as-organism as more than an interesting metaphor. But the related metaphor of the world-as-process has received more serious attention. In the nineteenth century, Herbert Spencer's application of evolution to ethics and social behavior rested upon the conviction that evolution was real and not just a tentative theory. And this belief continues as most educated people do affirm the reality of evolution in a way that is close to mythical.

Perhaps the most widespread religious root-metaphor until the rise of modern science was the presumption that religion was founded on objective, miraculous, divine occurrences. This assumption was allied with the notion that the Bible was literally true and miracles were to be believed to have been witnessed conclusively. For centuries the biblical stories were considered to be the supreme truth. Two forces undermined the status which the metaphor religion-is-the-objective-truth-in-the-Bible had occupied for so long. Both the rise of modern science with its rational explanations of natural events and the discovery of the nature of biblical literature brought about a series of changes in the root-metaphors used by religion.

For many, the shift was to theologies erected upon the root-metaphor of religion as the experience-of-the-divine-in-human-life. Although Schleiermacher was the foremost modern exponent of this view, religious experience had been a part of the Christian tradition (and other traditions) for centuries. In the West, Christians looked to religious experience as the confirmation of their beliefs whether biblically founded or given to them in the life of the church. The tension in this metaphor is well known. The experience is said to point beyond itself to a being unavailable directly. If the metaphor is taken literally, then it reduces religion to human experience alone.

A related root-metaphor is: religion-is-personal-experience. This metaphor is used to defend religious experience from the attacks made upon it by philosophers, psychologists, and sociologists. If religion really is personal and related to the language of "I," then it is unfair to criticize it with third person arguments. It is difficult to convince a mystic that he is wrong since he can always claim that his experience is self-authenticating. If you try his methods and do not achieve the same results, he can retort, "Keep trying and maybe you will have the experience and see the truth." This root-metaphor is different from the others that have been discussed in that it is more suggestive that it is expressive of human experience.

The root-metaphors of both science and religion involve human experience. When the scientist starts with the assumption that the world is mathematical, he knows that this is not literally true, but that it is an hypothesis which will produce enormously fruitful results in scientific theories. The successes of his predictions as confirmed by experiments convince him that he was correct in making this assumption. The theologian may similarly know that the metaphor of religion-is-the-divine-in-human-life is not completely correct as he wishes to retain the notion that God is also transcendent, but if this root-metaphor yields a theology influencing human actions, then he feels confirmed in his adoption of it.

That science as well as theology rests upon tentative and hypothetical metaphors may be disturbing to those who have always believed that it was only religion that could be considered to be speculative while they held science to be erected upon the solid foundation of concrete fact. But science properly done never claims to be infallible and dogmatic; scientists are always willing to consider new evidence and formulate new theories. Sometimes the nature of the new theory is so radical a departure from the old that an entirely new way of viewing the world is necessary so that a new root-metaphor is selected and an old one discarded. Among theologians, it was only after the root-metaphor of religion as divine-miraculous-occurrences had been overthrown that the tentative and speculative status of the discipline came to be recognized. Some theologians still tend to be dogmatic, basing their attitude upon the earlier notion that religion was in fact objective. Objectivity, however, for both science and religion always involves the subject as he selects the aspects of human experience from which he will make, by analogy, assumptions about the nature of the world and human experience. These analogies expressed in root-metaphors then influence the way in which his explanations are constructed to describe the world and his experience in it. The categories selected and his theory of truth all must be in accord with the basic way of looking at the world that the root-metaphor provides.

QUESTIONS FOR STUDY

1. Why does Mac Cormack say that "it has been seriously doubted that metaphor could be a legitimate device for the expression of genuine knowledge"?

2. What is the tension theory of metaphor? Identify the tenor and the vehicle in the metaphor "God is light."

3. What is a dead or faded metaphor? Illustrate.

4. What power does metaphor provide that literal, ordinary language does not?

5. What is Mac Cormack's definition of *root metaphor*?

6. Give two examples of root metaphor in science or cosmology and two in theology.

QUESTIONS FOR REFLECTION

1. Turn to the entry for *positivism* in the Glossary. Would a positivist reject metaphorical language? Explain.

2. Height or "upness" is often a metaphor for excellence, power, or authority. Can you think of three common expressions that illustrate this? Example: "She makes high grades."

3. Explain the tension involved in the claim that "The Lord is my shepherd." In what sense suggested by Mac Cormack would the biblical figure of Job take exception to this metaphor?

4. What metaphor is applied to God in the creation account found in the book of Genesis? Can you see any advantages to the image? Would this metaphor be as revealing today as it was 2,500 years ago?

5. Give three characteristics of a world understood according to the root metaphor "the world is a living organism" and according to the root metaphor "the world is a machine." A current metaphor for the planet earth is that it is a living system. What are the consequences of this metaphor for our behavior toward the planet?

6. Tradition and theology often claim that God is "wholly other," a being who cannot be known in any independent way because no similarity exists between God and anything in the world of our experience. If this is so, how can metaphorical speech, which depends on some resemblance, be applied to God in any useful way, and how could any metaphor, once applied, be tested for its accuracy?

NETWORKING

The subject of *metaphor* may be found in Barbour (Part I), Schmidt, McFague, and Roach. *Root metaphor* or *world view* is discussed in Swimme, Hick, McFague, and Berry, while *mechanism and Newtonianism* are topics in Bube and Dillard. Fuller, McFague, Cobb, Lovelock, and Berry advocate notions of *organicism*.

EVER RETHINKING THE LORD'S PRAYER
R. BUCKMINSTER FULLER

Buckminster Fuller (1925–1983) is perhaps the best-known American engineer of the twentieth century. He attended Harvard University and the U.S. Naval Academy. His accomplishments include architectural and automotive designs. His most popular invention is the geodesic dome, the primary example of which was a major attraction in the Seattle World's Fair in 1962. Fuller wrote prodigiously and with a unique style that self-consciously attempted to integrate the technical language of geometry and systems engineering into philosophical and social concepts. Perhaps his most popular book is *Operating Manual for Spaceship Earth,* published originally by the University of Southern Illinois where he was a research professor for many years.

Since 1927, whenever I am going to sleep, I always concentrate my thinking on what I call "Ever Rethinking the Lord's Prayer." The Lord's Prayer had obviously been evolved by a plurality of deeply earnest and thoughtful individuals whose names we will never know. My latest rethinking of it follows. . . .

EVER RETHINKING THE LORD'S PRAYER
July 12, 1979

To be satisfactory to science
all definitions
must be stated
in terms of experience.

I define Universe as
all of humanity's
in-all-known-time
consciously apprehended
and communicated (to self or others)
experiences.

In using the word, God,
I am consciously employing
four clearly differentiated
from one another
experience-engendered thoughts.

Firstly I mean:—
those experience-engendered thoughts
which are predicated upon past successions
of unexpected, human discoveries
of mathematically incisive,
physically demonstrable answers
to what theretofore had been misassumed
to be forever unanswerable
cosmic magnitude questions
wherefore I now assume it to be
scientifically manifest,
and therefore experientially reasonable that

scientifically explainable answers
may and probably will
eventually be given
to all questions
as engendered in all human thoughts
by the sum total
of all human experiences;
wherefore my first meaning for God is:—

all the experientially explained
or explainable answers
to all questions
of all time—

Secondly I mean:—
The individual's memory
of many surprising moments
of dawning comprehensions
of an interrelated significance
to be existent
amongst a number
of what had previously seemed to be
entirely uninterrelated experiences
all of which remembered experiences
engender the reasonable assumption
of the possible existence
of a total comprehension
of the integrated significance—
the meaning—
of all experiences.

Thirdly, I mean:—
the only intellectually discoverable

a priori, intellectual integrity
indisputably manifest as
the only mathematically statable
family
of generalized principles—
cosmic laws—
thus far discovered and codified
and ever physically redemonstrable
by scientists
to be not only unfailingly operative
but to be in eternal,
omni-interconsiderate,
omni-interaccommodative governance
of the complex
of everyday, naked-eye experiences
as well as of the multi-millions-fold greater range
of only instrumentally explored
infra- and ultra-tunable
micro- and macro-Universe events.

Fourthly, I mean:—
All the mystery inherent
in all human experience,
which, as a lifetime ratioed to eternity,
is individually limited
to almost negligible
twixt sleepings, glimpses
of only a few local episodes
of one of the infinite myriads
of concurrently and overlappingly operative
sum-totally never-ending
cosmic scenario serials

With these four meanings I now directly
address God.
*   "Our God—*
Since omni-experience is your identity
You have given us
overwhelming manifest:—
of Your complete knowledge
of Your complete comprehension
of Your complete concern
of Your complete coordination
of Your complete responsibility
of Your complete capability to cope
in absolute wisdom and effectiveness

with all problems and events
and of Your eternally unfailing reliability
so to do

Yours, Dear God,
is the only and complete glory.

By Glory *I mean*
the synergetic totality
of all physical and metaphysical radiation
and of all physical and metaphysical gravity
of finite
but nonunitarily conceptual
scenario Universe
in whose synergetic totality
the a priori energy potentials
of both radiation and gravity
are initially equal
but whose respective
behavioral patterns are such
that radiation's entropic, redundant disintegratings
is always less effective
than gravity's nonredundant
syntropic integrating

Radiation is plural and differentiable,
radiation is focusable, beamable, and self-sinusing,
is interceptible, separatist, and biasable—
ergo, has shadowed voids and vulnerabilities;

Gravity is unit and undifferentiable
Gravity is comprehensive
inclusively embracing and permeative
is non-focusable and shadowless,
and is omni-integrative;
all of which characteristics of gravity
are also the characteristics of love.
Love is metaphysical gravity.

You, Dear God,
are the totally loving intellect
ever designing
and ever daring to test
and thereby irrefutably proving
to the uncompromising satisfaction
of Your own comprehensive and incisive

knowledge of the absolute truth
that Your generalized principles
adequately accommodate any and all
special case developments,
involvements, and side effects;
wherefore Your absolutely courageous
omnirigorous and ruthless self-testing
alone can and does absolutely guarantee
total conservation
of the integrity
of eternally regenerative Universe

Your eternally regenerative scenario Universe
is the minimum complex
of totally intercomplementary
totally intertransforming
nonsimultaneous, differently frequenced
and differently enduring
feedback closures
of a finite
but nonunitarily
nonsimultaneously conceptual system
in which naught is created
and naught is lost
and all occurs
in optimum efficiency.

Total accountability and total feedback
constitute the minimum and only
perpetual motion system.
Universe is the one and only
eternally regenerative system.

To accomplish Your regenerative integrity
You give Yourself the responsibility
of eternal, absolutely continuous,
tirelessly vigilant wisdom.

Wherefore we have absolute faith and trust in You,
and we worship You

awe-inspiredly,
all-thankfully,
rejoicingly,
lovingly,
Amen.

QUESTIONS FOR STUDY

1. What single criterion must all definitions satisfy?

2. What are the four meanings or images of God given by Fuller?

3. What is Fuller's understanding of *glory*?

4. Fuller claims that "love is metaphysical gravity." Explain his metaphor.

QUESTIONS FOR REFLECTION

1. Does Fuller's model of God possess any personal characteristics?

2. What traditional religious language does Fuller use? In your estimate, is it compatible with his scientific and technological terminology? Does this terminology lend additional insight into the nature of God?

3. Is Fuller's essential metaphor of God that of a cosmic "mind"?

4. Does the imagery of Fuller's version of the Lord's Prayer reflect or parallel the original version of Jesus? Compare the two.

NETWORKING

The systems or process view of God is a subject in Barbour (Part I), Dyson, Burhoe, Haught, McFague, Cobb, and Berry.

STORIES

UNDERSTANDING MYTH   SUSANNE K. LANGER

Susanne Langer, born in 1895, studied at Radcliffe College and the University of Vienna. She taught at Radcliffe, Columbia, Northwestern, Ohio State, and several other institutions before going to Connecticut College where she stayed until her retirement in 1961. Her thought was influenced by Alfred North Whitehead and Ernst Cassirer. This selection is from her most widely known work, *Philosophy in a New Key.*

Myth, . . . is a recognition of natural conflicts, of human desire frustrated by nonhuman powers, hostile oppression, or contrary desires; it is a story of the birth, passion, and defeat by death which is man's common fate. Its ultimate end is not wishful distortion of the world, but serious envisagement of its fundamental truths; moral orientation, not escape. That is why it does not exhaust its whole function in the telling, and why separate myths cannot be left entirely unrelated to any others. Because it presents, however metaphorically, a world-picture, an insight into life generally, not a personal imaginary biography, myth tends to become systematized; figures with the same poetic meaning are blended into one, and characters of quite separate origin enter into definite relations with each other. Moreover, because the mythical hero is not the subject of an egocentric day-dream, but a subject greater than any individual, he is always felt to be superhuman, even if not quite divine. He is at least a descendant of the gods, something more than a man. His sphere of activity is the real world, because what he symbolizes belongs to the real world, no matter how fantastic its expression may be (this is exactly contrary to the fairytale technique, which transports a natural individual to a fairyland outside reality).

The material of myth is, indeed, just the familiar symbolism of dream—image and fantasy. No wonder psychologists have discovered that it is the same material as that of fairytale; that both have symbols for father and son, maiden and wife and mother, possession and passion, birth and death. The difference is in the two respective *uses* of that material: the one, primarily for supplying vicarious experience, the other essentially for understanding actual experience. Both interests may be served in one and the same fiction; their complete separation belongs only to classic cases. Semi-mythical motives occur in sheer day-dream and even night-dream, and an element of compensation-fantasy may persist in the most universalized, perfected myths. That is inevitable, because the latter type has grown at some point out of the former, as all realistic thinking springs from self-centered fancy. There is no clean dividing line. Yet the two are as distinct as summer and winter, night and day, or any other extremes that have no exact zero-point between them.

We do not know just where, in the evolution of human thought, myth-making begins, but it begins somewhere with the recognition of *realistic significance* in a story. In every fantasy, no matter how utopian, there are elements that represent real human relations, real needs and fears, the quandaries and conflicts which the "happy ending" resolves. Even if the real situation is symbolized rather than stated (a shocking condition may well be disguised, or a mysterious one strangely conceived), a certain importance, an emotional interest, attaches to those elements. The ogre, the dragon, the witch, are intriguing figures in fairy-lore. Unlike the hero, they are usually ancient beings, that have troubled the land for many generations. They have their castles or caves or hermitages, their magic cook-pots and sorcerer's wands; they have evil deeds laid up against them, and extremely bad habits, usually of a cannibalistic turn. Their records are merely suggested in the story, which hastens to get on with the fortunes of the hero; but the suggestion is enough to activate a mind which is, after all, committed to some interests besides dream-spinning. Because they represent the realistic setting from which the dream starts its fanciful escape, they command a serious sort of contemplation.

It is significant that people who refuse to tell their children fairytales do not fear that the children will believe in princes and princesses, but that they will believe in witches and bogeys. Prince or princess, to whom the wish-fulfilment happens, we find in ourselves, and need not seek in the outer world; their reference is subjective, their history is our dream, and we know well enough that it is "make-believe." But the incidental figures are material for superstition, because their meanings are in the real world. They represent those same powers that are conceived, first perhaps through "dreadful" objects like corpses or skulls or hideous idols, as ghosts, keres, hoodoos, and similar spooks. The ogres of literature and the ghouls of popular conception embody the same mysterious Powers; therefore the fairytale, which even most children will not credit as a narrative, may carry with it a whole cargo of ideas, purely secondary to its own purpose, that are most convincing elements for superstition. The awful ancestor in the grave goes abroad as the goblin of story: that is the god of superstition. The world-picture of spook-religion is a reflection of fairytale, a dream whose nightmare elements become attached to visible cult objects and thus taken seriously.

There is nothing cosmological about the being such a symbol can embody. Deities in the classical sense cannot be born of tales whose significance is personal, because the setting of such tales is necessarily a *genre* picture, a local, temporal, human environment, no matter how distorted and disguised. The forces that play into an individual's dream are social forces, not world-powers. So long as the hero is the self, the metaphorical dragons he slays are his elders, his rivals, or his personal enemies; their projection into the real world as sacred beings can yield only ancestors, cave-monsters, manitos, and capricious demigods.

It is noteworthy that when these secondary characters of day-dream or story are incorporated into our picture of the external world as objects of superstition, they represent a generalized, heightened conception of the social forces in question: not a man's father, but his *fathers,* the paternal power in all generations, may be seen in the fabulous animal-ancestor he reveres; not his brother, but a "Great Brother," in the manito-bear that is his familiar of the forest. The process of symbolization, while it often obscures the origin of our ideas, enhances their conceptual form. The demon, therefore, presents to us not a specific person, but the human estate of such a person, by virtue of which we are oppressed, challenged, tempted, or triumphant. Though he is born of a purely self-centered imagination, he is super-personal; a product not only of particular experience, but of *social insight.* He is the envisagement of a vital factor in life; that is why he is projected into reality by the symbolism of religion.

The great step from fairytale to myth is taken when not only social forces—persons, customs, laws, traditions—but also cosmic forces surrounding mankind, are expressed in the story; when not only relationships of an individual to society, but of mankind to nature, are conceived through the spontaneous metaphor of poetic fantasy.

Perhaps this transition from subjectively oriented stories, separate and self-contained, to the organized and permanent envisagement of a world-drama could never be made if creative thought were not helped by the presence of permanent, obvious symbols, supplied by nature: the heavenly bodies, the changes of day and night, the seasons, and the tides. Just as the social framework of personal life, first conceived in dream-like, inchoate forms, is gradually given enduring recognition through religious symbols, so the cosmic setting of man's existence is imponderable, or at best a mere nightmare, until the sun and the moon, the procession of stars, the winds and waters of earth, exhibit a divine rule, and define the realm of human activity. When these gods arrive, whose names connote heavenly powers and natural processes, the deities of local caves and groves become mere vassals and lesser lights.

It has often been asked, not without justification, how men of sane observant minds—however unschooled or innocent—can be led to identify sun, moon, or stars with the anthropomorphic agents of sacred story. Yet the interpretation of gods and heroes as nature-symbols is very ancient; it has been variously accepted and rejected, disputed, exploded, and reëstablished, by Hellenic philosophers, medieval scholars, modern philologists, archeologists, and theologians, over a period of twenty-five hundred years. Mystifying as it is to psychology, it challenges us as a fact. . . .

It is a peculiar fact that every major advance in thinking, every epoch-making new insight, springs from a new type of symbolic transformation. A higher level of thought is primarily a new activity; its course is opened up by a new departure in semantic. The step from mere sign-using to symbol-using marked the crossing of the line between animal and man; this initiated the natural growth of language. The birth of symbolic gesture from emotional and practical movement probably begot the whole order of ritual, as well as the discursive mode of pantomime. The recognition of vague, vital meanings in physical forms—perhaps the first dawn of symbolism—gave us our idols, emblems, and totems; the primitive function of dream permits our first envisagement of events. The momentous discovery of nature-symbolism, of the pattern of life reflected in natural phenomena, produced the first universal insights. Every mode of thought is bestowed on us, like a gift, with some new principle of symbolic expression. It has a logical development, which is simply the exploitation of all the uses to which that symbolism lends itself; and when these uses are exhausted, the mental activity in question has found its limit. Either it serves its purpose and becomes truistic, like our orientation in "Euclidean space" or our appreciation of objects and their accidents (on the pattern of language-structure, significantly called "logic"); or it is superseded by some more powerful symbolic mode which opens new avenues of thought.

The origin of myth is dynamic, but its purpose is philosophical. It is the primitive phase of metaphysical thought, the first embodiment of *general ideas.* It can do no more than initiate and present them; for it is a non-discursive symbolism, it does not lend itself to analytic and genuinely abstractive techniques. The highest development of which myth is capable is the exhibition of human life and cosmic order that epic poetry reveals. We cannot abstract and manipulate its concepts any further *within the mythical mode*. When this mode is exhausted, natural religion is superseded by a discursive and more literal form of thought, namely philosophy.

Language, in its literal capacity, is a stiff and conventional medium, unadapted to the expression of genuinely new ideas, which usually have to break in upon the mind through some great and bewildering metaphor. But bare denotative language is a most excellent instrument of exact reason; it is, in fact, the only general precision instrument the human brain has ever evolved. Ideas first adumbrated in fantastic form become real intellectual property only when discursive language rises to their expression. That is why myth is the indispensable forerunner of metaphysics; and metaphysics is the literal formulation of basic abstractions, on which our comprehension of sober facts is based. All detail of knowledge, all exact distinction, measure, and practical manipulation, are possible only on a basis of truly abstract concepts, and a framework of such concepts constitutes a philosophy of nature, literal, denotative, and systematic. Only language has the power to effect such an analysis of experience, such a rationalization of knowledge. But it is only where experience is already presented—through some other formative medium, some vehicle of apprehension and memory—that the canons of literal thought have any application. We must have ideas before we can make literal analyses of them; and really new ideas have their own modes of appearance in the unpredictable creative mind.

The first inquiry as to the literal truth of a myth marks the change from poetic to discursive thinking. As soon as the interest in factual values awakes, the mythical mode of world-envisagement is on the wane. But emotional attitudes that have long centered on a myth are not easily broken; the vital ideas embodied in it cannot be repudiated because someone discovers that the myth does not constitute a *fact*. Poetic significance and factual reference, which are two entirely different relations in the general symbol-and-meaning pattern, become identified under the one name of "truth." People who discover the obvious discrepancy between fantasy and fact deny that myths are true; those who recognize the truth of myths claim that they register facts. There is the silly conflict of religion and science, in which science must triumph, not because what it says about religion is just, but because religion rests on a young and provisional form of thought, to which philosophy of nature—proudly called "science," or "knowledge"—must succeed if thinking is to go on. There must be a rationalistic period from this point onward. Some day when the vision is totally rationalized, the ideas exploited and exhausted, there will be another vision, a new mythology.

QUESTIONS FOR STUDY

1. Are myths about the lives and problems of specific persons, or do they refer to something broader?

2. Langer grants that myths share material and themes with dreams and fairy tales. What is the major distinction between these types?

3. Why, according to Langer, is it significant that some people refuse to tell their children fairy tales? What do they fear?

4. What is the role of nature in the transition from personal dreams and fairy tales to myths?

5. Langer says that "the origin of myth is dynamic, but its purpose is philosophical." Explain.

6. How do the symbols of myth give rise to rational thought and even to logic?

7. Why is the conflict between religion and science "silly"?

QUESTIONS FOR REFLECTION

1. Heroes are major figures in mythology. Name several traditional heroes and the characteristics they share. Who would qualify as a hero in the contemporary world: the astronaut, the statesman, the revolutionary? Do we even have heroes today? If not, is this situation a matter for concern?

2. Have scientists, including Galileo, Newton, and Einstein, become "mythologized" in history? Examine the various symbolic uses of Einstein's image and his discoveries, such as $E=mc^2$ and relativity, in modern culture. Describe the mythic figure of the scientist as the isolated "great man." Given the nature of "big science" today, is this image accurate?

3. As Langer notes, natural objects, such as the sun, moon, and stars, have often become anthropomorphic agents in myths. How did science reverse this process? Is science in any way responsible for the alienation of society from nature?

4. In the following selection, Brian Swimme claims that we are composing a new cosmic story or myth based upon the world picture revealed by modern science. Would Langer support this project?

NETWORKING

Swimme, Tillich, and Roach also deal with the issue of *myth and symbol in science and religion.*

A COSMIC CREATION STORY   BRIAN SWIMME

Brian Swimme is a physicist, lecturer, and author of *The Universe is a Green Dragon*. He teaches at the Institute in Culture and Creation Spirituality in Oakland, California.

Our planetary difficulties: our technologies have resulted in 50,000 nuclear warheads; our industrial economies have given us ecocide on every continent; our social distribution of goods and services has given us a billion underdeveloped and starving humans. One thing we can conclude without argument: as a species and as a planet we are in terrible shape. So as we consider proposals for leading us out of this dying world, we need to bear in mind that only proposals promising an immense efficacy need be considered. Anything less than a fundamental transformation of our situation is hardly worth talking about.

And yet, given this demand, my own suggestion is that we tell stories—in particular, that we tell the many stories that comprise the great cosmic story. I am suggesting that this activity of cosmic storytelling is the central political and economic act of our time. My basic claim is that by telling our cosmic creation story, we inaugurate a new era of human and planetary health, for we initiate a transformation out of a world that is—to use David Griffin's thorough formulation—mechanistic, scientistic, dualistic, patriarchal, Eurocentric, anthropocentric, militaristic, and reductionistic.

A *cosmic creation story* is that which satisfies the questions asked by humans fresh out of the womb. As soon as they get here and learn the language, children ask the cosmic questions. Where did everything come from? What is going on? Why are you doing such and such anyway? The young of our species desire to learn where they are and what they are about in this life. That is, they express an inherent desire to hear their cosmic story.

By *cosmic creation story* I also mean to indicate those accounts of the universe we told each other around the evening fires for most of the last 50,000 years. These cosmic stories were the way the first humans chose to initiate and install their young into the universe. The rituals, the traditions, the taboos, the ethics, the techniques, the customs, and the values all had as their core a cosmic story. The story provided the central cohesion for each society. *Story* in this sense is "world-interpretation"—a likely account of the development and nature and value of things in this world.

Why story? Why should "story" be fundamental? Because without storytelling, we lose contact with our basic realities in this world. We lose contact because *only* through story can we fully recognize our existence in time.

To be human is to be in a story. To forget one's story is to go insane. All the tribal peoples show an awareness of the connection between health and storytelling. The original humans will have their cosmic stories just as surely as they will have their food and drink. Our ancestors recognized that the universe, at its most basic level, is story. Each creature is story. Humans enter this world and awaken to a simple truth: "We must find our story within this great epic of being."

What about our situation today? Do we tell stories? We most certainly do, even if we do not call them stories. In our century's textbooks—for use in grade schools and high schools—we learn that it all began with impoverished primitives, marched through the technical inventions of the scientific period, and culminated—this is usually only implied, but there is never much doubt—in the United States of America, in its political freedom and, most of all, in its superior modes of production. For proof, graphs of industrial output compare the United States with other countries. Throughout our educational experiences, we were drawn into an emotional bonding with our society, so that it was only natural we would want to support, defend, and extend our society's values and accomplishments. Of course, this was not considered story; we were learning the facts.

Obviously, Soviets reflecting on their educational process recall a different story, one that began with the same denigration of the primal peoples, continued through a critique of bourgeois societies, and culminated in the USSR. And the French or British, reflecting on *their* educations, remember learning that, in fact, *they* were the important societies, for they were extending the European cultural tradition, while avoiding both the superficiality of the Americans and the lugubriousness of the Soviets.

Although we told ourselves such human stories, none of us in the industrial countries taught our children cosmic stories. We focused entirely on the human world when telling our stories of value and meaning. The universe and Earth taken together were merely backdrop. The oceans were large, the species many, yes—but these immensities were just the stage for the humans. This mistake is the fundamental mistake of our era. In a sentence, I summarize my position this way: *all our disasters today are directly related to our having been raised in cultures that ignored the cosmos for an exclusive focus on the human.* Our uses of land, our uses of technology, our uses of each other are flawed in many ways but due fundamentally to the same folly. We fail in so grotesque a manner because we were never initiated into the realities and values of the universe. Without the benefit of a cosmic story that provided meaning to our existence as Earthlings, we were stranded in an abstract world and left to invent nuclear weapons and chemical biocides and ruinous exploitations and waste.

How could this have happened? How could modern Western culture escape a 50,000-year-old tradition of telling cosmic stories? We discovered science. So impressed were we with this blinding light, we simply threw out the cosmic stories for the knowledge that the sciences provided. Why tell the story of the Sun as a God when we knew the sun was a locus of thermonuclear reactions? We pursued "scientific law," relegating "story" and "myth" to the nurseries and tribes. Science gave us the real, and the best science was mathematical science. We traded myth for mathematics and, without realizing it, we entered upon an intellectual quest that had for its goal a complete escape from the shifting sands of the temporal world. As Ilya Prigogine summarizes: "For most of the founders of classical science—even for Einstein—science was an attempt to go beyond the world of appearances, to reach a timeless world of supreme rationality—the world of Spinoza."

What a shock it has been to have *story reappear,* and this time right in the very center of the mathematical sciences! Someday someone will tell the full story of how "story" forced its way into the most antistory domain of modern science—I mean mathematical physics. Here I would like to indicate in broad strokes what has happened.

For physicists during the modern period, "reality" meant the fundamental interactions of the universe. In a sense, the world's physical essence was considered captured by the right group of mathematical equations. Gravity and the Strong Nuclear Interaction were the real actors in the universe. The actual course of events was seen as of secondary importance, as the "details" structured by the fundamental dynamics of physical reality. The Story of Time was regarded as secondary, even illusory—time was simply a parameter that appeared in the equations. That is, nothing was special about the time today, as opposed to some time one billion years from now. Each time was the same, for the mathematical equations showed no difference between any two times.

The best story I know concerning this dismissal of time concerns Albert Einstein. Out of his own amazing genius, he arrived at his famous field equations, the mathematical laws governing the universe in its physical macrodimensions. What most alarmed Einstein—and we must remember that here was a man who had the courage to stick to his mathematical insights no matter how shocking they might seem to the world—what most disturbed Einstein about his own equations was their implication that the universe was expanding. Such a notion made no sense in the Newtonian cosmology of a static universe, which held that the universe today is essentially the same as the universe at any other time. In Newton's universe motion could exist *in* the universe, but the idea that the universe as a whole was changing was hardly thinkable. For these reasons, Einstein's equations stunned him when they whispered their secret—that the universe is not static; that the universe is expanding each moment into a previously nonexistent space; that the universe is a dynamic developing reality.

To avoid these alarming implications, Einstein altered his equations to eliminate their predictions. If only the truth of the universe could be so easily contained! Soon after Einstein published his equations, the Russian mathematician Alexander Friedmann found solutions to Einstein's equations—these solutions were theoretical universes, some of which expanded, some of which contracted, and some of which oscillated in and out. Einstein's response to Friedmann's communication was a polite dismissal of what seemed to be an utterly preposterous mathematical fiction.

But when Edwin Hubble later showed the empirical evidence for an expanding universe, Einstein realized his failure of nerve. He later came to regard his doctoring of the field equations as the "biggest blunder of my life." My point is the complete surprise this discovery was for the scientists involved. If Einstein had left the equations as he had come to them, he would have made the greatest prediction in the entire history of science. But such a leap out of a static universe into a cosmic story was simply beyond the pale for our century's greatest scientist.

Even so, we now realize—following the work of Einstein, Hubble, and others—that ours is a universe that had a beginning in time and has been developing from 15 to 20 billion years. And every moment of this universe is new. That is, we now realize that we live not in a static Newtonian space; we live within an ongoing cosmic story.

Story forced its way still further into physics when in recent decades scientists discovered that even the fundamental interactions of the universe evolved into their present forms. *The laws that govern the physical universe today and that were thought to be immutable are themselves the results of developments over time.* We had always assumed that the laws were fixed, absolute, eternal. Now we discover that even the laws tell their own story of the universe. That is, the Cosmic Story, rather than being simply governed by fixed underlying laws, draws these laws into its drama.

Story inserts itself still further into the consciousness of contemporary physicists when the very status of physical law is put into a new perspective. Where once we listed a set of laws that, we were certain, held everywhere and at all times, we now ponder the violations of each of these laws. A preeminent physicist of our time, John Archibald Wheeler, concludes that in nature "there is no law except the law that there is no law." Wheeler's inclination is to question our fixation with law; he demands that the details of nature be given the same attention we give to the unifying ideas. As Wheeler sings, "Individual events. Events beyond law. Events so numerous and so uncoordinated that, flaunting their freedom from formula, they yet fabricate firm form."

What happens when physicists begin to value not just the repeatable experiment but history's unrepeatable events, no longer regarding each event as simply another datum useful for arriving at mathematical law but as a revelation all by itself? A reenchantment with the universe happens. A new love affair between humans and the universe happens.

Only when we are surprised in the presence of a person or a thing are we truly in love. And regardless how intimate we become, our surprise continues. Without question we come to know the beloved better and are able to speak central truths about her or him or it, but never do we arrive at a statement that is the final word. Further surprises always occur, for to be in love is to be in awe of the infinite depths of things. What I am suggesting by remembering Einstein's astonishment at the time-developmental nature of the universe and by underlining Wheeler's fascination with the individual event is that scientists have entered a new enchantment. Having been raised and trained in the disenchanted world of classical Newtonian physics, they are suddenly astonished and fascinated in an altogether new way by the infinite elegance which gathers us into its life and existence.

A central desire of scientists in the future will be to explore and celebrate the enveloping Great Mystery—the story of the universe, the journey of the galaxies, the adventure of the planet Earth and all of its life forms. Scientific theories will no longer be seen simply as objective laws. Scientific understanding will be valued as that power capable of evoking in humans a deep intimacy with reality. That is, the value of the electromagnetic interaction as objectively true will be deepened by our awareness that study and contemplation of the electromagnetic interaction allows humans to enter a rich communion experience with the contours of reality in the stellar cores, as well as in the unfolding dynamics of our sun and forests.

I am convinced, finally, that the story of the universe that has come out of three centuries of modern scientific work will be recognized as a supreme human achievement, the scientific enterprise's central gift to humanity, a revelation having a status equal to that of the great religious revelations of the past.

Of course, these are my speculations. I may be wrong. Instead of scientists devoting themselves to a further exploration and celebration of the cosmic story, they may be entirely captured by the militaries of the planet. But I do not think so, and for a number of reasons. The one reason I mention here concerns the planetary implications of the cosmic creation story.

I discussed Einstein's resistance to highlight an obvious and significant fact of the cosmic creation story—*its power to draw humans into itself.* Einstein did not want to discover an expanding, time-developmental universe. Another famous physicist, Arthur Eddington, found the whole notion "abhorrent." But the story convinces regardless. Its appeal to humans is virtually irresistible. The cosmic creation story has the potency to offset and even to displace entirely every previous worldview. Often, this displacing of traditional stories has resulted in cultural tragedy, and this reality must be discussed. What I want to bring to the readers' attention here is that the human being, as constituted today, finds the cosmic story undeniably tied to the truth, and this is great news indeed.

For suddenly, the human species as a whole has a common cosmic story. Islamic people, Hopi people, Christian people, Marxist people, and Hindu people can all agree in a basic sense on the birth of the Sun, on the development of the Earth, the species of life, and human cultures. For the first time in human existence, we have a cosmic story that is not tied to one cultural tradition, or to a political ideology, but instead gathers every human group into its meanings. Certainly we must not be naive about this claim of universality. Every statement of the cosmic story will be placed in its own cultural context, and each context is, to varying degrees, expressive of political, religious, and cultural perspectives. But given that fact, we have even so broken through to a story that is panhuman; a story that is already taught and developed on every continent and within every major cultural setting.

What does this mean? Every tribe knows the central value of its cosmic story in uniting its people. The same will be true for us. We are now creating the common story which will enable *Homo sapiens* to become a cohesive community. Instead of structuring American society on its own human story, or Soviet society on its own human story, and so on, we have the opportunity to tell instead the cosmic story, and the oceanic story, and the mammalian story, so that instead of building our lives and our society's meanings around the various human stories alone, we can build our lives and societies around the Earth story.

This is a good place to make my final comment on the meaning of *cosmic creation story.* Although with this phrase I refer in general to the account of our emergence out of the fireball and into galaxies and stars and Earth's life, I also think of the cosmic story as something that has not yet emerged. I think we will only have a common story for the human community when poets tell us the story. For until artists, poets, mystics, nature lovers tell the story—or until the poetic and mystical dimensions of humans are drawn forth in every person who sets out to tell us our story—we have only facts and theories.

Most tribal communities understand the necessity of developing storytellers—people who spend their lives learning the cosmic story and celebrating it in poetry, chant, dance, painting, music. The life of the tribe is woven around such celebrations. The telling of the story is understood both as that which installs the young and that which regenerates creation. The ritual of telling the story is understood as a cosmic event.

Unless the story is sung and danced, the universe suffers from decay and fatigue. Everything depends on telling the story—the health of the people, the health of the soil, the health of the sun, the health of the soul, the health of the sky.

We need to keep the tribal perspective in mind when we examine our situation in the modern period. Instead of poets, we had one-eyed scientists and theologians. Neither of these high priests nor any of the rest of us was capable of celebrating the cosmic story. It is no wonder then that so many of us are sick and disabled, that the soils have gone bad, that the sky is covered with soot, and that the waters are filled with evils. Because we had no celebrations inaugurating us into the universe, the whole world has become diseased.

But what will happen when the storytellers emerge? What will happen when "the primal mind," to use Jamake Highwater's term, sings of our common origin, our stupendous journey, our immense good fortune? We will become Earthlings. We will have evoked out of the depths of the human psyche those qualities enabling our transformation from disease to health. They will sing our epic of being, and stirring up from our roots will be a vast awe, an enduring gratitude, the astonishment of communion experiences, and the realization of cosmic adventure.

We must encourage cosmic storytellers because our dominant culture is blind to their value. Is it not remarkable that we can obtain several hundred books on how to get a divorce, how to invest money, how to lose fat, and yet there is nothing available to assist those destined to sing to us the great epic of reality?

I suggest that when the artists of the cosmic story arrive, our monoindustrial assault and suicide will end and the new beginnings of the Earth will be at hand. Our situation is similar to that of the early Christians. They had nothing—nothing but a profound revelatory experience. They did nothing—nothing but wander about telling a new story. And yet the Western world entered a transformation from which it has never recovered.

So too with our moment. We have nothing compared to the massive accumulation of hate, fear, and arrogance that the intercontinental ballistic missiles, the third world debt, and the chemical toxins represents. But we are in the midst of a revelatory experience of the universe that must be compared in its magnitude with those of the great religious revelations. And we need only wander about telling this new story to ignite a transformation of humanity. For this story has the power to undo the mighty and arrogant and to ignite the creativity of the oppressed and forgotten. As the Great Journey of the Universe breaks into human self-awareness, nothing can dam up our desire to shake off the suffocation of nationalism, anthropocentrism, and exploitation and to plunge instead into the adventure of the cosmos.

Let me end with an imaginary event—a moment in the future when children are taught by a cosmic storyteller. We can imagine a small group gathered around a fire in a hillside meadow. The woman in the middle is the oldest, a grandmother to some of the children present. If we can today already imagine such an event, we can be assured that tomorrow someone will begin the journey of bringing such dreams into practice.

The old woman might begin by picking up a chunk of granite. "At one time, at the beginning of the Earth, the whole planet was a boiling sea of molten rock. We revere rocks because everything has come from them—not just the continents and the mountains, but the trees, the oceans and your bodies. The rocks are your grandmother and your grandfather. When you remember all those who have helped you in this life, you begin with the rocks, for if not for them, you would not be."

She holds the rock before them in silence, showing each person in turn. "Do you hear the rock singing? In the last era, people thought there was no music in rocks. But we know that is not true. After all, some rocks became Mozart and showed their music as Mozart. Or did you think that the Earth had to go to Mars to learn how to play its music? No, Mozart is rocks, Mozart is the music of the Earth's rocks."

Now she slowly sinks her hands into the ground and holds the rich loamy soil before her. "Every rock is a symphony, but the music of soil soars beyond capture in human language. We had to go into outer space to realize how rare and unique soil is. Only the Earth created soil. There is no soil on the moon. There are minerals on the moon, but no soil. There is no soil on Mars. There is no soil on Venus, or on Sun, or on Jupiter, or anywhere else in the surrounding trillion miles. Even the Earth, the most extraordinarily creative being of the solar system, required four billion years to create topsoil. We worship and nurture and protect the soils of the Earth because all music and all life and all happiness come from the soil. The soils are the matrix of human joy."

She points now to a low-hanging star in the great bowl of the nightsky. "Right now, that star is at work creating the elements that will one day live as sentient beings. All the matter of the Earth was created by the Grandmother Star that preceded our Sun. She fashioned the carbon and nitrogen and all the elements that would later become all the bodies and things of Earth. And when she was done with her immense creativity, she exploded in celebration of her achievement, sharing her riches with the universe and enabling our birth.

"Her destiny is your destiny. In the center of your being you too will create, and you too will shower the world with your creativity. Your lives will be filled with both suffering and joy; you will often be faced with death and hardship. But all of this finds its meaning in your participation in the great life of Earth. It is because of your creativity that the cosmic journey deepens."

She stares into the distance. In the long silence, she hears the thundering breakers on the ocean shore, just visible in the evening's light. They listen as the vast tonnage of saltwater is lifted up in silence, then again pounds up the sand.

"Think of how tired we were when we arrived here, and all we had to do was carry our little bodies up the hills! Now think of the work that is being done ceaselessly as all the oceans of the world curl into breakers against the shores. And think of all the work that is done ceaselessly as the Earth is pulled around the Sun. Think of all the work that is done ceaselessly as all 100 billion stars of the Milky Way are pulled around the center of the galaxy.

"And yet the stars don't think of this as work. Nor do the oceans think of their ceaseless tides as work. They are drawn irresistibly into their activities, moment after moment. The Earth finds itself drawn irresistibly to the Sun, and would find any other path in life utterly intolerable. What amazing work the stars and the planets accomplish, and never do we hear them complain!

"We humans and we animals are no different at all. For we find ourselves just as irresistibly drawn to follow certain paths in life. And if we pursue these paths, our lives—even should they become filled with suffering and hardship—are filled as well with the quality of effortlessness. Once we respond to our deepest allurements in the universe, we find ourselves carried away, we find ourselves on the edge of a wave passing through the cosmos that had its beginning 15 to 20 billion years ago in the fiery explosion of the beginning of time. The great joy of human being is to enter this allurement which pervades everything and to empower others—including the soil and the grasses and all the forgotten—so that they might enter their own path into their deepest allurement."

The light of dusk has gone. She sits with them in the deepening silence of the dark. The fire has died down to become a series of glowing points, mirroring the ocean of starlight all above them.

"You will be tempted at times to abandon your dreams, to settle for cynicism or greed, so great will your anxieties and fears appear to you.

"But no matter what happens, remember that our universe is a universe of surprise. We put our confidence not in our human egos but in the power that gathered the stars and living cells together. Remember that you are here through the creativity of others. You have awakened in a great epic of being, a drama that is 15 to 20 billion years in the making. The intelligence that ignited the first minds, the care that spaced the notes of the nightingale, the power that heaved all 100 billion galaxies across the sky now awakens as you, too, and permeates your life no less thoroughly.

"We do not know what mystery awaits us in the very next moment. But we can be sure we will be astonished and enchanted. This entire universe sprang into existence from a single *numinous* speck. Our origin is mystery; our destiny is intimate community with all that is; and our common species' aim is to celebrate the Great Joy which has drawn us into itself."

Rocks, soils, waves, stars—as they tell their story in 10,000 languages throughout the planet, they bind us to them in our emotions, our spirits, our minds, and our bodies. The Earth and the universe speak in all this. The cosmic creation story is the way in which the universe is inaugurating the next era of its ongoing journey.

QUESTIONS FOR STUDY

1. What are some of the questions that a cosmic creation story is intended to answer?

2. Swimme claims that "to be human is to be in a story." Explain.

3. What social force or movement is most responsible for having eliminated the story-telling tradition?

4. What point is the author making in recounting the incident of "Einstein's biggest blunder"?

5. The cosmic story is "panhuman." What does this mean and why is it desirable?

QUESTIONS FOR REFLECTION

1. How does a story differ from a scientific theory? Identify and compare some elements of each. If stories and theories differ greatly, how can Swimme claim that the vision of contemporary science is the beginning of a new awareness of our cosmic story?

2. Swimme insists that storytelling heals the rift between human life and nature. How so?

3. How does our situation resemble that of the early Christians? Could Swimme have taken Hinduism or Buddhism as equally useful examples?

NETWORKING

Swimme and Berry share common opinions on the importance of a *unifying cosmic myth*. The *disenchantment of nature* is discussed in Bube and Gray.

SUGGESTIONS FOR FURTHER READING

Barbour, Ian G. *Myths, Models, and Paradigms: A Comparative Study in Science and Religion*. New York: Harper and Row Publishers, 1974. Perhaps the best discussion of the nature of myths and models in religion and science. Barbour offers numerous illustrations taken from both fields.

Campbell, Joseph. *Myths to Live By*. New York: Viking Press, 1972. A series of nontechnical essays written by this foremost scholar who has helped to popularize myth over the last several decades.

_____, with Bill Moyers. *The Power of Myth*. New York: Doubleday and Company, 1988. The edited transcript of the immensely popular series of interviews for public television that Bill Moyers conducted with Campbell before Campbell's death. Also available on videotape.

Ferre, Frederick. *Language, Logic and God*. New York: Harper and Row Publishers, 1961. A clear survey of linguistic philosophy and its implications for theistic discourse.

Fuller, R. Buckminster. *No More Secondhand God and Other Writings*. New York: Doubleday, 1963. Some of the more accessible thoughts of the great, somewhat eccentric inventor and philosopher. Fuller's religious faith emerges in several of his essays and especially in his poetry.

Gilkey, Langdon. *Naming the Whirlwind: The Renewal of God-Talk.* Indianapolis: Bobs-Merrill, 1969. An excellent resource for the dynamics of language and religion within the context of modern culture.

Harrison, Edward. *Masks of the Universe.* New York: Macmillan Publishing Company, 1985. Harrison's "masks" of the universe are the historical world views or fundamental metaphorical images of the world that enable a culture to locate itself in the universe.

McFague, Sallie. *Models of God: A Theology for an Ecological and Nuclear Age.* Philadelphia: Fortress Press, 1987. In this award-winning book, McFague examines the metaphors of God as mother, lover, and friend as she labors to construct a theology that will fit in the postmodern world. A fine example of the theological imagination at work.

Slater, Peter. *The Dynamics of Religion: Meaning and Change in Religious Traditions.* San Francisco: Harper and Row Publishers, 1978. Slater develops a model of symbols that allows him to discuss the central position of symbol and story in religious and personal transformation.

Wiggans, James B., ed. *Religion as Story.* San Francisco: Harper and Row Publishers, 1975. Valuable study for understanding the fundamental role of dramatic narrative, biography, and myth in religion and culture.

PART III

The Two-Storied Universe

THIS COMMANDMENT, FROM CHAPTER 20 OF THE BOOK OF EXODUS, IS A PILLAR OF
MONOTHEISM FOR JUDAISM, CHRISTIANITY, AND ISLAM, AND A SUCCINCT EXPRESSION
OF THE ULTIMATE AND SOVEREIGN NATURE OF GOD. IT CONTRIBUTES TO THE
IMAGE OF GOD AS A BEING WHO STANDS APART FROM THE WORLD AND DIRECTS
IT ACCORDING TO DIVINE WILL. THIS IS A POSITION THAT TROUBLES MANY
SCIENTISTS WHO WOULD RATHER SEE THE PHYSICAL WORLD AS AUTONOMOUS
OR NOT SUBJECT TO SUPERNATURAL INTERVENTION.

INTRODUCTION   *The Two-Storied Universe*

Traditional monotheistic religions, including Judaism, Christianity, and Islam, subscribe to the common proposition that there exists a single ultimate being, known variously as Yahweh, God the Father, and Allah, who stands beyond the world as its creator, sustainer, and director. In this perspective, reality is divided sharply into two very distinct realms: the natural and the supernatural. Nature consists of the creation, the realm of all finite creatures that is available to scientific inquiry and subjected to technological exploitation. Supernature is the realm of the holy, of God the Creator, who, of course, is not available to humans on their terms and is subject to no greater power or authority. This means that, while God acts unilaterally upon the realm of nature, creatures do not enjoy equal say or influence with respect to God.

This great divide of reality is necessary if monotheism is to preserve the absolute sovereignty or aseity of God (from the Latin *a se,* meaning "in himself"). For the purposes of scientific inquiry, however, the supernatural does not exist. The world is itself sovereign. Anything that happens, anything at all, does so as a consequence of other things that have happened. All happenings are the effects of previous natural happenings and will themselves serve as causes for future happenings. The natural universe is constituted by these countless cause-and-effect relationships and any explanation must be in terms of them. One can use geology, biology, psychology, anthropology, and historiography, but never theology, to explain mundane or this-worldly events. If science is by definition the search for an intelligible network of natural cause-and-effect relationships, then it cannot admit to the possibility of a supernatural cause influencing this network in any way. And even if science could admit to this hypothesis, confirmation would be impossible. The approach of science, limited to the investigation of natural causes, could never identify supernatural ones.

The readings in this part are intended to explore the nature-supernature split and its implications. The first section, "Principles and Problems," includes a definition of the split and examines some methodological issues that arise in theology when the philosophy of science scrutinizes the notion of the supernatural. This sets the stage in the second section, "Einstein and the Transcendent God," for a discussion of Einstein's rejection of supernaturalism and his suggestion to religion on how to live without it. The direct response of the theologian Paul Tillich reveals the underlying religious persuasion of the great scientist. Finally, the four selections in the third section, "Miracles," set up the debate about the existence and character of miracles by taking a critical look at the interruption of the supernatural into the natural.

The keynote selection for Part III is the attempt by C. S. Lewis to define naturalism and supernaturalism. For those who subscribe to naturalism, the world is a vast interlocking system of parts that operates on its own and requires no further explanation. For those who subscribe to supernaturalism, there is, in addition to this cosmic system, a power or being residing outside the sphere of time and space. This being is not coequal with the world system. Rather this being (God) is its initiator and sustainer. If the world goes on its own, then there can be no transcendent governor. If there is a transcendent governor, then the world cannot go on its own. In "The Naturalist and the Supernaturalist," Lewis' descriptions show clearly that, given the conditions he provides, the two positions are irreconcilable.

A major consequence of this situation is described in the subsequent selection, Richard Bube's "The Failure of the God-of-the-Gaps." These "gaps" are areas of scientific ignorance or phenomena which have not yet been adequately explained. Believers often take comfort by arguing that if science cannot explain why certain things happen, then God's actions may be inserted to fill the gap.

Bube sees that the God-of-the-Gaps position suffers from a simple but fatal weakness: any gap is vulnerable to scientific advance. Science may well progress to a point where any particular gap vanishes in the light of new knowledge. As soon as an occurrence can be scientifically explained, it is removed from direct divine influence.

As God retreats along the frontier of advancing knowledge, the principle of parsimony, sometimes called "Occam's Razor" after the medieval philosopher who first stated it, comes into play. Simply put, parsimony instructs science never to multiply explanations beyond what is minimally necessary to explain an event. Keep theories simple and stingy.

The application of this principle eliminates the idea that God acts directly in nature. If a phenomenon can be explained completely with reference only to the action of natural causes, then the addition of a supernatural cause violates the principle of parsimony. When asked how God the Creator fit into his closed and complete theory about the birth of the universe, the nineteenth-century French astronomer Pierre-Simon Laplace summed it up nicely when he answered, "I have no need of that hypothesis." The God-of-the-Gaps seems to be the unwilling victim of parsimony.

In addition to the God-of-the-Gaps and parsimony, a third principle applies to the nature-supernature distinction. Led by Karl Popper, the author of the third selection, philosophers of science have long known that nothing can be proved conclusively by scientific induction because no theory can be exhaustively tested, that is, submitted to every possible instance for verification. Science is therefore fated always to be a kind of hasty generalization. Of course, the confidence that scientists have in theories grows over time as more and more conforming instances are observed.

It is, however, possible to falsify a theory simply by discovering a single disconfirming instance. Indeed, the strength of a good scientific hypothesis is its naked vulnerability, its openness to any and all comers who would falsify it by discovering counter instances. This vulnerability comes in the form of testability, a critical experiment or a set of observations that might decide against the theory. A theory is considerably weakened in its claims to be scientific by the absence of any such decisive test.

When seen in the light of this criterion, many laws of physics are strong theories. The laws of buoyancy and the inverse relationship of pressure and volume of a gas in a closed container can be tested with precision by any eighth-grade student. Astrology, however, is a different story. In "Falsification" Karl Popper insightfully concludes that predictions made by astrologers are often so vague that they can seldom fail. It is always possible to reinterpret a prediction by introducing new assumptions so as to rescue it from refutation by disconfirming evidence. Hence, astrology becomes foolproof.

As a theory it does not rule out anything and can never be falsified. No situation can exist for which it cannot, in principle, account. It is immune to refutation. Ironically, however, this same power forever denies astrology the status of a scientific theory.

Sometimes the "hypothesis" of a supernatural being who acts in the world of human experience appears to be irrefutable as well. Any possible state of affairs can be explained or explained away as a disconfirming instance simply by modifying the God hypothesis to disallow it.

The selections in the second section revolve around one of Albert Einstein's rare statements about religion. In "Science and Religion," the father of relativity theory and other important discoveries of contemporary physics subscribes, on the one hand, to the position that science and religion are separate and independent enterprises. On the other hand, he sees the possibility of useful cooperation between them. But he then goes further to question the commitment of religion to the notion of a personal and transcendent God. Einstein's reasons are various and include the rejection of an external or other-worldly cause interfering with the rational set of causes found in the universe. Two ultimate causal agencies is one too many. In these remarks, Einstein fits Lewis's definition of a naturalist. He counsels religion to attend to its proper task, which is essentially ethical, a commitment to "superpersonal values." Finally, Einstein reveals his own deep cosmic experience, his "profound reverence for the rationality made manifest in existence."

Paul Tillich responds to Einstein in "Science and Religion: A Discussion with Einstein." Tillich criticizes each of Einstein's arguments in turn. But he reserves much of his attention for the idea of a personal God, which, interestingly enough, Tillich himself also rejects. The target of a personal and supernatural deity is a false one, claims Tillich. God cannot exist. An existing God would be just an object among objects and certainly God is more than that. God is the ground of existence, the creator of all existing things, but not to be found among them. For this reason, belief in a personal and otherworldly deity should be rejected. Personhood, at best, is a symbol for the holy ground of existence, but it should never be taken literally. Einstein makes that mistake, or so Tillich contends.

Tillich points out that Einstein's sense of mystical awe and reverence for the deep rationality of nature is itself a fundamental religious experience. Einstein is plumbing the "inexhaustible depths" of the ground of existence and hence is coming very close to an encounter with Tillich's understanding of what he calls elsewhere "the God beyond God."

One bone of contention between science and religion or between naturalists and supernaturalists is the existence of miracles, the subject of the third section. If miracles are defined in the traditional way as dramatic interruptions of lawful natural processes, then science certainly has a stake in their existence.

Such interference is unacceptable to the naturalist in a world that "goes on its own," in Lewis's words. The existence of miracles violates the principle of uniformity, the claim of science that the most general laws of nature apply everywhere and always, in the depths of the earth and in the most distant galaxy. Science would not be possible if uniformity were violated arbitrarily and sporadically by an unknown and probably unknowable causal agent originating from beyond the universe. If the universe is a complete interlocking set of cause-and-effect relationships, then anything that happens in the universe should be explicable in terms of consistent laws that describe these relationships. But the cause of a miracle lies beyond the universe, beyond the powers of science to discover it, while the miracle itself takes place within the universe. This situation of having a known effect with an unknowable cause is understandably intolerable to science.

"Miracles," is taken from John Hick, a highly regarded philosopher of religion. Hick begins with his understanding of the testimony of biblical writers as they bore witness to the acts of God, including miracles, in their history and community. These accounts, Hick claims, should not be taken literally because they arise out of a prescientific world view. Surely, the authors did the best they could and it clearly satisfied the contemporary audiences for which their narratives were intended. But the three-storied biblical cosmology, the sun circling the earth to be halted in its course, the six-day creation account in Genesis, and the bodily resurrection of all persons at the end of history, are simply no longer plausible beliefs for modern men and women. We should recognize here that Hick's conclusions are rejected by conservative theologians who find no problem acknowledging that an all-powerful God could have done all these things, primitive world views notwithstanding.

What, then, of miracles? Are they to go the way of all the other prescientific accounts in scripture? Hick deals with this question by redefining miracle so as to eliminate its intrusive character. He questions the traditional mythological accounts of miracles and seeks to replace them with a version more acceptable to the modern mind, a mind shaped by the authority of science. Thus, a miracle may be alternatively understood as an act of God which reveals the divine will and intentions in a striking way but without breaking the order of nature. In this understanding, nature is the medium of divine communication. No laws are violated, so uniformity is preserved.

The seventh selection, by biblical scholars Robert Spivey and D. Moody Smith, is an effort to explore the miracles reported in the New Testament accounts of Jesus of Nazareth within the cultural and religious context of the first century. In "The New Testament Understanding of Miracles," the authors claim that miracles were not understood to be violations of laws of nature. Rather they were seen to be strange and wondrous events intended to serve as signs of personal authority or indications of future events. The gospel writers emphasized the accounts of Jesus' miracles in order to confirm their understanding of him as the Messiah, as one with authority over the powers of the worldly realm. The authors go on to examine three types of miracles attributed to Jesus as evidence of this insight and conclude that to assess them fairly we must reenter the consciousness of the contemporaries of Jesus and determine what they thought about the phenomenon in terms of faith and impending eschatological events.

The eighth short reading is taken from Richard Dawkins' "Miracles and Probability." Dawkins focuses on the strong version of miracle as an apparent violation of natural law, the version Hick sees as obsolete. Dawkins offers an alternative understanding even for this kind of miracle. A miracle, he says, is a highly improbable event, a coincidence whose mathematical possibility approaches but does not equal zero. However unlikely the event is to happen, its occurrence is still within the realm of possibility, so that, if it does happen, divine intervention is not required to explain it. Dawkin's argument cuts both ways. The believer could still argue that the chances of such a thing actually happening are so infinitesimally small as to be virtually impossible. Thus, if the event does occur, a miracle may be properly inferred.

The final selection of this section, "Do Miracles Exist?" by Paul Davies, is a debate between a believer and a skeptic that underscores the complex issues involved in the notion of miracle. The debate is interesting because it raises questions about miracles that the other readings do not raise, and because it is a good illustration of the application of the God-of-the-Gaps concept and the principles of parsimony, falsifiability, and uniformity. The character of the skeptic in the disputation is somewhat strident and the believer theologically unsophisticated, but the issues are clear. Davies' summary in his final paragraph is a fair account of the conflict over miracles.

The perspective of a two-storied universe places great emphasis upon the discontinuity rather than the continuity of God and creation. However, it neglects the intimate dimension of God's involvement in the world, known to theologians as the divine "immanence." Our intention is not to be one-sided, but rather to recognize the contribution of the two-story image in traditional monotheism to the science-religion discussion. Numerous theologians and scientists advocate a picture of God and world that places greater emphasis upon the connectedness between them. Proponents of this position are well represented in Parts IV, V, and VI.

PRINCIPLES AND PROBLEMS
THE NATURALIST AND THE SUPERNATURALIST
C. S. LEWIS

C. S. Lewis (1898-1963) was professor of medieval and renaissance literature at Cambridge University. Following his conversion from atheism to Christianity in 1931, Lewis became known as one of the premier apologists for the faith in the modern world. His very readable books in the rational defense of Christianity are too numerous to list but include *The Great Divorce, The Screwtape Letters, Mere Christianity, The Problem of Pain, Surprised by Joy,* and *Miracles,* from which this selection is taken.

I use the word *Miracle* to mean an interference with Nature by supernatural power.[1] Unless there exists, in addition to Nature, something else which we may call the supernatural, there can be no miracles. Some people believe that nothing exists except Nature; I call these people *Naturalists*. Others think that, besides Nature, there exists something else: I call them *Supernaturalists*. Our first question, therefore, is whether the Naturalists or the Supernaturalists are right. And here comes our first difficulty.

Before the Naturalist and the Supernaturalist can begin to discuss their difference of opinion, they must surely have an agreed definition both of Nature and of Supernature. But unfortunately it is almost impossible to get such a definition. Just because the Naturalist thinks that nothing but Nature exists, the word *Nature* means to him merely "everything" or "the whole show" or "whatever there is." And if that is what we mean by Nature, then of course nothing else exists. The real question between him and the Supernaturalist has evaded us. Some philosophers have defined Nature as "What we perceive with our five senses." But this also is unsatisfactory; for we do not perceive our own emotions in that way, and yet they are presumably "natural" events. In order to avoid this deadlock and to discover what the Naturalist and the Supernaturalist are really differing about, we must approach our problem in a more roundabout way.

I begin by considering the following sentences. (1) Are those his natural teeth or a set? (2) The dog in his natural state is covered with fleas. (3) I love to get away from tilled lands and metalled roads and be alone with Nature. (4) Do be natural. Why are you so affected? (5) It may have been wrong to kiss her but it was very natural.

A common thread of meaning in all these usages can easily be discovered. The natural teeth are those which grow in the mouth; we do not have to design them, make them, or fit them. The dog's natural state is the one he will be in if no one takes soap and water and prevents it. The countryside where Nature reigns supreme is the one where soil, weather and vegetation produce their results unhelped and unimpeded by man. Natural behaviour is the behaviour which people would exhibit if they were not at the pains to alter it. The natural kiss is the kiss which will be given if moral or prudential considerations do not intervene. In all the examples Nature means what happens "of itself" or "of its own accord": what you do not need to labour for; what you will get if you take no measures to stop it. The Greek word for Nature (Physis) is connected with the Greek verb for "to grow"; Latin *Natura,* with the verb "to be born." The Natural is what springs up, or comes forth, or arrives, or goes on, *of its own accord:* the given, what is there already: the spontaneous, the unintended, the unsolicited.

What the Naturalist believes is that the ultimate Fact, the thing you can't go behind, is a vast process in space and time which is *going on of its own accord.* Inside that total system every particular event (such as your sitting reading this book) happens because some other event has happened; in the long run, because the Total Event is happening. Each particular thing (such as this page) is what it is because other things are what they are; and so, eventually, because the whole system is what it is. All the things and events are so completely interlocked that no one of them can claim the slightest independence from "the whole show." None of them exists "on its own" or "goes on of its own accord" except in the sense that it exhibits, at some particular place and time, that general "existence on its own" or "behaviour of its own accord" which belongs to "Nature" (the great total interlocked event) as a whole. Thus no thoroughgoing Naturalist believes in free will: for free will would mean that human beings have the power of independent action, the power of doing something more or other than what was involved by the total series of events. And any such separate power of originating events is what the Naturalist denies. Spontaneity, originality, action "on its own," is a privilege reserved for "the whole show," which he calls *Nature.*

The Supernaturalist agrees with the Naturalist that there must be something which exists in its own right; some basic Fact whose existence it would be nonsensical to try to explain because this Fact is itself the ground or starting-point of all explanations. But he does not identify this Fact with "the whole show." He thinks that things fall into two classes. In the first class we find either things or (more probably) One Thing which is basic and original, which exists on its own. In the second we find things which are merely derivative from that One Thing. The one basic Thing has caused all the other things to be. It exists on its own; they exist because it exists. They will cease to exist if it ever ceases to maintain them in existence; they will be altered if it ever alters them.

The difference between the two views might be expressed by saying that Naturalism gives us a democratic, Supernaturalism a monarchical, picture of reality. The Naturalist thinks that the privilege of "being on its own" resides in the total mass of things, just as in a democracy sovereignty resides in the whole mass of the people. The Supernaturalist thinks that this privilege belongs to some things or (more probably) One Thing and not to others—just as, in a real monarchy, the king has sovereignty and the people have not. And just as, in a democracy, all citizens are equal, so for the Naturalist one thing or event is as good as another, in the sense that they are all equally dependent on the total system of things. Indeed each of them is only the way in which the character of that total system exhibits itself at a particular point in space and time. The Supernaturalist, on the other hand, believes that the one original or self-existent thing is on a different level from, and more important than, all other things.

At this point a suspicion may occur that Supernaturalism first arose from reading into the universe the structure of monarchical societies. But then of course it may with equal reason be suspected that Naturalism has arisen from reading into it the structure of

modern democracies. The two suspicions thus cancel out and give us no help in deciding which theory is more likely to be true. They do indeed remind us that Supernaturalism is the characteristic philosophy of a monarchical age and Naturalism of a
democratic, in the sense that Supernaturalism, even if false, would have been believed
by the great mass of unthinking people four hundred years ago, just as Naturalism, even
if false, will be believed by the great mass of unthinking people to-day.

Everyone will have seen that the One Self-existent Thing—or the small class of
self-existent things—in which Supernaturalists believe, is what we call God or the gods.
I propose for the rest of this book to treat only that form of Supernaturalism which
believes in one God; partly because polytheism is not likely to be a live issue for most
of my readers, and partly because those who believed in many gods very seldom, in
fact, regarded their gods as creators of the universe and as self-existent. The gods of
Greece were not really supernatural in the strict sense which I am giving to the word.
They were products of the total system of things and included within it. This introduces
an important distinction.

The difference between Naturalism and Supernaturalism is not exactly the same as
the difference between belief in a God and disbelief. Naturalism, without ceasing to be
itself, could admit a certain kind of God. The great interlocking event called Nature
might be such as to produce at some stage a great cosmic consciousness, an indwelling
"God" arising from the whole process as human mind arises (according to the
Naturalists) from human organisms. A Naturalist would not object to that sort of God.
The reason is this. Such a God would not stand outside Nature or the total system,
would not be existing "on his own." It would still be "the whole show" which was the
basic Fact, and such a God would merely be one of the things (even if he were the most
interesting) which the basic Fact contained. What Naturalism cannot accept is the idea
of a God who stands outside Nature and made it.

We are now in a position to state the difference between the Naturalist and the
Supernaturalist despite the fact that they do not mean the same by the word Nature. The
Naturalist believes that a great process, or "becoming," exists "on its own" in space and
time, and that nothing else exists—what we call particular things and events being only
the parts into which we analyse the great process or the shapes which that process takes
at given moments and given points in space. This single, total reality he calls Nature.
The Supernaturalist believes that one Thing exists on its own and has produced the
framework of space and time and the procession of systematically connected events
which fill them. This framework, and this filling, he calls Nature. . . .

If we decide that Nature is not the only thing there is, then we cannot say in
advance whether she is safe from miracles or not. There are things outside her: we do
not yet know whether they can get in. The gates may be barred, or they may not. But if
Naturalism is true, then we do know in advance that miracles are impossible: nothing
can come into Nature from the outside because there is nothing outside to come in,
Nature being everything. No doubt, events which we in our ignorance should mistake
for miracles might occur: but they would in reality be (just like the commonest events)
an inevitable result of the character of the whole system.

Our first choice, therefore, must be between Naturalism and Supernaturalism.

NOTE

1. This definition is not that which would be given by many theologians. I am adopting it not because I think it an improvement upon theirs but precisely because, being crude and "popular," it enables me most easily to treat those questions which "the common reader" probably has in mind when he takes up a book on Miracles.

QUESTIONS FOR STUDY

1. Give two essential characteristics of "Nature" in Lewis' description.

2. Why can no thoroughgoing naturalist believe in free will?

3. Supernaturalists believe in this worldly reality *and* some others. Are these two worlds equal?

4. What does Lewis mean when he says that "Naturalism gives us a democratic, Supernaturalism a monarchical, picture of reality"?

5. Can one be a naturalist and believe in God? How?

QUESTIONS FOR REFLECTION

1. Is it necessary, as Lewis maintains, for a naturalist to deny free will? If nature is "spontaneous" and "goes on its own," does it follow that the parts of nature (creatures) be deprived of these features?

2. Why should a Supernaturalist insist that nature is derivative from Supernature? Is it illogical to assume that the two are equals? See process philosophy on this point in Cobb's selection, Part VI.

3. If God or Supernature exists, are miracles possible? Are they necessary?

NETWORKING

Other authors who focus on *naturalism and supernaturalism* include Gilkey, Einstein, Davies, Jastrow, Gish, Burhoe, and Peacocke. Teilhard and Cobb discuss *divine immanence* and Bube explores *Deism. Miracles* are in the last section of this part.

THE FAILURE OF THE GOD-OF-THE-GAPS
RICHARD H. BUBE

Richard Bube is associate chair of the Department of Materials Science and Electrical Engineering at Stanford University. Before coming to Stanford, he was senior staff scientist at the Radio Corporation of America laboratories in Princeton, New Jersey. Dr. Bube is the author of several books both on engineering and on science and religion.

In earlier days it was both possible and common to sustain a religious interpretation of the world by looking directly to God as the immediate Cause of those physical and biological events which man was then unable to describe or understand. In the historical context of growing scientific description of the world, this religious interpretation became known as a concern with a *God-of-the-Gaps*. The practical consequence of the view that God's existence could be proved by man's ignorance of certain key physical and biological mechanisms was that evidence for God's existence decreased as man's scientific knowledge grew; the more man knew of the creation, the less reason he had to believe in the Creator.

It is a common belief that traditional Christianity had no alternative but to commit itself to a God-of-the-Gaps. Ralph W. Burhoe, for example, writes: "The mainstream of Christian theology properly avoided that solution [the Deist position], but, to do so, it had to separate its realm of spiritual and moral values from the scientific world view and thus remove itself to a 'God of the gaps' position in which it has been withering as the scientific world view proceeds to fill the gaps."[1]

Although they may not have actually represented the mainstream of Christian theology, enough influential Christian apologists have espoused a God-of-the-Gaps to require a careful appraisal of their position. Such consideration involves both a re-evaluation of God's relationship to the physical world in the light of biblical insights, and an understanding of the nature of scientific and alternative descriptions. Earlier in this century the choice seemed to be between God-as-an-Exile and God-of-the-Gaps; this essay claims that biblical Christianity affirms instead that God-at-the-Center best correlates with the totality of life and experience.

HISTORICAL BACKGROUND

A defense of a God-of-the-Gaps developed over many years in a series of events in which each stage seemed to follow in a direct way from the preceding. Before the sixteenth century a comfortable relationship could be maintained between contemporary religious and scientific descriptions of the world. In the Aristotelian heritage, "how" questions and "why" questions were answered in much the same way. Purpose was inherent in descriptions of events in the natural world. An acorn fell to the earth so that a new oak might arise. Rain came so that crops might grow and people might be fed. A moving wagon came to rest because a state of rest was the normal condition for a body on earth. In this context the direct participation of God in the daily affairs of life was easy to accept. God was the Good, the One who made all things to function in such a way that His purpose might be fulfilled. God's revelation was the ultimate source of wisdom, and the role of man's reason was to interpret that revelation and to apply it to daily life.

But Christian thought profoundly influenced human thinking in other ways as well. Through emphasis on the world as the creation of God the Creator, earthly things were effectively desacralized. What had been worshiped, or at least regarded with awe as representing the immediate presence of a god in the world, was now understood instead to be a created thing, event or process. The spirits of animism were exorcised; the familiar spirits of rocks, trees and rivers were stripped of reality. It was right and proper for man to find out for himself how the world functioned. Instead of attempting to settle scientific questions on the basis of conjectural reasoning or tradition alone, it now became appropriate to "think God's thoughts after Him" by attempting to understand the natural mechanisms that control the created universe.

As a consequence, Galileo, Newton and other devout scientists contributed to the development of a new scientific approach to descriptions of natural events and processes. The ranks of seventeenth and eighteenth century scientists are replete with men who were driven to understand the natural mechanisms of the world as a way of glorifying the God they served.

But as they developed the experimental method and mathematical models of the world, they introduced radical changes in the way questions about the world were answered. Now an acorn fell because of the force of gravity. Rain came because of the interaction of warm and cold air fronts, high and low pressure areas. A moving wagon with no force acting on it came to rest because of the friction of its axle. Teleological "explanations" gave way to mechanistic descriptions. Recognition of God's immediate activity in the world began to fade. The view in which evidence for the existence and activity of God depended upon His direct intervention in the world was increasingly threatened.

This threat was accentuated by philosophical conclusions that seemed to be demanded by a growing scientific understanding. Initially a special creature made in God's image to rule over the very center of the universe, man found himself displaced to a small planet somewhere in a vast machinelike universe. The concept of God was altered from that of God the Good to God the Mechanic, the Master Architect, the Clockmaker *par excellence*. If it could no longer be maintained that God was directly active in events of this world, then it could still be maintained that God had made the clockwork that scientists were describing. But once God is relegated to the position of First Cause, His significance for the present is swallowed up by His activity in the distant past. Despite the firm intention of many theistic scientists to defend God's significance, the way they did so seemed inevitably to lead to a perspective in which God played little role in contemporary life. It was argued that what once could be found only in revelation, could now at least be duplicated by human reasoning. And if thus duplicated, why could not human reasoning finally replace revelation altogether? While revelation may have been necessary in a time of man's intellectual infancy, now that man was growing up, why could he not take over and work out his own system, without dependence on ancient mysticism?

The final blow in this sequence of events seemed to occur with the appearance of Darwin's *Origin of Species* in 1859. Although now demoted positionally in the universe and deprived of a teleological perspective on the physical world, man could still gain religious comfort from the fact that he alone was made directly in the image of God and hence in complete discontinuity with the rest of the creation. But the theory of evolution toppled this final refuge; man was, so it now appeared, nothing more than a highly developed animal. He existed without ultimate significance or enduring purpose, being presumably the end product of impersonal chance operating throughout time. In the words of Bertrand Russell, "That Man is the product of causes which had no prevision of the end they were achieving; that his origin, his growth, his hopes and fears, his loves and his beliefs, are but the outcome of accidental collocations of atoms . . . if not quite beyond dispute, are yet so nearly certain, that no philosophy which rejects them can hope to stand.[2] Born without choice, man was destined to die without choice, with no more meaning in the sequences of human history than in the dropping of a leaf in autumn.

Our concern now is to ask whether the philosophical and religious conclusions drawn from these scientific developments were actually the appropriate ones. Must one conclude that only in the shrinking areas of our persisting ignorance can modern man still hope to find evidence of God and His work in the world, and that He has been decisively squeezed out everywhere else? Are we forced to invent dichotomies in order to maintain that, although we have apparently lost our evidence for God in the physical dimension, that evidence can still be found in the spiritual, where science cannot penetrate and religion has safe anchorage? Or have these philosophical and religious conclusions no necessary connection at all with our increased scientific understanding, finding their origin, rather, in presuppositions that have always been alienated from historic Christian thought and have been simply waiting for opportunities to find suitable arguments? Can we argue that, after all, the God-of-the-Gaps is the result of a faulty understanding of the biblical revelation and that those Christians who have fallen into this trap have failed to distinguish cultural influences from a truly biblical theology?

RESPONSES TO MAN'S INCREASING KNOWLEDGE

The application of science has staggeringly increased man's knowledge of the universe in the last few centuries. At least three basic responses have been made to this vast growth of knowledge. Two of them, one commonly made by non-Christians and one commonly made by Christians, agree in accepting a God-of-the-Gaps. Only the third view is able to integrate modern scientific understanding with a biblical perspective on the relationship between God and the universe.

The first response to man's increasing scientific knowledge of the world and of himself is to hail this knowledge as the foundation of man's liberation from the chains of ignorance. When man was ignorant of what *really* was happening in the world, he readily fell victim to myths and superstitions. Instead of exercising his reason, he was subjected to the ritual of priests. As a result, he had a false perception of reality. He fell easy prey to exploiters who made use of his weakness for religion to control him for their own benefit, and he could not develop his full potential. Our understanding of scientific mechanisms has liberated mankind from the anthropomorphic projection of a cosmic deity. Instead of being led astray and handicapped by subjective illusions, man is now able autonomously to face the reality of the world and to develop his own future.

Such a response to the growth in man's knowledge is common to many non-Christian interpreters who find a God-of-the-Gaps increasingly expandable as those gaps are closed by an extension of scientific understanding. For them, the circumstance that modern knowledge banishes a God-of-the-Gaps is a cause for rejoicing.

The second response is to regard man's increasing scientific understanding as a threat to faith in God. It is argued that there are aspects of life where only God has the power and the right to act; human encroachment on these areas recreates a modern Babel where men seek to exalt themselves and to bring God down. Christian faith rests, so it is believed, upon the existence of areas of human ignorance and impotence, areas that can properly be described only as the direct activity of God in the world, without involving any phenomena capable of natural description. It is essential that man shrink from further encroachment of this kind and, wherever possible, combat the impression that increases in scientific understanding are indeed firmly established. God is accepted as a God-of-the-Gaps; evidence for His existence is to be found primarily in human limitations. Here, the recognition that a God-of-the-Gaps is being squeezed out by modern knowledge is a cause for lamentation.

The third response to man's increasing understanding rejects the idea that God is a God-of-the-Gaps. It is God who brought man to his new level of understanding, and it is God who can bring man the ability to make responsible decisions thrust upon him by this understanding. It is possible for Christians to accept responsibly their new position of knowledge and choice—but only with trembling, and as sustained by a vision of God as the Lord of all reality. God is to be found at the center of life, as Dietrich Bonhoeffer declared:

> Religious people speak of God when human knowledge...has come to an end, or when human resources fail—in fact it is always the *deus ex machina* that they bring on to the scene, either for the apparent solution of insoluble problems, or as strength in human failure....It always seems to me that we are trying anxiously in this way to reserve some place for God; I should like to speak of God not on the boundaries but at the center, not in weakness but in strength; and therefore not in death and guilt but in man's life and goodness.[3]

It is therefore right and appropriate that the God-of-the-Gaps has been dislodged by man's increasing knowledge, for this "God" never was the God of the Bible. It is possible to rejoice, therefore, that the God-of-the-Gaps has been squeezed out, to refrain from attempts to restore this God-of-the-Gaps, and to seek to glorify the Lord of all created reality by placing Him at the very center of life.

CHRISTIAN DEFENSE OF A GOD-OF-THE-GAPS

To characterize God as a God-of-the-Gaps is to attempt to prove or defend belief in the existence and activity of God by proposing that it is God alone who acts in areas in which man is ignorant of any scientific basis. There is a long history of Christian acceptance and use of this position. Such a choice ironically has allied the Christian with the non-Christian who also sees God as a God-of-the-Gaps, and has thus served to obscure the Christian witness to biblical theism.

The argument runs this way: Man may now know much about physics, chemistry, biology and the like, but certain key physical, chemical or biological mechanisms must forever elude him because such mechanisms do not in fact even exist. These gaps in the description of natural events and processes can be filled only by recognizing that God acts in these gaps above and beyond any physical, chemical or biological mechanism. In this interpretation God remains the Great Mechanic, and His very existence and activity forever rule out the possibility of a complete physical, chemical or biological description—even in principle.

Newton invoked the God-of-the-Gaps when certain irregularities in the motion of the planets could not be explained by his theory of gravitation. Since the mechanics of the theory of gravity could not explain the irregularities, Newton inferred that it was a direct manifestation of the intervention of God. Newton was wrong; subsequent analysis of the planetary system provided a natural explanation for these irregularities. Supposed evidence for the intervention of God was discredited.

The list of phenomena invoked by Christians to defend the God-of-the-Gaps is very long and still with us. The healing of physical sicknesses continues to be an area of special interest. Fifty years ago many diseases now curable had no known treatment; confronted with an incurable disease, doctors would tell the patient's relatives that nothing further could be done by medical science. The ill person was now completely in the hands of God, who could heal the sickness if He so willed. If the ill person recovered, the relatives thanked God for having intervened. Today if doctors are confronted with the same disease, they consider it wrong to withhold treatment and tell relatives that only prayer can meet the patient's needs. Instead they administer treatment. If the relatives have been influenced by the God-of-the-Gaps fallacy, they will now thank the doctor and forget God completely. Insofar as it has become possible to heal by natural methods what formerly could be healed only by supernatural means, another area of evidence for the existence and activity of the God-of-the-Gaps is lost. If the relatives have not been trapped by the God-of-the-Gaps fallacy, they will thank the doctor *and* they will thank God for the wisdom and skill of modern medicine. These remarks should not be construed to be an argument against the *possibility* of God healing by direct action nor against the historical *fact* of such action; rather, they are a warning that if supernatural action is our only, or even our primary, evidence for the existence and activity of God, we have committed ourselves to a God-of-the-Gaps.

The supernatural intervention of God was advanced as the direct cause of weather patterns; now that we know that such weather patterns are meteorological phenomena, this evidence for a God-of-the-Gaps is gone. A place was reserved for the God-of-the-Gaps by some Christians who objected to human space travel on the grounds that earth was man's proper domain, whereas the heavens were reserved for God. A large portion of the battle over evolution centered on the need to reserve the origin of life, or at least the origin of human life, for the domain of supernatural intervention; the theory of evolution that advanced natural mechanisms as the means by which life and human beings came into existence was an obvious threat to the God-of-the-Gaps. The possibility that laboratory scientists may construct a living creature from nonliving substances is seen as another threat to the God-of-the-Gaps, whose existence and activity demand that human beings be unable to accomplish this goal.

In many areas human beings today are called upon to confront responsibly a variety of dilemmas that our ancestors did not have to face and to exercise new capabilities. Those committed to a God-of-the-Gaps see these areas as ones in which God has the right of direct intervention, and they therefore contend that humans should leave these areas totally alone in order to give God His due. But may not God rather be bringing us to the point where we have the ability and knowledge to respond to more and more human needs, as well as to situations where our previous efforts to improve life have only created new dilemmas? If this is the case, then it is not only possible for man today to make more informed decisions than ever before, but it also is wrong for him to shirk this responsibility. A retreat to making no choice is no longer possible; in many areas, not to make a choice is already to have made one.

Bernard Ramm has stressed the need to understand that God is active in all areas of life. Having indicated that man must supply some answer to a host of problems previously ignored or left "in the hands of God"—for example, genetic engineering, the definition of death, and the electrical, chemical and surgical alterations of human behavior—Ramm continues:

> In the light of developments in behavioral sciences and psychiatry we need to take a second look at our doctrine of the Holy Spirit. Put in simplest and most direct terms, many of the things we now claim *only* the Holy Spirit can do with man supernaturally, man will do for himself. We see no ceiling to the control, shaping and modulation of human behavior in the future.[4]

Ramm argues that we must reflect on what it means to speak of the immanence of the Holy Spirit in every dimension of the universe. While maintaining clearly the uniqueness and discontinuity of the work of the Holy Spirit in the appropriate context, we must also be careful to maintain the continuity between the Holy Spirit's work and the natural mechanisms of man's increased technological control over the world. It is in this direction that a response to the God-of-the-Gaps must be found.

RETHINKING THE GOD-OF-THE-GAPS

Two quotations are helpful in setting the stage for what it means to rethink the God-of-the-Gaps and replace this concept with the biblical emphasis. The first is a statement by Malcolm Jeeves: "God, to the theist, while being the cause of everything, is scientifically the explanation of nothing."[5] The second, somewhat enigmatic, statement is by Bonhoeffer: "Before God, and with God, we live without God."[6]

The thrust of Jeeves' remark is that God is to be conceived as the underlying cause of *all* created reality. One way to describe the world is in terms of natural science; in such a description God does not systematically enter at places where natural mechanisms are absent in order to provide a supernatural explanation. The God-of-the-Gaps is therefore avoided, not by giving up the witness for the activity of God in the world, but by seeing this activity in the context of all of created reality—not simply in those aspects where we presently lack a scientific description.

Bonhoeffer's statement can best be understood by focusing on the meaning of the three prepositions he uses with respect to God: (1) *Before*—our life is lived in the created universe that God has called into being and sustains in being; we are constantly in the presence of God. (2) *With*—our lives are joined to God in constant fellowship in Jesus Christ, so that we are never alone but rest wholly in the arms of God. (3) *Without*—while not denying the possibility of God's activity in the world without us, we do not use this possibility as an excuse or stopgap for our own ignorance or apathy; instead we seek to serve God fully in all of life without constantly invoking Him to deliver us from the need to serve Him.

Bonhoeffer draws sharp distinction between religion in general and Christian commitment. He argues that human beings are intrinsically and incurably religious. Without a Christian commitment and the personal relationship of faith in Christ, humans will use religion to answer to insoluble problems when they are in trouble, or they will exalt and deify religion itself when they are successful. Both responses are God-of-the-Gaps responses. Only commitment to Christ permits man to escape from what amounts to a religious denial of God's reality in the world in order fully to participate in the world as a servant of Christ.

Any perspective, therefore, that limits the evidence for the existence and activity of God to a particular sphere of experience—the peripheral, the miraculous, the unique, the spiritual, the sacred—is a perspective built on a God-of-the-Gaps. If there is evidence for God in the rare events known as miracles, there is as great evidence for Him in the constant normal events known as natural. Unless a person's commitment to God embraces the ordinary as well as the special aspects of life, the physical as well as the spiritual, and the secular as well as the sacred—unless, indeed, he sees that distinction within these pairs is not a distinction of kind but of convenience—he will be under the limitations of belief in God-of-the-Gaps.

THE RELATIONSHIP BETWEEN GOD AND THE WORLD

The uneasiness engendered when Christians are called upon to give up the God-of-the-Gaps is typified by remarks such as, "If the development of man can be described in terms of natural categories according to the theory of evolution, then what becomes of the biblical picture of God as Creator?" Or, "If human beings can put together nonliving matter and produce living creatures, then what becomes of the biblical picture of God as the Giver of life?"

Such uneasiness can be dissipated only by realizing that the concept of God giving rise to these questions is too limited and nonbiblical. What is involved is our fundamental concept of the way in which God and the world are related. This is a theological question, and our answer must come from the biblical revelation that God Himself has provided.

> By faith we understand that the world was created by the word of God, so that what is seen was made out of things which do not appear (Heb. 11:3, RSV).

He [Jesus] reflects the glory of God and bears the very stamp of his nature, upholding the universe by his word of power (Heb. 1:3, RSV).

He [Jesus] is before all things, and in him all things hold together (Col. 1:17, RSV).

In his hand is the life of every living thing and the breath of all mankind (Job 12:10, RSV).

In him we live and move and have our being (Acts 17:28, RSV).

There is one God, the Father, from whom are all things and for whom we exist, and one Lord, Jesus Christ, through whom are all things and through whom we exist (1 Cor. 8:6, RSV).

From these and many other passages it is clear that the Bible teaches that we depend moment by moment upon God for our very existence. There is nothing *natural* that can happen without God's free activity. To describe events in terms of natural categories is not to explain God's activity *away;* it is rather a fuller exposition of the ways in which we perceive this activity.

It is true that the world has an existence *separate* from God—it is not a part of God, as pantheism would maintain—but it has no existence *independent* of God. Only because the continuing free activity of God maintains it in being does the totality of our universe remain in existence at all. It is not just the order of the universe, or the design of the universe, or the stability or moral character of the universe that depends on God's own existence and activity. He sustains the very *existence* of the universe on a moment-by-moment basis. There is no event, either natural or supernatural, either physical or spiritual, either secular or sacred, which does not depend ultimately and completely upon the sustaining power of God. Every particle of created matter is as instantaneously in relationship to God as is every point on a two-dimensional circle to a three-dimensional creature.

The God-of-the-Gaps is a god who intervenes in the world in order to effect his purpose. But the God of the Bible does not *intervene in* the world. There is no world for Him to intervene in except for that world whose being and character is constantly maintained by His free activity. We describe what God does in terms of processes and laws, but these are modes of our description of God's activity. Neither does the God of the Bible "use natural processes" or "work through natural law." Again, natural processes and natural laws are *our* descriptions of God's activity, not independent tools that God makes use of. To perform a miracle, God needs only to act in a manner different from His "regular" or "normal" action; He does not need to suspend natural law to do something "unnatural." The God of the Bible is not a Master Craftsman who adjusts a former creation that exists independently of Him; the God of the Bible is the Creator and Sustainer who holds all things "in the palm of His hand."

The existence of the God-of-the-Gaps can be debated. If he were not there, the gaps would be empty, but the rest of the universe would continue as before. The God of the Bible is the very foundation of creaturely existence itself. The Bible accepts His reality but does not debate His existence, if indeed that term can be properly applied to God.

The God-of-the-Gaps makes his presence known primarily through the performance of miracles; it is departure from the natural that provides the evidence for his existence. But the God of the Bible is attested as well by every aspect of the created order. The natural cries out to the Psalmist as loudly as the supernatural; in fact, this distinction, so often sharply drawn, turns out to be a good deal less sharp than commonly believed. A natural event presupposes God's activity, no less than a supernatural act. If, for example, the development of a human being could be consistently described in terms of a set of evolutionary natural mechanisms, such a possibility would pose no necessary threat to the Christian. The uniqueness of man as a creature made in the image of God does not necessarily *demand* a nonevolutionary development. What we describe as evolutionary natural mechanisms in the created world are themselves, if valid, the evidence of God's activity. The normal mode of God's free activity in sustaining the world is what we term *natural process*. Unusual modes of God's free activity in sustaining the world, undertaken for the purposes of special revelation, are what we term *miracles*.

DIFFERENT LEVELS OF DESCRIPTION

A second response to the God-of-the-Gaps is the realization that a scientific description is only one of a number of possible types of descriptions of reality, each drawing on categories of experience different from the others. Even if we could give a complete description of the universe using the categories of physics and chemistry, for example (i.e., even if there were no gaps in our physical and chemical descriptions), we would still need other descriptions for dimensions of life not encompassed by the physical and chemical. We either accept the need for such other kinds of description, or we deny the need to symbolize experience in categories other than the physical and chemical; in the latter case, we choose to reduce man to an organic machine.

Reflection on this question shows that it is both possible and necessary to describe reality on several levels corresponding, for example, to the physical sciences, to biology, psychology, sociology and to theology. Every phenomenon that occurs in the world can, at least in principle, be described on every one of these levels. Furthermore, to be able to provide even an exhaustive description on one level (i.e., with no gaps *on that level*) does not rule out the necessity or utility of descriptions on other levels. Complete knowledge would require exhaustive descriptions on every level simultaneously.

The understanding of this rule of multilevel descriptions rescues one from many of the dilemmas that give rise to a defense of the God-of-the-Gaps. The theologian, seeking to describe reality in terms of a relationship between man and God, need not reject scientific descriptions of the same aspects of reality in order to "reserve room for God." Similarly, the scientist, seeking to describe reality in terms of natural categories, need not reject theological descriptions of the same aspects of reality in order to preserve intellectual integrity from supernatural mythology; having found a scientific description of a phenomenon or event, the scientist has neither the need nor the grounds to claim that this discovery in itself does away with evidence for the existence and activity of God.

An understanding of the possibility and the necessity of multilevel descriptions of reality removes many kinds of false dichotomies that frequently give rise to arguments involving a God-of-the-Gaps. It is no longer necessary to debate whether Christian conversion, for example, is a psychological or a theological phenomenon. A significant contribution to understanding the totality of phenomena involved in conversion can be made by providing descriptions on a variety of levels, including the sociological, psychological and even the physical, along with the theological.

Multilevel descriptions make it possible to admit that man is a highly developed animal and a complex organic machine—as those terms are commonly used. Such descriptions, however, do not exhaust the nature of man and must be supplemented with other types of description, including, of course, that of man as a creature made in the image of God. As Vernon Grounds has pointed out,[7] man can truly be described as garbage, machine or animal, depending on whether we focus our attention on chemical, mechanical or biological descriptions, but that a full description of man must include the fact that he is also a unique creature of God, made in His image, with the possibility of fellowship with God shared by no other creature.

NOTES

1. Ralph Wendell Burhoe, "The Human Prospect and the 'Lord of History,'" *Zygon* 10, No. 3 (1975): 333.
2. Bertrand Russell, "A Free Man's Worship," in *Mysticism and Logic and Other Essays* (New York: Norton, 1929).
3. Dietrich Bonhoeffer, *Letters and Papers from Prison,* rev. ed., ed. Eberhard Bethge (New York: Macmillan Co., 1968), p. 142.
4. Bernard Ramm, "Evangelical Theology and Technological Shock," *Journal of the American Scientific Affiliation* 23, No. 2 (1971): 52.
5. Malcolm A. Jeeves, *The Scientific Enterprise and Christian Faith* (London: Tyndale Press, 1969), p. 103.
6. Bonhoeffer, *loc. cit.*, p. 188.
7. Vernon C. Grounds, "God's Perspective on Man," *Journal of the American Scientific Affiliation* 28, No. 4 (1976): 145.

QUESTIONS FOR STUDY

1. What is Bube's definition of the God-of-the-Gaps?

2. Trace briefly the development of the God-of-the-Gaps mentality as science moved away from "teleological" to "mechanistic" explanations.

3. Bube examines three basic responses, both positive and negative, to the "vast growth of scientific knowledge." What are they?

4. Give two examples of a Christian use of the God-of-the-Gaps.

QUESTIONS FOR REFLECTION

1. How did Christianity contribute to the development of science? How does modern science view the world such that this contribution is no longer acknowledged? See Barbour in Part I for further discussion.

2. Look up *Deus ex machina* in the Glossary and in a dictionary of philosophy. What are the origins of the terms in Greek drama? How was it used in the seventeenth century?

3. Examine the life and thought of Dietrich Bonhoeffer. What was his understanding of God's presence in an increasingly secular world?

4. Explain the quotation from Malcolm Jeeves: "God, to the theist, while being the cause of everything, is scientifically the explanation of nothing." Compare with Gilkey's understanding of how God acts in Part I.

NETWORKING

The *God-of-the-Gaps* is an issue for Einstein, Tillich, Asimov, and Polkinghorne. Hick reenforces Bube's approval of the *autonomy of humankind and nature*. Gilkey discusses the *how/why questions in science and religion*. The idea of *levels of description* or *hierarchy* may be found defended by Haught and criticized by Gray and Roach. Swimme concurs with Bube's description of the *disenchantment of nature*.

FALSIFICATION   KARL POPPER

Karl Popper is a renowned philosopher of science. His accomplishments and honors are too numerous to be listed here. They include, however, several honorary degrees and prizes as well as membership in the Royal Society and the British Academy. In 1965 he was knighted in recognition of these achievements. Popper received his doctorate in Vienna in 1928. His books include *The Logic of Scientific Discovery, The Open Society and its Enemies,* and *Conjectures and Refutations*

When I received the list of participants in this course and realized that I had been asked to speak to philosophical colleagues I thought, after some hesitation and consultation, that you would probably prefer me to speak about those problems which interest me most, and about those developments with which I am most intimately acquainted. I therefore decided to do what I have never done before: to give you a report on my own work in the philosophy of science, since the autumn of 1919 when I first began to grapple with the problem, *"When should a theory be ranked as scientific?"* or *"Is there a criterion for the scientific character or status of a theory?"*

The problem which troubled me at the time was neither, "When is a theory true?" nor, "When is a theory acceptable?" My problem was different. I *wished to distinguish between science and pseudo-science;* knowing very well that science often errs, and that pseudo-science may happen to stumble on the truth.

I knew, of course, the most widely accepted answer to my problem: that science is distinguished from pseudo-science—or from "metaphysics"—by its *empirical method,* which is essentially *inductive,* proceeding from observation or experiment. But this did not satisfy me. On the contrary, I often formulated my problem as one of distinguishing between a genuinely empirical method and a non-empirical or even a pseudo-empirical method—that is to say, a method which, although it appeals to observation and experiment, nevertheless does not come up to scientific standards. The latter method may be exemplified by astrology, with its stupendous mass of empirical evidence based on observation—on horoscopes and on biographies.

But as it was not the example of astrology which led me to my problem I should perhaps briefly describe the atmosphere in which my problem arose and the examples by which it was stimulated. After the collapse of the Austrian Empire there had been a revolution in Austria: the air was full of revolutionary slogans and ideas, and new and often wild theories. Among the theories which interested me Einstein's theory of relativity was no doubt by far the most important. Three others were Marx's theory of history, Freud's psycho-analysis, and Alfred Adler's so-called "individual psychology."

There was a lot of popular nonsense talked about these theories, and especially about relativity (as still happens even today), but I was fortunate in those who introduced me to the study of this theory. We all—the small circle of students to which I belonged—were thrilled with the result of Eddington's eclipse observations which in 1919 brought the first important confirmation of Einstein's theory of gravitation. It was a great experience for us, and one which had a lasting influence on my intellectual development.

The three other theories I have mentioned were also widely discussed among students at that time. I myself happened to come into personal contact with Alfred Adler, and even to co-operate with him in his social work among the children and young people in the working-class districts of Vienna where he had established social guidance clinics.

It was during the summer of 1919 that I began to feel more and more dissatisfied with these three theories—the Marxist theory of history, psycho-analysis, and individual psychology; and I began to feel dubious about their claims to scientific status. My problem perhaps first took the simple form, "What is wrong with Marxism, psycho-analysis, and individual psychology? Why are they so different from physical theories, from Newton's theory, and especially from the theory of relativity?"

To make this contrast clear I should explain that few of us at the time would have said that we believed in the *truth* of Einstein's theory of gravitation. This shows that it was not my doubting the *truth* of those other three theories which bothered me, but something else. Yet neither was it that I merely felt mathematical physics to be more *exact* than the sociological or psychological type of theory. Thus what worried me was neither the problem of truth, at that stage at least, nor the problem of exactness or measurability. It was rather that I felt that these other three theories, though posing as sciences, had in fact more in common with primitive myths than with science; that they resembled astrology rather than astronomy.

I found that those of my friends who were admirers of Marx, Freud, and Adler, were impressed by a number of points common to these theories, and especially by their apparent *explanatory power*. These theories appeared to be able to explain practically everything that happened within the fields to which they referred. The study of any of them seemed to have the effect of an intellectual conversion or revelation, opening your eyes to a new truth hidden from those not yet initiated. Once your eyes were thus opened you saw confirming instances everywhere: the world was full of *verifications* of the theory. Whatever happened always confirmed it. Thus its truth appeared manifest; and unbelievers were clearly people who did not want to see the manifest truth; who refused to see it, either because it was against their class interest, or because of their repressions which were still "un-analysed" and crying aloud for treatment.

The most characteristic element in this situation seemed to me the incessant stream of confirmations, of observations which "verified" the theories in question; and this point was constantly emphasized by their adherents. A Marxist could not open a newspaper without finding on every page confirming evidence for his interpretation of history; not only in the news, but also in its presentation—which revealed the class bias of the paper—and especially of course in what the paper did *not* say. The Freudian analysts emphasized that their theories were constantly verified by their "clinical observations." As for Adler, I was much impressed by a personal experience. Once, in 1919,

I reported to him a case which to me did not seem particularly Adlerian, but which he found no difficulty in analysing in terms of his theory of inferiority feelings, although he had not even seen the child. Slightly shocked, I asked him how he could be so sure. "Because of my thousandfold experience," he replied; whereupon I could not help saying: "And with this new case, I suppose, your experience has become thousand-and-one-fold."

What I had in mind was that his previous observations may not have been much sounder than this new one; that each in its turn had been interpreted in the light of "previous experience," and at the same time counted as additional confirmation. What, I asked myself, did it confirm? No more than that a case could be interpreted in the light of the theory. But this meant very little, I reflected, since every conceivable case could be interpreted in the light of Adler's theory, or equally of Freud's. I may illustrate this by two very different examples of human behaviour: that of a man who pushes a child into the water with the intention of drowning it; and that of a man who sacrifices his life in an attempt to save the child. Each of these two cases can be explained with equal ease in Freudian and in Adlerian terms. According to Freud the first man suffered from repression (say, of some component of his Oedipus complex), while the second man had achieved sublimation. According to Adler the first man suffered from feelings of inferiority (producing perhaps the need to prove to himself that he dared to commit some crime), and so did the second man (whose need was to prove to himself that he dared to rescue the child). I could not think of any human behaviour which could not be interpreted in terms of either theory. It was precisely this fact—that they always fitted, that they were always confirmed—which in the eyes of their admirers constituted the strongest argument in favour of these theories. It began to dawn on me that this apparent strength was in fact their weakness.

With Einstein's theory the situation was strikingly different. Take one typical instance—Einstein's prediction, just then confirmed by the findings of Eddington's expedition. Einstein's gravitational theory had led to the result that light must be attracted by heavy bodies (such as the sun), precisely as material bodies were attracted. As a consequence it could be calculated that light from a distant fixed star whose apparent position was close to the sun would reach the earth from such a direction that the star would seem to be slightly shifted away from the sun; or, in other words, that stars close to the sun would look as if they had moved a little away from the sun, and from one another. This is a thing which cannot normally be observed since such stars are rendered invisible in daytime by the sun's overwhelming brightness; but during an eclipse it is possible to take photographs of them. If the same constellation is photographed at night one can measure the distances on the two photographs, and check the predicted effect.

Now the impressive thing about this case is the *risk* involved in a prediction of this kind. If observation shows that the predicted effect is definitely absent, then the theory is simply refuted. The theory is *incompatible with certain possible results of observation*—in fact with results which everybody before Einstein would have expected. This is quite different from the situation I have previously described, when it turned out that the theories in question were compatible with the most divergent human behaviour, so that it was practically impossible to describe any human behaviour that might not be claimed to be a verification of these theories.

These considerations led me in the winter of 1919–20 to conclusions which I may now reformulate as follows.

1. It is easy to obtain confirmations, or verifications, for nearly every theory—if we look for confirmations.

2. Confirmations should count only if they are the result of *risky predictions;* that is to say, if, unenlightened by the theory in question, we should have expected an event which was incompatible with the theory—an event which would have refuted the theory.

3. Every "good" scientific theory is a prohibition: it forbids certain things to happen. The more a theory forbids, the better it is.

4. A theory which is not refutable by any conceivable event is nonscientific. Irrefutability is not a virtue of a theory (as people often think) but a vice.

5. Every genuine *test* of a theory is an attempt to falsify it, or to refute it. Testability is falsifiability; but there are degrees of testability: some theories are more testable, more exposed to refutation, than others; they take, as it were, greater risks.

6. Confirming evidence should not count *except when it is the result of a genuine test of the theory;* and this means that it can be presented as a serious but unsuccessful attempt to falsify the theory. (I now speak in such cases of "corroborating evidence.")

7. Some genuinely testable theories, when found to be false, are still upheld by their admirers—for example by introducing *ad hoc* some auxiliary assumption, or by re-interpreting the theory *ad hoc* in such a way that it escapes refutation. Such a procedure is always possible, but it rescues the theory from refutation only at the price of destroy-ing, or a least lowering, its scientific status. (I later described such a rescuing operation as a *"conventionalist twist"* or a *"conventionalist stratagem."*)

One can sum up all this by saying that *the criterion of the scientific status of a the-ory is its falsifiability, or refutability, or testability.*

II

I may perhaps exemplify this with the help of the various theories so far mentioned. Einstein's theory of gravitation clearly satisfied the criterion of falsifiability. Even if our measuring instruments at the time did not allow us to pronounce on the results of the tests with complete assurance, there was clearly a possibility of refuting the theory.

Astrology did not pass the test. Astrologers were greatly impressed, and misled, by what they believed to be confirming evidence—so much so that they were quite unim-pressed by any unfavourable evidence. Moreover, by making their interpretations and prophecies sufficiently vague they were able to explain away anything that might have been a refutation of the theory had the theory and the prophecies been more precise. In order to escape falsification they destroyed the testability of their theory. It is a typical soothsayer's trick to predict things so vaguely that the predictions can hardly fail: that they become irrefutable.

The Marxist theory of history, in spite of the serious efforts of some of its founders and followers, ultimately adopted this soothsaying practice. In some of its earlier formulations (for example in Marx's analysis of the character of the "coming social revolution") their predictions were testable, and in fact falsified. Yet instead of accepting the refutations the followers of Marx re-interpreted both the theory and the evidence in order to make them agree. In this way they rescued the theory from refutation; but they did so at the price of adopting a device which made it irrefutable. They thus gave a "conventionalist twist" to the theory; and by this stratagem they destroyed its much advertised claim to scientific status.

The two psycho-analytic theories were in a different class. They were simply non-testable, irrefutable. There was no conceivable human behaviour which could contradict them. This does not mean that Freud and Adler were not seeing certain things correctly: I personally do not doubt that much of what they say is of considerable importance, and may well play its part one day in a psychological science which is testable. But it does mean that those "clinical observations" which analysts naïvely believe confirm their theory cannot do this any more than the daily confirmations which astrologers find in their practice. And as for Freud's epic of the Ego, the Super-ego, and the Id, no substantially stronger claim to scientific status can be made for it than for Homer's collected stories from Olympus. These theories describe some facts, but in the manner of myths. They contain most interesting psychological suggestions, but not in a testable form.

At the same time I realized that such myths may be developed, and become testable; that historically speaking all—or very nearly all—scientific theories originate from myths, and that a myth may contain important anticipations of scientific theories. Examples are Empedocles' theory of evolution by trial and error, or Parmenides' myth of the unchanging block universe in which nothing ever happens and which, if we add another dimension, becomes Einstein's block universe (in which, too, nothing ever happens, since everything is, four-dimensionally speaking, determined and laid down from the beginning). I thus felt that if a theory is found to be non-scientific, or "metaphysical" (as we might say), it is not thereby found to be unimportant, or insignificant, or "meaningless," or "nonsensical." But it cannot claim to be backed by empirical evidence in the scientific sense—although it may easily be, in some genetic sense, the "result of observation."

(There were a great many other theories of this pre-scientific or pseudo-scientific character, some of them, unfortunately, as influential as the Marxist interpretation of history; for example, the racialist interpretation of history—another of those impressive and all-explanatory theories which act upon weak minds like revelations.)

Thus the problem which I tried to solve by proposing the criterion of falsifiability was neither a problem of meaningfulness or significance, nor a problem of truth or acceptability. It was the problem of drawing a line (as well as this can be done) between the statements, or systems of statements, of the empirical sciences, and all other statements—whether they are of a religious or of a metaphysical character, or simply pseudo-scientific. Years later—it must have been in 1928 or 1929—I called this first problem of mine the '*problem of demarcation*.' The criterion of falsifiability is a solution to this 'problem of demarcation,' for it says that statements or systems of statements, in order to be ranked as scientific, must be capable of conflicting with possible, or conceivable, observations.

QUESTIONS FOR STUDY

1. What problem "troubled" Popper and encouraged his development of the principle of falsification?

2. What three popular "scientific" theories led Popper to suspect something was wrong with their claims?

3. What "virtue" did these theories have that, according to Popper, is really a vice?

4. How is the principle of falsification the solution to the problem of demarcation?

QUESTIONS FOR REFLECTION

1. Do you agree that both Freud and astrology are in some sense "pseudosciences"? Why is Einstein's theory of relativity not a pseudoscience?

2. Read the horoscope section in your newspaper. Do any of the readings seem to satisfy the criterion of falsifiability or testability? Why or why not? What steps could astrology take to avoid this difficulty? Would it then qualify as a legitimate science?

3. In what ways do myths and pseudoscientific claims resemble one another? Can myth be "true" in any scientific sense? If not, what possible purpose can it have?

4. Explain Popper's third conclusion: "Every 'good' scientific theory is a prohibition: it forbids certain things to happen. The more a theory forbids the better it is."

NETWORKING

Further discussion of *methodological issues concerning theory and the idea of total explanation in science and religion* is to be found in Schilling, Gilkey, Küng, Schmidt, Davies, and Gish.

EINSTEIN AND THE TRANSCENDENT GOD

SCIENCE AND RELIGION   ALBERT EINSTEIN

Albert Einstein (1879–1955), the greatest theoretical physicist of the twentieth century, wrote little about science and religion. This selection, delivered originally to a conference on the topic in 1940, is one of his most focused attempts to address the subject.

It would not be difficult to come to an agreement as to what we understand by science. Science is the century-old endeavor to bring together by means of systematic thought the perceptible phenomena of this world into as thoroughgoing an association as possible. To put it boldly, it is the attempt at the posterior reconstruction of existence by the process of conceptualization. But when asking myself what religion is I cannot think of the answer so easily. And even after finding an answer which may satisfy me at this particular moment, I still remain convinced that I can never under any circumstances bring together, even to a slight extent, the thoughts of all those who have given this question serious consideration.

At first, then, instead of asking what religion is I should prefer to ask what characterizes the aspirations of a person who gives me the impression of being religious: a person who is religiously enlightened appears to me to be one who has, to the best of his ability, liberated himself from the fetters of his selfish desires and is preoccupied with thoughts, feelings, and aspirations to which he clings because of their superpersonal value. It seems to me that what is important is the force of this superpersonal content and the depth of the conviction concerning its overpowering meaningfulness, regardless of whether any attempt is made to unite this content with a divine Being, for otherwise it would not be possible to count Buddha and Spinoza as religious personalities. Accordingly, a religious person is devout in the sense that he has no doubt of the significance and loftiness of those superpersonal objects and goals which neither require nor are capable of rational foundation. They exist with the same necessity and matter-of-factness as he himself. In this sense religion is the age-old endeavor of mankind to become clearly and completely conscious of these values and goals and constantly to strengthen and extend their effect. If one conceives of religion and science according to these definitions then a conflict between them appears impossible. For science can only ascertain what *is,* but not what *should be,* and outside of its domain value judgments of all kinds remain necessary. Religion, on the other hand, deals only with evaluations of human thought and action: it cannot justifiably speak of facts and relationships between facts. According to this interpretation the well-known conflicts between religion and science in the past must all be ascribed to a misapprehension of the situation which has been described.

For example, a conflict arises when a religious community insists on the absolute truthfulness of all statements recorded in the Bible. This means an intervention on the part of religion into the sphere of science; this is where the struggle of the Church against the doctrines of Galileo and Darwin belongs. On the other hand, representatives of science have often made an attempt to arrive at fundamental judgments with respect to values and ends on the basis of scientific method, and in this way have set themselves in opposition to religion. These conflicts have all sprung from fatal errors.

Now, even though the realms of religion and science in themselves are clearly marked off from each other, nevertheless there exist between the two strong reciprocal relationships and dependencies. Though religion may be that which determines the goal, it has, nevertheless, learned from science, in the broadest sense, what means will contribute to the attainment of the goals it has set up. But science can only be created by those who are thoroughly imbued with the aspiration toward truth and understanding. This source of feeling, however, springs from the sphere of religion. To this there also belongs the faith in the possibility that the regulations valid for the world of existence are rational, that is, comprehensible to reason. I cannot conceive of a genuine scientist without that profound faith. The situation may be expressed by an image: science without religion is lame, religion without science is blind.

Though I have asserted above that in truth a legitimate conflict between religion and science cannot exist, I must nevertheless qualify this assertion once again on an essential point, with reference to the actual content of historical religions. This qualification has to do with the concept of God. During the youthful period of mankind's spiritual evolution human fantasy created gods in man's own image, who, by the operations of their will were supposed to determine, or at any rate to influence, the phenomenal world. Man sought to alter the disposition of these gods in his own favor by means of magic and prayer. The idea of God in the religions taught at present is a sublimation of that old concept of the gods. Its anthropomorphic character is shown, for instance, by the fact that men appeal to the Divine Being in prayers and plead for the fulfillment of their wishes.

Nobody, certainly, will deny that the idea of the existence of an omnipotent, just, and omnibeneficent personal God is able to accord man solace, help, and guidance; also, by virtue of its simplicity it is accessible to the most undeveloped mind. But, on the other hand, there are decisive weaknesses attached to this idea in itself, which have been painfully felt since the beginning of history. That is, if this being is omnipotent, then every occurrence, including every human action, every human thought, and every human feeling and aspiration is also His work; how is it possible to think of holding men responsible for their deeds and thoughts before such an almighty Being? In giving out punishment and rewards He would to a certain extent be passing judgment on Himself. How can this be combined with the goodness and righteousness ascribed to Him?

The main source of the present-day conflicts between the spheres of religion and of science lies in this concept of a personal God. It is the aim of science to establish general rules which determine the reciprocal connection of objects and events in time and space. For these rules, or laws of nature, absolutely general validity is required—not proven. It is mainly a program, and faith in the possibility of its accomplishment in principle is only founded on partial successes. But hardly anyone could be found who would deny these partial successes and ascribe them to human self-deception. The fact that on the basis of such laws we are able to predict the temporal behavior of phenomena in certain domains with great precision and certainty is deeply embedded in the consciousness of the modern man, even though he may have grasped very little of the contents of those laws. He need only consider that planetary courses within the solar system may be calculated in advance with great exactitude on the basis of a limited number of simple laws. In a similar way, though not with the same precision, it is possible to calculate in advance the mode of operation of an electric motor, a transmission system, or of a wireless apparatus, even when dealing with a novel development.

To be sure, when the number of factors coming into play in a phenomenological complex is too large, scientific method in most cases fails us. One need only think of the weather, in which case prediction even for a few days ahead is impossible. Nevertheless no one doubts that we are confronted with a causal connection whose causal components are in the main known to us. Occurrences in this domain are beyond the reach of exact prediction because of the variety of factors in operation, not because of any lack of order in nature.

We have penetrated far less deeply into the regularities obtaining within the realm of living things, but deeply enough nevertheless to sense at least the rule of fixed necessity. One need only think of the systematic order in heredity, and in the effect of poisons, as for instance alcohol, on the behavior of organic beings. What is still lacking here is a grasp of connections of profound generality, but not a knowledge of order in itself.

The more a man is imbued with the ordered regularity of all events the firmer becomes his conviction that there is no room left by the side of this ordered regularity for causes of a different nature. For him neither the rule of human nor the rule of divine will exists as an independent cause of natural events. To be sure, the doctrine of a personal God interfering with natural events could never be *refuted,* in the real sense, by science, for this doctrine can always take refuge in those domains in which scientific knowledge has not yet been able to set foot.

But I am persuaded that such behavior on the part of the representatives of religion would not only be unworthy but also fatal. For a doctrine which is able to maintain itself not in clear light but only in the dark, will of necessity lose its effect on mankind, with incalculable harm to human progress. In their struggle for the ethical good, teachers of religion must have the stature to give up the doctrine of a personal God, that is, give up that source of fear and hope which in the past placed such vast power in the hands of priests. In their labors they will have to avail themselves of those forces which are capable of cultivating the Good, the True, and the Beautiful in humanity itself. This is, to be sure, a more difficult but an incomparably more worthy task.[1] After religious teachers accomplish the refining process indicated they will surely recognize with joy that true religion has been ennobled and made more profound by scientific knowledge.

If it is one of the goals of religion to liberate mankind as far as possible from the bondage of egocentric cravings, desires, and fears, scientific reasoning can aid religion in yet another sense. Although it is true that it is the goal of science to discover rules which permit the association and foretelling of facts, this is not its only aim. It also seeks to reduce the connections discovered to the smallest possible number of mutually independent conceptual elements. It is in this striving after the rational unification of the manifold that it encounters its greatest successes, even though it is precisely this attempt which causes it to run the greatest risk of falling a prey to illusions. But whoever has undergone the intense experience of successful advances made in this domain is moved by profound reverence for the rationality made manifest in existence. By way of the understanding he achieves a far-reaching emancipation from the shackles of personal hopes and desires, and thereby attains that humble attitude of mind toward the grandeur of reason incarnate in existence, and which, in its profoundest depths, is inaccessible to man. This attitude, however, appears to me to be religious, in the highest sense of the word. And so it seems to me that science not only purifies the religious impulse of the dross of its anthropomorphism but also contributes to a religious spiritualization of our understanding of life.

The further the spiritual evolution of mankind advances, the more certain it seems to me that the path to genuine religiosity does not lie through the fear of life, and the fear of death, and blind faith, but through striving after rational knowledge. In this sense I believe that the priest must become a teacher if he wishes to do justice to his lofty educational mission.

NOTE

1. This thought is convincingly presented in Herbert Samuel's book, *Belief and Action*.

QUESTIONS FOR STUDY

1. What are Einstein's definitions of science and religion?

2. In Einstein's opinion is it possible to be religious without believing in a divine being?

3. Does Einstein believe that science and religion can legitimately conflict? Why or why not?

4. Does Einstein see any mutually beneficial relationships between science and religion? If so, how are they expressed in the quote, "Science without religion is lame, religion without science is blind"?

5. How is the concept of a personal God the main source of conflict between science and religion?

QUESTIONS FOR REFLECTION

1. Is Einstein himself religious in accordance with his own definition of religion?

2. Do you agree with Einstein that the chief task of religion is inspired ethical living? Is he right in claiming a necessary connection between religion and ethics? Can one be moral without being religious? Is ethical guidance the only service that religion renders to a society?

NETWORKING

Various opinions on a *supernatural deity* may be found in Gilkey, Lewis, Tillich, Davies, Lackey, Geisler and Anderson, Updike, and Burhoe. The *problem of evil* is discussed in Tillich and Davies, *ethics* in Neibuhr and Updike, and the *intelligibility of the cosmos* in Polkinghorne.

SCIENCE AND RELIGION: A DISCUSSION WITH EINSTEIN

PAUL TILLICH

Paul Tillich (1886–1965) is considered to be one of the most influential Protestant theologians of the twentieth century. Born and educated in Germany where he earned two doctorates, one in philosophy and another in theology, Tillich came to the United States after Hitler's rise to power. He taught at Union Theological School in New York City, Harvard University, and the University of Chicago. His works include *Systematic Theology* in three volumes; *The Courage to Be; The Shaking of the Foundations* and *The New Being,* which are collections of sermons; and an autobiography, *On the Boundary.*

Several years ago Albert Einstein delivered an address on "Science and Religion," which aroused considerable opposition among religious people and theologians because of his rejection of the idea of the Personal God. If it had not been Einstein, the great transformer of our physical world view, his arguments probably would not have produced any excitement, for they were neither new nor powerful in themselves. But in the mouth of Einstein, as an expression of his intellectual and moral character, they became significant. Therefore it is justified that philosophical or apologetic theology not only deals with Einstein's criticism but tries to sketch a solution in which this criticism is accepted and overcome at the same time.

Einstein attacked the idea of a Personal God from four angles: The idea is not essential for religion. It is the creation of primitive superstition. It is self-contradictory. It contradicts the scientific world view.

The first argument presupposes a definition of the nature of religion leaving out everything in which religion differs from ethics: Religion is the acceptance of and devotion to superpersonal values. But the question whether this is an adequate definition of religion cannot be answered before the question is answered whether the idea of the Personal God has some objective meaning or not. Therefore we must turn to the second argument, the historical.

It does not show and cannot show why primitive imagination created just the idea of *God.* There is no doubt that this idea has been used and abused by all kinds of superstition and immorality. But in order to be abused it first must have been used. Its abuse does not tell anything about its genesis. Looking at the tremendous impact the idea of God always has made on human thought and behavior, the theory that all this was a product of an uneducated arbitrary imagination appears utterly inadequate. Mythological phantasy can create stories about gods, but it cannot create the idea of God itself, because the idea transcends all the elements of experience which constitute mythology. As Descartes argues: the infinite in our mind presupposes the infinite itself.

The third argument of Einstein challenges the idea of an omnipotent God who creates moral and physical evil although, on the other hand, he is supposed to be good and righteous. This criticism presupposes a concept of omnipotence which identifies omnipotence with omni-activity in terms of physical causality. But it is an old, and always emphasized, theological doctrine that God acts in all beings according to their special nature; in man according to his rational nature, in animals and plants according to their organic nature, in stones according to their inorganic nature. The symbol of omnipotence expresses the religious experience that no structure of reality and no event in nature and history has the power of removing us from community with the infinite and inexhaustible ground of meaning and being. What "omnipotence" means should be found in the words Deutero-Isaiah (Is. 40) speaks to the exiled in Babylon when he describes the nothingness of the world-empires in comparison with the divine power to fulfill its historical aim through an infinitely small group of exiled people. Or what "omnipotence" means can be found in the words Paul (Rom. 8) speaks to the few Christians in the slums of the big cities when he pronounces that neither natural nor political powers, neither earthly nor heavenly forces can separate us from the "Love of God." If the idea of omnipotence is taken out of this context and transformed into the description of a special form of causality, it becomes not only self-contradicting—as Einstein rightly states—but also absurd and irreligious.

This leads to the last and most important argument of Einstein: The idea of a Personal God contradicts the scientific interpretation of nature. Before dealing with this argument, we should make two methodological remarks: Firstly we can agree entirely with Einstein when he warns the theologians not to build their doctrines in the dark spots of scientific research. This was the bad method of some apologetic fanatics of nineteenth-century theology, but it never was the attitude of any great theologian. Theology, above all, must leave to science the description of the whole of objects and their interdependence in nature and history, in man and his world. And beyond this, theology must leave to philosophy the description of the structures and categories of being itself and of the *logos* in which being becomes manifest. Any interference of theology with these tasks of philosophy and science is destructive for theology itself.

Secondly we must ask every critic of theology to deal with theology with the same fairness which is demanded from everyone who deals, for instance, with physics—namely, to attack the most advanced and not some obsolete forms of a discipline. After Schleiermacher and Hegel had received Spinoza's doctrine of God as an intrinsic element of any theological doctrine of God, just as the early theologians, Origen and Augustine, had received Plato's idea of God as an inherent element in their doctrine of God, it became impossible to use the most primitive pattern of the concept of the Personal God in order to challenge the idea itself. The concept of a "Personal God," interfering with natural events, or being "an independent cause of natural events," makes God a natural object beside others, an object among objects, a being among beings, maybe the highest, but nevertheless *a* being. This, indeed, is the destruction, not only of the physical system, but even more the destruction of any meaningful idea of

God. It is the impure mixture of mythological elements (which are justified in their place, namely, in the concrete religious life) and of rational elements (which are justified in their place, namely, in the theological interpretation of religious experience). No criticism of this distorted idea of God can be sharp enough.

In order to indicate an idea of the Personal God, which by no means can interfere with science or philosophy as such, we can turn to some beautiful words of Einstein: the true scientist "attains that humble attitude of mind towards the grandeur of reason incarnate in existence, which, in its profoundest depths, is inaccessible to man." If we interpret these words rightly, they point to a common ground of the whole of the physical world and of suprapersonal values; a ground which, on the one hand, is manifest in the structure of being (the physical world) and meaning (the good, true, and beautiful), and which, on the other hand, is hidden in its inexhaustible depth.

Now this is the first and basic element of any developed idea of God from the earliest Greek philosophers to present-day theology. The manifestation of this ground and abyss of being and meaning creates what modern theology calls "the experience of the numinous." Such an experience can occur in connection with the intuition of the "grandeur of reason incarnate in existence"; it can occur in connection with the belief in "the significance and loftiness of those suprapersonal objects and goals which neither require nor are capable of rational foundation," as Einstein says. The same experience can occur, and occurs for the large majority of men, in connection with the impression some persons, historical or natural events, objects, words, pictures, tunes, dreams, etc. make on the human soul, creating the feeling of the holy, that is, of the presence of the "numinous." In such experiences religion lives and tries to maintain the presence of, and community with, this divine depth of our existence. But since it is "inaccessible" to any objectifying concept it must be expressed in symbols.

One of these symbols is Personal God. It is the common opinion of classical theology, practically in all periods of Church history, that the predicate "personal" can be said of the Divine only symbolically or by analogy or if affirmed and negated at the same time. It is obvious that in the daily life of religion the symbolic character of the idea of the Personal God is not always realized. This is dangerous only if distorting theoretical or practical consequences are derived from the failure to realize it. Then attacks from outside and criticism from inside follow and must follow. They are demanded by religion itself. Without an element of "atheism" no "theism" can be maintained.

But why must the symbol of the personal be used at all? The answer can be given through a term used by Einstein himself: the supra-personal. The depth of being cannot be symbolized by objects taken from a realm which is lower than the personal, from the realm of things or sub-personal living beings. The supra-personal is not an "It," or more exactly, it is a "He" as much as it is an "It," and it is above both of them. But if the "He" element is left out, the "It" element transforms the alleged supra-personal into a sub-personal, as usually happens in monism and pantheism. And such a neutral sub-personal cannot grasp the center of our personality; it can satisfy our aesthetic feeling or our intellectual needs, but it cannot convert our will, it cannot overcome our loneliness, anxiety, and despair. For as the philosopher Schelling says: "Only a person can heal a person." This is the reason that the symbol of the Personal God is indispensable for living religion. It is a symbol, not an object, and it never should be interpreted as an object. And it is one symbol beside others indicating that our personal center is grasped by the manifestation of the inaccessible ground and abyss of being.

QUESTIONS FOR STUDY

1. How does Tillich respond to Einstein's argument that belief in a personal God is a primitive hangover?

2. If Tillich rejects the idea of a literal personal God, with what does he replace it?

3. How does the idea of a personal God serve as a symbol? Why is it useful, even if risky?

QUESTIONS FOR REFLECTION

1. What does Tillich mean when he says that "Without atheism, no theism can be maintained"?

2. Tillich agrees with Einstein's reasons for dismissing "the concept of a 'personal God,' interfering with natural events," or being, "an independent cause of natural events." He goes on to say that "No criticism of this distorted idea of God can be sharp enough." Explain this important point.

3. Pantheism is the belief that the world is God. Are Einstein and Tillich pantheists?

NETWORKING

Niebuhr shares Tillich's account of *God as the ground or principle of being*. For the *numinous or mystical,* see Buber and Dillard. For the *role of symbol,* see Schmidt and Langer.

MIRACLES

MIRACLES JOHN HICK

John Hick is a widely known philosopher of religion. He was an assistant professor of philosophy at Cornell, Stuart Professor of Christian Philosophy at Princeton Theological Seminary, and, for many years, H. G. Wood Professor of Theology at the University of Birmingham, England. He now teaches at the Claremont Graduate School in California. Hick is the author of numerous books, including *The Existence of God, Evil and the God of Love,* and *God Has Many Names.*

THE CHALLENGE OF MODERN SCIENCE

The tremendous expansion of scientific knowledge in the modern era has had a profound influence upon religious belief. Further, this influence has been at a maximum within the Judaic-Christian tradition, with which we are mainly concerned. . . . There have been a series of specific jurisdictional disputes between the claims of scientific and religious knowledge, and also a more general cumulative effect which constitutes a major element, critical of religion, in the contemporary intellectual climate.

Since the Renaissance, scientific information about the world has steadily expanded in fields such as astronomy, geology, zoology, chemistry, biology, and physics; contradicting assertions in the same fields, derived from the Bible rather than from direct observation and experiment, have increasingly been discarded. In each of the great battles between scientists and churchmen the validity of the scientific method was vindicated by its practical fruitfulness. Necessary adjustments were eventually made in the aspects of religious belief that had conflicted with the scientists' discoveries. As a result of this long debate it has become apparent that the biblical writers, recording their experience of God's activity in human history, inevitably clothed their testimony with their own contemporary prescientific understanding of the world. Advancing knowledge has made it possible and indeed necessary to distinguish between their record of the divine presence and calling, and the primitive world view that formed the framework of their thinking. Having made this distinction, the modern reader can learn to recognize the aspects of the scriptures that reflect the prescientific culture prevailing at the human end of any divine-human encounter. Accordingly, we find that the three-storied universe of biblical cosmology, with heaven in the sky above our heads, hell in the ground beneath our feet, and the sun circling the earth but halting in its course at Joshua's command, is no longer credible in the light of modern knowledge. That the world was created some 6,000 years ago and that humanity and the other animal species came into being at that time in their present forms can no longer be regarded as a reasonable belief. Again, the expectation that at some future date the decomposed corpses of mankind through the ages will rise from the earth in pristine health for judgment has largely ceased to be entertained. Yet, in all of these cases, churchmen initially resisted, often with great vehemence and passion, scientific evidence that conflicted with their customary beliefs. In part, this resistance represented the natural reaction of conservative-minded people who preferred established and familiar scientific theories to new and disturbing ones. But this reaction was supported and reinforced by an unquestioning acceptance of the propositional conception of revelation. . . . This conception assumes that all statements in the scriptures are God's statements; consequently, to question any of them is either to accuse God of lying or to deny that the Bible is divinely inspired.

The more general legacy of this long history of interlocking scientific advance and theological retreat is the assumption, which is part of the climate of thought in our twentieth-century western world, that even though the sciences have not specifically disproved the claims of religion, they have thrown such a flood of light upon the world (without at any point encountering that of which religion speaks) that faith can now be regarded only as a harmless private fantasy. Religion is seen as a losing cause, destined to be ousted from more and more areas of human knowledge until at last it arrives at a status akin to that of astrology—a cultural "fifth wheel," persisting only as a survival from previous ages in which our empirical knowledge was much less extensive.

The sciences have cumulatively established the autonomy of the natural order. From the galaxies whose vastness numbs the mind to the unimaginably small events and entities of the subatomic universe, and throughout the endless complexities of our own world, which lies between these virtual infinities, nature can be studied without any reference to God. The universe investigated by the sciences proceeds exactly as though no God exists.

Does it follow from this fact that there is, indeed, no God?

There are forms of theistic belief from which this negative conclusion follows and others from which it does not.

If belief in the reality of God is tied to the cultural presuppositions of a prescientific era, this set of beliefs, taken as a whole, is no longer valid. But the situation is otherwise if we suppose (with much contemporary theology) that God has created this universe, insofar as its creation relates to humanity, as a neutral sphere in which we are endowed with a sufficient degree of autonomy to be able to enter into a freely accepted relationship with our Maker. From this point of view, God maintains a certain distance from us, a certain margin for a creaturely independence which, although always relative and conditioned, is nevertheless adequate for our existence as responsible personal beings. This "distance" is epistemic rather than spatial. It consists of the circumstance that God, being not inescapably evident to the human mind, is known only by means of an uncompelled response of faith. . . . This circumstance requires that the human environment should have the kind of autonomy that, in fact, we find it to have. The environment must constitute a working system capable of being investigated indefinitely without the investigator's being driven to postulate God as an element within it or behind it. From the point of view of this conception of God, the autonomy of nature, as it is increasingly confirmed by the sciences, offers no contradiction to religious faith. The sciences are exploring a universe that is divinely created and sustained, but with its own God-given autonomy and integrity. Such an understanding of God and of the divine purpose for the world is able to absorb scientific discoveries, both accomplished and projected, that had initially seemed to many religious believers to be profoundly threatening. The tracing back of man's continuity with the animal kingdom; the locating of the origin of organic life in natural chemical reactions taking place on the earth's surface, with the consequent prospect of reproducing these reactions in the laboratory; the exploration of outer space and the possibility of encountering advanced forms of life on other planets; the probing of the chemistry of personality and the perfecting of the sinister techniques of "brainwashing"; the contemporary biomedical revolution, creating new possibilities for the control of the human genetic material through, for example, gene deletion and cloning; the harnessing of nuclear energy and the dread possibility of human self-destruction in a nuclear war—all these facts and possibilities, with their immense potentialities for good or evil, are aspects of a natural order that possesses its own autonomous structure. According to religious faith, God created this order as an environment in which human beings, living as free and responsible agents, might enter into a relationship with God. All that can be said about the bearing of scientific knowledge upon this religious claim is that it does not fall within the province of any of the special sciences: science can neither confirm nor deny it.

From this theological point of view, what is the status of the miracle stories and the accounts of answered prayer that abound in the scriptures and in human records from the earliest to the present time? Must these be considered incompatible with a recognition that an autonomous natural order is the proper province of the sciences?

The answer to this question depends upon the way in which we define "miracle." It is possible to define the term in either purely physical and nonreligious terms, as a breach or suspension of natural law, or in religious terms, as an unusual and striking event that evokes and mediates a vivid awareness of God. If "miracle" is defined as a breach of natural law, one can declare *a priori* that there are no miracles. It does not follow, however, that there are no miracles in the religious sense of the term, for the principle that nothing happens in conflict with natural law does not entail that there are no unusual and striking events evoking and mediating a vivid awareness of God. Natural law consists of generalizations formulated retrospectively to cover whatever has, in fact, happened. When events take place that are not covered by the generalizations accepted thus far, the properly scientific response is not to deny that they occurred but to seek to revise and extend the current understanding of nature in order to include them. Without regard to the relevant evidence, it cannot be said that the story, for example, of Jesus's healing the man with the withered hand (Luke 6:6–11) is untrue, or that comparable stories from later ages or from the present day are untrue. It is not scientifically impossible that unusual and striking events of this kind have occurred. Events with religious significance, evoking and mediating a vivid sense of the presence and activity of God, may have occurred, even though their continuity with the general course of nature cannot be traced in our present very limited state of human knowledge.

In the apologetic systems of former centuries miracles have played an important part. They have been supposed to empower religion to demand and compel belief. In opposition to this traditional view many theologians today believe that, far from providing the original foundation of religious faith, miracles presuppose such faith. The religious response, which senses the purpose of God in the inexplicable coincidence or the improbable and unexpected occurrence, makes an event a miracle. Thus, miracles belong to the internal life of a community of faith; they are not the means by which the religious community can seek to evangelize the world outside. . . .

QUESTIONS FOR STUDY

1. What ancient beliefs does Hick see as disconfirmed by science?

2. According to Hick, how did God create the world so that science could flourish without necessarily jeopardizing faith?

3. Give four examples of progress in science that appear "profoundly threatening" to many religious believers.

4. Give two definitions of miracle. Which of these is incompatible with the view of science?

QUESTIONS FOR REFLECTION

1. Many religious conservatives refuse to accept the understanding of the world view of the Bible as outdated. What arguments can you think of for their position?

2. Hick states that God's distance from his Creation "is epistemic rather than special." What does he mean?

3. Do Hick's remarks have anything to contribute to the principle of parsimony or the God-of-the-Gaps argument?

4. Hick insists that "if 'miracle' is defined as a breach of natural law, one can declare *a priori* that there are no miracles." What does he mean?

5. If science comes across an event it cannot easily explain, is it permissible to classify that event as a miracle? What other response does science have?

6. Is it truer to say that miracles compel faith or that faith confirms miracles? Explain.

NETWORKING

World views are important for Swimme, Bube, Gray, McFague, and Berry. See Bube and Updike for a discussion of the *hiddenness of God* and *human autonomy*.

THE NEW TESTAMENT UNDERSTANDING OF MIRACLES

ROBERT A. SPIVEY AND D. MOODY SMITH

Robert Spivey is a New Testament scholar and educator. He is president of Randolph Macon College in Lynchburg, Virginia. D. Moody Smith teaches the New Testament in the Divinity School of Duke University.

Doubtless to many early Christians Jesus' miracles were crucially important. The most characteristic miracles in the Synoptics are Jesus' healings, especially the exorcism of demons, which Mark emphasizes. Miracle stories comprise a large part of each of the Gospels. Nearly one third of the Gospel of Mark is devoted to healings. Matthew and Luke report practically all the Markan miracles and add others. Depending on how one counts, between thirty and forty miracles are reported in all the Gospels. In Peter's first speech to the Gentiles, no mention is made of Jesus' teaching, but the good news includes "how God anointed Jesus of Nazareth with the Holy Spirit and with power; how he went about doing good and healing all that were oppressed by the devil" (Acts 10:38). Even the Talmud . . . acknowledges that Jesus healed, but dismisses his work as that of a sorcerer.[1] Contemporary stress on Jesus' teachings has to reckon with the unequivocal Gospel evidence that one of Jesus' principal activities was healing.

Yet there has always been a certain ambiguity about miracles. When the crowds gathered around Jesus after many healings, his family "went out to seize him, for they said, 'He is beside himself.' And the scribes who came down from Jerusalem said, 'He is possessed by Beelzebub, and by the prince of demons he casts out demons'" (Mark 3:21 f.). Thus healing miracles could be the work of God or the devil; they do not prove messiahship. Indeed, according to one major New Testament strain Jesus' power is not in mighty works, but in his crucifixion and death. Christ crucified is "to those who are called, both Jews and Greeks . . . the *power* of God and the wisdom of God" (1 Cor. 1:24). Moreover, to desire miracles as proof of Jesus' messiahship would be to seek after signs (cf. 1 Cor. 1:22). When the Pharisees come to Jesus asking for a sign, he replies, "An evil and adulterous generation seeks for a sign; but no sign shall be given to it except the sign of the prophet Jonah" (Matt. 12:39; see Mark 8:12). Despite such reservations about signs in the Synoptics and Paul, miracles do function as signs of who Jesus is in the Gospel of John. This is only one of the many differences that exist between the Fourth Gospel and the others. In all probability the Synoptics are closer to Jesus' own view, whereas in John later controversy about Jesus' identity has led to the use of the miracle tradition in this polemical way.

Before looking more closely at miracles in the Gospels, we need to understand the first century's view of miracles so that the miracle tradition is set within its environment. This, in turn, will set the stage for our final section when we look at miracles from the modern perspective.

MIRACLES IN THE FIRST CENTURY

Were Miracles Common in the Ancient World?

In the first century, indeed in the New Testament itself, Jesus is not the only miracle worker. Simon the Magician is said to have done great wonders and to have amazed people by his magic. Moreover, he tried to buy the Spirit from the apostles and was refused because according to Peter the gift of God could not be obtained with money (Acts 8:9–24). Simon desired the Spirit because the disciples performed signs and great miracles (Acts 5:12). The apostle Paul himself performed wonders (2 Cor. 12:12). Even the rabbis, who were known primarily as teachers, performed miracles. Onias, the Circlemaker, a rabbi in the first century B.C., is reported to have made it rain for Israel neither too fiercely nor too gently, but in moderation. A famous miracle worker in Hellenistic literature was Apollonius of Tyana, a Pythagorean philosopher who lived during the first Christian century.[2] He is reported to have miraculously exorcised a demon from a young man who later became a philosopher and a miracle worker himself.

Within this context the miracles of Jesus are not quite so unusual. In fact, some early Christians felt constrained to enlarge the miracle activity of Jesus beyond what is reported in the Gospels. Consequently, in the apocryphal Gospels bigger and better miracles are attributed to Jesus. According to the infancy Gospel of Thomas, Jesus fetches water for his mother with a garment instead of a pitcher. When the carpenter Joseph discovers that one of the boards for a bed is too short, his son Jesus corrects the situation by stretching the board to the proper length. In the same Gospel, Jesus makes twelve clay birds that become real birds after he claps his hands. When a young boy disturbs a pool of water in which Jesus is playing, Jesus withers him as if he were a tree. Under the influence of popular piety Jesus became a real magician. Miracle stories served both to entertain the pious and to support their belief that Jesus was the Christ, the Son of God.

It is understandable, therefore, that Jesus should have been portrayed as a miracle worker in the Gospels, especially because he had been known as a healer during his lifetime. Very likely his healings and exorcisms first attracted attention to him. The tendency to enlarge upon the miracles of Jesus, which we observe in the apocryphal Gospels, may have already been at work in the earliest tradition. Whether the Gospels have furthered or checked this tendency is a good question. John obviously highlights Jesus' miracle-working power. Matthew, on the other hand, reduces the dimensions of the miraculous by abbreviating Mark's miracle stories.

MIRACLES IN THE SYNOPTIC GOSPELS

Did the Miracles Reported in the Gospels All Actually Happen?

Miracle in modern usage is an occurrence contrary to known scientific laws. Because the evangelists wrote at a time in which there was no commonly accepted concept of "known scientific laws," they understood miracles as powers, wonders, mighty works, signs. These strange, remarkable happenings caused people to be amazed and terrified, and to wonder whether these occurrences were the power of God (the good) or of Satan (the evil). Remembering this, we may nevertheless, for convenience's sake, speak about miracles in the Gospels. The term corresponds roughly to the reported events.

To understand miracles in Jesus' ministry, we must first take account of the view of the world and history in which they are set, then attempt to classify the miracles according to type, and finally explore the relation of miracles to faith. We deal primarily with the Synoptics rather than with John because in all probability they are closer to Jesus' own position in their estimate of miracles.

The Eschatological Context

The proclamation of the kingdom of God was central to the preaching and teaching of Jesus (cf. Mark 1:14). Jesus himself appears to have linked his mighty works to the coming of the kingdom: "But if it is by the finger of God that I cast out demons, then the kingdom of God has come upon you" (Luke 11:20; cf. Matt. 12:28). His work is at the same time a manifestation of his having overcome the powers of Satan, i.e., evil: "When a strong man, fully armed, guards his own palace, his goods are in peace; but when one stronger than he assails him and overcomes him, he takes away his armor in which he trusted, and divides his spoil" (Luke 11:20–21; cf. Mark 3:27). When Jesus is asked on behalf of John the Baptist whether he is the coming one, that is, the Messiah or charismatic leader who would inaugurate the rule of God, he responds: "Go and tell John what you have seen and heard: the blind receive their sight, the lame walk, lepers are cleaned, the dead are raised up, the poor have good news preached to them" (Luke 7:22; cf. Matt 11:4–5). He instructs his disciples that in healing the sick they should say to them, "The kingdom of God has come near to you" (Luke 10:9). In Jesus' own view, then, his miracles are signs of the breaking in of the eschatological kingdom.

The breaking in of the kingdom of God in the miracle activity of Jesus is not, however, the kingdom's final realization. The miracles signify an inaugurated kingdom, not a completed one. This setting of Jesus' miracles within the context of "inaugurated eschatology" has two implications: First, the nature of the irrupting kingdom defines the meaning of the miracles rather than the reverse; the kingdom's promise includes and extends beyond physical healing, as the exorcisms already suggest. Second, the miracles point to the working of God rather than to the status of Jesus. God's kingdom, not the rule of Jesus, is inaugurated. Moreover, from the standpoint of Jesus' opponents these miracles or wonders are ambiguous and could be viewed as the work of Satan as well as of God. Jesus refuses to use the miracles as signs to validate himself (Mark 8:11 f.; Matt. 12:39). Similarly, the temptation stories show Jesus' declining to elicit support by the performance of miracles or spectacular feats (Matt. 4:1–11; Luke 4:1–13). The healings bear witness to the kingdom's appearance, and this extraordinary presence of God Jesus consistently and continually proclaims in his message.

Three Types of Miracles

Now that we have discerned the framework of the proclamation of the kingdom in which the miracles occur, we turn for a closer look at the actual miracle stories themselves. The Synoptic Gospels contain basically four types: exorcisms, healings, resuscitations, and nature miracles. All except exorcism are found also in John. The first three have to do with changes in human subjects; the fourth involves changes in inanimate matter. Generally speaking, the exorcisms pertain to what we would call mental disorders and the healings to physical diseases; for our purposes they both can be treated under one heading—healings.

In the Gospel of Mark exorcisms (1:21–28; cf. 32–34) and healings (1:29–31, 40–45; cf. 32–34) are narrated in rapid succession; it becomes clear that these acts are closely related and that both belong to the essence of Jesus' saving, or healing, work. In the exorcism of the demon at the synagogue of Capernaum and the cleansing of the leper, similar elements characterize each narrative. There is a forceful approach to Jesus (vss. 23–24; cf. vs. 40); Jesus responds vigorously or compassionately (vs. 25; cf. vss. 41, 43); the evil spirit or force departs (vs. 26; cf. vs. 42). Although in the one case there is an immediate crowd reaction (vs. 27) and in the other none is reported, in both stories Jesus' fame is said to spread throughout the area (vss. 28, 45). In both Jesus is portrayed as responding immediately to a dire situation or need, albeit one that has presumably existed for some time prior to the encounter with him. In both Jesus acts, and speaks, decisively so as to overcome the evil spirit or disease.

Even though Jesus in both stories acts as an authoritative, charismatic figure, in neither case does the question of his messiahship arise at all. Whether the command to silence (vs. 44; cf. vss. 25, 34) originates with Mark or Jesus himself, its effect is to subordinate the role of Jesus' healing to his primary proclamation of the nearness of the kingdom of God. As best we can tell, this order of priorities goes back to Jesus himself.

The question of whether the miracle actually happened should be considered in light of the fact that the "leprosy" spoken of need not have been the incurable disease called by that name. Moreover, similar miracles have been attributed to others.[3] Nevertheless, such considerations are not decisive in determining what may have occurred. There is an overall impression of authenticity that stems from the fact that the miracle does not call attention to itself. The restraint in detail bespeaks its probable historicity. But it is pointless to offer scientific or psychological explanations of what happened; although these are not ruled out in principle, they are purely speculation in light of the silence of the text about most matters of detail.

Two examples of *nature miracles* are the feeding of five thousand (Mark 6:30–44; cf. Matt. 14:13–21; Luke 9:10–17 and John 6:1–14) and the stilling of the storm (Mark 4:35–41; cf. Matt. 8:18–27 and Luke 8:22–25). In comparing the Gospels' accounts of the feeding of the five thousand, we note that the evangelists have exercised freedom in detail regarding the occasion of the miracle. They agree, however, that Jesus is surrounded by hungry throngs at a place where food is not accessible. We cannot isolate an earlier, nonmiraculous version of the story; the central point is that of a miraculous feeding, possibly with eucharistic overtones. It is beside the point to explain this story as some kind of picnic in which Jesus and his disciples encouraged the people to generosity. Yet the question of whether such an incredible miracle took place remains still unanswered. The form of this story clearly reflects the eucharistic practice of the early church (see Mark 6:41). Therefore, the miracle may be a post-resurrection story, based upon the Christians' experience in the Lord's Supper that the living Christ feeds the hungry multitudes (cf. John 21:9–14; Luke 24:28–35). Such a conjecture is supported by the fact that this nature miracle concentrates more upon the person and action of Jesus than do most other miracle stories. The kind of emphasis on Jesus may reflect a concern of the early church more than the attitude of the historical Jesus and is characteristic of the Fourth Gospel (see 6:15 ff.). But again, the compassion upon the multitudes is what we would expect of Jesus of Nazareth. The essence of the story agrees with our evolving picture of the historical Jesus. The form, however, reflects the interests of the early church.The historical critic is justified in questioning the historical probability of this miraculous feeding even apart from considerations of whether the event could have happened. This does not necessarily mean that no event (no actual meal) lies at the root of this story; however, that event is inaccessible to us.

The stilling of the storm on the Sea of Galilee also belongs in the category of nature miracles (Mark 4:35–41 parr.). Its present form may obscure an earlier story about the exorcism of a storm demon (4:39; cf. 1:25). As it now reads, however, it demonstrates Jesus' authority over nature and challenges the disciples' lack of faith (4:40 f.). Moreover, this action by Jesus seems to embody that salvation ascribed to God in the Old Testament: "Who dost still the roaring of the seas, the roaring of their waves, the tumult of the people" (Psalm 65:7; cf. 89:9). The entire miracle story makes Jesus the object of religious awe. Probably we have here a Christological confession, occasioned not by an incident out of Jesus' life but by the total impact of Jesus, particularly his death and resurrection. Again this conclusion does not mean that no actual historical event lies at the root of this story.

As example of *resuscitations* is the story of the raising of Jairus' daughter (Mark 5:21–43; cf. Matt. 9:18–26 and Luke 8:40–56).[4] It is strangely interrupted by an account of the healing of the woman with the hemorrhage (Mark 5:25–34 parr.). Yet this break in the story of the resuscitation is not accidental, for the interlude illustrates the power of believing (cf. 5:36). The striking thing about the healing of the woman with the hemorrhage is its occurrence without Jesus' being aware of her presence. Consequently, Jesus did not intend the miracle (see 5:28–30). If the miracle happens without Jesus' intent, then in a sense the miracle happened to Jesus as well as to the woman. The healing of the woman makes the implicit point that belief in Jesus is actually faith in the power that works through Jesus rather than in Jesus himself (5:30, 34).

This understanding of belief is then taken up in the raising of Jairus' daughter (5:36). Jesus' raising of the dead girl might rest upon an actual incident in which he aroused a girl who was in a coma (cf. vss. 35 f., 39). As it now stands, however, it raises the question of whether belief in God goes so far as to affirm the victory of Jesus over death. Thus the story of Jesus' raising of Jairus' daughter uses an actual incident of healing to affirm a central matter of faith, God's power to raise the dead. Such faith becomes the center of attention in the Fourth Gospel. There Jesus first claims the God-given power to raise the dead (5:25–29), then most dramatically exercises that power as he restores Lazarus to life, calling him forth from the grave (11:43).

Miracles and Faith

A consistent theme of all three types of miracle story is the response of faith. But what is the relation between faith and miracles? In many instances faith seems to be the triggering mechanism that produces miracles. God is always ready to perform miracles; consequently, if a person has faith, miracles occur. Support from the Gospels for this understanding is found especially in such statements as, "And he [Jesus] could do no mighty work there, except that he laid his hands upon a few sick people and healed them. And he marveled because of their unbelief" (Mark 6:5 f.; cf. Matt. 13:58). Furthermore, Jesus replies to the woman with the hemorrhage, "Daughter, your faith has made you well; go in peace and be healed of your disease" (Mark 5:34 parr.). The disciples' astonishment at the withered fig tree prompts Jesus to say, "Have faith in God. Truly I say to you, whoever says to this mountain, 'Be taken up and cast into the sea,' and does not doubt in his heart, but believes that what he says will come to pass, it will be done for him" (Mark 11:22 f. and Matt. 21:21; cf. 1 Cor. 13:2). In John, of course, it is the other way around. Miracles as signs lead to faith, although they sometimes meet resistance (John 9; cf. 2:23–25). But traces of the other view of the relation of miracles and faith appear even there (4:48–50; 5:6; cf. 14:13 f.).

Yet before we conclude that according to Jesus faith produces miracles or whatever the believer wishes, we should remember that in the Gospels even Jesus did not have his own way. The temptation stories set the tempo for Jesus' entire life in that he denies his natural impulses. Moreover, in Gethsemane Jesus prays, "Abba, Father, all things are possible to thee, remove this cup from me; yet not what I will, but what thou wilt" (Mark 14:36 parr.). Because the cup was not removed, we can only conclude that faith is not an automatic device for accomplishing the will of Jesus or of the believer. Faith's ultimate object is God and His will. In the Gospels, faith means that man trusts, accepts, and responds affirmatively to the coming of God. If in some instances faith appears as the condition for a miracle, or vice versa, the reader ought not to conclude that this represents the fundamental understanding of faith in the Gospels or in the ministry of Jesus. The faith that Jesus demands is belief in the good news of his announcement of the coming of God and His kingdom. Everything else depends on such faith (Mark 1:15; 8:34–38; Matt. 12:28; and so on).

Undoubtedly Jesus did perform "miracles": demons were cast out, the sick were healed, the people were terrified and amazed at his actions (see Mark 1:27; 2:12; 9:15). Yet these extraordinary acts were ambiguous and did not prove that Jesus was the Messiah. Some people saw this as the work of the devil; others saw and did not believe (cf. Mark 3:22). These events, like many at that time and many since, aroused temporary wonder, amazement, and faith. But in themselves, the miracles did not produce the faith that changed "sinners" into persons who radically obeyed, trusted God instead of themselves, forgave their enemies, and lived out of the assurance of God's favor.

MIRACLES IN A MODERN PERSPECTIVE

Many people regard a miracle as a "breach of scientific, natural law." Taken literally, however, such language can be misleading, because scientific laws are statements about cause and effect based upon empirical observation. Out of observation and experiment a law is formed, then with more testing it is found to be inadequate, so the law is reformulated; then it is again found to be inadequate, reformulated again, and so forth. We need to keep in mind that scientists themselves realize that the models or laws that the scientific process constructs are only aids toward understanding reality. The laws are impersonal oversimplifications that are useful in a pragmatic way but are not determinative of reality. To mistake these scientific, natural laws for reality itself pushes the observer into a flat scientific (actually unscientific) view of the world in which all complexity and mystery are abolished for the sake of certain solutions.

Miracle stories convey mystery; they speak about extraordinary events, situations in which things are more than they seem. Miracle stories claim that a power is at work which is personal concern—understood in the New Testament as the will of God. The point of miracle stories is not scientific explanation; their point is beyond all such explanation.

It has been thought possible to reconcile Biblical miracles with a modern view of the world by assigning them to those areas of experience that have not yet been explored or explained by science. Thus all conflict with the sciences is avoided. But the increase of scientific knowledge threatens radically to reduce such areas, and thus the scope of the miraculous activity of God. Conversely, it is possible to regard all events as miraculous because they stem from God. This notion is usually associated with pantheism (from the Greek words *pan,* "all," and *theos,* "God"; God is all). The first option views a miracle as an event contrary to nature and reduces God's activity to peripheral, occasional interventions. The second option, pantheism, asserts God's activity in every event and hence renders human activity insignificant. Yet neither of these viewpoints corresponds with the Biblical perspective, and each threatens to dissolve miracles either into remote and barely conceivable possibilities or into everyday occurrences.

According to the Gospels, Jesus' miracles were real, specific, and discernible events. Yet they occurred in an atmosphere of eschatological expectation and faith. When wrenched from this context, they look like the works of a magician or a sorcerer. In his own time and in the earliest church the question of miracle could not be separated from faith in Jesus' preaching and power, both of which had to do with the dawning kingdom of God. Faith could not, and cannot, prove the miracles happened; faith provides the context in which their meaning can be discussed. Apart from their eschatological context, Jesus' miracles, if they are not rejected outright, must be viewed as occult phenomena with certain parallels in ancient and modern times. If however, one believes that the new age was really dawning in Jesus, a basis is provided for understanding the miracles. Early Christians believed this was happening. In their time and subsequently, such faith has lent reality and meaning to accounts of the miraculous.

NOTES

1. See Klausner, *Jesus of Nazareth,* pp. 27 f.
2. C. K. Barrett, *The New Testament Background: Selected Documents* (London: SPCK, 1957), pp. 150 f., 76–79. See Cartlidge and Dungan, *Documents for the Study of the Gospels,* pp. 205–242, where extensive portions of Philostratus' *Life of Apollonios of Tyana* are reproduced.

3. See R. Bultmann, *History of the Synoptic Tradition*, trans. J. Marsh (New York: Harper & Row, 1968), pp. 218–44. Also F. W. Beare, *The Earliest Records of Jesus* (Nashville: Abingdon, 1972), pp. 72–74.

4. Only two other resuscitations are reported by the Gospels, the raising of the widow of Nain's son (Luke 7:11–17) and of Lazarus (John 11:1–44). For parallels, see Bultmann, *History of the Synoptic Tradition*, p. 233.

QUESTIONS FOR STUDY

1. Which of the four Gospels is most concerned with the miracles of Jesus? Which is least concerned?

2. How were miracles understood in the first century? Who besides Jesus performed miracles included in scriptural accounts?

3. How did Jesus himself probably understand his miracles?

4. Classify the miracle stories in the Gospels. Give one possible reason for each type.

QUESTIONS FOR REFLECTION

1. The authors claim that miracles have "a certain ambiguity." What is this ambiguity? Even if miracles as a violation of the laws of nature actually occur, is it ever possible to be certain about their origin? Does this uncertainty make them useless as "signs"?

2. Would the absence of the idea of scientific laws governing nature in the ancient world serve to enhance or reduce belief in the possibility of miracles?

3. New Testament scholars often interpret the miracles of Jesus as stories that reflect the interests and understanding of the early church rather than eye witness accounts of what Jesus actually did. How important is it that Jesus be understood as a miracle worker? Would his status in history be reduced if the Gospel accounts said nothing about miracles?

4. Is it truer to say that faith is a condition for miracles or that miracles produce faith? If faith produces miracles one might suspect self-deception or credulity: the faithful are seeing things that are not really there. However, faith produced by miracles does not even qualify as faith since it is based on evidence or proof. Is there any way around this dilemma?

5. The authors reject the idea that miracles are spectacular violations of the laws of nature, and they also reject the contention that all events are miracles because "they stem from God." The first concept is Deism (see Bube's selection in Part III) and the second is pantheism. What is the problem with each?

NETWORKING

The issues associated with *miracles* are the subjects of other articles in the second section of Part III. The spector of *pantheism* arises with Tillich and Einstein; with advocates of the Anthropic Principle, including Wald and Dyson; and in the Gaia hypothesis of James Lovelock. Even Martin Buber has been accused of pantheistic inclinations.

MIRACLES AND PROBABILITY
RICHARD DAWKINS

Richard Dawkins is a lecturer in animal behavior at Oxford University and the author of *The Selfish Gene,* a popular book on sociobiology. This selection is taken from his recent book on the mechanisms of evolution, *The Blind Watchmaker.*

So, what do we mean by a miracle? A miracle is something that happens, but which is exceedingly surprising. If a marble statue of the Virgin Mary suddenly waved its hand at us we should treat it as a miracle, because all our experience and knowledge tells us that marble doesn't behave like that. I have just uttered the words "May I be struck by lightning this minute." If lightning did strike me in the same minute, it would be treated as a miracle. But actually neither of these two occurrences would be classified by science as utterly impossible. They would simply be judged very improbable, the waving statue much more improbable than the lightning. Lightning does strike people. Any one of us might be struck by lightning, but the probability is pretty low in any one minute (although the *Guinness Book of Records* has a charming picture of a Virginian man, nicknamed the human lightning conductor, recovering in hospital from his seventh lightning strike, with an expression of apprehensive bewilderment on his face). The only thing miraculous about my hypothetical story is the *coincidence* between my being struck by lightning and my verbal invocation of the disaster.

Coincidence means multiplied improbability. The probability of my being struck by lightning in any one minute of my life is perhaps 1 in 10 million as a conservative estimate. The probability of my inviting a lightning strike in any particular minute is also very low. I have just done it for the only time in the 390,000 minutes of my life so far, and I doubt if I'll do it again, so call these odds one in half a million. To calculate the joint probability of the coincidence occurring in any one minute we multiply the two separate probabilities. For my rough calculation this comes to about one in five trillion. If a coincidence of this magnitude happened to me, I should call it a miracle and would watch my language in the future. But although the odds against the coincidence are extremely high, we can still calculate them. They are not literally zero.

In the case of the marble statue, molecules in solid marble are continuously jostling against one another in random directions. The jostlings of the different molecules cancel one another out, so the whole hand of the statue stays still. But if, by sheer coincidence, all the molecules just happened to move in the same direction at the same moment, the hand would move. If they then all reversed direction at the same moment the hand would move back. In this way it is *possible* for a marble statue to wave at us. It could happen. The odds against such a coincidence are unimaginably great but they are not incalculably great. A physicist colleague has kindly calculated them for me. The number is so large that the entire age of the universe so far is too short a time to write out all the noughts! It is theoretically possible for a cow to jump over the moon with something like the same improbability. The conclusion to this part of the argument is that we can *calculate* our way into regions of miraculous improbability far greater than we can *imagine* as plausible.

Let's look at this matter of what we think is plausible. What we can imagine as plausible is a narrow band in the middle of a much broader spectrum of what is actually possible. Sometimes it is narrower than what is actually there. There is a good analogy with light. Our eyes are built to cope with a narrow band of electromagnetic frequencies (the ones we call light), somewhere in the middle of the spectrum from long radio waves at one end to short X-rays at the other. We can't see the rays outside the narrow light band, but we can do calculations about them, and we can build instruments to detect them. In the same way, we know that the scales of size and time extend in both directions far outside the realm of what we can visualize. Our minds can't cope with the large distances that astronomy deals in or with the small distances that atomic physics deals in, but we can represent those distances in mathematical symbols. Our minds can't imagine a time span as short as a picosecond, but we can do calculations about picoseconds, and we can build computers that can complete calculations within picoseconds. Our minds can't imagine a timespan as long as a million years, let alone the thousands of millions of years that geologists routinely compute.

Just as our eyes can see only that narrow band of electromagnetic frequencies that natural selection equipped our ancestors to see, so our brains are built to cope with narrow bands of sizes and times. Presumably there was no need for our ancestors to cope with sizes and times outside the narrow range of everyday practicality, so our brains never evolved the capacity to imagine them. It is probably significant that our own body size of a few feet is roughly in the middle of the range of sizes we can imagine. And our own lifetime of a few decades is roughly in the middle of the range of times we can imagine.

We can say the same kind of thing about improbabilities and miracles. Picture a graduated scale of improbabilities, analogous to the scale of sizes from atoms to galaxies, or to the scale of times from picoseconds to aeons. On the scale we mark off various landmark points. At the far left-hand end of the scale are events which are all but certain, such as the probability that the sun will rise tomorrow—the subject of G. H. Hardy's halfpenny bet. Near this left-hand end of the scale are things that are only slightly improbable, such as shaking a double six in a single throw of a pair of dice. The odds of this happening are 1 in 36. I expect we've all done it quite often. Moving towards the right-hand end of the spectrum, another landmark point is the probability of a perfect deal in bridge, where each of the four players receives a complete suit of cards. The odds against this happening are 2,236,197,406,895,366,368,301,559,999 to 1. Let us call this one dealion, the unit of improbability. If something with an improbability of one dealion was predicted and then happened, we should diagnose a miracle unless, which is more probable, we suspected fraud. But it *could* happen with a fair deal, and it is far far far more probable than the marble statue's waving at us. Nevertheless, even this latter event, as we have seen, has its rightful place along the spectrum of events that could happen. It is measurable, albeit in units far larger than gigadealions. Between the double-six dice throw, and the perfect deal at bridge, is a range of more or less improbable events that do sometimes happen, including any one individual's being struck by lightning, winning a big prize on the football pools, scoring a hole-in-one at golf, and so on. Somewhere in this range, too, are those coincidences that give us an eerie spine-tingling feeling, like dreaming of a particular person for the first time in decades, then waking up to find that they died in the night. These eerie coincidences are very impressive when they happen to us or to one of our friends, but their improbability is measured in only picodealions.

QUESTIONS FOR STUDY

1. What is Dawkins' definition of a miracle? Does it include any supernatural components?

2. How may a highly improbable coincidence be mistaken for a miracle?

3. What is Dawkins' definition of a picodealion?

4. How is the human tendency to respond to a highly improbable occurrence as if it were a miracle to be explained as the result of evolution?

QUESTIONS FOR REFLECTION

1. Dawkins has an unspoken understanding of miracle that he is trying to reject with his modified definition. What is this hidden definition?

2. What would Hick have to say to Dawkins' argument "naturalizing miracle"? In what sense is it beside the point?

3. Could a believer in miracles turn Dawkins' argument against him by claiming that God manipulates the odds?

NETWORKING

For more on *chance and probability,* see Barbour (Part V), Peacocke, and Polkinghorne.

DO MIRACLES EXIST?   PAUL DAVIES

Paul Davies is a British theoretical physicist at the University of Newcastle-Upon-Tyne who writes widely in contemporary physics. One of his most successful titles is *God and the New Physics,* from which this selection is taken.

"I THINK YOU SHOULD BE MORE EXPLICIT HERE IN STEP TWO."

Believer: In my opinion, miracles are the best proof that God exists.

Sceptic: I'm not sure I know what a miracle is supposed to be.

Believer: Well, something extraordinary and unpredictable.

Sceptic: The fall of a large meteorite, or the eruption of a volcano is extraordinary and unpredictable. You aren't suggesting they are miraculous surely?

Believer: Of course not. Such phenomena are natural events. Miracles are *supernatural*.

Sceptic: What do you mean by supernatural? Isn't it just another word for miraculous? (Consults Oxford dictionary.) It says here: "Supernatural. Outside the ordinary operation of cause and effect." Hmm. It all depends on what you mean by "ordinary."

Believer: I would say ordinary meant familiar or well understood.

Sceptic: A dynamo or a radio would have been regarded as miraculous by our ancestors, who were not familiar with electromagnetism.

Believer: I agree they probably would have regarded these devices as miraculous, but erroneously, for we know they operate according to natural laws. A truly supernatural event is one whose cause cannot be found in any natural law, *known* or *unknown*.

Sceptic: Surely that is a useless definition? How do you know which laws might be unknown? There may be totally bizarre and unexpected laws that we may simply happen not to have stumbled across. Suppose you saw a rock float in the air. Would you regard that as a miracle?

Believer: It depends. . . . I would have to be sure there was no illusion, or trickery.

Sceptic: But there may be natural processes that produce super illusions that nobody would suspect.

Believer: Or perhaps all our experience is an illusion and we might as well give up discussing anything?

Sceptic: O.K., let's not take that route. But you still can't be sure that some quirky magnetic or gravitational effect isn't making the rock levitate.

Believer: But it's easier to believe in God than outlandish magnetic phenomena. It's all a question of credibility.

Sceptic: Ah! So by a miracle you really mean 'something caused by God'?

Believer: Absolutely! Though he may sometimes use human intermediaries.

Sceptic: Then you cannot present miracles as evidence for God, or your argument is circular. 'Miracles prove the existence of an agency which produces miracles.' What it really boils down to, as you admitted, is belief. You have to believe in God already for miracles to have any meaning. Apparently miraculous events in themselves cannot prove the existence of God. They might be freak natural events.

Believer: I concede that levitating rocks are dubious from the miracle point of view, but consider some of the famous miracles: Jesus' feeding of the multitude, for example. You can't tell me any sort of natural law would duplicate loaves and fishes!

Sceptic: But what possible reason can you have for believing a story written hundreds of years ago by a lot of superstitious zealots with a vested interest in promoting their own brand of religion?

Believer: You are remarkably cynical. Taken in isolation, the loaves and fishes story is nothing. You have to see it in the context of the whole Bible. It was not the only miracle reported there.

Sceptic: Remind me of another.

Believer: Jesus walked on the water.

Sceptic: Levitation! I thought you'd dismissed that sort of miracle as "dubious."

Believer: For a rock yes, for Jesus, no.

Sceptic: Why not?

Believer: Because Jesus was the Son of God and so possessed supernatural powers.

Sceptic: But you're begging the question again. I don't believe Jesus had supernatural powers. If he did walk on water I would rather suppose it to have been a freak natural event. However, I don't believe the story anyway. Why should I?

Believer: The Bible has been a source of inspiration to millions. Don't dismiss it lightly.

Sceptic: So have the works of Karl Marx. I wouldn't believe any account of his about miracles either.

Believer: You may refuse to accept the word of the Bible, but you can't dismiss the claims of hundreds of people who have experienced miracles even in recent years.

Sceptic: People claim all sorts of things: meetings with aliens, teleportations, clairvoyance. Only a fool or a madman would listen to such nonsense.

Believer: I concede that many wild and fanciful claims are made, but the evidence for faith healing is compelling. Think of Lourdes.

Sceptic: Psychosomatic! Let me quote you: "It's all a question of credibility." I agree. Surely it's easier to believe in a few freak medical events than to invoke a Deity?

Believer: You can't debunk all miracles as psychosomatic. What does that term mean anyway? It's just a euphemism for "medically inexplicable." Why should so many people be so convinced by miracles if they were just natural freaks?

Sceptic: It's all a hang-over from the age of magic. Before the rise of science, or the great world religions, primitive peoples believed that almost anything which happened was caused by magic—the action of some minor god or demon. As science explained more and more, and religion groped towards the idea of one God, so the magical explanations became moribund. But a vestige lives on.

Believer: You're not suggesting that Lourdes pilgrims are demon worshippers!

Sceptic: Not overtly. But their belief in faith healing differs very little, maybe not at all, from the beliefs concerning African witch-doctors, or spirit contacts, for example. Atavistic superstitions from the age of magic have simply been institutionalized by the great religions. Talk of miracles is just sanitized magic-mongering.

Believer: There are powers of good and evil. They manifest themselves in many ways.

Sceptic: And do you take evil supernatural events as evidence for God too? Does he also wield evil powers?

Believer: The relation between good and evil is a delicate theological subject. There are many shades of opinion about your questions. Man's wickedness can act as a channel for evil, whatever its ultimate origin.

Sceptic: So you would not necessarily make God responsible for the so-called occult powers, if they exist?

Believer: Not necessarily, no.

Sceptic: So there are at least two types of supernatural events, then: those that originate with God—what you have called miracles—and the nasty ones—the black arts, shall we say—the origin of which is controversial. Then there would be the neutral ones, I suppose. Like psychokinesis and precognition? It all sounds a bit complicated to me. I'd rather believe that all these topics are just primitive fantasies, a relic of the age of magic, a vestige of polytheism. Your belief in miracles is just the respectable end of a spectrum of neurotic primeval superstitions, and quite unworthy of a God of the majesty and power that you describe.

Believer: It seems to me to be not at all unreasonable to suppose that supernatural powers exist, and can be manipulated in a variety of ways, for good or evil. Faith healing is the good side.

Sceptic: And provides evidence for God?

Believer: I believe so.

Sceptic: What about the failures, the unfortunate ones who don't respond to the healing? Doesn't God care about them? Or does his power waver occasionally?

Believer: God moves in mysterious ways, but his power is absolute.

Sceptic: That's just a platitudinous way of saying you don't know. And if God's power is absolute why does he need miracles anyway?

Believer: I don't understand.

Sceptic: An omnipotent God, who rules the entire universe, and who can make anything happen, has no need of miracles. If he wants to avoid somebody dying of cancer he could prevent them contracting the disease in the first place. In fact, I would regard a miracle as evidence that any God had lost control of the world, and was clumsily trying to patch up the damage. What is the point of God doing all these miracles?

Believer: Through miracles, God demonstrates his divine power.

Sceptic: But why is he so obscure about it? Why does he not write a clear proclamation in the sky, or turn the moon tartan, or something else utterly incontrovertible? Better still, why not avert some major natural disaster, or prevent the spread of devastating epidemics? However wonderful a few cures at Lourdes may be, the stock of human misery is enormous. I repeat, the miracles you describe seem unworthy of an omnipotent God. Levitation, multiplying fishes—they have the air of a cosmic conjuring act. Surely they are just products of puerile human imagination?

Believer: Perhaps God *is* averting disasters all the time.

Sceptic: That's no reply! Anyone could claim the same. Suppose I say that by pronouncing an incantation each morning I prevent world war, and cite as evidence the fact that world war has indeed not broken out? In fact a group of UFO buffs claim just that.

Believer: Christians believe that God continually holds the world in being, so in a sense everything that happens is a miracle, and all this talk of distinction between natural and supernatural is actually a red herring.

Sceptic: Now you're shifting ground. You seem to be saying God *is* nature.

Believer: I'm saying God causes everything in the natural world, though not necessarily in the temporal sense. He doesn't just set the whole thing going and then sit back. God is outside the world, and *above* the laws of nature, sustaining all of existence.

Sceptic: It seems to me we have a semantic quibble here. Nature has a beautiful set of laws and the universe runs along a pathway of evolution mapped out by those laws. You describe exactly the same thing in theistic terms by talk of 'upholding.' Your God is only a mode of speaking, surely? What does it mean to say God upholds the universe? How is that different from simply saying that the universe continues to exist?

Believer: You cannot be content with the bald fact that the universe exists. It must have an *explanation*. I believe God is that explanation, and his power is employed at every moment sustaining the miracle of existence. In most cases he does this in an orderly way—what you would call the laws of physics—but from time to time he departs from this order and produces dramatic events as warnings or signs to human beings, or to assist the faithful, such as when he parted the Red Sea for the Hebrews.

Sceptic: What I find hard to understand is why you think that this supernatural miracle-worker is the *same* as the being who created the universe, who answers prayers, who invented the laws of physics, who will sit in judgement and so on. Why can't all these individuals be different supernatural agents? I should have thought that with so many miracles apparently supporting many different and conflicting religions, a believer in miracles would be obliged to concede the existence of a whole host of supernatural beings in competition.

Believer: One God is simpler than many.

Sceptic: I still don't see how so-called miraculous events, however remarkable, can be regarded as evidence of God's existence. It seems to me you are simply exploiting the fairy godmother instinct we all have, turning "Lady Luck" into a real being and calling her God. How can you take these "miracles" seriously?

Believer: I don't find anything incredible in God, who is creator of all, manipulating material objects. Compared to the miracle of his universe, what is so remarkable about God parting the Red Sea?

Sceptic: But you are still basing your argument on the assumption that God exists. I agree that if a God of the sort you describe—infinite, omnipotent, benevolent, omniscient, and so on—does exist, the Red Sea would be a triviality for him. But how do we know he does exist?

Believer: It's all a question of faith.

Sceptic: Precisely!

This inconclusive dialogue I hope brings out the essence of the conflict between science and religion when it comes to supernatural matters. The religious person, who is comfortable with the notion of God's activity and sees God's work all around him every day, finds nothing incongruous about miraculous events because they are simply another facet of God's action in the world. In contrast the scientist, who prefers to think of the world as operating according to natural laws, would regard a miracle as "misbehaviour," a pathological event which mars the elegance and beauty of nature. Miracles are something that most scientists would rather do without.

QUESTIONS FOR STUDY

1. The skeptic charges that the argument establishing God's existence through the existence of miracles is circular. What does he mean?

2. How does God's selective use of healing miracles raise questions about God's goodness?

3. How do miracles raise questions about God's omnipotence?

QUESTIONS FOR REFLECTION

1. A chair levitates. Scientists are called in to investigate but, after exhaustive tests, they cannot explain the phenomenon. Since they are limited to the assumptions of naturalism, what conclusions can these scientists reach about the floating chair? What alternative explanations, if any, are possible?

2. If a person believes in God, is it irrational not to believe in miracles too?

3. Would you agree that Davies is a deist in his assumptions about God's relation to the world?

NETWORKING

Gilkey, Spivey and Smith, Dillard, Polkinghorne, and Haught also discuss *laws of nature,* and Gilkey, Bube, Einstein, Hick, and Updike express reservations concerning *divine interference in natural processes.* For *falsification and verification,* see Popper, Gish, and Asimov.

SUGGESTIONS FOR FURTHER READING

Beversluis, John. *C. S. Lewis and the Search for Rational Religion*. Grand Rapids, Michigan: William B. Erdmans Publishing Company, 1985. A revealing philosophical portrait of the influential Christian apologist.

Bonhoeffer, Detrich. *Letters and Papers from Prison*. Translated and edited by Eberhard Bethge. New York: Macmillan Publishing Company, 1967. The correspondence of the German theologian while in a Nazi prison before his execution in 1945. Contains Bonhoeffer's developing theological insights which were to lead to the secular theology of the 1960s.

Diamond, Malcolm L. *Contemporary Philosophy and Religious Thought*. New York: McGraw-Hill Book Company, 1974. One of the better introductions to the philosophy of religion. Includes discussions of Buber and Tillich.

Einstein, Albert. *Ideas and Opinions*. Edited by Carl Seelig, trans. by Sonja Bargmann. New York: Bonanza Books, 1954. A rich collection of Einstein's letters, short essays, and comments. Very revealing of the scientist's personal philosophy.

Flew, Anthony, and Alasdair MacIntyre. *New Essays in Philosophical Theology*. London: SCM Press, 1955. A critique of modern theology from the point of view of linguistic philosophy. Includes an application of the notion of falsification to the concept of God.

Geisler, Norman L. *Miracles and Modern Thought*. Grand Rapids: Zondervan, 1982. A defense by a conservative theologian of the traditional concept of miracles.

Hick, John. *Philosophy of Religion*. 3rd ed. Englewood Cliffs, N.J.: Prentice-Hall, 1982. An excellent survey of the field with an emphasis on Christian theology.

Hume, David. *Dialogues Concerning Natural Religion*. Edited by Nelson Pike. Indianapolis, Indiana: The Bobbs Merrill Company, Inc. Includes Hume's classic criticism of the existence of miracles.

Robinson, John A. T. *Honest to God*. Philadelphia: Westminster Press, 1963. A thoughtful exploration into the idea of the supernatural God as an outmoded theological concept. Intended for a wide audience.

Swineburne, Richard. *The Concept of Miracle*. London: Macmillan, 1970. Thorough examination of the subject by a highly respected and very capable philosopher of religion.

Tillich, Paul. *The Courage to Be*. New Haven, Connecticut: Yale University Press, 1952. A good example of Tillich's existential theology. The final section of the book, "Theism Transcended," is a clear expression of Tillich's notion of God.

PART IV

The Cosmos

MODERN ASTRONOMY REVEALS THE UNIVERSE AS A PLACE OF ASTONISHING GRANDEUR, ORDER, AND COMPLEXITY. THE ANDROMEDA SPIRAL IS THE SISTER GALAXY OF OUR MILKY WAY. ALTHOUGH WONDROUSLY IMPRESSIVE, WITH A DIAMETER OF TWO HUNDRED THOUSAND LIGHT YEARS AND CONTAINING MORE THAN A TRILLION STARS, ANDROMEDA IS BUT ONE OF MORE THAN A BILLION ISLAND UNIVERSES POPULATING THE KNOWN PHYSICAL UNIVERSE. IN THE PRESENCE OF SUCH IMMENSITIES, IT IS NO WONDER THAT BOTH SCIENCE AND RELIGION HAVE ALWAYS LOOKED TO THE HEAVENS FOR INSPIRATION AS WELL AS EXPLANATION.

INTRODUCTION   *The Cosmos*

The twentieth century has witnessed a revolution in the physical sciences, including astronomy, physics, and chemistry, that rivals or even exceeds the Scientific Revolution of the sixteenth and seventeenth centuries. The revolutionaries of those days, whose names include Copernicus, Kepler, Galileo, and Newton, contributed to the overthrow of the medieval world and opened the way for the modern era. This second revolution is no less impressive. Einstein, Bohr, Heisenberg, Hubble, Hawking, Wheeler, and Guth are names associated with its discoveries. The consequences of their labors are every bit as significant as those of their forebears, and the cultural revolution they have triggered may prove to be equally monumental.

The first Scientific Revolution resulted in a reorientation of religion. In the secular society that followed, religion was but one option for those who sought universal answers. Truth also could be sought outside the authorities of revelation—the church, theology, and scripture—and the ideal person was not one fulfilled necessarily in relation to God, but one fulfilled in relation to society or to himself or herself alone. This radical, self-centered autonomy was called *individualism*.

Because the second scientific revolution continues, its consequences are not yet settled, but the clues are there. The selections of this part are chosen to highlight several of the discoveries of twentieth-century astronomy and physics that have contributed to the dialogue between science and religion.

The first section, "Cosmology and Creation," examines the theory that the universe had its beginning in time during a primordial explosion—the Big Bang. Is this hypothesis a clear confirmation of the account of creation found in scripture? If there were a beginning, is it *The Beginning* recorded in the first chapters of the book of Genesis, or something else that may forever remain a mystery to both science and theology? The second section, "A Universe by Design?," explores the controversy surrounding God's alleged implication in the growth of the cosmos following its violent birth. Since that original event, the universe has continuously organized itself at ever higher levels of complexity. The cosmos displays overall direction, but is it *directed?* Is its development through physical evolution an intelligent design that aims to produce ever higher life forms despite incredible odds? In the third section, "Microcosmos," we move from the immense to the infinitesimal, with the contention that discoveries about the nature of the smallest existing things, including sub-atomic particles and quanta, reveal a reality that is far different from the reality we encounter in our daily lives. These discoveries force religious thought to face the task of reconciling its traditional views of God, creation, and creaturehood with the new picture of the physical world.

We in the West have inherited a legacy of rational speculation about the existence of God based on evidence taken from the creation. Such attempts take the form of arguments known as *natural theology*. Several such speculations may be found in the works of Greek philosophers, including Aristotle, who lived before the Christian era, but they are best articulated by medieval theologians, especially Thomas Aquinas (1224/5–1274) and by modern proponents and detractors. Two of these arguments, known as the *cosmological* and the *teleological* arguments, come closest to reflecting theological interests in scientific cosmology. This distinctively Western tradition undergirds each of the authors in the first two sections as they attempt to draw theological conclusions from scientific accounts of the physical world.

The first section begins with "The Big Bang and the Cosmological Argument" by philosopher Douglas Lackey, who explains the inner logical workings of the traditional cosmological argument for the existence of God and then relates it to the most recent discoveries in the astronomical sciences.

While the assumptions and claims of the cosmological argument may be questioned, it is clear that science has provided considerable data in support of its initial premise: the universe had a beginning in time. Lackey details the fascinating story of this discovery and raises several questions for a religious interpretation of the data.

In the next selection, "God and the Astronomers," the astrophysicist Walter Jastrow reports that many leading astronomers find the idea that the entire universe had a sudden and inexplicable beginning to be perplexing, even repugnant. Something suddenly appears out of nothing for no apparent reason. Furthermore, that "something" is everything! Science was far more comfortable seeing the cosmos as an everlasting static entity. An essentially changeless or immutable universe requires no explanation for the simple reason that it has no originating cause. Scientists could then proceed with their program of investigating causes *in* the universe without troubling themselves about the cause *of* the universe.

Another implication of the Big Bang hypothesis is equally important for Jastrow. Evidence strongly suggests that the creation of the world was an act of unprecedented violence, a primordial explosion that virtually annihilated any preceding state of affairs. If there were a physical First Cause we can never determine its character from the evidence because none remains. The first creation resembles the perfect crime: the perpetrator cannot be traced. None of this succors scientists who, in Einstein's definition of their calling, aim "to establish general rules which determine the . . . relation of objects and events in space and time." The pursuit of absolute generality may have reached its end with this one glaring exception—the universe itself.

Norman Geisler and Kerby Anderson share Jastrow's apparent pleasure at the chagrin of astronomers. In the third selection, "Origin Science," these authors go further to argue that the Big Bang is clear evidence for a supernatural cause of creation and that this is a true scientific hypothesis.

Their argument is based on a unique understanding of scientific method. Science, they claim, is of two sorts. The first sort, called *operation science,* endeavors to discover the laws of nature by observing patterns of action, described mathematically, which reveal themselves in the consistent behavior of things when they interact with other things under similar conditions. These repeated patterns of action are the results of secondary or natural causes at work. Most scientists would readily admit that their task is to do operation science.

Science of the second sort is more controversial. *Origin science,* as the authors term it, concerns events that occur only once. Such events are not subject to the procedures of operation science because they are not repeatable. One event never establishes a pattern that can be generalized. Operation science alone simply misses singular events in its bias toward repeatability.

The author of the next selection, John Robert Russell, is more cautious than either Jastrow or Geisler and Anderson about the ramifications of modern cosmology for Christian theology. In "Cosmology and Theology," Russell recognizes the potential for insight, but he insists that great care must be exercised lest theology hitch its wagon to a falling star of a scientific theory made obsolete by future discoveries.

Perhaps it is possible to reconstruct the circumstances preceding the Big Bang despite Jastrow's denial. At the very least it is not irrational to speculate upon what might happen if the universe turns out to be "closed" in spacetime. The result of a collapse back upon itself would be a supercollision that would throw cosmic material outward in a repeat of the original explosion. A new universe would then appear phoenix-like from the ashes of the old only to slow and collapse back upon itself again, thereby repeating the eternal cycle of birth and rebirth. Explosion leads eventually to implosion and that to another explosion and so on conceivably in an infinite number of such cycles.

For the sake of their argument, Geisler and Anderson embrace a scientific option that will not allow them to consider the picture of a closed and oscillating universe. It seems that they are forced to do this because the latter alternative removes the Big Bang from the category of a singular and irrepeatable event and places it squarely in the category of operation science. God is thereby removed from consideration as a primary cause. This dependence of theology upon scientific theory is exactly the situation that Russell wants to avoid.

Theoretical progress in cosmology is rapid and accelerating. Tremendous advances in instrumentation and space science open up new possibilities with every shuttle launch. New discoveries are tough on old theories, and the newer theories that replace them are more exotic than ever. Russell believes that prudent theologians should not commit themselves to any one attractive but precarious theory.

The cosmological argument is but one of several popular arguments for the existence of God. Another is the teleological argument, also called the argument from design. Its popularity stems from its appeal to intuition, to common sense. A classic statement of the position is found in *Dialogues Concerning Natural Religion* by David Hume, the skeptical Scottish philosopher of the eighteenth century who is credited with mounting a devastating critique of the argument in its traditional form.

Look around the world, contemplate the whole and every part of it: you will find it to be nothing but one great machine, subdivided into an infinite number of lesser machines, which again admit of subdivisions to a degree beyond what human senses and faculties can trace and explain. All these various machines, and even their most minute parts, are adjusted to each other with an accuracy that ravishes into admiration all men who have ever contemplated them. The curious adapting of means to ends, throughout all nature, resembles exactly, though it much exceeds, the productions of human contrivance—of human design, thought, wisdom, and intelligence. Since therefore the effects resemble each other, we are led to infer, by all the rules of analogy, that the causes also resemble, and that the Author of nature is somewhat similar to the mind of man, though possessed of much larger facilities,

proportioned to the grandeur of the work which He has executed. By this argument a posteriori, and by argument alone, do we prove at once the existence of a Deity and His similarity
to human mind and intelligence.

Despite his clear, elegant, and apparently sympathetic account, Hume launches into
a series of criticisms which effectively demolish this form of the argument. Hume's critique and the subsequent discovery of the mechanism of evolution by Charles Darwin
should have laid the argument from design permanently to rest, but they did not.
Ironically, the evolutionary model, coupled with significant advances in our knowledge
of the birth and development of the entire universe, has revived speculations about teleology. The selections in the third section are examples of these speculations.

Freeman Dyson is a renowned theoretical physicist who ably draws out the implications of modern science for our self-understanding. In "A Growing God" Dyson also
reveals how receptive he is to theological counsel as part and parcel of his perspective.
His focus is primarily upon understanding the role of purpose in the organization and
development of the physical universe.

Dyson appeals frequently to a "Socinian" view of how God orders and directs the
world. Socinus was an Italian heretic. His error lay in denying God the traits of total
power (omnipotence) and knowledge (omniscience) by giving some of each to the
world of creation. This compromised the prevailing view of theology that God is
absolutely superior to the world that, without divine guidance and support, would fall
into chaos and nothingness. In the eyes of traditionalists, a limited Socinian God hardly
seems worthy of worship.

Dyson is not constrained by the concerns of medieval theologians. Socinus is
attractive because he allows us to understand how science, on the one hand, can speak
of randomness in the world and how theology, on the other hand, can speak of God's
directive activity in that same world. Dyson concludes that God's purposes or plans for
the creation are enhanced, not frustrated, by the existence of chance. The play of chance
in the world means that God's influence is limited or that the world expresses it freedom through the operations of events which are not directed by God. However, God is
not a passive witness of the proceedings; God learns from experience and works always
to adjust earlier plans and expectations to fit the prevailing situation. God's final aim is
therefore not to dictate the future of the creation but to work along with it in producing
the greatest possible diversity and richness.

In one of its several forms, the Anthropic Principle is a recent revision of the teleological argument for the existence of God. Dyson's version of the Anthropic Principle,
which differs in detail from the one presented by George Wald in the sixth selection, is
that the design and development of the universe must be congenial to the existence of
creaturely minds which know that universe. We can imagine countless alternative universes that might have been but which could never have supported the evolution of conscious creatures. It seems odd that just this universe was realized, a universe productive
of creatures who could marvel at this mystery. The implication is that the universe was
designed with the purpose of producing minds like our own, human minds, fully capable of appreciating it. Thus the title "Anthropic Principle."

The next selection, "Life and Mind in the Universe," by the famous research biologist George Wald, is a further development of the Anthropic Principle. Wald contends that cosmic evolution depends upon a series of critical thresholds where events of incredible improbability occurred. Because these events built upon one another, the universe was led to ever greater levels of complexity, culminating finally (or most recently) in the emergence of at least one intelligent species, *Homo sapiens,* capable of envisioning the whole process and asking "why?"

Certainly, Wald admits, our astonishment derives from a self-centered view that we represent the best of all of the immense number of possible worlds, most of them desolate, that could have resulted had any one of these critical quantities assumed an ever-so-slightly different value than it actually did. In fact, however, none of the results varied at all and we were the end product. The cosmos seems to have prepared for our arrival; we were expected. We are special. So be it. The final question, the most important one, thus becomes, "how did the universe find out?"

The seventh selection, a short story by Gerald Feinberg and Robert Shapiro, is a response to Wald's version of the Anthropic Principle. In "A Puddlian Fable," the little rotifers who know only the world of puddles are led by their limited perspective and some self-serving logic to conclude that the universe is made exclusively for their kind. They reason that the physical and chemical conditions of the universe are optimal for the existence and flourishing of rotifer societies. Other life forms requiring other conditions are worse than unfortunate—they cannot even exist.

The authors' selection of puddle dwellers is itself intended to satirize advocates of the Anthropic Principle who share one thing in common with the puddlian philosopher—a sense of hubris or pride about their place in the universe. Their folly is to believe that this vast and varied cosmos was intended to prepare for the coming of a single privileged life form. The numerous and unlikely evolutionary coincidences specified by both Wald and Philo, the rotifer philosopher, are difficult to dismiss. But the claim that we are special because the universe has intentionally produced us as intelligent observers of its own design seems suspiciously circular, since it assumes that we are special as a premise for the argument that concludes that we are special.

Those who subscribe to the design argument have found a new tool for searching out the infinitely subtle underlying order of God's intentions in his physical creation. The eighth selection is taken from the novel *Roger's Version* by John Updike. In this scene a young and very ambitious graduate student, Dale Kohler, appears before a grants committee consisting of several sophisticated professors for the purpose of persuading them to fund his search for evidence that would implicate God in the act of creation. Kohler argues with passion that God may be found in the unlikely events of the Big Bang and its subsequent developments as well as in the relationships between the physical constants of the cosmos as revealed by the computer.

The dialogue advances through questions raised by the committee members and concludes with a comment by Roger, the main character and follower of the theologian Karl Barth, that Dale's project is "a kind of obscene cosmological prying."

Once again pride enters the picture, not in the self-centered appraisal of our special place as the aim of cosmic evolution, but in the assumption that we are perfectly capable of exposing God with our unassisted cunning. To this kind of hubris, Barth shouts "Nein!"

The excursions of twentieth-century science into the world of atoms and particles have shown that our assumptions about the common sense nature of reality fail when extended to the realm of the very small. The major parts of atoms—electrons, protons, and neutrons—do not behave like tiny baseballs. Other particles populating these regions are even more bizarre, and efforts to observe them introduce further shocks to the very nature of scientific inquiry.

The selections found in the third section, "The Microcosmos," explore some of the implications of this new picture for religion. The range of alternative pictures of realities offered by physicists as they try to make sense of their experience is indeed great. The claim of the dominant school, the Copenhagen interpretation, is that there simply is *no* underlying reality, no matter what, so that the observer is left to create the world he witnesses and measures. Other physicists concur in their own way. Reality is the product of consciousness and nothing else; or at the very least, reality is only some shadowy set of possibilities suspended in the limbo of the world of pure potential as it awaits the call to actualization by the attention of an observer, who by looking or measuring, calls only one member of the set into actuality (Heisenberg, Wheeler). Or perhaps reality is an undivided whole, just one single entity rather than the many things located in space and persisting over time (Bohm). Or maybe reality is made of an infinite number of universes, each in its own space/time/place paralleling the others and yet blithely unaware of their existence (Everett). When compared to these fantastic options, the classic Newtonian world picture with its simple intuitive intelligibility is tidy and comfortable.

Fritjof Capra enters the discussion and makes his contributions precisely at this point. In "Beyond Language" Capra's contention is simple: reality as revealed in atomic physics is paradoxical and beyond the logic of common sense that we apply to our everyday world, the same world examined by classic Newtonian physics. Capra advises us to abandon our ingrained rational understanding of nature and replace it with the deeper intuitive awareness of Eastern mysticism.

In "All Nature Is Touch and Go," naturalist writer Annie Dillard discloses a similar interest in mysticism and particle physics. Her approach, however, is not the same as Capra's. Dillard's contribution is neither hard science nor pure theology. Rather it represents an effort, primarily literary, to relate symbolically one of the more important discoveries of the new physics to the larger world of our everyday experience.

Dillard revels in the discovery of uncertainty in the behavior of particles first stated by Werner Heisenberg in his principle of uncertainty. Heisenberg's principle claims that our efforts to acquire total knowledge about a particle are doomed to failure. The complete description of an electron's motion and position is indeterminable. The principle does not claim that the behavior of the electron itself is necessarily undetermined, that is, that the electron moves and positions itself by its own free will or by chance alone. The laws of nature may well continue to influence the lowly and elusive electron. We human observers, however, are fated to remain partially ignorant of these influences.

Other subatomic phenomena—the spontaneous decay of unstable atoms, the coming and going of particles in high-energy accelerators, and the description of the particle's position as a wave function or "fog of probabilities"—suggest, nonetheless, that true freedom exists for particles in nature. These instances provide other evidence for Dillard's claims.

On the basis of her conclusions, Dillard describes physicists as mystics. *Mystic* is derived from the Greek word *muein,* meaning to close the mouth, to become mute. The mystic seeks to encounter the deeper levels of reality that lie behind the veil of the senses. When successful, the mystic is often rendered speechless in her wonder and in her subsequent efforts to communicate the marvelous and direct experience of this fundamental reality in terms of the logic and language of those who have never known it.

Modern physics has acquired this deeper reality, but it has done so at the price of surrendering the convenient images, vocabulary, and reasoning of classic physics and its investigation of the everyday world. In this limited sense physicists qualify as mystics.

Dillard returns to the scene at Tinker Creek and indulges in a few mystical observations of her own. She makes a final connection; the natural community of the creek shares in the radical freedom and hiddenness to be found in the tiniest particle.

In the final selection, John Polkinghorne provides a summative statement for most of the issues of this part. In "More to the World Than Meets the Eye," Polkinghorne looks at the discoveries of modern physics for both the contributions and threats they provide to religious thought. On the positive side, he marvels at the intelligibility of the physical cosmos. Its fundamental patterns can be expressed in mathematical abstractions accessible to the human mind. This correspondence suggests that God managed the creation so as to provide for the existence of creatures who are capable of understanding the order of that creation. Polkinghorne also takes seriously the data of evolution which suggest that God fine-tuned the developing cosmos by adjusting "the knobs of the universe" so as to direct the process toward the emergence of intelligent life forms. This, of course, is a restatement of the Anthropic Principle.

These efforts at a "revised natural theology" are chastined by three threats. The first is the "fitful" world of subatomic particles. Does God play dice with the world after all? Conclusions about Heisenberg's principle that excite Dillard bother Polkinghorne. The second threat is related to the first. True chance is at work in evolution, which means either that God does not control the process entirely or that God twiddles some knobs randomly. Polkinghorne relates the play of chance to the reliability of order and sees freedom as the product. He is one with Dyson on this point. Freedom is good. Therefore, chance is good. The final and most severe threat is the "ultimate futility of the universe" as revealed in the laws of thermodynamics. Entropy, the inevitable decline of all order into static chaos, leads to the prognosis of an eventual death of the cosmos. All this is nothing new to religion, which has always recognized the corruption of the material world. At this point Polkinghorne, like Ralph Burhoe in Part V, relies upon hope—a basic theological virtue—that all this waste and decay has significance in the sight of God who will act to redeem Creation from its irreversible terminal condition.

The perplexity and the imagination expressed by the authors in this part suggest that Western theology has not yet fully incorporated the insights and discoveries of twentieth-century physics into its traditional doctrines of God and creation. The reason lies, perhaps, in the difficulty of the subject itself; modern physics is abstract, mathematically oriented, and counterintuitive. It is a daunting subject for even the educated

layperson. Or the reason could lie in the accounts it offers of the exotic nature of particles. They seem to have about as much to do with the world of our lives as the figures
of Alice's Wonderland have to do with real life as it proceeds on this side of the
Looking Glass. It may be that the God of the middle-level reality between the very
small and the very large, between peek-a-boo quanta and all-consuming black holes,
suffices to meet the religious needs of society. However, as the worlds of cosmology
and quantum physics begin to have impact upon society in further advances in technology and science and in the education of new generations, theology will probably be prudent by continuing in its efforts to give an account of itself in the terms they provide.

COSMOLOGY AND CREATION
THE BIG BANG AND THE
COSMOLOGICAL ARGUMENT
DOUGLAS P. LACKEY

Douglas Lackey teaches at Baruch College and the Graduate Center of New York. In the introduction of the book from which this selection was taken, Professor Lackey identifies as one of his tasks "to determine how much religious hope the scientific attitude can tolerate."

Perhaps the most popular argument for God for the ordinary person is the cosmological argument—the argument that God must exist because only God could have created the universe. In outline the cosmological argument reads:

1. The universe had a beginning in time (Premise 1);
2. Everything that has a beginning in time must have a cause (Premise 2); so,
3. There exists a cause of the universe; and
4. *The cause of the universe could only be God* (Premise 3); so,
5. God exists.

God, in short, is the first cause of everything in the physical universe.

Premise 1

The first premise of the cosmological argument—that the universe had a beginning in time—implies that the physical history of the universe does not stretch infinitely far into the past. For people accustomed to the story of the Book of Genesis, nothing could be more natural than thinking that there was some moment at which the universe *began*. But many eminent philosophers, Aristotle (384–322 B.C.) for example, have thought that the idea of a beginning of the universe is absurd (because "nothing can come from nothing"). Thus, Aristotle believed that the universe had no beginning and that the past history of the universe is infinite. Is there any evidence that the past history of the universe is *finite*?

Evidence that the universe *does* have a beginning has been provided in recent years by the branch of astronomy called *cosmology*. The data from cosmology are worth describing in detail.

In the 1920s, astronomers established for the first time that certain fuzzy patterns of light in the sky were actually large clusters of stars, or galaxies, located at distances from Earth far greater than the distances of the stars in the night sky. The stars in the night sky, in fact, were themselves part of the Milky Way, a local galaxy, the center of which is visible as a filmy streak in the night sky in summer.

In the 1930s, astronomers discovered that the light from the galaxies was shifted toward the red, that is, the frequencies of light obtained from the stars in distant galaxies were lower than one would expect if those galaxies were stationary relative to the earth. There are various explanations of this Red Shift, but the one that made the most scientific sense was that the galaxies are all moving away from the earth. More precisely (since the earth is not at the center of the universe), the Red Shift shows that the average distance between the galaxies is increasing with time.

Now, if the average distance between the galaxies is increasing as time goes on, it follows that if we go *backward* in time, the average distance between the galaxies is *decreasing*. If we could put the history of the universe on film and then run the film backward, we would see the galaxies all converging in a small volume of space. By the late 1940s, various astronomers were suggesting the expansion of the universe from the past to the present was caused by a gigantic explosion, named the Big Bang, which hurled the matter of the galaxies outward in all directions. In 1966, evidence for the existence of the Big Bang was discovered in background radiation evenly distributed throughout the universe—the residual heat of the early great explosion.

In the astronomy of the 1960s, there was no theory as to what the matter of the universe was doing during or before the Big Bang. For all cosmology knew, the matter of the universe could have been in a tight ball for eons and then suddenly exploded. In short, the Big Bang theory of the 1960s was at least *compatible* with the idea that the physical universe is infinitely old.

In the early 1970s, physicists Steven Hawking and Roger Penrose proved that the matter of the present universe could *not* be infinitely old. They demonstrated—if you imagine time running backward once again—that as the galaxies approached one another in the distant past, they came together into a single dense ball. The great forces acting inside this ball broke down the normal resistance of matter to compression, so the ball steadily became denser and denser. At one point in the past, all the matter of our universe was compressed into an object the size of a basketball; still earlier, the size of a golf ball. If we look at still earlier and earlier moments, at one projected point in the past, the density of the universe is infinite and its volume is zero. This hypothetical moment of infinite density is located by astronomers between 10 and 20 billion years B.C.

Contemporary Big Bang theory, then, does not merely say that the *galaxies* are not more than 20 billion years old. It says that the matter and energy *of which the galaxies are made* are not more than 20 billion years old.

What was going on before the Big Bang? According to Einstein's General Theory of Relativity, developed as a theory of gravity in 1915 and applied by Einstein to cosmology in 1917, nothing whatsoever, not even time. In the General Theory, space and time are *features of* the physical universe, not dimensions that *contain* the universe. The universe is all there is of space and time, and the beginning of the Big Bang is the beginning of time itself. There are no moments of time before the Big Bang, and nothing has ever happened that should be dated before the Big Bang. If this theory is right, then the cosmological argument is correct in saying that the universe has a beginning in time.

Premise 2

The claim that *everything with a beginning in time must have a cause* is called the Law of Universal Causation or the Principle of Sufficient Reason. As the German philosopher Gottfried Leibniz (1646–1716) explained it, if there is no cause that makes something happen, then nothing will happen, because "nothing is simpler and easier than something." The law applies to all events, so it applies to the Big Bang. Unless there was something that made the Big Bang happen, it never would have happened at all.

Why should we believe the Law of Universal Causation? To begin with, we already know that a great many events do have causes because we know what these causes are. The remaining events either have *unknown* causes or have *no causes at all*. Take any such event: should we assume that it has no cause or that we simply don't know what its cause is?

Many times in the past, when people have assumed that an event E has no cause, science has eventually discovered the cause of E. We can prove events have causes, but we can never prove an event has no cause, since we can never be sure what the future science will be able to explain. For any event E for which no cause is proven, it is always more reasonable to assume that E has a real but unknown cause than that E has no cause.

Another argument for the Law of Universal Causation comes from Immanuel Kant. Kant wondered how it was possible, in general, to distinguish perceptions of the real world from other sorts of perceptions, like hallucinations, which provide no knowledge of the world at all. He argued that the Law of Universal Causation was a tool we must use in order to distinguish genuine experiences from nongenuine ones. Genuine experiences are experiences of objects *connected to* other objects by relations of cause and effect. Hallucinations are experiences of objects *not* connected to other objects by relations of cause and effect. Thus, any event that has no causes is something we would have to classify as *unreal*. Because of the way we must think about the world when we know anything about it, the Law of Universal Causation applies to all worldly events.

Premise 3

Even if we have established that the Big Bang must have a cause, we still must show what the first cause is. We cannot simply assume that the Creator of the universe is God, since Creator of the Heavens and the Earth is not an essential property of God. To show that the Creator is God, we must show that the Creator is all-powerful and all-good.

Obviously, any creator of the universe must have great power. But why should we think the Creator is *all*-powerful? Why can't we just say the Creator is *very* powerful but not *all*-powerful? One reason might be that any being who is powerful enough to create a universe is powerful enough to do anything at all. Notice that the cause of the universe has created matter and energy from nothing, or at least from something that is not itself matter and energy. It seems reasonable to think a being who could create matter and energy from nothing could do anything whatsoever.

Why should we think the Creator of the universe is supremely good? One reason is that if the Creator is the cause of all things, then all good things come from the Creator. Furthermore, the Creator could have chosen not to create these good things. It follows that the Creator must have wanted to create them, and his desire to create what is good shows that the Creator *is* good. But since the Creator is all-powerful, his desire to create the good knows no bounds. He will create an infinite amount of good, and thereby show that He is infinitely good.

Thus, the Creator, infinitely powerful and infinitely good, must be none other than God.

CRITICISM OF THE COSMOLOGICAL ARGUMENT

The Universe Might Have Begun Spontaneously.

It would not be wise for critics of the cosmological argument to challenge the Big Bang theory that supports the first premise of the argument. Though a few cosmologists reject the theory, most think the evidence in its favor is overwhelming. The point to attack in the cosmological argument is the point at which it claims the universe must have a cause. The critic can argue the Big Bang was an event that had no cause at all. It happened spontaneously, without cause.

If we say this, we are rejecting the Law of Universal Causation. But many philosophers and many scientists believe the Law of Universal Causation is false. The reason lies in the theory of *quantum physics*, the physics developed between 1900 and 1930 by Max Planck, Albert Einstein, Nils Bohr, Louis de Broglie, Werner Heisenberg, Erwin Schrodinger, Paul Dirac, and others to explain the behavior of the tiniest bits of matter and energy. According to quantum physics, the behavior of atomic particles is not determined precisely by prior conditions. It is to some degree spontaneous. For example, it is not possible to predict when a given radioactive atom will decay, and this difficulty in prediction is not due to our ignorance of the atom. It springs from the nature of the atom itself.

Thus, the Law of Universal Causation is rejected in quantum physics. Some events don't have causes. But perhaps the Law of Universal Causation only fails for little things like radioactive atoms. Can we say that the law also fails for the Big Bang, and that the creation of the universe was as spontaneous an event as the decay of a radioactive atom?

There are two reasons for thinking the Law of Universal Causation fails for the Big Bang. First, the Law of Universal Causation says that every event has a cause, and this means that every event has a cause *that is another earlier event.* Since the Big Bang is the first moment of time, nothing can be earlier than it. Second, according to Big Bang cosmology, at some past point in time the entire universe was no larger than an atomic particle. Whatever rules apply to atomic particles would apply to the universe at that time. The behavior of a universe of such small size could be as spontaneous as the decay of a radioactive atom.

So the big bang might have no cause. How then did it happen? One explanation provided by quantum theory depends on the fact that in quantum physics the energy levels of particles and systems can never be precisely measured, but oscillate spontaneously between certain levels. For the smallest particles, this oscillation between energy levels may cause the energy level to drop to zero, at which point the particle ceases to exist. Conversely, the oscillation can raise a particle from zero to some finite level; that is, it brings a particle into existence. Such particles, usually called virtual particles, are literally coming into existence from a vacuum, that is, from nothing. A few physicists, Heinz Pagels for one, have suggested that one could explain the Big Bang as a fluctuation in a vacuum, like the fluctuations that bring virtual particles into existence. But if the fluctuations are spontaneous, then the creation of the universe from a vacuum is also spontaneous.

The Creator Might Not Be God.

Suppose the preceding objection is mistaken and the universe does indeed have a cause. All we know about this cause is that it has the power to create our universe. This is far from showing that the Creator of the universe is all-powerful. An all-powerful being must be able to create an infinite number of universes. We cannot tell, if a being has made one universe, whether it has the power to create any more. For all we know, the Creator of the universe might have died in the effort of making it.

There is still less reason to think that the Creator of the universe *must* be all-good. If one argues that all good things come from the Creator, then one must argue that all bad things come from the Creator as well. But bad things cannot come from a supremely good being. Even if the universe has a Creator, the fact of creation is not sufficient to show that this Creator must be God.

QUESTIONS FOR STUDY

1. Put the cosmological argument in your own words.

2. Briefly describe the scientific evidence for the theory that the universe had a beginning in time.

3. Why is it inaccurate to say that the universe had a beginning in time?

4. What is the Law of Universal Causation?

5. How may we argue that the First Cause of the universe must be God? What is the argument that the First Cause may not be God?

QUESTIONS FOR REFLECTION

1. Which appears more natural to you, that the universe is eternal (of infinite duration in time) or that it had a beginning? What biblical source explains the evident Western preference for the latter opinion?

2. Is it accurate to claim that, "nothing has ever happened that should be dated before the Big Bang"? See Russell, "Cosmology and Theology" later in this part.

3. Lackey notes that virtual particles can arise from fluctuations in a vacuum, and he uses this fact to support the spontaneous uncaused nature of the Big Bang. Is a vacuum the same as an absolute "nothing"?

NETWORKING

The importance of *natural theology* is found in selections by Barbour (Part I), Bube, Dyson, and Polkinghorne. Gilkey, Bube, and Geisler and Anderson discuss *primary and secondary causation.*

GOD AND THE ASTRONOMERS
WALTER JASTROW

Walter Jastrow is a leading atmospheric physicist and professor of physics and earth science at Dartmouth College in New Hampshire. At one time he headed the Theoretical Division of NASA's Goddard Space Flight Center. Dr. Jastrow is the noted author of numerous books.

Now three lines of evidence—the motions of the galaxies, the laws of thermodynamics, and the life story of the stars—pointed to one conclusion; all indicated that the Universe had a beginning. A few scientists bit the bullet and dared to ask "What came before the beginning?" Edmund Whittaker, a British physicist, wrote a book on religion and the new astronomy called *The Beginning and End of the World,* in which he said, "There is no ground for supposing that matter and energy existed before and was suddenly galvanized into action. For what could distinguish that moment from all other moments in eternity?" Whittaker concluded, "It is simpler to postulate creation *ex nihilo*—Divine will constituting Nature from nothingness." Some were even bolder, and asked "Who was the Prime Mover?" The British theorist, Edward Milne, wrote a mathematical treatise on relativity which concluded by saying, "As to the first cause of the Universe, in the context of expansion, that is left for the reader to insert, but our picture is incomplete without Him."

But the views of most physicists and astronomers are closer to that of Saint Augustine, who, asking himself what God was doing before he made Heaven and Earth, gave the reply, "He was creating Hell for people who asked questions like that." In fact, some prominent scientists began to feel the same irritation over the expanding Universe that Einstein had expressed earlier. Eddington wrote in 1931, "I have no axe to grind in this discussion," but "the notion of a beginning is repugnant to me . . . I simply do not believe that the present order of things started off with a bang . . . the expanding Universe is preposterous . . . incredible . . . *it leaves me cold.*" The German chemist, Walter Nernst, wrote, "To deny the infinite duration of time would be to betray the very foundations of science." More recently, Phillip Morrison of MIT said in a BBC film on cosmology, "I find it hard to accept the Big Bang theory; *I would like to reject it.*" And Allan Sandage of Palomar Observatory, who established the uniformity of the expansion of the Universe out to nearly ten billion light years, said, "It is such a strange conclusion . . . *it cannot really be true.*" (The italics are mine.)

There is a strange ring of feeling and emotion in these reactions. They come from the heart, whereas you would expect the judgments to come from the brain. Why?

I think part of the answer is that scientists cannot bear the thought of a natural phenomenon which cannot be explained, even with unlimited time and money. There is a kind of religion in science; it is the religion of a person who believes there is order and harmony in the Universe, and every event can be explained in a rational way as the product of some previous event; every effect must have its cause; there is no First Cause. Einstein wrote, "The scientist is possessed by the sense of universal causation." This religious faith of the scientist is violated by the discovery that the world had a beginning under conditions in which the known laws of physics are not valid, and as a product of forces or circumstances we cannot discover. When that happens, the scientist has lost control. If he really examined the implications, he would be traumatized. As usual when faced with trauma, the mind reacts by ignoring the implications—in science this is known as "refusing to speculate"—or trivializing the origin of the world by calling it the Big Bang, as if the Universe were a firecracker.

Consider the enormity of the problem. Science has proven that the Universe exploded into being at a certain moment. It asks, What cause produced this effect? Who or what put the matter and energy into the Universe? Was the Universe created out of nothing, or was it gathered together out of pre-existing materials? And science cannot answer these questions, because, according to the astronomers, in the first moments of its existence the Universe was compressed to an extraordinary degree, and consumed by the heat of a fire beyond human imagination. The shock of that instant must have destroyed every particle of evidence that could have yielded a clue to the cause of the great explosion. An entire world, rich in structure and history, may have existed before our Universe appeared; but if it did, science cannot tell what kind of world it was. A sound explanation may exist for the explosive birth of our Universe; but if it does, science cannot find out what the explanation is. The scientist's pursuit of the past ends in the moment of creation.

This is an exceedingly strange development, unexpected by all but the theologians. They have always accepted the word of the Bible: In the beginning God created heaven and earth. To which St. Augustine added, "Who can understand this mystery or explain it to others?" It is unexpected because science has had such extraordinary success in tracing the chain of cause and effect backward in time. We have been able to connect the appearance of man on this planet to the crossing of the threshold of life, the manufacture of the chemical ingredients of life within stars that have long since expired, the formation of those stars out of the primal mists, and the expansion and cooling of the parent cloud of gases out of the cosmic fireball.

Now we would like to pursue that inquiry farther back in time, but the barrier to further progress seems insurmountable. It is not a matter of another year, another decade of work, another measurement, or another theory; at this moment it seems as though science will never be able to raise the curtain on the mystery of creation. For the scientist who has lived by his faith in the power of reason, the story ends like a bad dream. He has scaled the mountains of ignorance; he is about to conquer the highest peak; as he pulls himself over the final rock, he is greeted by a band of theologians who have been sitting there for centuries.

QUESTIONS FOR STUDY

1. According to the author, what is the general response of science to the discovery of the originating Big Bang?

2. Why is this discovery so traumatic to scientists?

3. Is science now forever forbidden from pursuing its goal of obtaining complete knowledge of the world? Explain.

4. In what sense may theologians say to scientists, "We told you so"?

QUESTIONS FOR REFLECTION

1. What is creation *ex nihilo?* Why does theology object to the idea that God could have created the world out of some preexisting material? Read carefully the first verses of the book of Genesis. Do you find the concept there?

2. Is it necessary to postulate a personal cause for the physical origin of the cosmos— a "He" or "She" rather than an "It"?

3. Does theology risk its integrity when it takes credit for prior knowledge about the beginning of the world? Does it really matter if the discoveries of science, such as the Big Bang, confirm or deny the accounts of scripture? Do theologians have privileged insight denied to scientists in these matters?

NETWORKING

For *naturalism as a belief system,* see Gilkey, Niebuhr, Bube, and Gish.

ORIGIN SCIENCE
NORMAN L. GEISLER AND J. KERBY ANDERSON

Norman Geisler earned his Ph.D. from Loyola University and has taught systematic theology at the Dallas Theological Seminary and Liberty University. He has written more
than twenty books from the conservative Christian perspective. Kerby Anderson has
published in the field of creationism.

A FORENSIC SCIENCE

The investigation of origins may be compared to researching an unwitnessed murder.
Clues can be pieced together to give a plausible reconstruction of what occurred. But
the reconstructed scenario is still speculation, no matter how plausible it is.

Because a murder (or origin) does not recur, hypotheses about it cannot be empirically tested. We may re-enact the crime (or origin) and test the reconstruction or model
against data collected in experiments. But we cannot test our model against the original
event. There is thus no direct way to know whether the results from these experiments
give information about the particular unique event in question. Origin science then
functions more like a forensic science than an empirical science.

A PLACE FOR PRIMARY CAUSES

Operation scientists succeeded in discovering secondary causes and understanding the
operation of the universe. This success led them to apply similar principles to origin
questions. Nature was conceived of as a continuous web of natural (secondary) causes
and effects. Primary causes were interpreted as having no intervening role in the ongoing processes of nature. The reasoning went like this: if nature is a seamless web in
which God does not interfere, then it must be that natural causes account for the beginning; secondary causes extend back further and further until the beginning. This, scientists believed, would give a true scientific explanation of origins. . . .

The modern search for the beginning, however, has turned into a nightmare.
Astrophysicist Robert Jastrow tells the story in *God and the Astronomers*: "For the scientist who has lived by his faith in the power of reason, the story ends like a bad
dream." A scientist who is committed to philosophical naturalism finds it difficult to
accept that the data indicate a beginning of the universe. Philosophical naturalism has
implicit within it the notion that there never was a beginning. So, for example, the
steady state hypothesis which denied a beginning had an intuitive appeal to committed
naturalists. The strange thing is that even when scientists have looked through a naturalistic lens, the data still seemed to point to a beginning. This seems to be an instance

where in spite of a naturalistic bias the door was opened to a supernatural explanation. For the notion of a beginning has theistic implications, including the possibility of a primary supernatural cause. This has undoubtedly troubled many committed naturalists; hence the "bad dream" Jastrow referred to.

Contemporary approaches to the origin of the universe have taken a radical turn with the widespread acceptance of a big bang cosmogony. According to Jastrow, "Three lines of evidence—the motions of the galaxies, the laws of thermodynamics, and the life story of the stars—pointed to one conclusion: all indicated that the Universe had a beginning." In short, "science has proven that the Universe exploded into being at a certain moment." Thus "the scientist's pursuit of the past ends in the moment of creation."

Although some scientists believe the big bang is only the most recent explosion in an endless series of explosions and contractions, a current body of evidence supports the scientific model of a beginning of the universe. The second law of thermodynamics affirms that in a closed isolated system (such as the whole universe) the amount of usable energy is decreasing. So it is argued that even if the universe did have enough mass to rebound, nevertheless, like a bounding ball in reverse, it would rebound less and less until it could rebound no more. Thus, according to big bang cosmogony, the regular laws of the universe (thermodynamics, measurable expansion) point to a unique singular beginning.

Whether or not the big bang theory is correct is not the point here. What is significant is that a scientific hypothesis has been developed in which the regularities of the present are used as a key to formulating a scientific view suggesting a past singularity of origin. Without these observable laws there would be no way to construct a scientific model about a past unobserved singularity. So regularities (constant conjunctions) in the present are the key to a scientific approach to this singularity in the past. By using observed regularities from the present it is possible to construct a scientific model about a past singularity which has no parallel in the present.

Most scientists have acknowledged the scientific plausibility of the big bang hypothesis. However, it is an example of origin science. For by using the principles of causality and uniformity one can make a plausible case in support of a particular view about the singularity of the origin of the universe. Observed regular events of the present (such as the second law of thermodynamics), which can be described by known law, can aid in understanding an unobserved singular event of the past. And if this is so, then it is possible to posit a primary cause for the origin of the universe.

SOME KEY DIFFERENCES BETWEEN ORIGIN SCIENCE AND OPERATION SCIENCE

Origin science does not involve an unbroken continuity of causes. For the scientific evidence points to a beginning of the universe. And if there was a beginning then the need to seek an endless series of causes is gone. As Jastrow aptly put it,

Astronomers now find they have painted themselves into a corner because they have proven, by their own methods, that the world began abruptly in an act of creation to which you can trace the seeds of every star, every planet, every living thing in this cosmos and on the earth.

And they have found that all this happened as a product of forces they cannot hope to discover. . . .

One reason scientists are surprised that uniform laws point to a singular beginning is that there has been such a widespread confusion of operation science and origin science. They failed to keep in mind that only the *operation* of the universe, not its *origin*, demands regularity. Only the *basis* for science needs to be a constant conjunction or regularity; its *object* can be a singularity. In short, they did not recognize the difference between a scientific analysis of singularities and that of regularities.

So the big bang theory of the origin of the universe has brought into sharp focus the need to clearly distinguish between the cause of origin and the cause of operation of the universe. This only reminds us of the distinction between cosmogony (study of origin of the cosmos) and cosmology (study of the operation of the cosmos). Both are legitimate studies. Hence, while scientists rightly rule miracles out of regularity science, of which operation science is the application in the present . . . , they cannot thereby eliminate them from singularity science, of which origin science is an application to the past. The supernatural is correctly ruled out of operation science because operation science is based on regular events which must have secondary causes. Because origins, like miracles . . . , are singularities, it remains possible that a primary cause was involved. Indeed, according to the big bang hypothesis, no regularly observed causes operative in the world were involved in the origin of the universe. Hence, the big bang model illustrates that a discontinuity at the moment of beginning can be a legitimate characteristic of origin science.

Jastrow notes that not all scientists were happy with the conclusion that the universe had a beginning. Arthur Stanley Eddington wrote . . . , "The notion of a beginning is repugnant to me . . . I simply do not believe that the present order of things started off with a bang. . . ." Walter Nernst said, "To deny the infinite duration of time would be to betray the very foundations of science." More recently Phillip Morrison of MIT said, "I find it hard to accept the Big Bang theory; I would *like* to reject it" . . . , (emphasis added). Allan Sandage of Palomar Observatory once said, "It is such a strange conclusion . . . it cannot really be true."

Why did scientists react in this unusual and unscientific way to the mounting evidence for a radical and singular beginning of our universe? Jastrow offers this response:

I think part of the answer is that scientists cannot bear the thought of a natural phenomenon which cannot be explained, even with unlimited time and money. There is a kind of religion in science; it is the religion of a person who believes there is order and harmony in the Universe. Every event can be explained in a rational way as the product of some previous event; every effect must have its cause; there is no First Cause. . . .

But in spite of the fact that many scientists find the results of the scientific evidence for a singular beginning of the universe to be undesirable, nevertheless the scientific evidence is strong that there was a beginning of the universe. Indeed it results from following the principle of uniformity, which is the key to understanding the past. Thus unexpectedly the principle of uniformity has led to a break in the scientific community with the long-standing principle of endless continuity. And with this break, the door has been reopened for origin science.

In view of this development we suggest that just as applying secondary causes to astronomical explanations of origin opened the door to the decline of a special creationist view, so the big bang theory of the origin of the universe has resurrected the possibility of a creationist view of origins in astronomy. Likewise, just as a secondary cause was extended from astronomy to geology and biology, there is now no reason why a primary-cause explanation of origins cannot be applied in these areas to re-establish a creationist view. In short, it appears that while in the nineteenth century the application of secondary causes moved from astronomy to geology and biology, thus leading to the decline of creationist views, now the plausibility of a primary cause for the origin of the universe can be extended from astronomy to geology and biology,[1] thus reopening the door for a special creationist view.

THE POSSIBILITY OF A PRIMARY SUPERNATURAL CAUSE

An important lesson that origin science learned from big bang cosmogony is that the principle of continuity does not apply to origin science either. Thus the universe may have a primary cause. For one cannot demand on purely scientific grounds that there is an endless series of physical causes. This is especially so in view of the scientific evidence which points to a beginning of the physical series of causes.

Further, the primary cause may be a supernatural cause. Science is based on the principle of causality: every event has an adequate cause. This means that the scientific evidence for the big bang leaves open the possibility of a primary cause of the origin of the cosmos. For the scientific evidence points to a beginning of the natural (space-time) world. And if every event needs an adequate cause, then it naturally suggests a primary cause of the beginning of the universe. As Jastrow put it, many scientists were surprised "by the discovery that the world had a beginning under conditions in which the known laws of physics are not valid, and as a product of forces or circumstances we cannot discover." Jastrow even went so far as to say "that there are what I or anyone would call supernatural forces at work is now, I think, a scientifically proven fact."

To be sure, not all scientists understand "supernatural" to mean a creator. Some simply look at it as a "mystery." Be that as it may, at least current theory in astronomy has opened the door for considering a possible primary cause of the origin of the universe. That is, it is conceivable in origin science to consider a primary cause that is beyond the physical universe and independent of it, and that produced singularities such as bringing the physical universe into existence. Despite his self-proclaimed agnosticism, even Jastrow acknowledges what he calls the "theistic" implications of his speculative scenario of origins. . . .

So in big-bang cosmogony there is a singularity for which it is valid to posit an unknown, unobserved primary force to account for it. Of course this scientific evidence for a beginning does not in itself make it necessary to conclude there is a primary cause of the material universe. One could simply posit that the material universe began, but without a cause. As Anthony Kenny put it, "According to the big bang theory, the whole matter of the universe began to exist at a particular time in the remote past. A proponent of such a theory, at least if he is an atheist, must believe that the matter of the universe came from nothing and by nothing."

Such a view would kill operation science as well as origin science, for it is inherently irrational to suppose events occur willy-nilly without a cause. In response we note that even Hume said, "I never asserted so absurd a proposition as that anything might arise without a cause." Likewise, Laplace believed it was absurd to assume "an event without a cause." Indeed the whole of modern science from Bacon on is based on the search for adequate causes of events.

So this well-established scientific practice of positing an adequate cause of an event leads to positing a cause of the beginning of the whole physical universe. Thus the big bang hypothesis in origin science illustrates that one can have a scientific approach to understanding singularities and discontinuities, and also that a primary cause is possible.

NOTE

1. Actually, discontinuity has always existed in the fossil record, as evolutionists from Darwin to Gould have acknowledged. . . . So in this sense the big bang cosmology is only the occasional cause which enables scientists to view anew what has always been there in the fossil record. The difference between evolutionist and creationist perspectives is a matter not of facts but of interpretation.

QUESTIONS FOR STUDY

1. According to the authors, how is origin science similar to the forensic investigation of a murder?

2. Define *operation science.*

3. What is the difference between a first or primary cause of origin science and the secondary causes of operation science?

4. How does a study of regular secondary causes lead the scientist to a unique original cause?

5. In what way does the Big Bang, the first effect of some unique and unknown primary cause, point to theism?

QUESTIONS FOR REFLECTION

1. Is it accurate to say that there are two kinds of science—"origin" and "operation"? Are the procedures used in forensic science, the study of criminal investigations, really different from the procedures of normal operation science?

2. If unique, irrepeatable causes are allowed in geology and biology as well as astronomy, is the door opened for literally any speculation on the reasons for natural events? How?

3. Does Big Bang cosmology require a supernatural or theistic first cause, or is it possible to understand the cause as purely natural—very big, to be sure, but nonetheless natural?

NETWORKING

Barbour (Part I), Gilkey, and Bube concur with the authors' views on *primary and secondary causation*. Other remarks on *method* may be found in Barbour (Part I), Schilling, Gilkey, and Popper.

COSMOLOGY AND THEOLOGY
JOHN ROBERT RUSSELL

Robert Russell is Associate Professor of Theology and Science in Residence at the Graduate Theological Union and the director for the Center for Theology and the Natural Sciences in Berkeley, California. With training in both the physical sciences and theology, he works to understand the implications of modern physics, including quantum mechanics and cosmology, for religious thought. Russell coedited and contributed to the recent anthology *Physics, Philosophy and Theology*.

In his special theory of relativity (1905), Einstein took the first step in establishing modern cosmology. In this theory, space and time are put on an equal mathematical footing, combined as a four-dimensional continuum called spacetime. Einstein's general theory of relativity (c. 1915) extends the notion of spacetime to include gravity. For Newton gravity was a force exerted between masses as they moved about in space. Einstein took a radically new approach in which particles follow curved paths of curved spacetime. What determines the curvature of spacetime? For this Einstein turned back to matter and created a "closed circuit" between the two great ideals of natural order: form and content. In Einstein's view, the structure of spacetime, its size, shape, and texture, is dependent on the distribution of matter, while the motion of matter is determined by the local curvature of spacetime. Hence spacetime itself is physical and contingent, no longer the absolute container of Newton or the unalterable category of Kant.

Given general relativity and Edwin Hubble's discovery in 1926 that light from distant galaxies is redshifted, and hence that galaxies are receding from us and from each other, we obtain the most staggering fact of twentieth century science: the age of the universe is finite and it is expanding from an initial singularity. Moreover its expansion is slowing down. Now the mathematics of Einstein's theory presents us with two types of dust models, both of which are expanding in time from a moment of zero size and infinite density when $t=0$ (where t is physical time). In the open model, a saddle-shaped surface expands forever, while in the closed model, a spherical-shaped surface expands up to a maximum size, then recontracts. If the closed model is correct, the slow-down will continue until the universe reaches a maximum size, after which contraction will begin until the universe is once again arbitrarily small some 50–100 billion years from now. If however the universe is open, as most evidence currently suggests, it will continue expanding forever, growing steadily colder and more dilute. . . .

In its doctrine of creation, theology has most often taken the position of distinguishing between God and the world in several ways: God is infinite, the world finite; God is eternal, the world, temporal; God is free, the world is dependent, and so on. With Einsteinian cosmology each of these questions needs to be reformulated and the theological language altered. We must ask again whether the universe is finite, what we are to make of the absolute beginning suggested by $t=0$, whether the universe is contingent or necessary, and what the universe will be like in the far future.

Let us take the question of origins and begin by restricting ourselves to standard Big Bang cosmology. This model of the universe gives little room for speculation for what could lie before the Big Bang, for $t<0$. Its equations as they currently stand cannot probe it. Yet, to many physicists, the embarrassing thing about modern cosmology is its inability to "eternalize" matter. All that is seems contingent on an initial starting point which itself is without physical precedent or cause, and which therefore seems outside of scientific study. Does this suggest that theology be enlisted as part of the explanatory agenda of science or that the "event" $t=0$ be assumed within a theological program?

We must be very cautious here. The June 1978 issue of *The New York Times* contained an article by NASA's Robert Jastrow entitled "Found God?", in which theologians were reportedly "delighted" that astronomical evidence "leads to a biblical view of Genesis." The article ends by describing the beleaguered scientist who, as in a bad dream, after scaling the highest peak of discovery finds a "band of theologians . . . (who) have been sitting there for centuries."

Though some theologians and clerics have taken encouragement from the Big Bang theory, it is well to keep in mind that *any* physical cosmology which science generates, including one without an initial singularity or a finite age (such as in Hoyle's steady state cosmology) might be equally compatible with the heart of the Christian creation tradition. There are philosophical and scientific grounds for caution, too. If the method of science is based on causal explanations, then in principle no scientific model could describe an uncaused first event. Hence "$t=0$" is not part of the physical picture but merely a description of the boundary of the physical model. Moreover, with a suitable redefinition of the time parameter, the age of the universe could appear infinite, as McMullin and Barbour have pointed out.

It is equally important to remember that scientific ideas themselves change, both at the immediate level of working models and at the longer-term level of broad interpretative paradigms. Newtonian cosmology gave way to Einsteinian, and the latter are being replaced by "inflationary" models which may take into account quantum effects—the physics of the microscopic which we discussed previously. Ironically, the effects of quantum gravity become critically important precisely at the initial moments of the universe, since then the size of the universe is microscopic and hence subject to indeterminacy. Some of these new cosmological models predict that the universe never contracts to zero size, but rather that it "bounces" and hence "oscillates" into another expansion *ad infinitum*. What would an infinitely old universe with an infinite set of oscillations in the future imply theologically?

Coupled to the issue of the age of the universe is the question of its size. Returning to the standard Big Bang cosmologies, we found that in the closed model the universe is finite in size. Since it also has a finite past and a finite future, as a *spacetime* model it can be classified as homogeneous or strictly finite. The open model, however, raises an intriguing paradox. In this model the universe is spatially infinite. However though its future is infinite, its past age is finite. Therefore as a *spacetime* model it is heterogeneous or mixed, displaying both finite and infinite characteristics. The occurrence of a heterogeneous model of the universe raises intriguing theological questions for the doctrine of creation. Still like the preceding discussion of time the details are highly model dependent, limiting its general relevance to theology. I expect that the fruitfulness of any of these sorts of questions will depend strongly on how such results in science, such as a heterogeneous model of the universe, are actively grafted into specific theological research programs.

That it should be pursued is underscored by Max Wildiers. In his book, *The Theologian and His Universe,* Wildiers warns those who would shrug their shoulders at efforts to relate science and religion. In his words, "It is at our peril that we neglect the invisible bond between cosmology and theology.". . . Fortunately, some of the leading research programs in theology today take contemporary cosmology seriously. J. Moltmann, writing on "Creation and Redemption," stresses that the universe is "open and in the process of being created." He urges theologians to "speak of creation not only at the beginning but also in history, at the end, and in relation to the totality of divine creative activity. . .". . .

How strong a correlation ought we to expect between creation theology and physical cosmology? According to Notre Dame philosopher Ernan McMullin, "what one *could* readily say . . . is that if the universe began in time through the act of a Creator, from our vantage point it would look something like the Big Bang that cosmologists are talking about. What one cannot say is, first, that the Christian doctrine of creation "supports" the Big Bang model, or second, that the Big Bang model "supports" the Christian doctrine of creation.". . .

Given McMullin's suggestions and the fundamental importance of a theology of creation to the project of science and religion, I expect that physical cosmology holds real promise for a new creative theological vision of God as "maker of heaven and earth."

QUESTIONS FOR STUDY

1. How did Einstein link space and time so that they mutually affect one another?

2. According to Russell, what is "the most staggering fact of twentieth century science"?

3. Describe both the 'closed model' of cosmic expansion and the 'open model'.

4. Does Russell encourage or discourage efforts to relate cosmology to theology?

QUESTIONS FOR REFLECTION

1. Explain Russell's claim that any physical cosmology may be equally compatable with the Christian creation tradition.

2. Geisler and Anderson claim that science sees no alternative to the universe created for the first and only time with the Big Bang event. Russell speaks, however, of the possibility of an oscillating universe. If he is correct, would origin science and its possible supernatural cause be weakened?

3. Do you agree with Russell's quote from McMullin that "if the universe began in time through the act of a Creator, from our vantage point it would look something like a Big Bang"?

NETWORKING

The other selections in this part deal with *God and the Big Bang*. See Gilkey for *Further Reservations on Theology Taking Comfort from the Discoveries of Science.*

A UNIVERSE BY DESIGN?

A GROWING GOD FREEMAN DYSON

Freeman Dyson is professor of physics at the Institute for Advanced Studies in Princeton University. Before coming to Princeton, the English-born scientist studied at Cornell. During World War II he conducted research for the Royal Air Force and later served as an arms-control consultant for the U.S. government. Dyson has written two books on science and society: *Disturbing the Universe* and *Infinite in all Directions,* from which this selection is taken.

Like the majority of scientists in this century, I have not concerned myself seriously with theology. Theology is a foreign language which we have not taken the trouble to learn. My personal theology is the theology of an amateur. But I did once have some help from a professional theologian in formulating my ideas in an intellectually coherent fashion. I happened to meet Charles Hartshorne at a meeting in Minnesota and we had a serious conversation. After we had talked for a while he informed me that my theological standpoint is Socinian. Socinus was an Italian heretic who lived in the sixteenth century. If I remember correctly what Hartshorne said, the main tenet of the Socinian heresy is that God is neither omniscient nor omnipotent. He learns and grows as the universe unfolds. I do not pretend to understand the theological subtleties to which this doctrine leads if one analyzes it in detail. I merely find it congenial, and consistent with scientific common sense. I do not make any clear distinction between mind and God. God is what mind becomes when it has passed beyond the scale of our comprehension. God may be considered to be either a world-soul or a collection of world-souls. We are the chief inlets of God on this planet at the present stage of his development. We may later grow with him as he grows, or we may be left behind. As Bernal said: "That may be an end or a beginning, but from here it is out of sight." If we are left behind, it is an end. If we keep growing, it is a beginning.

The great virtue of my version of the Socinian theology is that it leaves room at the top for diversity. Just as the greatness of the creation lies in its diversity, so does also the greatness of the creator. Many world-souls are better than one. When mind grows to fill the universe, it comes as a diversifier as well as a unifier.

Another theologian, with whom I have a more distant acquaintance, is St. Paul. St. Paul had some good things to say about diversity. "Now there are diversities of gifts, but the same spirit. And there are differences of administrations, but the same Lord. And there are diversities of operations, but it is the same God which worketh all in all." That passage from First Corinthians would make a good text for my sermon if I were preaching in church. But I am not preaching a Christian sermon. I am describing the universe as I encounter it in my life as a scientist and as a politically engaged citizen. I should not pretend to agree with St. Paul when in fact I find his point of view alien. For St. Paul, the diversity of the creation is less important than the unity of the creator. For me, it is the other way round. I do not know or particularly care whether the same God is working all in all. I care deeply for the diversity of his working. . . .

In the no-man's-land between science and theology, there are five specific points at which faith and reason may appear to clash. The five points are the origin of life, the human experience of free will, the prohibition of teleological explanations in science, the argument from design as an explanatory principle, and the question of ultimate aims. Each of these points could be the subject of a whole chapter, but fortunately I have only a few pages for all five. I will deal with each of them in turn as well as I can in a few lines.

First, the origin of life. This is not the most difficult problem from a philosophical point of view. Life in its earliest stages was little removed from ordinary chemistry. We can at least imagine life originating by ordinary processes which chemists know how to calculate. Much more serious problems for philosophy arise at a later stage with the development of mind and consciousness and language. As the physicist Wigner once said: "Where in the Schrödinger equation do you put the joy of being alive?" The problem with the origin of life is only this: How do you reconcile a theory which makes life originate by a process of chance with the doctrine that life is a part of God's plan for the universe? There are three possible answers to this question. Answer 1. Deny that God has a plan and say that everything is accidental. This is the answer of Jacques Monod, and of the majority of modern biologists. But then Wigner will ask: Is consciousness also an accident? Answer 2. Deny that chance exists and say that God knows how the dice will fall. This is the answer of Einstein, who believed that chance is a human concept arising from our ignorance of the exact working of nature. But then, why do statistical laws play such a fundamental role in physics, if chance is only a cover for our ignorance? Answer 3. Say that chance exists because God shares our ignorance. This is the answer of Hartshorne, the Socinian heresy. God is not omniscient. He grows with the universe and learns as it develops. Chance is a part of his plan. He uses it as we do to achieve his ends.

The second clash between faith and reason is the problem of free will. It was formulated most clearly by Schrödinger in the epilogue at the end of his little book *What Is Life?* The problem is to reconcile the direct human experience of free will with a belief in scientific causality. Here again we have the same three alternative answers to deal with the conflict. But now both narrow-minded science and narrow-minded theology stand opposed to free will. The Jacques Monod view of the universe as pure "Chance and Necessity" denies free will. The orthodox theology of an omniscient and omnipotent God also denies it. For those of us who would like to believe both in God and in free will, the Socinian answer is the best way out. The philosophical problems of chance and of free will are closely related. The Socinian theology deals with both together. Free will is the coupling of a human mind to otherwise random processes inside a brain. God's will is the coupling of a universal mind to otherwise random processes in the world at large.

My third problem is the problem of forbidden teleology, the conflict between human notions of purpose and the operational rules of science. Science does not accept Aristotelian styles of explanation, that a stone falls because its nature is earthy and so it likes to be on Earth, or that man's brain evolves because man's nature is to be intelligent. Within science, all causes must be local and instrumental. Purpose is not acceptable as an explanation of scientific phenomena. Action at a distance, either in space or time, is forbidden. Especially, teleological influences of final goals upon phenomena are forbidden. How do we reconcile this prohibition with our human experience of purpose and with our faith in a universal purpose? I make the reconciliation possible by restricting the scope of science. The choice of laws of nature, and the choice of initial conditions for the universe, are questions belonging to meta-science and not to science. Science is restricted to the explanation of phenomena within the universe. Teleology is not forbidden when explanations go beyond science into meta-science.

The most familiar example of a meta-scientific explanation is the so-called Anthropic Principle. The Anthropic Principle says that laws of nature are explained if it can be established that they must be as they are in order to allow the existence of theoretical physicists to speculate about them. We know that theoretical physicists exist: ergo, the laws of nature must be such as to allow their existence. This mode of explanation is frankly teleological. It leads to non-trivial consequences, restrictions on the possible building blocks of the universe, which I have no space to discuss in detail. Many scientists dislike the Anthropic Principle because it seems to be a throwback to a pre-Copernican, Aristotelian style of reasoning. It seems to imply an anthropocentric view of the cosmos. Whether you like the Anthropic Principle or not is a matter of taste. I personally find it illuminating. It accords with the spirit of modern science that we have two complementary styles of explanation, the teleological style allowing a role for purpose in the universe at large, and the non-teleological style excluding purpose from phenomena within the strict jurisdiction of science.

The argument from design is the fourth on my short list of philosophical problems. The argument was one of the classic proofs of the existence of God. The existence of a watch implies the existence of a watchmaker. This argument was at the heart of the battle between creationists and evolutionists in nineteenth-century biology. The evolutionists won the battle. Random genetic variations plus Darwinian selection were shown to be sufficient causes of biological evolution. The argument from design was excluded from science because it makes use of teleological causes. For a hundred years the biologists have been zealously stamping out all attempts to revive the old creationist doctrines. Nevertheless, the argument from design still has some merit as a philosophical principle. I propose that we allow the argument from design the same status as the Anthropic Principle, expelled from science but tolerated in meta-science.

The argument from design is a theological and not a scientific argument. It is a mistake to try to squeeze theology into the mold of science. I consider the argument from design to be valid in the following sense. The universe shows evidence of the operations of mind on three levels. The first level is the level of elementary physical processes in quantum mechanics. Matter in quantum mechanics is not an inert substance but an active agent, constantly making choices between alternative possibilities according to probabilistic laws. Every quantum experiment forces nature to make choices. It appears that mind, as manifested by the capacity to make choices, is to some extent inherent in every electron. The second level at which we detect the operations of mind is the level of direct human experience. Our brains appear to be devices for the amplification of the mental component of the quantum choices made by molecules inside our heads. We are the second big step in the development of mind. Now comes the argument from design. There is evidence from peculiar features of the laws of nature that the universe as a whole is hospitable to the growth of mind. The argument here is merely an extension of the Anthropic Principle up to a universal scale. Therefore it is reasonable to believe in the existence of a third level of mind, a mental component of the universe. If we believe in this mental component and call it God, then we can say that we are small pieces of God's mental apparatus.

The last of the five philosophical problems is the problem of final aims. The problem here is to try to formulate some statement of the ultimate purpose of the universe. In other words, the problem is to read God's mind. Previous attempts to read God's mind have not been notably successful. One of the more penetrating of such attempts is recorded in the Book of Job. God's answer to Job out of the whirlwind was not encouraging. Nevertheless I stand in good company when I ask again the questions Job asked. Why do we suffer? Why is the world so unjust? What is the purpose of pain and tragedy? I would like to have answers to these questions, answers which are valid at our childish level of understanding even if they do not penetrate far into the mind of God. My answers are based on a hypothesis which is an extension both of the Anthropic Principle and of the argument from design. The hypothesis is that the universe is constructed according to a principle of maximum diversity. The principle of maximum diversity operates both at the physical and at the mental level. It says that the laws of nature and the initial conditions are such as to make the universe as interesting as possible. As a result, life is possible but not too easy. Always when things are dull, something new turns up to challenge us and to stop us from settling into a rut. Examples of things which make life difficult are all around us: comet impacts, ice ages, weapons, plagues, nuclear fission, computers, sex, sin and death. Not all challenges can be overcome, and so we have tragedy. Maximum diversity often leads to maximum stress. In the end we survive, but only by the skin of our teeth.

The expansion of life and of mankind into the universe will lead to a vast diversification of ecologies and of cultures. As in the past, so in the future, the extension of our living space will bring opportunities for tragedy as well as achievement. To this process of growth and diversification I see no end. It is useless for us to try to imagine the varieties of experience, physical and intellectual and religious, to which mankind may attain. To describe the metamorphosis of mankind as we embark on our immense journey into the universe, I return to the humble image of the butterfly. All that can be said was said long ago by Dante in Canto 10 of the *Purgatorio:*

> *O you proud Christians, wretched souls and small,*
> *Who by the dim lights of your twisted minds*
> *Believe you prosper even as you fall,*
> *Can you not see that we are worms, each one*
> *Born to become the angelic butterfly*
> *That flies defenseless to the judgment Throne?*

QUESTIONS FOR STUDY

1. Who was Socinus? What were his ideas? Why were they declared heretical?

2. What is the main problem with the origin of life as it refers to faith and reason? What are the three possible solutions?

3. Why is teleology forbidden in science?

4. What is Dyson's description of the Anthropic Principle?

5. Describe the author's three levels of mind. In which level would you place the mind of God?

6. What is the principle of maximum diversity?

QUESTIONS FOR REFLECTION

1. How does the idea of a limited God solve the problem of chance for Dyson?

2. In what sense did traditional science, with its idea of the laws of nature, and traditional theology, with its idea that God directs all events, team up to cancel out free human will? Were the two ideas compatible?

3. The faith of science includes the proposition that the universe is intelligible. How does Dyson see this proposition as evidence for the Anthropic Principle?

4. How is the claim that the universe has a final aim serve as a possible response to the problem of the existence of suffering and evil? Is it an adequate response? What is the relevance of the quotation from Dante?

NETWORKING

For a detailed account of *process thought,* see Barbour (Part I) and Cobb. Polkinghorne is the other author who explores *points of conflict between science and religion,* although Gilkey also clearly distinguishes several ways in which the two enterprises differ significantly on the notion of *theory.* For *natural theology,* see Barbour (Part I), Lackey, Updike, and Polkinghorne.

LIFE AND MIND IN THE UNIVERSE
GEORGE WALD

George Wald is the Emeritus Professor of Biology at Harvard University. He received the Nobel Prize in physiology in 1967 for his work in the biochemistry of vision. Dr. Wald has long been interested in the place of mind in cosmology. These reflections were given as the keynote address for a conference in creativity, science, and society held in Honolulu, Hawaii, in 1985.

We find ourselves in a peculiarly life-breeding universe. If any one of a considerable number of the physical properties of our universe that we know were other than it is, then this universe might exist, might be stable, but life would have become impossible in it, here or anywhere.

This universe is made of four so-called elementary particles—protons, electrons, neutrons, and photons—which are particles of radiation. I neglect the neutrinos; they do not interest us here since they do not interact with matter. The only gloss one need make to such a simple statement is that the first three of those particles, the protons, electrons, and neutrons, exist also as anti-particles, the particles constituting matter, the anti-particles constituting anti-matter.

As we look quite far out into this universe we cannot as yet be wholly sure that what we are seeing is matter rather than anti-matter. All our observations are made with photons, with radiation, and photons don't care. They don't discriminate. They are, as we say, their own anti-particles.

About thirty years ago, I was giving the Vanuxem Lectures at Princeton, and Albert Einstein was so good as to come. We walked up and down the street chatting before the first lecture. He turned to me and said, "Why do you think that all the natural amino acids are left handed?"

For those of you who don't know about these amino acids, they can come in two shapes that are mirror images of each other, left (L-) and right-handed (D-). All the natural ones are left-handed (L-).

I had my mind on the coming lecture and just mumbled something.

Then he said, "You know, I've wondered for many years how the electron came out to be negative. Negative, positive, those are perfectly symmetrical concepts. So why is the electron negative? I've thought about this a long time and all I can think at last is, it won in the fight."

I said, "That's exactly what I think about these L-amino acids. They won in the fight."

The fight that Einstein was talking about was the fight between matter and anti-matter. And now I must tell you the first of many strange things.

A few years ago at the Bell Laboratories in New Jersey, two men, Penzias and Wilson, discovered a radiation that had not been known before though there had been some prediction that it would exist. It was a very cold radiation, radiation that represents something less than three degrees above absolute zero. It permeates the universe. It comes from all directions and goes to all directions. It is the fundamental radiation that travels in this universe, and it turns out that there are a billion times as many photons in that radiation as there are particles that we call matter. The matter is only one part in a billion of that radiation. The nicest thought is this: as Einstein said, positive and negative are perfectly symmetrical. So matter and anti-matter are perfectly symmetrical. The neatest idea would be that if one were going to start a universe in the Big Bang, one would start it with exactly equal amounts of matter and anti-matter. Of course, the big principle is that if matter makes contact with anti-matter they mutually annihilate one another and come out as radiation. In that primitive fireball of the Big Bang, with the matter and anti-matter all packed together, there must have been a fantastic explosion of mutual annihilation, and all that should have come out at the end is radiation. But the idea we have is that there was a little mistake in the equality, of one part in one billion. And when all the mutual annihilation had finished, one part in one billion remained, and that's the matter of this universe.

Now I am going to just sample what is a longer argument, and to give the sampling some structure I shall meanwhile climb up the scale of states of organization of matter. So I'll begin with the elementary particles.

I want to say two things about protons, neutrons, and electrons. First—their masses. The nuclei of all atoms are made of protons and neutrons. These are both almost two thousand times the mass of the electron: 1,845 when I last looked. The five is uncertain. So almost two thousand times. The result is that the nucleus of an atom is so much heavier than those electrons weaving around it that its motions are not at all disturbed by whatever the electrons are doing. So an atom can take and hold a position. The position of an atom is the position of its nucleus regardless of what its electrons are doing, and it's only for that reason that we can have solid matter in the universe. If those particles that made up the atoms were anything nearer in mass, whether both heavy or both light, they'd revolve around each other. Nothing would stay put, nothing would be fixed. One couldn't have crystals. It's doubtful whether one could even have chemical combinations, surely not the big molecules that are the heart of our own construction.

I want to say something also about the charges on these particles. The electron and the proton—the proton, of course, plus-charged, the electron minus-charged (and so unlike in mass and every other regard) have exactly numerically equal charges. That is, the proton is exactly as plus as the electron is minus. How come?

It will help you to accept this as a legitimate question if I tell you that two of the most distinguished astro-physicists we have, R. A. Lyttleton and Herman Bondi, both in London, in 1959 published a long paper in the *Proceedings* of the Royal Society of London, proposing that, in fact, the proton and the neutron differ in charge by the infinitesimal amount: $2 \times 10^{-18}e$, where e is the tiny charge on either the proton or the electron. Two times ten to the minus eighteenth: that's two billion billionths. Your first thought is, Who gives a damn? But they explain that with that almost infinitesimal difference in charge, all the matter in the universe would be electrically charged, and in the same sense plus or minus; and since like charges repel, all the matter in the universe would repel all the other matter. So the universe would expand, as all of us believe that it is doing. The only trouble is that as far as I can see (and I've corresponded with both these gentlemen) it wouldn't do anything else. It would expand, yes, but nothing else. And even that almost infinitesimal difference in charge would be enough to overwhelm all the forces of gravitation that bring matter together in our universe. So we would have no galaxies, no stars, no planets, and worst of all, no physicists.

Let me go a step up to atoms, to elements. Of the ninety-two natural elements, ninety-nine percent of the living material we know is made of just four: hydrogen, oxygen, nitrogen, and carbon. Why? Those four elements possess absolutely unique properties not repeated by any other elements in the Periodic System of the elements. And those happen to be the properties on which the existence of life depends.

Biology professors tell their students foolish things, which the students carefully learn and reproduce on exams and eventually teach the next generation. Chemistry professors do that too. When one teaches the Periodic System of elements, one has those horizontal periods of the elements and the professors say, "If you go down vertically, the elements repeat their same properties." That's just utter nonsense, as any kid with a chemistry set would know. For under oxygen comes sulfur. Try breathing sulfur sometime. Under nitrogen comes phosphorus. There isn't any phosphorus in that kid's chemistry set. It's too dangerous. It bursts into flame spontaneously on exposure to air. And under carbon comes silicon.

If that chemistry professor were talking sense, two molecules should be very much alike: carbon dioxide, CO_2, and silicon dioxide, SiO_2. Well, in carbon dioxide the central carbon atom is attached to both of the oxygens by double chemical bonds: $O=C=O$. Those double bonds completely saturate the combining tendencies of all three atoms; so carbon dioxide is a fine, happy, independent molecule. It goes off into the air as a gas and dissolves in all the waters of the earth; and those are the places where living organisms ultimately find their carbon. But silicon (I was never taught this by my chemistry professors but found it in a book many years later, so perhaps if you've studied chemistry you haven't been taught this either) *cannot form a double bond*. Out of all the ninety-two natural elements, only carbon, nitrogen, and oxygen have the regular habit of forming multiple chemical bonds. Silicon cannot form a double bond as carbon does, so silicon is tied to those two oxygens next to it by single bonds, O-Si-O, leaving two half-formed bonds on the silicon and one on each of the oxygens, just dying to combine with something. What are they going to combine with? Nothing other than the next silicon dioxide, and that with the next, and that with the next, and on and on, until you end up with a rock. That's exactly what quartz is. It's silicon dioxides bound to one another to form a great super-molecule that is a quartz crystal. The reason quartz is so hard is that to break quartz you have to break numerous chemical bonds. And that is why silicon is great for making rocks, but if you want to make living organisms you have to use carbon. I could make a parallel argument for oxygen and nitrogen.

Let's go up a step, to molecules. By far the most essential molecule to life is water. No water, no life anywhere in the universe. And water is the strangest molecule in the whole of chemistry. Its strangest property is that ice floats; and if ice did not float, I doubt that there would be life in the universe.

You know that everything contracts on cooling. That's how we make thermometers; a bit of red-dyed alcohol, mercury if you can afford it, put in a capillary tube contracts on cooling, and you read the temperature. Everything does this. So does water, down to four degrees centigrade. But between four degrees centigrade and zero, where it freezes, it expands so rapidly that the ice that forms is lighter than liquid water, and it floats.

Just think what it would be like if water were like everything else—because practically nothing else does this. It's crazy. If water were more regular and just kept contracting as it cooled, that denser, contracted water would keep sinking to the bottom. Freezing, instead of beginning at the top as now, would begin at the bottom, and it would end by freezing the water all the way through. A really big lump of ice takes forever to melt. That would be the end of life on any planet in the universe if it happened once in a million years; and that would also mean a good chance that life would not develop on planets where life had not yet formed.

In my region of the United States, New England, the fishermen wait all winter for the ponds to freeze over. That's the best time to go fishing. They take their fishing equipment in one hand, a bottle of whiskey in the other, and cut themselves a round hole in the ice. Up to that point the fish were getting along fine. These creatures live through winter with no trouble at all. As soon as the warm weather comes, that skin of ice on the surface melts and with that everything's free again.

Let's go a step up, to planets. What does it take for a planet to be suitable for life? Well, it wants to be about the right temperature, about the right size, and to receive the right kind and amount of radiation from its sun. What's the size condition about? Well, you see, it's only the mass of a planet that by gravitation holds an atmosphere. Our planet is big enough, massy enough, to hold the gases of our atmosphere; though it started with lots of hydrogen, ammonia, and methane, lighter gases, which the Earth wasn't massy enough to hold. They leaked away long ago. It's only the rather heavier gases that even the Earth can hold. Mars is too small to hold an atmosphere. You didn't have to spend all that money, my fellow Americans, to find out that there is no life on Mars. There couldn't be any life on Mars. There is no life on Jupiter. Why? Because it's too heavy. It's so heavy that most of Jupiter is a solid atmosphere, and life is difficult in a solid atmosphere.

How about temperature? Life can tolerate any range of temperature that allows water to remain liquid. No liquid water, no life, as I've told you. As for the radiation, that's an interesting story too. But we won't go into that much, except that I will tell you in passing that for a long time on this planet, living things had to stay under water, because the radiation from the sun contains ultraviolet radiation that's killing. Not only would it kill all living organisms, it kills the really big molecules, the proteins and nucleic acids. But later in its evolution, life developed the process of photosynthesis in green plants, which produces as a by-product, oxygen. I don't know if all of you realize it, but all of the oxygen in our atmosphere was produced by green plants and is kept in the atmosphere only by green plants. Twenty-five miles up, the radiation from the sun turns some of that oxygen into ozone, which forms a layer that won't let the hard, killing, ultraviolet light through. Then life could emerge from under water and occupy the earth and air. The moral of what I've told you about planets is that the overwhelming probability is that any solar system in the universe will have only one planet that fulfills the conditions that support life. In our solar system, ours is that planet. One planet per solar system. There is a faint possibility that here and there two planets might satisfy those conditions, but in general just one.

And now, another step up, to stars. What does it take in a star to have a planet that supports life?

First, its mass. Our sun is just an ordinary run-of-the-mill middle-aged star. It has existed for five or six billion years and, barring accidents, has another five or six billion years to run. But a star twice the mass of the sun would stay put on what we call the Main Sequence (and only Main Sequence stars can have planets that bear life) only about two billion years. It took nearly two billion years for life to form upon the earth. So any star much massier than the sun would probably never have a planet bearing life, no matter what the other circumstances. A star half the mass of the sun would stay on the Main Sequence some forty billion years, instead of the . . . paltry ten to twelve billion that we're going to get out of our sun.

Finally, there is a cosmic condition. And these things (I hope you understand what I'm saying, and I'm just sampling them very briefly and in a very elementary way), these are very strange things. And I'm about to tell you one of the strangest.

You see, we live in an expanding universe. Everyone has pretty well agreed to that. But there are two forces at work in it. One is the force of expansion, dispersion; the other is the force of gravitation. The force of expansion is powered by the Big Bang. It pushes matter apart after that great explosion, in the midst of which we are still living. The force of gravitation brings matter together, and these two forces are both at work in our universe. If gravitation dominated our universe, after the Big Bang the expansion would come to an end, the matter would begin to fall together again, perhaps ready for the next Big Bang. There wouldn't be *time* for life to arise and evolve. If dispersion dominated the situation, then all the matter would be flying apart ever since the Big Bang, and there'd be no galaxies, stars, or planets. There'd be no *place* for life. We live in a universe in which it's just very lately been realized that those two forces are in exact balance, so that the universe as a whole is expanding wherever one looks, so everything very distant is going away from us. But locally, there are so-called local groups and clusters, where whole clusters of galaxies are held together by gravitation.

For example, our own galaxy, the Milky Way, has a sister galaxy, Andromeda. It's called by astronomers M-31. It's very much like our galaxy but a little smaller. There is also a still smaller galaxy, all part of our smallish local group.

All of you have probably heard that the reason we believe that the universe is expanding is because of the so-called "red shift." The further one looks out into space, the redder the light is, compared to the same sources here on earth. This is believed to be an expression of the so-called Doppler Effect and would mean that the further one looks out from us, the faster distant astronomical bodies are leaving, in all directions. But the first such color shift ever to be discovered, by the astronomer Slipher back in 1912, was not a red shift, but a *blue* shift. Slipher was looking at our sister galaxy Andromeda; he observed a blue shift because Andromeda isn't going away from us, it's coming *towards us* at something like a hundred miles a second. So we find ourselves in a universe in which these forces are in exact balance. And hence, though at large distances everything is uniformly going away, locally large bodies, whole galaxies, are held together by gravitation. That's very strange because those forces could take any value, but they take this exactly equal value.

So to summarize, we find ourselves in a very curious universe. It possesses exactly those properties that breed life. It takes no great imagination or intelligence to dream up any number of other universes that could be perfectly good, stable universes, but lifeless. With so many options, how did it come about that our universe has turned out this way? From our self-centered point of view, that's the best way to make a universe. But I want to know, how did the universe find that *out?*

QUESTIONS FOR STUDY

1. Wald describes a series of improbable occurrences in the history of the cosmos. What is his point?

2. Make a chart listing each of Wald's stages or critical events in cosmic evolution and the unexpected property or event of that stage that moved evolution along.

3. What is the significance of the unique fact that ice has a density less than water, its liquid state?

QUESTIONS FOR REFLECTION

1. Is Wald arguing for supernatural intervention in natural processes?

2. Wald's version of the Anthropic Principle concludes that, despite incredible odds, the universe evolved to create conscious and intelligent beings. Is this a valid conclusion, or would any possible universe, even one barren and devoid of life, qualify as equally improbable?

NETWORKING

General issues in *teleology and design* may be found in Bube, Dyson, Updike, Barbour (Parts I and V), Gish, Asimov, Teilhard, Peacocke, and Lovelock. *The Anthropic Principle* is a subject for Barbour (Part I), Dyson, and Feinberg and Shapiro, Updike, and Polkingborne. *Chance and necessity* are discussed in Barbour (Part I), Peacocke, and Polkinghorne.

A PUDDLIAN FABLE
GERALD FEINBERG AND ROBERT SHAPIRO

Gerald Feinberg is a professor of physics at Columbia University, where he conducts research primarily in subparticle physics. He is also the author of *Solid Clues* and coeditor of *Cosmological Constants*. Robert Shapiro is a professor of chemistry at New York University where he performs cancer research. He has two recent books: *Origin: A Skeptic's Guide to the Creation of Life on Earth* and *The Human Blueprint*. This selection is reprinted from *Life Beyond Earth*.

The members of the Little Puddlian Philosophical Society were engaged in a debate about the possibility of life outside of Little Puddle. The chief advocate of the unrivaled fitness of their own environment for life, a medium-sized male rotifer named Philo, was speaking. This he accomplished by wriggling three of his many cilia, producing sound waves in the water of Little Puddle.

"It is obvious that life is impossible outside the confines of Little Puddle. The environment we inhabit is optimally designed for life. Its water remains at about the same temperature at all times, whereas even a small change would be lethal to us. The balance of acidity and alkalinity is exactly right for living things because of the small amounts of nitrates and phosphates dissolved in the water. The mud at the bottom of the Puddle contains just the right amount of sulfate to furnish an essential element of our metabolism. There are periodic infusions of liquid into Little Puddle containing small amounts of dissolved carbon compounds which we use in constructing our bodies. Furthermore, the lower forms of life that inhabit our Puddle and form the basis of our food supply also depend on these same conditions. How could the beneficial methane-producing bacteria exist without the mud that shields them from the outer oxygen and gives them the raw materials for their metabolism? Where would the algae that live on the surface of Little Puddle go if the Puddle were much greater in extent, so that the surface was much farther from the mud-cushioned bottom? There may be other environments in the Universe, but it is impossible to imagine any form of life that could be adapted to the differences that exist between them and Little Puddle.

"We rotifers are so well adapted to Little Puddle," he continued, "that in any environment which did not possess all of the same qualities in exactly these proper amounts, rotiferian life could not exist. Since we are an essential part of the ecology of Little Puddle, if we could not survive in another environment, neither could the whole Puddlian biosphere.

"The conclusion is inescapable," he stated with finality. "Life is only possible in Little Puddle, or in other identical Puddles. The rest of the Universe is barren."

Another rotifer rose to second Philo and extend his argument.

"Since that is so," said the second, "it must be that the whole Universe is designed to ensure the existence of our home. Were there no depression in the surrounding rock, Little Puddle would not have formed, and we would not be here to appreciate it. If water were to freeze at a slightly higher temperature, Little Puddle would ice over and the nutrient rain that fructifies it could not get down to us. By using a new idea that I call the 'rotiferic principle', I can demonstrate that the laws of nature must be exactly what they are and no different. Otherwise there would be no rotifers here to know about them. For example, if the heat necessary to vaporize water were slightly lower, then after the Big Rain created it, Little Puddle would have evaporated before the many hours that were needed for the first generation of rotifers to emerge from their eggs.

"So," he concluded, "but for the providentially high value of the heat of vaporization of water, the Universe would be empty of any life that could philosophize about it."

The listeners applauded this dazzling display of the power of rotifer reasoning, as did all the other inhabitants of Little Puddle, with the exception of a few insects on its surface who had seen some of their fellows eaten by a passing frog. Meanwhile, outside of Little Puddle, 10^{30} living beings followed their life-styles in a variety of Earth environments, oblivious to the rotifers' proofs of their nonexistence.

QUESTIONS FOR STUDY

1. What point is Philo, the rotifer philosopher, attempting to establish in his discussion about the environment of Little Puddle?

2. Where in the fable is the argument from design introduced?

QUESTIONS FOR REFLECTION

1. Compare the arguments for the 'rotiferian principle' with Wald's version of the Anthropic Principle. Do the points match?

2. One intention of satire is to expose the absurdity of a position by exaggeration. Does this fable qualify as satire? Why is the rotifer society chosen for this story?

3. Is it necessary to deny the existence of other life forms in order to accept the Anthropic (or 'rotiferian') Principle?

NETWORKING

For *teleology and design,* see Bube, Dyson, Updike, Barbour, Asimov, Peacocke, and Lovelock. In defense of the *Anthropic Principle,* see Barbour, Dyson, Updike, and Polkinghorne. *Human life and aim of the cosmos* is discussed in both Wald and Teilhard.

ROGER'S VERSION   JOHN UPDIKE

John Updike is one of the most renowned novelists in contemporary American literature. He has written over a dozen novels, several of which have been best sellers. Other
works include collections of short fiction and four volumes of poetry.

Dale described to the committee, as he had to me, the remarkable unlikelihood of the
extremely delicate balance of fundamental forces evidently struck in the instant of the
Big Bang, a balance of forces which alone could have produced a universe sustained
and stable enough to evolve life and, in the case of our planet's leading primates, consciousness, abstract thinking, and morality.

The committee listened in shadowy silence, beneath the flickering bright feet.
When Dale got a little lost in the relation of the strong force to deuterium production
and thence to nuclear reaction, Jeremy Vanderluyten, out of conversational mercy,
cleared his throat and with his elegant and grave elocution observed, "That's all of indubitable interest, Mr. Kohler, but—correct me if I'm wrong—these figures have been on
the table quite a few years now. Cosmologies change, and I expect have changed not for
the last time. What strikes *me,* if I may interject, is the manner in which our ethical and
religious concerns persist no matter what the prevailing cosmology. Think of the eighteenth century and how convinced its scientists were that mechanistic materialism had
all the answers. The universe was like a wound-up watch, they said, and Newtonian
physics was deemed airtight. Yet what happened within the Judaeo-Christian faith?
Pietism, and the Wesley revival, and the great missionary surge to every part of the
globe. Look at the young people today, when the so-called death of God has been certi-
fied over and over: the most religious generation in a century, and all out of inner
imperatives." The black man laid his hand across his rep necktie, and his iron face,
deeply creased, seemed on the verge of smiling. "The stars alone won't do it; it's the
stars *plus.* Plus ethics. Do you remember what Kant said?"

"*Der bestirnte Himmel über mir,*" Jeremy pronounced in ringing tones, "*und das
moralische Gesetz in mir.* 'The starry heavens over me,'" he obligingly translated, holding up a lengthy forefinger, then tapping his necktie, "'and the moral law within me.'
The two things together, you see."

"I see, of course," poor Dale said, impatient in his fatigue, and out of his field. "It's
just that people should *know,* you see, that the universe has these kinks, these telltale
signs, so the moral impulse and our will to believe have a place to grab hold, if you follow me."

"We follow you, Mr. Kohler," Rebecca Abrams said tartly. "We're here to follow
you. So where else are you leading?". . .

. . . "I'd like to see religion get away from all this hiding inside the human, this sort
of cowardly appeal to so-called subjective reality—to wishful thinking, in a way. What

I'm trying to offer, since you ask me what I'm trying to offer, is what science is trying to tell us, objectively, in its numbers, since the scientists themselves don't want to, they want to stay out of it, they want to stay pure. There are these numerical coincidences," he explained, and he told the committee about ten to the fortieth power, how it recurs in widely varied contexts, from the number of charged particles in the observable universe to the ratio of electrical force to gravitational, not to mention the ratio between the age of the universe and the time it takes light to travel across a proton. He tried to explain the remarkable coincidence whereby the difference between the masses of the neutron and the proton almost equals the mass of the electron, and furthermore whereby this difference times the speed of light squared equals the temperature at which protons and neutrons cease transmuting into one another and the numbers of both in the universe are frozen. Equally marvellous, to him, was another equation, which showed how the temperature at which matter decoupled from radiation equalled that at which the energy density of photons equalled that of matter, mainly protons. Also, the element carbon, so crucial to the forms of life, is synthesized in stars through an extraordinary set of nuclear resonances that apparently just happen—. . .

"Mah friend," Ed Snea pronounced, as if calling a jabbering lawn party to order, "what do these interrelations between these numbers *mean?* Aren't you adding apples and oranges, as they say, and then dividing by grapefruit?"

"These aren't just numbers, they are the basic physical constants," Dale told him. "These are the terms of Creation."

"Oh I *like* that," Rebecca gushed. She was, I realized, Dale's first ally on the committee, and he realized it too.

He turned his head to face her, one on one. "These numbers," he said intently, with an almost paternal earnestness and yearning for understanding, as the feet flickered over her head, "are the words in which God has chosen to speak. He could have chosen a whole other set, ma'am, but He chose these. Maybe our measurements are still imperfect, maybe my transformations weren't the most intelligent. . . . I was getting so tired, and nervous because of this meeting today; there might be a differential equation that would yield something definitive, I just don't know. But there has to be something here, if anywhere. . . ."

Closson cleared his throat once more and turned his big overstuffed box of a head toward me. "Roger, do you have any insights or thoughts you'd like to share with us before we excuse Mr. Kohler?" One of his cover-over strands had come unstuck and waved out from the side of his head like an inquisitive antenna.

It shocked me, to be called out of my apartness, my existence as purely a shadow. "You know me, Jesse," I said, with a false jocosity that barked in my own ears. "A Barthian all the way. Barth, I fear, would have regarded Dale's project as the most futile and insolent sort of natural theology. I also agree with Jere: apologetics mustn't leave ground where it's somewhat safe for ground where religion has been made to look ridiculous time and time again. Like Rebecca, I don't think God should be reduced purely to human subjectivity; but His objectivity must be of a totally other sort than that of these physical equations. Even if this were not so, there are additional problems with provability. Wouldn't a God Who let Himself be proven—more exactly, a God Who can't *help* being proven—be too submissive, too passive and beholden to human ingenuity, a helpless and contingent God, in short? I also see a problem with His facticity, as it would be demonstrated to us. We all know, as teachers, what happens to facts: they get ignored, forgotten. Facts are *boring*. Facts are inert, impersonal. A god Who is a mere fact will just sit there on the table with all the other facts: we can take Him or leave Him. The way it is, we are always in motion *toward* the God Who flees, the *Deus absconditus;* He by His apparent absence is always with us. What is being proposed here for us to finance, I'm sorry, just strikes me as a kind of obscene cosmological prying that has little to do with religion as I understand it. As Barth himself says somewhere—I can't give you the exact reference offhand—'What manner of God is He Who has to be proved?'"

QUESTIONS FOR STUDY

1. What point is Dale Kohler attempting to make with all of his references to the apparent correspondences between numerical constants of physical relationships in the cosmos?

2. How does the committee member, Jeremy Vanderluyten, argue against Dale's proposal?

3. According to Dale, what language does God use when he speaks through Creation?

QUESTIONS FOR REFLECTION

1. Johanne Kepler, an early pioneer of science, said that, in his efforts to discover the mathematical patterns of the planets in their orbits, he was "thinking God's thoughts after Him." How is Kepler's sentiment echoed in Dale's proposal?

2. In his final rejection of Dale's idea, Roger introduces the German theologian Karl Barth. Examine Barth's basic thought to better understand how Roger could appeal to him in support of the conclusion that Dale's project is "futile and insolent." See Suggestions for Further Reading.

3. According to Roger, why is it a virtue for God to be hidden from the prying eyes of science? Do you agree? Does this render any attempt to argue for God's existence from scientific evidence a futile exercise? See John Hick in Part III for further comments.

NETWORKING

Barbour (Part I), Bube, Dyson, and Polkinghorne are more positive in their appraisal of *natural theology*. For background on the *theology of the neo-orthodox theologian Karl Barth,* see Barbour (Part I).

MICROCOSMOS
BEYOND LANGUAGE   FRITJOF CAPRA

Fritjof Capra is a nuclear physicist with a Ph.D. from the University of Vienna. His fame did not come from physics, however, but rather in the integration of physics and Eastern mysticism and in his efforts to shape a world view for the twenty-first century. Capra's most famous book, *The Tao of Physics,* addresses the first topic, and his *Turning Point* addresses the second. He is presently director of the Elmwood Institute in Berkeley, California.

The contradiction so puzzling to the ordinary way of thinking comes from the fact that we have to use language to communicate our inner experience which in its very nature transcends linguistics.

D.T. Suzuki

The problems of language here are really serious. We wish to speak in some way about the structure of the atoms. . . . But we cannot speak about atoms in ordinary language.

W. Heisenberg

The notion that all scientific models and theories are approximate and that their verbal interpretations always suffer from the inaccuracy of our language was already commonly accepted by scientists at the beginning of this century, when a new and completely unexpected development took place. The study of the world of atoms forced physicists to realize that our common language is not only inaccurate, but totally inadequate to describe the atomic and subatomic reality. Quantum theory and relativity theory, the two bases of modern physics, have made it clear that this reality transcends classical logic and that we cannot talk about it in ordinary language. Thus Heisenberg writes:

> The most difficult problem . . . concerning the use of the language arises in quantum theory. Here we have at first no simple guide for correlating the mathematical symbols with concepts of ordinary language; and the only thing we know from the start is the fact that our common concepts cannot be applied to the structure of the atoms.

From a philosophical point of view, this has certainly been the most interesting development in modern physics, and here lies one of the roots of its relation to Eastern philosophy. In the schools of Western philosophy, logic and reasoning have always been the main tools used to formulate philosophical ideas and this is true, according to Bertrand Russell, even of religious philosophies. In Eastern mysticism, on the other hand, it has always been realized that reality transcends ordinary language, and the sages of the East were not afraid to go beyond logic and common concepts. This is the main reason, I think, why their models of reality constitute a more appropriate philosophical background to modern physics than the models of Western philosophy.

The problem of language encountered by the Eastern mystic is exactly the same as the problem the modern physicist faces. In the two passages quoted at the beginning of this chapter, D. T. Suzuki speaks about Buddhism and Werner Heisenberg speaks about atomic physics, and yet the two passages are almost identical. Both the physicist and the mystic want to communicate their knowledge, and when they do so with words their statements are paradoxical and full of logical contradictions. These paradoxes are characteristic of all mysticism, from Heraclitus to Don Juan, and since the beginning of this century they are also characteristic of physics.

In atomic physics, many of the paradoxical situations are connected with the dual nature of light or—more generally—of electromagnetic radiation. On the one hand, it is clear that this radiation must consist of waves because it produces the well-known interference phenomena associated with waves: when there are two sources of light, the intensity of the light to be found at some other place will not necessarily be just the sum of that which comes from the two sources, but may be more or less. This can easily be explained by the interference of the waves emanating from the two sources: in those places where two crests coincide, we shall have more light than the sum of the two; where a crest and a trough coincide, we shall have less. The precise amount of interference can easily be calculated. Interference phenomena of this kind can be observed whenever one deals with electromagnetic radiation, and force us to conclude that this radiation consists of waves.

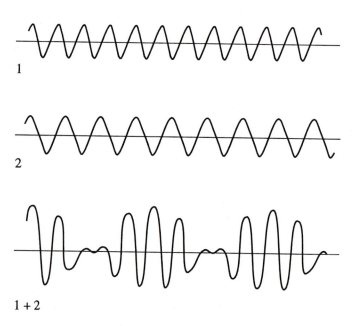

1

2

1 + 2

INTERFERENCE OF TWO WAVES

On the other hand, electromagnetic radiation also produces the so-called photoelectric effect: when ultraviolet light is shone on the surface of some metals it can "kick out" electrons from the surface of the metal, and therefore it must consist of moving particles. A similar situation occurs in the "scattering" experiments of X rays. These experiments can be interpreted correctly only if they are described as collisions of "light particles" with electrons. And yet, they show the interference patterns characteristic of waves. The question which puzzled physicists so much in the early stages of atomic theory was how electromagnetic radiation could simultaneously consist of particles (i.e., of entities confined to a very small volume) and of waves, which are spread out over a large area of space. Neither language nor imagination could deal with this kind of reality very well.

Eastern mysticism has developed several different ways of dealing with the paradoxical aspects of reality. Whereas they are bypassed in Hinduism through the use of mythical language, Buddhism and Taoism tend to emphasize the paradoxes rather than conceal them. The main Taoist scripture, Lao Tzu's *Tao Te Ching*, is written in an extremely puzzling, seemingly illogical style. It is full of intriguing contradictions and its compact, powerful, and extremely poetic language is meant to arrest the reader's mind and throw it off its familiar tracks of logical reasoning.

Chinese and Japanese Buddhists have adopted this Taoist technique of communicating the mystical experience by simply exposing its paradoxical character. When the Zen master Daito saw the Emperor Godaigo, who was a student of Zen, the master said:

> We were parted many thousands of *kalpas* ago, yet we have not been separated even for a moment. We are facing each other all day long, yet we have never met.

Zen Buddhists have a particular knack for making a virtue out of the inconsistencies arising from verbal communication, and with the *koan* system they have developed a unique way of transmitting their teachings completely nonverbally. *Koans* are carefully devised nonsensical riddles which are meant to make the student of Zen realize the limitations of logic and reasoning in the most dramatic way. The irrational wording and paradoxical content of these riddles makes it impossible to solve them by thinking. They are designed precisely to stop the thought process and thus to make the student ready for the nonverbal experience of reality. The contemporary Zen master Yasutani introduced a Western student to one of the most famous *koans* with the following words:

> One of the best *koans*, because the simplest, is *Mu*. This is its background: A monk came to Joshu, a renowned Zen master in China hundreds of years ago, and asked: "Has a dog Buddha-nature or not?" Joshu retorted, "*Mu!*" Literally, the expression means "no" or "not," but the significance of Joshu's answer does not lie in this. *Mu* is the expression of the living, functioning, dynamic Buddha-nature. What you must do is discover the spirit or essence of this *Mu*, not through intellectual analysis but by search into your innermost being. Then you must demonstrate before me, concretely and vividly, that you understand *Mu* as living truth, without recourse to conceptions, theories, or abstract explanations. Remember, you can't understand *Mu* through ordinary cognition; you must grasp it directly with your whole being.

To a beginner, the Zen master will normally present either this *Mu-koan* or one of the following two:

"What was your original face—the one you had before your parents gave birth to you?"

"You can make the sound of two hands clapping. Now what is the sound of one hand?"

All these *koans* have more or less unique solutions which a competent master recognizes immediately. Once the solution is found, the *koan* ceases to be paradoxical and becomes a profoundly meaningful statement made from the state of consciousness which it has helped to awaken.

In the Rinzai school, the student has to solve a long series of *koans*, each of them dealing with a particular aspect of Zen. This is the only way this school transmits its teachings. It does not use any positive statements, but leaves it entirely to the student to grasp the truth through the *koans*.

Here we find a striking parallel to the paradoxical situations which confronted physicists at the beginning of atomic physics. As in Zen, the truth was hidden in paradoxes that could not be solved by logical reasoning, but had to be understood in the terms of a new awareness; the awareness of the atomic reality. The teacher here was, of course, nature, who, like the Zen masters, does not provide any statements. She just provides the riddles.

The solving of a *koan* demands a supreme effort of concentration and involvement from the student. In books about Zen we read that the *koan* grips the student's heart and mind and creates a true mental impasse, a state of sustained tension in which the whole world becomes an enormous mass of doubt and questioning. The founders of quantum theory experienced exactly the same situation, described here most vividly by Heisenberg:

> I remember discussions with Bohr which went through many hours till very late at night and ended almost in despair; and when at the end of the discussion I went alone for a walk in the neighboring park I repeated to myself again and again the question: Can nature possibly be so absurd as it seemed to us in these atomic experiments?

Whenever the essential nature of things is analyzed by the intellect, it must seem absurd or paradoxical. This has always been recognized by the mystics, but has become a problem in science only very recently. For centuries, scientists were searching for the "fundamental laws of nature" underlying the great variety of natural phenomena. Those phenomena belonged to the scientists' macroscopic environment and thus to the realm of their sensory experience. Since the images and intellectual concepts of their language were abstracted from this very experience, they were sufficient and adequate to describe the natural phenomena.

Questions about the essential nature of things were answered in classical physics by the Newtonian mechanistic model of the universe which, much in the same way as the Democritean model in ancient Greece, reduced all phenomena to the motions and interactions of hard, indestructible atoms. The properties of these atoms were abstracted from the macroscopic notion of billiard balls, and thus from sensory experience. Whether this notion could actually be applied to the world of atoms was not questioned. Indeed, it could not be investigated experimentally.

In the twentieth century, however, physicists were able to tackle the question about the ultimate nature of matter experimentally. With the help of a most sophisticated technology they were able to probe deeper and deeper into nature, uncovering one layer of matter after the other in search for its ultimate "building blocks." Thus the existence of atoms was verified, then their constituents were discovered—the nuclei and electrons—and finally the components of the nucleus—the protons and neutrons—and many other subatomic particles.

The delicate and complicated instruments of modern experimental physics penetrate deep into the submicroscopic world, into realms of nature far removed from our macroscopic environment, and make this world accessible to our senses. However, they can do so only through a chain of processes ending, for example, in the audible click of a Geiger counter, or in a dark spot on a photographic plate. What we see, or hear, are never the investigated phenomena themselves but always their consequences. The atomic and subatomic world itself lies beyond our sensory perception.

It is, then, with the help of modern instrumentation that we are able to "observe" the properties of atoms and their constituents in an indirect way, and thus to "experience" the subatomic world to some extent. This experience, however, is not an ordinary one, comparable to that of our daily environment. The knowledge about matter at this level is no longer derived from direct sensory experience, and therefore our ordinary language, which takes its images from the world of the senses, is no longer adequate to describe the observed phenomena. As we penetrate deeper and deeper into nature, we have to abandon more and more of the images and concepts of ordinary language.

On this journey to the world of the infinitely small, the most important step, from a philosophical point of view, was the first one: the step into the world of atoms. Probing inside the atom and investigating its structure, science transcended the limits of our sensory imagination. From this point on, it could no longer rely with absolute certainty on logic and common sense. Atomic physics provided the scientists with the first glimpses of the essential nature of things. Like the mystics, physicists were now dealing with a nonsensory experience of reality and, like the mystics, they had to face the paradoxical aspects of this experience. From then on therefore, the models and images of modern physics became akin to those of Eastern philosophy.

QUESTIONS FOR STUDY

1. Why does Capra say that models of reality found in Eastern thought are more appropriate than models taken from Western philosophy?

2. What is the "dual nature of light"? Why is it so puzzling to scientists?

3. What is a koan? How is it used in the Rinzai school of Zen Buddhism?

4. In what ways were atoms understood to be similar to billiard balls in Newtonian physics?

5. Does modern science experience the existence of atoms and particles directly? Explain.

QUESTIONS FOR REFLECTION

1. Capra insists that ordinary logic is inadequate to account for the nature of sub-atomic reality, yet physicists use mathematics all the time for this purpose and mathematics is clearly logical. Is Capra wrong in his claim?

2. Is the dual nature of light a kind of Zen koan, like *Mu,* or is it an effort to employ metaphorical language in a flexible way?

3. What is a paradox? Is the dual nature of light a true paradox?

4. According to Capra, the Zen *koan* is capable of solution in a deeper transformation of personal awareness. Does he make the same claim for the koan of the dual nature of light? Are *Mu* and the dual nature of light as similar as he claims?

5. Physicists are forced to use ordinary language in extraordinary ways to describe their discoveries, but does this mean that they abandon the rationality and method that led to these discoveries in the first place? If not, how is mysticism a real response to the problems of complementarity and paradox?

NETWORKING

MacCormack's discussion of metaphor sheds light on the idea of *complementarity in physics. Heisenberg and his principle* are discussed in Dillard and Polkinghorne. Schmidt describes the *koan and the nature of paradox in Zen Buddhism.*

ALL NATURE IS TOUCH AND GO
ANNIE DILLARD

Annie Dillard has served as contributing editor to Harper's magazine and has written columns for the Wilderness Society. She is widely known, however, for her first book of prose, *Pilgrim at Tinker Creek,* a classic example of nature writing and as winner of the Pulitzer Prize for Non-Fiction in 1974. Her other books include *Holy the Firm, American Childhood,* and *Writing Life.* She currently teaches at Wesleyan University.

Living this way by the creek, where the light appears and vanishes on the water, where muskrats surface and dive, and redwings scatter, I have come to know a special side of nature. I look to the mountains, and the mountains still slumber, blue and mute and rapt. I say, it gathers; the world abides. But I look to the creek, and I say: it scatters, it comes and goes. When I leave the house the sparrows flee and hush; on the banks of the creek jays scream in alarm, squirrels race for cover, tadpoles dive, frogs leap, snakes freeze, warblers vanish. Why do they hide? I will not hurt them. They simply do not want to be seen. "Nature," said Heraclitus, "is wont to hide herself." A fleeing mockingbird unfurls for a second a dazzling array of white fans . . . and disappears in the leaves. Shane! . . . Shane! Nature flashes the old mighty glance—the come-hither look—drops the handkerchief, turns tail, and is gone. The nature I know is old touch-and-go.

I wonder whether what I see and seem to understand about nature is merely one of the accidents of freedom, repeated by chance before my eyes, or whether it has any counterpart in the worlds beyond Tinker Creek. I find in quantum mechanics a world symbolically similar to my world at the creek.

Many of us are still living in the universe of Newtonian physics, and fondly imagine that real, hard scientists have no use for these misty ramblings, dealing as scientists do with the measurable and known. We think that at least the physical causes of physical events are perfectly knowable, and that, as the results of various experiments keep coming in, we gradually roll back the cloud of unknowing. We remove the veils one by one, painstakingly, adding knowledge to knowledge and whisking away veil after veil, until at last we reveal the nub of things, the sparkling equation from whom all blessings flow. Even wildman Emerson accepted the truly pathetic fallacy of the old science when he wrote grudgingly towards the end of his life, "When the microscope is improved, we shall have the cells analysed, and all will be electricity, or somewhat else." All we need to do is perfect our instruments and our methods, and we can collect enough data like birds on a string to predict physical events from physical causes.

But in 1927 Werner Heisenberg pulled out the rug, and our whole understanding of the universe toppled and collapsed. For some reason it has not yet trickled down to the man on the street that some physicists now are a bunch of wild-eyed, raving mystics. For they have perfected their instruments and methods just enough to whisk away the crucial vein, and what stands revealed is the Cheshire cat's grin.

The Principle of Indeterminacy, which saw the light in the summer of 1927, says in effect that you cannot know both a particle's velocity and position. You can guess statistically what any batch of electrons might do, but you cannot predict the career of any one particle. They seem to be as free as dragonflies. You can perfect your instruments and your methods till the cows come home, and you will never ever be able to measure this one basic thing. It cannot be done. The electron is a muskrat; it cannot be perfectly stalked. And nature is a fan dancer born with a fan; you can wrestle her down, throw her on the stage and grapple with her for the fan with all your might, but it will never quit her grip. She comes that way; the fan is attached.

It is not that we lack sufficient information to know both a particle's velocity and its position; that would have been a perfectly ordinary situation well within the understanding of classical physics. Rather, we know now for sure that there is no knowing. You can determine the position, and your figure for the velocity blurs into vagueness; or, you can determine velocity, but whoops, there goes the position. The use of instru-

ments and the very fact of an observer seem to bollix the observations; as a consequence, physicists are saying that they cannot study nature per se, but only their own investigation of nature. And I can only see bluegills within my own blue shadow, from which they immediately flee.

The Principle of Indeterminacy turned science inside-out. Suddenly determinism goes, causality goes, and we are left with a universe composed of what Eddington calls, "mindstuff." Listen to these physicists: Sir James Jeans, Eddington's successor, invokes "fate," saying that the future "may rest on the knees of whatever gods there be." Eddington says that "the physical world is entirely abstract and without 'actuality' apart from its linkage to consciousness." Heisenberg himself says, "method and object can no longer be separated. *The scientific world-view has ceased to be a scientific view in the true sense of the word.*" Jeans says that science can no longer remain opposed to the notion of free will. Heisenberg says, "there is a higher power, not influenced by our wishes, which finally decides and judges." Eddington says that our dropping causality as a result of the Principle of Indeterminacy "leaves us with no clear distinction between the Natural and the Supernatural." And so forth.

These physicists are once again mystics, as Kepler was, standing on a rarefied mountain pass, gazing transfixed into an abyss of freedom. And they got there by experimental method and a few wild leaps such as Einstein made. What a pretty pass!

All this means is that the physical world as we understand it now is more like the touch-and-go creek world I see than it is like the abiding world of which the mountains seem to speak. The physicists' particles whiz and shift like rotifers in and out of my microscope's field, and that this valley's ring of granite mountains is an airy haze of those same particles I must believe. The whole universe is a swarm of those wild, wary energies, the sun that glistens from the wet hairs on a muskrat's back and the stars which the mountains obscure on the horizon but which catch from on high in Tinker Creek. It is all touch and go. The heron flaps away; the dragonfly departs at thirty miles an hour; the water strider vanishes under a screen of grass; the muskrat dives, and the ripples roll from the bank, and flatten, and cease altogether.

QUESTIONS FOR STUDY

1. What examples does the author use to illustrate the elusiveness of reality around Tinker Creek?

2. Who does Dillard credit with "pulling out the rug" from beneath classical physics?

3. Describe Heisenberg's Principle of Indeterminacy.

4. What are the direct consequences of this discovery for the scientific enterprise?

QUESTIONS FOR REFLECTION

1. Dillard contrasts the mountains and the creek. In what major way do they differ?

2. Was the world of Newtonian physics optimistic or pessimistic about its prospects for success? Explain.

3. Using the responses to the first two questions as your basis, express the theme of this selection in your own words.

4. Explain Heisenberg's statement that "the scientific world view has ceased to be a scientific view in the true sense of the word."

5. Heisenberg's principle asserts that we cannot know everything we need to know about a particle to be able to predict its future behavior. Does this mean that the particle is truly free, spontaneous, and "uncertain," or does it simply mean that we are ignorant, "uncertain" of its determined behavior?

NETWORKING

The arguments of Capra and Polkinghorne include references to *Heisenberg and his Principle of Uncertainty*. The case for the *spontaneous character of natural processes* is described by Lewis and argued by Lackey, Dyson, and Polkinghorne.

MORE TO THE WORLD THAN MEETS THE EYE
JOHN POLKINGHORNE

John Polkinghorne is both a theologian and a physicist. He is vicar of St. Cosmas and St. Damian in Kent, England, and Fellow of Trinity College. He is also Honorary Professor of Theoretical Physics at the University of Kent. Polkinghorne has authored several books on science and religion including *One World: The Interaction of Science and Theology* and *Science and Providence*.

. . . . The feeling that there is more to the world than meets the eye finds its scientific motivation at two different levels. The first is that fundamental intelligibility of the physical universe which makes science possible. The fact that we can understand the world is so familiar that most of the time we take it for granted. Nevertheless, it seems to me that it is a highly significant fact about the way things are. What is perhaps more to the point, it also seemed so to Einstein. He once remarked that the only incomprehensible thing about the universe is that it is comprehensible.

At the articulate level of thought, it is mathematics that provides the perfect language with which to describe the pattern and structure of the physical world, the key to unlock its mysteries. Time and again, successful theories in fundamental physics have proved to be characterized by that unmistakable quality of economy and elegance which the mathematicians rightly call beauty. So frequently has this proved to be the case that a theoretical physicist, offered a putative theory which is clumsy or contrived in its mathematical character, will instinctively feel that it cannot be right. This power of mathematics to mirror physical reality has survived crises so grave that they might have seemed to threaten the subversion of science's rationality. The dilemma of the early years of this century that faced physicists when they realized that light behaved sometimes as a wave and sometimes as if [it were] composed of particles is a case in point. One might have thought that this was a clash of contrarities which would have defied rational synthesis. However, Dirac worked the necessary dialectical trick by his invention of the formalism of quantum field theory.

Human reason has always proved equal to the tasks set it by the phenomena of physics. It could so easily have been otherwise. Suppose we had access only to the geometrical rationality of the circle and that the analytic rationality of the calculus and the inverse square law was closed to us. Then our gropings after the structure of the solar system would have been condemned to an endless proliferation of epicycle upon epicycle (whether in the spirit of Ptolemy or in the spirit of Copernicus) with the pattern of Newton's great theory forever hidden from us. But it has not proved so. There is a remarkable congruence between the experienced rationality of our minds and the perceived rationality of the world around us. Dirac expressed his faith in this congruity when he wrote:

> It is more important to have beauty in one's equations than to have them fit experiment . . . because the discrepancy may be due to minor features which are not properly taken into account and which will get cleared up with further developments in the theory. . . . It seems that if one is working from the point of view of getting beauty in one's equations, and if one has a really sound instinct, one is on a sure line of success.[1]

In this passage, he draws our attention to a second aspect of the way in which human reason is so successful in exploring the physical world. The reference to "a really sound instinct"—something which Dirac himself possessed in abundance—reminds us of that tacit side to scientific activity which Polanyi emphasized in his account of the scientific method.[2] The choice of questions to ask, the interpretation of experimental results, the elimination of spurious "background" effects, the judgment when a discrepancy is serious or venial, all these call for the exercise of skills which are not exhaustively specifiable but which are essential for the scientific enterprise. I would wish to add to that list the skillful exercise of induction, for I do not think that mere falsifiability gives an account of scientific method which is adequate to actual scientific experience, whose fundamental character is that of discovery. The great success of science in settling questions to universal satisfaction (Is matter composed of atoms? Are atoms composed of electrons and nuclei? Are nuclei composed of protons and neutrons? Are protons and neutrons composed of quarks and gluons?), this success indicates that our tacit powers of judgment are as adequate for the successful discernment of the pattern and structure of the physical world as are our explicit mathematical abilities.

Some may feel that I am in danger of being carried away in scientifically triumphalist euphoria. Well, in my professional lifetime as a physicist, I lived through the advance in our understanding of the structure of matter which took us from protons and neutrons to quarks and gluons. It was a heady experience. And that experience was made possible by the marvelous intelligibility of the world, its transparency to human reason.

Is that just our luck or has it a deeper significance about the way things are? Let me return to Einstein. He once said:

> In every true searcher of nature there is a kind of religious reverence; for he finds it impossible to imagine that he is the first to have thought out the exceedingly delicate threads that connect his perceptions. The aspect of knowledge which has not yet been laid bare gives the investigator a feeling akin to that of a child who seeks to grasp the masterly way in which elders manipulate things.[3]

Although not a conventionally religious man, Einstein often spoke of God, whom he referred to in comradely terms as "the Old One."

If the congruence between the experienced rationality of our minds and the perceived rationality of the world is to find a deeper explanation, it must lie in some rational basis which is common to both. An elegant and persuasive understanding would be provided by recognizing the undergirding reason of the Creator, who is the ground of all that is. To refuse to take that step would be to leave oneself with an unresolved coincidence, an action which is contrary to all the instincts of the scientist. If the search for rational understanding is so successful in our exploration of the physical world, must it not also be pursued beyond that world of science into realms of wider metaphysical coherence? I am greatly in sympathy with the Bishop of Birmingham when he writes:

> Here I must declare myself and say that I believe very strongly in the Principle of Sufficient Explanation. . . . It seems to me extraordinary that many who spend their lives exercising their minds on human problems or on the investigation of the natural world . . . should state categorically that the mind has no right to ask "Why" questions about the universe in which we live. To me, this is a dogma every bit as objectionable as religious dogma appears to rationalists.[4]

The great expositor of such a point of view has been the Jesuit philosopher, Bernard Lonergan. His whole metaphysics is built upon the analysis of, the centrality of, and ultimately the apotheosis of understanding. He does not hesitate to declare that "since we define being by its relation to intelligence, necessarily our ultimate is not being but intelligence."[5] That sounds like the creed of a professor! It often seems that for Lonergan God is the Great Explanation, so that he proclaims that "God is the unrestricted act of understanding, the eternal rapture glimpsed in every Archimedean cry of Eureka."[6] Certainly, it is part of the attractiveness and coherence of theism that it offers insight into the rationality of the world, as well as into such features, indispensable to a whole view of reality, as the existence of beauty and of the moral order. . . .

The second level of thought which motivates our feeling that there is more to the world than meets the scientific eye pertains to the character of the laws and circumstance revealed to rational inquiry. We have become aware in recent years of what appears to be a very delicate balance necessary in the *data* of our world if it is to be capable, in the course of its unfolding process, of evolving such interesting systems as you and me. In other words, if we played at God and wrote down a prescription for a universe—dictated its fundamental physical laws, prescribed the values of the physical constants which control the balance between the different forces described by those laws, specified the initial conditions from which the world derived its particular character—then, unless we had been meticulously careful in the mutual adjustment of the *data* of that prescription, our world would be one in which nothing interesting would happen. That is to say, it would not through its evolution prove capable of producing systems of the complexity which seems necessary if conscious beings are to appear upon its scene. Random twiddling of the "knobs of the universe" will get you nowhere as a Creator. Fine tuning is necessary if humans are to come into being. This insight is sometimes called the anthropic principle.

Let me give some examples of the considerations which lead to this conclusion. In the very early stages of its existence, the whole universe was hot enough to be a gigantic arena for nuclear reactions. However, quite quickly—after about three minutes, in fact—the expansion of the universe had so cooled it down that nuclear reactions ceased, only to start up again much later in the interiors of stars, formed by local condensation. Thus, those hectic first three minutes[7] fixed the gross nuclear structure of the universe as we still find it today: three-quarter hydrogen and one-quarter helium. The precise proportion of these two elements depends upon the mutual relationship of the fundamental forces of physics, in particular the balance between the weak nuclear force, which causes some nuclei to disintegrate, and the other forces. Had this balance been only a little different from its actual value, then we should not be here, for either the world would be all helium and no hydrogen or there would be no supernova explosions in stars. Either would have disastrous consequences for the possibility of the existence of life. In the first case, if there were no hydrogen, there would be no water, and we cannot imagine life evolving without that vital substance. On the other hand, if supernovae did not explode, then the heavier elements, such as carbon and iron, which are also essential for life and which are only made by localized nuclear processes in the interiors of stars, would have remained locked up forever in dying stellar cores and so would have been unavailable for incorporation into living systems. We are all made of the ashes of dead stars. Thus, without that particular balance between strong and weak nuclear forces that we actually observe, we should not be here today.

A second example relates to the circumstance of the world, namely that it is very big. Our sun is just an ordinary star among the hundred thousand million stars of our galaxy, which itself is nothing to speak about among the thousand million galaxies of the observable universe. We sometimes feel daunted at the thought of such immensity. We should not. If the world were not about that big, we should not be here to be dismayed by it. A smaller universe would have run its course before we had time to appear upon its scene. It takes about eighteen thousand million years to make us the way we are.

A third example may relate either to the character of universal law or to particular circumstance, according to how things work out. The phenomenon to which it draws attention is the incredibly delicate balance between two competing effects in the early universe. One is the force of expansion, present in the singular explosion of the big bang, driving matter apart. The other is the force of gravity, pulling matter together. At a very early epoch (the Planck time), these two competing effects, expansion and contraction, were so closely balanced that they differed from each other by just one part in 10^{60}. The numerate will marvel at such accuracy. For our innumerate friends, let us translate that into pictorial terms. If I took a target an inch wide and placed it on the other side of the observable universe, eighteen thousand million light years away, and took aim and hit the target, then I would have achieved an accuracy for one in 10^{60}. Remarkable! But once again, if there were not this delicate balance between expansive effects and contractive effects, then we would not be here to be astonished at it. In a universe in which expansion predominated even a little bit more, matter would fly apart too quickly for it to be able to condense into stars and galaxies. In so dilute a world, nothing interesting would happen. On the other hand, if the forces of contraction predominated even a little bit more, then the universe would have collapsed in on itself again before there had been time for anything interesting to happen. Therefore, if you are going to play at Creator and set up a universe, make sure that you get the balance between expansion and contraction right if you want your world to have a fruitful history.

It is possible that this balance can be achieved, not by having to put it into the specification of initial circumstance but by a suitable choice of the universe's basic physical laws. An ingenious young American, Alan Guth, has suggested that there might have been what he calls "an inflationary scenario" for the universe.[8] This is a process rather like the "boiling" of space, in which a very rapid expansion of the world takes place. If that is correct, it would not only explain the delicate balance between expansion and contraction but also other puzzling properties of the universe, such as its high degree of isotropy. (It looks the same in all directions.) Guth's suggestion is highly speculative, and it would be wise to bear in mind the warning about cosmologists uttered by the great Russian theoretical physicist, Lev Landau, that they are "often in error but never in doubt." However, even if Guth is right, his inflationary scenario depends for its possibility on the form and balance of the basic laws of physics, so once again one would have to be careful in framing one's prescription for the world.

As with the intelligibility of the world, so with the anthropic principle: is it just our luck or has it a deeper significance about the way things are? Scientists have certainly felt uneasy about the question and have sought to carry its discussion further. Various lines of attack have been pursued.

One suggests that if we understood things properly, we should find that there is only one rationally coherent theory of the physical world that is actually possible, completely specified in all its characteristics. In other words, the cosmic "knobs" cannot be twiddled after all. Relativistic quantum theory is very subtle and perhaps what seem like arbitrary quantities—the balance of strong and weak nuclear forces, for instance—may have to be exactly as they are if the theory is really to be totally consistent. Such a suggestion, if it were successful, would simply reduce our second consideration (the laws and circumstance of the world) to the first (the rationality of the world). The claim being made goes far beyond our present knowledge, and it also seems to me to be intrinsically improbable. Quantum electrodynamics, which describes the interaction of electrons and protons, is a beautiful and highly successful theory. I cannot see any rational impossibility in a world made up solely of electrons and photons though we should not be part of it to enjoy its intellectual coherence.

A second suggestion is that perhaps there is a portfolio of different universes, each with a different setting of the cosmic "knobs." Then, if there were enough of them, it would scarcely be surprising if by chance in one of them the tuning were fine enough for us to appear on its scene. Of course, that is the one in which we live because we could not turn up anywhere else. This ample proposition is sometimes alleged to be supported by the notion of an oscillating universe, endlessly collapsing into a sort of cosmic melting pot and reemerging thence, it is suggested, with its parameters changed by a mysterious process beyond the present power of science to investigate. Thus, a temporal succession of possible worlds would be generated. Alternatively, the highly contentious "many worlds" interpretation of quantum mechanics is invoked.[9] This proposes that at every act of quantum measurement, the world divides into a series of "parallel" universes, in each of which one of the possible results of the measurement actually occurs. However, that bizarre theory in no way suggests changes in cosmic parameters. The fact is that none of these ideas about multiple worlds is part of physics; they have no motivation at all in terms of our understanding of the pattern and structure of the physical world that we actually experience. In the strictest sense of the word they are metaphysical speculation.

The same can be said for the even cloudier proposition of the strong anthropic principle, which declares that in some unexplained way the emergence of human beings as observers forces the parameters of the world to assume values that permit that emergence. Here we would, with a vengeance, be hoisting ourselves by our own bootstraps.

There is nothing wrong with metaphysical speculation, but it should be recognized as such and not tricked out as pseudo-science. It seems to me that a metaphysical idea of much more economy and elegance is that there is just one world, which is the way it is, in its order and delicate balance, because it is the creation of a Creator who wills it to be capable of fruitful evolution. . . .

The intelligibility and tightly-knit structure of the world provide the basis of a revived natural theology.[10] The feeling that there is more to the world than meets the scientific eye encourages the thought of an Intelligence behind its processes. It is the scientists themselves who have seen things that way while their theological colleagues have remained surprisingly unconcerned. The theologians are mostly either ignorant of what modern science has to say, or are so confident in revelation that they feel no need of ancillary help from general reason, or—mindful of the fate of Paley and the authors of the Bridgewater treatises—they are excessively wary of the whole enterprise of natural theology.

Such wariness fails to recognize that a revived natural theology is also a revised natural theology. It differs from its predecessors in two respects. Firstly, it is more modest in its claims. It presents itself, not as a demonstrative discipline, but as an insightful inquiry into the nature of the world. It does not assert that God's existence can be proved, but it seeks to persuade us that God provides that sufficient reason which can make satisfying sense of the remarkable world revealed to our investigations. It is in this search for an understanding of the world through and through, to its very fundamentals, that we discover the meaning of Augustine's claim that we must believe in order that we may understand.

Secondly, a revised natural theology looks for the source of its insight, not to particulars—the emergence of life, the structure of the eye, even the complexity of the human brain—but to the root structure of the physical world, the *data* of scientific inquiry. Its concern, therefore, is with laws and not with occurrences. Its God is not a God of the Gaps, competing with science as the explanation of events and continually being jostled off the stage of the world by the advance of knowledge. Rather, God the Sustainer of the World, whose faithful will for material creation is expressed in those patterns of regularity which are the given of scientific inquiry. God is found, not in the gaps of knowledge, but in the fact of knowledge. William Temple once said that the fact of knowledge is more important than all known facts.

My case for a revived and revised natural theology rests ultimately on the order of the world. It would not be candid of me if I did not acknowledge the existence of three threats to that picture of wonderful order that I have presented. The first might seem to be posed by quantum theory, for it has dissolved the clear and determinate world of everyday into a cloudy, fitful world at its constituent roots.[11] For a subatomic particle, such as an electron, if I know where it is I do not know what it is doing, and if I know what it is doing, I do not know where it is. That is Heisenberg's uncertainty principle in a nutshell. Can the appeal to order survive such strange elusiveness in nature? Quantum theory deals in probabilities rather than certainties. At the level of elementary particles, it seems that God does indeed play at dice. In general, no cause is to be assigned to individual quantum mechanical events; their regularities are purely statistical.

There is a peculiar insubstantiality in the world. We may think that Dr. Johnson had a point, in his bluff way, when he kicked the stone and asserted that he refuted Bishop Berkeley thus. However, that solid-seeming stone is mostly empty space and what is not is a weaving of wave mechanical patterns. Even logic is subject to modification in the quantum world. You tell me that Bill is at home and that he is either drunk or sober. Neatly employing the distributive law of classical logic, I conclude that I will either find Bill at home drunk or I will find him at home sober. Who could doubt so transparent a conclusion? Yet a similar argument applied to electrons would, in fact, be fallacious and von Neumann and Birkoff had to invent a special quantum logic to apply to their behavior.

I could go on telling weird travellers' tales of those who voyage in the quantum world. Its elusive and counter-intuitive character has seemed to some more suggestive of the dancing, dissolving thought of the religions of the Far East[12] than the sternly realist tone of the religions of the Near East. I do not agree. However idiosyncratic elementary particles may prove to be in their behavior, they have their own essential reality, even if it differs from the naive objectivity of everyday experience.

I reject the positivist views of people like Niels Bohr who treated quantum theory as just a highly successful manner of speaking about the behavior of laboratory apparatus. Such a view is an inadequate account of scientific experience. When physicists at CERN got very excited in 1983 because they considered that they had discovered the heavy W and Z particles predicted by elementary particle theory, they were not just rejoicing at an ingenious account of the behavior of an elaborate and expensive array of electronic detectors. They believed—and rightly in my opinion—that they had added to our knowledge of what *is*. If I am to defend this realist position about quantum entities, I think that ultimately I have to do so by asserting that it is our ability to understand them that assures us of their reality. In the unpicturable quantum world, we have to rely on intelligibility as the criterion of reality. That gives physics something in common with Western theology as the latter pursues its quest for insight into the nature of the Unpicturable, transcendent as well as imminent in the rational ordering of the process of the world.

A more serious threat might be thought to be posed by the realization that that evolving process of the world depends for its fruitfulness upon a delicate interplay between chance and necessity.[13] Chance—the random congregation of atoms or the mutation of a gene—is the source of novelty. Without its operation, nothing new would happen. But without the presence of a lawfully regular environment to preserve and select these fortuitous variations, all would vanish again like smoke in the wind. The role of chance has been held by some to preclude the possibility of meaning in the workings of the world. Its end point is not foreseeable from its beginning. Jacques Monod expressed this with Gallic intensity when he wrote: "Pure chance, absolutely free but blind, is at the very root of the stupendous edifice of evolution."[14] For Monod the universe is a tale told by an idiot.

Monod reaches this conclusion by his concentration on the chance half of the partnership. Let us consider for a moment the sphere of lawful necessity. The aspects of the behavior of atoms, relevant to the coming-into-being of life and its subsequent elaboration, are adequately accounted for by the laws of electromagnetism (which is the controlling force of interaction in this regime) and the laws of quantum theory (which is the appropriate form of dynamics describing the effects of that force).

When I first read of the speculations of biochemists like Monod about the origin of replicating molecules and life, I was bowled over by the thought of the astonishing fruitfulness of these simple laws—the thought that such equations could eventually lead to you and me. It spoke to me of a deep-seated potentiality present in the structure of the world, an insight of design which gripped my imagination. I am not a natural Teilhardian, but, for once, I could follow de Chardin in apostrophizing matter: "You I acclaim as inexhaustible potentiality for existence and transformation."[15]

The role of chance is to explore and realize that potentiality present in the pattern and structure of the physical world. To be sure, the final details of the end are not prescribed in the beginning. No doubt there are accidental features in humankind, such as the precise number of toes. But we have no reason to suppose that it is an accident that the raw material of matter is capable of evolving, in one form or another, into conscious beings, transcending their origin and capable of communion with their Creator.

I would argue that the balance between chance and necessity that we observe in the workings of the world is consonant with that balance between the gift of freedom and the reliability of purpose which should characterize Love's act of creation. I have written elsewhere:

> Theology has always been in danger of a double bind in relation to physical causation. A tightly deterministic universe, evolving along predetermined lines, seems to leave little room for freedom and responsibility. It is congenial only to deistic indifference or the iron grip of Calvinistic predestination. On the other hand, too loose a structure dissolves significance. Meaning can drown in the rising waters of chaos. A world capable of sustaining freedom and order requires an equilibrium between these rigidifying and dissolving tendencies.[16]

Chance signifies the vulnerability accepted by the Creator in making room for creation; necessity reflects the divine steadfastness in relation to it. No scientific umpire can adjudicate between Monod and my own view in our different judgments of the world. We agree on the physical circumstances (though he understood them much better than I do) but find conflicting significance in them. Both natural theology and natural atheism partake of the nature of faith and find their motivations from wider realms of understanding than the strictly scientific. . . .

The most severe threat to claimed significance is posed by the third matter which we must consider, namely the ultimate futility of the physical universe. We do not know for sure the future fate of the world. It depends on the precise nature of the near balance between expansion and contraction in the cosmic process. If the forces of expansion prove just to be the victors, then the matter of the world will continue to fly apart for ever. Within galaxies, however, it will contract under gravity to form gigantic black holes which, after almost inconceivable lengths of time, will decay by Hawking radiation. If, as some modern speculative theories in elementary particle physics suppose, the proton is an unstable particle with a lifetime in excess of 10^{31} years, then the nuclear pattern of the world will already have disintegrated long before this happens. By one route or another, according to this scenario, the universe will decay.

No less dismal is the prospect if the forces of contraction gain a marginal victory. Then the expansion that we presently observe will eventually be halted and reversed. The universe which began in the fiery explosion of the big bang will collapse in upon itself again to terminate in the fiery implosion of the big crunch.

Neither scenario that I have sketched seems encouraging to those who look for an ultimate purpose fulfilled within the history of the physical universe. Macquarrie was sufficiently dismayed by such a prospect to write: "Let me say frankly, however, that if it were shown that the universe is indeed headed for an all-enveloping death, then this might seem to constitute a state of affairs so negative that it might be held to falsify Christian faith and abolish Christian hope."[17]

Such a reaction strikes me as extreme. After all, Christian faith and hope have never been centered on utopian expectations for this present world. We cannot suppose that Macquarrie has never heard of the resurrection from the dead and the life of the world to come. Modern science simply makes plain with deadly earnestness the fact that if in this life only we have hope, the prospect is pretty bleak, not just for us individually but also for the whole of the physical universe. If there is a purpose at work in the world, it can only find its lasting fulfillment in a destiny beyond what we now experience. Such a destiny is unimaginable, but I do not think that it is an incoherent possibility. We know that what counts is pattern—not the particular realization of that pattern but the pattern itself. Our material bodies change their physical constituents every few years. It is the information content of their organization that is preserved as the expression of our personal continuity. It does not seem in the least irrational to suppose that the pattern might be reconstituted in a new environment of God's choosing. For us, that would be the resurrection of the body. For the universe, it might be what Paul was groping after in those mysterious words in Romans when he spoke of the creation "subjected to futility" but also "subjected in hope" that it might "be set free from its bondage to decay and obtain the glorious liberty of the children of God."[18] I think the empty tomb might have something to say to us here if we would be willing to listen to its story, submitting ourselves to its insight rather than subjecting it to our prejudgment.

But if it's all going to be changed, why bother with the whole unsatisfactory process up to now? If fulfillment is in the new creation, what is the purpose of the old creation? Is not Macquarrie right after all to suggest that the decay of this present world is so negative a fate that it puts in question the hope of better things beyond it? The answer must lie in the preparatory processes of a God who chooses to work by unfolding development rather than by instantaneous decree. There is work for theologians to do in digesting these matters. I do not think the task is without clue or promise. Most of us Christians are content to face the prospect of the discarding and decay of our bodies without feeling that that denies the hope of a destiny beyond death. If that is true for us cosmic atoms, might it not be true for the cosmic whole?

It is time to face the question of what sort of God it is who is made known to us in the particularity of creation. Certainly this is not a God in a hurry. When one thinks of those eighteen thousand million years which elapsed from the big bang until conscious beings appeared, one can see that God is patient, content to achieve purposes through the slow unfolding of process. In that realization lies the small contribution that natural theology can make to that most agonizing of theological questions, the problem of the apparently wasteful suffering of the world.

The intelligible regularity of the universe reflects the rational reliability of its Creator. Its delicately balanced structure, intricately knit, evinces the subtlety of God's purpose to be achieved through the evolution of the world. The freedom which Love gives to its creation means that the potentiality with which the universe has been endowed is to be explored by the precarious interaction of chance and necessity and realized, not by the pronouncement of magical fiat, but by evolving development. If God's faithfulness implies that creation is orderly rather than fitfully manipulated; if the divine wisdom implies that creative purpose will be achieved by the anthropic potentiality inherent in the carefully adjusted balance of the universe; if love implies the acceptance of vulnerability by endowing the world with an independence which will find its way of development through the shuffling operations of chance rather than by rigid divine control; if all these things are true, then the world that such a God creates will have to look very much like the one in which we live, not only in its beautiful structure but also in its evolutionary blind alleys and genetic malfunctions.

We all tend to think that it would have been easy to have made things very differently, to have "twiddled the knobs" of the universe so as to have preserved the good and eliminated the bad. The anthropic principle gives pause to such facile speculation. I am not quite daring to say with Leibnitz that this is the best of all possible worlds, but the idea is not as manifestly foolish as one might at first sight have supposed, if the world is to be one of lawful process. . . .

What are the implications for theology generally of what we have been considering? I think they are considerable and need a sustained dialogue between scientists and theologians for their evaluation and digestion. If we believe in the unity of knowledge and experience, then advances in understanding in one realm of knowledge modify the tone and limit the range of acceptable insight in all others. There is an inescapable interaction between science and theology, as the whole of intellectual history from Copernicus through Darwin to the present day makes abundantly clear. That history is by no means one of continual warfare. Einstein once said that religion without science is blind and science without religion is lame. The two disciplines need each other.

Natural theology is alive and well and being practiced by scientists, however much it may be neglected or despised by theologians. It is important to recognize that there are reasons for believing in God which lie wholly outside our psyches. Such a realization would release contemporary theology from an undue dependence on existential analysis—a concern which, however necessary as part of a balanced exploration of experience, is, in isolation, always liable to threaten to reduce theology to anthropology. Natural theology also poses questions about the nature of God which general theological thought needs to take into account. For example, Bartholomew, in his important discussion of the role of randomness in the processes of the world, calls for "a doctrine of providence which, while allowing that God is ultimately responsible for everything that happens, does not require ultimate involvement in all things."[19] In other words, God willed a world in which chance has a role to play, thereby both being responsible for the consequences accruing and also accepting limitation of God's power to control.

Natural theology is valuable, but it can only take us so far. People like Paul Davies, while they claim that physics provides a road to God, usually go on to say that they detect no sign of the personal God of Jews and Christians. The most they can assent to is the Divine Mathematician or the Grand Intelligence. We need hardly be surprised. Limited investigation yields limited insight. If one wishes to encounter the God and Father of Our Lord Jesus Christ, then one must be willing to take the risk of leaving the clear, beautiful, lunar landscape of science for the untidy, perplexing world of personal encounter. But to pursue that matter belongs to a different discourse.

NOTES

1. P.A.M. Dirac, *Scientific American* (May, 1963).
2. M. Polanyi, *Personal Knowledge* (Routledge and Kegan Paul, 1958).
3. A. Einstein quoted in A. Moszokowski, *Conversations with Einstein* (Horizon, 1970).
4. H. Montefiore, *The Probability of God* (SCM Press, 1985), p. 8.
5. B. Lonergan, *Insight* (Longman, 1957), p. 677.
6. Lonergan, *ibid.*, p. 684.
7. S. Weinberg, *The First Three Minutes* (Andre Deutsch, 1977).
8. A.H. Guth and P.J. Steinhardt, *Scientific American* (May, 1984).
9. J.C. Polkinghorne, *The Quantum World* (Longman, 1984), Chapter 6.
10. For a fuller discussion, see J.C. Polkinghorne, *One World—The Interaction of Science and Theology* (SPCK, 1986).
11. See Polkinghorne, *Quantum World*.
12. F. Capra, *The Tao of Physics* (Wildwood House, 1975) and G. Zukav, *The Dancing Wu Li Masters* (Rider/Hutchinson, 1979).
13. D.J. Bartholomew, *God of Chance* (SCM Press, 1984).
14. J. Monod, *Chance and Necessity* (E.T.: Collins, 1972), p. 110.
15. T. de Chardin, *Hymn to the Universe* (E.T.: Fontana, 1970), p. 64.
16. Polkinghorne, *One World*.
17. J. Macquarrie, *Principles of Christian Theology* (SCM Press, 1977), p. 256.
18. Romans 8:20–21.
19. Bartholomew, *op. cit.*, p. 145.

QUESTIONS FOR STUDY

1. In what two major ways does the scientific study of the physical world reveal that "there is more to the world than meets the eye"?

2. How is the success of mathematics in describing the universe a good example of the amazing correlation of human thought to the basic principles that govern the universe?

3. How do these major ways lead to speculation about God?

4. Describe briefly the three threats arising from science for Polkinghorne's "revised natural theology."

QUESTIONS FOR REFLECTION

1. Within the context of Polkinghorne's essay, what is the significance of Einstein's claim that "the only incomprehensible thing about the universe is that it is comprehensible"?

2. Explain Polkinghorne's image of God twiddling the knobs of the universe? What point is he attempting to make? If God is allowed to adjust basic physical constants at will, how is science, which depends utterly on the reliability of these constants, possible? Is deism (See *deism* in Glossary) a possible way out of this problem?

3. How does a "revised natural theology" differ from its predecessors? Does Polkinghorne's proposal for salvaging natural theology meet the objections of Updike's characters in the earlier selection, "Roger's Version"?

4. Explain the author's claim that quantum mechanics and theology have something in common: "[the] quest for insight into the nature of the unpicturable."

5. Does Polkinghorne agree that the end of the universe is a real threat to the theological doctrine that God will redeem and fulfill the creation?

NETWORKING

Polkinghorne's broad essay touches on a number of important issues, including the following: *intelligibility of the universe:* Einstein, Tillich, Updike; *polanyi:* Barbour (I) and Haught; *anthropic principle:* Barbour, Dyson, Wald, and Updike; *natural theology:* Barbour (Part I), Hick and Lackey; *quantum physics:* Herbert, Capra, and Dillard; and *entropy:* Asimov, Teilhard, and Burhoe. A similar opinion on the *Interaction of Chance and Necessity* is voiced by Dyson.

SUGGESTIONS FOR FURTHER READING

Barrow, John D., and Frank J. Tipler. *The Anthropic Principle.* New York: Oxford University Press, 1986. A thorough investigation of the teleological or design argument through an examination of its history and recent discussion, especially concerning cosmology and quantum physics.

Barth, Karl. *Evangelical Theology: An Introduction*. Grand Rapids, Michigan: W. B. Eerdmans Publishing Company, 1963. A succinct statement of the theology of this most famous and influential twentieth-century Protestant theologian.

Davies, Paul. *God and the New Physics*. New York: Simon and Schuster, 1983. Davies is a physicist with excellent skills in communicating developments in the physical sciences to the lay public. While his theological skills are not of equal quality, the combination provides us with one of the few works of its kind in the field of science and religion.

____. *The Cosmic Blueprint: New Discoveries in Nature's Creative Ability to Order the Universe*. New York: Simon and Schuster, 1988. A more recent and mature effort by Davies to describe the newer accounts of the self-organizing powers of the universe. A good second volume to *God and the New Physics*.

Hartshorne, Charles. *A Natural Theology for Our Time*. La Salle, Illinois: Open Court Publishing Company, 1967. A short, readily accessible statement of the ideas of the most famous student of A. N. Whitehead. Dedicated to the memory of Socinus.

Hawkins, Stephen W. *A Brief History of Time: From the Big Bang to Black Holes*. New York: Bantam Books, 1988. The surprise best seller by a brilliant astrophysicist. A challenging yet rewarding introductory survey of the physical universe.

Herbert, Nick. *Quantum Reality: Beyond the New Physics*. New York: Doubleday and Company, 1985. A good exposition of quantum physics, especially the alternative theories or schools of thought that try to make sense of the bizarre behavior of particles.

Pine, Ronald. *Science and the Human Prospect*. Belmont, California: Wadsworth Publishing Company, 1989. A very good survey of modern science for students who have little prior exposure to its technical side. Also strong on science and its interaction with culture.

Row, William. *The Cosmological Argument*. Princeton, N.J.: Princeton University Press, 1975. A thorough examination and critique of several versions of the argument.

Russell, John Robert, *et al. Physics, Philosophy and Theology: A Common Quest for Understanding*. South Bend, Indiana: University of Notre Dame Press, 1988. Perhaps the best anthology on the subject. Advanced and often difficult, but thorough and rewarding.

Sagan, Carl. *Contact*. New York: Simon and Schuster, 1985. A best-selling novel by the noted exobiologist. The book's heroine, a SETI scientist, engages in occasional extensive theological disputes with various fundamentalists. Overall, the book reveals Sagan's own mystical or spiritual naturalism.

Tennant, R. R. *Philosophical Theology*. Cambridge, England: Cambridge University Press, 1928. Tennant recasts the teleological argument in response to its critics, especially Hume, and provides a basis for the entrance of scientific cosmology and evolution into the discussion.

Wilber, Ken, ed. *Quantum Questions: Mystical Writings of the World's Great Physicists*. Boston: Shambala Publications, Inc., 1984. A short collection of the philosophical reflections of Bohr, Heisenberg, Einstein, and others mostly confirming Eastern (Hindu and Buddhist) intuition about the nature of reality and the observer's role in it.

Zukav, Gary. *The Dancing Wu Li Masters: An Overview of the New Physics*. New York: William Morrow and Company, 1979. Description of twentieth-century atomic physics from an Eastern perspective. Less difficult than Capra's *The Tao of Physics*.

PART V

Life

THE PEACOCK'S DISPLAY CONSISTS OF AN INTRICATE ARRAY OF PRECISELY REPEATING PATTERNS.
IN THE PRESENCE OF SUCH BEAUTY, QUESTIONS ARE RAISED ABOUT THE PROCESSES AND GOALS
OF EVOLUTION THAT PROVIDE THE REASON FOR THIS DISPLAY—TO ATTRACT A SUITABLE MATE
AND PERPETUATE THE SPECIES BY MAXIMIZING PROGENY. DOES BIOLOGICAL EVOLUTION
CONSIST ONLY OF THE BLIND OPERATION OF GENETIC MUTATION AND NATURAL SELECTION
ALONG WITH OTHER SUBTLE BUT NATURAL FACTORS? OR IS IT A PROCESS INTENDED IN
SOME OTHER WAY TO PRODUCE BOTH THE PEACOCK'S BEAUTY AND CREATURES
LIKE OURSELVES CAPABLE OF APPRECIATING IT?

INTRODUCTION *Life*

Biology, literally "the study of life," raises questions and paradoxes that never appear in the study of matter itself. For one, living things are configured specifically to fulfill certain tasks or functions whose overall goal is to keep life going, even to advance it. Birds have wings, primates have hands, humans have a neocortex; whence and wherefore these attributes? How do living things come by functional organs that seem so ably and precisely fitted to accomplish just those tasks required by the organism to survive?

Another question specific to the life sciences is the nature of life itself. Clearly, living things fundamentally consist of the same stuff that other things consist of: atoms, molecules, substances of all kinds readily identified by physics and chemistry. A living protoplasmic entity is easily analyzed into parts and these parts into their subsequent parts until one arrives at a place where a chemist feels quite at home. The living body lends itself to a description based on physical and engineering principles, especially those that work so well in helping us understand the operations of machines. Even the brain is likened to an immensely complex organic computer. What, then, is life in and of itself?

Most of us resist the explanation for life in all its myriad dimensions, including moving, feeling, thinking, valuing, and hoping, that reduces it to a phenomenon of immense electrochemical complexity. Is life, and especially *my* life or *your* life, more than or different from its material composition in that each of us consists of something that is simply not totally accounted for by physics and chemistry?

The selections in Part V explore these issues and their consequences for religious ideas.

The first half of this part, "Creation and Evolution," explores the ongoing "war" between those who would see the grand order of life as the consequence of billions of years of dynamic development based on clearly understood principles and those who argue for a much shorter period of development in which the world is the product of divine fiat, a creative miracle of God. The world of life is therefore either the outcome of its own independent operation or the outcome of some intelligent external agency, an artifact of deity.

Evolutionists and creationists realize that much more than scientific truth is at stake in this debate. The values and principles of modern society are reflected, to a significant degree, in the unfettered, critical approach of science and the applications of its discoveries to our lives. Many scientists perceive these values and principles to be threatened by those who would return us to the dark ages of a dogmatic authority. Creationists see science and its ally humanism attacking on its flanks and seeking to demolish the foundations of tradition and faith by systematically removing God from the center of life. Both camps agree: if the *other* side emerges as victor the way is open to disaster.

In the first selection, "Theological Issues in Evolution," Ian Barbour examines several challenges that evolution has posed for religion. These challenges first emerged in the last century, but things have changed very little, and they remain as the chief concerns of creationists today.

From the perspective of those who feel threatened, evolution is a blind and automatic process that produces organized living things without the services of a designer. Evolution is directional but not directed. If this is so, then the human species is nothing special. We are continuous with all the rest of life. No special theological pleading intending to establish our exclusive status can overcome the harsh facts of our beastly origins. It follows that our ideals of good and evil, right and wrong, are best explained in terms of the evolutionary struggle for survival. This struggle encourages unfettered competition, even in human society, as the way nature eliminates the weak and establishes the strong or "fit." Finally, the evolutionary vision of life developing over vast periods of time measured in units of billions of years challenges the approach of scripture which insists that the Genesis account of creation (that creation occurred relatively recently and took a period of six days) is factual, not mythological. The Bible, God's Word, cannot be both inspired and in error. Protestant fundamentalism sees no compromise of its belief about scripture that does not entail the surrender of its basic position altogether.

The second selection, "Evolution—A Philosophy, Not a Science" by the biochemist Duane Gish, is a frontal attack on evolution as a science and as a naturalistic philosophy. Gish's merciless probing of alleged weaknesses in evolutionary science and his aggressive rhetorical style demonstrate clearly why the scientific community has galvanized its resources to counter creationism and why Isaac Asimov in the next selection characterizes the movement as a "threat."

Gish's angle of attack is ingenious. Only two possibilities exist for theoretically understanding living things in their abundance, variety, and harmony with the natural environment. One is evolution and the other is creation. Furthermore, these theories are both exhaustive and mutually exclusive. Both *cannot* be true but one *must* be true. Armed with these assumptions, Gish may pursue one of two strategies. He may attempt to show how all the evidence favors creation or he may attempt to show that the theory of evolution is fatally flawed. If he is successful in either strategy, creationism emerges victorious. Gish seems to prefer the latter strategy of eliminating his opponent, perhaps because it is almost always easier to attack rather than to defend a position. It is the reason why he relentlessly probes the alleged weaknesses of the evolutionary model and strives to give the impression of fragmentation within the scientific community by quoting the doubts that scientists themselves sometimes express about the explanatory power of evolutionary theory.

Gish's overriding intention in this selection is to disallow evolution as a scientific theory because its claims fail to satisfy the basic standards for any scientific theory. Scientists and philosophers of science would dispute each of Gish's contentions, beginning with his proposition that evolution is not observable and hence unfalsifiable. A sequence of fossil remains that demonstrate chronologically the development of some species or capability—anatomical developments that make hearing possible, for example—qualifies both as indirect observation and as evidence supporting the existence of evolutionary processes. Evolutionists continually voice the position that evolution itself is an established *fact*. The theory of *how* it occurs is what remains open for speculation, experiment, and the testimony of further evidence.

Gish's final thoughts reveal his deepest concerns and motives. The dispute is not primarily between true science and false science, but between the faith of nonbelieving, materialistic humanists and the faith of those who confess God's power and revelation found in the Bible preserved free from error. Gish is an excellent example of the perspective described by Barbour in the first selection.

The title of Isaac Asimov's contribution, "The 'Threat' of Creationism," clearly expresses his concern that creationists are out to turn the tables on evolutionary science. The challenges posed for religion by Darwin as described by Barbour have been complicated by the challenges posed for science by religion. Asimov responds to several of the major challenges before expressing his real concern in the matter; if creationists are successful in their efforts to win the day through legislation and courtroom battles, then the autonomy of the scientific enterprise, not to mention free speech and open educational inquiry, is threatened. The precedent raises the specter of governmental control and may eventually lead to the decline of American power and civilization.

On one level, the battle between creationism and evolution is joined on the field of facts and evidence. On another level, each camp fears the consequences for society if its opponent comes to dominate the field exclusively. Both levels are evident in the positions of Gish and Asimov.

In this debate the middle frequently falls victim to the extremes. Numerous attempts have been made to reconcile religion and evolution by constructing ideas that show how one is an expression of the other. The next two selections represent efforts to mediate between the positions represented by Gish and Asimov. "Some Reflections on Progress" by Pierre Teilhard de Chardin, is an account of divine energy at work in evolution. Here God gives meaning to evolution. In "Attributes of God in an Evolutionary Universe," Ralph Burhoe redefines God and other religious concepts in terms of evolutionary processes. Evolution gives meaning to God. In both cases religion and evolution are harmonized.

In his selection, Teilhard de Chardin responds to "realists," those pessimists who are disenchanted about the prospects of the human race for long-term advance. Teilhard wishes to show not only that progress is still possible, but that it is the major consequence of the nearly inevitable advance of evolution. Paleontology has discovered that developmental movement over vast epochs of time is a major fact of the cosmos. Biological life is part of this slow, massive movement. Life moves in a definite direction by organizing itself into larger and more complex systems of ever-increasing consciousness or spirit. A critical threshold is crossed with the emergence of the human species. For the first time, thought bursts forth as a controlling form of energy in a living species. We alone are capable of self-reflection and, therefore, of true freedom to command our destiny. We have accelerated the pace of evolution in the progress of science, technology, and culture. Our responsibility is to continue the evolutionary advance beyond ourselves by unifying our species into a great social system with a single consciousness. The force of attraction bringing about this unification, or *noogenesis,* is the spiritual energy of love.

Dedication to this project is dedication to God. God is both the directive impulse of evolution and its goal. "God creates and shapes us through the process of evolution," says Teilhard and achieves fulfillment in that process. It follows that the church is the perfect example of a voluntary human community gathered in love and sharing a unified consciousness. The institution of the church becomes the prototype for the next evolutionary advance.

In the fifth selection, Ralph W. Burhoe makes a conscious effort to construct a new foundation for Judeo-Christian theology by scooping out the mythic and metaphysical content of its most important symbols and replacing it with the established concepts of evolutionary science.

Since God is the central symbol of Western religion, our attention should be directed to a reconstruction of symbols associated with God's reality. These begin with the reality intended by title "god" (note the lowercase *g*) and proceed down the list of the divine attributes and activities that necessarily follow from that reality. The old model for God as a transcendent, sovereign person sustaining and directing Creation is unworkable. Science knows of no such being and, indeed, finds God's existence to be incompatible with the enterprise of science itself.

The theistic image of divinity is replaced by the notion that God is "the sovereign system of reality," "the totality of the natural world." Once this new model for God is clear, then all the other divine attributes and actions are easily translated according to its requirements. Each feature is reduced to an equivalent process in nature as disclosed by science. These are usually in accord with evolutionary biology, especially genetics and sociobiology.

The human response Burhoe hopes for is a renewed devotion to God to carry out the cosmic plan of evolutionary progress based on a clear understanding of what God is and what the divine will is for us. The enduring questions, especially those related to suffering and evil, are given new answers in this scientific theology.

The four selections in the second half of this part, "The Approach of Sociobiology," are about a very important issue arising from evolutionary theory. This is the determination of social conduct, and especially moral conduct, based on natural selection and genetic influences. In fact, a recent, optimistic but highly speculative science, *sociobiology,* is based on the theory that the human species is "wired" or genetically programmed by evolution toward predispositions (called *epigenetic rules*) to behave in certain ways in society. These tendencies are the result of natural selection at work on our ancestors in ancient and difficult times when people gathered in small communities and barely subsisted in a harsh environment. Social activities of "inclusive fitness," which favored survival, were retained and transmitted genetically because those groups that practiced these activities lived longer and produced more offspring to carry on the useful dispositions.

Sociobiology obviously questions the Western ideal of human nature shared by religion and humanism, namely that persons are guided by objective moral principles to decide freely for themselves on issues of right and wrong, and that these decisions are followed by appropriate conduct. Of course, everyone falls short of this ideal in practice, but it is considered to be an accurate and true account of our potential as responsible individuals. These latter selections explore this issue as understood by sociobiologists and by those who offer other alternatives for understanding the role of genes in human behavior.

For Michael Ruse, a philosopher, and Edward O. Wilson, a Harvard biologist and the acknowledged father of sociobiology, even ethics is to be reinterpreted in the light of this new science. Traditionally, we are led to understand that we are moral because of reason, virtue, and good will. Actually, as the authors explain in "The Evolution of Ethics," we are moral because doing or being good favored the survival of our ancestors. It seems to follow that morality, which is "merely an adaption put in place to further our reproductive ends," loses the whole point of being good for goodness sake. Even the belief that honesty, truth-telling, and courage are good and that we should conform to their requirements is a useful illusion with probable genetic origins. This is a radical point of view, one which strikes at the very foundations of the moral impulse.

The seventh article, by the Australian philosopher Peter Singer, questions these claims. In "Ethics and Sociobiology," Singer acknowledges the power of sociobiology to explain some forms of social behavior, especially those observed in other species. Altruistic or self-sacrificial conduct on the part of ants, bees, and crows is a good example.

But problems arise when these ideas are extrapolated to human societies. The very fact that moral behavior is the result of biological processes has the effect of discrediting that behavior by making it optional for the person who is aware of its evolutionary origins. For this person, moral principles are relative and free floating, deprived of deeper foundations. They no longer carry any power or authority as binding duties. Why should we in the modern world, living in an entirely different environment, be restricted by the moral codes of our cave-dwelling ancestors?

Another problem recognized by Singer is that a large number of these innate behavioral tendencies are understood to be offensive and immoral by modern society. They include double standards of sexist behavior and xenophobia—fear of strangers—that can lead to racism. Sociobiology seems to strengthen these social practices by showing that they are natural and probably unavoidable.

Finally, Singer argues that the very knowledge provided by sociobiologists may be employed against behaviors shaped by evolution. Now that we are aware of the "trickery" of our biology, we can act to defeat it and then go our own "good" way.

In the eighth selection, "God and the Selfish Genes," Arthur Peacocke examines the possible responses of theology to the claims of sociobiology. The new science works out of the assumptions of "evolutionary naturalism." These tend to be "deterministic, reductionistic, and functionalistic." That is, they explain complex human activities in terms of the "contribution to the survival of the genes." Rather than attacking this notion, Peacocke concedes its basic truth. But he then adds that God the Creator made it so. Thus, religion's response to sociobiology is not to deny its findings, but to take the essence of its message purified of methodological distortions (determinism, reductionism, functionalism) and of its hastily made claims (that altruism or charity is primarily directed toward one's kin for genetic reasons), and to use that message to enlighten theological inquiry.

Peacocke's points about reductionism are echoed in the final selection. John Haught's "Is Human Life Only Chemistry?" bridges the earlier discussion of evolution and of sociobiology by addressing the larger issue of material reductionism. Reductionism is the effort to explain higher human activities, like thinking, feeling, doing good, creating, loving, and worshiping in terms of the operations of lower level realities, such as atoms, molecules, the accidents of history, and the blind determinations of the laws of nature.

Haught is not sanguine about the ultimate success of the reductionist aim, which is, in the words of Francis Crick, "to explain all life in terms of physics and chemistry." In support of his reservations he refers to the thought of Michael Polanyi, who was a philosopher of science and a chemist. Polanyi maintains that reality is a series of levels or strata. Each level gives rise to the one above it and provides its foundation. But the principles that operate at higher levels cannot be reduced to those which operate at lower levels.

I am preparing these thoughts on a word processor. If the computer failed to function properly, my words would not register on its screen or in its memory. But someone who wants to know how English grammar works or how words are strung together to make meaningful statements would be foolish to dismantle this machine and seek the answers somewhere in its inner wiring. The two realities are hierarchically associated—they "interface," so to speak—but the higher (the words and the thoughts they express) is not reducible to the lower (the material substance and order of the machine and the flow of electricity that makes it work).

Where, then, does the hierarchy of ascending levels finally end: with mind, spirit, God, or, as Haught seems to suggest, with mystery? For the scientist bent on explaining all phenomena in terms of the behavior of their parts, the existence of various hierarchical realities is already mystery enough. But mystery does not mean ignorance. Each level depends upon its own laws and processes. It may easily be explained by simply understanding how those fundamentals work. One may speculate that God is the highest or most inclusive level, which is itself not included in any subsequent level—the nonincluded all-inclusive. It would then seem to follow that theology, the science of God, is as appropriate as physics and chemistry as an exercise of the human intellect.

CREATION AND EVOLUTION
THEOLOGICAL ISSUES IN EVOLUTION
IAN G. BARBOUR

Barbour's biographical sketch may be found in the first selection of Part I. This selection is taken from his classic *Issues in Science and Religion.*

In considering the debate that followed the publication of Darwin's *Origin,* it is not easy to disentangle the various issues involved, and in much of the controversy the levels of discussion were intermingled. Evolution as a biological theory was confused with evolutionary naturalism as an interpretive philosophy; some men supported both, others opposed both. An increasing group, however, accepted evolution but viewed it within a theistic context. We will postpone until the subsequent section a delineation of these patterns of interpretation—varieties of traditionalism, modernism, and naturalism—and try to list here some of the underlying issues raised by Darwin's work. Four problems that fall within the topics introduced in earlier chapters have been selected for comment:

(1) God and Nature: The Challenge to Design; (2) Man and Nature: The Challenge to Human Dignity; (3) Methods in Science: The Challenge of Evolutionary Ethics; and (4) Methods in Theology: The Challenge to Scripture.

GOD AND NATURE: THE CHALLENGE TO DESIGN

The prevalent version of the argument from design was particularly vulnerable, for it had started from the observed *adaptation of organic structures to useful functions.* But such adaptation could be accounted for by natural selection without invoking any pre-conceived plan. Usefulness was an effect and not a cause; it was the end product of an impersonal process. The species in existence are present simply because they have survived while thousands of others lost out in the struggle for existence. Instead of marveling that a fish has an eye that can see under water, we should have reason to be surprised only if this were *not* the case. Moreover, some of the facts that had always created difficulties for the advocates of design—such as useless rudimentary organs and traces of long-vanished limbs—could now be readily explained.

In some of his writings Darwin expressed the view that the *laws* by which life evolved were created by God, though the particular species resulting were the product of *chance* rather than design:

> There seems no more design in the variability of organic beings and in the action of natural science than in the course which the wind blows. [Everything in nature is the result of fixed laws.] . . . On the other hand, I cannot anyhow be contented to view this wonderful universe, and especially the nature of man, and to conclude that everything is the result of brute force. I am inclined to look at everything as resulting from designed laws, with the details, whether good or bad, left to the working out of what we may call chance.[1]

Chance seemed to be the antithesis of design. Darwin assumed that organic change is the product of a very large number of random spontaneous variations occurring entirely independently of each other, so the final result is accidental and unpremeditated. But the element of lawfulness, which received greater emphasis than the idea of chance, was also understood in a way which denied design. To earlier generations, scientific laws expressed the wisdom and constancy of God and were instruments of his purposes. Now they were increasingly taken as the autonomous and mechanical operation of impersonal forces. Law as well as chance appeared to be blind and purposeless.

Darwin at one point indicated that lawfulness does not exclude the concept of *God as primary cause;* he even spoke of natural laws as the "secondary means" by which God created.[2] He came close to recognizing that the scientist studies the domain of secondary causes and cannot ask why nature works as it does. But the following passage suggests that his own epistemology was undermined by the admission of the lowly origins of man's mind, so that in his later years he took a more agnostic position. He maintains

> . . . the impossibility of conceiving this immense and wonderful universe, including man with his capacity for looking far backwards and far into futurity, as the result of blind chance or necessity. When thus reflecting I feel compelled to look to a First Cause having an intelligent mind in some degree analogous to that of man: and I deserve to be called a Theist. . . .

But then arises the doubt, can the mind of man, which has, as I fully believe, been developed from a mind as low as that possessed by the lowest animals, be trusted when it draws such grand conclusions.[3]

Neither in the typical formulations of the design argument, such as Paley's, nor in the rejection of it by Darwin and others of his time, was the nature of divine causality discussed. Usually God's activity had simply been assumed to be like that of a workman; and evolution made this simple "maker" analogy untenable.

One way out of this dilemma was to *broaden the concept of design* by applying it not to specific organs or organisms but to the evolutionary process as a whole. Asa Gray, Harvard botanist and leading interpreter of scientific opinion to the American public, maintained that the over-all history of nature could be understood in purposeful terms, despite the occurrence of waste and struggle. "Emergence is design by wholesale, the direction of the process by which mind and moral personality arose, which are not explainable by matter in random motion." Gray defended the idea of a Creator working through evolution to produce a gradually unfolding design; he also argued that God providentially supplies the new variations in the right direction. Other scientists held that God does not intervene, but has built design into the very structure of the process through which higher forms of life and eventually man could come into being. The anthropologist Eiseley has recently written:

> Darwin did not destroy the argument from design. He destroyed only the watchmaker and the watch. . . . Darwin had delivered a death blow to a simple, a naively simple, form of the design argument, but as Huxley himself came to realize, it is still possible to argue for directivity in the process of life.[4]

MAN AND NATURE: THE CHALLENGE TO HUMAN DIGNITY

In the Western tradition, *man was set apart* from all other creatures. Man alone was a rational being; human reason was considered totally different in kind from whatever intelligence animals have. Man alone possessed an immortal soul, which defined his true being and his relationship to God. Man's distinctiveness put him in many respects "outside" nature, despite his sharing with other creatures a common dependence on God and a common finitude and temporality. This uniqueness of status now appeared to be denied by the theory of evolution. Distinctions between human and animal characteristics were indeed minimized by Darwin and his followers. Surviving primitive tribes, as Darwin portrayed them, almost closed the gap between man and animal. Huxley claimed that there is less difference between man and the highest apes than between higher and lower apes. Man himself, absorbed into nature, seemed to be the product of accidental variations and the struggle for survival, a child of blind chance and law.

Man's moral sense had always been considered one of his most distinctive capacities, but Darwin claimed that it too had originated by selection. In the early history of mankind a tribe whose members had strong social instincts, such as fidelity and self-sacrifice for the common good, would have had an advantage over other tribes. If morality conferred survival value, standards of conscience would have tended to rise. In the extinction of savage races in conflict with more civilized ones Darwin saw further evidence of built-in ethical advance. In a similar fashion he traced each of man's emotional and intellectual characteristics back to origins in the earlier stages of human and subhuman development.

There were other biologists, however, who gave greater emphasis to the *distinctive characteristics of man.* A. R. Wallace, who had formulated the principle of natural selection independently of Darwin, recognized that the presence of the human brain radically altered the character of evolution; with the development of intellect, bodily specialization and changes in physical organs were outmoded. Wallace also recognized that the gap in intellect between man and ape was far greater than Darwin had acknowledged; nor could "primitive" tribes fill the gap, for their inherent mental capacities are actually as great as those of civilized peoples. Again, he saw the distinctiveness of language as symbolic communication, where Darwin had seen little difference between animal signals and human speech. At each of these points, subsequent investigation has tended to vindicate Wallace's contributions.

In his later writing, Wallace went further and claimed that natural selection cannot account for *man's higher faculties.* He pointed out that the brain size in very primitive tribes, which is comparable to that in highly civilized groups, actually provides a mental capacity far beyond the simple needs of their aboriginal patterns of life, for which a much smaller brain would have sufficed. "Natural selection could only have endowed savage man with a brain a little superior to that of an ape, whereas he actually possesses one very little inferior to that of a philosopher."[5] And how can one explain musical, artistic, or ethical capacities that contribute nothing to survival? Wallace felt that such "latent powers" possessed in advance of the need to employ them indicate that "some higher intelligence may have directed the process by which the human race was developed." More recent opinion has not supported Wallace's idea of "latent powers," but it has tended to agree with him in holding that man's evolution involved distinctive processes which Darwin's purely biological framework ignored.

It is perhaps understandable that Darwin overemphasized *the continuity of man and animal.* The earlier tradition had portrayed such an absolute discontinuity that to establish man's rootedness in nature Darwin looked for all the similarities he could find, overlooking the differences. The tremendous scope of the theory of evolution had been amply demonstrated, and it was easy to assume that all human phenomena could be exhaustively interpreted in essentially biological terms. It is also understandable that there were both scientists and theologians who, in reaction to such claims, insisted that natural selection could not account for man. Today we can see that in the long history of the world, man's emergence marks a genuinely new chapter—one not disconnected from previous chapters, and yet involving factors not previously present. Something radically different takes place when culture rather than the genes becomes the principal means by which the past is transmitted to the future, and when conscious choice alters man's development.

Moreover, both opponents and proponents of evolution often seem to have made the implicit assumption that *man's descent determines his nature.* Much of the emotion accompanying the rejection of the idea that "we have apes in our family tree" can be traced to this notion that source fixes meaning. Belief in evolution was equated with belief that man is "nothing but an animal." Man's origins were too readily taken by both sides to be the chief clue to his significance; a subhuman past somehow came to imply a less than fully human present. This is a genetic or temporal form of "reductionism," which finds the significance of an entity not in its smallest parts, as with eighteenth-century materialism, but in its most primitive beginning; it is a philosophical assumption equally destructive to the dignity of man, and equally unwarranted as a conclusion from the data.

METHODS IN SCIENCE: THE CHALLENGE OF EVOLUTIONARY ETHICS

If Darwin and his defenders believed that the theory of evolution had undermined the argument from design and the traditional status of man, it might be expected that their attitudes toward the future would have been pessimistic. But amid the optimism of the late nineteenth-century the total evolutionary picture seemed to convey a hopeful message. In the climate of the Victorian era the idea of *evolutionary progress* became a secular substitute for providence; blind fate was transformed into beneficent cosmic process, which was taken to guarantee the final fruition of history and even the perfectibility of man. Faith in progress replaced the doctrines of creation and providence as assurance that the universe is not really purposeless. Neither uniform law nor accidental chance is any threat if it leads to inevitable advance and if nature is a coherent and intelligible system. The Harvard philosopher John Fiske wrote that man was reinstated because evolution "shows us distinctly, for the first time, how the creation and perfection of man is the goal toward which nature's work has been tending from the first." The Enlightenment faith in social progress had been expanded to confidence in a progressive universe.

Was this concept of progress a conclusion reached *by the methods of science?* Darwin himself was evidently aware of the ambiguity at this point. He recognized that in speaking of "the fittest to survive," a biologist is not rendering a moral judgment, but only referring to physical endurance. The "improvement" of a species means only an advantage in competition in a given environment; it might appear to be "retrogression" in a different environment or when viewed against the whole pattern of organic development. If Darwin and Spencer nevertheless often used "progress" in a way that implied a value judgment, they did so, says J. C. Greene,

> . . . because in their heart of hearts they believed that the processes of nature operated, however slowly and sporadically, to produce ever higher forms of existence. As naturalists they tried to define "improvement," "fitness," "highness," and the like in biological terms, but their use of the terms was subtly colored by the indomitable optimism of their age. The nineteenth century believed in progress, but it was not very careful to define what it meant by progress.[6]

The problem of *the relation of ethical norms to evolution* becomes acute if man's free and conscious choice guides his own future evolution. In some passages, Darwin implied that anything man does is an expression of natural selection, and that if progress is inherent in the process no human decision can hinder it. In other passages, he urged man to choose deliberately the pattern which the rest of nature exemplifies. He warned that future progress would be hindered by sentimental policies which protect weaker individuals, such as the sick or maimed, who would be eliminated under more competitive conditions. "There should be open competition for all men; and the most able should not be prevented by laws or customs from succeeding best and rearing the largest number of offspring." But Darwin was not altogether consistent, for there was "deep in his character a warm humanitarianism and a strong holdover of the Christian ethic in which he had been trained."[7] He recognized "a higher morality" which would encourage respect and love toward all men, including the weak; but such a morality would lessen the competitive struggle and thus undermine what he had taken to be the source of progress. He also pointed out that even among animals brute strength is often not the most important factor in survival.

The belief that *competition promotes progress* fitted in well, however, with the predominantly individualistic social philosophy common in this period. Biological and political ideas merged in what has been called *"social Darwinism."*[8] Even before he read Darwin, Herbert Spencer had tried to show that laissez faire private enterprise was in keeping with the stern disciplines of nature that produce biological improvement. He found in the evolutionary struggle as Darwin described it a justification for his claim that economic competition unhampered by government regulation fosters human welfare. The survival of the fittest was to be the instrument for the evolution of society also; here, too, rugged individualism would bring beneficial results. Competition between groups and the conflict of races had been valuable historically, "a continuous overrunning of the less powerful or less adapted by the more powerful or more adapted, a driving of inferior varieties into undesirable habitats, and, occasionally, an extermination of inferior varieties." But Spencer, like Darwin, faced difficulties in his attempt to derive ethical norms from evolution. Having made biological survival his criterion of progress, Spencer could provide no satisfactory basis for rejecting an appeal to arms, such as that of Prussian militarism which would try to prove a nation's fitness on the battlefield.

T. H. Huxley, taking issue with both Darwin and Spencer, held that valid *ethical norms cannot be derived from evolution*. Standards appropriate for human conduct simply cannot be obtained from examining natural selection or copying the law of the jungle: "Let us understand, once for all, that the ethical progress of society depends not on imitating the cosmic process, still less in running away from it, but in combating it."[9] Huxley asserted:

> The practice of that which is ethically best—what we call goodness or virtue—involves a course of conduct which in all respects is opposed to that which leads to success in the cosmic struggle for existence. In place of ruthless self-assertion, it demands self-restraint; in place of thrusting aside or treading down all competitors, it requires that the individual shall not merely respect, but shall help his fellows; its influence is directed, not so much to the survival of the fittest, as to the fitting of as many as possible to survive. It repudiates the gladiatorial theory of existence.[10]

Having rejected both "evolutionary ethics" and revealed religion, Huxley fell back on a sort of moral intuitionism as the source of ethical norms—though the goals he actually defended seem principally to reflect his religious upbringing and surrounding culture.

We will find this discussion of the relation between evolution, progress, and ethics continuing vigorously today, accompanied by a more careful analysis of the methodological distinctions between scientific and ethical questions.

METHODS IN THEOLOGY: THE CHALLENGE TO SCRIPTURE

Long before Darwin, *biblical literalism* had been cast in doubt by scientific knowledge— from Copernican astronomy to the new geology. Moreover, the scholarly analysis of biblical texts—the historical and literary research known as "higher criticism"—had already on completely different grounds begun to call the inerrancy of scripture into question. It appears surprising therefore that part of the popular outcry against evolution centered on the challenge to biblical authority. One reason was that, for the first time, central biblical beliefs—the purposefulness of the world, the dignity of man, and the drama of man's creation and fall—seemed to be threatened. Many Christians knew only one way to defend these religious convictions, namely to reassert the doctrine of biblical infallibility that had been typical of the "scholastic" period of Protestant orthodoxy.

Besides, some of the leading scientists had linked evolution with their own *atheistic viewpoints,* and conservative churchmen opposed both indiscriminately. Such a liaison between a scientific theory and a sweeping attack on religion had occurred previously among the French skeptics, but it was a less familiar phenomenon in England and America. Darwin himself was cautious in his criticism of religion, but some of his defenders—most notably Huxley—went on the offensive against Christianity in the name of the freedom of science. Again, a number of assumptions that had been part of the *intellectual milieu* of the West for centuries were closely associated with particular biblical passages, as we have seen; familiar patterns of thought were defended by appeals to scripture. For example, the traditional view of man's status seemed to many people inseparable from the biblical account of Adam's creation in a unique act of God.

For the biblical literalists, then, there could be *no compromise with evolution.* Genesis describes the once-for-all creation of species in their present form, and if Darwin maintained that species change he was simply mistaken. Philip Gosse proposed that God had put all those fossils in a plausibly misleading pattern in order to test man's faith. From the ages of Adam's descendants, Archbishop Ussher had calculated that creation must have occurred in 4004 B.C. Others pointed out that evolution is "only a theory, not a fact," and that "it has not been proved"—remarks that are valid but show an inadequate understanding of the character of scientific inquiry, for no scientific theory can ever be proved with certainty to be true or immune to future modification. There was abundant opportunity for appeal to prejudice—or to sentiment, as when Wilberforce asked Huxley whether he traced his descent from an ape on his grandfather's side or his grandmother's.

But there were many others whose view of scripture *allowed the acceptance of evolution.* The majority of Protestant authors distinguished between the religious ideas of Genesis and the ancient cosmology in which these ideas were expressed. They interpreted the biblical account as a symbolic and poetic rendition of affirmations about the dependence of the world on God—affirmations they found not incompatible with the picture of evolution as God's way of creating. The modernists went further; for them the Bible was a purely human document, a record of man's evolving religious insight.

The evolutionary view of nature molded the modernist understanding of God; the divine was now an immanent force at work within the process, an indwelling spirit manifest in the creative advance of life to ever higher levels. Catholic thought avoided the extremes of both literalism and modernism. Though Rome was at first reluctant to accept evolution, a position was gradually defined which acknowledged man's physical derivation from animal ancestry but preserved his uniqueness as a spiritual being. . . .

NOTES

1. F. Darwin, *Life and Letters,* Vol. I, 279; Vol. II, 105. The sentence in brackets is found only in Nora Barlow, ed., *The Autobiography of Charles Darwin, 1809–1882, with Original Omissions Restored* (New York: Harcourt, Brace, 1959), p. 87.
2. M. Mandelbaum, "Darwin's Religious Views," *Journal of The History of Ideas,* Vol. 19 (1958), 363; J. C. Greene, "Darwin and Religion," *Proceedings of American Philosophical Society,* Vol. 103 (1959), 715.
3. F. Darwin, ed., *Life and Letters,* Vol. I, 282.
4. From p. 198 of *Darwin's Century* by Loren C. Eiseley. Copyright © 1958 by Loren C. Eiseley. Reprinted by permission of Doubleday & Company, Inc., and Victor Gollancz, Ltd.
5. A. R. Wallace, *Contributions to the Theory of Natural Selection,* 2nd ed. (New York: The Macmillan Company, 1871), p. 356.
6. Quoted by permission from *The Death of Adam* by John C. Greene, © 1959 by the Iowa State University Press, p. 301. Mentor PB.
7. *Ibid.,* p. 81.
8. See Richard Hofstadter, *Social Darwinism in American Thought,* rev. ed. (Boston: Beacon Press, 1955; PB).
9. Thomas H. Huxley, *Evolution and Ethics* (New York: D. Appleton & Co., 1896), p. 83.
10. *Ibid.,* p. 81.

QUESTIONS FOR STUDY

1. How was the argument from design weakened by Darwin's theories?

2. How may the human species be understood as "set apart from all other creatures"? In what way did Darwin's theories undermine this human uniqueness?

3. How may one argue from evolutionary theory to the conclusion that competition in society—in the economy and in personal relationships—is right and good?

4. What alternative to the strict interpretation of the Bible, sometimes known as *biblical literalism,* exists for understanding scripture and avoiding conflict with evolution?

QUESTIONS FOR REFLECTION

1. Explain how the design argument may be salvaged by a broader understanding of the ways God works in creation.

2. Argue for the proposition that the continuity of human life with all life as the most recent product of evolution affirms rather than denies human dignity.

3. Do evolutionary processes in nature, especially strong competition between species, provide good reasons for making such behavior the moral norm for human society? Is following nature, "doing what is natural," the best foundation for moral action?

NETWORKING

Barbour explores many concepts discussed elsewhere. Some of the more important include *design* in Bube, Hick, Dyson, Polkinghorne, Asimov, Teilhard, and Lovelock; *law and chance* in Davies, Dawkins, and Polkinghorne; *primary and secondary causation* in Gilkey, Lackey, and Geisler and Anderson; *status of humankind in nature* in Teilhard, Peacocke, Haught, Dobel, Gray, and Berry; *progressive evolution* in Swimme, Wald, Teilhard, and Burhoe; *ethics* in Einstein, Updike, Ruse and Wilson, Singer, and Burhoe; *the Bible* in Barbour (Part I), Niebuhr, Gish, Asimov; and *divine immanence* in Teilhard, Burhoe, and Cobb.

EVOLUTION—A PHILOSOPHY, NOT A SCIENCE
DUANE T. GISH

Duane Gish is associate director of the Institute for Creation Research in El Cajon, California. His Ph.D. in biochemistry is from the University of California at Berkeley. He has conducted research at Berkeley and with the Upjohn Company. Dr. Gish has lectured widely on creation science and is known especially for his public debates with scientists. He is also the author of numerous books and articles on this subject.

The general theory of organic evolution is the theory that all living things have arisen by a materialistic, naturalistic evolutionary process from a single source which itself arose by a similar process from a dead, inanimate world. This theory may also be called the molecule-to-man theory of evolution.

The creation account found in Genesis, on the other hand, records the fact that all basic animal and plant types (the created kinds) were brought into existence by acts of God using special processes which are not operative today.

Most scientists accept evolution, not as a theory, but as an established fact. Theodosius Dobzhansky, geneticist and widely-known evolutionist, formerly Professor of Zoology at Columbia University and . . . at the University of California, Davis, has said that, "The occurrence of the evolution of life in the history of the earth is established about as well as events not witnessed by human observers can be."[1] Richard B. Goldschmidt, a Professor at the University of California before his death, has stated dogmatically that "Evolution of the animal and plant world is considered by all those entitled to judgment to be a fact for which no further proof is needed."[2] Almost all science books and school and university texts present evolution as an established fact. These considerations alone convince many people that molecule-to-man evolution has actually occurred.

The proponents of evolution theory adamantly insist that special creation be excluded from any possible consideration as an explanation for origins on the basis that it does not qualify as a scientific theory. On the other hand, they would view as unthinkable the consideration of evolution as anything less than pure science. In fact, as already mentioned, most evolutionists insist that evolution must no longer be thought of as a theory but must be considered to be a fact. In spite of this attitude, however, not only is there a wealth of scientific support for rejecting evolution as a fact, but evolution does not even qualify as a scientific theory according to a strict definition of the latter.

What criteria must be met for a theory to be considered as scientific in the usually accepted sense? George Gaylord Simpson has stated that, "It is inherent in any definition of science that statements that cannot be checked by observation are not really about anything . . . or at the very least, they are not science."[3] A definition of science given by the Oxford Dictionary is:

A branch of study which is concerned either with a connected body of *demonstrated truths* or with *observed facts* systematically classified and more or less colligated by being brought under general laws, and which includes trustworthy methods for the discovery of new truth within its own domain.

Thus, for a theory to qualify as a scientific theory, it must be supported by events, processes, or properties which can be observed, and the theory must be useful in predicting the outcome of future natural phenomena or laboratory experiments. An additional limitation usually imposed is that the theory must be capable of falsification. That is, it must be possible to conceive some experiment the failure of which would disprove the theory.

It is on the basis of such criteria that most evolutionists insist that creation be refused consideration as a possible explanation for origins. Creation has not been witnessed by human observers, it cannot be tested experimentally, and as a theory it is non-falsifiable.

The general theory of evolution also fails to meet all three of these criteria, however. It is obvious, for example, that no one observed the origin of the universe, the origin of life, the conversion of a fish into an amphibian, or an ape into a man. No one, as a matter of fact, has even observed the origin of a species by naturally occurring processes. Evolution has been *postulated*, but it has never been *observed*.

This has been affirmed by both Dobzhansky and Goldschmidt, whom, as it has been noted, are wholly committed to faith in evolution. In the quotation cited earlier in this chapter, Dobzhansky clearly states that *evolution has not been witnessed by human observers.*

Goldschmidt, after outlining his postulated systemic mutation, or "hopeful monster," mechanism for evolution, stated, "Such an assumption is violently opposed by the majority of geneticists, who claim that the facts found on the sub-specific level must apply also to the higher categories. Incessant repetition of this *unproved claim*, glossing lightly over the difficulties, and the assumption of an arrogant attitude toward those who are not so easily swayed by fashions in science, are considered to afford scientific proof of the doctrine. It is true that nobody thus far has produced a new species or genus, etc., by macro-mutation. *It is equally true that nobody has produced even a species by the selection of micromutations."* [4] Later on in this same paper, he stated, "Neither has anyone witnessed the production of a new specimen of a higher taxonomic category by selection of micromutants." [5] Goldschmidt has thus affirmed that, in the molecules-to-man context, only the most trivial change, or that at the sub-species level, has actually ever been observed.

Since evolution has not been observed in nature, and even a species cannot be produced by the selection of mutants, it is apparent that evolution is not subject to experimental test. This was admitted by Dobzhansky when he said, "These evolutionary happenings are unique, unrepeatable, and irreversible. It is as impossible to turn a land vertebrate into a fish as it is to effect the reverse transformation. The applicability of the experimental method to the study of such unique historical processes is severely restricted before all else by the time intervals involved, which far exceed the lifetime of any human experimenter. And yet it is just such *impossibility* that is demanded by antievolutionists when they ask for 'proofs' of evolution which they would magnanimously accept as satisfactory."[6]

Dobzhansky thus states that the applicability of the experimental method to evolution is an "impossibility." One reason given by Dobzhansky and other evolutionists for rejecting creation as a possible explanation for origins is because it is not subject to the experimental method. At the same time, however, they consider it wholly unreasonable for creationists to place the same demand on evolution theory!

It can be seen that evolutionists seek to excuse the fact that evolution cannot be observed nor tested experimentally on the basis that real evolutionary events require great lengths of time for their consummation. Yes, it is true that the evolutionary process postulated would require more time than we have available for human observation. But then, evolution can never be more than just a postulate.

While evolutionists deny the miraculous in the origin of living things, the evolutionary process, given enough time, supposedly produces miracles. Thus,

$$\text{FROG} \xrightarrow{\;t = \text{instantaneous}\;} \text{PRINCE} = \text{NURSERY TALE}$$

but

$$\text{FROG} \xrightarrow{\;t = 300 \text{ million years}\;} \text{PRINCE} = \text{SCIENCE}$$

Furthermore, the architects of the modern synthetic theory of evolution have so skillfully constructed their theory that it is not capable of falsification. The theory is so plastic that it is capable of explaining anything. This is the complaint of Olson[7] and of several participants in the Wistar Symposium on Mathematical Challenges to the Neo Darwinian Interpretation of Evolution.[8]

Eden, one of the mathematicians, put it this way, with reference to falsifiability: "This cannot be done in evolution, taking it in its broad sense, and this is really all I meant when I called it tautologous in the first place. It can, indeed, explain anything. You may be ingenious or not in proposing a mechanism which looks plausible to human beings and mechanisms which are consistent with other mechanisms which you have discovered, but it is still an unfalsifiable theory."[9]

In addition to scientists who are creationists, a growing number of other scientists have expressed doubts that modern evolution theory could explain more than trivial change. Eden became so discouraged after computerized calculations showed that the probability of certain evolutionary changes occurring (according to mechanisms postulated by modern evolutionists) was essentially zero that he proclaimed, ". . . an adequate scientific theory of evolution must await the discovery and elucidation of new natural laws,—physical, physico-chemical, and biological."[10] Salisbury has similarly stated his doubts based on probabilistic considerations.[11]

The attack on the theory by French scientists has been intense in recent years. A review of the French situation stated, "This year saw the controversy rapidly growing, until recently it culminated in the title 'Should We Burn Darwin?' spread over two pages of the magazine *Science et Vie*. The article, by the science writer Aime Michel, was based on the author's interviews with such specialists as Mrs. Andree Tetry, professor at the famous *Ecole des Hautes Etudes*, and a world authority on problems of evolution, Professor Rene Chauvin, and other noted French biologists; and on his thorough study of some 600 pages of biological data collected, in collaboration with Mrs. Tetry, by the late Michael Cuenot, a biologist of international fame. Aime Michel's conclusion is significant: The classical theory of evolution in its strict sense belongs to the past. Even if they do not publicly take a definite stand, almost all French specialists hold today strong mental reservations as to the validity of natural selection."[12]

E. C. Olson, one of the speakers at the Darwinian Centennial Celebration at Chicago, made the following statement on that occasion, "There exists, as well, a generally silent group of students engaged in biological pursuits who tend to disagree with much of the current thought but say and write little because they are not particularly interested, do not see that controversy over evolution is of any particular importance, or are so strongly in disagreement that it seems futile to undertake the monumental task of controverting the immense body of information and theory that exists in the formulation of modern thinking. It is, of course, difficult to judge the size and composition of this silent segment, but there is no doubt that the numbers are not inconsiderable."[13]

Fothergill refers to what he calls "the paucity of evolutionary theory as a whole."[14] Erhlich and Holm have stated their reservations in the following way, "Finally, consider the third question posed earlier: 'What accounts for the observed patterns in nature?' It has become fashionable to regard modern evolutionary theory as the *only* possible explanation of these patterns rather than just the best explanation that has been developed so far. It is conceivable, even likely, that what one might facetiously call a non-Euclidean theory of evolution lies over the horizon. Perpetuation of today's theory as dogma will not encourage progress toward more satisfactory explanations of observed phenomena."[15]

Sometimes the attacks are openly critical, such as Danson's letter which appeared recently in *New Scientist* and stated in part, ". . . the Theory of Evolution is no longer with us, because neo-Darwinism is now acknowledged as being unable to explain anything more than trivial change, and in default of some other theory we have none . . . despite the hostility of the witness provided by the fossil record, despite the innumerable difficulties, and despite the lack of even a credible theory, evolution survives . . . Can there be any other area of science, for instance, in which a concept as intellectually barren as embryonic recapitulation could be used as evidence for a theory?"[16]

Macbeth has recently published an especially incisive criticism of evolution theory.[17] He points out that although evolutionists have abandoned classical Darwinism, the modern synthetic theory they have proposed as a substitute is equally inadequate to explain progressive change as the result of natural selection, and, as a matter of fact, they cannot even define natural selection in nontautologous terms. Inadequacies of the present theory and failure of the fossil record to substantiate its predictions leave macro-evolution, and even micro-evolution, intractable mysteries according to Macbeth. Macbeth suggests that no theory at all may be preferable to the existing one.

In view of the above, it is incredible that most leading scientists dogmatically insist that the molecules-to-man evolution theory be taught as a fact to the exclusion of all other postulates. Evolution in this broad sense is unproven and unprovable and thus cannot be considered as fact. It is not subject to test by the ordinary methods of experimental science—observation and falsification. It thus does not, in a strict sense, even qualify as a scientific theory. It is a postulate, and may serve as a model within which attempts may be made to explain and correlate the evidence from the historical record, that is, the fossil record, and to make predictions concerning the nature of future discoveries.

Creation is, of course, unproven and unprovable by the methods of experimental science. Neither can it qualify, according to the above criteria, as a scientific theory, since creation would have been unobservable, and would as a theory be non-falsifiable. In the scientific realm, creation is, therefore, as is evolution, a postulate which may serve as a model to explain and correlate the evidence related to origins. Creation is, in this sense, no more religious nor less scientific than evolution. In fact, to many well-informed scientists, creation seems to be far superior to the evolution model as an explanation for origins.

It is often stated that there are no reputable scientists who do not accept the theory of evolution. This is just one more false argument used to win converts to the theory. While it is true that creationists among scientists definitely constitute a minority, there are *many* creation scientists, and their number is growing. Among these may be numbered such well-established scientists as Dr. A. E. Wilder-Smith, Professor of Pharmacology in Boggern, Switzerland, and author or co-author of more than 50 technical publications; Dr. W. R. Thompson, world-famous biologist and former Director of the Commonwealth Institute of Biological Control of Canada; Dr. Melvin A. Cook, winner of the 1968 E. G. Murphee Award in Industrial and Engineering Chemistry from the American Chemical Society and also winner of the Nobel Nitro Award, now president of the Ireco Chemical Company, Salt Lake City; Dr. Henry M. Morris, for 13 years Professor of Hydraulic Engineering and Head of the Civil Engineering Department at Virginia Polytechnic Institute and University, one of the largest in the U.S., now Director of the Institute for Creation Research and Academic Vice-President of Christian Heritage College, San Diego; Dr. Walter Lammerts, geneticist and famous plant-breeder; Dr. Frank Marsh, Professor of Biology at Andrews University until his retirement; and the late Dr. J. J. Duyvene De Wit, Professor of Zoology at the University of the Orange Free State, South Africa, at the time of his death.

The Creation Research Society, a recently formed organization of Christian men of science, all of whom hold advanced degrees and are fully committed to the acceptance of Biblical and scientific creationism as opposed to evolution, now numbers over 400 in membership.[18] There is yet a vastly larger number of scientists who do not accept the theory but choose to remain silent for a variety of reasons.

Why have most scientists accepted the theory of evolution? Is the evidence really that convincing? This seems to be the clear implication. On the other hand, is it possible for that many scientists to be wrong? The answer is an emphatic "YES!" Consider for a moment some historical examples. For centuries the accepted scientific view was that all planets revolved around the earth. This was the Ptolemaic geocentric theory of the universe. Only after a prolonged and bitter controversy did the efforts of Copernicus, Galileo, and others succeed in convincing the scientific world that the Ptolemaic system was wrong and that Copernicus was right in his contention that the planets in the solar system revolved around the sun.

At one time most people with scientific training who rejected the Biblical record of creation accepted as fact the idea that life spontaneously arose from non-life. Thus, frogs supposedly spontaneously arose from swamps, decaying matter generated flies, and rats were brought to life out of matter found in debris, etc. A series of carefully designed and executed experiments by Redi, Spallanzani, and Pasteur spanning 200 years were required to put to rest the theory of the spontaneous generation of life.

In recent times, a theory dealing with weak interactions of atomic particles became so widely accepted by physicists that it won the status of a law, the Law of Parity. During the 1950's, two brilliant Chinese-American scientists performed a series of experiments that disproved the theory and deposed the "Law."

In all of the above examples, the vast majority of scientists was wrong and a small minority was right. No doubt, strong preconceived ideas and prejudices were powerful factors in accounting for the fact that scientists were reluctant to give up the geocentric theory of the universe and the theory of the spontaneous generation of life.

The effects of prejudice and preconceived ideas is of overwhelming importance in the acceptance of the theory of evolution. The reason most scientists accept evolution has nothing to do, primarily, with the evidence. The reason that most scientists accept the theory of evolution is that *most scientists are unbelievers, and unbelieving, materialistic men are forced to accept a materialistic, naturalistic explanation for the origin of all living things.* Watson, for example, has referred to the theory of evolution as "a theory universally accepted not because it can be proved by logically coherent evidence to be true, but because the only alternative, special creation, is clearly incredible."[19] That this is the philosophy held by most biologists has been recently emphasized by Dobzhansky. In his review of Monod's book, *Chance and Necessity,* Dobzhansky said, "He has stated with admirable clarity, and eloquence often verging on pathos, *the mechanistic materialist philosophy shared by most of the present 'establishment'* in the biological sciences."[20]

Sir Julian Huxley, British evolutionist and grandson of Thomas Huxley, one of Darwin's strongest supporters when he first published his theory, has said that " Gods are peripheral phenomena produced by evolution."[21] What Huxley meant was that the idea of God merely evolved as man evolved from lower animals. Huxley would like to establish a humanistic religion based on evolution. Humanism has been defined as "the belief that man shapes his own destiny. It is a constructive philosophy, *a non-theistic religion, a way of life.* "[22] This same publication quotes Huxley as saying, "I use the word 'Humanist' to mean someone who believes that man is just as much a natural phenomenon as an animal or plant; that his body, mind, and soul were not supernaturally created but are products of *evolution,* and that he is not under the control or guidance of any supernatural being or beings, but has to rely on himself and his own powers." The inseparable link between this non-theistic humanistic religion and belief in evolution is evident.

Dr. George Gaylord Simpson, Professor of Vertebrate Paleontology at Harvard University until his retirement and one of the world's best known evolutionists, has said that the Christian faith, which he calls the "higher superstition" (in contrast to the "lower superstition" of pagan tribes of South America and Africa) is intellectually unacceptable.[23] Simpson concludes his book, *Life of the Past,*[24] with what Sir Julian Huxley has called "a splendid assertion of the evolutionist view of man."[25] "Man," Simpson writes, "stands alone in the universe, a unique product of a long, unconscious, impersonal, material process with unique understanding and potentialities. These he owes to no one but himself, and it is to himself that he is responsible. He is not the creature of uncontrollable and undeterminable forces, but his own master. He can and must decide and manage his own destiny."

Thus, according to Simpson, man is alone in the Universe (there is no God), he is the result of an impersonal, unconscious process (no one directed his origin or creation), and he is his own master and must manage his own destiny (there is no God who is man's Lord and Master and who determines man's destiny). That, according to Simpson and Huxley, is *the evolutionist's view of man.*

No doubt a large majority of the scientific community embraces the mechanistic materialistic philosophy of Simpson, Huxley, and Monod. Many of these men are highly intelligent, and they have woven the fabric of evolution theory in an ingenious fashion. They have then combined this evolution theory with humanistic philosophy and have clothed the whole with the term "science." The product, a non-theistic religion, with evolutionary philosophy as its creed under the guise of "science," is being taught in most public schools, colleges and universities of the United States. It has become our unofficial state-sanctioned religion.

The evolutionist's view of man as expressed by Simpson and Huxley is in direct contrast to the Biblical view of man, found, for example, in Psalm 100, verse 3: "Know ye that the Lord he is God: it is he that hath made us and not we ourselves; we are his people and the sheep of his pasture." The Bible does indeed reveal that there is a living God who has created us and who controls our destiny.

Furthermore, a God who is great enough to create and control this universe is great enough, once having given His revelation to man, to preserve that revelation free from error. This preservation was not dependent upon man, but succeeded in spite of man. In this revelation, found in the Bible, is recorded in the first two chapters of Genesis the account of creation in a grand but concise fashion.

Not all evolutionists are materialistic atheists or agnostics. Many evolutionists believe in God, and some even believe the Bible to be the Word of God. They believe that evolution was God's method of creation, that God initiated the process at the molecular level and then allowed it to follow its natural course. The Biblical and scientific evidence, however, tells just as strongly against theistic evolution as it does against any other form of evolution.

The first two chapters of Genesis were not written in the form of parables or poetry but present the broad outlines of creation in the form of simple historical facts. These facts directly contradict evolution theory. The Bible tells us that at one time in history there was a single human being upon the earth—a male by the name of Adam. This is in basic contradiction to evolution theory because, according to that theory, populations evolve, not individuals. After God had formed Adam from the dust of the ground, the Bible tells us that He used some portion from Adam's side (in the King James version this is translated as "rib") to form Eve. This, of course, cannot be reconciled with any possible evolutionary theory concerning the origin of man.

The New Testament Scriptures fully support this Genesis account. For example, in I Corinthians 11:8 we read, "Man is not of the woman, but the woman of the man." By any natural reproductive process, man is always born of a woman. We all have mothers. This Biblical account can, therefore, be referring only to that unique time in history when God created woman from man, just as described in Genesis 2:21, 22.

It is apparent that acceptance of creation requires an important element of faith. Yes, it is true, creationists do have faith, and that faith is vitally important. In Hebrews 11:6 we read "But without faith it is impossible to please Him, for he that cometh unto God must believe that He is, and that He is a rewarder of them that diligently seek Him." This faith is an intelligent faith, supported both by Biblical revelation and the revelation found in nature. While the *theories* and *opinions* of some scientists may contradict the Bible, there is no contradiction between the *facts* of science and the Bible.

Of course, belief in evolution also requires a vitally important element of faith. According to one of the most popular theories on the origin of the universe, all energy and matter of the universe was once contained in a plasma ball of electrons. protons, and neutrons (how it got there, no one has the faintest notion). This huge cosmic egg then exploded—and here we are today, several billion years later, human beings with a three-pound brain composed of 12 billion neurons each connected to about 10 thousand other neurons in the most complicated arrangement of matter known to man.

If this is true, then what we are and how we came to be was due solely to the properties inherent in electrons, protons, and neutrons. To believe *this* obviously requires a tremendous exercise of faith. Evolution theory is indeed no less religious nor more scientific than creation.

The question is, then, who has more evidence for his faith, the creationist or the evolutionist? Even after laying aside the powerful evidence offered by revelation, the scientific case for special creation . . . is much stronger than the case for evolution. The more I study and the more I learn, the more I become convinced that evolution is a false scientific theory and that special creation offers a much more satisfactory interpretive framework for correlating and explaining the scientific evidence related to origins.

NOTES

1. T. Dobzhansky, *Science,* Vol. 127, p. 1091 (1958).
2. R. B. Goldschmidt, *American Scientist,* Vol. 40, p. 84 (1952).
3. G. G. Simpson, *Science,* Vol. 143, p. 769 (1964).
4. R. B. Goldschmidt, Ref. 2, p. 94.
5. R. B. Goldschmidt, Ref. 2, p. 97.
6. T. Dobzhansky, *American Scientist,* Vol. 45, p. 388 (1957).
7. E. C. Olson, in *Evolution after Darwin,* Vol. 1: *The Evolution of Life,* ed. by Sol Tax, University of Chicago Press, Chicago, (1960).
8. P. S. Moorhead and M. M. Kaplan, eds., *Mathematical Challenge to the Neo-Darwinian Interpretation of Evolution,* Wistar Institute Press, Philadelphia, pp. 47, 64, 67, 71 (1967).
9. M. Eden, Ref. 8, p. 71.
10. M. Eden, Ref. 8, p. 109.
11. F. Salisbury, *Nature,* Vol. 224, p. 342 (1969); *American Biology Teacher,* Vol. 33, p. 335 (1971).
12. L. Litynski, *Science Digest,* Vol. 49, p. 61 (1961).
13. E. C. Olson, Ref. 7, p. 523.

14. P. G. Fothergill, *Nature,* Vol. 189, p. 425 (1961).
15. P. R. Ehrlich and R. W. Holm, *Science,* Vol. 137, p. 655 (1962).
16. R. Danson, *New Scientist,* Vol. 49, p. 35 (1971).
17. N. Macbeth, *Darwin Retried,* Gambit, Inc., Boston, 1971.
18. Creation Research Society, 2717 Cranbrook Road, Ann Arbor, Michigan 48104.
19. D. M. S. Watson, *Nature,* Vol. 124, p. 233 (1929).
20. T. Dobzhansky, *Science,* Vol. 175, p. 49 (1972).
21. J. Huxley, *The Observer,* July 17, 1960, p. 17.
22. *What is Humanism?* A pamphlet published by The Humanist Community of San Jose, San Jose, California 95106.
23. G. G. Simpson, *Science,* Vol. 131, p. 966 (1960).
24. G. G. Simpson, *Life of the Past,* Yale University Press, New Haven, 1953.
25. J. Huxley, *Scientific American,* Vol. 189, p. 90 (1953).

QUESTIONS FOR STUDY

1. What three conditions must be met before a theory qualifies as a true scientific theory?

2. In what sense, according to Gish, is evolution "unfalsifiable"?

3. In the author's opinion, is creationism a scientific theory?

4. What basic philosophical outlook of most scientists does Gish identify as responsible for their easy or uncritical acceptance of evolution?

5. What is the "faith" of the evolutionist?

QUESTIONS FOR REFLECTION

1. Why would the mutation of an insect species that provided it with adaptive resistance to a particular insecticide be discounted by Gish as a genuine example of evolution in action?

2. Gish quotes a number of scientists who express reservations about orthodox evolutionary theory. Would the scientific community defend such dissent?

3. Would Gish accept the "theistic evolution" of Teilhard de Chardin in the fourth selection as an acceptable compromise?

4. Is the faith of a believer in the inerrancy of scripture really identical with the faith of an evolutionist? What are some possible differences between these two kinds of faith?

5. Can you see any practical result, for example in public schooling, that Gish would achieve by establishing that neither evolution nor creation is a true scientific theory?

NETWORKING

For *materialism,* see Barbour (Part I) and Haught. *Falsification* is the subject of Popper's essay. Gish offers illustrations of Niebuhr's *closed community* orientation in science. And, of course, as a creationist, he defends *biblical literalism* as described in both of Barbour's selections (I and V).

THE "THREAT" OF CREATIONISM   ISAAC ASIMOV

Isaac Asimov (1920–1992) was a biochemist and writer. He is best known as an author of science fiction and fact with several hundred books and hundreds more articles to his credit in subjects ranging from biochemistry to the Bible. He was a tireless apologist of the scientific approach.

Scientists thought it was settled.

The universe, they had decided, is about 20 billion years old, and Earth itself is 4.5 billion years old. Simple forms of life came into being more than three billion years ago, having formed spontaneously from nonliving matter. They grew more complex through slow evolutionary processes and the first hominid ancestors of humanity appeared more than four million years ago. *Homo sapiens* itself—the present human species, people like you and me—has walked the earth for at least 50,000 years.

But apparently it isn't settled. There are Americans who believe that the earth is only about 6,000 years old; that human beings and all other species were brought into existence by a divine Creator as eternally separate varieties of beings; and that there has been no evolutionary process.

They are creationists—they call themselves "scientific" creationists—and they are a growing power in the land, demanding that schools be forced to teach their views. State legislatures, mindful of votes, are beginning to succumb to the pressure. In perhaps 15 states, bills have been introduced, putting forth the creationist point of view, and in others, strong movements are gaining momentum. In Arkansas, a law requiring that the teaching of creationism receive equal time was passed this spring and is scheduled to go into effect in September 1982, though the American Civil Liberties Union has filed suit on behalf of a group of clergymen, teachers, and parents to overturn it. And a California father named Kelly Segraves, the director of the Creation-Science Research Center, sued to have public-school science classes taught that there are other theories of creation besides evolution, and that one of them was the Biblical version. The suit came to trial in March, and the judge ruled that educators must distribute a policy statement to schools and textbook publishers explaining that the theory of evolution should not be seen as "the ultimate cause of origins." Even in New York the Board of Education has delayed since January in making a final decision, expected this month, on whether schools will be required to include the teaching of creationism in their curriculums.

The Rev. Jerry Falwell, the head of the Moral Majority, who supports the creationist view from his television pulpit, claims that he has 17 million to 25 million viewers (though Arbitron places the figure at a much more modest 1.6 million). But there are 66 electronic ministries which have a total audience of about 20 million. And in parts of the country where the Fundamentalists predominate—the so-called Bible Belt—creationists are in the majority.

They make up a fervid and dedicated group, convinced beyond argument of both their rightness and righteousness. Faced with an apathetic and falsely secure majority, smaller groups have used intense pressure and forceful campaigning—as the creationists do—and have succeeded in disrupting and taking over whole societies.

Yet, though creationists seem to accept the literal truth of the Biblical story of creation, this does not mean that all religious people are creationists. There are millions of Catholics, Protestants, and Jews who think of the Bible as a source of spiritual truth and accept much of it as symbolically rather than literally true. They do not consider the Bible to be a textbook of science, even in intent, and have no problem teaching evolution in their secular institutions.

To those who are trained in science, creationism seems like a bad dream, a sudden reliving of a nightmare, a renewed march of an army of the night risen to challenge free thought and enlightenment.

The scientific evidence for the age of the earth and for the evolutionary development of life seems overwhelming to scientists. How can anyone question it? What are the arguments the creationists use? What is the "science" that makes their views "scientific"? Here are some of them:

THE ARGUMENT FROM ANALOGY

A watch implies a watchmaker, say the creationists. If you were to find a beautifully intricate watch in the desert, far from habitation, you would be sure that it had been fashioned by human hands and somehow left there. It would pass the bounds of credibility that it had simply formed, spontaneously, from the sands of the desert.

By analogy, then, if you consider humanity, life, Earth, and the universe, all infinitely more intricate than a watch, you can believe far less easily that it "just happened." It, too, like the watch, must have been fashioned, but by more-than-human hands—in short by a divine Creator.

This argument seems unanswerable, and it has been used (even though not often explicitly expressed) ever since the dawn of consciousness. To have explained to prescientific human beings that the wind and the rain and the sun follow the laws of nature and do so blindly and without a guiding hand would have been utterly unconvincing to them. In fact, it might well have gotten you stoned to death as a blasphemer.

There are many aspects of the universe that still cannot be explained satisfactorily by science; but ignorance implies only ignorance that may someday be conquered. To surrender to ignorance and call it God has always been premature, and it remains premature today.

In short, the complexity of the universe—and one's inability to explain it in full—is not in itself an argument for a Creator.

THE ARGUMENT FROM GENERAL CONSENT

Some creationists point out that belief in a Creator is general among all peoples and all cultures. Surely this unanimous craving hints at a great truth. There would be no unanimous belief in a lie.

General belief, however, is not really surprising. Nearly every people on earth that considers the existence of the world assumes it to have been created by a god or gods. And each group invents full details for the story. No two creation tales are alike. The Greeks, the Norsemen, the Japanese, the Hindus, the American Indians, and so on and so on all have their own creation myths, and all of these are recognized by Americans of Judeo-Christian heritage as "just myths."

The ancient Hebrews also had a creation tale—two of them, in fact. There is a primitive Adam-and-Eve-in-Paradise story, with man created first, then animals, then woman. There is also a poetic tale of God fashioning the universe in six days, with animals preceding man, and man and woman created together.

These Hebrew myths are not inherently more credible than any of the others, but they are our myths. General consent, of course, proves nothing: There can be a unanimous belief in something that isn't so. The universal opinion over thousands of years that the earth was flat never flattened its spherical shape by one inch.

THE ARGUMENT BY BELITTLEMENT

Creationists frequently stress the fact that evolution is "only a theory," giving the impression that a theory is an idle guess. A scientist, one gathers, arising one morning with nothing particular to do, decides that perhaps the moon is made of Roquefort cheese and instantly advances the Roquefort-cheese theory.

A theory (as the word is used by scientists) is a detailed description of some facet of the universe's workings that is based on long observation and, where possible, experiment. It is the result of careful reasoning from those observations and experiments and has survived the critical study of scientists generally.

For example, we have the description of the cellular nature of living organisms (the "cell theory"); of objects attracting each other according to a fixed rule (the "theory of gravitation"); of energy behaving in discrete bits (the "quantum theory"); of light traveling through a vacuum at a fixed measurable velocity (the "theory of relativity"), and so on.

All are theories; all are firmly founded; all are accepted as valid descriptions of this or that aspect of the universe. They are neither guesses nor speculations. And no theory is better founded, more closely examined, more critically argued and more thoroughly accepted, than the theory of evolution. If it is "only" a theory, that is all it has to be.

Creationism, on the other hand, is not a theory. There is no evidence, in the scientific sense, that supports it. Creationism, or at least the particular variety accepted by many Americans, is an expression of early Middle Eastern legend. It is fairly described as "only a myth."

THE ARGUMENT FROM IMPERFECTION

Creationists, in recent years, have stressed the "scientific" background of their beliefs. They point out that there are scientists who base their creationist beliefs on a careful study of geology, paleontology, and biology and produce "textbooks" that embody those beliefs.

Virtually the whole scientific corpus of creationism, however, consists of the pointing out of imperfections in the evolutionary view. The creationists insist, for example, that evolutionists cannot show true transition states between species in the fossil evidence; that age determinations through radioactive breakdown are uncertain; that alternate interpretations of this or that piece of evidence are possible and so on.

Because the evolutionary view is not perfect and is not agreed upon in every detail by all scientists, creationists argue that evolution is false and that scientists, in supporting evolution, are basing their views on blind faith and dogmatism.

To an extent, the creationists are right here: The details of evolution are not perfectly known. Scientists have been adjusting and modifying Charles Darwin's suggestions since he advanced his theory of the origin of species through natural selection back in 1859. After all, much has been learned about the fossil record and about physiology, microbiology, biochemistry, ethology, and various other branches of life science in the last 125 years, and it is to be expected that we can improve on Darwin. In fact, we have improved on him.

Nor is the process finished. It can never be, as long as human beings continue to question and to strive for better answers.

The details of evolutionary theory are in dispute precisely because scientists are not devotees of blind faith and dogmatism. They do not accept even as great a thinker as Darwin without question, nor do they accept any idea, new or old, without thorough argument. Even after accepting an idea, they stand ready to overrule it, if appropriate new evidence arrives. If, however, we grant that a theory is imperfect and that details remain in dispute, does that disprove the theory as a whole?

Consider. I drive a car, and you drive a car. I do not know exactly how an engine works. Perhaps you do not either. And it may be that our hazy and approximate ideas of the workings of an automobile are in conflict. Must we then conclude from this disagreement that an automobile does not run, or that it does not exist? Or, if our senses force us to conclude that an automobile does exist and run, does that mean it is pulled by an invisible horse, since our engine theory is imperfect?

However much scientists argue their differing beliefs in details of evolutionary theory, or in the interpretation of the necessarily imperfect fossil record, they firmly accept the evolutionary process itself.

THE ARGUMENT FROM DISTORTED SCIENCE

Creationists have learned enough scientific terminology to use it in their attempts to disprove evolution. They do this in numerous ways, but the most common example, at least in the mail I receive, is the repeated assertion that the second law of thermodynamics demonstrates the evolutionary process to be impossible.

In kindergarten terms, the second law of thermodynamics says that all spontaneous change is in the direction of increasing disorder—that is, in a "downhill" direction. There can be no spontaneous buildup of the complex from the simple, therefore, because that would he moving "uphill." According to the creationist argument, since, by the evolutionary process, complex forms of life evolve from simple forms, that process defies the second law, so creationism must be true.

Such an argument implies that this clearly visible fallacy is somehow invisible to scientists, who must therefore be flying in the face of the second law through sheer perversity.

Scientists, however, do know about the second law and they are not blind. It's just that an argument based on kindergarten terms is suitable only for kindergartens.

To lift the argument a notch above the kindergarten level, the second law of thermodynamics applies to a "closed system"—that is, to a system that does not gain energy from without, or lose energy to the outside. The only truly closed system we know of is the universe as a whole.

Within a closed system, there are subsystems that can gain complexity spontaneously, provided there is a greater loss of complexity in another interlocking subsystem. The overall change then is a complexity loss in line with the dictates of the second law.

Evolution can proceed and build up the complex from the simple, thus moving uphill, without violating the second law, as long as another interlocking part of the system—the sun, which delivers energy to the earth continually—moves downhill (as it does) at a much faster rate than evolution moves uphill.

If the sun were to cease shining, evolution would stop and so, eventually, would life.

Unfortunately, the second law is a subtle concept which most people are not accustomed to dealing with, and it is not easy to see the fallacy in the creationist distortion.

There are many other "scientific" arguments used by creationists, some taking quite clever advantage of present areas of dispute in evolutionary theory, but every one of them is as disingenuous as the second-law argument.

The "scientific" arguments are organized into special creationist textbooks, which have all the surface appearance of the real thing, and which school systems are being heavily pressured to accept. They are written by people who have not made any mark as scientists, and, while they discuss geology, paleontology and biology with correct scientific terminology, they are devoted almost entirely to raising doubts over the legitimacy of the evidence and reasoning underlying evolutionary thinking on the assumption that this leaves creationism as the only possible alternative.

Evidence actually in favor of creationism is not presented, of course, because none exists other than the word of the Bible, which it is current creationist strategy not to use.

THE ARGUMENT FROM IRRELEVANCE

Some creationists put all matters of scientific evidence to one side and consider all such things irrelevant. The Creator, they say, brought life and the earth and the entire universe into being 6,000 years ago or so, complete with all the evidence for an eons-long evolutionary development. The fossil record, the decaying radioactivity, the receding galaxies were all created as they are, and the evidence they present is an illusion.

Of course, this argument is itself irrelevant, for it can neither be proved nor disproved. It is not an argument, actually, but a statement. I can say that the entire universe was created two minutes ago, complete with all its history books describing a nonexistent past in detail, and with every living person equipped with a full memory: you, for instance, in the process of reading this article in midstream with a memory of what you had read in the beginning—which you had not really read.

What kind of a Creator would produce a universe containing so intricate an illusion? It would mean that the Creator formed a universe that contained human beings whom He had endowed with the faculty of curiosity and the ability to reason. He supplied those human beings with an enormous amount of subtle and cleverly consistent evidence designed to mislead them and cause them to be convinced that the universe was created 20 billion years ago and developed by evolutionary processes that included the creation and development of life on Earth.

Why?

Does the Creator take pleasure in fooling us? Does it amuse Him to watch us go wrong? Is it part of a test to see if human beings will deny their senses and their reason in order to cling to myth? Can it be that the Creator is a cruel and malicious prankster, with a vicious and adolescent sense of humor?

THE ARGUMENT FROM AUTHORITY

The Bible says that God created the world in six days, and the Bible is the inspired word of God. To the average creationist this is all that counts. All other arguments are merely a tedious way of countering the propaganda of all those wicked humanists, agnostics, and atheists who are not satisfied with the clear word of the Lord.

The creationist leaders do not actually use that argument because that would make their argument a religious one, and they would not be able to use it in fighting a secular school system. They have to borrow the clothing of science, no matter how badly it fits, and call themselves "scientific" creationists. They also speak only of the "Creator," and never mention that this Creator is the God of the Bible.

We cannot, however, take this sheep's clothing seriously. However much the creationist leaders might hammer away at their "scientific" and "philosophical" points, they would be helpless and a laughing stock if that were all they had.

It is religion that recruits their squadrons. Tens of millions of Americans, who neither know nor understand the actual arguments for—or even against—evolution, march in the army of the night with their Bibles held high. And they are a strong and frightening force, impervious to, and immunized against, the feeble lance of mere reason.

Even if I am right and the evolutionists' case is very strong, have not creationists, whatever the emptiness of their case, a right to be heard?

If their case is empty, isn't it perfectly safe to discuss it since the emptiness would then be apparent?

Why, then, are evolutionists so reluctant to have creationism taught in the public schools on an equal basis with evolutionary theory? Can it be that the evolutionists are not as confident of their case as they pretend. Are they afraid to allow youngsters a clear choice?

First, the creationists are somewhat less than honest in their demand for equal time. It is not their views that are repressed: Schools are by no means the only place in which the dispute between creationism and evolutionary theory is played out.

There are the churches, for instance, which are a much more serious influence on most Americans than the schools are. To be sure, many churches are quite liberal, have made their peace with science and find it easy to live with scientific advance—even with evolution. But many of the less modish and citified churches are bastions of creationism.

The influence of the church is naturally felt in the home, in the newspapers, and in all of surrounding society. It makes itself felt in the nation as a whole, even in religiously liberal areas, in thousands of subtle ways: in the nature of holiday observance, in expressions of patriotic fervor, even in total irrelevancies. In 1968, for example, a team of astronauts circling the moon were instructed to read the first few verses of Genesis as though NASA felt it had to placate the public lest they rage against the violation of the firmament. At the present time, even the current President of the United States has expressed his creationist sympathies.

It is only in school that American youngsters in general are ever likely to hear any reasoned exposition of the evolutionary viewpoint. They might find such a viewpoint in books, magazines, newspapers, or even, on occasion, on television. But church and family can easily censor printed matter or television. Only the school is beyond their control.

But only just barely beyond. Even though schools are now allowed to teach evolution, teachers are beginning to be apologetic about it, knowing full well their jobs are at the mercy of school boards upon which creationists are a stronger and stronger influence.

Then, too, in schools, students are not required to believe what they learn about evolution—merely to parrot it back on tests. If they fail to do so, their punishment is nothing more than the loss of a few points on a test or two.

In the creationist churches, however, the congregation is required to believe. Impressionable youngsters, taught that they will go to hell if they listen to the evolutionary doctrine, are not likely to listen in comfort or to believe if they do.

Therefore, creationists, who control the church and the society they live in and who face the public school as the only place where evolution is even briefly mentioned in a possibly favorable way, find they cannot stand even so minuscule a competition and demand "equal time."

Do you suppose their devotion to "fairness" is such that they will give equal time to evolution in their churches?

Second, the real danger is the manner in which creationists want their "equal time."

In the scientific world, there is free and open competition of ideas, and even a scientist whose suggestions are not accepted is nevertheless free to continue to argue his case.

In this free and open competition of ideas, creationism has clearly lost. It has been losing, in fact, since the time of Copernicus four and a half centuries ago. But creationists, placing myth above reason, refuse to accept the decision and are now calling on the Government to force their views on the schools in lieu of the free expression of ideas. Teachers must be forced to present creationism as though it has equal intellectual respectability with evolutionary doctrine.

What a precedent this sets.

If the Government can mobilize its policemen and its prisons to make certain that teachers give creationism equal time, they can next use force to make sure that teachers declare creationism the victor so that evolution will be evicted from the classroom altogether.

We will have established the full groundwork, in other words, for legally enforced ignorance and for totalitarian thought control.

And what if the creationists win? They might, you know, for there are millions who, faced with the choice between science and their interpretation of the Bible, will choose the Bible and reject science, regardless of the evidence.

This is not entirely because of a traditional and unthinking reverence for the literal words of the Bible; there is also a pervasive uneasiness—even an actual fear—of science that will drive even those who care little for Fundamentalism into the arms of the creationists. For one thing, science is uncertain. Theories are subject to revision; observations are open to a variety of interpretations, and scientists quarrel among themselves. This is disillusioning for those untrained in the scientific method, who thus turn to the rigid certainty of the Bible instead. There is something comfortable about a view that allows for no deviation and that spares you the painful necessity of having to think.

Second, science is complex and chilling. The mathematical language of science is understood by very few. The vistas it presents are scary—an enormous universe ruled by chance and impersonal rules, empty and uncaring, ungraspable and vertiginous. How comfortable to turn instead to a small world, only a few thousand years old, and under God's personal and immediate care; a world in which you are His peculiar concern and where He will not consign you to hell if you are careful to follow every word of the Bible as interpreted for you by your television preacher.

Third, science is dangerous. There is no question but that poison gas, genetic engineering, and nuclear weapons and power stations are terrifying. It may be that civilization is falling apart and the world we know is coming to an end. In that case, why not turn to religion and look forward to the Day of Judgment, in which you and your fellow believers will be lifted into eternal bliss and have the added joy of watching the scoffers and disbelievers writhe forever in torment.

So why might they not win?

There are numerous cases of societies in which the armies of the night have ridden triumphantly over minorities in order to establish a powerful orthodoxy which dictates official thought. Invariably, the triumphant ride is toward long-range disaster.

Spain dominated Europe and the world in the 16th century, but in Spain orthodoxy came first, and all divergence of opinion was ruthlessly suppressed. The result was that Spain settled back into blankness and did not share in the scientific, technological and commercial ferment that bubbled up in other nations of Western Europe. Spain remained an intellectual backwater for centuries.

In the late 17th century, France in the name of orthodoxy revoked the Edict of Nantes and drove out many thousands of Huguenots, who added their intellectual vigor to lands of refuge such as Great Britain, the Netherlands, and Prussia, while France was permanently weakened.

In more recent times, Germany hounded out the Jewish scientists of Europe. They arrived in the United States and contributed immeasurably to scientific advancement here, while Germany lost so heavily that there is no telling how long it will take it to regain its former scientific eminence. The Soviet Union, in its fascination with Lysenko, destroyed its geneticists, and set back its biological sciences for decades. China, during the Cultural Revolution, turned against Western science and is still laboring to overcome the devastation that resulted.

Are we now, with all these examples before us, to ride backward into the past under the same tattered banner of orthodoxy? With creationism in the saddle, American science will wither. We will raise a generation of ignoramuses ill-equipped to run the industry of tomorrow, much less to generate the new advances of the days after tomorrow.

We will inevitably recede into the backwater of civilization, and those nations that retain open scientific thought will take over the leadership of the world and the cutting edge of human advancement.

I don't suppose that the creationists really plan the decline of the United States, but their loudly expressed patriotism is as simple-minded as their "science." If they succeed, they will, in their folly, achieve the opposite of what they say they wish.

QUESTIONS FOR STUDY

1. Describe the creationist "argument from analogy." Does Asimov attack the argument directly? What is his response?

2. Describe the creationist position that evolution is "only a theory"? What is Asimov's account of the concept of theory in science?

3. Describe the creationist use of the second law of thermodynamics. In Asimov's mind how is this a distortion of science?

4. Why, according to Asimov, is the argument that God created the world just as we see it in six days irrelevant? In what way does it detract from the goodness of God?

5. Where is the influence of creationism in American life primarily exerted?

6. What three characteristics of science are disadvantageous in its struggle with creationism?

QUESTIONS FOR REFLECTION

1. How may Asimov's statement, "to surrender to ignorance and call it God is always immature," be understood as a reference to the God-of-the-Gaps? See Bube in Part III.

2. Why do you think that "virtually the whole scientific corpus of creationism . . . consists of the pointing out of imperfections in the evolutionary view," rather than developing scientific evidence to support its own position?

3. Relate Asimov's "argument from irrevelance" to Popper's "principle of falsification." See Popper in Part III.

4. If creationism were taught in public school science courses, why should astrology or Buddhist cosmology be denied the same privilege?

5. Who should have the authority to decide what is to be taught in science classrooms: parents, scientists, or the legislature? Defend your choice.

NETWORKING

See MacCormack for a detailed discussion of *analogy and metaphor*. Bube, Tillich, and Polkinghorne include the concept of the *God-of-the-Gaps* in their analyses. The *role of theory in science and religion* is to be found in selections by Schilling, Gilkey, Popper, and Davies. Burhoe, Teilhard, and Polkinghorne have concerns about the *theological implications of entropy*. For *the Bible*, see Barbour (Part I) and Niebuhr.

SOME REFLECTIONS ON PROGRESS
PIERRE TEILHARD DE CHARDIN

Pierre Teilhard de Chardin (1881–1955) was a French Jesuit and scientist whose life passion was to construct a synthesis of evolutionary science and the Christian faith. As a professional paleontologist, he undertook numerous expeditions seeking fossils of the earliest human beings. He spent years in China where he was, in effect, exiled by the church for his heterodox opinions on matters of faith. While in China during World War II, he was held in a Japanese camp for foreigners. There he composed *The Phenomenon of Man*, the most complete statement of his position. Teilhard's many essays and speeches went unpublished during his lifetime because of church disapproval. Following his death, however, they were collected and appeared as several volumes of his *Oeuvres* or "Works." Many are available in translation.

PART I. THE FUTURE OF MAN SEEN BY A PALAEONTOLOGIST

Introduction

When little more than a century ago, Man first discovered the abyss of time that lies behind him, and therefore the abyss that lies ahead, his first feeling was a tremendous hope, a sense of wonderment at the progress our fathers had made.

But now the wind seems to have changed. Following many setbacks a wave of troubled scepticism (adorned with the name of "realism") is sweeping through the world. Whether from immobilist reaction, sick pessimism or simply pose, it has become "good form" to deride or mistrust anything that looks like faith in the future.

"Have we ever moved? Are we still moving? And if so, are we going forward or back or simply in a circle?"

This is an attitude of doubt that will prove fatal if we do not take care, because in destroying the love of life it also destroys the life-force of Mankind.

I wish to show in this paper that, however bitter our disillusionment with human goodness in recent years, there are stronger scientific reasons than ever before for believing that we do really progress and that we can advance much further still, provided we are clear about the direction in which progress lies and are resolved to take the right road.

Preliminary Observations: The Slow Movements

To understand what follows we must first thoroughly assimilate the idea that there are movements in the Universe so slow that we cannot directly detect them. The idea of slow movement is in itself very simple and commonplace—we have all looked at the hour-hand of a watch. But it took us a long time to realise that the more stable and immobile a given object in Nature may appear to be, the greater is the likelihood that it represents a profound and majestic process of movement. We know now that the vast system of stars in our own sky is composed of a single nebula, the Milky Way, in course of granulation and deployment; and that this nebula, in association with millions of other spiral units, forms a single, immense super-system which is also in process of expansion and organization. We know that the continents tremble and that the mountains continue to rise beneath our feet . . . and so on.

It can be said that Science today progresses only by peeling away, one after another, all the coverings of apparent stability in the world; disclosing beneath the immobility of the infinitely small, movement of extra rapidity, and beneath the immobility of the Immense, movement of extra slowness.

We are concerned here with the second of these effects, which may be expressed as follows: everything in the Universe moves; but *the larger a thing is, the slower is its movement*.

The Case of Life

This being posited let us leave the nebulae and the mountains and turn to Life itself, of which Mankind is a fragment.

Life, by our time-scale, is a phenomenon of prodigious age—over 300 million years. Moreover it is composed of myriads of separate elements and it covers the earth. In terms of space-time Life comes in the category of immensely large things. It is part of the Immense, and if it moves at all it moves like the Immense.

Our object is to determine whether Life and Mankind move. We can only find out by observing them (like the hour-hand of our watch) over a *very great length of time*. Here it is that we see the part played by palaeontology, as well as the secret vice of our critics.

The Role of Palaeontology

It might seem that palaeontology is a science of pure speculation or inquisitiveness, and the palaeontologist the most unreal and useless of researchers; a man dedicated to retrospection, plunged living into the past, where he spends his days collecting the debris of all kinds of dead things. That is certainly what many laymen think, and it may well be the view humbly taken by many palaeontologists of themselves.

But in this the instinct that prompts our work sees more clearly than reason. The reconstruction of 'that which was' may rationally appear to be merely a fantasy for idle minds; but in fact the meticulous work accomplished in the past hundred years by the collectors of fossils, the results which they have patiently recorded in innumerable papers and in barbarous language, perfectly incomprehensible to non-initiates, the paraphernalia of systematised knowledge and the clutter on the museum shelves, all this has made a contribution of the utmost importance to the world's thinking. It has added to the sum of human knowledge an item of extraordinary interest—*a segment of the past extending over some three hundred million years.*

Do we fully realise its value?

We are trying, let me repeat, for vital reasons to determine whether the world, Mankind, is the seat of any kind of progress. Let us put aside all metaphysical speculation, all sentimental impressions and arguments. We are dealing with a question of fact and we must look at the facts. If we confine ourselves to short periods of time on which progress makes no mark our argument will drag on and get nowhere. But if we contemplate a depth of time such as this one that we have been able to reconstruct in the laboratory, any movement of Life, if such exists, must of necessity show itself.

Instead of arguing fruitlessly within the over-brief space of a few generations, let us look at the broad vista which science offers us. What do we see?

The Growth of Consciousness

For various psychological and technical reasons which I need not examine here, the reading or decipherment of the tract of time disclosed by palaeontology is still not free of difficulty. Indeed it continues to be a matter of vehement dispute. The interpretation which I am about to put forward must therefore not be regarded as 'accepted.' Nevertheless it seems to me so self-evident that I have no hesitation in offering it as the correct interpretation and the one destined sooner or later to win general scientific agreement.

It may be stated thus: when observed through a sufficient depth of time (millions of years) Life can be seen to move. Not only does it move but it advances in a definite direction. And not only does it advance, but in observing its progress we can discern the process or practical mechanism whereby it does so.

These are three propositions which may be briefly developed as follows.

a. Life moves. This calls for no demonstration. Everyone in these days knows how greatly all living forms have changed if we compare two moments in the earth's history sufficiently separated in time. In any period of ten million years Life practically grows a new skin.

b. In a definite direction. This is the crucial point which has to be clearly understood. While accepting the undeniable fact of the general evolution of Life in the course of time, many biologists still maintain that these changes take place without following any defined course, in any direction and at random. This contention, disastrous to any idea of progress, is refuted, in my view, by the tremendous fact of the continuing "cerebralisation" of living creatures. Research shows that from the lowest to the highest level of the organic world there is a persistent and clearly defined thrust of animal forms towards species with more sensitive and elaborate nervous systems. A growing "innervation" and "cephalisation" of organisms: the working of this law is visible in every living group known to us, the smallest no less than the largest. We can follow it in insects as in vertebrates; and among the vertebrates we can follow it from class to class, from order to order, and from family to family. There is an amphibian phase of the brain, a reptilian phase, a mammalian phase. In mammals we see the brain grow as time passes and become more complex among the ungulates, the carnivores and above all the primates. So much so that one could draw a steadily rising Curve of Life taking Time as one co-ordinate and, as the other, the quantity (and quality) of nervous tissue existing on earth at each geological stage.

What else can this mean except that, as shown by the development of nervous systems, there is a continual heightening, a rising tide of consciousness which visibly manifests itself on our planet in the course of the ages?

c. We come to the third point. What is the *underlying process* whose existence we can perceive in this continual heightening of consciousness, as revealed by the organic evolution of the nervous system and the brain? Let us look more closely in the light of the latest data supplied by the combined ingenuity of an army of research workers. As we are beginning to realise, there are probably tens of thousands of atoms grouped in a single virus molecule. There are certainly tens of thousands of molecules grouped in a single cell. There are millions of brains in a single ant-hill. . . .

What does this atomism signify except that Cosmic Matter, governed at its lower end (as we already know) by forces of dispersal which slowly cause it to dissolve into atoms, now shows itself to be subjected, at the other end, to an extraordinary power of enforced coalescence, of which the outcome is the emergence, *pari passu*, of an ever-increasing amount of spiritual energy in matter that is ever more powerfully synthesized? Let me note that there is nothing metaphysical in this. I am not seeking to define either Spirit or Matter. I am simply saying, without leaving the physical field, that the greatest discovery made in this century is probably the realisation that the passage of Time may best be measured by the gradual gathering of Matter in superposed groups, of which the arrangement, ever richer and more centralised, radiates outwards from an ever more luminous fringe of liberty and interiority. The phenomenon of growing consciousness on earth, in short, is directly due to the increasingly advanced organisation of more and more complicated elements, successively created by the working of chemistry and of Life. At the present time I can see no more satisfactory solution of the enigma presented to us by the physical progress of the Universe.

The Place of Man in the Forefront of Life

In what I have said thus far I have been looking at Life in general, in its entirety. We come now to the particular case which interests us most—the problem of Man.

The existence of an ascendant movement in the Universe has been revealed to us by the study of palaeontology. Where is Man to be situated in this line of progress?

The answer is clear. If, as I maintain, the movement of the cosmos towards the highest degree of consciousness is not an optical illusion, but represents the essence of biological evolution, then, in the curve traced by Life, Man is unquestionably situated at the topmost point; and it is he, by his emergence and existence, who finally proves the reality and defines the direction of the trajectory—"the dot on the i" . . .

Indeed, within the field accessible to our experience, does not the birth of Thought stand out as a critical point through which all the striving of previous ages passes and is consummated—the critical point traversed by consciousness, when, by force of concentration, it ends by reflecting upon itself?

Prior to Galileo science thought of Man as the mathematical and moral centre of a World composed of spheres turning statically upon themselves. But in terms of our modern neo-anthropocentricity, Man, both diminished and enlarged, becomes the *head* (terrestrial) of a Universe that is in the process of psychic transformation—Man, the last-formed, most complex and most conscious of "molecules." From which it follows that, borne on the tide of millions of years of psychogenesis, we have the right to consider ourselves the fruit of a progression—the children of progress.

The world did at least progress to the point where the first-born of our race appeared. Here we have a fixed and solid point on which to base our philosophy of life.

Let us now take a further step.

We may agree that zoological evolution culminated in Man. But having reached this peak did it come to a stop? Life continued to move until Thought entered the world, this we may admit. But has it advanced since then? Can it make any further progress?

The Movement of Mankind upon Itself

Ancient though prehistory may make it seem to our eyes, Mankind is still very young. We can trace its existence for not much more than a hundred thousand years, a period so short that it has left no mark on the majority of the animal forms that preceded us on the earth and which still surround us. It may seem impossible, and it is certainly a very delicate matter, to measure any movement of Life in so slender a fragment of the past. Nevertheless, owing to the exceptionally rapid development which is a characteristic of the human wave, a direct assessment of the advance of our own group in terms of consciousness is possible to the practised eye, even within this limited tract of time.

a. It seems in the first place that, anatomically, a gradual evolution of the brain can be discerned during the earliest phases of our phylogenesis. Pithecanthropus and Sinanthropus possessed intelligence, but there are solid grounds for supposing that they were not cerebrally as well developed as ourselves.

b. We may accept that the human brain reached the limit of its development at the stage which anthropologists call *Homo sapiens;* or at least, if it has continued to develop since then, that the change cannot be detected by our present methods of observation. But although, since the Age of the Reindeer (that is to say, within a period of twenty or thirty thousand years) no progress is perceptible in either the physical or the mental faculties of Individual Man, the fact of organo-psychic development seems to be clearly manifest in Collective Man: and this, whatever we may think of it, represents as true an advance as the acquisition of an added convolution by the brain.

Let me here repeat the two fundamental equations or equivalents which we have established:

Progress = growth of consciousness

Growth of Consciousness = effect of organization

Taken together these mean that, in order to discover or verify the existence of biological progress within a given system, we have only to observe, for the period of time and the field we are considering, how far the state of organization varies within that system.

This being posited we may compare the world of the cave-dweller with the world of today. Setting all theory aside there can be no question but that, within this period of 30,000 years, Mankind has advanced almost unbelievably in its state of concentration.

Economic concentration, manifest in the unification of the earth's energies.

Intellectual concentration, manifest in the unification of our knowledge in a coherent system (science).

Social concentration, manifest in the unification of the human mass as a thinking whole.

To those who have not studied its implications, this slow and irresistible flow of our history in the direction of more and more unified groupings has no particular meaning; they relegate it to the trivial category of surface and incidental phenomena, no more. But to the enlightened eye this human development, succeeding all the twists and turns of pre-human consciousness, assumes a dazzling significance. *For the two curves are a prolongation one of the other.* Tremendous events such as those through which we are now passing are seen to take shape, and with a brilliant clarity. This tremendous war which so afflicts us, this remoulding, this universal longing for a new order, what are they but the shock, the tremor and the crisis, beyond which we may glimpse a more synthetic organization of the human world? And this new order, the thought of which is in all our minds, what form can it take other than a higher degree of self-awareness on the part of a Mankind become at once more complex and more centred upon itself?

No, truly: Life in emerging into Thought did not come to a stop. Not only has it moved and progressed from the protozoa to Man, but since the coming of Man it has continued to advance along its most essential path. We can feel it at this moment quivering beneath our feet! The ship that bears us is still making headway.

And it is here that the ultimate and decisive question arises, finally the only question that interests us. Thus far Life, and Man himself, has progressed. So be it. But what of the future? We are still moving, but can we continue much longer to advance?

Have we not reached a dead-end? Can we talk seriously of a future for Mankind?

The Future of Mankind

I make no claim to be a prophet. Moreover I know, as a scientist, how dangerous it is to extend a curve beyond the facts, that is to say, to extrapolate. Nevertheless I believe that, basing the argument upon our general knowledge of the world's history over a period of 300 million years, we can advance the following two propositions without losing ourselves in a fog of speculation:

a. Firstly, Mankind still shows itself to possess a *reserve*, a formidable potential of concentration, i.e. of progress. We have only to think of the immensity of the forces, ideas and human beings that have still to be born or discovered or applied or synthesized. . . .

"Energetically" as well as biologically the human group is still young, still fresh. If we are to judge by what history teaches us about other living groups, it still has, organically speaking, some millions of years in which to live and develop.

b. Everything leads us to believe that it really does dispose of this vast reservoir of time, which is necessary for the normal achievement of its evolution. The earth is far from having completed its sidereal evolution. We may envisage all kinds of mischance (disaster or disease) which might in theory put an end to our evolutionary progress: but the fact remains that for 300 million years Life has paradoxically flourished in the Improbable. Does not this suggest that its advance may be sustained by *some sort of complicity on the part of the "blind" forces of the Universe*—that is to say, that it is inexorable?

The more we ponder these matters the more must we realise that, scientifically speaking, the real difficulty presented by Man is not the problem of whether he is a centre of constant progress: it is far more the question of how long this progress can continue, at the speed at which it is going, without Life blowing up upon itself or causing the earth on which it was born to explode. Our modern world was created in less than 10,000 years, and in the past 200 years it has changed more than in all the preceding millennia. Have we ever thought of what our planet may be like, psychologically, in a million years' time? It is finally the Utopians, not the "realists," who make scientific sense. They at least, though their flights of fancy may cause us to smile, have a feeling for the true dimensions of the phenomenon of Man.

The Advance

Having clarified our ideas, let us see what action they require of us. If progress is to continue, it will not do so of its own accord. *Evolution, by the very mechanism of its syntheses, charges itself with an ever-growing measure of freedom.*

If indeed an almost limitless field of action lies open to us in the future, what shall our moral dispositions be, as we contemplate this march ahead?

I can think of two, which may be summarised in six words: *a great hope held in common.*

a. First, the hope. This must spring to life spontaneously in every generous spirit faced by the task that awaits us; and it is also the essential *impulse,* without which nothing can be done. A passionate longing to grow, to be, is what we need. There can be no place for the poor in spirit, the sceptics, the pessimists, the sad of heart, the weary and the immobilists. Life is ceaseless discovery. Life is movement.

b. A hope held in common. Here again the history of Life is decisive. Not all directions are good for our advance: one alone leads upward, that which through increasing organization leads to greater synthesis and unity. Here we part company with the whole-hearted individualists, the egoists who seek to grow by excluding or diminishing their fellows, individually, nationally or racially. Life moves towards unification. Our hope can only be realised if it finds its expression in greater cohesion and greater human solidarity.

This double point is finally established by the verdict of the Past.

The Crossroads

But here there is a grave uncertainty to be resolved. The future, I have said, depends on the courage and resourcefulness which men display in overcoming the forces of isolationism, even of repulsion, which seem to drive them apart rather than draw them together. How is the drawing together to be accomplished? How shall we so contrive matters that the human mass merges in a single whole, instead of ceaselessly scattering in dust?

A priori, there seem to be two methods, two possible roads.

a. The first is a process of tightening-up in response to external pressures. We are in any case inescapably subject to this through the negative action of terrestrial causes. The human mass, because on the confined surface of this planet it is in a state of continuous additive growth, in numbers and inter-connections, must automatically become more and more tightly concentrated upon itself. To this formidable process of natural compression there may well be added the artificial constraint imposed by a stronger human group upon a weaker; we have only to look about us at the present time to see how this idea is seeking, indeed rushing towards, its realisation.

b. But there is another way. This is that, *prompted by some favouring influence,* the elements of Mankind should succeed in making effective a profound force of mutual attraction, deeper and more powerful than the surface-repulsion which causes them to diverge. Forced upon one another by the dimensions and mechanics of the earth, men will purposefully bring to life a common soul in this vast body.

Unification by external or by internal force? Compulsion or Unanimity?

I spoke earlier of the present war. Does it not precisely express the tension and interior dislocation of Mankind shaken to its roots as it stands at the crossroads, faced by the need to decide upon its future?

The Choice

Gloriously situated by life at this critical point in the evolution of Mankind, what ought we to do? We hold Earth's future in our hands. What shall we decide?

In my view the road to be followed is clearly revealed by the teaching of all the past.

We can progress only by uniting: this, as we have seen, is the law of Life. But unification through coercion leads only to a superficial pseudo-unity. It may establish a mechanism, but it does not achieve any fundamental synthesis; and in consequence it engenders no growth of consciousness. It materialises, in short, instead of spiritualising. Only unification through unanimity is biologically valid. This alone can work the miracle of causing heightened personality to emerge from the forces of collectivity. It alone represents a genuine extension of the psychogenesis that gave us birth.

Therefore it is inwardly that we must come together, and in entire freedom.

But this brings us to the last question of all. To create this unanimity we need the bond, as I said, the cement of a favouring influence. Where shall we look for it; how shall we conceive of this principle of togetherness, this soul of the Earth?

Is it to be in the development of a common *vision,* that is to say, the establishment of a universally accepted body of knowledge, in which all intelligences will join in knowing the same facts interpreted in the same way?

Or will it rather be in common *action,* in the determination of an Objective universally recognised as being so desirable that all activity will naturally converge towards it under the impulse of a common fear and a common ambition?

These two kinds of unanimity are undoubtedly real, and will, I believe, have their place in our future progress. But they need to be complemented by something else if they are not to remain precarious, insufficient and incomplete. A common body of knowledge brings together nothing but the geometrical point of intelligences. A common aspiration, no matter how ardent, can only touch individuals indirectly and in an impersonal way that is depersonalizing in itself.

It is not a *tête-à-tête* or a *corps-à-corps* that we need; it is a heart-to-heart.

This being so, the more I consider the fundamental question of the future of the earth, the more it appears to me that the generative principle of its unification is finally to be sought, not in the sole contemplation of a single Truth or in the sole desire for a single Thing, but in the common attraction exercised by a single *Being.* For on the one hand, if the synthesis of the Spirit is to be brought about in its entirety (and this is the only possible definition of progress) it can only be done, in the last resort, through the meeting, *centre to centre,* of human units, such as can only be realised in a universal, mutual love. And on the other hand there is but one possible way in which human elements, innumerably diverse by nature, can love one another: it is by knowing themselves all to be centred upon a single "super-centre" common to all, to which they can only attain, each at the extreme of himself, through their unity.

"Love one another, recognising in the heart of each of you the same God who is being born." Those words, first spoken two thousand years ago, now begin to reveal themselves as the essential structural law of what we call progress and evolution. They enter the scientific field of cosmic energy and its necessary laws.

Indeed, the more I strive, in love and wonder, to measure the huge movements of past Life in the light of palaeontology, the more I am convinced that this majestic process, which nothing can arrest, can achieve its consummation only in becoming Christianised.

PART II. ON THE POSSIBLE BASES OF A
UNIVERSAL HUMAN CREED

The purpose of the New York meetings, if I understand it right, is not merely to seek a superficial reconciliation between the diverse forms of Faith which divide the human spirit and make it at odds with itself, but to find what they have fundamentally in common. We seek a new spirit for a new order.

I beg to be allowed to offer a brief contribution and personal testimony, the fruit of thirty years spent in close and sincere contact with scientific and religious circles in Europe, America and the Far East.

The Precise Point of Divergence . . . God or the World?

It seems to me clear above all else, setting aside the countless minor divergences, and ignoring the dull, inert mass of those who believe in nothing at all, that the spiritual conflict afflicting Mankind today arises out of the division of minds and hearts into the two profoundly separated categories of:

a. Those whose hopes are directed towards a spiritual state or an absolute finality situated beyond and outside this world.

b. Those who hope for the perfection of the tangible Universe within itself.

The first of these groups, by far the older, is preeminently represented in these days by the Christians, protagonists of a transcendent and personal God.

The second group, comprising those who for a variety of reasons have dedicated their lives to the service of a Universe which they conceive as eventually culminating in some form of impersonal and immanent Reality, is of very recent origin. Throughout human history this conflict between the "servants of Heaven" and the "servants of earth" has gone on; but only since the birth of the idea of Evolution (in some sort divinising the Universe) have the devotees of earth bestirred themselves and made of their worship a true form of religion, charged with limitless hope, striving and renunciation.

Are we to disdain the world and put it behind us, or live in it in order to master and perfect it? Mankind is rent asunder at this moment by these two concepts or rival mysticisms; and in consequence its vital power of adoration is disastrously weakened.

Such in my view is the nature of the crisis, more profound than any economic, political or social struggle, through which we are passing.

A Principle of Convergence; The Concept of Noogenesis

Any two forces, provided both are positive, must *a priori* be capable of growth by merging together. Faith in God and faith in the World: these two springs of energy, each the source of a magnificent spiritual impulse, must certainly be capable of effectively uniting in such a way as to produce a resulting upward movement. But in practical terms where are we to look for the principle and the generative medium which will bring about this most desirable evolutionary step?

I believe that the principle and the medium are to be found in the idea, duly "realised," that there is in progress, within us and around us, a continual heightening of consciousness in the Universe.

For a century and a half the science of physics, preoccupied with analytical researches, was dominated by the idea of the dissipation of energy and the disintegration of matter. Being now called upon by biology to consider the effects of synthesis, it is beginning to perceive that, parallel with the phenomenon of corpuscular disintegration, the Universe historically displays a second process as generalised and fundamental as the first: I mean that of the gradual concentration of its physico-chemical elements in nuclei of increasing complexity, each succeeding stage of material concentration and differentiation being accompanied by a more advanced form of spontaneity and spiritual energy.

The outflowing flood of Entropy equalled and offset by the rising tide of a Noogenesis! . . .

The greater and more revolutionary an idea, the more does it encounter resistance at its inception. Despite the number and importance of the facts that it explains, the theory of Noogenesis is still far from having established itself as a stronghold in the scientific field. However, let us assume that, as all the observable evidence suggests, it will succeed before long in gaining in one form or another the place it deserves at the head of the structural laws of our Universe. Plainly the first result will be precisely to bring about the *rapprochement* and automatic convergence of the two opposed forms of worship into which, as I said, the religious impulse of Mankind is at present divided.

Once he has been brought to accept the reality of a Noogenesis, the believer in this World will find himself compelled to allow increasing room, in his vision of the future, for the values of personalisation and transcendency. Of Personalisation, because a Universe in process of psychic concentration is *identical* with a Universe that is acquiring a personality. And a transcendency because the ultimate stage of "cosmic" personalisation, if it is to be supremely consistent and unifying, cannot be conceived otherwise than as having emerged by its summit from the elements it super-personalises as it unites them to itself.

On the other hand, the believer in Heaven, accepting this same reality of a cosmic genesis of the Spirit, must perceive that the mystical evolution of which he dreams presupposes and consecrates all the tangible realities and all the arduous conditions of human progress. If it is to be super-spiritualised in God, must not Mankind first be born and grow *in conformity with the entire system* of what we call "evolution"? Whence, for the Christian in particular, there follows a radical incorporation of terrestrial values in the most fundamental concepts of his Faith, those of Divine Omnipotence, detachment and charity. First, Divine Omnipotence: God creates and shapes us through the process of evolution: how can we suppose, or fear, that He will arbitrarily interfere with the very means whereby He fulfils His purpose? Then, detachment: God awaits us when the evolutionary process is complete: to rise above the World, therefore, does not mean to despise or reject it, but to pass through it and sublime it. Finally, charity: the love of God expresses and crowns the basic affinity which, from the beginnings of Time and Space, has drawn together and concentrated the spiritualisable elements of the Universe. To love God and our neighbour is therefore not merely an act of worship and compassion superimposed on our other individual preoccupations. For the Christian, if he be truly Christian, it is Life itself, Life in the integrity of its aspirations, its struggles and its conquests, that he must embrace in a spirit of togetherness and personalizing unification with all things.

The sense of the earth opening and exploding upwards into God; and the sense of God taking root and finding nourishment downwards into Earth. A personal, transcendent God and an evolving Universe no longer forming two hostile centres of attraction, but entering into hierarchic conjunction to raise the human mass on a single tide. Such is the sublime transformation which we may with justice foresee, and which *in fact* is beginning to have its effect upon a growing number of minds, free-thinkers as well as believers: the idea of a spiritual evolution of the Universe. The very transformation we have been seeking!

A New Soul for a New World: Faith Renewed in the Progress of Mankind

From this standpoint it is at once apparent that, to unify the living forces of humanity, at present so painfully at odds, the direct and effective method is simply to sound the call-to-arms and form a solid block of all those, whether of the right or the left, who believe that the principal business of present-day Mankind is to achieve a breakthrough straight ahead by forcing its way over the threshold of some higher level of consciousness. Whether Christian or non-Christian, the people inspired by this particular conviction constitute a homogeneous category. Though they may be situated at the two extreme wings of Mankind on the march, they can advance unequivocally side by side because their attitudes, far from being mutually exclusive, are virtually an extension one of the other and ask only to be completed. What more do they need that they may know and love one another? The *union sacrée,* the Common Front of all those who believe that the World is still advancing: what is this but the active minority, the solid core around which the unanimity of tomorrow must harden?

Despite the wave of scepticism which seems to have swept away the hopes (too ingenuous, no doubt, and too materialistic) on which the nineteenth century lived, faith in the future is not dead in our hearts. Indeed, it is this faith, deepened and purified, which must save us. Not only does the idea of a possible raising of our consciousness to a state of super-consciousness show itself daily, in the light of scientific experience, to be better founded and psychologically more necessary for preserving in Man his will to act; but furthermore this idea, carried to its logical extreme, appears to be the only one capable of paving the way for the great event we look for—the manifestation of a unified impulse of worship in which will be joined and mutually exalted both a passionate desire to conquer the World and a passionate longing to be united with God: the vital act, specifically new, corresponding to a new age in the history of Earth.

I am convinced that finally it is upon the idea of progress, and faith in progress, that Mankind, today so divided, must rely and can reshape itself.

QUESTIONS FOR STUDY

1. Describe Teilhard's account of the slow movement of the universe over time. Why is it important to him?

2. Where does Teilhard locate the human species on the advancing curve of evolution?

3. What is distinctive about the human species when it is compared with all other living species?

4. What two ways does Teilhard see for unifying human society? Which of these does he prefer?

QUESTIONS FOR REFLECTION

1. Teilhard subscribes to the concept of progress. By what standard does he measure evolutionary progress so that, when comparing an earlier stage with a later one, he can show that advancement has taken place?

2. Define *noogenesis* from its context in the selection.

3. What role does God play in Teilhard's vision of evolution? Does his approach to God through evolution resemble the attempt of the young graduate student in Updike's selection in Part IV? Can Teilhard be criticized in the same way?

4. What "is the principal business of present-day mankind"? How is this goal consistent with the "business of evolution"?

5. Do you see evidence for Teilhard's thesis that human society is unifying itself on a global scale through increased communication and contact? What inventions from the past half century have encouraged a heightened global consciousness or "noosphere"? Are efforts to solve the present global environmental crisis—for example, the Rio Summit Conference of 1992—contributing to this unity?

NETWORKING

Human destiny is a subject for Cobb, McFague, and Berry. Teilhard's overall commitment to *evolution* is shared by many authors from Wald, Polkinghorne, Asimov, and Burhoe, to Cobb, McFague, and Berry. He has a unique reading of *cosmic teleology* discussed by Bube, Updike, Barbour (Parts I and V), Gish, Asimov, Peacocke, and Lovelock. *Noosphere* is mentioned by Berry. The ravages of *entropy* are a concern for Burhoe and Polkinghorne.

ATTRIBUTES OF GOD IN AN EVOLUTIONARY UNIVERSE
RALPH WENDELL BURHOE

Ralph Burhoe is a leading pioneer in the field of interdisciplinary studies in science and religion. He attended Harvard University and Andover Newton Theological School before spending twelve years with Harvard's Bluehill meteorological observatory. In 1947 he became the executive officer of the American Academy of Arts and Sciences, and in 1964 he assumed the position of Research Professor of Theology and Science at Meadville/Lombard Theological School in Chicago. Burhoe went on to found the Institute of Religion in an Age of Science, the Center for Advanced Study in Religion and Science, and *Zygon: The Journal of Religion and Science.* In 1980 he received the Templeton Prize for Progress in Religion. Further writings by Burhoe can be found in the pages of *Zygon,* of which he was executive editor for a number of years.

God is the name for the "absolute and underlying power of the universe," according to one recent authority. In science the search is always on for ever more invariant formulations which explain or predict the manifold events of the universe in terms of the underlying power or forces. . . .

I shall not attempt to deal here with the failure of the scientific model of reality to provide an attribute of "personhood" to *god;* such personhood may not be necessary. In many religions, the ultimate power is not anthropomorphically conceived, and even in the Christian tradition the "three persons" that made up the trinitarian *god* did not identify "person as a self-conscious being as modern usage does." Even the Old Testament or Judaic tradition sought to deanthropomorphize God, whose ways should not be confused with man's ways.

Today, the nature of the sovereign system of reality which created man—and within which and according to which man lives and moves and has his being—has become dim in the minds of men. Many have come to feel that man is master of his own destiny, and they have lost their belief in the practical reality of a transhuman sovereignty. Even theologians have been granting the death of God, and the secular culture has been broadcasting a view, misrepresented as coming from the sciences, that man is in charge of his own destiny, master of his own fate, and king of the world. The recently aroused concern for the ecosystem is a sign that in some degree the scientific information or revelation that there is such a transcendent and sovereign reality is beginning to penetrate public understanding. But this beginning is a long way from an adequate vision of the sovereign power that rules us. . . .

There may be a lot of detailed interpretation necessary to make it clear that the reality system revealed by the sciences is the same as what the ultimate or sovereign realities pictured by the traditional religions sought to designate as the gods. Some of the characteristics and attributes of the traditional gods may need to be revised if they are to accord with the new scientific revelations; but their main features seem to remain significant. As I said, I shall use the term *god* to denote the total sovereign system, which in scientific language may be said to be the total cosmic ecosystem including the details of local ecosystems on earth.

Though the exercise could be done for many religious traditions, I shall limit myself here to giving some attributes of *god* that have been presented in the Judeo-Christian tradition because members of this symposium and most of our readers (initially, at least) will be from that tradition, not because I feel it could not be done for other religious traditions.

Among the main features of traditional attributes or characteristics of *god* as the ultimate reality that determines human destiny are:

1. *God* is the one and only ultimate reality surrounding and infusing man, which created man, and upon which man is utterly dependent.

2. *God* has revealed in part *god*'s requirement of and *god*'s disposition to men; hence, *god* is not wholly hidden, alien, or mysterious.

3. Yet *god* is in large part hidden, transcendent, beyond what man can fully understand—"supernatural"; hence, the ultimate mystery of *god*.

4. *God* is lawgiver, the reality or power that determines what is right and wrong, and has incarnated or revealed in large measure (by a grace sufficient for the day) the requirements for good and evil in the hearts and traditions of creatures.

5. But *god*'s continuing program of creation of ever-new stages calls upon most evolving creatures to seek the new as well as abide by the established requirements that are still valid—or else disappear from the scene.

6. The guarantee or justification for the hope of the ultimate triumph of *god*'s purposes and of all creatures who participate in them, even though any present situation may seem to be disastrously short of this triumph, is revealed by a careful reading of *god*'s mighty acts in the past 6×10^3 years.

7. *God* is gracious to man; that is, without any merit on man's part, man has been raised up from the dust and perennially sustained and redeemed from his errancy and given the opportunity to be a conscious cocreator of *god*'s evolving Kingdom of Life, as long as man seeks, finds, and executes *god*'s requirements.

The characteristics listed here of our creator and sustainer are not wholly separate, but overlap one another. They may be listed in other ways, but these ways are helpful for certain purposes. I shall give more detail *seriatim*.

1

I think it self-evident that the first characteristic of deity or the ultimate reality listed above is recognizably a part of the scientific picture of the source of man's being. Man is the utterly dependent creature of the transcendent and omnipotent source of flow patterns in the cosmos. The biological term "adaptation" portrays man's historical relation to these characteristics of the superior nature, which has selected the evolving patterns of life from the most primitive to man. Many different sciences have begun to reveal in new detail how man was fashioned literally out of the dust (small particles) or molecules of the earth by the ultimate powers that be. The ecologists are rapidly bringing a generation who have forgotten the supremacy of transcendent reality up against the sharp fact that we cannot in the end violate the ordained requirements and still continue to have life on earth.

The modern sciences go a good deal further than any previous revelations in making clear and valid the hypothesis that *god* is one, or a single system of related parts whose interrelationships in time and space we can increasingly describe in ever-simpler symbols that logically account for ever-larger domains of what we can experience. The sciences make ever clearer that we can never escape from *god*'s judgment (selection), even if we flee to the farthest corners of the universe. The different domains of the different sciences are increasingly shown to be different levels of description, describing increasingly interconnectible aspects of our experience of a single system of reality. New areas of science in the past few decades, such as molecular biology and brain studies, are revealing the essential inseparability or oneness of the reality designated by the two domains called "life" and "matter" and the two domains called "mind" and "matter."

Many will be disturbed by the seeming impropriety of my using the term *god* as the totality of the natural world rather than as a being beyond nature, a supernatural being. Without going into great detail, let me say that one can interpret the ancient usage of "supernatural" as referring to a hidden "nature" which is just as "real" as the tangible, visible world "out there" which everyone can see. Hence, "supernatural" means essentially the hidden, subtle forces not immediately obvious to common sense. During the past few centuries the changes in physics have quite obliterated this distinction between nature and supernature. Physicists have themselves become the best revealers of the hidden aspects of the entities and forces not immediately available to common sense, not readily found in what the world presents to the eyes, ears, touch, and other sense receptors. In modern science, "nature" includes the unperceptible ranges of electromagnetic radiations and entities from the invisible and intangible cosmic rays and subatomic particles to the great generalizations such as the laws of thermodynamics. The new "nature" of physics includes and describes the invisible "spirits" that animate men and shape men's "visions"—describes them as "natural" and "material" entities such as complex patterns of molecular structures and behaviors. These supersensory and super-commonsense entities commonly dealt with by contemporary science as "nature" are precisely the kinds of things that earlier usage meant by "supernatural." Hence, the sovereign system presiding over the world and human destiny described by the sciences is properly "supernatural" if the word is used in its former meaning, and is properly "natural" if the word is used in the sense now common among scientists. I do not recall that even the "linguistic" theologians have straightened out this problem of the meaning of "supernatural." Since for most scientists the natural universe includes all that really is, it includes all that was real for the earlier theologians who may have used the word "supernatural" to refer to some special class of reality that was not "naturally" observable. For many scientists there is commonly no meaning left for the term "supernatural" since for them all reality is classed as "natural"—even the still hidden and unknown characteristics of the cosmos.

2

The revelation to or the incarnation in man of information about the nature and requirements of the ultimate and sovereign reality which created man is a patent fact of genetic and cultural evolution. At every stage of evolving life, so scientists suppose, the surrounding reality has selected and presented to each new generation the information of the essential requirements that this reality ordains for living systems. The genotype is the scientific name for revelation at one level; it is literally incarnated within man in the DNA molecular alphabet. The culturetype or socially transmitted wisdom is the name for revelation at another level of scientific analysis of human life; and it is widely believed that this is also incarnated in the central nervous system by transmissions of information that are received both with and without conscious awareness, and which, along with the already incarnated genotypic information, shapes the molecular structures of the brain and hence the feelings, thoughts, and behaviors of men in such ways that men respond to the environment as a living system. Within the evolution of cultures, it seems clear that all populations are indebted to the critically significant revelations (about man and his relation to *god*) that have been made in the past by men who are sometimes symbolized as the *god*-sent saviors.

3

The third characteristic of *god* is clear, especially to those at the forefront of the sciences, namely, that we do not and probably even cannot know or fully prove the ultimate nature of reality. Much of contemporary philosophy of science, as well as the logic of the Gödel theorem, suggests why. While man has been given much useful knowledge, through what has been selected in his genetic and cultural heritage, the creative process and its creations ever remain a wonderful mystery for further exploration. While we sometimes feel bound by our finite capacity for counting to speak of a beginning and an ending, an alpha and an omega, this is only a symbol of the finitude of our brains and not necessarily a proper model of the reality we contemplate. The scientific theories of the cosmos, like their earlier predecessors in religious cosmic poetry, present the possible logical alternatives of either a finite or an infinite series in space and time. Likewise, while the scientific community is proud that it knows something about the world, its pioneers, at least, are certain that what now seems quite reasonable and true may tomorrow become a discarded theory or paradigm. "Reality" is not necessarily fully symbolized in what men happen to think or feel about it. In the evolution of our understanding, as well as in the evolution of prehuman information about how to live, we must forever adapt ourselves to the new and extended conditions of reality presented to us.

4

The fourth attribute of *god* stems from the first three and states how the omnipotent whole, (1) of which man is a part and which created man and sustains him, (2) whose law for having life is partially inscribed in man's heart, and (3) whose further requirements we must continue to seek, all adds up to (4) providing man with a "divine" or "cosmic" purpose—a goal or aim implied in the evolving character of the life system in which we participate. The laws or norms of life (selected and sustained by the nature of the total reality of the larger ecosystem—including at least the solar system—and inscribed in DNA and in culture) were given us as a heritage of unearned grace, which has defined the purposes of our lives. Like the sparrows and the lilies, we have goals and norms which we delight in carrying out and which yield the rich complexities of our lives. We like to breathe, to eat and drink, to keep suitably warm or cool, to procreate, and to do most of the other things that the sovereign creator of life requires for the maintenance and advancement of living systems. This is a sort of Garden of Eden picture before we consider the problem of our continuing consciously—after eating of the fruit of the Tree of Knowledge that makes us aware of the future—to adapt to the new requirements for the further building or evolving of the life system.

5

The fifth attribute of *god* is the continuing program of creation of life to raise it to ever-higher levels of complexity and wonder. It is here that man, already endowed by grace with a complex system of tried and tested norms, aims, goals, or purposes that yield life, must now adventure beyond the already known and revealed into discovering new patterns of life adapted to future requirements. In the advanced stages of human culture, after man began eating from the Tree of Knowledge, cultural evolution of *god*'s kingdom of life began, and man was called to participate in it consciously.

Hence, a prime purpose of man is to risk himself and suffer in serving to help build *god*'s future Kingdom of Life. This is a new level of purpose, a higher order of purpose which is a program for seeking new norms, aims, or goals required for a higher, more complex level of life. It is only as man participates on the exploratory and developing edge of evolving life systems that he has to unlearn or revise inherited information and search for better patterns of living. When man is at this edge—beyond the protective and nourishing circle of the already established grace that *god* has provided up to the point where man's phenotypic living starts—he has the necessity to question, not *god*'s goodness or power, but man's own completeness. Both theology and science explain man's perennial incompleteness.

At this point, if man wishes to continue in the forefront of building *god*'s Kingdom of Life on earth, he must let perish or die the inadequate elements of his prior-existing state and reform or replace them by entering on a further search for states acceptable to *god*'s coming Kingdom or purpose. This is by ordination a path of suffering and confusion (symbolized by the way of the cross) for the body or phenotype and for the associated perceptions of self and world provided by the brain. It will mean the death of certain of the present patterns of the organized system of the brain or body. Sooner or later it requires a discarding of the existing phenotype altogether. This is the way our creator has ordained that we evolve to our present stage of life, and there do not appear to be any alternatives but continual struggle with suffering and death of the phenotype forever in the future.

This would be a rather bleak and hopeless view if we did not have an insight into the immortal or eternal nature of the human *soul* and the potential joy and triumph of man, even on the cross, even in renouncing all his worldly goods and pleasures, even in the midst of the nastiest and otherwise most discouraging circumstances. Because the present phenotype is only a transient part of the full system or nature we call man, I shall later introduce a scientifically based doctrine of man's larger nature or *soul* that transcends death and defeat, since upon such a notion we are dependent for psychological and social viability in the world.

6

The sixth characteristic of the sovereign power in our cosmos, the surety that *god* will ultimately triumph over all evil and that his Kingdom will grow and prevail forever, implies that if we are to remain as partners in bringing about the Kingdom, we then can be sure that our *souls* shall live and that our purposes shall prevail and triumph over death and evil. While I shall deal with the reality of our *soul*'s participation later, I shall indicate here something of the scientific evidence for the ultimate triumph of the Kingdom of the sovereign power. It is essentially one of those scientific truisms that are tautological: If there is a scheme or system of things that is in fact inevitably moving in some direction, then it certainly will move in that direction. The increase of entropy in time is such a statement. We make this kind of tautological statement meaningful in history insofar as we are able to point to and empirically confirm real trends that actually take place according to such a law. We can and do find formulas or models of the reality system that enable our prophecy or prediction of events in ways which then are confirmed or validated in experience.

Our scientific expansion of the history of our evolution to more than a billion years ago is such a basis for understanding that things are happening in some orderly program or process of development that accounts for a certain direction thus far. Our discernment of evolution's laws or modes of operation offers some perspective on the future. It is important to note some recent developments that say something about the general overall trends of this evolutionary history. Today we have a much longer history and in much more detail than was available when the cosmologies of traditional religions were created.

Within the nineteenth century the scientists extended our historical perspective from a few thousand to a few million years, and within the past few decades they have revealed much about another thousandfold extension of our time span. They have given evidence of the creation of life from the dust of the cosmos and have detailed something of how it has been done. One of the findings has been that life has been evolving in a direction from disorder to order, from chaos and void to form. This trend from chaos to order is not a new observation or hypothesis; but it is now given in much greater detail, with more grounds for credibility, and for a much longer time span. Both Erwin

Schrödinger and Norbert Wiener noted this movement of life in a direction they called negentropic. Yet they and most other good scientists also noted that a very plausible interpretation of the second law of thermodynamics spells the doom of life and order in the end. This has raised a difficult problem for understanding the purpose of human life.

There has been in the past two decades a good deal of effort to understand why life *seems* to be running counter to this basic physical law. The most general interpretation of the second law by scientists for the past century is made with the assumption that the universe is a closed system and that increased entropy and the death of all further life by the eventual exhaustion of available energy is inevitable. One of the most significant breakthroughs to a better physical interpretation and a better ground for theological interpretation in my opinion has been that of J. Bronowski, who pointed out that while the second law of thermodynamics "is a *true theorem in combinatorial arithmetic,* and (like other statistical laws) *a fair guess at the behavior of long runs . . .* it tells us little about the natural world which, in the years since the Second Law seemed exciting, has turned out to be full of preferred configurations and hidden stabilities, even at the most basic and inanimate level of atomic structure."

In Bronowski's interpretation, as for biological theory in general, the movement of evolution is determined by processes of small steps. But his interpretation suggests that each step to a new level is a step provided by random fluctuations around an existing norm, some of which fluctuations are bound to hit upon new hidden stabilities or preferred configurations that are characteristics inherent in the universe. In some respects, Bronowski's theory is similar to that of Herbert Simon and that of Ross Ashby, where evolution of complexity takes place as the result of random variations in level A finding stable or preferred states at a new level B within the limits of a narrow spread of variability. Then variations around step B produce the discovery of a new level, C, and so on up a ladder of stable states that are intrinsic to the nature of the various levels of the hierarchies of evolving systems. If the universe were indeed a closed system, evolution toward successively higher levels of complexity by random variations discovering stable niches would be doomed eventually to cease further evolving by the second law of thermodynamics, for eventually the supply of energy to generate variations to achieve higher levels of complexity would become exhausted. This cosmology might give us a frozen heaven of some final perfection of complex forms never to be disrupted because all the available energy of the closed-system cosmos will have been exhausted.

But we do not have any way to prove the ultimate character of the cosmos. What is significant is that the character of the cosmos does provide grounds for discerning the direction of evolution, for that frontier of events in time which represents the penetration to ever-new states of realization of the hidden preferences intrinsic to the nature of the cosmos or *god*. As far as man is concerned, this can continue for as long a time in the future as in the past under our present cosmologies. The period of time is at least as long as our information about events in it is secure. For all practical purposes, this is indefinitely long. And hence man today, even with the present high levels of scientific information, must remain as unsure about *god*'s ultimates as are some theologians. If we postulate our plans on what to do for a million or a billion years, we shall have enough to keep us busy. What is important is our knowledge that there is a direction in time, a purpose, pointing to goals to be attained in the future. The scientific reality of cosmic evolution and its direction is more certain than the hypotheses about ultimate parameters, whether of finite or infinite character. *God*'s kingdom is a kingdom of development, evolution, or process—not merely random motions in a static frame. About the ultimate nature of *god,* or the total reality, we probably will remain uncertain, and we can say "sufficient unto the next millennium are the problems thereof."

Most scientific cosmologies or world systems indicate the essentially inevitable or predestined motion from one level to another in evolution according to nature's intrinsic, hidden preferences. If we cast our lot to continue working for *god*'s kingdom thus defined, we are bound to triumph with it. If we wish to opt out, we shall merely cease to be. Trust in *god* we must.

This *god* which is utterly transcendent, impassible, and triumphant, seems to imply little significance or room for man's independent efforts in the larger cosmos of *god* or nature. In prescientific language it poses the question of whether man has any freedom or power of his own, any responsibilities at all, or whether he is a puppet. It raises a host of other questions about man's relation to the creator and operator of the cosmic process within which we live and move and have our being.

7

This brings us to the seventh attribute or characteristic I have ascribed to the nature of the ultimate ecosystem: *god*'s essential "graciousness." I am here referring to the important element of Christian thought called "grace." Other religions have different ways and terms for allowing man to have hope for his future in spite of his present inadequacies (sin) and wretchedness. I shall not here enter into the varying views of *god*'s grace within Christendom, nor attempt evaluation of their relative validity, nor seek to compare their validity with related views in other religions. I shall simply seek to show how this rather important religious function—to provide men with salvation in spite of their errors and misery—can be ascribed to the sovereign nature revealed by the sciences. In this task I shall confine myself to the Judeo-Christian views.

The scientific pictures, it seems to me, support the biblical view that man is an image or reflection of the cosmic reality which created him, and man has been made one with it, a partner or steward in the program of bringing about the kingdom of advancing life.

Man, in the scientific picture, is seen as especially endowed with powers to carry on the work of *god*'s program of evolving—we may say, of evolving toward higher levels of complexity of life in a direction roughly implied by evolution thus far from molecules to man. Human endowments for this task are especially manifest in cultural evolution. Instead of *god*'s power overwhelming man and making no place for man's efforts in the scheme of things, it seems that *god*'s selection of a creature capable of cultural evolution has endowed man with special powers and freedom to discover new levels of hidden preferences in the scheme of things. In this man is the most highly endowed creature on earth for the most rapid further evolutionary development.

The scientific picture helps us with the old theological problem of theodicy, the problem of a good and omnipotent *god* as creator of evil in the world. This is related to the old query of whether there was also an evil *god* or devil, and the related ancient debate as to whether sinners might be damned forever.

The answer I read from the scientific revelations (literally, unveilings) is that there is no eternal hell. The living systems that fail to meet the requirements for survival simply cease to be. Patterns that do not exist can hardly experience suffering. The patterns that survive and evolve to more complex levels are all that count in any measurement of progress in that direction. The other patterns simply are unstable and disappear from the ecosystem. Each error, each random mutation that does not discover a new level of stability, is erased and a new opportunity to try again is provided to all that remains in being. Suffering is reserved for the righteous or living.

It is true that living men and animals fear, and rightly so, being caught in the forces that destroy life. This fear, however, is a good, for purposes of remaining alive, in that it enables the living to move from evil toward good, from destruction and death to life. The movement toward the good and away from the evil is the source of hope, joy, and pleasure, just as the movement toward evil is the source of the fears and pains that warn against evil and death and thus provide man with his capacity to distinguish good from evil. These homeostatic mechanisms have already been selected and abound in a hierarchy throughout all levels of living systems as a grace already granted. But, since they are homeostatic, negative-feedback mechanisms, the neurological patterns (and correlated consciously experienced patterns) are "symbols" or models of the reality system. These models disappear when the lethal event—which is ultimate judgment—hits the living system. The living system and the self-guiding purposes or models it produces by neural configurations disappear when the system disintegrates. At least this is my understanding of what most scientists dealing with these phenomena believe. In such a system there is no eternal hell.

It is only for the living that there can be joy and fear, and in the living the *selected* mechanisms that produce joy and fear are balanced in such a way that life tends to be a desired and sometimes exciting venture toward the building of a kingdom of a more complex hierarchy or ecosystem, whose ultimate triumph as far in the future as we can project is assured by the ultimate nature and power of the almighty cosmic sovereignty evolving in time. . . .

QUESTIONS FOR STUDY

1. What is Burhoe's definition of "god"?

2. How does the author define the supernatural?

3. Define *genotype*, *phenotype*, and *culturetype*.

4. Where in the human biological makeup are the laws of God "inscribed"?

5. What is the central purpose of human life?

6. In what sense does God triumph over evil?

QUESTIONS FOR REFLECTION

1. Using C. S. Lewis' description in Part III as your standard, is Burhoe a naturalist or a supernaturalist?

2. Why does Burhoe not use "god" as a proper noun?

3. Does the author's depersonalization of the idea of God reduce deity to a blind cosmic process? What happens to traditional religious practices, including prayer, worship, and thanksgiving, when God is understood this way?

4. Overall, does Burhoe have a positive view of human freedom? Are we in charge of our destiny? What are the consequences of refusing to follow our destiny?

5. What major role does genetics play in Burhoe's doctrines of revelation, judgment, and grace?

6. Why does the scientific concept of entropy pose a serious problem for Burhoe? Is his response adequate, given his reliance on the discoveries of science to inform his understanding of "god"? See also Polkinghorne in Part IV.

7. In what way does the "phenotype" or individual "bear his cross" and contribute to God's Kingdom?

NETWORKING

For further remarks on a *personal God,* see Einstein, Tillich, and Teilhard. The selections in the remainder of Part V focus on *sociobiology. Entropy* is a concern for Polkinghorne, Asimov, and Teilhard, and *reductionism* concerns Barbour (Part I), Peacocke, and Haught.

THE APPROACH OF SOCIOBIOLOGY
THE EVOLUTION OF ETHICS
MICHAEL RUSE AND EDWARD O. WILSON

Michael Ruse is a professor of philosophy at the University of Guelph in Canada. He has published widely on the philosophy of evolution. A recent book is *The Darwinian Paradigm: Essays in its History, Philosophy, and Religious Implications.* Edward O. Wilson is the Frank B. Baird Professor of Science at Harvard where he teaches and conducts research in behavioral and evolutionary biology. His books on sociobiology, including *Sociobiology: The New Synthesis* and *On Human Nature*, have had considerable impact, both within the profession and with the broader public.

Attempts to link evolution and ethics first sprang up in the middle of the last century, as people turned to alternative foundations in response to what they perceived as the collapse of Christianity. If God does not stand behind the Sermon on the Mount, then what does? Such attempts at evolutionary ethicising became known collectively as "social Darwinism," although they owed less to Charles Darwin and more to that quintessentially Victorian man of ideas, Herbert Spencer. Finding worth in what he perceived to be the upward progress of evolution from amoeba to human, from savage to *Homo britannicus*, Spencer argued that right conduct lies in the cherishing of the evolutionary process, in order that the best or fittest be able to survive and the inadequate be rigorously eliminated.

While Spencer's ideas attracted strong support in some quarters, for example the North American barons of industry, evolutionary ethics in this mode never really caught fire. On the one hand, social Darwinism seems so immoral! Right conduct surely cannot entail stamping on widows and babies. And no amount of tinkering by revisionists, such as Prince Peter Kropotkin in the last century and Sir Julian Huxley and C. H. Waddington in this, changes the fact. On the other hand, the very basis of a Spencerian-type approach is shaky. There is no progress to evolution. In a purely Darwinian sense, an amoeba is as good as a person.

Most people, therefore, have happily agreed with the 18th-century philosopher David Hume that there is an impassable gulf between matters of fact (for example, evolution) and matters of morality (disinterested help of others). To use phrasing made popular in this century by the Cambridge philosopher G. E. Moore, evolutionary ethics commits "the naturalistic fallacy" by trying to translate *is* into *ought*.

It is true that past efforts to create an evolutionary ethics have come to very little. Yet to revert to the opposite conclusion, that evolution and ethics have nothing to say to each other, is altogether too quick. Recent advances in evolutionary theory have cast a new light on the matter, giving substance to the dreams of the old theorisers, although not in the way or for the reasons they thought.

Our starting point is with the science. Two propositions appear to have been established beyond any reasonable doubt. First, the social behaviour of animals is firmly under the control of the genes, and has been shaped into forms that give reproductive advantages. Secondly, humans are animals. Darwin knew that the first claim was true, and a multitude of recent studies, from fruit flies to frogs, have affirmed it repeatedly. Darwin knew also that the second claim is true, and positive evidence continues to pour in from virtually every biological discipline. Genetically, we are a sibling species to the chimpanzee, having evolved with them for more than 3 1/2 billion years, parting a mere 6 million or so years ago.

What do these facts have to with morality? A chain of reasoning leads us to a distinctly human but still biologically based ethical sense. First, note that we are not just talking about behaviour, but about *social* behaviour. Today's students of this subject, sociobiologists, know that it is often in an individual's biological self-interest to cooperate with its fellows rather than (as traditional evolutionary ethicists thought) to fight flat out. After all, a loaf shared is better than a whole loaf, if the latter carries the risk of being killed or seriously hurt.

Secondly, and less obviously, there are ways in which nature can bring about "altruism," in the sense of self-sacrifice for the benefit of others. If those benefited are relatives, the altruist is still favouring genes identical to his own, even if he dies without leaving any direct offspring. Thus we say that the individual is altruistic but his genes are "selfish." Note that such behaviour implies nothing about good intentions or other ways of being "nice." To get altruism you can go the way of the ants. They are genetically hardwired, performing their duties in perfect cooperative harmony. They have no thoughts, at least of a human kind, only actions. Alternatively, you could go to the other extreme, and evolve super-brains, where every possible action is first weighed and assessed, and a policy of rationally assessed self-interest is always followed.

Neither of these options has proved attractive to animals like humans, and we have avoided both. If we had become hardwired in the course of evolution, we could never deviate from our course. Were something untoward to happen, we would be stuck with maladaptive behaviour. Worker ants are relatively cheap to produce, so this rigidity matters relatively little to their colonies. Humans require a great deal of parental investment, and it would be stupid in the literal sense of the word if we were to go wrong at the slightest environmental quiver. Alternatively, if we possessed super-brains, we would require even more resources than we do now; such as parental care stretched over many more years. Additionally, like those chess machines that survey every move, we would be forever making up our minds. Crises would be upon us, and we would still be thinking.

NATURE'S MORAL IMPERATIVE

How then has nature made humans "altruistic"? The clue lies in the chess machines we just mentioned. The new breed, those that can beat grandmasters, forgo omnipotence for utility. They follow certain strategies that have proved successful. So with humans. Our minds are not tabulae rasae, but moulded according to certain innate dispositions. These dispositions, known technically as "epigenetic rules," incline us to particular courses of action, such as learning rapidly to fear heights and snakes, although they certainly do not lock us, ant-like, into undeviating behaviour.

The best studied epigenetic rules, such as those affecting fears or the avoidance of incest, appear to have been put into place because of their biological virtues. Although altruism is less well documented (there is some evidence, for example, that varying degrees of its expression have a genetic component), such behaviour is also adaptive— at least when directed in appropriate measure toward kin and allies. We need to be altruistic. Thus, we have rules inclining us to such courses of behaviour. The key question is then: how are these rules expressed in our conscious awareness? We need something to spur us against our usual selfish dispositions. Nature, therefore, has made us (via the rules) believe in a disinterested moral code, according to which we *ought* to help our fellows. Thus, we are inclined to go out and work with our fellows. In short, to make us altruistic in the adaptive, biological sense, our biology makes us altruistic in the more conventionally understood sense of acting on deeply held beliefs about right and wrong.

Such is the modern scientific account of morality; at least the one most consistent with biology. But, what has any of this to do with the concerns of the traditional evolutionary ethicist? Even if the explanation were proved to be entirely true, it does not reveal whether in some ultimate, absolute sense, evolution stands behind morality. Does the sociobiological scenario just sketched justify the same moral code that religionists believe to be decreed by God? Or that some philosophers believe to exist apart from humanity, like a mathematical theorem?

It used to be thought, in the bad old days of social Darwinism when evolution was poorly understood, that life is an uninterrupted struggle—"nature red in tooth and claw." But this is only one side of natural selection. What we have just seen is that the same process also leads to altruism and reciprocity in highly social groups. Thus the human species has evolved genuine sentiments of obligation, of the duty to be loving and kind. In no way does this materialist explanation imply that we are hypocrites, consciously trying to further our biological ends and paying lip-service to ethics. We function better because we believe. In this sense, evolution is consistent with conventional views of morality

On the other hand, the question of ultimate foundations requires a different and more subtle answer. As evolutionists, we see that no justification of the traditional kind is possible. Morality, or more strictly our belief in morality, is merely an adaptation put in place to further our reproductive ends. Hence the basis of ethics does not lie in God's will—or in the metaphorical roots of evolution or any other part of the framework of the Universe. In an important sense, ethics as we understand it is an illusion fobbed off on us by our genes to get us to cooperate. It is without external grounding. Ethics is produced by evolution but not justified by it, because, like Macbeth's dagger, it serves a powerful purpose without existing in substance.

In speaking thus of illusion, we are not saying that ethics is nothing, and should now be thought of as purely dreamlike. Unlike Macbeth's dagger, ethics is a *shared* illusion of the human race. If it were not so, it would not work. The moral ones among us would be outbred by the immoral. For this reason, since all human beings are dependent on the "ethics game," evolutionary reasoning emphatically does not lead to moral relativism. Human minds develop according to epigenetic rules that distinguish between proper moral claims like "Be kind to children" and crazy imperatives like "Treat cabbages with the respect you show your mother."

Ethical codes work because they drive us to go against our selfish day-to-day impulses in favour of long-term group survival and harmony and thus, over our lifetimes, the multiplication of our genes many times. Furthermore, the way our biology enforces its ends is by making us think that there is an objective higher code, to which we are all subject. If we thought ethics to be no more than a question of personal desires, we would tend to ignore it. Why should we base our life's plan on your love of French cuisine? Because we think that ethics is objectively based, we are inclined to obey moral rules. We help small children because it is right, even though it is personally inconvenient to us.

If this perception of human evolution is correct, it provides a new basis for moral reasoning. Ethics is seen to have a solid foundation, not in divine guidance or pure moral imperatives, but in the shared qualities of human nature and the desperate need for reciprocity. The key is the deeper, more objective study of human nature, and for this reason we need to turn ethical philosophy into an applied science.

Some philosophers have argued that even if ethics could be explained wholly in such a materialist fashion, this alone would not eliminate the possibility that moral imperatives exist, sitting apart like mathematical truths. Perhaps human evolution is moving toward such celestial perfection, and the apprehension of such truths. There are biological reasons for seeing and hearing the moving train, but it still exists!

Unfortunately, the cases of mathematical principles, material objects and ethics are not parallel. Natural selection is above all opportunistic. Suppose that, instead of evolving from savannah-dwelling primates, we had evolved in a very different way. If, like the termites, we needed to dwell in darkness, eat each other's faeces and cannibalise the dead, our epigenetic rules would be very different from what they are now. Our minds would be strongly prone to extol such acts as beautiful and moral. And we would find it morally disgusting to live in the open air, dispose of body waste and bury the dead. Termite ayatollahs would surely declare such things to be against the will of God. Termite social theorists would surely argue for a stricter caste system.

Ethics does not have the objective foundation our biology leads us to think it has. But this is no negative conclusion. Human beings face incredible social problems, primarily because their biology cannot cope with the effects of their technology. A deeper understanding of this biology is surely a first step towards solving some of these pressing worries. Seeing morality for what it is, a legacy of evolution rather than a reflection of eternal, divinely inspired verities, is part of this understanding.

QUESTIONS FOR STUDY

1. What is the connection of sociology and biology in the new hybrid science of sociobiology?

2. Define *altruism*. Give the sociobiological explanation for altruism.

3. What is the connection between epigenetic rules and moral virtues?

4. What do the authors mean when they claim that ethics is a "shared illusion"?

QUESTIONS FOR REFLECTION

1. Sociobiology is a reductionist science. What is reductionism? How is the term applicable to sociobiology?

2. Now that sociobiology has told us that ethics is an illusion, why do we persist in behaving morally? Are we hypocrites? Explain.

3. If morality is not adaptive behavior programmed in the genes, what else could it be? That is, what are possible objective sources for moral values? Why, according to the authors, do we believe in objective morality?

4. Is it true that, had our species evolved differently, as termites for example, our morality would be far different from what it is?

5. If moral behavior is genetically determined for the entire human species, why do moral codes appear to vary so widely in different cultures?

6. Ethics is often associated with religion. Is it possible for sociobiology to argue that epigenetic rules exist for religious faith, practice, and beliefs?

7. Is sociobiology falsifiable? See Karl Popper in Part III.

NETWORKING

Alternative views on *reductionism as a method* may be found in Barbour (Part I), Peacocke, and Haught. Barbour (Part I), Burhoe, Singer, and Peacocke discuss *evolutionary morality*. For the *'Is-Ought' problem* and *altruism*, see Peacocke and Singer in this section.

ETHICS AND SOCIOBIOLOGY   PETER SINGER

Peter Singer is best known for his pioneering work in the field of animal rights. His *Animal Liberation*, Second Edition, is considered to be a charter document of the movement. Singer also authored *The Expanding Circle: Ethics and Sociobiology*. He is professor of philosophy and director of the Centre for Human Bioethics, Monash University, Melbourne, Australia.

The highest point of a people's development is the rational consciousness of its life and conditions, the scientific understanding of its laws, its system of justice, its morality.

G. W. F. Hegel, *The Philosophy of History*

Hegel thought that with the unfolding of his own system of philosophy, our civilization had attained rational consciousness of its life and conditions, and hence had reached the highest point of its development. He was wrong. He knew nothing about genes. Edward O. Wilson, Richard Dawkins, David Barash, and others who write in the field now known as sociobiology know a lot about genes. They know more about genes than anyone who lived before them ever knew. They believe that knowing about genes is absolutely essential for a proper understanding of human nature as well as human life and its conditions, laws, justice, and morality. If they are right, the efforts of Plato, Aristotle, Aquinas, Hobbes, Hume, Rousseau, Kant, Hegel, Marx, and all the other great figures of the past to achieve this understanding have been built on ignorance. It is only now, with the gains just made in our knowledge of how genes work, that we can truly see ourselves for what we are. It is only now that we have found the right path toward that rational consciousness of our life and conditions that Hegel considered to be the highest point of our development.

Wilson is not coy about the territorial ambitions of the new endeavor he has helped to found. These ambitions go beyond the social sciences and the provision of accurate explanations of human behavior which would follow from an adequate account of human nature. In *Sociobiology* Wilson suggests that perhaps "the time has come for ethics to be removed temporarily from the hands of the philosophers and biologicized" (1975, 562), while in *On Human Nature* he looks forward to the day when sociobiology will "fashion a biology of ethics, which will make possible the selection of a more deeply understood and enduring code of moral values" (1978, 196).

So far, the reaction to sociobiology has not been as uniformly grateful as might be expected by those who finally answer such ancient and difficult questions. "It is not surprising," says the Sociobiology Study Group of Science for the People, "that the model of society that turns out to be 'natural' bears a remarkable resemblance to the institutions of modern market society, since the theorists who produce these models are themselves privileged members of just such a society" (1977, 133). Far from accepting it as the science it claims to be, critics have seen sociobiology as part of the ideological underpinning of the resurgence of the political Right, and as a means of justifying individualism, ethical egoism, hierarchy, inequality, male dominance, double standards in sexual morality, the nuclear family, the dismantling of social welfare programs, nationalism, xenophobia, and war.

The debate between those who regard sociobiology as the first real science of human nature and those who regard it as the latest fad of capitalist ideologues is continuing. Books by sociobiologists flow from the presses, greeted by critical reviews written by social scientists, philosophers, or left-wing biologists. Arthur Caplan's *The Sociobiology Debate*, a collection of readings that appeared in 1978, is already in need of a second edition to bring it up to date.

This essay is intended to offer some thoughts on the aspects of sociobiology mostly likely to be of interest. Three questions shape the following survey. First, what is sociobiology? Second, what is its significance for ethics in general? Finally, what relevance does it have to specific social and political issues like sexual morality, economic distribution, and feminism?

WHAT IS SOCIOBIOLOGY?

The key to the sociobiological approach is the belief that all social behavior, including that of humans, has a biological basis and is the outcome of an evolutionary process that selects some genes or groups of genes in preference to others. If the evidence and arguments supporting this belief were not strong, there would be no point in looking further into sociobiology; but once we abandon Divine Creation and accept that Homo sapiens is one among several species of social mammals, the key tenet of sociobiology must be taken seriously.

We can, of course, immediately add that although human beings are social animals, they are different from other animals in several crucially important respects. Even so, we have conceded enough to the sociobiologists to require us to take their views seriously. Whatever the differences between humans and other animals may turn out to be, once we have recognized that we *are* social animals (which, as Mary Midgley points out in her splendid book *Beast and Man: The Roots of Human Nature,* is saying more than that we are *like* animals [1978, xiii]) it becomes an open question *how much* of human social life can be explained in biological terms and how much is resistant to this form of explanation, requiring to be accounted for in terms of, say, the particular culture of the group we are investigating. If this is accepted as a question open for scientific investigation, the legitimacy of seeking sociobiological explanations can scarcely be denied, even by those prepared to bet that no such explanations will prove credible in the long run.

On this basis it is worth approaching sociobiology with an open mind and attempting to assess its implications. I trust it will be obvious that in saying this I am not committed to accepting the detailed explanations of various social phenomena offered by sociobiologists. Nor am I committed to the general thesis that human social behavior can be adequately explained in biological terms. My position is only that here we have a new discipline, or rather a multidisciplinary form of enquiry, trying to answer some of the most fundamental questions about human affairs. As long as we continue to study and cite Hobbes, Rousseau, and Marx—none of whose views of human nature can today be ranked as scientific—it would be perversely backward-looking to refuse even to consider sociobiology and what follows from it.

THE SIGNIFICANCE OF SOCIOBIOLOGY FOR ETHICS

Does sociobiology have anything to tell us about ethics? Leaving aside for the moment any implications sociobiology may have for specific practical ethical issues, does it tell us anything new and significant about the nature of the entire field of ethical thought and action?

As we have already seen, Wilson thinks it does. *Sociobiology* begins with the following passage:

> The biologist, who is concerned with questions of physiology and evolutionary history, realizes that self-knowledge is constrained and shaped by the emotional control centers in the hypothalamus and limbic system of the brain. These centers flood our consciousness with all the emotions—hate, love, guilt, fear and others—that are consulted by ethical philosophers who wish to intuit the standards of good and evil. What, we are then compelled to ask, made the hypothalamus and limbic system? They evolved by natural selection. That simple biological statement must he pursued to explain ethics and ethical philosophers, if not epistemology and epistemologists, at all depths.

The way to an understanding of ethics, Wilson believes, is through an understanding of the origins of altruism. Altruism is, Wilson says, "the central theoretical problem of sociobiology." If altruism benefits others at some cost to oneself, why hasn't it been weeded out in the evolutionary struggle for survival?

When a hawk flies overhead, blackbirds utter warning cries, thereby risking attracting the predator's attention to themselves. Why? The popular answer is that it is for the good of the species. Though the individual blackbird may fall, the species itself survives because of such selfless behavior.

But think about this for a moment. If behavior evolves by natural selection, how could such selfless activity endure? Though it might be good for the species, the altruistic individual would, on average, die younger and leave fewer descendents. In competition within the species, altruism would be selected out; the fact that it might help the species in competition with other species would be of no avail to individual altruistic blackbirds, since individuals come in and out of existence so much more frequently than does the species.

The idea that altruistic behavior can spread by group selection was given its fullest statement in V. C. Wynne-Edwards's *Animal Dispersion in Relation to Social Behavior* (1962), and was defended by the popular writer Robert Ardrey in his best-selling book *The Social Contract* (1972, 192–98). Wynne-Edwards's book was cogently attacked by W. D. Hamilton in a number of articles in scientific journals, and by George C.

Williams in *Adaptation and Natural Selection* (1966). The current crop of sociobiologists is united in rejecting group selection, though some allow that in small, closely knit, isolated groups (not whole species) it could play some role.

If altruism could not have evolved because it benefits the group, how is it that we are not all ruthless individual egoists? The sociobiologists' answer is that it is not the individual, either, that is the unit of selection. The individual cannot survive more than a few years anyway. It is the genes the individual possesses that are immortal. (Here "gene" does not mean the particular bits of DNA in our bodies, but the type of gene.) Those genes that are best able to replicate themselves in subsequent generations will be selected by the evolutionary process; the others will disappear. Thus the title of Dawkins's book, though misleading insofar as it implies that genes can have motivations, is apt to the extent that it forces us to see evolution in terms of the survival or disappearance of kinds of genes.

Our kin share many of our genes with us. Here lies the clue to one important form of altruism. My children bear half of my genes; my full siblings on average have a similar share; my nieces and nephews have a quarter, and my first cousins one-eighth. Hence there is no puzzle in the survival and spread of a set of genes that leads me to make sacrifices to benefit my kin, in rough proportion to their closeness to me. J. B. S. Haldane once joked that he would be ready to lay down his life for two of his brothers, four of his nephews, or eight of his first cousins. In doing so, he would have been doing no harm to his genes' prospects of survival.

Yet altruism seems to extend beyond the circle of kinship. In a paper often quoted by sociobiologists, Robert L. Trivers suggested that altruistic behavior could develop in circumstances in which it was likely to be reciprocated, with gains for both parties. If monkeys cannot scratch the lice out of their own backs, they will be better off if they scratch each other. Of course, they would be *best* off if they could get others to scratch them without having to waste time on the chore of picking the lice out of another monkey's back; therefore reciprocal altruism can only be expected to occur among animals capable of recognizing each other and refusing to do unto others what those others will not do unto them (Trivers 1971, 35–57).

Kin altruism plus reciprocal altruism, with perhaps a little group altruism too, seems a slender basis on which to explain human ethics. Any sociobiologist who did not allow for a major cultural component would be a dogmatic fool. Still, obligations to kin and obligations of reciprocity are quite central among ethical obligations in virtually all human societies. In *The Origin and Development of the Moral Ideas,* published in 1906 but still the most comprehensive collection of anthropological data on morality, Edward Westermarck notes the near universal prevalence among human societies of recognized obligations to kin, and notes that the obligations weaken as the degree of kinship becomes less close (1908, chap. 23). More recently the anthropologist Marshall Sahlins has said: "Kinship is the dominant structure of many of the peoples anthropologists have studied, the prevailing code not only in the domestic sphere but generally of economic, political and ritual action." This quotation comes from *The Use and Abuse of Biology,* a slim volume devoted to attacking sociobiology; Sahlins goes on to deny that the dominance of kinship supports sociobiology. His argument rests on the claim that what is recognized as kinship in different societies does not always follow strict degrees of genetic proximity. Sahlins's argument could only succeed, however, against a doctrinaire sociobiologist who denied culture any role at all. Sahlins's own examples show a high correlation between genetic relationship and what various human societies regard as kinship (1976, 18). The correlation is presumably not accidental.

Reciprocal altruism can also be linked plausibly with central features of human ethics. Here too Westermarck finds that "to requite a benefit, or to be grateful to him who bestows it, is probably everywhere, at least under certain circumstances, regarded as a duty" (1908, 2: 155). Anthropologists from Mauss to Levi-Strauss have written at length of the importance of reciprocity, and the sociologist Alvin Gouldner concluded a survey of several recent studies by suggesting that "contrary to some cultural relativists, it can be hypothesized that a norm of reciprocity is universal" (1960, 171).

So perhaps sociobiological theories about altruism do tell us something about the origin of human ethics, or at least some central features of it. But how does this enhance our understanding of ethics as it now is?

Though Wilson clearly thinks that the light thrown on ethics by sociobiology is tremendously important, he is less clear about why it is so important. In *Sociobiology* the only contemporary moral philosopher he mentions is John Rawls, whom he describes as an "intuitionist." About this position, Wilson writes: "The Achilles heel of the intuitionist position is that it relies on the emotive judgment of the brain as though that organ must be treated as a black box. While few will disagree that justice as fairness is an ideal state for disembodied spirits, the conception is in no way explanatory or predictive with reference to human beings. Consequently it does not consider the ultimate ecological or genetic consequences of the rigorous prosecution of its conclusions" (Wilson 1975, 562).

Though defending Rawls is not a role that comes easily to me, it has to be said that Wilson's criticisms are a mess. The first sentence assumes without argument that Rawls's position is based on "emotive judgment" rather than rational considerations. The antecedent clause of the second sentence is false, because utilitarians, for example, would not agree that "justice as fairness" is an ideal state for disembodied spirits or for more normal beings. The remainder of the second sentence implies that Rawls's conception is somehow intended to be or should be "explanatory or predictive" for human beings. No reason is given for this suggestion, which seems quite out of keeping with the aim of Rawls's theory of justice, or of normative theories of ethics in general. The last sentence is false, because what Rawls's theory directs us to do will depend upon the information we have available about the consequences of our actions, and this will include information about ecological or genetic consequences.

Thus sociobiological criticism of contemporary moral philosophy did not get off to a promising start. But what, more positively, does Wilson hope to do for ethics? In *Sociobiology* there are only brief hints, such as the following: "In the first chapter of this book I argued that ethical philosophers intuit the deontological canons of morality by consulting the emotive centers of their own hypothalmic-limbic system. . . . Only by interpreting the activity of the emotive centers as a biological adaptation can the meaning of the canons be deciphered" (Wilson 1975, 563).

Then comes a sketch of an interpretation of the activity of the emotional centers as a biological adaptation. Some emotional activity will be, Wilson suggests, an outdated relic of earlier forms of tribal life. In other ways our emotions may be in the process of adapting to urban life. Impulses arising from altruistic genes established by group selection will be opposed by more egoistic impulses arising from genes favored by individual selection. Age and sex differences may cause further moral ambivalence. Evolution selects more strongly against altruism in young children than it does in older people who have already reproduced. Females who must bear, and in the past had to feed, the infants have a stronger genetic interest in a durable relationship with a sexual partner than do males.

All this Wilson sees as leading to a theory of "innate moral pluralism" according to which no single set of moral standards is applicable either to all human populations or to all the different age and sex groups within each population. It is also supposed to show that "the requirement for an evolutionary approach to ethics is self-evident" (1975, 564).

In *On Human Nature* Wilson is more explicit about the ethical conclusions to be drawn from biology. In the final chapter he anticipates "a biology of ethics, which will make possible the selection of a more deeply understood and enduring code of moral values." Although Wilson does not think we have quite reached the day when we can deduce all our moral values from our knowledge of the biological facts, he thinks he can already discern three values that the coming biology of ethics will lead us to embrace. These are the cardinal value of the entire human gene pool, the value of diversity in the gene pool, and universal human rights.

Taken together, the two books by Wilson seem to be saying three things about what sociobiology can do for ethics. First, it can provide information about the ultimate genetic consequences of putting ethical ideas into practice. Second, it can explain why we have certain ethical ideas by relating them to our evolutionary history. And third, it can establish certain moral values.

Of these three points, the first makes no difference to the way in which philosophers study ethics since philosophers who hold consequentialist theories of ethics have always been aware of the need to have the best possible information about the consequences of actions. Philosophers who are not consequentialists, on the other hand, have generally been indifferent to information about the consequences of what they consider to be morally right, and no doubt they will continue to be indifferent to such information even when it comes from sociobiology.

I shall postpone discussion of the second point, the explanation of our ethical ideas, in order to deal beforehand with the third and most fundamental challenge to accepted tenets of contemporary moral philosophy, the idea that biology can lead us to, in Wilson's phrase, "ethical premises inherent in man's biological nature" (1978, 5).

Although many people have claimed the gulf between facts and values can be bridged, few have given concrete examples of how it is to be done. Wilson is one of the few; we should therefore look at how he does it. I shall take as an example the most far-reaching of the values that he believes can be supported by our new biological knowledge, that of universal human rights. Here, complete and unabridged, is the passage in which Wilson defends this value:

Universal human rights might properly be regarded as a third primary value. The idea is not general; it is largely the invention of recent European-American civilization. I suggest that we will want to give it primary status not because it is a divine ordinance (kings used to rule by divine right) or through obedience to an abstract principle of unknown extraneous origin, but because we are mammals. Our societies are based on the mammalian plan: the individual strives for personal reproductive success foremost and that of his immediate kin secondarily; further grudging cooperation represents a compromise struck in order to enjoy the benefits of group membership. A rational ant—let us imagine for a moment that ants and other social insects had succeeded in evolving high intelligence—would find such an arrangement biologically unsound and the very concept of individual freedom intrinsically evil. We will accede to universal rights because power is too fluid in advanced technological societies to circumvent this mammalian imperative; the long-term consequences of inequity will always be visibly dangerous to its temporary beneficiaries. I suggest that this is the true reason for the universal rights movement and that an understanding of its raw biological causation will be more compelling in the end than any rationalization contrived by culture to reinforce and euphemize it (1978, 198–99).

Wilson's argument here is not as clear as it might be. In part he seems to be explaining why the idea of universal human rights is popular among humans, and in part he seems to be saying that we ought to adopt the idea of universal human rights to avoid the dangers of a less equitable system. Yet neither of these lines of argument sits comfortably with the opening sentences of the paragraph in which Wilson suggests that we should give universal human rights "primary status." An explanation of why a value is popular is not a reason for adopting it—slavery has also been popular—and to say that we should adopt an idea to avoid the dangers of not adopting it is to give the avoidance of those dangers primary status, and only a secondary or derivative status to the idea we adopt as a means of avoiding them.

Whichever way we take it, the argument fails. It fails as an explanation of the popularity of universal human rights. Human beings have been mammals at all times and in all places. The "recent European-American civilization" which, as Wilson says, has invented the idea of universal human rights amounts to only a minute fraction of all these eons of human existence; hence the present popularity of the idea can hardly be explained by our mammalian nature. Nor is the argument any more successful if taken as a moral justification of human rights. It is, as I noted, a justification which makes universal rights a means to some ultimate end, rather than rights which are intrinsic to autonomous or rational beings simply because of what they are. Since I am a consequentialist, that does not disturb me, though it would cost Wilson the support of many advocates of human rights. But even as a consequentialist justification, what Wilson says is peculiar. The "long-term consequences of inequity," he states, "will always be visibly dangerous to its temporary beneficiaries." This is a factual claim that would seem to be refuted by the existence of advanced technological societies in which the "temporary beneficiaries" of inequity do not see the dangers of denying universal human rights. (Choose your own example, according to your political slant, from the following advanced technological societies which have been accused of violating universal human rights: Argentina, Uruguay, East Germany, South Africa, the Soviet Union, the United States). In any case the factual claim, even if true, would not provide a moral justification of universal human rights; it would provide grounds on which those who believe that it would pay them to deny human rights to others might be made to think again. It becomes clear that it is not a moral justification Wilson is offering once we recognize that there are two possible responses that could be made by those interested in denying human rights to some underprivileged group: they might give up the attempt because of the dangers Wilson points out, or they might find some new scheme, unforeseen by Wilson, of controlling power so as to eliminate the dangers—to them—of denying rights to others. The fact that Wilson's argument is equally well met by either response shows that Wilson is not putting up a moral case at all.

Wilson might reply—and it would be in keeping with a common line of sociobiological thinking if he did—that what we call "morality" can never be more than a pragmatic compromise between groups with different interests, and it is therefore a mistake to look for any "higher" justification of human rights than one in terms of the self-interest of the dominant group. (Readers of Plato's *Republic* will recognize that this attitude predates sociobiology.) Wilson does not argue for this view. Nor do other sociobiologists, but in their writings they often appear to assume it without considering alternatives. From the opening paragraph of *Sociobiology*, for instance, Wilson assumes that moral standards are "intuited" and these intuitions flow from the "emotional control centers" in the hypothalamus and limbic system of the brain. This means that although at first glance Wilson seems to be an ethical naturalist who is attempting to deduce moral values from biological facts, it is equally possible to see him as a moral subjectivist or skeptic who offers pragmatic justifications for action instead of moral ones. There is, however, no systematic argument for moral subjectivism or moral skepticism to be found in the work of Wilson or any other sociobiologist I have read. There is a real need for sociobiologists to show how they would reply to the arguments of philosophers, from Plato to R. M. Hare or Thomas Nagel, who claim that reason has an important role to play in ethics (Hare 1963, Nagel 1970). Perhaps sociobiologists can do this. They might begin by studying J. L. Mackie's *Ethics,* since Mackie's form of moral skepticism would fit neatly with evolutionary explanations of morality, as he himself suggests (1977, chap. 5 and p. 113). Moral skepticism that combined philosophically sophisticated argument with a sociobiological explanation of morality would need to be taken seriously; but thoroughgoing moral skepticism is not a very palatable position, and it would be interesting to see to what extent sociobiologists themselves would be prepared to accept the conclusions of their argument, once ethical naturalism is rejected and the skeptical implications of what they are saying become clear.

With that challenge I conclude my discussion of sociobiology's attempt to reveal new moral values. But before I finish surveying what sociobiology has to say about ethics in general, I still need to return to a point that was left aside earlier: the claim that sociobiology can provide explanations for certain ethical ideas by relating them to our evolutionary history. This may seem a minor claim, certainly much less dramatic than the attempt to bridge the gap between "is" and "ought"; yet there is, I think, something important here that no one with an interest in ethics should ignore.

I have already quoted Wilson's claim that "the Achilles heel of the intuitionist position is that it relies on the emotive judgment of the brain as though that organ must be treated as a black box." Though this is unfair to those philosophers Wilson calls intuitionists, since they do try to eliminate intuitions resulting from obvious cultural prejudices or self-interested biases, there is a serious point here. Philosophers in the analytic tradition have not made any systematic investigation into the origins of our common moral convictions. They have regarded that as a task for historians rather than philosophers. As a result analytic philosophy has been regarded as naively uncritical by many Continental thinkers, who have been more concerned with the social origins of our ideas. Now the sociobiologists have added a further perspective from which our common moral convictions may be scrutinized—the perspective of evolutionary theory. If our common moral convictions can be shown to have a biological basis we may have to think again about accepting them at face value as the self-evident starting points of moral inquiry.

Take, for example, the preference for our kin that leads us to pay less attention to the sufferings of strangers than to those of our relatives. Most of us, of course, simply care more about the welfare of our relatives than we do about the welfare of strangers. That may be a brute fact which cannot be altered by new insights into human nature. But many people also think that it is morally right to give priority to our families and to those close to us, and it would be wrong, whatever our feelings might be, to allow the welfare of strangers equal weight. Indeed this is, as we saw earlier, the accepted moral view in most human societies. It might therefore appear to be a moral conviction which, not being the result of any specific cultural prejudices, has some claim to acceptance as a self-evident principle of morality. A biological explanation of the prevalence of kin preference undermines this claim. If the moral conviction that it is right to give priority to our families rather than to strangers derives from the evolutionary process of gene selection, it loses whatever credence it seemed to possess as a self-evident moral truth. It might, of course, still be a desirable way of living; but that is now a question open for debate.

A demonstration that a specific form of behavior has a biological basis can thus have the opposite effect of that which many expect. Far from justifying principles that are shown to be "natural," a biological explanation can be a way of debunking what seemed to be eternal moral axioms. When a widely accepted moral principle is given a convincing biological explanation, we need to think again about whether we should accept the principle. In this way sociobiology could have major repercussions for our thinking about ethics.

Where does this debunking stop? I said earlier that there is no systematic argument for moral skepticism to be found in the writings of Wilson or other sociobiologists. We have now seen that there are arguments for skepticism about specific moral principles. What if all our moral judgments could thus be shown to be biologically explicable? Would they then all be equally discredited? Wouldn't we then have a general argument for moral skepticism?

Perhaps in this manner a general case for moral skepticism could after all be drawn out of the sociobiological program. For this case to succeed, however, it would need to do what, as I have already said, no sociobiologist tries to do: it would need to show that no moral judgments can be given a rational foundation.

THE SOCIAL AND POLITICAL RELEVANCE OF SOCIOBIOLOGY

Sociobiology, then, does have something to contribute to the study of ethics in general, although the effect of its contribution is not quite what it is usually taken to be. All this, however, will strike some readers as tame stuff. It is not, after all, for its attempt to link facts and values that sociobiology has been denounced as a pseudoscientific attempt to justify the inequalities of our sexist, elitist, capitalist society.

The political case against sociobiology can be found vehemently stated in "Sociobiology: A New Biological Determinism," written in a suitably collective manner by the Sociobiology Study Group of Science for the People, and included in *Biology as a Social Weapon,* edited by The Ann Arbor Science for the People Editorial Collective. The paper is also included in Arthur Caplan's *The Sociobiology Debate,* along with a reply by Wilson and comments by several others. The charges are of two distinct kinds: that sociobiology is bad science, and that it is politically reactionary. The two charges come together in the overall claim that sociobiology has gained so much attention— a cover story in *Time* being the crowning achievement—not because it is a genuine scientific breakthrough, but because sociobiology suits the conservative interests that rule our society.

It is not the purpose of this essay to evaluate the scientific merits of sociobiology, although obviously this is something that everyone interested in the subject should make an effort to do. Instead I shall consider the charge that sociobiology supports sexist prejudices and an unequal distribution of wealth and power.

Sociobiology's critics begin by pointing out that the forms of behavior said by sociobiology to be natural or innate resemble closely those forms of behavior central to modern capitalist society. Aggression, male dominance, competition, self-interested striving, battles over territory, a division of society into the few who struggle for leadership and the many who are led, double standards of sexual morality are all said to be, at least by some sociobiologists, the natural outcome of genetic selection. The implication is, their critics charge, that we should accept the world as it is rather than struggle in vain for peace, women's rights, participatory democracy, or a more equal distribution of wealth. Sociobiology is, therefore, "a new biological determinism" which threatens to persuade the public that our society cannot be improved.

To see what the implications of sociobiology in these controversial areas really are, I shall examine one example in detail. The example I have chosen is the intriguing claim that there is a biological basis for the double standard by which conventional sexual morality judges the extramarital sexual activity of males much more leniently than similar acts by females. One reason for selecting this example is that the argument presented by sociobiologists such as Dawkins and Freedman is easy to grasp (Dawkins 1976, chap. 6; Freedman 1979, chap. 2). Another reason is that the conventional double standard seem as obvious a piece of sexism as any; the sociobiological claim therefore threatens feminist views not in their wilder flights of Amazonian fantasy but on the solid ground that most progressively minded people no longer question.

Sociobiologists start by asking: how can human beings maximize the number of their descendants in future generations? It becomes apparent immediately that the strategy that would work best for a male would not necessarily work best for a female. The number of children a male can have is virtually limitless (Freedman quotes the *Guinness Book of World Records* as putting the highest number recorded at 886, but that could no doubt be exceeded). The number of children a female can have, on the other hand, is strictly limited by the duration of the pregnancy and the number of childbearing years (the *Guinness Book of World Records* puts the record at 69, which included several multiple births). Thus a female will have more grandchildren if she ensures that the chances of each of her children surviving to maturity are as high as possible. Where it requires effort to raise children, their chances of survival will be increased if the females mate only with a male who will assist in providing for their offspring. Hence a female can be expected to prefer a lasting relationship rather than a casual sexual encounter. A male, on the other hand, may have more descendants if, like a fish releasing millions of eggs, he places his sperm in the maximum possible number of females, without waiting around to care for any offspring that might result. Each of his children will have a lower chance of survival than they would have had if he had helped raise them, but the total number of his descendants could still be greater.

I have chosen this example because it illustrates nicely both the strengths and the limits of sociobiology. On the one hand, it provides us with a neat and plausible explanation of a widespread observable phenomenon, namely the greater proclivity of males for casual sexual encounters with a variety of partners, and the greater social acceptance of this practice in a wide variety of cultures. Of course, alternative explanations could be offered. It might be said that males have used their superior power to suppress female sexual appetites, which otherwise would be as indiscriminate as their own. Certainly there is evidence that in some cultures males have tried to suppress female sexuality, sometimes by physical means like clitorectomies and sometimes by social attitudes that are only a little more subtle. Yet it is doubtful if these cultural explanations can bear the full weight of explaining the observed facts. Why is it, for instance, that even in the most sexually liberated societies, female prostitutes have no difficulty obtaining male clients, whereas male heterosexual prostitution is rare? The existence of the market shows where the demand is greater than the freely available supply. One explanation would be that in the most sexually liberated societies females are still not so free of traditional social attitudes that they are prepared to buy sex; but my own guess is that even in the absence of such attitudes, males would be more interested in sex outside any lasting relationship than would females. An appreciation of the different ways in which the two sexes can pass on their genes removes the need for an explanation in terms of social attitudes.

Not everyone will share my views about the plausibility of the sociobiological explanation in this area. But suppose the sociobiologists are right. What follows? In particular, what follows for the traditional double standard of sexual morality, which viewed sexually promiscuous females as sluts or worse and similarly inclined males as just "sowing their wild oats"?

From what was said in the previous section of this essay, it should be clear that assuming the sociobiological explanation to be true does not do anything to justify the existence of the double standard. The fact, if it is a fact, that females generally prefer lasting sexual relationships to casual ones does not carry with it any implication that individual females who have many casual sexual relationships are doing anything wrong. Indeed, following on what I have said earlier about the debunking effect of a biological explanation, we might argue that by explaining the widespread acceptance of the double standard, we also remove any lingering idea that this standard is some sort of self-evident moral truth. Instead it can be seen as merely the result of the blind evolutionary process and, as such, something about which we should make a more deliberate decision, now that we have understood it.

In making decisions about sexual conduct it is commonplace to recognize that sex and reproduction are distinct. They always were distinct, but by developing modern contraceptives we have sharpened the distinction. In so doing we have thwarted the biological mechanisms that have evolved over the centuries as a means of passing on our genes. From the perspective of evolutionary history, the pleasure associated with sex is a means to the end of reproduction, not an end in itself. In this area evolution works by an indirect route. Humans do not desire to reproduce as much as they desire to have sex. Evolution might, of course, have produced beings with desires to reproduce but no desire for sex as such. These beings would then have regarded sex merely as a means to a desired end, much as we regard peeling an orange as a means to eating it. But, as it happened, evolution did not take that route, presumably because we have evolved out of creatures incapable of foreseeing consequences that lie so far in the future. We desire sex for its own sake at least partly because we evolved from creatures who saw no connection between sex and reproduction. The frequency of our use of contraception is an expression of the degree to which we desire sex rather than reproduction. It enables us to enjoy as an end in itself something that from an evolutionary perspective is merely a means. I take this to be a good thing.

Thus sociobiology does not necessarily lead to biological determinism. On the contrary, because we are beings capable of knowing the consequences of our actions and choosing accordingly, we can play tricks on evolution. Sociobiology can contribute to the success of our trickery by telling us more about what evolution is up to; the better we understand evolution, the better we can outfox it. This point was made long ago by T. H. Huxley in his Romanes Lecture "Ethics and Evolution" and has been reiterated by several sociobiologists (Huxley 1947, 82; Dawkins 1976, 3; Alexander 1977, 276–77).

Can the same general point be made in respect of other areas in which sociobiology has been thought to justify existing injustices? It will not always be so easy to circumvent the consequences of satisfying our desires, because the desires may be more directly related to their evolutionary function. For instance, assuming that sociobiologists are right to believe that aggression is at least partly a result of genetic factors, can we satisfy aggressive desires without some of us becoming victims of aggression? Maybe we can find other outlets for aggression, like competitive sports; but maybe these quasi-aggressive pastimes do more to reinforce aggression than to reduce it. We don't really know. On the other hand, it is obvious that sociobiological explanations of aggression do not justify it. Nor do they imply that we ought to sit back and accept it as inevitable. Wilson, for instance, suggests that the promotion of cultural ties may reduce aggression between nations (1978, 120). He may or may not be right, but he surely is right to suggest that the more we know about aggression, the better our prospects of controlling it.

Finally, what does sociobiology have to say about equality—both equality between the sexes and equality of power and wealth throughout society? Here the case for saying that sociobiology favors the status quo is stronger, but it is still not entirely accurate. What is true is that sociobiology is in opposition to the long line of political thought that regards human beings as naturally equal and all inequalities as the result of the corrupting effect of social conditions. Sociobiologists find hierarchies in virtually all social mammals, including humans. So when egalitarians like Rousseau or Marx or Bakunin tell us that all we have to do is destroy the old society and a new kind of egalitarian human being will emerge from the wreckage, sociobiologists warn us not to be so sure. They predict that we will find the old inequalities reappearing, as they have reappeared in the Soviet Union, and China, and in Israeli kibbutzim.

This does not mean that existing inequalities are inevitable and should be accepted; what it does suggest is that any move toward greater equality will have its price. The sociobiological argument is really a restatement of the old right-wing claim that equality and liberty are at odds with each other. Equality is not the natural condition of human society; hence it can only be achieved and, once achieved, maintained by stringent supervision and constant rectifying of inequalities as they crop up.

That claim is a factual one. It says nothing about whether the price of equality is worth paying. It is also a claim that takes "liberty" in a laissez-faire or anarchist sense, as the absence of state interference. It is certainly possible to argue, without raising the issue of the truth or falsity of the factual claim, that this is not the most important sense of liberty, and that there are other senses in which more liberty is lost by existing inequalities than would be lost by the controls needed to eliminate them (Cohen 1979, Taylor 1979). On that view there would not be a simple trade-off between equality and liberty, but rather a more complicated situation in which equality and the aspects of liberty that go with equality would have to be balanced against the loss of liberty in the laissez-faire or anarchist sense.

This conclusion holds for equality between the sexes as well as for equality in a society as a whole. Just as, if the sociobiologists are right, destroying the unequal class structure of the old society will not in itself ensure the birth of a new egalitarian society, so—if the sociobiologists are right—destroying the male chauvinist traditions and social attitudes of the old society and providing full equality of opportunity between the sexes will not in themselves ensure that power and wealth are equally distributed between males and females. After all the old prejudices have been cleared away, we may still find that males seek power and status more aggressively and more persistently than do females. Should this turn out to be the case, we can still pursue equality, but we shall have to do so by different methods.

This conclusion does have an implication for one controversial issue in applied ethics, the issue of reverse discrimination. The implication is that we are not justified in concluding from the mere fact that the government or a large corporation has more males than females at the top of its hierarchy that there has been overt discrimination against females. There may have been, of course; but it may also be the case that males have, on average, tried harder to reach the top than females. Hence one argument for reverse discrimination—that an imbalance is *ipso facto* evidence of discrimination—fails. There are, however, better arguments for reverse discrimination (Singer 1979, 40–47; Goldman 1979).

I conclude that of the standard positions in applied ethics and political philosophy, very few are directly attacked by sociobiology: the egalitarian form of anarchism is one of the few, but neither egalitarians who are prepared to use the state to achieve equality nor anarchists who are prepared to allow some to have more than others need abandon their positions, no matter how solid the evidence for a sociobiological approach to human behavior should become. Nevertheless if sociobiological theories do become firmly grounded, those of us who value equality will have to begin to face up to some hard questions about the best means of bringing about a more equitable society at the least cost in terms of our other values. Speculative as sociobiological theories now are, it may not be premature to start thinking about these issues. The worst thing that egalitarians could do would be to turn away from a sociobiological approach to human nature without even examining the evidence for it. As Mary Midgley writes in the introduction to *Beast and Man:* "For every political purpose, but particularly for reforming and revolutionary ones, we need to understand our genetic constitution. The notion that reformers can do without this understanding is a bizarre tactical aberration, closely comparable to that of the Christian church in the nineteenth century when it rejected the doctrine of evolution . . ." (1978, xix).

REFERENCES

Alexander, Richard. 1977. *Darwinism and Human Affairs*. Seattle: Univ. of Washington Press.

Ardrey, Robert. 1972. *The Social Contract*. London: Fontana.

Barash, David. 1977. *Sociobiology and Behavior*. New York: Elsevier.

Caplan, Arthur. 1978. *The Sociobiology Debate*. New York: Harper & Row.

Cohen, G. A. 1979. "Capitalism, Freedom and the Proletariat." In *The Idea of Freedom,* ed. Alan Ryan. Oxford: Univ. Press.

Dawkins, Richard. 1976. *The Selfish Gene*. Oxford: Univ. Press.

Freedman, Dan. 1979. *Human Sociobiology*. New York: Free Press.

Goldman, Alan H. 1979. *Justice and Reverse Discrimination*. Princeton, N.J.: Univ. Press.

Gouldner, Alvin. 1960. "The Norm of Reciprocity." *American Sociological Review* 25.

Gregory, Michael, Anita Silvers, and Diane Sutch, eds. 1979. *Sociobiology and Human Nature*. San Francisco: Jossey-Bass.

Hare, R. M. 1963. *Freedom and Reason*. Oxford: Univ. Press.

Huxley, T. H. 1947. "Ethics and Evolution." In *Evolution and Ethics,* ed. J. S. Huxley and T. H. Huxley. London: Pilot Press.

Mackie, J. L. 1977. *Ethics*. Harmondsworth, England: Penguin.

Midgley, Mary. 1978. *Beast and Man: The Roots of Human Nature*. Ithaca, N.Y.: Cornell Univ. Press.

Nagel, Thomas. 1970. *The Possibility of Altruism*. Oxford: Univ. Press.

Ruse, Michael. 1979. *Sociobiology: Sense or Nonsense?* Dordrecht, Holland: Reidel.

Sahlins, Marshall. 1976. *The Use and Abuse of Biology*. Ann Arbor: Univ. of Michigan.

Singer, Peter. 1979. *Practical Ethics*. Cambridge: Univ. Press.

Sociobiology Study Group. 1977. "Sociobiology: A New Biological Determinism." In *Biology as a Social Weapon,* ed. Ann Arbor Science for the People Editorial Collective. Minneapolis: Burgess Publishing.

Taylor, Charles. 1979. "What's Wrong with Negative Liberty?" In *The Idea of Freedom,* ed. Alan Ryan. Oxford: Univ. Press.

Trivers, Robert L. 1971. "The Evolution of Reciprocal Altruism." *Quarterly Review of Biology* 46:35–57.

Westermarck, Edward. 1908. *The Origin and Development of the Moral Ideas*. London: Macmillan.

Williams, George C. 1966. *Adaptation and Natural Selection*. Princeton, N.J.: Univ. Press.

Wilson, Edward O. 1975. *Sociobiology, The New Synthesis*. Cambridge, Mass.: Harvard Univ. Press.

____. 1978. *On Human Nature*. Cambridge, Mass.: Harvard Univ. Press.

Wilson, Edward O., and Charles J. Lumsden. 1981. *Genes, Mind, and Culture: The Coevolutionary Process*. Cambridge, Mass.: Harvard Univ. Press.

____. 1983. *Promethean Fire: Reflections on the Origin of Mind*. Cambridge, Mass.: Harvard Univ. Press.

Wynne-Edwards, V. C. 1962. *Animal Dispersion in Relation to Social Behavior*. Edinburgh: Oliver & Boyd.

QUESTIONS FOR STUDY

1. According to Edward O. Wilson, the father of sociobiology, the clue to ethics lies in the origins of altruism. Define *altruism* and two of its types—kin and reciprocal. Why is altruism so important? How does sociobiology account for it?

2. Some say that giving ethics a biological foundation provides it with a firm basis in nature and rescues it from charges of relativism. Singer is not so sure. What are his reservations?

3. Give one major criticism of sociobiology.

4. Singer uses sexual conduct to show that persons use their genetically disposed behavior in various ways as they see morally fit. How is this a counter-case to biological determinism?

5. What reservations does sociobiology have about equality among members of a society?

QUESTIONS FOR REFLECTION

1. Sociobiology has been accused of making up "just so" stories to account for various forms of widespread human practices. Make up a plausible story for the "fact" that most women students carry their books against their bosoms while most men students carry theirs in their hand, which swings freely as they walk along. Your account should, of course, attempt to show why such behavior in ancient times was

eventually programmed into our genes because it favored tribal societies in their relentless struggle to survive in an unforgiving environment.

2. Singer says that for sociobiology to succeed in its claim that ethics is nothing but genetically disposed social behavior shaped by evolution, one would have to show that "no moral judgments can be given a rational foundation." What does he mean? Would Ruse and Wilson take issue with this claim?

3. What evidence do we have that our actions are not determined completely by our genes? See Singer's interpretation of the separation of sex from reproduction for insight into this question.

4. What response is possible from a monotheist (a Christian, Jew, or Muslim) to sociobiological claims about the origins of morality? According to these faiths, what is the source of morality? How would a theologian from one of these traditions argue for an independent foundation for ethics?

5. Could the theist argue that God designed the world to evolve in the direction of producing creatures who have the divine law written on their hearts? Is this reformed design argument a way of having one's sociobiology and faith, too?

NETWORKING

The *role of evolution in morality* is discussed in Barbour (Parts I and V), Burhoe, Ruse and Wilson, and Peacocke. For the *'Is-Ought'* problem, see Ruse and Wilson and Peacocke.

GOD AND THE SELFISH GENES
ARTHUR R. PEACOCKE

Arthur Peacocke has long been involved in the interaction between science and religion. He is dean of Claire College, Cambridge University, and both a physical biochemist and theologian. His books include the award-winning *Science and the Christian Experiment* and *Creation and the World of Science,* the Bampton Lectures of 1978.

The advent of sociobiology accompanied, as in the case of Darwinism, by overtly reductionist and antireligious sentiments on the part of some of its proponents may likewise tempt the theologian into ill-advised and premature opposition. Not that this has indeed been the stance of many theological contributions. One has to be reminded that "sociobiology" as a distinctive biological discipline or, rather, programme is still a relative newcomer. It is still only a decade or so since E. O. Wilson's volume launched that title for his claimed 'new synthesis'. In this chapter we shall attempt to assess the core of sociobiological arguments that seem to be important for our understanding of man, God and evolution and to point to what might be appropriate responses to this new multifaceted activity.

Sociobiology is concerned with interpreting human social behaviour, with its rich cultural expression and variety, in the light of animal, bird and insect social behaviour, with their more fixed behaviour patterns (often entirely so in the case of insects) that are described in terms of genetic cost-benefit exchanges. By virtue of thus straddling the world of human culture and that of the behaviour of the nonhuman biological world, it inevitably touches, indeed sometimes forcibly strikes, upon many issues concerning the fundamental nature of man. The debate about sociobiology is not entirely a replay of the old controversy concerning the nature-nurture dichotomy as factors in human behaviour because there has been an enormous increase in knowledge of the complexity of the strategy of gene perpetuation and of the many-levelled character of any adequate interpretation of human behaviour (symbolic, psychological, hormonal, neurological, nutritional—not to mention the spiritual, ethical and intellectual). So many of the issues that the proponents of sociobiology touch upon are those that have again and again been raised by both science and philosophy for religion.

The emphatically evolutionary outlook of sociobiology does not, in itself, have any new implications for religion that have not been raised in relation to the general idea of biological (and indeed, cosmic) evolution, namely, questions concerning continuity, chance, emergence, and inter-connectedness, with their resulting renewed stress on the immanence of God in the natural processes of creation. However, it is true that the wide-ranging scope of sociobiology and the energy and zest with which its expositors apply and extend it, undoubtedly makes even more urgent the need for Christian (and indeed all) theology to become much clearer and explicit about its relation to such views, that is, to the world view of scientific 'evolutionary naturalism'. This latter is the dominant viewpoint of the contemporary scientific community and has been described by Karl E. Peters in the following terms:

> . . . evolutionary naturalism may be described as follows: First, the realm of nature is all there is; there is no supernatural in the sense of a realm of knowable reality totally other than that which is open to some possible interpretation of every-day experience by some possible scientific theories. Second, nature is dynamic; it evolves. Change is not merely an appearance or an indication of a second-class reality but is essential to the way things are. Third, at least at the level of life, the evolution of nature is best understood by updated Darwinian mechanisms: a continuing inheritance by the replication of major bodies of information; continual, essentially random, small variations of these information systems; and environmental selection pressures favoring the reproduction of some variations over others and thus modifying in small steps the information heritage.[1]

However incomplete we may regard these propositions (and Peters's first, namely "no supernatural . . .," is to be questioned,[2] . . .), the second and third are supported on scientific grounds and their religious implications require exploration. They will not go away, however uncongenial to traditional theology, and increasingly constitute the most widely, generally accepted account of at least how we arrived here, if not why. For myself, it is in its bare outline the best account we have of the natural world of which we now know we are part—and sociobiology, stripped of its reductionist overtones, is certainly a new and positive contribution to that evolutionary naturalism. As Peters points out, such evolutionary naturalism (except for the first clause in his account that I have already questioned) is not by itself definitive of any particular theistic or atheistic position and is, as a matter of observation, shared by at least liberal theists, religious humanists, and agnostic and atheistic humanists—if not always by some Christian theologians. But for anyone who believes that the natural world is the sphere of action of God the Creator, it makes new demands upon theological conceptualization.

Sociobiologists are not a uniform group with respect to their philosophical positions. However, I think it is fair to say that, by successfully delineating the genetic strategies underlying behaviour patterns and roles in many insect, bird, and animal societies, they have often been confidently and explicitly deterministic, reductionist and functionalistic in their interpretation of human behaviour—or, perhaps it is more accurate to say, they have shown a general tendency to favour interpretations of human behaviour that have been easily seized upon by those who are determinists, reductionists and functionalists. Some sociobiologists[3, 4] have gone out of their way to disavow such extreme positions, which at times their writings may have seemed to imply. Actually the net effect of sociobiology has been a renewed stress on reducing accounts of biological behaviour to a deterministic level that views it functionally in terms of its contribution to the survival of genes; behaviour is regarded as a strategy, however indirect, for gene survival.

There can be no doubt of the success of many such interpretations in the nonhuman biological field, but . . . it is with respect to their application to human behaviour that particular controversy arises. . . . The theological response to these ideas is, in their general import, that which must be made to any purely deterministic and reductionistic accounts of human behaviour.[5] But in making any such appropriate responses, theologians would do well to recognize, more explicitly than they have done in the past, the complexity of human nature and the fact that its basic foundational level is biological and genetic, however overlaid by nurture and culture. And they must couple this also with an acknowledgement that it is this kind of genetically based creature that God has actually created as a human being through the evolutionary process. God has made human beings thus with their genetically constrained behaviour—but, through the freedom God has allowed to evolve in such creatures, he has also opened up new possibilities of self-fulfilment, creativity, and openness to the future that requires a language other than that of genetics to elaborate and express.

The scientifically reductionist account has a limited range and needs to be incorporated into a larger theistic framework that has been constructed in response to questions of the kind, Why is there anything at all? and What kind of universe must it be if insentient matter can evolve naturally into self-conscious, thinking persons? and What is the meaning of personal life in such a cosmos? Scientists *per se* are unlikely to seek such incorporation, but at least they may be prepared to recognize that the scientific method is not of the kind that can be directed to answering such questions. Meanwhile theologians have to take more seriously the mode of God's actual creation of human beings through evolution and also our new understanding of the creature thus formed—even though, in the past, words such as *determinism, reductionism* and *functionalism* have been red rags to the theological bull! For the genetic constraints upon our nature and action are, from a theistic viewpoint, what God has determined shall provide the matrix within which freedom can operate. But is not this nothing other, in a new form, than the old theological chestnut of pre-destination and free will?

Where the Christian theist differs from the sociobiologist, as such, is in his affirmation of God as "primary cause" or ground of being of the whole evolutionary process and, indeed, of God as the agent in, with, and under this process of creation through time. What constitutes the challenge to theology is a new apprehension and explication of God's presence and agency in the processes that biology, in general, and sociobiology, in particular, have unveiled. Of course, many sociobiologists will be opposed to setting their science in such a wider, theistic framework; for Wilson, for example, "no species, our own included, possesses a purpose beyond the imperatives created by its genetic history. . . . If the brain evolved by natural selection, even the capacities to select particular esthetic judgments and religious beliefs must have arisen by the same mechanistic processes," and "scientists cannot in all honesty serve as priests."[6]

Here conflict between religion and a particular philosophical interpretation of biology is inevitable, but the theologian should not enter the lists with destructive ambitions. Indeed some theologians have even argued that theology must come to terms with the domination of the biological process by the prime requirement for *survival*, whether it be of genes, individuals, groups or species. Philip Hefner, for example, argues[7] that, in the light of biological evolution in general and the sociobiological critique in particular, the whole discussion of the is/ought dichotomy—which for too long (he thinks), as the naturalistic fallacy, has prevented us from seeing how the biological process generates human values—has moved into the arena of survival and nonsurvival. He uses the categories of A. J. Dyck[8] to elaborate the "ought" as 'moral requiredness' which is described as a 'gap-induced requiredness': moral requiredness is a gap we feel compels us (moral obligation) to act so as to fill it in order to improve some situation. So Hefner then argues that: "The most urgent gap experienced by humans [in relation to its value-requirements]—and therefore the most pressing gap-induced requiredness—is the gap created by the possibility of not surviving. Theology, therefore, has no alternative but to speak its truth about what is and ought to be in terms relevant to survival—the survival of the species, of the world, *of values, of human worth, of all the conditions upon which the human spirit is dependent*" (italics added).[9] But the question is: Can the values, and so on, whose survival is spoken of in the italicized end of this quotation, be regarded as derivable simply from contemplation of the sociobiological facts (if they are facts)? Mary Hesse comments on this prescription of theology's task by Hefner as follows: "But whatever facts may be discovered about the conditions of survival by sociobiology, the conclusion that the survival of the human species is the most urgent *value* may itself be regarded as *morally* repugnant. This is surely a sufficient rebuttal of the claim that the facts alone permit the 'ought' to be derived from the 'is' . . . God in his wisdom may have ordained values which are consistent with earthly extinction; to suppose otherwise is to embrace some form of materialism."[10] Whether or not this is a "sufficient rebuttal" will certainly be argued, but I quote this interchange as an example of a new kind of question regarding *survival* and what it means that is raised for theology by sociobiology.[11]

There is an application of sociobiology which is relevant to theology and which has been taken up by a number of evolutionary naturalists sympathetic to religion in general, if not especially to Christian theology as such. This is the view that the religions have had a function in enabling human societies (and genes?) to survive and, to that extent, can be justified as useful, functional mythologies—even if they are now ripe, according to Wilson, for replacement by "the evolutionary epic" as "probably the best myth we will ever have."[12] Donald T. Campbell[13] and Ralph Burhoe[14] both argue for a positively selected role for religion in the survival of cultures (which is their unit of survival, and so of selection); and Burhoe especially, unlike Wilson, argues for its continuing role in the development and survival of human culture, providing it can incorporate the scientific world view. No doubt Christian theologians will be grateful for this attribution of a survival function to religion in human culture, but the attribution again raises the questions of "Survival for what?" Is survival a value? What kind of survival? However, theologians will (or should, in my view) first want to ask questions about the *truth* of religious notions, regardless of the contribution of religion to the survival of human culture(s). And one could argue that it is the ultimate commitment to the truth which is in God and Jesus the Christ that characterises the Christian faith without regard to survival calculations—think too of Job's "Though he slay me, yet will I wait for him."[15] Is not that the core of a religion which has a cross as its central symbol and historical focus?[16]

A new nuance has recently[17] been given by Michael Ruse and Edward Wilson to these somewhat more sympathetic sociobiological interpretations of morality and its conventionally presumed religious basis. They urge[18] that the possession of a moral code, of moral beliefs, in short of ethics, is "an illusion fobbed off on us by our genes to get us to cooperate . . . ethics is a *shared* illusion of the human race"—albeit a useful illusion enforced by biology. For "by making us think that there is an objective higher code, to which we are all subject," biology inculcates the motivations that encourage altruism and reciprocity, and hence furthers our reproductive ends. "We function better [presumably biologically] because we believe [in an objective ethical code]."[19]

But, I wonder, does this really provide a new basis for understanding ethics as such, that is, the *content* of ethical codes, our actual ethical beliefs? For these latter can, in developed societies, be given, on reflection, some rational justification on bases other than that of reproductive efficiency in a purely biologically competitive milieu. And this is not surprising for evolution has now become "psychosocial," as Julian Huxley used to put it,[20] that is, the factors affecting the development of human culture now depend not only on the interaction of *homo sapiens* with the physical and biological environment, but also on the knowledge and customs transmitted by culture. Human beings radically alter their environment at their own will and so alter their own development in a way that transcends that of all other living organisms. Evolution has become history.

It may well be true that long ago in human history, natural selection operated to favour genes which gave us brains that disposed us to act in those ways the sociobiologists denote as "altruistic" and "reciprocal." However, it seems to be the case that this early stage of our biological history also, no doubt by the processes of natural selection, endowed us with brains that had the capacity to think rationally and to evolve belief systems of our own devising. The biologically selective process cannot of itself prescribe the *content* of these ratiocinations and reflections on our own behaviour, in the light of various belief systems that now constitute the ethical codes of humanity. For these develop by the procedures and constraints upon coherent, rational *thinking.*

The ethical codes so developed are, in any case, not uniform, and are often counter-biological, as in the Christian ethic which, while urging one to "love one's neighbour as oneself," explicates this in the classic parable of the Good Samaritan from which it becomes clear that our "neighbour" is anyone in need—and not at all our genetic kin. Indeed the story was told precisely to deny this latter. We may well have a capacity for acknowledging constraints on our behaviour "wired-in," as it were, by our early biological origins, but the justification of the content of beliefs about such constraints in developed cultures goes far beyond, and often does not at all correspond with, the prescriptions for survival of the individual, of the community and, least of all, of the genes as such, that biology alone would predict.[21] It seems that this new twist to "evolutionary ethics" is still guilty of the well-known, and in the circumstances ironically and ambiguously designated, "genetic fallacy," whereby the ultimate form of a human cultural development is thought to be reductively entirely explained in terms of its biological or cultural origins. Just as science is not magic, so ethics, on the same grounds, is not genetics.

A more fruitful way of relating our biological origins and constraints to our developed rationally informed perceptions of ourselves may well be found in the publications of those who wish to emphasise, in a positively holistic fashion, the physical and biological rooting of the mental and spiritual lives of human beings (in addition to those of Burhoe, Campbell, Crook, Midgley and even Wilson, one could also cite Altner,[22]

Jaynes,[23] Pugh[24] and Sagan[25]). To varying degrees these works see human mental and spiritual life as continuous with, and a development and elaboration of, the physical and biological (especially genetic) substratum through which evolution has operated. We have also witnessed the recognition by at least one eminent biologist, Sir Alister Hardy, of the religious experience of human beings as one of their natural characteristics and amenable to scientific investigation, at least in the style of natural history.[26] Our mental and spiritual life, it seems, must fulfil at least basic, evolutionary requirements long established, but we then go on to interpret ourselves to ourselves at our own culturally developed level. The pressure from the ideas of sociobiology in particular, and of biology and cosmic evolution in general, is towards a franker recognition of our natural relatedness to the physical and biological worlds and an acknowledgment that our mental and spiritual aspirations are so grounded. But what we should aspire to is not thereby prescribed and so it is that theology has, in my view, a new and exciting role to play if it will only recognise its new brief.

NOTES

1. K. Peters, *Zygon* 15 (1980), 213.
2. See A. R. Peacocke, *Intimations of Reality: critical realism in science and religion* (University of Notre Dame Press, Notre Dame, 1983), Chapter I.
3. E. O. Wilson, "Biology and the Social Sciences," *Daedalus* 106, 6 (Autumn 1977), 127–40.
4. R. Dawkins, *The Selfish Gene* (Oxford University Press, Oxford, 1976).
5. It needs, of course, much amplification along the lines I have developed elsewhere in *Creation and the World of Science,* 1979, which outlines the arguments against reductionist interpretation of human behaviour and attempts to establish a placing for theological discourse. See also *The Shaping of Man,* by R. Trigg (Blackwell, Oxford, 1982).
6. E. O. Wilson, *On Human Nature* (Harvard University Press, Cambridge, Mass., 1978), pp. 2, 193, respectively.
7. P. Hefner, "Is/Ought: a risky relationship between theology and science" in *The Sciences and Theology in the Twentieth Century,* ed. A. R. Peacocke (Oriel Press, Routledge & Kegan Paul, London and Notre Dame Press, Notre Dame, Indiana, 1981), pp. 58–78. The impossibility of deducing ethical norms from the character of the evolutionary process, what *ought* to be from what *is* (or has been) the case—the "naturalistic fallacy" of G. E. Moore (*Principia Ethica,* Cambridge University Press, Cambridge, 1903)—still continues to have the support of philosophers, e.g. A. M. Quinton, "Ethics and the theory of evolution," in I. T. Ramsey (ed.), *Biology and Personality* (Blackwell, Oxford, 1966) and A. G. N. Flew, *Evolutionary Ethics* (Macmillan, London, 1967). However, it does not bar us from allowing evolutionary considerations to bear upon our ethical judgments.
8. A. J. Dyck, "Moral Requiredness: Bridging the gap between 'Ought' and 'Is'— Part I," *J. Rel. Ethics* 6 (1978), 293–318; see also, Eileen Barker, "Value systems generated by biologists," *Contact* 55 (1976), 2–13.

9. P. Hefner, *op. cit.*, ref. 7, p. 76.
10. M. Hesse, "Retrospect" in *The Sciences and Theology in the Twentieth Century,* (ed.) A. R. Peacocke (Oriel Press, Routledge & Kegan Paul, London, and Notre Dame Press, Notre Dame, 1981), pp. 283–4.
11. For further discussion of this issue see P. Hefner, "Survival as a Human Value," *Zygon* 15 (1980), 203–12 and W. H. Austin, "Are Religious Beliefs 'Enabling Mechanisms for Survival'?," *ibid.*, pp. 193–201.
12. E. O. Wilson, ref. 40, p. 201.
13. D. T. Campbell, "On the conflicts between biological and social evolution and between psychology and moral tradition," *Amer. Psychologist* 30 (1975), 1103–26, reprinted in *Zygon* (Vol. 11, No. 3, 1976) is a discussion of Campbell's thesis.
14. R. W. Burhoe, "The Human Prospect and The Lord of History," *Zygon* 10 (1973), 299–375.
15. Job 13:15.
16. Hefner's reply to this question would be that "the most fundamental affirmation in the Judeo-Christian traditions concerning God is that of his faithfulness to and love for his creation. . . . The theologian has no alternative but to assume God's faithfulness will not allow creation, including the human portion of that creation, to go unconsummated . . . when the term 'survival' is incorporated within the theological perview, it takes on the meaning associated with consummation and destiny under God. . . . Christian faith gives the created order very significant status within the purposes of God: if therefore it is determined that the survival thrust is a major motif operative within that order, a motif that gives shape and dynamic to the created order, even where that order includes human beings, the theologian must make the effort to discern how that motif is related to God" (Hefner, ref. 35, pp. 209–10).
17. M. Ruse and E. O. Wilson, "The evolution of ethics," *New Scientist,* Oct. 17, 1985, pp. 50–2. See also M. Ruse, "The morality of the gene," *Monist* 67 (1984) 167–99; and Michael Ruse and Edward O. Wilson, "Ethics as applied science," *Philosophy,* 1986, in press.
18. M. Ruse and E. O. Wilson, "The evolution of ethics," *op. cit.*, p. 52.
19. *Ibid.*, p. 51.
20. J. Huxley, "The evolutionary process" in *Evolution as a Process,* ed. J. Huxley, A. C. Hardy, E. B. Ford (Allen & Unwin, London, 1954).
21. The incest taboo seems to be a case where a combination of its contra-genetic character and early conditioning render it a universal feature of all ethical codes.
22. G. Altner (ed.), *The Human Creature* (Anchor Books, Doubleday, Garden City, NY, 1974).
23. J. Jaynes, *The Origin of Consciousness and the Breakdown of the Bicameral Mind* (Houghton Mifflin, New York, 1976).
24. G. E. Pugh, *The Biological Origin of Human Values* (Basic Books, New York, 1977).
25. C. Sagan, *The Dragons of Eden: Speculations on the Evolution of Human Intelligence* (Hodder & Stoughton, London, 1977).
26. Sir Alister Hardy, *The Spiritual Nature of Man* (Clarendon Press, Oxford, 1979).

QUESTIONS FOR STUDY

1. Give the basic beliefs of "evolutionary naturalism" as described in the quote from Karl Peters.

2. Peacocke sees sociobiologists as tending toward *determinism, reductionism,* and *functionalism.* Define each of these terms.

3. How does sociobiology explain the role of religion in the survival of human societies?

4. What is the role played by ethics in sociobiological theory?

QUESTIONS FOR REFLECTION

1. Why does evolutionary naturalism appear to pose a threat to traditional religion?

2. Peacocke claims that ". . . the genetic constraints upon our nature and action are, from the theistic viewpoint, what God has determined shall provide the matrix within which freedom can operate." Explain his statement. Would a sociobiologist necessarily agree, especially with respect to the claim about freedom?

3. Why is survival such an important concept for evolutionary theory? How does Peacocke use the statement from the Book of Job, "Though he slay me, yet will I wait for him," to argue against survival as a central value in traditional religion?

4. What does the author mean when he concludes that "evolution has become history"?

5. Read the parable of the Good Samaritan from the New Testament. In what sense does it seem to deny the sociobiologist contention that altruistic or charitable human actions, even in religion, are primarily for the benefit of our genetic kin?

NETWORKING

In addition to the other selections in this section, Barbour (Part I) and Burhoe discuss *sociobiology. Naturalism* is a subject for Gilkey, Lewis, Bube, and Davies. *Human freedom in relation to God's actions and natural processes* is to be found in Haught and Burhoe. The allied issue of *ethics* is discussed by Teilhard, Burhoe, and Ruse and Wilson. For *reductionism,* see Barbour (Part I) and Haught.

IS HUMAN LIFE ONLY CHEMISTRY ?
JOHN F. HAUGHT

John F. Haught is professor of theology at Georgetown University. He holds a Ph.D. from Catholic University of America. A recent book is *The Cosmic Adventure: Science, Religion and the Quest for Purpose.*

Is the universe nothing but physical and chemical activity, devoid of life and mind as we have understood them for centuries? Many scientists and philosophers today think so. They believe that matter alone is real and that all phenomena in the universe, including life and mind, can be completely explained, at least in principle, in terms of chemistry and physics.

This view—"scientific materialism"—has posed a serious challenge to the traditional view of the universe common to the great religions It is the fundamental issue between science and religion today. But now other voices are being heard, arguing that life and mind are not reducible to matter and that a religious view of the universe is quite consistent with the scientific understanding of nature.

Any religious vision requires a hierarchical understanding of the universe. Traditionally, religious hierarchies differentiate various levels of reality and grade them according to degrees of importance. Matter is often the least real and least important; life is more real and more important than matter; and consciousness more significant than life. At the highest level is the ultimate reality—referred to as "God" in Western theism.

This hierarchical vision takes it for granted that something is going on at the levels of life and mind that is not happening at the level of matter. It also accepts as self-evident that while the higher levels can encompass and "comprehend" the lower, the lower cannot comprehend the higher. Thus if there is an overarching purpose or meaning to the universe, it cannot be adequately grasped at any of the lower levels. And whenever attempts are made to understand the higher levels in terms of the lower, something is inevitably lost in the translation.

The hierarchical world-view has shaped the consciousness (and continues to do so) of most people of most times and places. And it is compatible with the comforting hypothesis that we live in a purposeful or "teleological" universe even if mere mortals cannot comprehend such purposiveness.

But can we any longer think responsibly of our cosmos in this hierarchical way? Developments in science have caused many scientific thinkers to believe that only physical and chemical activity occur in the universe, not only at the level of matter, but also at the levels of life and mind. Indeed, adherents of scientific materialism question whether we can any longer view life and mind as being "real" in the sense assumed by the religious interpretation of things. To them, it seems more likely that they are mere "epiphenomena"—that is, secondary phenomena derived from matter.

We know today, for example, that the manipulation of molecules in a DNA chain will affect the shape of the organism it encodes. Life, it is clear, has a chemical basis. We also know that the introduction of a wide variety of chemical substances into the brain can alter the way we feel and think. So mind also has a chemical basis. But does this mean that mind and life are therefore reducible to chemistry? Is there anything going on in living and thinking entities that is not specifiable by objective scientific analysis? If so, how are we to understand it?

THE CASE FOR A CHEMICAL YOU

The historical basis for scientific materialism was set forth centuries ago in the atomism of Leucippus, Democritus and Lucretius. It was given its definitive modern formulation in the classical physics of Galileo, Descartes and Newton (though these men were not themselves materialists). And further weight was added in the 19th century in the laws of thermodynamics and in Darwin's evolutionary theory. With its view of the gradual rise of life and consciousness out of a purely material substrata, evolutionary theory suggests that life and mind are on an unbroken continuum with matter and that there is no reason why the latter two cannot be reduced to and explained adequately in terms of the first, out of which they evolved.

The apparent reducibility of life to matter was promoted still further by biological developments in this century. Molecular analysis of the living cell has revealed that the apparent "secret" of life lies in large molecules of nucleic and amino acids, which are composed of nothing more than chains of atoms. The most important molecule in the living cell, DNA, is the informational source of a replication and translation process that is apparently nothing more than a set of complex chemical reactions.

Biology appears to many today to be no more than a special application of principles formulated in the physical sciences. So exciting was the discovery of the chemistry of the cell that it led Francis Crick to exclaim that ". . . the ultimate aim of the modern movement in biology is to explain all of life in terms of chemistry and physics." More recently, the new science of sociobiology has attempted to account even for the larger world of culture in terms of the activity of genes, which are themselves segments of DNA.

As if the discovery of the molecular basis of life were not a sufficient basis for a materialistic philosophy of nature, the evidence is clear today that human mental activity does not occur apart from a complex set of physiological occurrences in the brain. We know that the breakdown or malfunctioning of chemical processes in the brain and central nervous system will result in the failure of mental life as well. It makes us wonder whether anything other than chemistry is going on in consciousness.

Scientific materialism sees these developments as entailing the complete collapse of the cosmic hierarchy that has been the basis of all religious visions. According to mechanism-materialism, which Alfred North Whitehead said has shaped the intellectual life of every university in the world, if everything is explicable in terms of the mass-energy continuum, then there is no basis for the sense of discontinuity required in a hierarchy. There is, therefore, no reasonable basis for a religious interpretation of the universe. If there is essentially only one level of reality, and that level is in principle completely open to scientific understanding, then there is no reason for positing a distinct, overarching, transcendent meaning to the totality of cosmic or historical events.

This, at any rate, is the anti-hierarchical conclusion of much modern and recent scientific philosophy. It may well be that the majority of scientists do not personally hold to this view. But where they express reservations about it, they do not usually give reasons for their dissent.

MACHINES AND MYSTERY

One significant dissenting view came from the late Hungarian-born scientist and philosopher Michael Polanyi, whose ideas are becoming in increasingly important part of discussions on science and religion. Polanyi challenged the methodological ideal of explaining mind and life in terms of the principles of chemistry and physics. Such reductionism he thought to be not only a sickness of contemporary intellectual culture, but, more important, fundamentally unreasonable and illogical. He was not afraid to ask some tough questions: Is biology logically reducible to physics and chemistry? To gain an adequate understanding of life (and mind), is it logically appropriate to consult the experts in physics and chemistry?

In answer, he began by noting the trend in biology toward trying to understand organisms in terms of machines performing tasks. The machine, of course, is a useful and fruitful model, and we need not immediately resort to shrieks of "mechanism" at its usage by biologists. However, if even a machine cannot be exhaustively explained in terms of chemistry and physics, should we expect that the organism it is modeling is itself reducible?

There are two distinct kinds of principles involved in the concept of a mechanism (a steam engine, for example): first, the invariant laws of chemistry and physics; and, second, the "boundary conditions" (determined by mechanical engineering) within which those laws operate. These boundary conditions impose a specific organizational pattern upon the operations of atoms and molecules—a pattern that is not reducible to, and is not the result of, the operation of physical and chemical laws.

A knowledge of the physics and chemistry of water and steel, therefore, will not add up to a knowledge of what a steam engine really is or how it works. We do not consult the chemist, but rather the mechanical engineer, for such insight. The steam engine is a hierarchically structured entity requiring distinct sciences to deal with each level, and for that reason we justifiably have separate departments of physics and mechanical engineering. There is no danger that departments of engineering will be collapsed into those of chemistry and physics.

But is the universe as a whole similarly structured hierarchically in such a way that the levels of life and mind cannot be understood in a purely chemical way? Or are these "higher levels," unlike a steam engine for example, fully specifiable in chemical terms?

Take the case of DNA, the most important molecule in the sphere of life. It is agreed by all, including materialist biologists, that this molecule is informational, that it is the carrier of a message. Is it reducible to, or fully understandable in terms of, chemistry?

Any code, in order to function as such, must be capable of an indefinite number of configurations if it is to convey information. It must be able to be broken down and put back together in a variety of sequences.

Thus, as Harry Prosch puts it in his new book "Michael Polanyi: A Critical Exposition," the carrier of a message must be chemically and physically neutral or indifferent to the message it carries. DNA is composed of four "letters" (the nitrogenous bases A, C, T, and G) arranged in a specific sequence that determines the kind and shape of any organism. But the *specific* arrangement of bases in DNA is not the product of chemical necessity; if it were, the letters in a DNA chain could not serve as informative. And if the order of items in a DNA molecule were chemically determined, there would be only one sort of DNA molecule, and so only one "message." DNA can serve as a code precisely because its *specific* order in any particular organism is not simply the result of chemical laws; the specific *informational* sequence of nitrogenous bases in DNA is somehow "extraneous" to the chemistry. Thus biology is not logically reducible to chemistry, and life is not reducible to matter. The universe may still plausibly be understood as a hierarchical structure.

In Polanyi's philosophy of nature, the universe is an emergent hierarchy of discontinuous "levels" in which the higher "in-dwell" and rely upon but are not totally explicable in terms of the lower. According to philosopher Marjorie Grene's interpretation of Polanyi, the levels may be continuous in terms of evolutionary history or in terms of atoms and molecules—and that is why they do not show up as hierarchically distinct when viewed by a science that seeks relentlessly to break them down to their lowest physical denominator. But historical and physical continuity do not logically rule out an "ontological discontinuity"—that is, a qualitative differentiation of matter from life and life from mind.

Polanyi's theories are finding unexpected support from science itself—in the form of a new emphasis in the sciences on the role of *information* in the constitution of things. In terms of Polanyi's thought each higher level of phenomena can be understood as consisting of organizational or informational principles which "harness" the lower levels, informing them with a pattern or order that cannot be derived from or explained by analysis of the physical components alone. The lower levels are necessary but not sufficient conditions for the successful performance of the higher. The failure of the lower can account for the failure of the higher, but the successful achievements of the higher (whether a snail's crawling or a person's writing an essay) cannot be accounted for simply on the basis of the deterministic movements of molecules.

Our knowledge that chemical aberrations can cause failures in the physiological basis of life and mind has unwarrantedly led scientific materialists to the belief that chemical processes alone can account as well for the successful achievements of lives and minds. For example, the dizzying knowledge that chemical substances can alleviate depression by redressing a chemical imbalance in the brain may easily tempt us to think that mind is therefore fully explainable in terms of brain chemistry. However, it is meaningless to speak of chemical processes failing or succeeding in themselves. What can fail or succeed is not chemical processes but the arrangement of "information" in a particular aggregate of molecules (or other physiological configurations).

Interestingly, the "higher levels" of a hierarchy do not interrupt or intrude into the lower, and so they will not be found or scientifically mastered by an analysis of the lower. Life and mind do not require any violations of the laws of physics and chemistry any more than my writing this sentence violates the laws of chemistry involved in the bonding of paper and ink. Yet I would be quite insulted to be told that there is nothing more going on here than chemical activity.

CAN WE EVER REALLY KNOW?

Still we remain troubled. Why, if they exist, do the "higher levels" seem so unverifiable? Why do they not show themselves to us with the same vividness as the objects of scientific investigation? Here we are thrown back upon a principle essential to hierarchical thinking: A higher level can comprehend a lower but the lower cannot encompass the higher. Put otherwise, an analysis of the lower does not yield a knowledge of the higher, but only some necessary conditions for the emergence of a higher.

Some thinkers are quite comfortable with this hierarchical principle. Others are not. For the latter, hierarchical thinking still allows too much untouchable mystery in the universe to make it palatable. A hierarchical cosmology renders reality incapable of being mastered by the objectivist ideal, for it situates the most important aspects of reality off-limits to scientific mastery. It leaves too much mystery, and the objective of science, it has been said, is to eliminate mystery.

Polanyi would suggest, however, that the objective of science is to solve problems, not to eliminate mystery.

QUESTIONS FOR STUDY

1. Describe the hierarchical understanding of the universe. Sketch several levels or strata involved in this understanding.

2. What are "epiphenomena"?

3. How does scientific materialism represent the collapse of the traditional cosmic hierarchy?

4. According to Michael Polanyi, why is it impossible for physics and chemistry to explain the working of a machine?

QUESTIONS FOR REFLECTION

1. Haught claims that the collapse of the cosmic hierarchy also destroys the religious interpretation of the universe. What is the connection between this hierarchy and religion that makes this destruction possible?

2. Haught quotes Francis Crick in his contention that the aim of biology is to explain life in terms of chemistry and physics, that is, in terms of matter, energy, and atoms. How is it possible for matter, energy, and atoms in the form of living things called biologists (Crick included) to have conscious aims? Is a hierarchical arrangement required to explain this apparent absurdity?

3. Is the mind fully explainable in terms of brain chemistry? If it is *not,* then what is thought?

4. If higher levels emerge from the operations of lower ones, does this mean that the mental and spiritual levels vanish with disruptions in the organization of lower material levels? If so, are spirit and soul now utterly dependent on material foundations? That is, does the idea of a detached or disembodied spirit make any sense in the hierarchical view?

5. To carry the concerns of the previous question further, if God is the highest level of the cosmic hierarchy, is God's existence tied inextricably to lower levels? If so, does this view represent an unacceptable compromise of God's absolute independence to divine sovereignty?

NETWORKING

Barbour (Part I), Dyson, Gish, and Peacocke deal directly with *scientific materialism and reductionism,* and Ruse and Wilson provide an illustration of its application in argument. The associated concept of *hierarchy* is to be found in Bube, Polkinghorne, Teilhard, Burhoe, and Gray. Expressions of *Polanyi's thought* are found in Barbour and Polkinghorne.

SUGGESTIONS FOR FURTHER READING

Birch, Charles, and John B. Cobb. *The Liberation of Life: From the Cell to the Community.* Cambridge: Cambridge University Press, 1981. Cobb, the process theologian, and Birch, an Australian biologist, team up to produce a statement promoting organicism as the successor to mechanism. Extensive application of the model to the human and natural worlds.

Christian Scholar's Review, vol. XXI, No. 1, September 1991. This special issue, "Creation/Evolution and Faith," is devoted entirely to evolution and Scripture with emphasis on the apparent conflict between evolutionary theory and the Genesis account. Includes excellent articles by the philosopher Alvan Plantinga, who defends special creation, and Ernan McMullin, who defends evolution.

Dawkins, Richard. *The Blind Watchmaker*. New York: W. W. Norton and Company, 1986. The author is an evolutionary naturalist who promotes a refined neo-Darwinianism against all comers. Informative and well argued.

Godfrey, Laurie R., ed. *Scientists Confront Creationism*. New York: W. W. Norton and Company, 1983. The response of the scientific community as it marshalled its forces against creationism in the early 1980s. A well-done handbook for opponents of that movement. Several excellent articles.

Monod, Jaques. *Chance and Necessity*. New York: Random House, 1972. A classic statement by the Nobel Laureate in biochemistry. Monod reduces all explanation to the operations of natural law and random occurrences in nature. He is left with an existential criterion of value and truth.

Peacocke, A. R. *Creation and the World of Science: the Bampton Lectures 1978*. Oxford, England: Clarendon Press, 1979. The view of a Christian biochemist who is also well versed in classic and contemporary theology. A counterbalance to Monod.

Teilhard de Chardin, Pierre. *The Phenomenon of Man*. New York: Harper and Row Publishing Company, 1959. The most complete single statement of the grand cosmic vision of the Jesuit paleontologist and mystic. Teilhard's style is rich, but difficult.

Thomas, Lewis. *The Lives of a Cell: Notes of a Biology Watcher*. Toronto: Bantam Books, 1974. Well-written and engaging essays by a microbiologist on the nature of life and our place in it.

Wilson, Edward O. *Biophilia*. Cambridge: Harvard University Press, 1984. Intended by the author, Harvard biologist and father of the sociobiology movement, for a larger audience than his previous technical writings. Argues for the centrality of life as a focal human value.

PART VI

Ecos and Gaia

THIS CONCAVE ALUMINUM MIRROR IS LOCATED IN THE ROTUNDA OF THE PHYSICAL SCIENCES BUILDING OF FLORIDA INTERNATIONAL UNIVERSITY IN MIAMI. IT IS ALIGNED TO CONCENTRATE THE RAYS OF THE SUN DURING THE VERNAL AND AUTUMNAL EQUINOX SO THEY FOCUS IN A POINT ON A GRANITE STRUCTURE LOCATED IN THE BUILDING'S COURTYARD. DESPITE APPEARANCES, THE STAR OF THIS SHOW IS NOT THE SUN BUT THE EARTH. THE TILT OF THE EARTH'S AXIS AND ITS ANNUAL PASSAGE AROUND ITS STELLAR PARENT COMBINE TO PRODUCE THE RELATIVE MOTION OF THE SUN IN THE SKY SO THAT ON TWO DAYS OF THE YEAR—ONE IN SPRING, THE OTHER IN AUTUMN (THE SOLAR EQUINOXES)—ITS RAYS FALL DIRECTLY UPON THE EQUATOR AND CONTRIBUTE TO THIS DRAMATIC EFFECT.

Ecos and Gaia

The selections in Part VI are reflections upon the mounting emergency with the environment—the chronic and progressive deterioration of the biosphere that is the legacy of our profligate behavior toward nature for the past three hundred years. Examples are easily cited. Some of these—pollution, solid waste disposal, rising temperatures due to trace elements in the atmosphere, vanishing habitats and species—are global issues requiring global solutions. A new understanding of deity emerges here because the energies of religion must contribute to any enduring restabilization of the open planetary system. The older theological doctrines of God and creation, some have claimed, are partially to blame for the current predicament. If this allegation is true, then religion has an important responsibility to contribute to the solution of problems it helped to create. New ideas are called for from every discipline, including theology, if our prospects are to improve. The selections in Part VI illustrate the variety of ways religion contributes to a constructive revision of our understanding of the natural world.

The selections in the first half of this part, *"Ecos"* (Greek for "household"), address the following question: In response to the environmental emergency, should we consider humankind to be apart *from* nature or to be a part *of* nature? The first selection, "Stewards of the Earth's Resources," by J. Patrick Dobel, is an argument for the former opinion that we somehow transcend nature by occupying a special status with unique responsibilities. Traditionally, this position has been best expressed in the doctrine of Christian stewardship. In this context, a steward is one who is entrusted with the responsibility of looking after another's property in the owner's absence. For Judaism and Christianity, Adam and Eve were the first stewards chosen by God from all original creatures to oversee the good order of paradise.

Despite historical evidence suggesting that the notion of stewardship has been abused by Western society and used as an excuse to despoil creation rather than protect it, Dobel is reluctant to abandon the special status of humans granted by God in the first chapters of Genesis. He sees grave risks in the alternatives: neopaganism and nature worship. But he sees real merit in the idea that each generation occupies the earth only temporarily. He concludes that we should leave the earth as neat and healthy as we found it for the sake of future generations who in all fairness deserve a habitable planet.

The next two selections call into question Dobel's theological model of the vertical relationship in which humans are slotted in a position above the natural order. In "A Holistic View of Reality," Sallie McFague insists that the boundaries of theology must be expanded to include all life. She admits that the completion of this task requires a radical act of the imagination because Western culture thinks only in terms of the hierarchical and dualistic categories permitted by the modern mechanistic world view. The idea of relationship must replace that of the cosmic machine if progress away from an anthropocentric world view and toward solidarity with nature is to occur. A "mutualistic" and "organic" metaphor emphasizing an ethic of justice and care is required if the needs of our time are to be addressed. It seems that the traditional notion of stewardship is not of great importance in this new model.

McFague's emphasis on relationship is echoed and further developed in "Process Theology and Environmental Issues" by John Cobb. The widely acknowledged father of process thought was the Anglo-American philosopher Alfred North Whitehead (1861–1947). Whitehead saw the world as a flowing river of events. God functions to give order to the world and to manage the stream of process continuously. To do this, God must receive information about the states of the world so that relevant adjustments can be made. God takes this information, compares it with the vision of the vast range of possible worlds, and then sends back instructions in the form of goals or ideals to be felt by every creature, each in its own proper way. The world responds to God's recommendations, but never perfectly, and God once again updates the divine experience for the sake of making further corrections in a never-ending cosmic process.

We might call Whitehead's deity the divine *Kybernetes* or "steersman," because that is God's function in the order of things. God accumulates experience and uses it to increase the variety and richness of creation. God and world constitute a coupled system with feedback, a neverending transactional event. The world is God's body or environment and a necessary component in the divine life. God is nothing more or less than the ongoing interaction with the world, which in turn is nothing more or less than its ongoing interaction with God.

Admittedly, process theology compromises the classic view of God as the all-powerful, perfect, and changeless being. But process theologians are confident that God's status is not compromised by sacrificing immutability. Indeed, the opposite is true. Because of this total involvement, the process deity is absolutely active, sympathetic, and loving in ways that the classic model of God could never match.

With this description of process philosophy, it is easy to see that Cobb's preferred term, "interconnectedness," is more than a mere description of the surface of things. It is a deep and pervasive feature of all reality; to be is to be connected. Things do not simply exist. They interexist. Unfortunately, our society sees things differently. The individual is the norm and fundamental unit of value. Connections between individuals are incidental and optional. This erroneous perspective has led to the assault on nature and the utter violation of essential environmental connectedness. The assault is enhanced by the limited vision of the fragmentation of knowledge into ever more concentrated specialties, so almost no one sees things whole. Individualism leads to anthropocentrism—the philosophy of the supremacy of the human species. Process theology would replace this destructive vision with one that slots our species into a spectrum of intrinsic value for all life. No longer are humans seen to possess supreme or exclusive value. All creatures are valuable both with respect to themselves (intrinsic value) and with respect to their contributions to the entire system of nature (holistic value). Biocentrism replaces anthropocentrism.

God is the creative source and the ultimate subject of all things. God alone is in a position to experience the whole of things for its own sake, and God alone can enjoy the contribution of each and every creature to that total worth. God and cosmos constitute a complete system with a common good. "The good for God is the good for creation and the good for creation is the good for God," says Cobb. Theocentrism replaces anthropocentrism and reenforces biocentrism.

The fourth selection, "A Critique of Dominion Theology" by Elizabeth Dodson Gray, is an argument for a modified Christian view of the world based on some of these same concerns. The villain is not so much monotheism as it is the picture of the universe incorporated into traditional Christian theology. This picture is decidedly hierarchical. The diverse creatures of the world are ranked from lower to higher in such a way that the lower, inferior beings are subjected to the higher, superior ones.

Gray identifies the culprit as patriarchy—a hierarchy based on the perceived superiority of a masculine figure, God, or the male. Men attempt to control and dominate the world, including women and nature, and fail to respond sensitively to the demands of the greater whole. The consequence of this unilateral action is the destruction of all the levels of the hierarchy, including that occupied by men themselves.

The selections in the second half of this part, "Gaia," have to do with the planet Earth as a subject in and of itself. For many centuries the earth provided the mere backdrop for the great events of Western history, the stage on which the drama of civilization played itself out. From the moment the first astronauts gazed back on the planet and saw it whole from space, things have not been the same. Since all life forms about which we have any knowledge live on this world, and since nearly all of our actions toward the environment take place here, the vague and indefinite realm of "nature" has now come to be synonymous with the planet itself. The Earth is the focus of human attention. It is as if we relate to the planet as a being separate from ourselves, a being which requires our concern and attention. In addition, far from being a cluster or crowd of unrelated activities, the Earth is a single integrated system of great complexity, an individual in the original sense of that term as "indivisible."

The consequences of this shift in the modern Western perspective are profound. They include the tendency to personify the planet as a she and then to reinterpret traditional notions of nature in terms of this new metaphor. As the selections in this part demonstrate, even religion is not immune to this tendency.

The first of these three selections is by James Lovelock, the British scientist who first employed the name "Gaia," the ancient Greek earth goddess, for our planet. In "God and Gaia," Lovelock's contribution is to see that the various activities of life upon the earth are in a state of mutual adjustment and balance. Gaia is a natural system with the capacity to aim for its own best state of equilibrium and to maintain that balance in the face of various disturbances. The planet, for all intents and purposes, behaves like a living organism with a repertoire of homeostatic mechanisms that allows her to be self-sustaining and self-managing.

This description suggests additional questions: Should we who endanger her well-being treat Gaia with the reverence normally reserved for a sacred being, a deity? Lovelock, the tough-minded scientist, rejects this option. He appears willing, however, to recover the enchantment of the Earth—that sense of a living, spiritual presence in the planet itself that provokes a response of awe, wonder, celebration, and even reverence.

Several major themes from the previous section, *"Ecos,"* are reiterated by Thomas Berry in the sixth selection, "Human Presence." These include "intimacy" (Berry's equivalent of McFague's "relationship" and Cobb's "interconnectedness") and "autism" (his equivalent of the alienation of our species from natural processes through mechanism, anthropocentrism, and individualism).

Berry shares a third and most important concept with these other authors. The call for a return to a holistic and biocentric perspective in previous selections becomes for him a call for a return to Mother Earth. The sources for our understanding of intimacy with the Earth are ancient religious traditions, including native American rituals and Chinese and Hindu wisdom, and modern science with its vast vision of cosmic evolution. Drawing on Teilhard de Chardin, a favorite author, Berry identifies five major components or layers of the Earth's life. The last of these, the noosphere or mindsphere, is the most recent to emerge. Its manifestation in the human species offers great opportunity and peril. The human community has "the power of life and death over its basic life systems." Returning again to ancient sources, Berry claims that the collective human response must be in the form of a cosmic caring, love or charity, a virtue expressed as the Chinese *jen* and *ch'eng* and the Hindu *bhakti* and Buddhist *karuna*. But most of all, he recommends the discoveries of modern science, especially Lovelock's notion of Gaia, about the Earth as a highly organized self-directing entity within which the human species is a component. Any successful solution to the environmental crisis must be based on this new perspective.

Lovelock and Berry share a common sense of reverence for planet Earth. For them, the planet possesses a numinous and maternal quality. She is close to becoming a divine mother. But in the final selection, "Loving Mother Earth: Some Reservations," Catherine Roach takes exception to this characterization. Lovelock and Berry would probably agree with the sentiment "Love Your Mother" appearing as a caption beneath a photograph of the planet taken from space. Roach, too, understands the appeal of the metaphor. The Earth does indeed function in some ways that resemble the traditional responsibilities of a mother. Her argument is with other suggestive aspects of the metaphor that are potentially damaging. Sex-typing the planet serves to extend the very ideas of gender discrimination that Roach finds so destructive in a patriarchical culture. The concept of motherhood is far more ambivalent than the image would suggest. Experiences of any child about its mother are often less than positive. Indeed, Roach shows that some images of mother are inimical to the environmental movement itself. Mother is a sacrificial provider. She gives unconditionally to her children and even cleans up after them. These are not helpful images for an environmental ethic that would encourage discipline, constraint, and mature responsible behavior toward nature.

Symbols and images not only allow for the articulation of ideas and relationships that would remain hidden without them, they also recommend norms of conduct. Ecofeminism reminds theologians and philosophers that they should watch their words lest they encourage courses of action that would be more damaging than helpful to the achievement of their desired goals.

ECOS

STEWARDS OF THE EARTH'S RESOURCES
J. PATRICK DOBEL

J. Patrick Dobel is an associate professor and director of the Graduate School of Public Affairs at the University of Washington in Seattle. This selection is taken from *The Christian Century,* a moderate, mainly Protestant weekly report and commentary on social and cultural issues.

Browsing in a local bookstore recently, I took down several of the more general books from the "Ecology" shelf. Scanning the tables of contents and indexes of 13 books, I discovered that nine of them made reference to "Christianity," "the Bible" or the "Judeo-Christian tradition." Examining their contents more closely, I found that seven of these books blamed specific Christian or Bible-based values as significant "causes" of the ecology crisis.

Over half these books referenced an article by Lynn White, Jr., titled "The Historical Roots of Our Ecologic Crisis" (*Science,* March 10, 1967). In this short, undocumented and simplistic article White argues that the root of the entire problem lies in "the Christian maxim that nature has no reason for existence save to serve man." From the Christians' penchant for cutting down sacred Druidic groves to the development of "modern science from natural theology," Christianity, White argues, laid the foundations of Western "arrogance towards nature" and "limitless rule of creation."

Almost all similar statements are indebted to White; they even cite the same examples: grief over the destruction of the sacred groves; respect for Saint Francis of Assisi. Although few of the authors have read anything about him except that he talked to birds, they have raised poor Francis to the rank of first "ecological saint," while conveniently ignoring his myriad admonitions about asceticism and communal ownership of property.

DOMINION OVER THE EARTH

The ecological indictment of Christianity boils down to two somewhat contradictory assertions: that the postulated transcendence and domination of humanity over nature encourages thoughtless exploitation of the earth and that the otherworldly orientation of Christianity encourages contempt and disregard for the earth. In documenting the first indictment authors often cite Genesis 1:26: "Let us make man in our image, after our likeness; and let them have dominion over the fish of the sea, and over the birds of the air, and over the cattle, and over every creeping thing that creeps upon the earth." Some also quote Genesis 1:29: "Be fruitful and multiply, and fill the earth and subdue it; and have dominion over the fish of the sea and over the birds of the air and over every living thing that moves upon the earth."

These texts lead to the conclusion that the Bible emphasizes the absolute superiority of humanity over the rest of creation. And this relation must be primarily one of antagonism and alienation, for "cursed is the ground because of you; in toil you shall eat of it all the days of your life . . . In the sweat of your face you shall eat bread" (Gen. 3:17).

Thus Christianity separates both humanity and God from the earth and destroys the inherent sacredness of the earth. This alienation is coupled with humanity's innate superiority over nature and the divine mandate to exploit nature limitlessly for human ends—a mandate that is carried out in the context of antagonism and an expectation that the earth must be treated harshly to gain the yield of human survival. Together these notions have shaped Western culture's spoliation of the earth.

In bringing the second indictment, critics point out that Christianity's otherworldly preoccupation also contributes to human abuse of the environment. Christians are instructed to "kill everything in you that belongs only to the earthly life" and to "let your thoughts be on heavenly things, not on the things that are on the earth" (Col. 3:2–5). The emphasis is upon awaiting "a new heaven and a new earth in which righteousness dwells" (II Pet. 3:13). In some ways this stress undercuts the mandates of superiority and rule since it implies that humanity rules nothing but a fallen and contemptible orb. If the contempt, however, is tied to an antagonistic human domination and to the need of people to discipline their unruly bodies through work, it can provide an ethical framework to support the thoughtless and arrogant exploitation which is part of the ecology crisis. The thesis linking Calvinism with the rise of industrialization reflects this ambivalent world-hating but smug and exploitative attitude.

The critics see modern science and technology along with notions of unbridled progress and exploitation emerging from this Judeo-Christian matrix. They conclude that Christianity must accept most of the "blame" for the unique "Western" perspectives which have led to the present state of affairs. This "blame" somehow rings false when the ecologists extend the link to the later implications of a secularized technology and a liberal view of human progress.

LOOKING FOR THE ROOTS

The attempt to discover historical roots is a dubious business at best, and in this case it borders on the ludicrous. Christianity's ecological critics consistently underestimate the economic, social and political influences on modern science and economy; their approach makes for good polemics but bad history. Their thesis lacks a careful historical analysis of the intellectual and practical attitudes toward the earth and its use in the consciously Christian Middle Ages. They disregard the earth-centered ideals of the Christian Renaissance and its concern with the delicate limitations of the Great Chain of Being, and they pay little attention to the emergence of a peculiarly non-Christian deism and theism which defined God in the 17th and 18th centuries to accommodate a newly secularized nature and new developments in science and trade. These critics neglect to mention the specifically Christian prohibitions which often made religion a detriment to economic and scientific development.

They also ignore the rise of the secularized nation-state from the decay of "Christendom"; yet these new government regimes provided much of the impetus to maximize the exploitation of resources and the discovery of new lands. Most of the operative "roots" of the present crisis are to be found in the far more secularized and non-Christian world of nationalism, science and liberalism in the 16th through the 19th centuries.

Given the unsoundness of the theory that blames Christianity for the environmental crisis, it is surprising that it has gained such remarkable currency. In light of this fact there are two distinct tasks which confront the Christian community. First, this thesis should be addressed in some detail, not only to show its flaws but to discover what ideas and practices the tradition can contribute to a concrete ecological program. Second, we must use the vast ethical and conceptual resources of the Judeo-Christian tradition to develop a God-centered ecological ethic which accounts for the sacredness of the earth without losing sight of human worth and justice. In addressing myself to this second task, I will try to develop appropriate responses to the following questions through textual exegesis of the Bible: What is the ethical status of the earth as an entity in creation? What is the proper relation of humanity to the earth and its resources?

Ecological critics have nostalgically lamented the decline of "nature worship" and have spoken wistfully of the need to import "Eastern" concepts of pantheism or quietist respect for the "equality of all life." Even some of the most secularized ecologists are calling for a rediscovery of the "sacredness" of nature.

Although it is hard to discover the enduring sacredness of anything in a totally secularized world, we must keep several points in mind about these calls. First, all cultures, regardless of religion, have abused or destroyed large areas of the world either because of economic or population pressures or from simple ignorance. Second, the ethical consequences of the new nature worship, neopantheism and the militant assertion of the equality of all creaturehood pose grave problems for establishing any prior claims of worth or inherent dignity for human beings. The more undifferentiated God and the world become, the harder it is to define individual humans as worthwhile with specific claims to social justice and care. Third, a sort of mindless ecological imperative based upon such notions is ultimately reactionary and antihuman, as well as anti-Christian. There are fundamental ethical differences between plants and animals and between animals and human beings. To resort simplistically to militantly pro-earth and antiprogress positions misses the vital Christian and humanistic point that our sojourn upon the earth is not yet completed and that we must continue to work unflaggingly toward social justice and the well-being of all people.

The unique contribution a Christian ecology can make to the earth is the assertion that we can insist on a reasonable harmony with our world without abandoning our commitment to social justice for all members of our unique and self-consciously alienated species. We can love and respect our environment without obliterating all ethical and technological distinctions, and without denying the demand that we cautiously but steadily use the earth for the benefit of all humanity.

"THE EARTH IS THE LORD'S"

The first question to address is the status of the earth and its resources. A different way of putting this is "Who owns the earth?" The answer of the entire Judeo-Christian tradition is clear: God. "In the beginning God created the heavens and the earth" (Gen. 1:3). In direct ethical terms God created the earth, and in distributive-justice terms it belongs to him: "The earth is the Lord's and the fullness thereof" (Ps. 24:1). As an act of pure love he created a world and he "founded the earth to endure" (Ps. 119:90–91).

What kind of world did God create? The answer has two dimensions: the physical or descriptive and the ethical. As a product of nature the world was created as a law-bound entity. The laws are derivative of God's will for all creation as "maintained by your rulings" (Ps. 119:90–91). Things coexist in intricate and regulated harmony—the basic postulate of science, mythology and reason. Although we have a world of laws, it is also a world of bounty and harmony. For it had been promised that "while the earth remains, seedtime and harvest shall not cease" (Gen. 8:22). It was arranged "in wisdom" so that in the balance of nature, "All creatures depend upon you to feed them . . . you provide the food with a generous hand." God's presence ultimately "holds all things in unity" (Col. 1:16–20) and constantly "renews" the world (Ps. 104:24–30). This world abounds in life and is held together in a seamless web maintained by God-willed laws.

In ethical terms, God saw that the world was "very good" (Gen. 1:31). In love and freedom he created the world and valued it as good. All the creatures of the world also share in this goodness (I Tim. 4:4). This does not mean that the world is "good for" some purpose or simply has utilitarian value to humanity. The world, in its bounty and multiplicity of life, is independently good and ought to be respected as such.

As an independent good, the earth possesses an autonomous status as an ethical and covenanted entity. In Genesis 9:8–17, God directly includes the earth and all the animals as participants in the covenant. He urges the animals to "be fruitful and multiply." Earlier in Genesis 1:30, he takes care specifically to grant the plant life of the earth to the creatures who possess "breath of life." In the great covenant with Noah and all humanity, he expressly includes all other creatures and the earth.

> And God said, "This is a sign of the covenant which I make between *me and you and every living creature* that is with you, for all future generations: I set my bow in the sky, and it shall be a sign of the *covenant between* me and the earth" [emphasis added].

The prophets, Isaiah especially, constantly address the earth and describe its independent travail. Paul describes the turmoil and travail of the earth as a midwife of all creation and redemption (Rom. 8:18–22). The earth must be regarded as an autonomous ethical entity bound not just by the restraints of physical law but also by respect for its inherent goodness and the covenanted limitations placed upon our sojourn. Perhaps we must think seriously of defining a category of "sins against the earth."

The proper relation between humanity and the bountiful earth is more complex. One fact is of outstanding moral relevance: the earth does not belong to humanity; it belongs to God. Jeremiah summarizes it quite succinctly: "I by my great power and outstretched arm made the earth, land and animals that are on the earth. And I can give them to whom I please" (Jer. 27:5). For an ecological ethic this fact cannot be ignored. The resources and environment of the earth are not ours in any sovereign or unlimited sense; they belong to someone else.

A TRUST FOR FUTURE GENERATIONS

Humanity's relation to the earth is dominated by the next fact: God "bestows" the earth upon all of humanity (Ps. 115:16). This gift does not, however, grant sovereign control. The prophets constantly remind us that God is still the "king" and the ruler/owner to whom the earth reverts. No one generation of people possesses the earth. The earth was made "to endure" and was given for all future generations. Consequently the texts constantly reaffirm that the gift comes under covenanted conditions, and that the covenant is "forever." The Bible is permeated with a careful concern for preserving the "land" and the "earth" as an "allotted heritage" (Ps. 2:7–12).

This point is central to the Judeo-Christian response to the world. The world is given to all. Its heritage is something of enduring value designed to benefit all future generations. Those who receive such a gift and benefit from it are duty-bound to conserve the resources and pass them on for future generations to enjoy. An "earth of abundance" (Judg. 18:10) provides for humanity's needs and survival (Gen. 1:26–28, 9:2–5). But the injunction "obey the covenant" (I Chron. 16:14–18) accompanies the gift.

There are some fairly clear principles that direct our covenanted responsibilities toward the earth. Each generation exists only as "sojourner" or "pilgrim." We hold the resources and the earth as a "trust" for future generations. Our covenanted relations to the earth—and for that matter, to all human beings—must be predicated upon the recognition and acceptance of the limits of reality. For there is a "limit upon all perfection" (Ps. 119:96), and we must discover and respect the limits upon ourselves, our use of resources, our consumption, our treatment of others and the environment with its delicate ecosystems. Abiding by the covenant means abiding by the laws of nature, both scientific and moral. In ecological terms the balance of nature embodies God's careful plan that the earth and its bounty shall provide for the needs and survival of all humanity of all generations.

The combined emphases upon God's ownership, our trusteeship and the limits of life call for an attitude of humility and care in dealing with the world. Only "the humble shall have the land for their own to enjoy untroubled peace" (Ps. 37:11). Knowledge of limits, especially of the intricacy of the ecosystems, makes humility and care a much more natural response. The transgression of limits usually brings either unknown or clearly dangerous consequences and ought to influence all actions with a singular sense of caution. Humility and respect do not mean simple awe, or withdrawal from all attempts to use or improve the bounty we are given. At the very least, they lead to the loss of arrogant ignorance which leads us to pursue policies in contradiction to the clear limits and laws of nature and particular ecosystems.

THE STEWARDSHIP IMPERATIVE

The New Testament distills these notions and adds a strong activist imperative with its account of stewardship. This activist element is a vital alternative to some of the more extreme ethical positions in reactionary ecological ethics. The parable of the good steward in Luke 12:41–48 and the parable of the talents in Matthew 25:14–30 summarize the concept. The preservation of what is given "in trust" demands a recognition of the owner's dictates for the resources. We must know the limits and laws of the world in order to use them wisely. Our actions must be guided, in part, by concerns for future generations. Above all, we must never knowingly exhaust or ruin what has been given to us. If doing so is absolutely necessary to sustain life, then equity demands that we must leave some equally accessible and beneficial legacy to replace what has been exhausted.

But there is more involved in being a "faithful and wise steward." Even the most conservative banker is obliged to improve the stock for the benefit of the heirs. The parable of the talents makes it abundantly clear that we who are entrusted with his property will be called to account for our obligation to improve the earth. The stewardship imperative assumes that the moral and ecological constraints are respected, and it adds the obligation to distribute the benefits justly. The steward must "give them their portion of the food at the proper time." Mistreating his charges, gorging himself on the resources in excess consumption, and not caring for the resources will all cause the stewards to be "cut off." True stewardship requires both respect for the trusteeship and covenanted imperatives and an active effort to improve the land for the future and to use it in a manner to benefit others. Ethical proportionality applies to all those responsible for the earth, for "when a man has had a great deal given him on trust, even more will be expected of him" (Luke 12:48–49).

AN INFORMED HUMILITY

The lessons are clear. Any ecological ethic which takes into account both God and humanity and does not reduce both to some extension of undifferentiated nature must begin with a rejection of the unbridled sovereignty of humanity over the earth. In this rejection is the recognition that all work upon the earth must be informed by a clear understanding of and respect for the earth as an autonomous and valuable entity and the laws of nature on which the bounty of the earth depends.

These are necessary but by no means sufficient within the Judeo-Christian tradition. For the earth, while it possesses its own moral autonomy, is not God and must not be confused as such. Our own relation to it must be predicated upon a careful understanding that earth and its resources are for any generation a restricted gift held in trust for future generations. We must never lose sight of the fact that a just and informed humility provides the framework for a working relationship with the earth.

Much more work remains to be done on the "ethics of stewardship"; I have merely suggested a few ethical considerations: the obligation not to exhaust nonrenewable resources, the imperative to provide accessible replacements, the necessity to improve our heritage modestly and carefully, the greater responsiblity of the advantaged to improve that which exists and to share, and the obligation to refrain from excessive consumption and waste. "Each of you has received a special gift, so like good stewards responsible for all the different gifts of God, put yourselves at the service of others" (I Pet. 4:10–11).

QUESTIONS FOR STUDY

1. The "ecological indictment of Christianity" is based on two charges. What are they?

2. Upon what biblical texts do opponents of Christianity base their criticisms?

3. What other causes of the environmental crisis does the author list?

4. Dobel claims that a Christian ecological ethic can be found in the answer to the question, Who owns the Earth? What is this answer?

5. If humans do not own the Earth, what is their status upon it?

QUESTIONS FOR REFLECTION

1. If Genesis 1:29 instructs us to subdue the Earth and fill it with our numbers, why should we act any differently?

2. Does a tension exist between the requirements for social justice and care for the Earth? Which is the primary responsibility of the human species?

3. Are humans merely higher animals whose task is to harmonize with the natural environment and their fellow creatures, or are we something more? If more, then what? If we are a superior or privileged species, are we not entitled to "lord it over the Earth" by virtue of that status?

4. The author claims that each generation is a "sojourner" or "pilgrim." What does he mean? Do you agree?

5. Dobel insists on the condition that the Earth "is not God and should not be treated as such." Why does he need to say this?

NETWORKING

The *disenchantment of nature* is lamented by Swimme, Bube, Gray, and Berry. Important discussion of the *status of the human species in nature* is to be found in many selections, including Dyson, Wald, Feinberg and Shapiro, Barbour (Part V), Teilhard, Burhoe, Ruse and Wilson, Haught, Peacocke, and the selections in this part. For *justice,* see McFague and Gray.

A HOLISTIC VIEW OF REALITY
SALLIE MCFAGUE

Sallie McFague is professor of theology and former dean of the Vanderbilt Divinity School of Vanderbilt University in Nashville, Tennessee. The titles of her books reveal a continuing interest in the role of figurative language in theology. They include *Speaking in Parables: A Study in Metaphor and Theology* and *Metaphorical Theology: Models of God in Religious Language*. This selection is taken from her recent *Models of God: Theology for a Nuclear Age*, which received the 1988 American Academy of Religion Award for Excellence.

During the last twenty years, feminist Christian theologians have made a strong case against the androcentric, hierarchical character of the Western religious tradition. They have insisted that the humanity of women be given equal status and that the divisions that separate people—male/female, rich/poor, old/young, white/colored, straight/gay, Christian/non-Christian—be minimized in order to create an inclusive vision. As Elisabeth Schussler Fiorenza puts it, "Not the holiness of the elect but the wholeness of *all* is the central vision of Jesus."[1] But only in a few instances has this vision been extended to the nonhuman world.[2] The feminist theologians who have given attention to the nonhuman world have been, for the most part, those involved in Goddess traditions and witchcraft, for whom the body, the earth, and nature's cycles are of critical importance.[3] Those of us within the Christian tradition have much to learn from these sources,[4] but even these feminists have not, I believe, focused primarily on the intrinsic value of the nonhuman in a way sufficient to bring about the needed change of consciousness. Nor have other forms of liberation theology, which generally speaking are more anthropocentric than is feminist theology. All forms of liberation theology insist on the "deprivatizing" of theology,[5] but to date this has been for the most part limited to human beings and has not included the destiny of the cosmos. The principal insight of liberation theologies—that redemption is not the rescue of certain individuals for eternal life in another world but the fulfillment of all humanity in the political and social realities of this world—must be further deprivatized to include the well-being of all life. This is the case not only because unless we adopt an ecological perspective recognizing human dependence on its environment, we may well not survive, but also, of equal theological if not pragmatic importance, because such a perspective is the dominant paradigm of our time and theology that is not done in conversation with this paradigm is not theology *for our time.*

What is at stake here is not a sentimental love of nature or a leveling of all distinctions between human beings and other forms of life but the realization, as Teilhard de Chardin says, that his and everyone else's "poor trifling existence" is "one with the immensity of all that is and all that is still in the process of becoming." We are not separate, static, substantial individuals relating in external ways—and in ways of our choice—to other individuals, mainly human ones, and in minor ways to other forms of life. On the contrary, the evolutionary, ecological perspective insists that we are, in the most profound ways, "not our own": we belong, from the cells of our bodies to the finest creations of our minds, to the intricate, constantly changing cosmos. The ecosystem of which we are part is a whole: the rocks and waters, atmosphere and soil, plants, animals, and human beings interact in dynamic, mutually supportive ways that make all talk of atomistic individualism indefensible. Relationship and interdependence, change and transformation, not substance, changelessness, and perfection, are the categories within which a theology for our day must function.

To appreciate the extent to which we are embedded in the evolutionary ecosystem requires an act of imagination, since the Western sensibility has traditionally been nurtured by an atomistic, reductionistic perspective that separates human beings from other beings and reduces all that is not human to objects for human use. But the example of the human mind shows that human development is both culture- and nature-dependent. Infants have brains, but the human mind depends not only on other human beings in order to develop the distinctive characteristics of human existence but also on the stimuli of nature such as light, sound, smell, and heat: without the "warbling birds, blossoming cherry trees, sighing wind, and speaking humans, there would be no sources of signals—and thus no intellects."[6] We do not ordinarily feel indebted to birds and trees for our minds, but recognizing and appreciating that debt is an aspect of the new sensibility necessary for today's theology.

All of this is a poetic way of expressing the most fundamental tenet of the evolutionary, ecological perspective: that the question of what an entity is most basically is answered in terms of its relationships.[7] Thus, for instance, electrons, protons, and neutrons are viewed not as substantial entities but on the models of waves and particles. It is how they behave within the system of which they are a part that determines, on any particular occasion, which model will be used to describe them. What is the case at the subatomic level becomes even clearer at the level of life: each living organism is part of a system, a system with levels.

> The life of the cell is best understood in terms of ecological relationships among molecules. The living organism is best seen in terms of its ecological relationship with its environment. The interdependence of each living organism with other living organisms and with other components of its environment is the principle of population ecology.[8]

To feel in the depths of our being that we are part and parcel of the evolutionary ecosystem of our cosmos is a prerequisite for contemporary Christian theology. It is the beginning of a turn from the anthropocentrism and individualism so deeply embedded in the Western religious tradition, which is nowhere more precisely put than in Augustine's statement in the *Confessions*: "God and the soul, nothing more, nothing at all." That tradition, with its stress on the human individual, continued in much of Protestantism, flowering in the existentialism of the twentieth century. To be sure, another more political context for theology, with deep roots in the Hebrew Scriptures and certainly also in Augustine's two cities, as well as in Calvin's insistence that God is sovereign over the secular state, emerges in our time in the liberation theologies. But what has received less attention—and that largely from the Greek cosmological rather than the Hebraic historical tradition—is the creation which also "groans" for fulfillment.[9] Such lack of attention leads at the very least to an attitude of unconcern for the earth that is not only our home but, if we accept the evolutionary, ecological paradigm, also the giver and sustainer of our lives in basic and concrete ways. It has created a mentality of human domination and ruthlessness aptly captured in a remark by Huston Smith contrasting Western and Eastern attitudes toward nature:

> When Mount Everest was scaled the phrase commonly used in the West to describe the feat was "the conquest of Everest." An Oriental whose writings have been deeply influenced by Taoism remarked, "We would put the matter differently. We would speak of 'the befriending of Everest.' "[10]

One is reminded of Oriental nature paintings, in which human beings are often depicted not only as diminutive in comparison with the surrounding water and trees but also in a pose of mutual deference with a mountain—each bent, as it were, toward the other.

The evolutionary, ecological perspective perhaps comes across most clearly by contrast with the picture of the world it is replacing: the mechanical model. The mechanical model, bequeathed to us by Newtonian physics and Leibnizian philosophy, informs not only our daily common-sense assumptions and values in the West but also much of traditional Christian theology. Darwin, in the life sciences, and Einstein, in physics, were to overturn this model, but many of its characteristics, sketched here by A. R. Peacocke, remain part of our sensibility:

> By the end of the nineteenth century the absolutes of space, time, object, and determinism were apparently securely enthroned in an unmysterious, mechanically determined world, basically simple in structure at the atomic level and, statistically at least, unchanging in form—for even geological and biological transformations operated under fixed laws.[11]

This picture, though based in the physical rather than the biological sciences, was assumed to cover both, so that life—and not only the most fundamental physical processes of the universe—was understood on the model of a machine. In the early years of the twentieth century there was a movement toward a model more aptly described as organic, even for the constituents with which physics deals, for there occurred a profound realization of the deep relations between space, time, and matter, which relativized them all. In other words, relationships and relativity, as well as process and openness, characterize reality as it is understood at present in all branches of science. It is a considerably more complex picture than the old view, with a hierarchy of levels of organization from the microworld of the subatomic through the macro-world of the biosphere to the megaworld of intergalactic space.[12] But the characteristics of all levels of reality in this picture are similar: the play of chance and necessity replaces determinism; events appear to be more basic than substances, or to phrase it differently, individuals or entities always exist within structures of relationship; process, change, transformation, and openness replace stasis, changelessness, and completeness as basic descriptive concepts. Whereas with the model of the machine, life is patterned on the nonliving, with the organic model the nonliving takes on characteristics of life. The model is most appropriate to life, and hence the qualities of life—openness, relationship, interdependence, change, novelty, and even mystery—become the basic ones for interpreting all reality.

It is obvious how this perspective breaks through the old dualisms generated by the mechanical model—spirit/flesh, human/nonhuman, objective/subjective, reason/passion, supernatural/natural—for in the organic model hard lines cannot be drawn between matter and energy, the organic and the inorganic, the mind and the body, human beings and other forms of life.[13] In addition, the organic or evolutionary, ecological model is one that unites entities in a way basically different from the mechanistic model: instead of bringing entities together by means of common laws that govern all, creating a pattern of external relations, it unites by symbiotic, mutual interdependencies, creating a pattern of internal relations. In the organic model, one does not "enter into relations" with others but finds oneself in such relationships as the most basic given of existence. What separates entities differs as well: whereas in the mechanistic model entities are separated dualistically and hierarchically, in the organic model (or "mutualistic" model—a term that avoids the suggestion of reducing life to bodies which is implied in "organic") all entities are considered to be subjects as well as objects, to have intrinsic value as well as instrumental worth. "The ecological model is a model of living things which are acted upon and which respond by acting in their turn. They are patients and agents. In short they are subjects."[14] To take this perspective does not mean granting consciousness to amoebas, let alone to rocks, but it is to relativize the differences that have in the past been viewed as absolutes. It is to adopt the view toward the world so well captured in Martin Buber's famous distinction between I-Thou and I-It. It is the difference between an aesthetic and a utilitarian perspective, between one that appreciates the other (*all* others) and one that merely uses the other. An aesthetic sensibility toward the cosmos is one that values what is unselfishly, with a sense of delight in others for their own sakes. Such appreciation and delight are a necessary step in turning from an anthropocentric to an ecological sensibility. Thus, in the evolutionary, mutualistic model, all entities are united symbiotically and internally in levels of interdependence but are also separated as centers of action and response, each valuable in its own "beingness," however minimal or momentary that may appear to us. The symbol of the mountain and the human being bent toward each other, if allowing more agency and response to the mountain than can be empirically defended, does express an attitude of respect for otherness rare in the traditional Western sensibility.

Moreover, such an attitude is a basic ingredient in the development of the kind of global consciousness and conscience in relation to human solidarity and solidarity with other levels of life which is the required sensibility for the twenty-first century. Although it is manifestly utopian to imagine that the appreciation of otherness, whether human or nonhuman, will revolutionize our national and international behavior, it is surely folly to continue to encourage in ourselves and those whom we influence individualistic, hierarchical, dualistic, and utilitarian ways of thinking that are outmoded and have proved to be destructive of life at all levels.

The evolutionary, ecological, mutualistic model suggests an ethic toward others, both human and nonhuman, characterized by both justice and care. Carol Gilligan in her work on male- and female-oriented studies of moral development contrasts the pattern of "competing rights," in which one assumes that self and other should be treated fairly in spite of differences in power, and that of "responsibility and care," in which one assumes that everyone will be responded to and included.[15] The first pattern, characteristic of Western male development, begins from a position of separation and works toward connection; the second, characteristic of Western female development, begins from a position of relationship and works toward independence. The ethical pattern of the West has been principally the first, a logic of justice with emphasis on rights and rules and respect for the other. It is a noble ethic in many ways and underlies both the Western regard for the individual and the democratic form of government. But it is an "unfair" ethic, for it has been applied only to human beings—and even here, selectively. An ethic of justice in the evolutionary, ecological, mutualistic model would include the competing rights of other levels of life and would insist on these rights not simply from a utilitarian but also from an aesthetic point of view. That is to say, other levels of life deserve just treatment because of their intrinsic worth. Sorting out the rights of competing levels of life is, needless to say, a complex task, but to include the cosmos in the justice enterprise is essential. The second ethical pattern, that of care, has had a much slighter impact on Western thought. It has, as Gilligan points out, been seen as a weakness when individuals, usually women, understand moral response to focus on sensitivity to the needs of others, responsibility for including and caring for others, rather than on autonomous thinking and clear decision making in regard to the conflicting rights of separate parties.[16] But the model of reality we have sketched clearly demands not only the logic of justice but also the ethic of care. In fact, when the logic of justice is extended to include the nonhuman world, it moves naturally into such a mode, for appreciation for the cosmos *in our time* means responsibility for what is weaker and more vulnerable than human beings.

This is an important point and signals a significant change from the past. Until a few generations ago, nature appeared more powerful than we are. But this is no longer the case. Our ability to diminish if not destroy life through nuclear energy is perhaps the clearest proof of our power, but damage to other species and the ecosphere through a variety of pollutants and practices makes the point as well. In other words, the logic of justice, the acceptance of the rights of others, if applied (with meaningful distinctions and relativities) in our time to all others, does inevitably move into an ethic of care, for there is no way that such justice can be accorded except through care. It is for this reason that we need to imagine new models for the relationship between ourselves and our earth. We can no longer see ourselves as namers of and rulers over nature but must think of ourselves as gardeners, caretakers, mothers and fathers, stewards, trustees, lovers, priests, co-creators, and friends of a world that, while giving us life and sustenance, also depends increasingly on us in order to continue both for itself and for us.

If one were to do Christian theology from the holistic perspective, it is evident that some significant changes from traditional models and concepts would be necessary for expressing the relationships between God and the world and between ourselves and the world. Language that supports hierarchical, dualistic, external, unchanging, atomistic, anthropocentric, and deterministic ways of understanding these relationships is not appropriate *for our time,* whatever its appropriateness might have been for other times. It would appear that the appropriate language for our time, in the sense of being true to the paradigm of reality in which we actually live, would support ways of understanding the God-world and human-world relationships as open, caring, inclusive, interdependent, changing, mutual, and creative.

Needless to say, I am not proposing that the only criterion for theology is its fit with the reigning understanding of reality. But for theology to do *less* than fit our present understanding—for it to accept basic assumptions about reality from a very different time—seems blatantly wrongheaded. Nor am I suggesting that the holistic perspective and the guidelines it suggests for interpreting the relationships between God and the world and between ourselves and the world will necessarily be more permanent than earlier paradigms and guidelines. The evolutionary, ecological model insists above all else that the only permanence is change and hence that a theology appropriate to the holistic model will, at the very least, have to overcome what Rosemary Radford Ruether calls the "tyranny of the absolutizing imagination," which supposes that revolutions, theological or any other kind, are for all time.[17] What is needed is attention to the needs of one's own time. It is my contention that a theology that does not work within the context of the holistic view of reality cannot address the needs of our time.

NOTES

1. Elisabeth Schüssler Fiorenza, *In Memory of Her: A Feminist Theological Reconstruction of Christian Origins* (New York: Crossroad, 1983), 121.
2. A well-known exception is Rosemary Radford Ruether, who when stating her understanding of the biblical critical principle of renewal, invariably extends it to include a critique of "humanocentrism." "The 'brotherhood' of man needs to be widened to embrace not only women but also the whole community of life" (*Sexism and God-Talk: Toward a Feminist Theology* [Boston: Beacon Press, 1983], 87).
3. See, e.g., Ynestra King, "Making the World Live: Feminism and the Domination of Nature," in *Women's Spirit Bonding,* ed. Janet Kalven and Mary I. Buckley (New York: Pilgrim Press, 1984); Susan Griffin, *Woman and Nature: The Roaring inside Her* (New York: Harper & Row, 1978); Mary Daly, *Pure Lust: Elemental Feminist Theology* (Boston: Beacon Press, 1984); Starhawk, *Dreaming the Dark: Magic, Sex, and Politics* (Boston: Beacon Press, 1982); and idem, *The Spiral Dance: A Rebirth of the Ancient Religion of the Great Goddess* (San Francisco: Harper & Row, 1979).
4. See Chapter 4, pp. 99–100.
5. The phrase "the deprivatising of theology" comes from "Editorial Reflections," in *Cosmology and Theology,* ed. David Tracy and Nicholas Lash (New York: Seabury Press; Edinburgh: T. & T. Clark, 1983), 89.
6. Harold K. Schilling, "The Whole Earth Is the Lord's: Toward a Holistic Ethic," in *Earth Might Be Fair: Reflections on Ethics, Religion, and Ecology,* ed. Ian Barbour (Englewood Cliffs, N.J.: Prentice-Hall, 1972), 102. Schilling makes the further and related point that almost everything we value is of a social, relational sort: not only the obvious communities in which we exist, such as family, city, and country, but

also education, politics, the arts, science, and language. Moreover, the most basic, precious things we value are profoundly social and relational: friendship, love, parenthood, loyalty, wisdom.

7. Two recent sources (among the many available) that flesh out the implications of this statement for theology are Charles Birch and John B. Cobb, Jr., *The Liberation of Life: From the Cell to the Community* (Cambridge: At the Univ. Press, 1981), and A. R. Peacocke, *Creation and the World of Science* (Oxford: At the Clarendon Press, 1979). Another very interesting treatment by Stephen Toulmin depicts a postmodern cosmology in which human beings, in order to be "at home" in the world, must adopt not just a utilitarian but an appreciative attitude toward the other forms of life with which we are in relationship: "We can do our best to build up a conception of 'the overall scheme of things' which draws as heavily as it can on the results of scientific study, informed by a genuine piety in all its attitudes toward creatures of other kinds: a piety that goes beyond the consideration of their usefulness to Humanity as instruments for the fulfillment of human ends. That is an alternative within which human beings can both *feel,* and also *be,* at home. For to be at home in the world of nature does not just mean finding out how to utilize nature economically and efficiently—home is not a hotel! It means making sense of the relations that human beings and other living things have toward the overall patterns of nature in ways that give us some sense of their proper relations to one another, to ourselves, and to the whole" (*The Return to Cosmology: Postmodern Science and the Theology of Nature* [Berkeley and Los Angeles: Univ. of California Press, 1982], 272). Toulmin claims that postmodern science has more in common with the classical theory of "correspondences" among all aspects of the natural world—the various interlocking relations in creation—than it does with modern (Newtonian) science.
8. Birch and Cobb, *The Liberation of Life*, 42.
9. See George S. Hendry, *Theology of Nature* (Philadelphia: Westminster Press, 1980), for a treatment of what he calls the cosmological, political, and psychological contexts for presenting the saving activity of God.
10. Huston Smith, *The Religions of Man* (New York: Harper & Row, 1965), 209.
11. Peacocke, *Creation and the World of Science,* 54.
12. *Ibid.,* 61–62.
13. One illustration of this point is found in a number of studies with higher mammals, such as apes and dolphins, that reveal complex problem-solving abilities; other studies among a broad range of animals underscore that what could be called "spirit"—experiences of vitality, joy, and grief—is not limited to human beings. Anyone who has been in a "symbiotic relationship" with a pet for any length of time knows that there is communication across the dividing line of species.
14. Birch and Cobb, *The Liberation of Life,* 123.
15. Carol Gilligan, *In a Different Voice: Psychological Theory and Women's Development* (Cambridge: Harvard Univ. Press, 1982).
16. *Ibid.,* Chapter 1.
17. Rosemary Radford Ruether, "Envisioning Our Hopes: Some Models of the Future," in *Women's Spirit Bonding,* ed. Kalven and Buckley, 335.

QUESTIONS FOR STUDY

1. McFague argues that neither feminist nor liberation theologies go far enough. What does she mean?

2. The author quotes Augustine, "God and the soul, nothing more, nothing at all," to illustrate the anthropomorphism and individualism so deeply embedded in Western religious tradition. Why is this reference revealing?

3. What is the contrast between Western and Eastern attitudes toward nature?

4. What is the basic model of the world given by Newton and other originators of the modern world view? What model does McFague propose as its replacement?

QUESTIONS FOR REFLECTION

1. Explain the point of the quote, "without 'warbling birds, blossoming cherry trees, sighing wind, and speaking humans, there would be no source of signals—and thus no intellects.'" Compare it with this remark from Teilhard de Chardin: "We require the whole world just to be ourselves."

2. List several features of the mechanistic model of the world and several for the organic or mutualistic model. Why, according to McFague, is the latter to be preferred over the former?

3. Distinguish between the concepts of justice and care. What are the problems raised by an exclusive emphasis on justice? How does care correct these problems?

4. In the last paragraph of this selection, McFague attempts to relativize her own position by suggesting it is no more permanent than the view it hopes to replace. Does this qualification weaken her position or recommend it more highly? How can she claim it is true or even truer if it is subjected to the everchanging circumstances of history?

NETWORKING

Various versions of *holism/organicism* are found in Fuller, Capra, MacCormack, Cobb, and Lovelock. Discussions of its opposite, *mechanism,* are to be found in MacCormack and Bube. Gray and Roach are expressions of *ecofeminism.* The *future of the human species* is a subject for Dyson, Teilhard, Burhoe, and Cobb. See Buber for the *I-Thou principle. Models of God* are discussed in MacCormack, Fuller, and Bube. Dobel and Gray focus on the idea of *justice in the context of the environmental crisis.*

PROCESS THEOLOGY AND ENVIRONMENTAL ISSUES

JOHN B. COBB

John Cobb is best known for his advocacy of Alfred North Whitehead's process philosophy within the context of Christian theology. He has done with Whitehead's thought what Thomas Aquinas did with Aristotle's. Cobb is Ingraham Professor of Theology at the Clarement School of Theology in California, Avery Professor in the Clarement Graduate School, and director of the Center for Process Studies, an area in which he is widely published. One statement on theology and ecology is his *Is it too Late?: A Theology of Ecology.*

I

The central message of the ecological consciousness that caught the imagination of the late sixties was the interconnectedness and interdependence of living things with each other and with the inorganic world. Rapid alterations of major elements of this interconnected system by human activities were already threatening the support systems necessary for human enjoyment and even for human life itself. Insecticides were poisoning fish and threatening the survival of those species of birds that fed on them. Long-term consequences appeared damaging to human health as well. Eventually in the United States the use of such poisons was drastically curtailed.

To some extent the realization has entered the public consciousness that this kind of interconnectedness is a general characteristic of our world. We can see that dumping wastes in rivers not only destroys fish life there but also affects the breeding grounds of ocean fish and reduces the supply for the dining table. We recognize that the killing of animal predators leads to the excessive multiplication of their prey, members of which then overgraze the vegetation and hasten the erosion of the soil. But for the most part these are still treated as specific, isolable problems rather than as dramatic clues to the nature of reality. Our laws still allow the development of all sorts of new products unless they can be shown to cause specific, measurable harm. Since in most cases the resultant harm is neither dramatic nor immediate, there is no way to prevent continuing dangerous tampering with our environment.

The narrow limits within which the ecological consciousness has become effective express very deep-seated features of our Western mode of thinking. We think of what is most real as individual, physical entities, more or less self-contained, and only secondarily entering into relations with other entities. We accept the importance of these relations only as they are individually proved. Newtonian science and laissez-faire economics are both expressive of this sense of reality. In philosophy, it is most systematically formulated in analyses which take substances and their attributes as primary, but it also appears wherever philosophy seeks the essences of things. In both cases, relations become a secondary issue. With regard to human self-understanding, this basic view of reality is expressed wherever the self is understood to transcend experience as its agent or patient, as in most forms of idealism and in Husserl's phenomenology. It is not fully overcome in the existential analyses of either Heidegger or Sartre.

In theology, this sense of individual human beings alone with themselves and with God has played an important role in the way both this-worldly and otherworldly salvation have been conceived. Even in the doctrine of the church, despite the organic images in the New Testament, we have not overcome this tendency to view persons primarily in their self-existence and only secondarily in their relations. These generalizations are supported by such major exceptions as Buber's stress that the I of the I-thou relation is different from the I of the I-it relation; for even he failed to generalize his insight fully.

Physics found that it could not interpret its data by use of the particle model. Particles dissolved into waves which became functions of field. Change in any part of the field changes the entire field. It is no more true to say that the field is made up of the parts than to say that the parts of the field are constituted by their place in the field. In short, there are no entities in abstraction from the relations to all the other entities. Relations are fundamentally constitutive of entities.

It was the particular contribution of Alfred North Whitehead to have grasped the meaning of this and to have seen that it reversed our usual habits of mind. Science had been trying to understand organisms as patterns of organization of entities that are not organic. Thus the obvious dependence of organisms on their environment was dismissed as a clue to the fundamental nature of reality. Now physics discovered that its most basic units are more like organisms than like self-contained particles. Large organisms are societies of small organisms. Relations are primary at both levels.

The point of this excursus into "the philosophy of organism" is to show that the adoption of this philosophy, as by process theology, reverses the perception of things and relations. We see a world of interrelated things such that alteration of any one affects all. Important practical consequences follow from this vision. The currently dominant world view places the burden of proof on those who would stop alterations in the environment. They must show that such "development" has serious negative consequences in the readily foreseeable future. A society that adopted the view of all things as interconnected would place the burden of proof on those who would introduce changes. They must show both that their projects are really needed and that the risks run in these alterations are relatively minor, even when the indefinite future is considered. The results of such a shift in the burden of proof would be enormous.

II

The interconnectedness of things crosses all the lines of demarcation established by our academic and professional disciplines. Each of these investigates that aspect of the whole sphere of organic relations amenable to its methods and grasped by its concepts. In the past, philosophy and theology have attempted to maintain some unifying overview to counteract this fragmentation, but recently dominant schools in both disciplines have accepted the compartmentalized model. Philosophy limits itself to epistemology, or logic, or phenomenology, or the analysis of language. Theology attempts to become one science alongside others by identifying its specific subject matter as Scripture and its contemporary meaning.

The result is that the world of contemporary thought is incapable of dealing appropriately with the interconnected world of real things. For the contemporary intellect to apply itself to the solution of environmental problems, these have to be formulated in the categories of existing disciplines. In some instances, the need may be recognized for an interdisciplinary approach. The extreme difficulty of genuine interdisciplinary work is already recognized, but even when cooperation is achieved, at best a problem is dealt with by several fragmentary disciplines. Its real nature still eludes such an approach.

This is a highly practical problem which presents itself in even the best achievements of recent times, such as the "Green Revolution." The problem of insufficient food in the tropical world was approached by agronomists, who were brilliantly successful in producing hybrid grains which have greatly increased food production. To do this they concentrated on quite specific tasks in the appropriate scientific manner. They could not consider all the consequences of introducing grains that had not developed resistance to all the possible diseases and blights. They could not calculate the risks that such grains would rapidly displace disease- and blight-resistant native varieties so that recovery from a disaster may prove extremely difficult. They could not consider the effects of the new agriculture on the existing structure of peasant communities. Hence a profound change has been introduced which makes important gains in one direction while running great risks in other ways.

There is another approach to development in the tropical world which much better reflects the organic nature of reality. It tends to be supported by amateurs rather than specialists. It is possible for peasant villages to take control of their own destiny and find ways of improving their agricultural output as part of the improvement of their corporate life. This can be done with full sensitivity to the long-term effects upon the ecology. Tom Takami's Asian Rural Institute is an example. Paolo Freire's conscientization of Brazilian villagers—until it was stopped by the military government—was another. But as long as the mind-set of the intellectual leadership is governed by academic and professional specialization, the vast majority of the resources directed to development will neglect the organic character of human society and of its relation to nature. The results are an ever more precarious human condition.

It is difficult to conceive of a reversal of the long trend to intellectual fragmentation. But the beginning of such a reversal must be the will to reverse it. This is difficult to attain without some sense as to what a holistic vision would be like. At this point Whitehead is immensely valuable. He is the one great thinker of our century who produced a cosmology based both on the results of the natural sciences and on the examination of multifaceted human experience. He proved that holistic vision is still possible in our time. Process theology participates in this vision and tries to encourage its wider adoption. To do so, in even a minimal way, provides a perspective from which the dangers of currently dominant approaches are apparent. In an organically interconnected world, we cannot accept policy formation by specialized expertise. We can encourage the subordination of expertise to such human wisdom as can be mustered. We can also encourage new efforts to root the discrete disciplines in a common vision so that the interconnectedness of the sciences is built into their self-understanding, their methods, and their concepts. We can at least begin by abandoning the ideal of an autonomous theology and make its interdependence with all other aspects of thought explicit in our Christian reflections.

III

A third limitation of our present approach to environmental problems may be conceived as an aspect of the second, but it is sufficiently important to warrant separate treatment. We not only fragment our problems so that they conform to our established disciplines; we also treat them in too limited space-time horizons. A very minor example illustrated this vividly for me.

In my hometown of Claremont, California, the city council became concerned about environmental issues around 1970. It established a commission to draw up a plan for the future of the city. The commission planned for green belts and low-density housing to preserve and enhance the parklike atmosphere of the city. If implemented, the plan would make Claremont a very attractive place to live; but this solution to the problem of future growth is counterproductive in a wider context. It converts more farmland into city; it is extravagant in its use of utilities; and it creates a greater dependence on private automobiles—one of the chief environmental curses of the American way of life.

The dilemma is that the solution of problems as defined by a limited horizon exports problems to other times and places. We seem to be forced to choose between urban crowding and suburban sprawl. The advantages of the former in terms of efficiency are matched by its negative social consequences. But organic thinking which sees the limited problem in global perspective is possible. The vision of Paolo Soleri is of this sort. He designs possible cities or "arcologies" which could accommodate larger populations with less impact on the environment and greater possibilities for human community. Yet his proposals will not receive serious attention until problems are viewed in organic, global perspective. From every other perspective they appear "fantastic."

The negative global consequences of otherwise positive policies can be illustrated in other ways. Perhaps the most immediately critical problem in the United States is unemployment, especially as it affects minority communities. The well-established method of reducing unemployment is by accelerating economic growth. Now we find that this cannot be done without an undesirable level of inflation. But let us suppose that our economic experts could solve that problem, too. Surely the results in terms of genuine and urgent social needs in the United States would be admirable!

Nevertheless, viewed in global perspective, the evaluation changes. Our Latin American friends, for example, tell us that a major obstacle to their liberation is United States economic colonialism. There can be no speeding up the U.S. economy that does not retain and heighten its dependence on the international economic system that inhibits freedom in Latin America. Furthermore, all growth in the economies of the developed nations, and especially the United States, accelerates the exhaustion of global resources, intensifies the problems of waste disposal and pollution, and increases the

dependence on nuclear energy, which may well prove the greatest crime of our generation against the future. In global perspective an entirely different approach to unemployment is needed, but as yet this global perspective has hardly affected the thinking of
those most likely to be able to propose practical alternatives.

Christian theology as a whole suggests, in principle, a global perspective. That is,
Christians recognize that they are called to consider the totality of God's creation and
especially the planet earth. But as long as the intimate interconnectedness of the parts is
not deeply realized, the habit of identifying and solving problems in terms of very limited contexts prevails. Process thinking clarifies how the planet as a whole functions as
the context that defines our problems.

IV

Western thought, when compared with archaic and Eastern thinking, is strikingly
anthropocentric. Bernard Meland has long recognized the power and the limitations of
this anthropocentric stance. As early as 1933 he interpreted this as "a fallacy of misplaced valuation" and called on human beings to find our place in the world "not as
plunderers and exploiters of nature's resources, but as creatures of earth, born of its
processes, nurtured and sustained by the subtle and intricate interchange as humanly
evolved organisms. . . ." But of course this protest of what was then called neonatural-
ism was little heard and less heeded. In the decades since, at least until the late sixties,
anthropocentrism strengthened its hold.

In this dominant Western vision all things are viewed from the perspective of
human beings. In one sense this is, of course, simply inevitable. Human beings can view
the world only as human beings. In another and more important sense, it is an ideal not
yet attained; for we in fact view many things as bourgeoisie, as whites, as males, as
Americans, or even from a completely selfish individual point of view. This diversity
suggests that the human perspective is not simply given. Instead, it constitutes a norm
we have adopted and strive for. This norm provides leverage for those who are concerned for the poor, the black, and the female. It has without doubt been a basically positive factor in modern society.

Our ethics and our economics are based on this anthropocentric norm. Human
beings are to be respected as ends in themselves. We teach that the need of another
human being lays a claim upon each of us quite apart from any special relationship such
as commonality of race or language. Even nations pay lip service to concern for the
well-being of humanity. Economics offers theories as to how scarce commodities can
be distributed in such a way as to satisfy human wants in general.

The limitations of our anthropocentric norms appear when we ask about the value
of other animal species. In economics that question can only mean the value of other
species to human beings—and finally, what human beings will pay for them. Our dominant ethics supports this view. What is not human is merely means to human ends. Our
dominant philosophical traditions have grounded this in the nature of reality. For
Descartes, animals are only material objects. For Kant, they exist only as phenomena in
human observation. Obviously, material objects and mere phenomena can lay no moral
claim upon us.

There remains a natural sympathy with animals, an unreasoned belief that they too suffer and that their suffering is an evil in itself—not only for the human who chances to sympathize. This assumes that animals are not mere objects or phenomena but also subjects with their own intrinsic value. Process theology supports and systematizes these natural beliefs and shares in their implicit critique of our inherited anthropocentrism.

This stance has practical importance for our response to the environmental problem. Indeed, it alters the definition of the problem. The term "environmental problem" is already too anthropocentric. It suggests that there are human beings and that everything else exists only as our environment. The problem is that this environment may not continue to serve human needs adequately.

A more inclusive view sees the problem as that of a decaying biosphere. Despite vast natural catastrophes, drastic changes in climate, and the disappearance of many species of living things, over billions of years the planetary biosphere grew richer. The high point came with the emergence of the remarkable human species. Our species introduced new capacities for destructiveness and was probably responsible for the destruction of many other species even during the Paleolithic period. Nevertheless, for hundreds of thousands of years we basically participated in the enrichment of the value of the whole.

With the domestication of animals and the plowing of the land for agriculture ten thousand years ago, a new level of destructiveness was introduced. Human action became the major instrument of the extension of deserts into once fertile land. By now it has resulted in the loss of half of the land that was arable at that time. During that same period, on the other hand, civilization has introduced whole new dimensions of value into the whole. For thousands of years one might appraise the gains as outweighing the losses. But at last the decline of the biosphere threatens the substructure of human culture itself on a global basis. To continue to "progress" along the lines of our past development is now suicidal.

This picture appeals for response not only to biocentric motives but also to anthropocentric ones. In most cases there is convergence between enlightened anthropocentrism and biocentrism so far as the implications for policy are concerned. One main argument for biocentrism is that it is a check on the shortsightedness of most policies proposed from anthropocentric motives—a check that is needed also from the perspective of enlightened anthropocentrism. However, there are issues on which judgments will differ according to whether they are made from the biocentric perspective or the anthropocentric—even the most enlightened.

From the biocentric perspective of process theology, there are other remarkable achievements of the evolutionary process besides the human species. The porpoise and the elephant will serve as examples. The porpoise and the elephant are of value in and for themselves as well as for reality as a whole. They would be of value whether or not human beings existed. If we ignore or deny this and measure their value only by their use to human beings, we will probably destroy all except for a few exhibited in shows and zoos: porpoises compete with fishermen for fish; and elephants in the wild, even if they can be protected from the many poachers, require space whose use an increasing human population will want for itself. It will be difficult to argue from an anthropocentric perspective that these species are of particular importance to the ecology as a whole. Hence, we must expect a continuing struggle between those humans who believe all value is value for humans and those who believe there is intrinsic worth in animals of other species and accordingly seek to protect them for their own sake and the sake of the whole.

Confusion arises at this point if we suppose that, when we deal with what has intrinsic value, we must simply reverence and never calculate. Albert Schweitzer, with whose principle of reverence for life process theology otherwise agrees, seems to have allowed this confusion. Schweitzer was, of course, forced to destroy some creatures in order that others might live, and he always favored human life, but theoretically he did not provide any basis for judgments of relative value.

The theoretical problem is as follows. In dealing with human beings we have argued that each should be treated equally as an end of immeasurable worth. Hence, no measurement of the objective value of persons has been possible or desirable. If we then argue that all living things are ends in themselves, we seem to elevate them all to the same status as humans. Or if we practically recognize that a hierarchy of value obtains, we value other creatures according to their resemblance to humans. But this seems to introduce a new form of anthropocentrism.

Process theology proposes that we be clear that the locus of intrinsic value is, not in persons as such, but in experience. All experience has intrinsic value. But we prize some forms of experience more than others. Joy is preferable to misery, intensity to dullness, depth to superficiality, complexity to simplicity, harmony to discord. The situation is complex because the practical alternatives may be superficial joy and intense pain, or simple harmony and complex discord.

This is not the place to elaborate a theory of comparative intrinsic values. My point is only that, although there are many instances in which very diverse experiences are of roughly equal value, there are others in which great differences of value are apparent. For example, there is every indication that most experiences of dogs are of more value than any of those of bacteria. To kill a considerable number of bacteria to restore the health of a dog is justified.

The human prejudice as to the superior value of human beings seems justified by considerations of this sort. However, the question is always to be kept open. There may well be creatures of greater worth. Among our fellow species on this planet there are probably some respects in which we are excelled by some marine mammals. Many of our fantasies of creatures from other planets, as in *Close Encounters of the Third Kind*, envision them as superior, and this is quite possible in theory. Traditionally, the superior position has been attributed to angels. The point here is that only human beings can conceive a scale of values that does not make their own experience the criterion. We can transcend anthropocentricity to some extent in determining what is of value in itself and hence also for God. Of course, our judgments in this area, as in all areas, are highly fallible, but rejection of anthropocentrism need not involve the abandonment of ethical thinking. It calls instead for its revision and extension.

In these comments I have not been explicitly theological. However, a doctrine of God is presupposed. The appeal to an inclusive perspective is implicitly an appeal to God. Apart from God the whole cannot constitute a perspective from which valuing can occur. The theological conviction is that God is the creative source of all things and especially of all living beings, that God's purposes are realized through all types of creatures, and that God finds good all that exists. Unnecessarily to destroy species that God has created and now enjoys is to impoverish God. To waste the inanimate resources of the planet is to limit the possibilities for future creation. Process theology rejects anthropocentrism for theocentrism, but there can be for it no contrast between seeking the good of God and seeking the good of creation. The good for God is the good for creation and the good for creation is the good for God. For practical purposes there is a coincidence of the implications of theocentrism and biocentrism. . . .

QUESTIONS FOR STUDY

1. According to Cobb, what was the central message of the ecological consciousness of the late sixties? How does he illustrate its importance and truth?

2. In what sense is the interconnectedness of things violated by academic disciplines?

3. Cobb argues that "Western thought . . . is strikingly anthropocentric." What does he mean? In what ways is anthropocentrism damaging to the world around us?

4. Describe Cobb's understanding of individualism. What are some of its advantages? Its problems?

5. What are the positions of traditional theism and humanism with respect to the role of God in assuring the future? How does process theology mediate between the two extremes?

QUESTIONS FOR REFLECTION

1. Cobb asserts that "a society that adopted the view of all things as interconnected would place the burden of proof on those who would introduce changes." Why is this so? Do you see a possible danger in this position?

2. Examine the organization of your school. Is it divided neatly into professional schools and disciplines within a college? What interdisciplinary programs exist? Speak to one or two program directors. How do they understand the notion of autonomous specialization as compared with that of interdisciplinary emphasis?

3. The author describes attempts to improve his hometown and the problems they produce. What point is he making?

4. What is the distinction between anthropocentrism and biocentrism? What are some of the problems of biocentrism? How does Cobb propose to solve them?

5. How does the concept of God enter into the argument for the preservation of the natural world in which anthropocentrism is replaced by theocentrism?

NETWORKING

Fuller, McFague, and Gray deal with various aspects of *interconnectedness*. Barbour (Part I) discusses and Dyson applies the ideas of *process thought*. Discussions of *hierarchy and levels of existence* are contained in Bube, Haught, and Gray. *Evil* is a subject for Einstein, Burhoe, and Davies. The *future and destiny of the human species with respect to nature* is discussed in Dyson, Teilhard, and Burhoe.

A CRITIQUE OF DOMINION THEOLOGY
ELIZABETH DODSON GRAY

Elizabeth Dodson Gray and her husband, David, are founders and directors of the Bolton Institute of Wellesley, Massachusetts. The institute focuses on contemporary issues of economics, the environment, and woman's identity. She also teaches in the Theological Opportunities Program of the Harvard Divinity School and lectures widely. Her most influential book is *Green Paradise Lost: Re-mything Genesis.*

I want to challenge us to rethink some current assumptions about eco-justice as an issue for Christians and the churches. I want to challenge the assumption that we already have a perfectly adequate basis for eco-justice preaching in our hebrew Scriptures and our New Testament. I want to show you why I don't think that's so. Then I want to challenge the assumption that we have in our Jewish and Christian traditions an adequate creation theology. By creation theology I mean an adequate mental picture and conceptual grasp of ourselves, our world, and our relationship to the Creator. And finally I want to challenge the scope of the current issues usually thought of as eco-justice issues. Let me deal briefly with this last one, and then spend most of my time with my first two concerns.

In the call to this conference about eco-justice preaching there was a good list of "eco-justice issues"—hunger, employment, caring for the earth, and so on. All of these are good things, important things. Nowhere was there mention of the women's movement as an eco-justice issue. But think of the enormous women's involvement in the environmental movements, such as those for clean air and stopping nuclear power, in the currents of thought called eco-feminism, in the peace movement and the nuclear freeze movement. Think of Rachel Carson, Helen Caldicott, Randy Forsberg—already almost forgotten as the author of the idea of the nuclear freeze. Think of Greenham Common, and you think of women. Think of Hazel Henderson, who began her career as a counter-economist by working as a mother for clean air. When you start thinking of specific events, places, people—many in the eco-justice movement involve women taking unheard-of roles in challenging male madness over eco-justice issues. In short, the women's movement is perhaps the largest movement today for eco-justice.

The reason I am bothered by the invisibility of all these women activists "as women" is that I hear people talk about the 1970s as a time of apathy, a time when "nothing was happening." To those people, the 1960s and the civil rights movement and the anti-Vietnam War movement was a time of action, but nothing happened in the '70s. Well, what happened in the 1970s was the women's movement. It has taken many forms. And it is usually invisible to men and to male historians and to our male church. But unless you can see the women's movement and women's concerns and organizing skills and leadership and energies and emerging moral judgment in eco-justice movements ranging from Green politics in Western Europe to liberation movements in Central and Latin America, as well as in the economies and politics of developing countries in Africa and in the Middle East, then you haven't seen much of the eco-justice movement of today and tomorrow.

WHERE ARE WE IN GOD'S CREATION?

Our sense today of where we are in God's creation is very different from what it was a century, or even a few decades, ago. Today we know we live and move and have our being on a small planet in one galaxy among 193 billion such galaxies. And we know that, like all that is alive here, we live on the outer skin of this planet, within a five- to seven-mile-thick layer ecologists call the biosphere. The biosphere contains all the biological life-supporting systems and cycles of the earth, and these systems and cycles keep alive all that grows. That includes us.

But we as Christians, when we are thinking as Christians, have blinded ourselves to much of this. We have been helped in dissociating our sense of self from this biological understanding of ourselves by Christian theologians both past and present who have helped us think that just as far as God is removed from creation, we humans are removed from the rest of creation: we are created in God's image and are spirit. And we get very upset when we are reminded of our biological similarity to mammals or other animals. Our theologians have emphasized God's transcendence and our own capacities for self-transcendence and being different from the rest of God's creation. Yes, we are different—in the sense of being distinct and unique as a species. But we are kept alive by the air we breathe and in the other ways we participate in the biosphere, just as much as any of the rest of creation.

Think of our planet as like a gigantic tennis ball that has a five- to seven-mile-high coat of fuzz on it. We exist within that fuzz very much the way the "Whos" did in the Doctor Seuss book *Horton Hears a Who*. We are like the Whos in the fuzz of the tennis ball. And when we talk about creation, when we preach about creation, when we teach creation in our Sunday schools, we never mention important little things like the biosphere and ecological cycles. They somehow don't seem to fit in.

But whether we preach about them or not, whether we are moved to religious awe and wonder before these latter-day burning bushes or not, the creation of God on this planet does everything by the interaction of the carbon cycle, the oxygen cycle, the nitrogen cycle, the hydrological cycle, and about a dozen other cycles or round-and-round processes. What's terrific about these cycles—and about the magnificence of God's design, if you will—is that each part of them takes its essential raw materials from the waste products of other parts of the cycle. Each part then does its special thing, dumps its own wastes, and—in the wonderful mystery of God's ecology—those wastes are precisely the raw materials another part of the cycle needs in order to do its thing. Contemplate a cow in a grassy field and you're witnessing, among other things, a part of the nitrogen cycle at work, for the cow eats the grass and, in turn, the cow provides manure that fertilizes the field of grass. As long as there is rain and the sun continues to shine, then the cow and the grass are good for each other and provide for each other. What you are contemplating is a small ecosystem or community of life and interdependence.

You can see the same sort of thing happening around the process of photosynthesis, the sunlight-into-sugars process that goes on in green plants when the sun is shining. A waste product of photosynthesis is the oxygen you and I breathe. We tend to think that oxygen is always there in the air for human beings to breathe. Economists talk about air and water as "free goods." Free, baloney! Oxygen to breathe is there only because it is breathed out by all the green things on the planet, from the blue-green algae in the ocean to the plants and trees of tropical rain forests and the ivy growing on your windowsill at home. In the miracle of photosynthesis, plants, when the sun shines, breathe out oxygen to us. We in turn breathe out carbon dioxide back to them. Once again, it is a never-ending cycle of cooperative community or relationship. We and the plants are totally dependent on each other, each to breathe out so the other can breathe in. But most of us don't feel a sense of community with the trees outside or the blue-green algae in the ocean; we don't have the faintest clue that we can breathe only because plants and trees are breathing too.

LIFE IN HUMAN SOCIETY

Now consider how differently things usually go within the circle of human activity. There is energy coming in that we use, which usually someone dug up from the biosphere in the form of a fossil fuel (actually fossil sunshine, stored from photosynthesis long ago). Within this circle of human activity there are also metals and minerals coming in, many of which we also dig up, such as copper and zinc, from the earth's crust or seabed.

What happens to our wastes? Keep in mind now that we're speaking of the contrast between our ways and those of the biosphere. The more our human populations increase, the more wastes we are likely to pour out, and the more the pace of our economic system picks up in growth, and the more and the faster our wastes go back out into the systems of the biosphere—into the air, into the streams, into the soils, into the oceans—until like a house with an inadequate septic-tank system it can't handle so much so fast. The capacity of biospheric systems to use these wastes is overwhelmed.

MEMBERS ONE OF ANOTHER

Look outside your window and you just see plants and buildings and trees and sidewalks and sky. You don't see ecosystems because you have not been trained in ecology. Most of us haven't. But what is really out there are these communities of life that scientists call ecosystems, in which the wastes of one part of the ecosystem are essential raw materials that other parts of the system need. It's all interconnected and it is all mutually interdependent, and it does its thing and keeps on going indefinitely.

Now about 1942 we got the great idea of producing DDT in the laboratory to get rid of malaria. It was a good thing to do, a great idea: DDT knocked out mosquitoes that carried malaria to humans. But you can't knock out mosquitoes with DDT without also knocking out all the insects you expose to DDT. So you killed all the insects in an ecosystem, and pretty soon Rachel Carson wrote *Silent Spring,* calling attention to how DDT had killed off the food for the birds or, alternatively, how you had poisoned the birds because they ate the poisoned insects.

For a while we thought this was all we had done. But DDT is a persistent pesticide, what today we'd call "nonbiodegradable." DDT is washed by rain into rivers and lakes and oceans. Little fish who feed on algae also get DDT with supper, and the DDT stays in their flesh. Then the little fish and their DDT are eaten by bigger fish, who in turn are eaten by still bigger fish—and the DDT gets "biologically concentrated" and is stored in fatty tissue. In three species—the bald eagle, the peregrine falcon, and the Pacific pelican—the DDT from a fish diet ends up, scientists have learned, in the liver of the female bird, where it interferes with production of an enzyme which determines the thickness of the shell of the eggs the female lays. So for the first time in evolution mother birds laid eggs and sat on them—and the eggs went splat because the shell wasn't thick enough.

Now the point here is not just one of concern for these three endangered species, though we should be concerned, but that we are regularly producing substances in the laboratory and the chemical plant—and we do not have the faintest idea what ripple effects they will have upon our larger life-support systems.

HOW DID WE EVER THINK WE COULD GET AWAY WITH IT?

When you really get into this, you begin to think there is something really bizarre about the way we have treated the planet. I argue in my book *Green Paradise Lost* that our view of our place in creation came to us as part of our Judeo-Christian tradition. Our whole Western civilization with its science and industrial system is built upon this cultural foundation and is still very much shaped by it. What's been taken for granted in this heritage and in our heads is conveniently summarized by an illustration from a curriculum developed by the Educational Development Center in Newton, Massachusetts. The accompanying text reads: "People in the Old Testament believed in only one God who created a divine order [i.e., hierarchy] that placed people above nature and gave people dominion over the fish of the sea, the fowl of the air," and so on.

What that creation theology from the Bible translates into is a set of relationships we hold in our heads and which we have been deeply socialized into. I've found it useful to diagram those relationships like this:

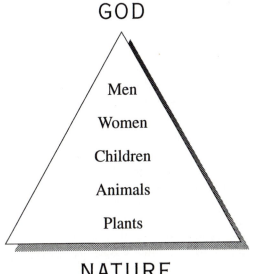

GOD

Men

Women

Children

Animals

Plants

NATURE

Note first of all that this is a hierarchy being diagramed here. By that I mean it is a picture of diversity being "ranked." It depends upon the illusion that there is some magic standing point you can taken and then, according to your values, say this is higher and more important and of more value than that. What is of highest value is always visualized by us as "up." God is up, above, lofty, high and mighty, and so on. And what is of next value is arranged below. I think you see this most clearly presented in Scripture not in the Genesis accounts of creation but in Psalm 8, which says:

> When I consider thy heavens, the work of thy fingers,
> The moon and the stars, which thou hast ordained;
> What is man, that thou art mindful of him?
> And the son of man, that thou visitest him?
> For thou *hast made him a little lower than the angels,*
> And hast crowned him with glory and honor.
> Thou *madest him to have dominion* over the works of
>   thy hands;
> Thou *hast put all things under his feet:*
> All sheep and oxen,
> Yea, and the beasts of the field;
> The fowl of the air, and the fish of the sea,
> And whatsoever passeth through the paths of the seas.
>   (Psalm 8:3–8, KJV)

What we're given here is a nifty little snapshot in which God is above, highest in value. Angels are next and just slightly higher than humans. Then come humans. And everything else is underneath our feet.

And it's not just that these are of higher worth and value but that all things and all creatures in this great ladder of things are supposed to obey their higher-ups. Man and creation are supposed to obey God, or else. Women are supposed to obey men, and children are certainly supposed to obey their parents and obey God. Most of us call pets and other animals subhuman—not nonhuman—and we assume we can train animals, torture them for our medical experiments, do horrible things to them as we raise them to be our food. We can relate to cats, dogs, horses in terms of personalities with consciousness. They are at least more like us. But plants I don't think we can relate to at all. They're simply rooted in the ground in one place. What in this context we call "nature" is finally on the very bottom of this pyramid of value and obedience and who-is-supposed-to-adapt-to-whom.

Paul Santmire, who wrote *Brother Earth,* has said that in Christian theology nature has been a theological noncategory. It has had all the importance of the stage—or wall or floor; nature is simply the context in which the really important thing, the drama of salvation, takes place between man and God.

THREE MYTHS

What I'm saying is that we have embedded in our heads this pyramidal picture of our place in creation, and we confront nature with three myths. The first myth is that *reality is hierarchical*. If there's anything I want you to understand, it is that reality is an interrelated system. A system is something in which everything affects everything else. Most of us don't have a clue what that means, so instead we conceptualize reality in hierarchies.

The second myth is that *man is "above" nature in dominion* or control. Once again, this is rooted in our Judeo-Christian tradition. It is very clearly said in our biblical creation tradition that God has given us dominion, rule. Dominion is a kingly metaphor, and just as God is king in the heavens, we're supposed to reign, in God's name of course, here on earth. And the earth is supposed to obey and adapt to what we say and do. Presumably we're supposed to listen to God up there and only do what God says we should down here.

But the whole mental picture is wrong because nature is not below us, is not awaiting our commands, and is managing itself very nicely unless we go around messing it up.

Let's talk about stewardship at this point. There is considerable effort nowadays to whitewash our tradition and avoid taking a look at what is really happening in the Old Testament and in our hierarchical theological tradition. We are attempting to say that dominion is all right as long as it is done with stewardship. We think our problem has been that we've done it wrong because we made "dominion" into "domination." We did it wrong and tomorrow we'll do it right. That is a fantasy!

We won't do it right, because we don't know enough to do it right. If there's anything I've learned, it is that we don't know enough of the intricacies of the way things work always to do it right. Whether it is DES or EDB or DDT or Love Canal or TMI or AIDS or genetic engineering, we are discovering every day new little intricacies we didn't know existed yesterday. Stewardship assumes we have perfect knowledge as well as a desire to do right by the planet. I don't think we've got either the knowledge or the desire, because we still in our gut feel we're above and we do not have to fit in.

I talk about "fitting in" when people say, "What do you want to substitute for dominion?" My answer is "attunement," or fitting in. That means you've got to listen. It's like what I consider good parenting to be—cybernetic. It means being guided by information feedback: you do one thing tentatively and you wait to see what happens. You monitor it very carefully (which we do not bother to do). If it looks like it's not doing well, you pull back and you change your behavior, trying something else. Attunement means listening, it means adapting yourself. It means fitting in. And it will never be done by us as a culture unless we, as a culture, realize we are not above. We are not going to do that, I don't think we are, until we Jews and Christians take a hard honest look at what we have received from our tradition. Or until we as a culture become more secular, more distant from our religious tradition.

The third myth is that *nature is feminine,* as in "Mother Nature" and "virgin resources." That, at least, did not come from our religious tradition. On the contrary, our creation mythology in Genesis 1 and 2 worked very hard to rule out all attempts to say the original creation of the world had anything to do with female sexuality. If you've compared Genesis with earlier creation myths of the ancient Middle East, you know that's true. Genesis was a polemic that said there's simply no way the procreation by women in bringing new life into this world had anything to do with the creation of the world, the creation of people.

It's not accidental that in Genesis Eve is born out of the body of Adam, the body of a man, which is the reverse of what happens in real life. That is no accident, just the way the only starring role allowed to women practically in the entire Old Testament is Eve in the creation, bringing evil into the world. That's no accident either. But the idea that nature is feminine does not come to us from this religious heritage. It comes to us in other ways. But it is nevertheless very firmly ensconced in our heads and in the ways we function toward nature, even without all that religious legitimation.

Our problem is not that these are myths, because I think humans always create myths, mental capsule-accounts which are simplifications. The problem comes when your myths are so out of touch with reality that you're functioning as though you were on angel dust, PCP, which convinces adolescent children they can swim when they can't, and they jump into swimming pools and drown. Or that they can fly, and they hurl themselves off buildings trying to. Myths that are so incongruent with the facts of life on our planet are a danger to your health. Hierarchical myths in an interrelated planet are dangerous to your health, and to your future.

DARWIN'S REVISION

When Darwin wrote *The Descent of Man,* the biblical pyramid of hierarchy (now called the Scale of Being) still shaped his thinking. To say that our real ancestors are related to monkeys is to drop us four steps down in the biblical hierarchy.

The evolutionary paradigm turns out to be exactly that same hierarchical pyramid, except that we've removed the action of God from the top. Evolution instead begins from the bottom in the primeval soup, and we envision ever divergent evolution as going up the levels from lower (simpler) to higher (complex) species, with humans occupying the top place. A hundred years after Darwin, Jacob Bronowski could turn the whole thing over in his book and television series entitled *The Ascent of Man,* and it remained believable. Why? Because the mental picture in our heads really hadn't changed, even though we thought we'd undergone an epoch-making transformation of thought.

We have confused our human uniqueness with our being superior. *Biologists view every species as unique.* A bioecological perspective views the human species as unique also, but not necessarily as the most important or the most adept. Certainly we don't have the best ears or the fleetest feet or the keenest sense of smell. We don't even have the largest brains, nor can we echolocate as do the dolphins. And we would be hard-pressed to show that what humans do is as important or as foundational to all life on this planet as what green plants do in photosynthesis.

THE ROLE OF ILLUSION

Attitudes like this coalesce into a pervasive "anthropocentric illusion," as I named it in my book *Green Paradise Lost.* We have seen only ourselves at the center of value and significance in God's creation. This assessment of our place and value in the scheme of things has been the basis of our Western science and technology, and it is going to kill us unless we abandon it. What I am suggesting is nothing less than that we finish the Copernican revolution. It felt theologically and religiously cozy to us to believe that we were at the center of the skies and that the sun and everything else went around us. All that is what Galileo and Copernicus overturned. When they discovered that what we see in the skies—our astronomy—requires a different assessment of the earth's place in the order of things, with difficulty we adjusted our astronomy. But we left in place the mental picture of a pyramid. We were still on top and therefore we could continue to do what we pleased.

Several centuries ago we adapted to a different astronomy. Today we must adapt to a different picture of our place in the orders of value and priority and importance of things. The diversity of this planet does not exist to be ranked. To ask of any differences, male/female, white/black, human/tree, Which of us is better? is to ask a dumb question, when viewed from the perspective of ecology and an understanding of systems.

RANKING DIVERSITY: THE CORE ISSUE

My contention, spelled out in more detail in *Patriarchy as a Conceptual Trap,* is that this ranking of diversity has come from patriarchy. Very early in human existence males created patriarchy because they as males did not produce life out of their bodies the way women did. In our early days as humans I don't think we understood how women managed to do that and what the male role in that was. Out of that male insecurity, I think males created a culture in which what men do is valued more and what women do is valued less—in short, patriarchy. It's a culture shaped to reassure males that they are terrific.

My problem with such a culture is that once you start ranking the primal difference between male and female and asking, Which of us is better? you then develop a mind-set that's always ranking things that are different or varied or diverse. Now, today it is almost impossible for us who have been deeply socialized into such a culture to encounter diversity—other humans or other species—and not immediately ask, Which of us is better? Which of us is smarter? Taller? Richer? More beautiful? Stronger?

So ultimately the problem of patriarchy is conceptual. It involves a fundamental mistake in how we think and organize what we perceive. What I want you to understand is that you are not going to deal with the problems of eco-justice until you deal with patriarchy. And what I find distressing again and again is that nowhere in the eco-justice dialogue and writings—except for what I say—is there any sense that patriarchy has any relationship to the eco-justice set of issues. When I say that ultimately the problem of patriarchy is conceptual, I mean that the problem which patriarchy poses for the human species is not simply that it oppresses women. Patriarchy has erroneously conceptualized and mythed Man's place in the universe. And thus, by the illusion of dominion that it legitimates, it endangers the entire planet.

QUESTIONS FOR STUDY

1. What is the importance of natural cycles for the author?

2. Briefly describe the cosmic hierarchy. How does Psalm 8 illustrate this ranking?

3. What three "myths" follow from this picture?

4. What is the problem of patriarchy?

QUESTIONS FOR REFLECTION

1. Some have claimed that nature goes in cycles while human history goes in a straight line and that a religion that emphasizes cycles is more in harmony with nature than one that emphasizes linearity. Which religions might qualify as cyclic and which as linear? Do you agree with this claim?

2. Why is Gray opposed to hierarchies? What abuses do they encourage? Would Haught in Part V agree?

3. With what concept would the author replace dominion? Why?

4. Is the theological notion of "stewardship" hierarchical? What is the problem with stewardship? Do you think the author is fair to the concept?

5. Why is Gray critical of the idea that nature is feminine? Why do you think it is often characterized as feminine?

6. "Myths that are so incongruent with the facts of life on our planet are a danger to your health." Explain.

7. What is *patriarchy?* How is the concept tied into hierarchy? Does a connection exist between patriarchy and the environmental crisis? What alternative do we have to the idea?

NETWORKING

Gray touches on a number of topics, including the following: Justice in Dobel and McFague; *status of human species* in McFague, Cobb, and Berry; *interconnectedness* in Fuller, McFague and Cobb; *hierarchy* in Bube, Peacocke, and Haught; *mythology* in Langer and Swimme; *stewardship* in Dobel; *nature as feminine* in McFague, Lovelock, Berry, and Roach; and *patriarchy* in Roach.

GAIA

GOD AND GAIA

JAMES LOVELOCK

In the 1970s, James Lovelock, a British physical and atmospheric chemist, worked on the unmanned Martian lander project for NASA. From this experience he developed the famous Gaia Hypothesis—that planetary bodies may be treated as complex systems for the purpose of understanding their geology, atmosphere, and capacity for evolving and sustaining life. His most complete and readable account of this idea is to be found in *The Ages of Gaia,* from which this selection is taken.

Gaia, mother of all, I sing, oldest of gods,
Firm of foundation, who feeds all creatures living on Earth,
As many as move on the radiant land and swim in the sea
And fly through the air—all these does she feed with her bounty.
Mistress, from you come our fine children and bountiful harvests,
Yours is the power to give mortals life and to take it away.
          J. DONALD HUGHES, *Gaia: An Ancient View of Our Planet*

Photographs, like biographies, often reveal more of the artist than of the subject. Maybe this is why passport photographs, taken in mechanically operated booths, look so lifeless. How could a mere machine capture the soul of its subject, stiffly sitting and gazing into the blind eye of the camera? Trying to write about God and Gaia, I share some of the limitations of a mechanical camera, and I know that this chapter will show more about myself than about my subjects. So why try? . . .

When I first saw Gaia in my mind I felt as an astronaut must have done as he stood on the Moon, gazing back at our home, the Earth. The feeling strengthens as theory and evidence come in to confirm the thought that the Earth may be a living organism. Thinking of the Earth as alive makes it seem, on happy days, in the right places, as if the whole planet were celebrating a sacred ceremony. Being on the Earth brings that same special feeling of comfort that attaches to the celebration of any religion when it is seemly and when one is fit to receive. It need not suspend the critical faculty, nor can it prevent one from singing the wrong hymn or the right one out of tune.

That is only what I feel about Gaia. What about God? I am too committed to the scientific way of thinking to feel comfortable when enunciating the Creed or the Lord's Prayer in a Christian Church. The insistence of the definition "I believe in God the Father Almighty, Maker of Heaven and Earth" seems to anesthetize the sense of wonder, as if one were committed to a single line of thought by a cosmic legal contract. It seems wrong also to take it merely as a metaphor. But I respect the intuition of those who do believe, and I am moved by the ceremony, the music, and most of all by the glory of the words of the prayer book that to me are the nearest to perfect expression of our language.

I have kept my doubts in a separate place for too long. Now that I write this chapter, I have to try somehow to explain, to myself as well as to you, what is my religious belief. I am happy with the thought that the Universe has properties that make the emergence of life and Gaia inevitable. But I react to the assertion that it was created with this purpose. It might have been; but how the Universe and life began are ineffable questions. When a scientist colleague uses evidence about the Earth eons ago to explain his theory of the origins of life it stirs a similar sense of doubt. How can the events so long ago that led to the emergence of anything so intricate as life be treated as a fact of science? It is human to be curious about antecedents, but expeditions into the remote past in search of origins is as supremely unimportant as was the hunting of the snark. The greater part of the information about our origins is with us here and now; so let us rejoice in it and be glad to be alive.

At a meeting in London recently, a wise man, Dr. Donald Braben, asked me: "Why do you stop with the Earth? Why not consider if the Solar System, the Galaxy, or even the Universe is alive?" My instant answer was that the concept of a living Earth, Gaia, is manageable. We know that there is no other life in this Solar System, and the nearest star is utterly remote. There must be other Gaias circling other docile long-lived stars but, curious though I may be about them and about the Universe, these are intangible— concepts for the intellect, not the senses. Until, if ever, we are visited from other parts of the Universe we are obliged to remain detached.

Many, I suspect, have trodden this same path through the mind. Those millions of Christians who make a special place in their hearts for the Virgin Mary possibly respond as I do. The concept of Jahweh as remote, all-powerful, all-seeing is either frightening or unapproachable. Even the sense of presence of a more contemporary God, a still, small voice within, may not be enough for those who need to communicate with someone outside. Mary is close and can be talked to. She is believable and manageable. It could be that the importance of the Virgin Mary in faith is something of this kind, but there may be more to it. What if Mary is another name for Gaia? Then her capacity for virgin birth is no miracle or parthenogenetic aberration, it is a role of Gaia since life began. Immortals do not need to reproduce an image of themselves; it is enough to renew continuously the life that constitutes them. Any living organism a quarter as old as the Universe itself and still full of vigor is as near immortal as we ever need to know. She is of this Universe and, conceivably, a part of God. On Earth she is the source of life everlasting and is alive now; she gave birth to humankind and we are a part of her.

This is why, for me, Gaia is a religious as well as a scientific concept, and in both spheres it is manageable. Theology is also a science, but if it is to operate by the same rules as the rest of science, there is no place for creeds or dogma. By this I mean theology should not state that God exists and then proceed to investigate his nature and his interactions with the Universe and living organisms. Such an approach is prescriptive, presupposes his existence, and closes the mind to such questions as: What would the Universe be like without God? How can we use the concept of God as a way to look at the Universe and ourselves? How can we use the concept of Gaia as a way to understanding God? Belief in God is an act of faith and will remain so. In the same way, it is otiose to try to prove that Gaia is alive. Instead, Gaia should be a way to view the Earth, ourselves, and our relationships with living things. . . .

A frequent misunderstanding of my vision of Gaia is that I champion complacence, that I claim feedback will always protect the environment from any serious harm that humans might do. It is sometimes more crudely put as "Lovelock's Gaia gives industry the green light to pollute at will." The truth is almost diametrically opposite. Gaia, as I see her, is no doting mother tolerant of misdemeanors, nor is she some fragile and delicate damsel in danger from brutal mankind. She is stern and tough, always keeping the world warm and comfortable for those who obey the rules, but ruthless in her destruction of those who transgress. Her unconscious goal is a planet fit for life. If humans stand in the way of this, we shall be eliminated with as little pity as would be shown by the micro-brain of an intercontinental ballistic nuclear missile in full flight to its target.

What I have written so far has been a testament built around the idea of Gaia. I have tried to show that God and Gaia, theology and science, even physics and biology are not separate but a single way of thought. . . .

In *The Self-Organizing Universe,* Erich Jantsch made a strong argument for the omnipresence of a self-organizing tendency; so that life, instead of being a chance event, was an inevitable consequence. Jantsch based his thoughts on the theories of those pioneers of what might be called the "thermodynamics of the unsteady state"— Max Eigen, Ilya Prigogine, Humberto Maturana, Francisco Varela, and their successors. As scientific evidence accumulates and theories are developed in this recondite topic, it may become possible to encompass the metaphor of a living Universe. The intuition of God could be rationalized; something of God could become as familiar as Gaia.

For the present, my belief in God rests at the stage of a positive agnosticism. I am too deeply committed to science for undiluted faith; equally unacceptable to me spiritually is the materialist world of undiluted fact. Art and science seem interconnected with each other and with religion, and to be mutually enlarging. That Gaia can be both spiritual and scientific is, for me, deeply satisfying. From letters and conversations I have learnt that a feeling for the organism, the Earth, has survived and that many feel a need to include those old faiths in their system of belief, both for themselves and because they feel that Earth of which they are a part is under threat. In no way do I see Gaia as a sentient being, a surrogate God. To me Gaia is alive and part of the ineffable Universe and I am part of her.

The belief that the Earth is alive and to be revered is still held in such remote places as the west of Ireland and the rural parts of some Latin countries. In these places, the shrines to the Virgin Mary seem to mean more, and to attract more loving care and attention, than does the church itself. The shrines are almost always in the open, exposed to the rain and to the sun, and surrounded by carefully tended flowers and shrubs. I cannot help but think that these country folk are worshipping something more than the Christian maiden. There is little time left to prevent the destruction of the forests of the humid tropics with consequences far-reaching both for Gaia and for humans. The country folk, who are destroying their own forests, are often Christians and venerate the Holy Virgin Mary. If their hearts and minds could be moved to see in her the embodiment of Gaia, then they might become aware that the victim of their destruction was indeed the Mother of humankind and the source of everlasting life.

When that great and good man Pope John Paul travels around the world, he, in an act of great humility and respect for the Mother or Father Land, bends down and kisses the airport tarmac. I sometimes imagine him walking those few steps beyond the dead concrete to kiss the living grass; part of our true Mother and of our ourselves.

QUESTIONS FOR STUDY

1. How does Lovelock himself respond to the idea that the Earth is alive?

2. The author speculates that Jahweh or God presents a problem to many Christians that makes Gaia an attractive alternative. What is this problem?

3. What Christian figure most closely resembles Gaia?

4. Does Lovelock believe that Gaia indulges her human progeny?

QUESTIONS FOR REFLECTION

1. Why does the idea of the Earth as a living organism evoke a religious response? If Lovelock had never referred to the planet as "Gaia," would this association have been avoided?

2. Is it possible to understand the tension between Gaia and the Judeo-Christian image of God, "Maker of Heaven and Earth," as a problem of patriarchy? See Gray, "A Critique of Dominion Theology," in this part.

3. Lovelock seems to oppose formalized institutional religion with its creeds and dogmas. Does he himself espouse a creed of sorts? Prepare a Lovelockian creed of Gaia beginning with the traditional words, "I believe. . ."

4. While he does not believe the Earth is really alive, Lovelock does not deny the possibility that someday science might establish that it is a living organism, at which time it might be appropriate to address the world as a deity. What is his definition of God that makes this assertion possible?

5. Lovelock's opposition to traditional monotheism and its emphasis on the supernatural resembles Einstein's opposition in "Science and Religion" (see Part III). What are these similarities? Are their religious attitudes similar as well?

6. Lovelock refers to the figure of Mary in Catholic piety. What point is he attempting to make with this reference? In your opinion, could the image of Mary provide a touchpoint between the Christian tradition and some new naturalistic religion?

NETWORKING

For discussions of the *characterization of nature as feminine,* see McFague, Gray, Berry, and Roach. *Teleology* may be found in Bube, Dyson, Polkinghorne, and Asimov. Fuller, Teilhard, and McFague use the *language and concepts of self-organizing systems* as an important dimension of their perspective.

HUMAN PRESENCE
THOMAS BERRY

Father Thomas Berry is an ecotheologian—that is, a theologian who self-consciously shapes the principles of the Christian religion in response to the natural world and our responsibilities toward it. He refers to himself as a "geologian" because of his focus on the planet Earth as the center of value and loyalty. He is known for his work in comparative religion and Asian Studies and taught for a number of years as director of the history and religion program in the Theology Department of Fordham University. In 1970, he founded the Center for Religious Research in Riverdale, New York. For twelve years he was president of the American Teilhard Association.

Our relationship with the earth involves something more than pragmatic use, academic understanding, or aesthetic appreciation. A truly human intimacy with the earth and with the entire natural world is needed. Our children should be properly introduced to the world in which they live, to the trees and grasses and flowers, to the birds and the insects and the various animals that roam over the land, to the entire range of natural phenomena.

Such intimacy with the universe we find with the Omaha Indians. When a child is born, the Omaha declare its newborn presence to the entire universe. First they address the sun, the moon, the stars, and every being that moves in the heavens, declaring: "Into your midst has come a new life. Consent ye, we implore! Make its path smooth, that it may reach the brow of the first hill." Then to the atmospheric world, to the winds, clouds, rain, mist, and all that moves in the air. Then to the hills, valleys, rivers, lakes, trees, and grasses. Finally, "Ye birds, great and small, that fly through the air. Ye animals, great and small, that dwell in the forest. Ye insects that creep among the grasses and burrow in the ground, I bid ye all to hear me. Consent ye all, we implore! Make its path smooth. Then shall it travel beyond the four hills."

This is an entrancing ritual for introducing a child to the world into which the child has been born. In our own thinking we are coming back to this once more out of our new mode of understanding the universe. We now experience ourselves as the latest arrivals, after some 15 billion years of universe history and after some 4.5 billion years of earth history. Here we are, born yesterday. We need to present ourselves to the planet as the planet presents itself to us, in an evocatory rather than a dominating relationship. There is need for a great courtesy toward the earth.

This courtesy we might learn from the Iroquois. Their thanksgiving ritual is one of the most superb ceremonies that humans have ever known. Too long to present in its entirety, it does have a refrain that is relevant here: "We return thanks"—first to our mother, the earth, which sustains us, then on to the rivers and streams, to the herbs, to the corn and beans and squashes, to bushes and trees, to the wind, to the moon and stars, to the sun, and finally to the Great Spirit who directs all things.

To experience the universe with such sensitivity and such gratitude! These are primary experiences of an awakening human consciousness. Such stupendous moments reveal a striking sense of the alluring earth. An intimacy wonderfully expressed in the famous Western Inscription of Chang Tsai, an eleventh-century administrative official in China. This inscription, placed on the west wall of his office, so that he would constantly have it before him, reads quite simply: "Heaven is my father and earth is my mother and even such a small creature as I finds an intimate place in its midst. That which extends throughout the universe, I regard as my body and that which directs the universe, I regard as my nature. All people are my brothers and sisters and all things are my companions."

Also, Wang Yang-ming, an early sixteenth-century Chinese writer, tells us that a truly developed person is someone who realizes that we form one body with heaven, earth, and all living things. He mentions "everything from ruler, minister, husband, wife, and friends to mountains, rivers, heavenly and earthly spirits, birds, animals, and plants; all should be truly loved in order to realize my humanity which forms a unity, and then my clear character will be completely manifested and I will really form one body with heaven, earth, and the myriad things."

India, too, has an intimacy with the natural world, as expressed in the epic poem, *The Ramayana*, with its touching scenes of Rama and Sita in exile, wandering in the forest with its flowering plants, fruit-bearing bushes, elephants, monkeys, deer, and brightly plumed birds. Also in India there are the familiar animal tales of the *Hitopadesa*, the teaching of wisdom through playful narratives of forest life.

Everywhere intimacy, the mutual presence of the life community in all its numinous qualities. We, too, have something of this in our own transcendental and romanticist traditions that arose in Germany in the late eighteenth century and came to the English-speaking world through Coleridge in England and Emerson in America. Within this context, we developed our own American feeling for the natural world, expressed in the writings of Walt Whitman, Henry Thoreau, and John Muir. These are the archetypal personalities whose work is continued in writers Aldo Leopold, Loren Eiseley, Mary Austin, Joseph Wood Krutch, Gary Snyder, Edward Abbey, Annie Dillard, Barry Lopez, and so many others, and through a multitude of artists and musicians.

With the more recent nature writers a new understanding of the universe begins to take shape. Our scientific understanding of the universe, when recounted as story, takes on the role formerly fulfilled by the mythic stories of creation. Our naturalists are no longer simply romanticists or transcendentalists in their interpretative vision; they have absorbed scientific data into their writings. A new intimacy with the universe has begun within the context of our scientific tradition. This is the most distinctive contribution presently being made toward renewal of our presence to the earth. Science is providing some of our most powerful poetic references and metaphoric expressions. Scientists suddenly have become aware of the magic quality of the earth and of the universe entire.

The physicist Brian Swimme tells us, "The universe shivers with wonder in the depths of the human." From the tiniest fragment of matter to the grand sweep of the galactic systems, we have a new clarity through our empirical modes of knowing. We are more intimate with every particle of the universe and with the vast design of the whole. We see it and hear it and commune with it as never before. Not only in its spatial extension, but in its emergent process, we are intimate with the world about us. We experience an identity with the entire cosmic order within our own beings. This sense of an emergent universe identical with ourselves gives new meaning to the Chinese sense of forming one body with all things.

This identity is expressed by physicists in terms of the anthropic principle. In this perception the human is seen as a mode of being of the universe as well as a distinctive being in the universe. Stated somewhat differently, the human is that being in whom the universe comes to itself in a special mode of conscious reflection. That some form of intelligent reflection on itself was implicit in the universe from the beginning is now granted by many scientists. The difficulty presently is with the mechanistic fixations in the human psyche, in our emotions and sensitivities as well as in our minds. Our scientific inquiries into the natural world have produced a certain atrophy in our human responses. Even when we recognize our intimacy, our family relations with all the forms of existence about us, we cannot speak to those forms. We have forgotten the language needed for such communication. We find ourselves in an autistic situation. Emotionally, we cannot get out of our confinement, nor can we let the outer world flow into our own beings. We cannot hear the voices or speak in response.

Yet the beginning of an intimacy can be observed. The very intensity of our inquiry into the structure and functioning of the natural world reveals an entrancement with this natural world. This attraction to the primordial splendor of the universe, however betrayed by our industrial exploitation, remains an overwhelming experience. We are constantly drawn toward a reverence for the mystery and the magic of the earth and the larger universe with a power that is leading us away from our anthropocentrism to this larger context as our norm of reality and value.

Perhaps nothing is more difficult for those of us who live within the Western biblical-classical tradition. Throughout the entire course of this tradition, the autism has deepened with our mechanism, our political nationalism, and our economic industrialism. Presently a new interpretation of the Western historical process seems to be indicated. Neither the liberal progressive nor the conservative traditionalist seems to fit the situation. The only suitable interpretation of Western history seems to be the ironic interpretation. This irony is best expressed, perhaps, by the observation that our supposed progress toward an ever-improving human situation is bringing us to wasteworld instead of wonderworld, a situation that found its finest expression in *Endgame* by Samuel Beckett.

The intimacy expressed in the Omaha celebration of a new life born into the earth community and in the Seneca thanksgiving ritual, in the Chinese feeling of presence to the universe—these experiences that formerly were so strangely distant and unreal—now begins to fascinate us with the promise of healing our estranged situation. This estrangement, however, must be overcome within our own sense of a time-developmental, as well as in a seasonal-renewing, universe. We have a new story of the universe. Our own presence to the universe depends on our human identity with the entire cosmic process. In its human expression the universe and the entire range of earthly and heavenly phenomena celebrate themselves and the ultimate mystery of their existence in a special mode of exaltation.

It has taken the entire course of some fourteen billion years for the universe, the earth, and all its living creatures to attain this mode of presence to itself through our empirical modes of knowing. Such is the culmination of the scientific effort. This endeavor over the past three centuries might be considered among the most sustained meditations on the universe carried out by any cultural tradition. Truly the Yoga of the West. If our science has gone through its difficulties, it has cured itself out of its own resources. Science has given us a new revelatory experience. It is now giving us a new intimacy with the earth.

In accord with the groping processes of nature itself, science has proceeded by an intense inquiry into the deep recesses of the universe by a special quality of empirical observation, analysis, and interpretation. This has brought us into the far depths of the heavens and into the inner spaces of the atom. Through this knowledge the very structure and functioning of life itself have been so affected that we can do very little anymore without this type of scientific understanding.

One of the finest moments in our new sensitivity to the natural world is our discovery of the earth as a living organism. This was clear in ancient times as an instinctive insight into the nature and functioning of the earth. But such insight expressed in mythic terms is no longer sufficient for an age of scientific inquiry. Quite naturally our scientific observation reveals first the physical aspects of the planet and its living forms. The genius of our sustained inquiry into the inner functioning of the planet finally brought us beyond a microphase perception into the larger macrophase awareness that the entire planet is a single organic reality that needs to be addressed in its spirit and person qualities as well as in its physical aspects.

Here the ancient mythic insight and our modern scientific perceptions discover their mutual confirmation. Personal designation of the earth as Gaia is no longer unacceptable in serious discussion. In considering the larger patterns in the earth functioning, we are now able to identify its five major components: the geosphere, the hydrosphere, the atmosphere, the biosphere, and the noosphere. These are present to each other in a comprehensive manner and are all infolded in the light and radiance of the sun. In this context we have a new mode of understanding our own intimacy with the earth and also of our total dependence on these other modes of earth expression. How appropriate, then, the traditional invocation of all these powers in any human endeavor. Appropriate, also, is our continuing gratitude to these powers for bringing us into being and for sustaining us in existence.

How great a marvel that these five forces in the light of the sun should bring forth the seas and the continents, the winds and the rain, and the profusion of blossoming flowers and other living forms that inhabit the earth. A magic world! Enchanting.

But while we present these thoughts, we need to reflect especially on the mindsphere—the latest of these five powers that constitute the earth functioning. The landsphere and the other three powers that formerly functioned with such exuberant creativity seem now to have given over to the mindsphere the major share of directing the course of earth development. The earth that directed itself instinctively in its former phases seems now to be entering a phase of conscious decision through its human expression. This is the ultimate daring venture for the earth, this confiding its destiny to human decision, the bestowal upon the human community of the power of life and death over its basic life systems.

Such an event is clearly something more than historical change or cultural transformation such as we have known them in the prior course of human history, much more than the change from the Paleolithic to the Neolithic or the rise of the classical civilizations. Perhaps nothing so significant has happened since the original shaping of the earth, the rise of life itself, or the appearance of the human. Something strange indeed is happening to the entire process, and we must wonder at ourselves and what we are doing and what is happening to the larger destinies of the earth, even perhaps of the universe.

Such consideration brings us back to the ancient sense of *Logos* in the Greek world, of *rita* in Hinduism, or *dharma* in Buddhism, of *tao*, *ch'eng*, and *jen* in the Chinese world. These are the ancient perceptions of the ordering, or the balancing, principles of the universe, the principles governing the interaction of all those basic forces constituting the earth process. To recognize and act according to these principles was the ultimate form of human wisdom.

What is remarkable throughout the Asian world is that terms designating supremely affectionate qualities carry ultimate cosmological significance. So in the Chinese world, *jen*, a term translated as love, benevolence, or affection, is not only an emotional-moral term, it is also a cosmic force. This can be said also of the virtue of *ch'eng*, translated as sincerity or integrity. In India the term *bhakti*, devotional love, was a cosmological as well as a spiritual force. In Buddhist tradition the term *karuna*, compassion, is a supreme cosmic power. Thus we find a pervasive intimacy and compassionate quality in the very structure of the universe and of the earth itself.

Our own quest for a more intimate and benevolent human presence to the earth in our times might reflect these precedents. But even more, perhaps, we might consider our intimate and compassionate presence to the earth as originating ultimately in the curvature of space, as it is presented in modern science. The entire earth community is infolded in this compassionate curve whereby the universe bends inwardly in a manner sufficiently closed to hold all things together and yet remains sufficiently open so that compassion does not confine, but fosters, the creative process.

This curve that finds its first expression in the physical bonding of the universe and later in the living process of the earth finds its most intimate expression in human thought and affection, as well as in our art, music, and dance. We can hear anew *The Creation* of Haydn and the *Ode to Joy* of Beethoven. We can read anew *Leaves of Grass* by Walt Whitman. We can understand the great intuitions the ancients had of the universe. We can dance anew to the rhythms of the earth.

This reenchantment with the earth as a living reality is the condition for our rescue of the earth from the impending destruction that we are imposing upon it. To carry this out effectively, we must now, in a sense, reinvent the human as species within the community of life species. Our sense of reality and of value must consciously shift from an anthropocentric to a biocentric norm of reference.

This anthropocentrism is largely consequent on our failure to think of ourselves as species. We talk about ourselves as nations. We think of ourselves as ethnic, cultural, language, or economic groups. We seldom consider ourselves as species among species. This might be referred to in biology, but it has never meant that much in real life. We must now do this deep reflection on ourselves. What earlier people did immediately and intuitively in establishing their human identity, we must do deliberately.

Although we are integral with the complex of life communities, we have never been willing to recognize this in law, economics, morality, education, or in other areas of human endeavor. We must do this now in the context of an emergent universe. What earlier peoples were doing, they were doing in a limited human world and in a spatial mode of consciousness. We have our experience in a dominant time-developmental mode of consciousness and with our empirical instruments of understanding. Within this context we can recognize ourselves not simply as a human community, but as genetically related to the entire community of living beings, since all species are descended from a single origin.

Perception of the earth itself as a living organism was first presented with scientific evidence by Lynn Margulis and James Lovelock. The idea itself, however, is not new. It has appeared in different cultural traditions at different historical periods. Although this belief was never central to Western thought tradition, it maintained itself consistently on the borders of Western consciousness as the *anima mundi* concept, "the soul of the world" concept of Plato. The influence of this concept continued through the hermetic teachings of Ficino, Pico della Mirandola, and Giordano Bruno. Later it passed on to the Cambridge Platonists of England. In Germany another expression of this vitalist tradition is found in the work of Silesius, Goethe, and Schelling, eventually reaching Bergson and all those influenced by him. Foremost among these were Vladimir Vernadsky and Teilhard de Chardin. Although these latter were primarily scientists and biologists, they were also deeply involved in the more profound philosophical currents of the West.

The scientific term *biosphere* was used in 1875 by an Austrian professor of geology, Edward Seuss (1831–1914). Later, also, he used the term in his four-volume study, which was completed in 1909—it was translated into English as *The Face of the Earth*. According to Jacques Grinevald in an unpublished paper entitled "The Forgotten Sources of the Concept of Biosphere," Teilhard read the work of Seuss in its French translation in 1920 and wrote a review of it in 1921. Already in the 1920s Vernadsky, Eduard Le Roy, and Teilhard were in contact with one another in Paris. Of these, Vernadsky was the one who wrote the first extensive treatise, entitled *La Biosphère*, in 1929. This term was quickly associated with the other term, *noosphere*, which was invented by Le Roy, but popularized by Teilhard. Later it was adopted by Vernadsky, who considered human thought as a "biospherical phenomenon."

Thus our general sense of the earth as a living planet has a twofold source. One is more visionary, the other more empirical. Even when the various cultures accepted the earth as a living entity, there were significant differences in their experiences. Grand as the other cultural traditions may be, and however helpful, they are not quite what we need presently in dealing with this question. We need the insight given by our own scientific study of the earth, for the planet is severely affected. Precisely as a living planet, the earth needs attention.

What is needed on our part is the capacity for listening to what the earth is telling us. As a unique organism the earth is self-directed. Our sense of the earth must be sufficiently sound so that it can support the dangerous future that is calling us. It is a decisive moment. Yet we would not feel that we alone are determining the future course of events. The future shaping of the community depends on the entire earth in the unity of its organic functioning, on its geological and biological as well as its human members.

QUESTIONS FOR STUDY

1. What attitude toward the Earth is Berry promoting in his references to various traditions found in the early part of this selection?

2. What discipline is contributing uniquely to our new "intimacy" with the natural world?

3. The opposite of this intimacy is *autism*. Define the term. What are its sources?

4. What is the "Yoga of the West"?

5. List the five major components of the Earth. What is the "noosphere"? See Teilhard de Chardin in Part V.

6. Describe the "twofold source" of the Earth as a living planet.

QUESTIONS FOR REFLECTION

1. In two of Berry's references the Earth is characterized as "mother." What is it about the planet that recommends this characterization? Would the image of "Father Earth" be misplaced? Why or why not?

2. Science has been accused of leading to the disenchantment of the world. Berry argues that it is the source of a reenchantment of the world. What is his argument? Do you agree?

3. Why is the birth of the 'mindsphere' so important for Berry?

4. As with Cobb and McFague, Berry sees anthropocentrism as the central problem. What are its sources? What alternative does he recommend? Can you suggest any other alternatives?

NETWORKING

McFague, Gray, and Roach have strong opinions concerning the *characterization of the planet or nature as feminine*. Barbour (Part I), MacCormack, McFague, and Cobb speak specifically and at length on the concept of *organicism*. For the general idea of the *noosphere,* see the selection by Teilhard de Chardin. Swimme, Bube, and Gray see the *disenchantment of nature* as a consequence of the rise of science.

LOVING MOTHER EARTH: SOME RESERVATIONS
CATHERINE ROACH

Catherine Roach is in the Ph.D. program in religion at Harvard University. Her interests lie in ecofeminism and psychoanalytic theory. This selection is taken from *Hypatia,* a women's journal, and was developed from her M.A. thesis at the University of Ottawa.

The environmental movement seems to have gathered such momentum these days that wherever one looks one finds posters, bumper-stickers, slogans, advertisements, and other eco-paraphernalia urging us to do this or that in the name of environmental soundness. In this essay I want to examine one such poster from an ecofeminist point of view. This poster (which I have also seen in T-shirt and bumper-sticker incarnations) consists of a picture and a short phrase. The picture is of the Earth as seen from outer space with the phrase, "Love Your Mother," printed beside it. I see this poster as a particularly interesting example of the relation that has often been posited between woman and nature and I will use the poster as an occasion to examine this relation in some detail.

. . .We speak of "Mother Nature" and "Mother Earth." How does the image of Earth as mother function in our patriarchal world, and how is the environment affected by this association with the female and the maternal? I argue that engendering the Earth as female mother, given the meaning and function traditionally assigned to "mother" and "motherhood" in patriarchal culture, will not achieve the desired aim of making our behaviour more environmentally sound, but will instead help to maintain the mutually supportive, exploitative stances we take toward our mothers and toward our environment. This analysis brings out one of the fundamental points of ecofeminism: the way we think about and treat the environment is related to the way we think about and treat women.

. . . The "mother" referred to in the poster is clearly "Mother Nature," the earth, the planet, the environment, the biosphere, or nature, whichever term one wishes to use (although, as I will discuss later, I think one's choice of terms is significant). The Earth is metaphorically equated with our mother. In directing us to love our mother, environmentalists employing this slogan communicate two messages to us. The first message, conveyed through the use of the imperative "love," is the exhortation to care for and maintain the health of the Earth. The second message, conveyed through the use of the term "mother," is that we are all closely tied to the environment, that our very existence derives from and depends on a healthy environment, as our existence once depended on a mother or mother-figures almost always female.

The question then arises: why, if this is what they want to say, do they not simply say it? Why do these environmentalists choose to pass through the metaphor of loving one's mother in order to express their message of environmental soundness? The text is deceptive to the extent that although it does not refer to our real-life mothers, it nevertheless does seek to take advantage of the fact that certain ideas about motherhood and about the connection between the Earth and motherhood are often assumed as part of the way motherhood functions. These generally assumed ideas lend the slogan its aura of aptness. Two of these ideas are that we all should and can love our real-life mothers and that we all can intuitively grasp how the Earth is, in a sense, our mother. By imaging Earth as mother, the poster plays on our love for our real-life mothers.

How well does the metaphor of "mother" apply to the Earth? How appropriate a metaphor is this? On first consideration, the Earth or nature does seem to fit reasonably enough into the metaphor of "mother." After all, it is from the environment that we draw our oxygen, food, water, and all of the raw materials out of which we fashion the endless items that make up the materiality of our culture. The Earth or the environment is certainly life-giving and life-sustaining, as were and are our mothers. And yet the Earth is not our mother. Sallie McFague discusses the "is" and "is not" function of metaphors (1987, 33–35). A metaphor should both shock us (the "is not") and evoke recognition (the "is"); a metaphor is not a definition but a likely account. While I do not deny that the Earth is like our mothers in certain ways, because mothering and motherhood function problematically in patriarchal culture, the metaphorical equation of Earth or nature with mother also becomes problematical and to a certain degree unhealthy, both for women and for the environment. For pragmatic reasons then, because of the exigencies of our environmental situation, I stress the "is not" of the Earth as our mother.

Since this stress rests on the problematical nature of the meaning and function of "mother" and "motherhood," and since the poster's text makes reference, through the "is" of its metaphor, to our actual mothers, we need to ask first how motherhood functions for us humans and how we understand our love for our mothers and our mothers' love for us. It strikes me that we do not unambiguously love our mothers. Mothers' housework and child-rearing are unpaid and seldom recognized or appreciated by society, except in condescending eulogies of the joys of motherhood or of the ideal mother and in platitudes about motherhood and apple pie. Mothers are too often abandoned and left to raise their children without a father. Dorothy Dinnerstein in *The Mermaid and The Minotaur* (1976) explains how the sexual arrangement of women providing almost all early childhood care results in mothers becoming the targets for deeply ambivalent feelings. To a baby the caretaker appears all-powerful and caring but also capricious and malevolent. The baby thus comes to love and desire but also to hate and fear the caretaker. Because the mother is usually this caretaker, she rarely is a "clean" parent like the father. According to Dinnerstein, then, mothers bear the burden of being too powerful and mysterious because we were too completely dependent on them. Loving one's mother is a difficult task and that love is often to some extent ambivalent. To change this, as Dinnerstein and others have argued, we need to have mothers and fathers share equally in the task of child-rearing in order that both might then bear the brunt of infants' ambivalent feelings toward the early parent or parents.

Along with this ambivalence, Dorothy Dinnerstein explains how our sexual arrangements for parenting result in a merging of the categories of "woman" and "nature." To the infant, mother appears as a "global, inchoate, all-embracing presence," as unbounded and amorphous, as the "monolithic representative of nature" (1976, 93, 95). Because of this all of us, men and women alike, have trouble perceiving mothers as autonomous subjects. As Jessica Benjamin points out, "the view of mother as object resounds throughout our culture" (1988, 77). Mothers and women remain for us closer to object than to subject, closer to nature than to culture. "We cannot believe," as Dinnerstein notes, "how accidental, unconscious, unconcerned—i.e., unmotherly—nature really is; and we cannot believe how vulnerable, conscious, autonomously wishful—i.e., human—the early mother really was" (1976, 108). Elizabeth Dodson Gray makes the same point about the objectification of women and the personification of the environment when she notes how "as adults we still have difficulty believing our surroundings really are impersonal or, on the other hand, that our mothers are really fully human persons" (1982, 105). Our parenting arrangements of women being responsible for almost all early child care ensure that we hold tight to the childhood belief that our first, magic parent was a semihuman force of nature and the idea that nature is our semihuman mother.

If it is difficult for us to love our mothers and to perceive them as fully human, equally problematic is the way we expect our mothers to love us. This point is especially significant for environmentalists using the "Love Your Mother" slogan, for we expect our mothers to love us in a way we can never expect the environment to love us. *There is no "Mother Nature" wanting to nurture and care for us, no "Mother Earth" who loves us.* As Elizabeth Dodson Gray (1989) insists, we must withdraw our weighty projections and try to see clearly the Earth as Earth and not as the mother or female we have imagined the Earth to be. Instead of leading us to greater environmental soundness, the strategy of picturing the Earth as our mother could have the exact opposite effect. Mother in patriarchal culture is she who provides all of our sustenance and who makes disappear all of our waste products, she who satisfies all of our wants and needs endlessly and without any cost to us. Mother is she who loves us and will take care of us no matter what (Gray 1982, 102–5). The last thing the environmental movement should do is encourage us to think of the environment in these terms. Our ecological breakdown has arisen, in part, precisely from our attitude that nature is a storehouse of riches which will never empty and which we may use at will for any purpose we desire, without incurring any debt or obligation of replacement.

Luce Irigaray makes this last point in her book *Sexes et parentés* (1987). She observes that we act in the environment as if there were no cost attached to our use of natural resources, as if they existed purely for our use, and as if they would never be depleted. Our behaviour can be explained in part, she suggests, by the fact that we assume the mother will, without charge and without limit, nourish and care for the child in particular and for the man and society in general. We expect the same from "Mother Earth" as we do from mother. In an environmental context, the "Love Your Mother" slogan keeps these expectations intact. I am reminded here of a quote by the scientist and science writer Richard Feynman: "Let's face it, nature is absurd so accept nature as she is" (1989, 6). If Feynman is correct, then nature is not only female but also inherently absurd. Feynman's choice of the word absurd is interesting, for its definition as "irrational and ridiculous" derives from an etymological meaning of "completely deaf." Do we feel that nature is deaf to our calls and unresponsive to our needs? Do we hear echoed in Feynman's statement the plaintive whine of children who feel ignored by their mothers? Given the way motherhood functions now, it currently is not possible for us to love unambiguously the Earth as our mothers, and loving the Earth as our mother would not necessarily help us to be more environmentally sound. For the slogan to be effective in encouraging environmentally sound behaviour, mothering would first have to be different.

The picture chosen to accompany the slogan "Love Your Mother" is itself significant. The picture is of the Earth as seen from outer space. It shows the full circle of the Earth swirled in its atmosphere, set alone in empty space. Although, on the positive side, this image reveals the oneness, beauty, and finiteness of the planet, it also shows the Earth as a remote ball, suspended in space in a way we never at firsthand see or experience the planet, unless we are participating in a multimillion dollar space project. This image is of the Earth as separate and very distant from our viewpoint, as an isolated object without context. Choosing this image of the Earth for the "Love Your Mother" slogan emphasizes for me those negative aspects of patriarchal motherhood I have discussed: mother as idealized, the perfectly round globe-breast; mother as mysterious, shrouded in cloud; mother as ambivalent love-object, abandoned up in space.

REFERENCES

Benjamin, Jessica. 1988. *The bonds of love: Psychoanalysis, feminism, and the problem of domination*. New York: Pantheon Books.

Dinnerstein, Dorothy. 1976. *The mermaid and the minotaur: Sexual arrangements and human malaise*. New York: Harper and Row.

Feynman, Richard. 1989. Quoted by Jerome Kagan. In A conversation with Jerome Kagan. *Harvard Gazette*. 22 September.

Gray, Elizabeth Dodson. 1982. *Patriarchy as a conceptual trap*. Wellesley, MA: Roundtable Press.

____. 1989. An ecofeminist critique of Christianity. Lecture delivered at Harvard Divinity School, Cambridge, Massachusetts. 29 November.

Irigaray, Luce. 1987. *Sexes et parentés*. Paris: Editions de Minuit.

McFague, Sallie. 1987. *Models of God: Theology for an ecological, nuclear age*. Philadelphia: Fortress Press.

QUESTIONS FOR STUDY

1. The slogan "Love your Mother [Earth]" communicates two messages. What are they?

2. In what ways does Roach admit that the metaphor of mother is appropriate for the Earth?

3. In what ways does she claim that the metaphor is inappropriate?

4. How does the view of the Earth taken from space suggest an inappropriate symbol of the planet as maternal?

QUESTIONS FOR REFLECTION

1. According to the author, one of the fundamental points of ecofeminism is that the environment and women are seen as similar and treated in similar ways. Do you agree that the environmental crisis is related to destructive sexist attitudes?

2. The ambivalence we feel toward our mothers is expressed in religion as well. The powerful figure of the goddess Kali in Hinduism is a clear example of this ambivalence. Examine the Kali sect and describe the two sides of the goddess. Can Gaia be described in a similar way? Do we have a double attitude toward "Mother Nature"?

3. How does sextyping the Earth in the hope that the image will alter our destructive behavior toward the planet conceivably lead to "the exact opposite effect"?

4. The pictures of the Earth returned from the early space flights have been heralded as a significant source of revised Western attitude toward nature. Is this claim justified? In your estimate, do the benefits of identifying the planet as maternal outweigh the disadvantages listed by Roach?

NETWORKING

Roach, like Gray, strongly objects to the *characterization of nature or the planet Earth, representing nature, as feminine.* See Lovelock and Berry for examples of this. MacCormack provides an excellent introduction to the notion of *metaphor.* Roach draws on Gray for her notion of *patriarchy.*

SUGGESTIONS FOR FURTHER READING

Cobb, John B., and David Ray Griffin. *Is It Too Late? A Theology of Ecology.* Beverly Hills, California: Bruce, 1972. An early statement by Cobb, but of continuing relevance because of the development of process principles in a theological context. Clear and nontechnical.

_____. *Process Theology: An Introductory Exposition.* Philadelphia: The Westminster Press, 1976. A clear and systematic survey of the ideas of process thought and their relevance for theology. Contains a chapter on the process interpretation of the environmental crisis and an excellent bibliography.

Devall, Bill, and George Sessions. *Deep Ecology: Living As If Nature Mattered.* Layton, Utah: Gibbs M. Smith, Inc. 1985. The authoritative handbook of the Deep Ecology movement. A survey of the ideas, resources, and principal figures of the movement.

Dubos, Rene. *So Human an Animal.* New York: Charles Scribner's Sons, 1968. Dubos was awarded the Pulitzer Prize for this statement of the intimate connection of the human species and the natural world.

Gray, Elizabeth Dodson. *Green Paradise Lost: Re-Mything Genesis.* Wellesley, Massachusetts: Roundtable Press, 1979. A good statement of ecofeminist philosophy based on the contention that masculine values dominate Western attitudes toward nature and that we treat women and nature according to the same hierarchical world view.

Joseph, Lawrence E. *Gaia: The Growth of an Idea.* New York: St. Martin's Press, 1990. An informative investigation of the concept of Gaia in history, science, and religion.

Leopold, Aldo. *A Sand County Almanac.* New York: Oxford University Press, 1949. The essential Leopold: his reflections on the place of human activity in the ecosystem. Leopold is a major prophet of the environmental movement and father of reformed ecology, which differs considerably from "Deep" ecology. One chapter, "The Land Ethic," is gospel for environmentalists.

Lønning, Per. *Creation—An Ecumenical Challenge.* Macon, Georgia: Mercer University Press, 1989. An excellent survey and critical study of the doctrine of creation in Christian theology, with an emphasis on how a theology of creation might contribute to new directions of religious action in response to challenges from culture and the environment.

Merchant, Carolyn. *The Death of Nature: Women, Ecology and The Scientific Revolution.* San Francisco: Harper and Row Publishers, 1980. An insightful feminist historical account of the destruction of the organic world view with its supportive mythological and symbolic structures, and its replacement by mechanism with special emphasis on the subjugation of women and the natural order.

Nash, Roderick Frazier. *The Rights of Nature: A History of Environmental Ethics.* Madison, Wisconsin: University of Wisconsin Press, 1989. An excellent historical survey of the history of environmental ethics, especially in the United States. His chapters on the "greening" of philosophy and religion are exhaustive annotated bibliographies. An indispensible resource.

Oates, David. *Earth Rising: Ecological Belief in an Age of Science.* Corvallis, Oregon: Oregon State University Press, 1989. Oates develops a philosophy and ethic of the environment based on the image of the Earth as a total organic system.

Rolston, Holmes. *Environmental Ethics.* Philadelphia: Temple University Press, 1988. Probably the most thorough and sustained statement on the value of the natural world and our responsibilities toward it.

Santmire, Paul. *The Travail of Nature: the Ambiguous Ecological Promise of Christian Theology*. Philadelphia: Fortress Press, 1985. Santmire traces the place of nature in the history of Christian thought and discovers, as the title suggests, that the religion is of two minds on the subject. Good, realistic critique.

White, Lynn, Jr. "The Historical Roots of Our Ecologic Crisis." *Science,* Vol. 155 (March 10, 1967): 1203–7. The seminal essay in religion and the environment. White traces our predicament to biblical origins. Theologians have been responding to White's thesis ever since this essay appeared.

GLOSSARY

Steve Toulmin, the philosopher and historian of science, has remarked that definitions are like belts: The shorter they are the more elastic they need to be. The terms in this glossary have been assembled in the spirit of this maxim. I have intentionally avoided technical detail in order to reduce confusion and to help satisfy the goal of a glossary in any introductory reader, which is to describe unfamiliar terms in a way that clarifies rather than obscures their meaning. **Since many of these terms appear repeatedly in the selections, they are not identified in the text in any special way.**

AGENT   A philosophical concept signifying anything that possesses power and that is capable of carrying out purposes. Persons are agents, as is the God of theism.

AGNOSTICISM   The view that God's existence is not known. The agnostic suspends both belief and disbelief in the existence of God because of insufficient evidence upon which to base a decision.

ANIMISM   The belief, found widely in ancestral or primal cultures, that a great many things in nature are "animated" by spirits. Some may even be addressed.

ANTHROPOCENTRISM   From the Greek *anthropos*, meaning "man." The position that the human creature is absolutely superior in the universe, that humans are without rival or peer in terms of value and worth. In medieval thought, anthropocentrism appears as the belief that all things in the creation are intended by God to serve the human species.

ANTHROPOMORPHISM   The tendency to model and understand nonhuman things and organisms in terms of human traits and behavior.

APOLOGETICS   A division of theology that defends the faith and promotes its doctrines through reason to the nonbeliever.

A POSTERIORI   A Latin term meaning that the truth of a statement can be known only by an appeal to evidence and the senses. For example, "All alligators are carnivores" can be established as true only by a survey of the feeding habits of real alligators and not through reason alone.

A PRIORI   An *a priori* statement is one whose truth can be known through reason alone without appeal to empirical evidence or verification. Euclidian geometry is *a priori*. Its conclusions are necessary: purely the function of logic and deduction. The theorem, "The sum of the interior angles of any triangle is 180 degrees," can be established exclusively through internal reasoning. No survey of triangles in the real world is required.

ATOMISM   A corollary to mechanism, materialism, and reductive analysis. The idea that all reality is composed of tiny, absolutely simple or indivisible parts called atoms. The world of our experience consists exclusively of combinations of these material atoms in obedience to the laws of nature.

CAUSALITY   Refers to cause-effect relationships. Causality is a widely held doctrine of science that all events are the products of prior causes or influences operating in a regular, predictable manner.

CLOSED-SOCIETY   Understood by H. R. Niebuhr to mean a social group—an institution or nation-state—so thoroughly controlled by an ideology that it is intolerant of new ideas or experiences.

COGNITIVE   Having to do with thinking. Includes perception, memory, judgement, and other mental processes.

CONTINGENT   In general, a being is contingent if it depends on powers outside of itself for its existence. In philosophy, a proposition is contingent if its truth claims can be denied without contradiction.

COSMOLOGY   The philosophical or scientific study of the nature and structure of the universe.

CULTURETYPE   Used by Ralph Burhoe to mean a specific human culture whose members share a similar cultural heritage just as members of a genotype share a common genetic heritage.

CYBERNETICS   The study of the self-regulating activities of living things, complex machines, and ecosystems.

DEISM   An influential theology of the seventeenth and eighteenth centuries that described God as having created a highly ordered world. Then, having nothing further to do, God retired, leaving the creation to go on its own. Since the deist God seldom interferes, science need not fear any disruption of its efforts to determine the uniform laws of nature.

DETERMINISM   The philosophy that every event is caused and directed entirely by outside forces.

DEUS ABSCONDITUS   Literally, "the God who hides." Refers to the theological teaching that God intentionally veils Himself so as to give human creatures ample room and opportunity to express their freedom and faith.

DEUS EX MACHINA   The "God from/of the machine." Title for the God of Deism.

DRYAD   In Greek mythology, a spirit or divinity found in the forests.

DUALISM   The philosophical belief that reality consists of two separate kinds of essences, each completely different from the other and not reducible to it. Mind and matter, mind and body, soul and body, and God and world are classic dualism.

ECOSYSTEM   An expanse of nature in which a number of plants and animals live in a balanced system of relationships. The "web of life" of a well-defined region: desert, tropical forest, savanna, mountain, lake, and ocean.

EIGHTFOLD PATH   A central teaching of the Buddha. Eight rules for living designed to lead the practitioner closer to achieving nirvana. See "Nirvana."

EMERGENCE   The process in biological evolution where new characteristics arise

MICROCOSM   A microcosm is a part of the universe that reflects or resembles the whole, the macrocosm. Frequently refers to the order of the human mind as analogous to the rational order and processes of the cosmos.

MONISM   The idea that reality consists of a single essence. All things are modification of this essence. Popular candidates have historically included mind (idealism), matter (materialism), and spirit (pantheism or panpsychism).

MYSTICISM   The practice of disciplining the body, mind, and spirit for the purpose of achieving inner union with the divine.

NATURAL SELECTION   An essential part of Darwin's theory of evolution that accounts for the power of the environment to sort out and favor only those species best prepared to fit into it. Natural selection is often blind and ruthless. Species with advantages live longer and produce more offspring that carry those advantageous traits on to later generations and larger populations. Species lacking these traits fail to compete and leave fewer progeny. Diminishment or even extinction may be their eventual fate.

NATURAL THEOLOGY   The attempt to discover knowledge about God's existence from the use of reason and evidence from the world. Contrasts with revealed theology, which insists that God and God alone can impart knowledge about himself.

NEGENTROPY   The tendency of nature, observed in cosmic and biological evolution, to achieve greater order by building complex systems over time and thus swimming against the descending flow of entropy.

NIRVANA   A major Buddhist concept meaning literally "to extinguish." Refers to the experience of the ineffable state of absolute reality achieved when the personal ego or self is destroyed through meditation—snuffed out as a candle is extinguished.

NOETIC   Having to do with the mind in its act of knowing. An experience possesses a noetic quality if it results in knowledge.

NOOGENESIS   From the Greek *nous* for "mind" and *genesis* for "birth." A neologism invented by Teilhard de Chardin that means the birth of self-conscious and thinking creatures, that is, humans, through the processes of biological evolution.

NOOSPHERE   Another term created by Teilhard. The thin layer of thought which, in addition to the geosphere, biosphere, and atmosphere, envelopes the earth. Consists of the collective and total awareness of all persons.

NORMATIVE   Having to do with standard, conventional, or accepted practice or beliefs.

NUMINOUS   From the Latin *numen*, meaning "divinity." Made famous by Rudolf Otto in his book *Das Heilige* (*The Idea of the Holy*) as the presence and experience of awesome and terrifying divine power and mystery.

PALEONTOLOGY   The study of ancient life forms, primarily through their fossil remains.

PANTHEISM   Belief that the world and God are a single reality. God (*theos*) is in all (*pan*).

PARADIGM   A set of principles and beliefs that serve as a model for practice. In physics, the Newtonian paradigm provided the basis for research until the twentieth century when it was modified by discoveries in atomic physics and astronomy.

PATRIARCHY   Any system, social, philosophical, or religious, that defines masculine characteristics and values as superior to and dominant over feminine ones.

PHENOMENON   An event or happening that appears to the senses before it is subjected to analysis or categorized according to some theory or idea.

PHENOTYPE   The genetic makeup of an individual organism in contrast to the genetic structure it shares with its group or species (its genotype).

PLEROMA   A theological term signifying the fulfillment or completion of history. The end of the age.

PLURALISM   A feature of any society that is not dominated by a single religious or cultural tradition. The situation of several traditions coexisting in one society. American society is pluralistic in this sense.

POSITIVISM   The scientific philosophy that asserts that no statement qualifies as true unless it is either capable of verification through scientific procedures or it is the valid conclusion of formal logic.

PRIMARY CAUSE   The originating cause, often identified with God, of the cosmos as a whole. Primary causality establishes the conditions under which secondary or natural causality operates. Sometimes referred to as "first cause."

PRINCIPLE OF BEING   The idea, found in H. R. Niebuhr, that to avoid the narrow-mindedness of closed-society henotheism, one must be open to all reality or "being" as an expression of God.

PROPITIATION   An act that attempts to gain the favor and attention or appease the wrath of a spirit or deity through offerings and sacrifice.

PSYCHISM   According to Schmidt, a mental state or condition.

RADICAL MONOTHEISM   Opposed to henotheism. The relativizing belief that all sources of power, value, and goodness are to be tested with respect to a single transcendent God, so that any effort to set up an earthly creature as superior or absolute is an act of idolatry.

RATIONALISM   The philosophical approach to truth based on the notion that reason and reason alone is the authority by which truth claims are tested. The belief that reason and not religious faith or dogma is the source of dependable knowledge.

REDUCTIONISM   A way of understanding an idea or an object by breaking it down to its simple components. Living creatures are "reduced" to chemical processes, to chemistry. A life becomes the sum of the atomic or molecular processes of the organism.

ROMANTICISM   An attitude characterized by an appeal to the authority of intuition and feelings in any response to immediate experience.

SCIENTISM   An ideology in which the procedures and aims of science are given absolute priority in the definition of and quest for truth.

SECULAR   A characteristic of modern society in which religion is seen to be only one of several sources of personal and corporate meaning in life and thus becomes optional.

SINGULARITY   The Standard Big Bang model of cosmic origins depicts the universe as arising explosively from a virtual dimensionless point in spacetime, a "singularity," containing all the mass and energy of the subsequent physical cosmos.

SPECIAL CREATION   The theological concept that God created the universe all at once and in a relatively short time. This creative act is "special" in the sense of being direct and miraculous as opposed to using laws and processes of nature, including evolution, to accomplish the task indirectly.

STEADY STATE   The description of a natural or social system that is neither growing nor decaying. A system that acts primarily to maintain itself.

SYNOPTICS   The first three Gospels in the New Testament—Matthew, Mark, and Luke—which are grouped together because of their similarities and shared materials. Synoptic is Greek for "seeing alike."

TABULAE RASAE   Latin for "blank slates." A description of the human mind at birth as a clear surface ready to receive anything that experience writes upon it.

TAO   The divine source and power of all existence, according to ancient Chinese philosophy. The Tao (meaning "way") is the infinitely creative and inexhaustible power of being, which is revealed primarily in nature.

TAO TE CHING   *The Way and Its Power*. The central scripture of classical Taoism. A book of eighty-one somewhat enigmatic and paradoxical "psalms" or poems. According to legend, these were composed by the Chinese master Lao Tzu (600 B.C.E.).

TELEOLOGY   From the Greek word *telos* meaning "purpose" or "end." The study of purpose or conscious intention. Also, philosophy that sees the world as the result of design and with purposes built into its creatures. Opposed to the belief that the world is the result exclusively of accident and blind chance.

THERMODYNAMICS   The study of the laws of heat flow in closed systems.

TRANSACTION   The act of communicating, exchanging, and relating in a give-and-take manner, often in a way that alters the parties involved in the dialogue.

ULTIMACY   Pertaining to the Ultimate, to that which is absolutely superior, having no competition or equal. Used by the theologian Paul Tillich as a synonym for God as unconditioned being.

VARIABLE   In mathematics, a sign ("*X*" or "*Y*") that can assume any one of a set or range of values, from 0 to 10, for example. More generally, that which changes in measure and degree in response to causal influence.

VERIFICATION One step in scientific method. The process of confirming a hypothesis by testing it empirically, usually by deducing its necessary consequences and seeing if they actually occur in experiment or observation.

VIA NEGATIVA Latin for "the negative way." A way of approaching God as one who shares absolutely no characteristics with anything humans can know. The only way, therefore, to speak of God is to say what God is not rather than what God is.

VITALISM A theory of early modern biology, now in disrepute, that living things possess a life energy or directive force that cannot be accounted for by mechanistic explanations.

WELTANSCHAUUNG German for "world picture" or "world view." The generalized understanding of the universe that prevails in a culture. A world view provides the essential values of the culture as well as its perspective on God, human nature, and the nonhuman world. The world view of modern Western culture is primarily scientific.

ILLUSTRATION CREDITS

COVER	Inset photo: Steve Dunwell / The Image Bank Background photo: © 1990 Tatsuhiko Shimada / Photonica
PART I, p. 1	Steve Dunwell / The Image Bank
PART II, p. 78	Temple Beth Am, Miami, Florida. Photo by Gaston de Cardenas
PART III, p. 121	Temple Beth Am, Miami, Florida. Photo by Gaston de Cardenas
PART IV, p. 180	By Jim Riffle, 12" F-5 Astromak, Astro Works, Cloudcroft, New Mexico
PART VI, p. 249	*Fountain II*, sculpture by Robert Thiele, assisted by Sid Smith, Florida International University, Miami, Florida. Photo by Gaston de Cardenas
Page 172	© 1977 by Sidney Harris—American Scientist Magazine
Page 190	© 1988 by Sidney Harris—American Scientist Magazine
Page 232	© 1987 by Sidney Harris—American Scientist Magazine
Page 256	© 1989 by Sidney Harris—American Scientist Magazine

ACKNOWLEDGMENTS

Asimov, Isaac "The Threat of Creationism"
Copyright 1981 by Isaac Asimov. From *The New York Times Magazine*, June 14, 1981. Reprinted by permission of the author.

Barbour, Ian "Theological Issues in Evolution"
From Ian G. Barbour, *Issues in Science and Religion,* copyright © 1966, pages 88–98. Reprinted by permission of Prentice Hall, Englewood Cliffs, New Jersey.

Barbour, Ian "Ways of Relating Science and Religion"
Excerpt from *Religion in an Age of Science* by Ian G. Barbour. Copyright © 1990 by Ian G. Barbour. Reprinted by permission of HarperCollins Publishers, Inc.

Berry, Thomas "Human Presence"
From *The Dream of the Earth*, by Thomas Berry. Copyright © 1988 by Thomas Berry. Reprinted with permission of Sierra Club Books.

Bube, Richard H. "The Failure of the God-of-the-Gaps"
Copyright © 1978 by Richard H. Bube. Pages 21–35 of Carl F.H. Henry's *Horizons of Science*, Harper and Row, Publishers, 1978. Reprinted with permission of the author.

Buber, Martin "I and You"
Reprinted with permission of Charles Scribner's Sons, an imprint of Macmillan Publishing Company from *I and Thou* by Martin Buber, translated by Walter Kaufmann. Translation copyright © 1970 Charles Scribner's Sons, and by T&T Clark, Ltd., Publishers, Edinburgh.

Burhoe, Ralph W. "Attributes of God in an Evolutionary Universe"
Copyright © 1973 by Ralph W. Burhoe. From "The Concepts of God and Soul in a Scientific View of Human Purpose," *Zygon: Journal of Religion and Science*, Vol. 8, No. 3–4 (September–December 1973), pp. 412–42. Reprinted by permission of *Zygon*.

Haught, John   "Is Human Life Only Chemistry?"
Copyright © 1987 by John Haught. From John Haught, "There's More to Adam than Atoms," *The Washington Post Outlook,* Sunday, March 15, 1987, page C3. Reprinted by permission of the author.

Hick, John   "Miracles"
Reprinted from John Hick, *Philosophy of Religion*, Third Edition, pages 38–39. Prentice Hall, Englewood Cliffs, New Jersey. Copyright © 1983. Used by permission of the publisher.

Jastrow, Walter   "God and the Astronomers"
Copyright by Walter Jastrow. From *God and the Astronomers*, W.W. Norton and Co., New York. Reprinted with permission of the author.

Küng, Hans   "On the Relationship of Theology and Science"
From *On Being a Christian* by Hans Küng. Copyright © 1976 by Doubleday, a division of Bantam Doubleday Dell Publishing, Inc. Used by permission of Doubleday, a division of Bantam Doubleday Publishing Group, Inc.

Lackey, Douglas P.   "The Big Bang and the Cosmological Argument"
From *God, Immortality and Ethics: A Concise Introduction to Philosophy* by Douglas P. Lackey, copyright © 1990 by Wadsworth, Inc. Reprinted by permission of the publisher.

Langer, Susanne K.   "Understanding Myth"
Reprinted by permission of the publishers from *Philosophy in a New Key: A Study in the Symbolism of Reason, Rite, and Art* by Susanne K. Langer, Cambridge, Mass.: Harvard University Press. Copyright © 1942, 1951, 1957 by the President and Fellows of Harvard College; renewed 1970, 1979 by Susanne Knaugh Langer; 1985 by Leonard C.R. Langer.

Lewis, C.S.   "The Naturalist and the Supernaturalist"
Copyright © 1960 by HarperCollins, Publisher, London. From the book *Miracles* by C. S. Lewis. Reprinted with special permission of the publishers.

Lovelock, James   "God and Gaia"
Reprinted from *The Ages of Gaia: A Biography of Our Living Earth*, by James Lovelock, with the permission of W.W. Norton and Co., Inc. Copyright © 1988 by the Commonwealth Fund Book Program of Memorial Sloan-Kettering Cancer Center.

MacCormack, Earl R.   "Metaphor in Science and Religion"
Earl R. MacCormack, *Metaphor and Myth in Science and Religion*, pages 73–101. Copyright © 1976, Duke University Press, Durham, NC. Reprinted by permission of the publisher.

McFague, Sallie   "A Holistic View of Reality"
Reprinted from *Models of God* by Sallie McFague. Copyright © 1987, Fortress Press. Used by permission of Augsburg Fortress.

Midgley, Mary   "Mixed Antitheses"
Reprinted from Mary Midgley, *Evolution As Religion*, pages 98–104. Copyright © Methuen & Company, 1985. Reprinted by permission of the publishers.

Niebuhr, H. Richard   "Radical Faith and Western Science"
Excerpt from *Radical Monotheism and Western Culture* by Richard Niebuhr. Reprinted by permission of Harper & Row, Publishers, Inc.

Peacocke, A. R.   "God and the Selfish Genes"
Excerpt from *God and the New Biology* by Arthur Peacocke. Copyright © 1986 by Arthur Peacocke. Reprinted by permission of HarperCollins Publishers.

Polkinghorne, John   "More to the World Than Meets the Eye"
From John C. Polkinghorne, "Creation and the Structure of the Physical World," *Theology Today,*

INDEX